Criminal Procedure in Scotland:
Cases & Materials

Criminal Procedure in Scotland: Cases & Materials

C. H. W. GANE,
LL.B.

*Lecturer in Law, University of Lancaster,
formerly Lecturer in Scots Law,
University of Edinburgh*

&

C. N. STODDART,
LL.B., LL.M.(McGill), Ph.D.

*Solicitor in the Supreme Courts,
formerly Lecturer in Scots Law,
University of Edinburgh*

EDINBURGH
W. GREEN & SON LTD
Law Publishers
St. Giles Street
1983

First published in 1983

© 1983. C. H. W. Gane and
C. N. Stoddart

ISBN 0 414 00711 5

Printed in Great Britain
by
John G. Eccles Printers Ltd, Inverness

PREFACE

The past few years has seen a proliferation of casebooks on various aspects of Scots law, a development in which the authors were involved with the publication in 1980 of their work *A Casebook on Scottish Criminal Law*. That volume received a most heartening response both from the legal profession and from the universities, so we decided to attempt a companion volume dealing this time with criminal procedure, a subject which we deliberately excluded from the earlier work. That exclusion was based in part on the belief that the Criminal Justice (Scotland) Act 1980 would produce a number of unforeseen problems in the revised procedural system and so it has turned out, although perhaps to a more limited extent than we had hoped or expected. For example it is regrettable that the Lord Advocate has not yet seen fit to use his powers under s.37 of the Act to refer a case to the High Court for its opinion on a point of law, whereas the comparable provision in England has been used regularly. Nor does it appear that there is so far much enthusiasm for leading evidence in replication, although judicial examination is beginning to produce new problems. But, having said all that, recent years have seen a number of leading cases on procedure, such as the first successful application for a Bill of Criminal Letters since 1909, a line of authority on pre-trial publicity and the first case on re-trials under the 1980 Act. These, together with many older but equally important authorities, comprise the subject-matter of the present work.

We deal with solemn, summary and appeal procedure, although not with the rules of evidence. We hope that this work will be of use particularly to students taking the Diploma in Legal Practice at the universities, where procedure is of course an essential subject. We also hope to attract a wider audience in the profession generally, where many more practitioners are specialising in criminal practice and where a ready reference to the authorities is essential. But in no way is this work a guide to all the procedural law; this year's edition of *Renton & Brown* fills that space on the lawyer's bookshelf. We simply deal with what we consider are the leading cases, with a short commentary on the points raised, where this seems appropriate.

We also include at various points throughout the work excerpts from the relative statutory provisions, particularly where there is little or no case law on the problems discussed, and particularly where the statutory material is of recent origin such as that relating to criminal appeals.

Once again we must record our thanks to Mr W. Howard and the staff at the Justiciary Office for all their help in making available much of the material necessary to complete our accounts of the cases. Our publishers and printers also deserve our special thanks for all their assistance. We would also like to thank Mr Robert Collinson for his assistance in the preparation of the tables. Finally we would like to thank the following for permission to reproduce copyright material: Sue Moody and Jacqueline Tombs; and Stevens and Sons Ltd., for permission to reproduce the extract from Lord Normand's article which originally appeared in the *Law Quarterly Review*. Needless to say, the responsibility for errors or omissions herein is to be laid at our door.

We have included cases decided up to May 31, 1983.

Edinburgh,   C.H.W. GANE
June, 1983.   C.N. STODDART

CONTENTS

TABLE OF CASES

Page numbers of cases set out in the text are in **bold** type.

ix

TABLE OF STATUTES

Page numbers of excerpted material are in **bold** type.

xx

INTERNATIONAL TREATIES AND CONVENTIONS

Page numbers of excerpted material are in **bold** type.

REPORTS OF COMMITTEES etc

Page numbers of excerpted material are in **bold** type.

CHAPTER 1

GENERAL AIMS AND PRINCIPLES OF
SCOTTISH CRIMINAL PROCEDURE

It has not been the practice of the standard works on criminal procedure to articulate or examine the general aims or guiding principles of Scottish criminal procedure. A similar reluctance to state explicitly any general philosophy seems to have been shared by the Thomson Committee (though one member of that Committee has since attempted to summarise the Committee's general aims: Gordon, *The Criminal Justice (Scotland) Act 1980*, p. xiii). This seems rather surprising. In the first place, criminal procedure has received considerably more attention from Parliament and the courts than has the substantive criminal law of Scotland, and one might have expected their activities to have provoked some general analysis of their efforts. Secondly, there now exists a substantial body of international and conventional guidelines for standards in criminal procedure, inviting comparison (critical or otherwise) with the present state of Scottish criminal procedure.

This chapter attempts to identify and illustrate some of these basic principles. However, certain issues which might be considered fundamental are not dealt with here, since they may be more aptly dealt with in the context of specific topics in later chapters. But it would perhaps be valuable to bear in mind these issues when considering the remainder of the topics in this book.

a.   Minimum standards for criminal procedures

**The European Convention on
Human Rights**
"Article 3
No one shall be subjected to torture or to inhuman or degrading treatment or punishment . . .
Article 5
1.   Everyone has the right to liberty and security of person. No one shall be deprived of his liberty save in the following cases and in accordance with a procedure prescribed by law:

(a) the lawful detention of a person after conviction by a competent court;

(b) the lawful arrest or detention of a person for non-compliance with the lawful order of a court or in order to secure the fulfilment of any obligation prescribed by law;

(c) the lawful arrest or detention of a person effected for the purpose of bringing him before the competent legal authority on reasonable suspicion of having committed an offence or when it is reasonably considered necessary to prevent his committing an offence or fleeing after having done so;

(d) the detention of a minor by lawful order for the purpose of educational supervision or his lawful detention for the purpose of bringing him before the competent legal authority;

(e) the lawful detention of persons for the prevention of the spreading of infectious diseases, of persons of unsound mind, alcoholics or drug addicts or vagrants;

(f) the lawful arrest or detention of a person to prevent his effecting an unauthorised entry into the country or of a person against whom action is being taken with a view to deportation or extradition.

2.   Everyone who is arrested shall be informed promptly, in a language which he understands, of the reasons for his arrest and of any charge against him.

3.   Everyone arrested or detained in accordance with the provisions of paragraph 1(c) of this Article shall be brought promptly before a judge or other officer authorised by law to exercise judicial power and shall be entitled to trial within a reasonable time or to release pending trial. Release may be conditioned by guarantees to appear for trial.

4.   Everyone who is deprived of his liberty by arrest or detention shall be entitled to take proceedings by which the lawfulness of his detention shall be decided speedily by a court and his release ordered if the detention is not lawful.

5.   Everyone who has been the victim of arrest or detention in contravention of the provisions of this Article shall have an enforceable right to compensation.

Article 6

1.   In the determination of his civil rights and obligations or of any criminal charge against him, everyone is entitled to a fair and public hearing within a reasonable time by an independent and impartial tribunal established by law. Judgment shall be pronounced publicly but the press and public may be excluded from all or part of the trial in the interests of morals, public order or national security in a democratic society, where the interests of juveniles or the protection of the private life of the parties so require, or to the extent strictly necessary in the opinion of the court in special circumstances where publicity would prejudice the interests of justice.

2.   Everyone charged with a criminal offence shall be presumed innocent until proved guilty according to law.

3. Everyone charged with a criminal offence has the following minimum rights:

(a) to be informed promptly, in a language which he understands and in detail, of the nature and cause of the accusation against him;

(b) to have adequate time and facilities for the preparation of his defence;

(c) to defend himself in person or through legal assistance of his own choosing or, if he has not sufficient means to pay for legal assistance, to be given it free when the interests of justice so require;

(d) to examine or have examined witnesses against him and to obtain the attendance and examination of witnesses on his behalf under the same conditions as witnesses against him;

(e) to have the free assistance of an interpreter if he cannot understand or speak the language used in court."

NOTES

1. The Convention does not form part of Scots law, nor can it be relied upon as an aid to the construction of a statute of the United Kingdom Parliament: *Surjit Kaur* v. *Lord Advocate,* 1981 S.L.T. 322. (For a discussion of this case see Finnie, "The European Convention on Human Rights: Domestic Status" (1980) 25 J.L.S. 434 and Gane, "The European Convention on Human Rights—A Scottish View," [1982] Liverpool Law Rev. (IV), 169). Nevertheless, the right of individual petition to the European Commission on Human Rights under article 25 of the Convention is recognised by the United Kingdom, and a failure to observe these minimum standards secured by the Convention could be made the subject of such a petition. (For an outline of the procedures governing such applications, see Chap. 18, *post.*)

2. Similar rights are guaranteed by other international conventions or declarations. See, for example Part III of the International Covenant on Civil and Political Rights, adopted by the General Assembly of the United Nations in 1966. (See Brownlie, *Basic Documents in Human Rights,* pp. 130 *et seq.*) The extent to which Scottish criminal procedure satisfies, or exceeds, these requirements is noted at relevant points in later chapters.

b. *The principle of fairness*

It has been said that the "central theme of Scots criminal procedure is the need for fairness." (Gordon, *The Criminal Justice (Scotland) Act 1980,* p. xii.) But what does "fairness" mean in this context?

1. Miln v. Cullen
1967 J.C. 21

An accused person challenged the admissibility in evidence of a reply which he was alleged to have made in response to a question put to him by a police officer after a road accident. The trial judge upheld his objection and he was acquitted. The prosecutor appealed:

LORD WHEATLEY: " . . . The legal principles in this field of evidence were exhaustively canvassed in *Chalmers* v. *H. M. Advocate,* and it would appear from the arguments addressed to us by counsel for the respondent and other expressions of opinion voiced elsewhere that certain misconceptions have arisen from the decision and opinions in that case. If that be so, then the sooner these misconceptions are cleared, the better it is for all concerned. For instance, counsel for the respondent submitted that once a person came under suspicion, no questions by a police officer and *a fortiori* no answers by the suspect were admissible in evidence. In *Chalmers* the Lord Justice-General, supported by a Full Bench, reviewed the legal position at three different and progressive stages, namely, (1) where routine investigations are being carried out and the person ultimately accused has not fallen under suspicion, (2) where that person has fallen under suspicion but has not been cautioned and charged, and (3) where that person has been cautioned and charged. I need not rehearse all that was said by Lord Cooper in that context, but I deem it important to stress that in the variety of circumstances which might attend cases in each of these categories the basic and ultimate test is fairness. While the law of Scotland has always very properly regarded fairness to an accused person as being an integral part of the administration of justice, fairness is not a unilateral consideration. Fairness to the public is also a legitimate consideration, and in so far as police officers in the exercise of their duties are prosecuting and protecting the public interest, it is the function of the Court to seek to provide a proper balance to secure that the rights of individuals are properly preserved, while not hamstringing the police in their investigations of crime with a series of academic vetoes which ignore the realities and practicalities of the situation and discount completely the public interest."

Appeal allowed.

NOTES

1. Lord Wheatley's remarks were made in the context of the admissibility of statements made to the police. This has been the area in which the "principle" has been most frequently invoked (see the cases on police questioning discussed *post,* Chap. 5), but it is not the only area in which it has been referred to. See, for example, *Wilson* v. *Milne,* 1975 S.L.T. (Notes) 26 (application for a warrant to take blood samples from a suspect); *Stirling* v. *Herron,* 1976

S.L.T. (Notes) 2 (same judge sitting in consecutive trials arising out of same offence).

2. If for "fairness" one reads "balance" then Scots law falls into line with those systems which postulate a "fundamental balance" between the interests of the accused and the interests of the community at large. This notion of "balance" was recently considered in England, as the following extract shows:

2. Royal Commission on Criminal Procedure

"The concept of a fundamental balance

1.11. The terms of reference require us to examine the pre-trial criminal process and in so doing have regard 'to the interests of the community in bringing offenders to justice and to the rights and liberties of persons suspected or accused of crime'. And in his statement in the House of Commons the then Prime Minister expressed the view that there was 'a balance to be struck here between the interest of the whole community and the rights and liberties of the individual citizen . . . The Government', he said, 'consider that the time has come for the whole criminal process, from investigation to trial, to be reviewed with the fundamental balance in mind'. This is the central challenge which the Royal Commission faces.

1.12. At first sight the notion of a fundamental balance of the kind specified may appear unarguable, almost axiomatic, a matter of common sense; but further consideration of the matter raises a number of difficult, and perhaps, in the last analysis, insoluble questions. Can there be in any strict sense an equation drawn between the individual on one side and society on the other? Is the balance some sort of social contract between the individual and society? What are the rights and liberties of the individual which are assumed to provide part of the balance? Who gives them and what justifies them? Are they all of equal weight; all equally and totally negotiable or are some natural, absolute, fundamental, above the law, part of the human being's birthright? On the other side of this assumed balance, especially in an increasingly heterogeneous and specialised society, how is the interest of the whole community to be defined with any useful precision? And where does one see, where do the police see, the role of the police being applied; in one or other of the scales, or at the fulcrum, or both? What is clear is that in speaking of a balance between the interests of the community and the rights of the individual issues are being formulated which should be the concern not only of lawyers or police officers but of every citizen."

c. The presumption of innocence and the burden of proof

1. Slater v. H.M. Advocate
1928 J.C. 94

The appellant was charged with the murder of an old woman by striking her on the head with a hammer. The alleged motive for the killing was theft, the old lady having in her home a large quantity of jewellery. Evidence was led that the appellant lived by gambling and dealing in jewels. There was also evidence that he was supported by the earnings of a prostitute. These circumstances were remarked upon by the Lord Advocate in his speech to the jury as indicating a character depraved enough to commit the crime in question. In his charge to the jury, the presiding judge (Lord Guthrie) made the following remarks (*inter alia*):

"That is the kind of man, and you will see at once that his character is double-edged. The Lord Advocate takes it in his own favour, and he may quite fairly do so because, in the first place, a man of that kind has not the presumption of innocence in his favour which is not only a form in the case of every man but is a reality in the case of the ordinary man. Not only is every man presumed to be innocent, but the ordinary man has a strong presumption in his favour. Such a man may be capable of having committed this offence, and that man also may be capable from his previous character of exhibiting a callous behaviour after the offence. That was founded upon by Mr McClure. A man of such character does not exhibit the symptoms that a respectable man who has been goaded into some serious crime of violence does after the crime is over, and so you will consider that matter from both points of view, telling in favour of the prisoner and telling against him. [After dealing with the prisoner's financial circumstances his Lordship continued]—Gentlemen, all these circumstances are relevant to the case, but I think if you make up your minds to convict the prisoner you will be wise to be in this position; to be able to say to yourselves, 'we have disregarded his character, we have disregarded his financial circumstances, we have convicted him without regard to these.' Having reached that conclusion, it might very well strengthen the conclusion to reflect on the two elements that I have mentioned, but I do not think they should be factors in enabling you to reach a conclusion, although they might support it after the conclusion had been reached."

The jury returned a verdict of guilty of murder. The appellant appealed on the ground, *inter alia*, of misdirection by the trial judge:

LORD JUSTICE-GENERAL (CLYDE): "It would be absurd to hold that a miscarriage of justice occurs whenever, in the report of a speech by counsel to the jury, anything is found which can be read as involving either a misstatement of some fact, or as presenting a wrong view of the relevancy of some piece of evidence; and there are many other passages in the prosecutor's speech which put the case against the appellant independently of any reference to any of the points in the evidence which were other than strictly relevant. But the specialty in this trial was that some of the aspects of the life which the appellant lived were relevant, while others were irrelevant, to the question of his guilt. Thus, the circumstances that the appellant never had a dentistry practice in Glasgow, but dealt in some way in articles of jewellery, was relevant to the motive which, according to the prosecution, drew the appellant to Miss Gilchrist's house in search of the valuables she kept there. But that other aspect of his life, with its peculiarly heinous implications, in which he was shown to be partly dependent on the proceeds of prostitution, was as remote from any bearing on the question of his guilt as it was suggestive of prejudice against his case. Both the former aspects of the appellants's mode of life, and latter aspect, unavoidably came—together and immixed—to the knowledge of the jury; and this made the possibility of misunderstanding on the jury's part the more likely if the odious (and irrelevant) aspect was referred to in the prosecutor's address to the jury for any other purpose than to distinguish it from the others as one which was irrelevant, and which must be put entirely out of their consideration. So far from this, it was unfortunately made the point of the opening passage of the presentation of the case for the prosecution.

We have already indicated our view that the decision of the case—particularly with regard to the vital point of satisfactory proof of identity—presented an unusually difficult and narrow issue, upon which the balance of judgment might easily be influenced in one direction or the other. It follows that the danger of allowing the minds of the jury to be distracted by considerations which were at once so irrelevant and so prejudicial as those connected with the relations of the appellant to his female associates was real and great; and in these circumstances we are of opinion that the clearest and most unambiguous instruction by the presiding judge was imperatively demanded, to prevent the possibility of any misunderstanding on the part of the jury with regard to so important a matter. As appears from the shorthand report of the judge's charge, however, the matter in question was the only one on which the directions given to the jury were open to serious criticism. They did nothing to remove the erroneous impression which the opening passages of the speech for the prosecution might so easily have produced in the minds of the jury. On the contrary, they were calculated to confirm them. No distinction was made between those aspects of the appellant's life which were relevant to the charge of murdering Miss Gilchrist, and those which were not. It was pointed out—quite justly—that the considerations arising out of the appellant's mode of life, as exhibited at the trial, were double-edged, and were founded on (for different purposes) by the prosecution and the defence alike. But the jury were told that what is familiarly known as the presumption of innocence in criminal cases applied to the appellant (in the light of his ambiguous character) with less effect than it would have applied to a man whose character was not open to suspicion. This amounted, in our opinion, to a clear misdirection in law. The presumption of innocence applies to every person charged with a criminal offence in precisely the same way, and it can be overcome only by evidence relevant to prove the crime with the commission of which he is charged. The presumption of innocence is fundamental to the whole system of criminal prosecution, and it was a radical error to suggest that the appellant did not have the benefit of it to the same effect as any other accused person. It is true that an accused person of evil repute has not the advantage, enjoyed by an accused person of proved good character, of being able to urge on the jury in his defence the improbability that a person of good character would commit the crime charged. The passage in the charge at present under discussion is suggestive that this was what was in the judge's mind. But, however that may be, he put the appellant's bad character as a consideration upon which the prosecution was entitled to found as qualifying the ordinary presumption of innocence . . . That a man should support himself on the proceeds of prostitution is regarded by all men as blackguardism, but by many people as a sign of almost inhuman depravity. It cannot be affirmed that any members of the jury were misled by feelings of this kind in weighing the question of the appellant's guilt, but neither can it be affirmed that none of them was. What is certain is that the judge's charge entirely failed to give the jury the essential warning against allowing themselves to be misled by any feelings of the kind referred to. It is manifestly possible that, but for the prejudicial effect of denying to the appellant the full benefit of the presumption of innocence, and of allowing the point of his dependence on the immoral earnings of his partner to go to the jury as a point not irrelevant to his guilt of Miss Gilchrist's murder, the proportion of nine to five, for 'guilty' and 'not proven' respectively, might have been reversed."

Appeal allowed: conviction quashed.

NOTES

1. It follows from the presumption of innocence that the burden of proof in criminal cases rests on the prosecution. Normally there is no onus on the accused to establish his or her innocence. See the notes following *McKenzie* v. *H.M. Advocate, infra.*

2. The presumption of innocence is reinforced in a number of ways in the Scottish system. Thus, for example, it is not normally permissible for the prosecution to introduce evidence of the accused's previous convictions, if any, prior to the verdict being returned. See the 1975 Act, ss. 141(*f*), 346(*f*), 160(1) and (2) and 357(1)(*b*). The effect of wrongly introducing evidence of previous convictions is discussed *post,* Chap. 14.

2. McKenzie v. H.M. Advocate
1959 J.C. 32

The appellant was charged, *inter alia*, with the culpable homicide of a police constable. He was alleged to have been the driver of a lorry which struck and killed the deceased. There was no dispute that he was travelling in the vehicle at the time of the accident, that he was drunk at that time, and that shortly before the accident he was driving the vehicle. The allegation that he was the driver of the vehicle at the material time was, however, disputed. The presiding judge omitted to give the jury any directions on the burden or standard of proof in a criminal case. On appeal on the ground of misdirection:

LORD JUSTICE-CLERK (THOMSON) "The presumption of innocence is a fundamental tenet of our criminal procedure. It follows that the burden of proof rests on the Crown to displace this presumption. It is further a fundamental tenet that the standard by which this burden falls to be discharged is the establishing of the guilt of the accused beyond reasonable doubt. As this is a fundamental matter, judges ought, as a matter of course, to tell the jury about it. The emphasis and elaboration called for will depend on the circumstances of the case and on whether the evidence is overwhelming or narrow. The bare minimum is to say that it is for the Crown to prove the guilt of the accused beyond reasonable doubt. It is better, however, to split the direction into its two stages, first, that the burden of proof is on the Crown and, second, that the standard of proof required of the Crown is the establishing of guilt beyond reasonable doubt. This tends to emphasise that the second is truly the more important element. Some judges like to tell the jury about the presumption of innocence as that helps to make the jury understand the reason behind the direction. Some like to underline that ordinarily no burden of proof rests on the accused. Most judges give some explanation of what is meant by a reasonable doubt generally by pointing out that a merely speculative or academic doubt is not enough. Others tell the jury that if they have a reasonable doubt on any matter of moment they must give the accused the benefit of the doubt. That is a popular way of putting it which most juries are able to understand and to apply. But as we have said the amount of elaboration and emphasis is dictated by the nature of the case and predilection of the individual judge. We add that in our view it is desirable to adhere so far as possible to the traditional formula and to avoid experiments in reformulation.

In charging the jury the presiding Judge began, as was natural, by explaining the indictment to them . . . . Having given the jury a lucid exposition of the problems which faced them, the Judge passed immediately to the facts which also raised complicated issues with which he dealt with his customary thoroughness and clarity. The natural point at which to say something to the jury about the burden of proof and the standard required would have been at the point of transition but his not having done so then or later meant that the jury had no guidance on what was a fundamental issue. There was therefore, to use the words of Lord Justice-Clerk Aitchison, 'Non-direction amounting to misdirection.' As the same Judge said in a later case, 'It is very easy in a serious case for the most experienced judge to omit to give some direction that ought to have been given.'

As the non-direction here was on a fundamental matter the conviction cannot be sustained unless the proviso to section 2 (1) of the Criminal Appeal Act can be applied. The test for its application has been variously formulated and we do not attempt to do it again. It is usefully and succinctly stated by Viscount Simon in *Stirland* [[1944] A.C. 315] that 'the provision that the Court of Criminal Appeal may dismiss the appeal if they consider that no substantial miscarriage of justice has actually occurred in convicting the accused assumes a situation where a reasonable jury, after being properly directed, would, on the evidence properly admissible, without doubt convict.' It is a high and exacting test and we have come to be of the view, that it has not been passed in the present case."

> Appeal allowed; conviction quashed;
> conviction of contravention of section 15 of
> the Road Traffic Act 1930 substituted.

NOTES

1.   The burden of proof remains on the Crown even when the accused tables a special defence (other than insanity): *Lambie* v. *H.M. Advocate*, 1973 S.L.T. 219, *post*, Chap. 9.

2.   There are cases in which the accused incurs a burden of proof. Here it is appropriate to distinguish between a "legal" or "persuasive" burden and an "evidential" burden of proof. The former may only be discharged by the accused leading evidence which satisfies the court or the jury *on a balance of probabilities*. The latter may be discharged by the accused pointing to any evidence (whether introduced by the defence or the prosecution) which supports his case, or would give rise to a reasonable doubt as to guilt.

3.   A "legal" burden is imposed on the accused when he tables a special defence of insanity, or a plea of diminished responsibility, to establish his mental abnormality. This is said to follow from a presumption of sanity: *Lambie* v. *H.M. Advocate, supra*; *H.M. Advocate* v. *Mitchell*, 1951 J.C. 53. The courts appear to adopt a similar approach under the "doctrine" of "recent possession":

3.   **Fox v. Patterson**
1948 J.C. 104

The appellant was convicted of reset of a quantity of phosphor bronze, on a complaint charging him with theft of the metal. The appellant apparently bought the metal from a stranger at a cattle market in Glasgow. He resold it, openly, to a third party. When he discovered that he was suspected of having stolen the metal, he offered to reimburse the purchaser. In convicting the appellant, the sheriff relied on the fact that the appellant had been in *de recenti* possession of stolen property without being able to give a satisfactory explanation of his possession. On appeal:

LORD JUSTICE-GENERAL (COOPER): "When applied with due regard to its limitations, the rule of recent possession of stolen goods is salutory and sensible: but, if its limitations are not observed, the cardinal presumption of innocence may easily be transformed into a rash assumption of guilt. The rule and its limitations are stated in substantially the same sense by Hume (Commentaries, vol. i, p. 111), Alison (Criminal Law, vol. i, pp. 320 *et seq.*) and Dickson (Evidence, (Grierson's ed.) vol. i, secs. 73 and 157); and to these classical citations I add a quotation aptly given by Dickson (sec. 73) from Bentham; 'Nothing can be more persuasive,' he says, 'than the circumstance of possession commonly is, when corroborated by other criminative circumstances; nothing more inconclusive, supposing it to stand alone. . . . Possession of the jewel, *actual* possession, may thus belong to half a dozen different persons at the same time; and as to *antecedent* possession, the number of possible successive possessors is manifestly beyond all limit.'

If the rule is to have full effect in shifting the onus from the prosecution to the accused and raising a presumption of guilt which the accused must redargue or fail, three conditions must concur:—(a) that the stolen goods should be found in the possession of the accused; (b) that the interval between the theft of the goods and their discovery in the accused's possession should be short—how short I need not in this case inquire; and (c) that there should be 'other criminative circumstances' over and above the bare fact of possession. If all these conditions are not present—if, for instance, the interval between the theft and the discovery is prolonged, or if the accused has only had temporary possession of the goods and has parted with them normally and openly—the facts which can be proved may well constitute ingredients (*quantum valeant*) in the case, and may combine with other factors to enable the Crown to establish guilt. But, unless all three conditions concur, the accused cannot be required to accept the full onus of positively excluding every element of guilt. Even when they concur, the weight of the resulting presumption, and the evidence required to elide it, will vary from case to case."

Conviction quashed.

NOTES

1.   For further examples of this approach see: *Simpson* v. *H.M. Advocate*, 1952 J.C. 1, *Brannan* v. *H.M. Advocate*, 1954 J.C. 87, *Cryans* v. *Nixon*, 1955 J.C. 1, *Wightman* v. *H.M. Advocate*, 1959 J.C. 44, *Cameron* v. *H.M. Advocate*, 1959 J.C. 59, *Cassidy* v. *McLeod*, 1981 S.C.C.R. 270. *Cf. McLeod* v. *Mason and Ors.*, 1981 S.L.T. (Notes) 109.

2.   The doctrine of recent possession is open to the fundamental objection that it converts a normal inference of fact into a rule of law. See, Gordon, "The Burden of Proof on the Accused," 1968 S.L.T. (News) 29, 37; Macphail, *Research Paper on the Law of Evidence of Scotland*, para. 22.13; Renton and Brown, para. 18-02. Indeed, it is even open to doubt if the "rule" exists at all, beyond imposing on the accused an "evidential" burden. Certainly, it is

difficult to see how "the weight of the resulting presumption, and the evidence required to elide it" could "vary from case to case" if a full "legal" burden is imposed upon the accused.

4. Earnshaw v. H.M. Advocate
1982 S.L.T. 179; 1981 S.C.C.R. 279

LORD JUSTICE-GENERAL (EMSLIE): "After trial on indictment the appellant was found guilty of five charges arising from a road accident with tragic consequences which took place on the night of 22nd December 1979 when the appellant, who was driving a badly loaded articulated lorry downhill into Hurlford, lost control of it at a left-hand bend. The lorry then 'jack-knifed' and travelled, partly on its side, to collide with, and roll over on top of, a motor-car coming in the opposite direction. The most serious of these charges was charge 1 in its alternative form, namely, contravention of section 1 of the Road Traffic Act 1972—causing the death, by reckless driving, of the three occupants of the motor-car. Charges 2, 3 and 4 libelled contraventions of section 5(1), section 25(1) and (4) and section 25(2) and (4) of the Act respectively, and charge 5 was a charge of contravention of section 9(3) of the Act. In particular charge 5 libelled that having been the driver of the lorry involved in the accident described in charge 1 and having been arrested following a positive breath test required under section 8(2) of the Act, the appellant failed without reasonable excuse to provide the specimen for a laboratory test lawfully required of him in terms of section 9.

This appeal against conviction relates only to charge 5 and the amended ground is in these terms:

'That there has been a miscarriage of justice in that the learned trial judge misdirected the jury in law in that he directed the jury that there was a burden of proof on the defence to prove that there was a reasonable excuse for failure under section 9 of the Road Traffic Act 1972 to provide a specimen for a laboratory test.'

In course of his directions to the jury upon the issues for their decision under charge 5 the trial judge referred to certain evidence which had been given and left it to the jury to say whether the appellant's admitted failure to provide the required specimen for a laboratory test was a failure with or without reasonable excuse. He then went on to say this: 'It is for the accused to show that he had a reasonable excuse, not for the Crown to show that he hadn't, but as in every case, whether there is a burden of proof on the defence, that burden can be satisfied on a lower standard of proof than that lying upon the Crown to establish guilt. If an accused satisfies you on a balance of probability that he had a reasonable excuse, that is enough for you to acquit him on this charge, but I am bound to say that if you accept that the requirement was properly made, it is difficult to see how what he said could be a reasonable excuse. You have also to consider of course whether he was too dazed to apply his mind properly to the matter and if you think he was, then of course you could acquit him on that ground.'

In the submission of counsel for the appellant the quoted passage contains a material misdirection in law. The offence created by section 9(3) is committed only if the accused person fails to provide the specimen of blood or urine 'without reasonable excuse'. It is for the Crown to establish this. In particular there is no onus upon an accused person who has failed to supply such a specimen to prove that he had a reasonable excuse for that failure. This has for long been settled in England where the matter of onus has been explained in various ways. For example, in *Regina v Clarke (Christopher)* [1969] 1 W.L.R. 1109 Geoffrey Lane J. (as he then was) giving the judgment of the court said this at p. 1113 G-H: 'It is true, of course, that there must be some evidence of such an excuse [and here he is referring to what might amount to a reasonable excuse in law] before the necessity arises of leaving the matter to the jury at all: however, once such evidence does emerge it is for the prosecution to eliminate the existence of such a defence to the satisfaction of the jury.' Further, for example, the matter was disposed of thus by Lord Parker C.J. in *Rowland v Thorpe* [1970] 3 All E.R. 192 at p. 197c: 'Of course, once the defence is raised of reasonable excuse, it is for the prosecution in every case to negative it. . . .' The question of the onus of proof in a section 9(3) case has never been the subject of judicial decision in Scotland but, as counsel for the appellant very properly pointed out, there are sentences in opinions in two Scots cases which, although clearly obiter, might at first sight appear to contradict his submission. The cases are *Milne v Elliot, 1974* S.L.T. (Notes) 71 and *MacDonald v McKenzie*, 1975 S.L.T. 190. In *Milne* the relevant passage which found its echo in *MacDonald* was this: 'If a conviction is not to follow a refusal to supply both blood and urine, it is for the accused to show that he had a reasonable excuse for not providing a sample of either blood or urine.' This passage was in the context of a case in which there was no suggestion in the evidence that there was any excuse at all for the accused's failure to supply a sample of urine and, properly understood, it means only that if a conviction is not to follow upon proof of *refusal* to supply a sample of either blood or urine it is for the accused to introduce the issue of alleged reasonable excuse. Upon the whole matter there was a misdirection by the trial judge in the present case and it was plainly a misdirection upon a fundamental matter. The verdict of guilt against the appellant on charge 5 was by a majority and that misdirection is fatal to the appellant's conviction on that charge.

For the Crown the learned advocate-depute accepted that it was for the Crown, in a charge laid under section 9(3), to establish that there has been a failure, without reasonable excuse, to supply the relevant specimens. It is no doubt for the accused to introduce the issue of reasonable excuse if he considers that there was such an excuse for an admitted failure, but the burden of proof of the commission of the offence, viz., failure to provide the required specimen 'without reasonable excuse', rests on the Crown throughout. In these circumstances it was accepted that the trial judge did misdirect the jury in the respect complained of. This, however, was not fatal to the conviction as the appellant has contended because there was no evidence of any circumstances capable in law of amounting to reasonable excuse. Whether any facts are capable of constituting a 'reasonable excuse' within the meaning of section 9(3) is a question of law and under reference to the case of *Glickman* v *MacKinnon*, 1978 J.C. 81 and the English cases therein considered the trial judge ought to have directed the jury that there was no evidence before them which they were entitled to treat as evidence of 'reasonable excuse' for the appellant's admitted failure to comply with the requirement made under section 9. Following the course taken in the case of *Regina* v *Clarke* it should be held that there was, accordingly, no miscarriage of justice in spite of the misdirection, and the conviction should be allowed to stand.

We have no difficulty at all in deciding that counsel for the appellant is well founded in his criticism of the charge of the trial judge. In section 9 Parliament did not make failure to provide the relevant laboratory specimen an offence subject to a statutory defence of reasonable excuse which it is for the accused to establish. The language of section 9(3) makes it clear that a person is guilty of the offence which it created only if, without reasonable excuse, he fails to provide the required specimen. In these circumstances, as the Crown accepts, no charge of contravention of section 9(3) will be relevant unless it libels failure to provide the specimen *without reasonable excuse* (the emphasis is ours). This is what must be established by the Crown in every such case and the burden of proof lies on the Crown throughout. In most or at least many cases there will be no suggestion that there was any excuse at all—far less any reasonable excuse—for a driver's failure or refusal to comply with his obligation under section 9(1) or (2). In those cases, however, in which there is some evidence of some fact or circumstance which could in law amount to 'reasonable excuse' the trial judge, where the charge is tried on indictment, should not only remind the jury that it is for the Crown to satisfy them beyond reasonable doubt that there was a failure without reasonable excuse, but should go on to direct them that if they accept that evidence, or if that evidence casts reasonable doubt on whether the alleged failure was without reasonable excuse they must acquit. In the result, upon this chapter of the appeal, we agree with the courts in England that it is not for the accused who has failed to provide a required specimen to prove that he had a reasonable excuse for that failure. We do not, however, with respect, adopt the language of Geoffrey Lane J. in *Clarke* or that of Lord Parker C.J. in *Rowland* to the effect that 'reasonable excuse' is a defence which it is for the Crown to negative or to eliminate."

Conviction of contravention
of section 9(3) quashed.

NOTES

1. A large number of statutes provide that the burden of proving certain matters (such as lawful authority or reasonable excuse for conduct otherwise unlawful) rests upon the accused. See, for example, the Prevention of Crime Act 1953, s. 1(1), the Misuse

of Drugs Act 1971, s. 28(2), and the Contempt of Court Act 1981, s. 3(3). The terminology of such provisions varies. Some create an offence, and add to it a defence. In such cases the defence must be established by the accused. Others, as here, include the absence of exculpation as a factor in the definition of the offence. In such cases there is only an "evidential" burden on the accused.

2. Section 66 of the 1975 Act provides:
"Any exception, exemption, proviso, excuse, or qualification, whether it does or does not accompany in the same section the description of the offence in the statute or order creating the offence, may be proved by the accused, but need not be specified or negatived in the indictment, and no proof in relation to such exception, exemption, proviso, excuse, or qualification shall be required on behalf of the prosecution."
Why did the Crown not rely on this provision? See *Kennedy* v *Clark*, 1970 J.C. 53.

3. Notwithstanding the general principle that the burden of proof rests generally on the prosecution, it may happen in some cases that the Crown case is so strong that conviction is inevitable unless the accused provides some explanation consistent with innocence. (See *Hardy* v. *H.M. Advocate*, 1938 J.C. 144; *McLeod* v. *Mason and Ors.*, *supra*; *Tallis* v. *H.M. Advocate*, 1982 S.C.C.R. 91. In such a case, however, only an evidential burden is imposed on the accused. It is a misdirection for the court to suggest that there is any legal onus on the accused to prove his innocence: *Tallis* v. *H.M. Advocate*, *supra*.

d. The right to a fair trial
Whatever else the rules of criminal procedure achieve, they must guarantee the right to a fair trial. But what is included in the notion of a fair trial? The principle is universally acknowledged, but when one examines its application wide variations appear. A tribunal free from bias may be axiomatic. But what about the right to legal representation, freedom from prejudicial publicity, or the effect of possibly oppressive conduct by the prosecutor?

1. McDevitt v. McLeod
1982 S.C.C.R. 282

LORD JUSTICE-CLERK (WHEATLEY): "The appellant was charged with a breach of the peace which was said to have taken place on board the vessel plying between Larne in Northern Ireland and Stranraer in Wigtownshire. It is accepted, and it could not have been otherwise, that there was abundant evidence before the bench of justices to warrant a conviction in the case. In particular there was a statement made by the appellant in answer to a caution and charge which can only be interpreted as an admission that he had committed a breach of the peace. The only point raised in the appeal is to be found in question 3 which relates to the fact that certain remarks were made by the chairman of the bench of justices which indicated that the appellant could not have had a fair trial and that accordingly the conviction recorded against him should be quashed. What happened was this. The chairman after the accused had been found guilty and sentenced said, 'I personally was a passenger on the boat that night and was in the public bar area from time to time. There were many supporters on board who were well behaved and a tribute to Scottish football. I may say that, to my mind, the police carried out their most onerous duties during the period in question in exemplary fashion.' The reference to the police was to the conduct of the police as found in findings in fact in relation to their apprehension of the appellant and the circumstances antecedent thereto that led to the charge of breach of peace. Before turning to consider whether or not those remarks were in the context and the circumstances of the case sufficient to vitiate the conviction, I would like to stress that it was most unfortunate and indeed improper for the chairman of the bench of justices to have sat in this case at all, in that he admittedly was present when the incidents took place which gave rise to the offence that was charged. Since the charge was defended and there was liable to be a conflict of evidence, as indeed there was, between witnesses for the prosecution in the form of the police officers and the defence, including at least the appellant himself, the chairman was not in a position to give the appearance of impartiality in that he himself had witnessed at least some of the incidents. It would have been much better if he had never sat at all, and I trust that such a situation will not occur again. However, that having been said, one has got to consider whether the fact that he did sit was in the circumstances here present sufficient to warrant the quashing of the conviction. In this particular case I am satisfied that the evidence was so clear that the appellant had committed the offence libelled including, as I have indicated, an admission by himself that he had committed it that I cannot think that the interests of justice would be served by quashing this conviction. In each case it is a balance whether or not conduct can so affect the conviction as to warrant its quashing. The balance here, in my opinion, remains in favour of sustaining the conviction, and accordingly I move you Lordships to answer question 3 in the negative and refuse the appeal."

Appeal refused.

NOTE

The interest of this case lies in the fact that there was no suggestion of malice or oppression on the part of the chairman of the justices. This was very much a case in which there was a risk of justice not being seen to be done.

What would have been required to tip the balance in favour of quashing the conviction? What would have been the outcome if the appellant had been acquitted at first instance? And what if he had been highly critical of the police action?

2. Atkins v. London Weekend Television Ltd.
1978 J.C. 48

The respondents were responsible for the transmission throughout the United Kingdom of a programme called *Weekend World* which contained a feature entitled "The Living Dead". This feature discussed the issues surrounding the provision of life-support measures for seriously brain-damaged patients. Reference was made in the feature to certain well-known cases of this kind. The feature began, however, with detailed references to the petitioner who was due to stand trial the following day at Edinburgh sheriff court on charges of assault to the danger of life. The petitioner, a nurse in Edinburgh Royal Infirmary, was charged with having twice attempted to stop the air supply to a patient in the hospital's intensive care unit. As well as giving details of the charge against the petitioner, the respondents also transmitted pictures of her taken admittedly without her permission.

The petitioner presented a petition to the *nobile officium* of the High Court craving that the court prohibit the respondents and others from broadcasting or publishing any material calculated to prejudice, or giving rise to possible prejudice to, any future trial of the petitioner.

LORD JUSTICE-GENERAL (EMSLIE): " . . . We come now to the question of whether the complaint of contempt of court has been made out. The offence alleged by the petitioner consists, to quote the words of Lord President Clyde in *Johnson* v. *Grant* 1923 S.C. 789 at p. 790, 'in interfering with the administration of the law, in impeding and perverting the course of justice'. It is the paramount duty of this Court to ensure that persons charged on indictment in Scotland shall receive a fair and impartial trial. Accordingly, where any person has been charged with crime and is awaiting trial 'the public dissemination of insinuations or suggestions capable of prejudicing the public mind and the minds of prospective jurors' with regard to the impending trial 'cannot be tolerated for it is in our view prejudicial to the interests of justice' [*vide* the opinion of the Lord Justice-General in *M'Alister*, p. 16]. The essence of a charge of contempt of the kind with which this petition is concerned is, therefore, the allegation that what was said and done was likely to prejudice the fair and impartial trial of the accused person and, thus, to be prejudicial to the interests of justice itself.

In this case the question for us is whether the contents of the programme complained of were such as to give rise to a real risk of prejudice to the fair and impartial trial of the petitioner on the charges on which she stood indicted . . . and we must approach this question as a jury would and examine the programme as it was likely to be understood by those who saw and heard it.

Mr Bruce with characteristic skill sought to persuade us that neither the feature as a whole nor any of its constituent parts created any such risk. Leaving aside the references to the petitioner the discussion was, he said, and we can readily accept this, quite unobjectionable in that it bore to be and was a serious debate upon a live question of immediate public concern. A reference to the impending trial of the petitioner and the nature of the charge against her could not by itself be an offence against the interests of justice for the charge and the fact that she was to be tried in Edinburgh on 14th November 1977 were public facts. We readily accept this also. The petitioner does not aver that the showing of her photograph was likely, by itself, to prejudice her in her defence and the feature as a whole involved no detailed discussion of the petitioner's case and it made no attempt to prejudge her guilt or innocence. Indeed express mention was made of her plea of not guilty. Even if there had been no reference made to the petitioner at all the feature might have had just the same effect upon the petitioner's trial.

The complaint is, however, that the showing of photographs of the petitioner and the particular references to her in sound made all the difference and converted a discussion of what was already a matter of public interest and comment into an act of contempt. So far as the photographs were concerned, said Mr Bruce, there is no hard and fast rule that the publication of a photograph of an accused person will always constitute contempt. We have no difficulty in accepting this proposition and we accept, too, the further proposition that the publication of a photograph of an accused person will only constitute contempt where a question of identification has arisen or may arise and where the publication is calculated to prejudice the prospects of a fair trial.

In our judgment there is not the slightest doubt that the references to the petitioner in the context of this particular feature as a whole were in the highest degree likely to prejudice the petitioner's prospects of a fair and impartial trial. We have seen and heard a videotape recording of the introduction to the programme and of the entire feature. For the purposes of considering the arguments of parties we have been supplied with, and we have had an opportunity of reading, the transcript of the sound track. The feature was specifically concerned, and no doubt properly concerned, to debate the serious issue on which medical opinion is divided, namely whether or not life support for certain patients who have suffered severe brain damage should, as matter of policy, be withdrawn. In course of that feature it was no doubt highly relevant and perfectly legitimate to refer to the two very recent cases, one in England and one in the United States, in which a decision to switch off the patient's breathing machine was deliberately taken. To introduce references to the case of Elizabeth Semple and to the petitioner's trial on the indictment the very next day was, however, utterly indefensible and irresponsible for the references were made in such a way as to imply that this was another case of the same kind as those of

Caroline Wilkinson and Karen Quinlan and, it may be, the latest example of actings by a nurse towards a patient in implement of a view held by eminent medical men in Scotland that withdrawal of life support for certain victims of severe brain damage is desirable and morally justifiable. 'A jury at the Sheriff's (*sic*) Court in the city will be told that Nurse Atkins twice tried to block the air supply to a 13-year-old girl in her care,' said the commentator. Contrary to Mr Bruce's submission that this would be understood as no more than a reference to the allegations in the charges this sentence was, in our judgment, calculated to convey and likely to convey to the public mind in Scotland, and to the minds of prospective jurors in Scotland, that the evidence would be that the petitioner had committed the acts charged, and the sting is not removed by the bare mention of the fact that she 'will plead not guilty to the charges' because the commentator immediately added but (the underlining is ours) 'by the middle of the week the whole country will be talking about the issues raised in this case.' We accept from Mr Bruce that the references to the petitioner were included for the sole purpose of giving topicality to the programme and, in short, we hold that this gratuitous introduction of the references to the petitioner, in the context of the feature as a whole and, in particular, in close company with the references to the Wilkinson and Quinlan cases, contained the clear insinuation that the real if not the only question which would arise out of the petitioner's trial would be whether she was medically and morally justified in committing the acts charged. In fact the petitioner's plea of not guilty necessarily raised the question of the identity of the person, if any, who attempted to block the child's air supply as well as the initial question whether any such acts as those charged were perpetrated at all by any person. It was therefore essential for the Crown to identify the petitioner as the perpetrator. In the whole circumstances the inclusion of the photographs but, more importantly, the verbal references to her in the context of the feature as a whole, were likely to be highly damaging to the prospects of a fair and impartial trial of the petitioner in Scotland. The Lord Advocate has informed us that in his opinion the conduct complained of on the part of those responsible for the feature 'The Living Dead' undoubtedly constituted a material interference with the due and proper administration of criminal justice in Scotland. We agree with him. Indeed, in our judgment, what was said and shown with reference to the petitioner in this feature was so prejudicial to the proper administration of justice in Scotland that we entertain the gravest doubt whether fair and impartial trial of the petitioner on the charges of assaulting Elizabeth Semple is now possible, however carefully the trial Judge may direct the jury. However that may be, and we are sure that the Lord Advocate will consider the question of further prosecution of the petitioner with anxious care, we say without hesitation that the complaint of contempt of court by those responsible for the feature 'The Living Dead' has been shown to be well founded."

Respondents held to be in contempt.

NOTES

1. The Contempt of Court Act 1981 now provides a statutory test for contempt by "publications" (which include "any speech, writing, broadcast or other communication which is addressed to the public at large or any section of the public": 1981 Act, s. 2(1)). The strict liability rule provided for by section 1 of the Act applies to any publication which "creates a substantial risk that the course of justice in the proceedings in question will be seriously impeded or prejudiced," provided that the "proceedings" are "active" 2(2), (3), and Schedule 1. The changed test does not, of course, affect the premises upon which this form of contempt is based.

2. By section 5 of the 1981 Act a publication made as or as part of a discussion in good faith of public affairs or other matters of general public interest will not be treated as a contempt under the strict liability rule "if the risk of impediment or prejudice to particular legal proceedings is merely incidental to the discussion". Although the test for contempt under the Act is now rather different from that put forward in *Atkins*, it seems likely that the respondents would still be held in contempt under the new test.

3. Prejudice arising from pre-trial publicity may be pleaded as a bar to trial: *Stuurman* v. *H.M. Advocate*, 1980 J.C. 111, *post*, Chap. 9. As yet, no such plea has been successfully maintained (and see the comments of Lord Avonside in *Stuurman* as to whether such a plea would have succeeded had the petitioner in *Atkins* been tried: *ibid.*, p.117). The new test for contempt requires a *substantial* risk that the course of justice will be *seriously* impeded or prejudiced. Could the court consistently hold that there had been contempt under that rule in a given case, and yet hold that it was not oppressive to insist in prosecuting the accused? (The risk of prejudice must, after all, mean a risk of prejudice which is in existence at the time of the trial.)

3. H.M. Advocate v. Waddell and Another
High Court, 1 December 1976, *unreported*

The accused were charged, *inter alia*, with the murder of an elderly woman. During the course of his charge to the jury the presiding judge, Lord Robertson, made the following remarks. The circumstances of the case are fully set out in his Lordship's charge. For earlier proceedings in this case, see *post*, Chap. 2

LORD ROBERTSON: "Members of the jury, this has been described by both counsel as a unique case, and it certainly has been a remarkable case, I think unprecedented in the annals of Scottish justice. The bald fact is that a crime was committed at 2 Blackburn Place, Ayr, on the night of 5, 6 July

1969, seven-and-a-half years ago, a vicious robbery following upon which Mrs Ross died. I shall deal later with the question of murder in law, but at the moment I assume, for the purposes of what I have to say that that is what happened, nobody in fact disputes it.

The remarkable thing about this is in the sequel. On 20 October 1969, at the High Court in Edinburgh there was a trial at which Patrick Meehan was charged with the robbery and, inter alia the murder of Mrs Ross, and after a long trial in which a large number of witnesses gave evidence for the Crown and also for the defence a jury returned a verdict of guilty upon the evidence which appeared amply to justify the verdict. An appeal was taken and was carefully considered by the Court of Criminal Appeal; the appeal failed. Thereafter the convicted man went to prison and from time to time tried to re-open the case in various ways, all of which attempts failed. But some public support was whipped up over a period of years and a campaign developed, from motives which are not entirely clear, but may be imagined, on behalf of Meehan. I shall deal later with some of the aspects of that campaign, but it appears that there have been undesirable consequences, most particularly in the use of money and inducements which have encouraged lying and fabricated stories, and also unscrupulous and biased questioning and the like, no doubt by well-meaning persons, which has interfered with due processes of law and the administration of justice in this country.

For a long time the Lord Advocate and the Crown authorities paid no attention to this clamour, but in 1976 a decision was apparently taken to advise the Queen to give a Free Pardon to Meehan. This was a quite unprecedented step which has had far-reaching consequences. The reasons for this decision have not become apparent in this trial. It is well to stress, ladies and gentlemen, that this decision was a decision by the executive, not reached by due process of law. Such action, ladies and gentlemen, runs counter to the whole basis of justice in Scotland, which is trial by jury and by proper process of law in independent courts. If the executive are going to interfere in such a way with the administration of justice by due process of law, there is no end to it and one of the great bulwarks of liberty in this country is threatened, because of course it could be done in every case or any case. This decision was all the more strange because the due processes of law were not exhausted before the decision was taken.

In a somewhat similar case, the celebrated case of Oscar Slater in 1928, this was not the procedure adopted by the then Secretary of State. The trial of Oscar Slater for the murder of an old lady in Glasgow in 1909 resulted in his conviction, sentence to death and reprieve. The evidence in that case against the accused it is safe to say was weak and the verdict marginal. At that time there was no Court of Criminal Appeal in Scotland and it is possible that had there been such a court the conviction might well not have stood at the time. Over the years there was a continual rumbling of criticism of the verdict, and after the Court of Criminal Appeal had been set up in 1926 the Secretary of State for Scotland remitted the case back to the new court for a reappraisal and reconsideration, including the hearing of fresh evidence which had become available in the interval. The court, after a prolonged hearing of the fresh evidence and reconsideration of the whole case, finally, in 1928 quashed the conviction of Oscar Slater, as it happened upon a legal point relating to the judge's charge and not on the effect of the new evidence. That procedure, ladies and gentlemen, was open to the Secretary of State in the present case and one might have thought would have been an appropriate step to take; at least the court might have been enabled to examine critically any new evidence placed before it with regard to the first verdict of the jury. But without exhausting this obvious process of law the Crown in the present case has seen fit to advise a pardon for the convicted man without due process of law, in itself a rare step, and then have gone on to charge a different person with the same crime. In other words, the Crown who had asked one jury to hold it proved beyond reasonable doubt that Meehan was guilty, now ask another jury to hold that Waddell is guilty or was guilty beyond reasonable doubt of the same crime.

This has created a most unusual and, I think, unfortunate situation. In the first place it has put into question the legal meaning and effect of the Free Pardon granted to Meehan about which there was extensive legal debate at the outset of this trial. The Lord Advocate has stated that this question has never been resolved before. For my part I have always thought, in the ordinary use of language, that if you pardon someone, you pardon them for something that they have done, and not for something that they haven't done. This indeed is an interpretation supported by the actual terms of the Free Pardon itself which appear to free Meehan from the consequences of the conviction and not from the conviction itself. It certainly doesn't quash the conviction by due process of law. This is borne out by the fact that the conviction against Meehan has been duly extracted and lodged in process in the present trial, so the Crown is endeavouring to persuade you to convict a man for a crime for which another man has been convicted by a proper process of law and whose conviction has never been quashed by due process of law.

Ladies and gentlemen, when this question was raised at the outset of the trial I considered it very carefully and, as you know, convened a larger court in order that the whole matter should be more fully argued. The result was that, with the assistance of two other judges, I reached the conclusion that the decision whether to prosecute a second man for a crime for which another man had been properly convicted by due process of law and his conviction had never been quashed was one for the Lord Advocate, in the exercise of his discretion, and was not a legal bar, but the circumstances in which an unprecedented step should be taken should only, in my view, be very exceptional. I understood the Lord Advocate to say repeatedly that save in very exceptional circumstances it would be unconscionable for him to proceed against a second man and I had rather expected that he would have acted accordingly, but he has not done so, and now asks you to convict another man for the same crime. This is a decision, ladies and gentlemen, which I think has far-reaching consequences. The most important of these is upon the basic fairness of any trial of Waddell, the second man, in these circumstances. It is of the very essence of the administration of justice in Scotland that an accused man comes into court without any previous publicity or speculation upon the crime and his responsibility for it. Thus in Scotland, before a criminal trial there is no preliminary hearing and no advance publicity of any kind.

Furthermore, it is fundamental that no reference is made to any previous convictions or criminal record that he may have. All this is contained on the vital principle known as the presumption of innocence. Some people think we go too far in this and that a man's previous record should be before a jury, but that isn't the present law. It is, for instance, an interesting speculation in the present case, what would have been the reaction of the jury in Meehan's trial if his life-long record of crime of housebreaking and proud claim to be an expert safeblower had been before them. Not a whisper of this of course was before them when they convicted him, but in this trial of Waddell he has very properly, and understandably put in a special defence of impeachment against Meehan, saying in effect that the murder was committed by Meehan and Griffiths and the Crown have gone on record some months ago, having taken steps publicly to free Meehan from the consequences of his conviction and has repeatedly stated, or impliedly rather, stated that Meehan did not commit the crime. Indeed, there has been in addition some extensive publicity in the media over a period of months, very often referring to Meehan, in terms such as—a man wrongly convicted of the murder. Members of the jury, there is no legal justification whatever in saying that Meehan was wrongly convicted of the murder, and indeed having heard all the evidence in this case you may well have come to the clear conclusion, although I don't pre-judge it because I will be dealing with this in detail later, but you may well have come to the clear conclusion that he was in fact rightly convicted as another jury found seven-and-a-half years ago. I shall deal of course with this later in some more detail, but at the moment I am stressing the basic background unfairness to this trial so far as Waddell is concerned and my belief that for this reason alone the Lord Advocate in the exercise of his discretion might well have not proceeded in this prosecution or asked you to convict Waddell.

This consideration is perhaps emphasised by the tendency which I think has become apparent from time to time in the course of the trial, for the Lord Advocate to treat the case as if it were a public inquiry into the death of Mrs Ross. Members of the jury, this is not a public inquiry, no doubt had the Secretary of State wanted, he could have set up a public inquiry of some sort into the whole affair, but he has not done so. This is the criminal trial of Waddell and he is entitled to all the rights of any other citizen accused of a crime. The presumption of innocence, proper observance of the rules of evidence, the rights to fairness, etc.

I also cannot refrain in passing from commenting upon the way in which this case has been handled in some particulars, especially in regard to the very senior and experienced policemen who have, over a period of years, been maligned, defamed and accused by Meehan of very grave dereliction of duty, perjury, planting of evidence, and the like, without as it has turned out any shred of justification whatsoever. I should have thought that in the absence of any evidence to support these allegations the Crown would have at least led these witnesses and supported them in their denial, instead, as we saw on Monday, forcing the defence to lead them as witnesses and then attempt to demean them by cross-examination.

Ladies and gentlemen, the discharge of its criminal duty by the Crown in Scotland has always been characterised by the highest standards of fairness and equity, and I can only hope that there will be no slipping from these standards.

Ladies and gentlemen, I should like you at the outset to remember that Waddell is entitled to be treated just like any other citizen, with complete fairness, bearing in mind the presumption of innocence, and I would invite you, if you think that all that has gone before has prevented him from receiving such treatment, to acquit him on that ground alone, without any further consideration, if you think he is prejudiced by what has gone before. If you do not take that step initially then I direct you to put out of your mind all considerations of the kind I have mentioned and, in particular, the decision of the Crown to proceed with the case after having apparently, with full publicity and without due process of law pre-judged it."

Verdict: not guilty.

NOTES

1. It is impossible to tell, of course, whether the jury's verdict was returned in response to Lord Robertson's invitation or on the basis of the evidence presented to them.

2. Just how far Lord Robertson's remarks could be developed is not clear. It should be remembered that the case was quite exceptional (as his Lordship pointed out), and many of his comments can be read as marks of censure on the conduct of the Crown as much as anything else. Certainly, the invitation to the jury to acquit if they thought Waddell had not been dealt with fairly seems a novel extension of the fairness principle, or of the right to a fair trial.

3. The whole ghastly affair of the "Ayr Murder" and its sequel(s) was made the subject of a searching inquiry by Lord Hunter: *Report of Inquiry into the whole circumstances of the murder of Mrs Rachel Ross*, etc., House of Commons Paper 444, July 1982.

e.   The right to a speedy trial

A guarantee of a speedy determination of the issue of guilt or innocence is generally regarded as a basic requirement of any system of criminal justice. (*Cf.* Gordon, *The Criminal Justice (Scotland) Act 1980*, p. xiii.) Various rules exist in Scots law, both in solemn and summary proceedings, to ensure that there is no undue delay in bringing an accused to trial. These rules are discussed at the relevant points in the examination of solemn and summary proceedings, *post*, Chaps. 7 and 11.

f. *The right to legal representation*

There are really two aspects to this issue. There is first of all the question of access to legal representation, and the extent to which such representation is available to those who cannot afford to pay for it. There is in Scotland a long tradition of the provision of free legal representation by the legal profession (the first statute in this area was passed in 1424). In *Thomson* v. *H.M. Advocate*, 1959 J.C. 15 the Lord Justice-Clerk suggested that the provision of free legal assistance for those unable to afford it was one aspect of ensuring a fair trial. Today, legal assistance in criminal cases is available under the duty solicitor scheme, provided for by the Legal Aid (Scotland) (Criminal Proceedings) Scheme 1975 and also under the Legal Aid (Scotland) Act 1967.

In a work of this size it is not possible to do more than note the existence of such provision. For a full discussion of legal aid in criminal proceedings see Stoddart, *The Law and Practice of Legal Aid in Scotland*.

The second question arises in connection with the person who has secured legal assistance. What guarantees are there of access to that assistance? In *Fraser* v. *Mackinnon*, 1981 S.C.C.R. 91 a sheriff insisted in proceeding with the trial of two accused persons in the absence of their legal adviser. The sheriff knew that he was in the building, acting as duty solicitor for that day, and that he would be released shortly from that duty. The solicitor arrived towards the close of the Crown case and moved for an adjournment. This too was refused, and the accused were convicted. In a suspension, the High Court held that in the circumstances of the case the sheriff's conduct amounted to oppression. What he had done was not necessary in the public interest, or to avoid prejudice to the prosecutor. It was, on the other hand, likely to prejudice the accused.

For the rights of persons in custody to consult with a solicitor, see *post*, Chap. 4.

CHAPTER 2

THE SYSTEM OF PROSECUTION

In keeping with most western legal systems Scots law regards the prosecution of crime as primarily a public function performed on behalf of the public by an official appointed for that purpose. Consequently, much of the material in this chapter concerns the powers and duties of the public prosecutor. The latter does not, however, enjoy exclusive title to prosecute. While public prosecution may be the norm, private prosecution is competent in both solemn and summary proceedings, and the rules governing such prosecutions may conveniently be considered in this chapter. Furthermore, Scottish criminal procedure appears to recognise a third "breed" of prosecutor, occupying a position midway between public and private prosecutor, known as the prosecutor in the public interest. The status of this prosecutor likewise deserves some examination.

a. Historical development — from private to public prosecution

Lord Normand, The Public Prosecutor in Scotland
[1938] L.Q.R. 345

"The prosecution of crime in Scotland is a public function exercised by the Lord Advocate with the assistance of the Solicitor-General, of other advocates depute nominated by the Lord Advocate and acting under deputations personally granted by him, and of procurators fiscal, who are local but permanent officials appointed as vacancies occur by the Lord Advocate.

This was not always the rule and there are still vestiges of an earlier system of private prosecution. It will be proper to trace briefly the history of criminal prosecution in Scotland before describing the practice of the present day.

Popular prosecution, by which *quivis e populo* might institute criminal proceedings, was unknown in Scotland. Scots law did not recognize at any time a general right of private individuals to prosecute for any offence that could be considered injurious to the public. Originally the person injured by the crime or certain of his relatives were entitled to prosecute the offender. That was a system of prosecution not unsuited to the primitive conditions of communication, the prevalence of sectional feuds, and the

26

weakness of the central authority of the Crown in Scottish history down to the sixteenth century. But it was rude and partial in operation and directed more to private vengeance than to the securing of public order. The powerful criminal escaped justice; the wealthy purchased immunity from punishment; and the poor and weak suffered wrongs without daring to bring the perpetrator to justice. Private arrangements by which criminals were left at liberty to repeat their offences were common, and money which should have come to the royal treasury from forfeitures and fines remained in the pockets of the wrong-doers or was divided between them and the parties whom they had injured. There were besides certain crimes against the State for which no private person could prosecute, and in these cases the right of the Lord Advocate to prosecute as the King's Advocate was recognized before 1579. In an Act of the Scottish Parliament of that year dealing with malicious and unnecessary prosecutions, provision was made for the punishment of unjust pursuers and of unjust informers where the King's Majesty's Advocate was the only pursuer. The crimes in which the King's Advocate was the only pursuer were mainly those of a public nature committed against the Crown or the State. In 1579 also the Privy Council directed the King's Advocate and the Treasurer to prosecute in certain cases though the private persons wronged declined to do so. The association of the Treasurer with the King's Advocate reveals the motive of the Privy Council's action. It was to prevent private arrangements by which the Treasury was deprived of fines and forfeitures. Eight years later the King's Advocate and the Treasurer are again associated in criminal prosecutions, this time by an Act of Parliament which marks an important step in the history of public prosecutions. The Act of 1587, cap. 77, provided that the Treasurer and Advocate pursue slaughters and other crimes although the parties be silent or would otherwise privily agree. Thus the Crown's right to prosecute, whether the private parties injured chose to prosecute or not, was clearly established, and immediately afterwards there are decisions by the Court affirming the Lord Advocate's title to prosecute in circumstances where it was formerly negatived. The position at the end of the sixteenth century is thus summed up in a judgment delivered in 1836 [*King's Advocate v. Lord Dunglas* (1836) 15 S. *per* Lord Medwyn at p.327]: 'The King's Advocate was authorised to act as public prosecutor of crimes in the time of James VI. This is implied in 1579, c. 78, and still more expressly by 1587, c. 77, which authorised the Treasurer and Advocate to pursue, although the private party did not. He may have had power previously from the Sovereign to prosecute in the pleas of the Crown; but in that large class of crimes, then prosecuted at the instance of the private party, his power was confirmed and firmly recognised by these statutes; so that, since the date of the latter Act, his right to prosecute all crimes has been unquestioned.' The Treasurer did not prosecute alone, and his association with the Lord Advocate as prosecutor ultimately ceased. Even after 1587 the Lord Advocate was frequently specially directed by the Privy Council to prosecute in certain cases. The explanation of this is probably to be found in the unruly condition of the country which made it unsafe for the Lord Advocate to act on his own initiative and caused him to seek such protection as a special order of Government might afford against the vindictiveness of powerful criminals and of their retainers or associates.

The Act of 1587 did not withdraw from the party injured his right to prosecute. But gradually the Lord Advocate assumed complete control of the administration of the criminal law. This change may have been favoured by decisions of the Court that the Lord Advocate could not be compelled to disclose the name of his informer [*James Connell*, 1599. Omond, *The Lord Advocates of Scotland*, 59; *Muirhead*, 1681. Fountainhall's *Decisions*, i, 136]. Under these decisions an injured party might well prefer that the Lord Advocate should act as prosecutor, for the private prosecutor, besides incurring the cost and trouble of conducting the prosecution, was exposed to a claim for expenses by the person accused if the trial resulted in an acquittal. So in time the private prosecutor almost disappeared, and his right to institute proceedings became so far subordinate to that of the Lord Advocate that he was required to obtain the Lord Advocate's concurrence. 'Prosecution [by the private prosecutor] is attended with this peculiarity', says a great institutional authority [Hume, ii, 125], 'that the libel [*i.e.* charge] cannot be raised at the pleasure of the individual; and bears, by ancient and invariable style, to be raised with the concourse of his Majesty's Advocate, for his Majesty's interest; and truly receives his concourse, by the subscription of that officer, or some one authorised by him, at the bill for the criminal letters' [the writ instituting proceedings]. 'This practice seems to be grounded on two considerations. First, his Majesty's interest in the fines, forfeitures, and confiscations, that accrue on occasion of convictions; which interest is guarded in this way, against any collusive dealings between the private accuser and the pannel' [the accused person]. 'And, next, that far superior interest which his Majesty has in the execution of his laws, and, especially, in the due and equal distribution of criminal justice to all his subjects.'"

NOTE

In common with many other commentators Lord Normand is critical of the haphazard enforcement of the criminal law in early times, and in particular of the way in which the guilty could purchase immunity from punishment. This could be achieved by informal arrangements made between the wrongdoer and his victim, but there was a recognised legal procedure whereby the wrongdoer offered compensation (known as *assythment*) to the victim (or in appropriate cases his relatives). In return for assythment the victim granted the offender forgiveness in a document known as a "letter of slaines" and thereby relinquished any interest in prosecuting the offender. (For a general account of the system, see R.B. Black, "A Historical Survey of Delictual Liability in Scotland for Personal Injuries and Death" (1975) 8 C.I.L.J.S.A. 46, at pp. 52 *et seq.*, and *McKendrick* v. *Sinclair*, 1971 S.L.T. 17, 234, and 1972 S.L.T. 110).

The increasing intervention of the Crown after 1587 did not lead to a reduction in the incidence of bought justice. Immunity from punishment at the hands of the Crown could be obtained by means of a pardon or remission. Such remissions were frequently obtained from the Crown in exchange for cash or favours, and the income from remissions figured prominently in the revenues of most of the Stuart monarchs.

b. Public prosecution

Responsibility for all public prosecutions in Scotland rests, ultimately, with the Lord Advocate who is the chief Law Officer of the Crown in Scotland, usually a Member of Parliament, and often a member of the ruling political party. In the discharge of his functions as public prosecutor the Lord Advocate is assisted by the second Law Officer, the Solicitor-General for Scotland, and a permanent staff of civil servants in the Crown Office in Edinburgh headed by the Crown Agent.

All prosecutions on indictment, whether in the High Court or the sheriff court, are conducted in the name of the Lord Advocate (1975 Act, s. 41). While the Lord Advocate may appear personally to prosecute it is customary today for him to be represented. In the High Court this task is performed by Crown counsel appointed by the Lord Advocate and known as advocates-depute. Prosecutions on indictment in the sheriff court are conducted on behalf of the Lord Advocate by the procurator fiscal of the court.

Summary prosecutions are conducted in the sheriff and district courts by the procurator fiscal of the appropriate court. In such cases the fiscal does not prosecute in the name of the Lord Advocate, but he remains responsible to him and acts under his general supervision and guidance.

All public prosecutors in Scotland enjoy, at least in principle, a considerable degree of discretion in the discharge of their functions as prosecutors, and a consideration of the limits of this discretion is the key to the appreciation of the role of the public prosecutor in the criminal justice system in Scotland.

(i) The basic principle: the public prosecutor as master of the instance

Boyle v. H.M. Advocate

1976 J.C. 32

(For the facts of this case see *post*, p. 423.)

LORD CAMERON:: ". . . In Scotland the master of the instance in all prosecutions for the public interest is the Lord Advocate. It is for him to decide when and against whom to launch prosecution and upon what charges. It is for him to decide in which court they shall be prosecuted. It is for him to decide what pleas of guilt he will accept and it is for him to decide when to withdraw or abandon proceedings. Not only so, even when a verdict of guilt has been returned and recorded it still lies with the Lord Advocate whether to move the court to pronounce sentence and without that motion no sentence can be pronounced or imposed."

NOTE

Lord Cameron's summary of the public prosecutor's powers is amplified in the following materials. It should be noted in particular that his Lordship gives no indications of the controls—judicial and extra-judicial—which may be brought to bear on the exercise of prosecutorial discretion. See also *Skeen* v *Fullarton*, 1980 S.L.T. (Notes) 46 for the position of the procurator fiscal as master of the instance of summary cases.

(ii) The decision to prosecute

The decision to prosecute rests, in theory at least, with the public prosecutor, and it is a commonly-held view that in Scotland the role of the police in bringing offenders to justice is restricted to the investigation of offences under the control or supervision of the prosecutor (see, *e.g.* Dickens, "The Control of Prosecutions in the United Kingdom" (1973) 22 N.I.L.Q. 1 at p. 21). It is also assumed, generally, that the separation of investigative and prosecution functions is a desirable objective. The accepted views, and challenges to them, are discussed in the following excerpts.

1. Smith v. H.M. Advocate
1952 J.C. 66

The appellant was convicted of assault and murder by stabbing a man at a dance hall. At the *locus* of the crime the police found, in addition to the murder weapon, a sheath knife. They did not disclose the discovery of the sheath knife to the procurator fiscal, with the result that it was not included on the Crown list of productions, nor was the name of the finder placed on the Crown list of witnesses. In disposing of the appeal the Lord Justic-Clerk made the following observations on the respective functions of the police and the procurator fiscal.

LORD JUSTICE-CLERK (THOMPSON): ". . . When a crime is committed it is the responsibility of the Procurator fiscal to investigate it. In actual practice much of the preliminary investigation is nowadays, especially in the larger centres of population with highly organised police forces, increasingly conducted by the police under the general supervision of the Fiscal. This is due to the remarkable development in recent years of the efficiency of the criminal investigation departments of the police forces, especially on the technical side of crime detection. However, the duty of the police is simply one of investigation under the supervision of the Procurator fiscal and the results of the investigation are communicated to the Procurator fiscal as the inquiries progress. It is for the Crown Office and not for the police to decide whether the results of the investigation justify prosecution. The two functions are quite distinct. In carrying out their initial investigation the police perform a public duty. Their investigation is entirely private and no one else is entitled to take part in it. As the police have a monopoly, two results follow. First, the manner in which they are allowed to carry out their investigation is regulated by certain rules. Second; as they are the sole investigators and no more than investigators, it is their duty to put before the Procurator fiscal everything which may be relevant and material to the issue of whether the suspected party is innocent or guilty. We repeat, it is not for the police to decide what is relevant and material but to give all the information which may be relevant and material.

Clearly, in reporting the results of their investigation, the police must exercise a power of selection. It would be absurd to suggest that all their results should be submitted. But a cautious officer will remember that he is not the judge of what is relevant and material and will tend to err on the safe side. If he is in doubt, he should consult the Procurator fiscal. He will also remember that, as he and he alone has the opportunity of the initial investigation in the public interest, he must put the result of his investigations fairly before the Fiscal in order that the Crown may have a fair basis on which to decide whether or not to prosecute.

On the basis of the information provided by the police the Crown prepare the precognition and carry out any necessary further investigation to enable them to decide whether to prosecute."

NOTE

Section 17(2) of the Police (Scotland) Act 1967 provides that in relation to the investigation of offences the chief constable of a police force shall comply with such lawful instructions as he may receive from the appropriate prosecutor. At a more general level, section 9 of the 1975 Act provides that the Lord Advocate may issue instructions to a chief constable with regard to the reporting of offences alleged to have been committed within this area "and it shall be the duty of a chief constable to whom such instruction is issued to secure compliance therewith." Compare, in this respect, the position of the Scottish chief constable with that of his English counterpart, as outlined by Lord Denning M.R. in *R*. v. *Metropolitan Police Commissioner, ex p. Blackburn* [1968] 1 All E.R. 763 at p. 769.

2. Moody and Tombs, Prosecution in the Public Interest, pp. 44-48

"While the powers of the fiscal appear to be very extensive and he is in theory given wide autonomy to make decisions independently, it is most important that he should not be regarded in isolation from the criminal justice process as a whole, since this exerts considerable pressure upon him to perform his work in particular ways and to strive for particular goals. For example, the fiscal does not himself collect the information upon which he relies in making marking decisions. This is in practice the prerogative of the police, even though the fiscal in theory is entitled to intervene and direct their investigations. There are other agencies which report directly to the fiscal but the vast majority of reports received for marking are submitted by the police. During the week of our Census 92 per cent of all reports received by fiscal offices were submitted by the police, 3 per cent from the Television Licence Records Office, 3 per cent from the Traffic Commissioners and 1 per cent from the Department of Health and Social Security. The remaining 1 per cent came from a wide variety of different agencies, including the Health and Safety at Work Executive and Local Environmental Health Offices.

Bundles of police reports, called police informations, are received by fiscal offices daily or more often in a larger office. This is generally the first intimation the fiscal will have of the alleged criminal incident unless the reporting police officer wishes to discuss the case with him before making a formal report. For example, in a complicated fraud case the CID officer involved in the investigation came to discuss with the fiscal the kind of information which would be needed to sustain a conviction. Again, a police officer sought a fiscal's advice regarding an allegation of rape where medical evidence was ambiguous. In that case, no report was submitted since the fiscal recommended that there was insufficient corroboration to support a prosecution. In a few offices there is a great deal of contact with the police before reports are actually submitted: 'where there is something specific which a reporting officer wishes to discuss with the fiscal, he will bring the report in himself . . . if it is something fairly serious he will want to speak to me about it.'

For the most part, however, fiscals do not speak to the reporting officer before marking a case and they rely on the police report solely in making decisions concerned with prosecution. If one accepts the premise that 'the quality of decision-making in most social contexts is directly related to the amount of relevant information available to decision-makers' [Bottomley: 1973: 98], it follows that the role of the police as reporters is a crucial one. Research on the creation of written records has shown that in encapsulating an actual event on paper ambiguities and inconsistencies are usually lost particularly where the writer is attempting to contain his description within a standard format and to suggest one course of action rather than another: 'in everyday life precise delineations are not made: vague stereotypes seem to be used. Control agencies in our society, however, in defining and classifying become responsible for drawing clearer lines than in fact exist in everyday life.' [Freidson: 1973: 125].

In the case of police reports, for example, most police forces present what they judge to be relevant information in a similar way. Cited cases, reports concerning an accused person who is not in custody, state the accused's name, sex, age and address, the charge or charges which the police deem appropriate and a summary of the alleged criminal incident. Use is sometimes made of a section headed *Comments* where the police may include some further observations about the accusèd or his family. Generally, however, the report focuses on the offence and the ingredients deemed necessary for proving the offence. The language is stereotyped and the thrust of the presentation is towards minimising uncertainty and maximising the strength of the case for the prosecution: 'reports are steroeotyped. In fact you will find out only that the accused is aged such and such, employed as so and so, has so many children.' Fiscals remark that only occasionally do the police express any doubts: 'two boys charged with assaulting X and X charged with assaulting one of these boys . . . the police clearly can't make up their own mind, that's why they have split this into two counterclaims'; 'occasionally we have cases where there is a charge and countercharge, the victim in one being the accused in the other, . . . we have a discussion with the police as to credibility, as to whom we should proceed against' . . .

Reports where an accused is in custody tend to be, if anything, briefer since the reporting officer may have apprehended the accused only hours before the fiscal receives his report: 'so many are drawn up—20, 30, 40 reports a night that obviously they must become stereotyped.' Under Scottish law the accused who has been arrested and held in custody by the police must be brought before a court on the next lawful day (excluding weekends and public holidays) or be released by the fiscal. The custody report contains the same information as in a cited case, though the police may also include *full statements*, verbatim accounts obtained from witnesses to the incident.

Statutory offences are more amenable to standardisation than Common Law crimes and this is reflected in the use of pro formas by the police in reporting such offences. For example, in a speeding case the reporting officer uses a standard form to report the offence. The form gives a statutory definition of the charge and the officer merely fills in the blanks left for name, age and address of the accused, the number of his car, the locus where he was stopped, the time of day when the incident took place and the speed at which the accused was alleged to be driving. The same is true for an increasing number of statutory offences under road traffic legislation, the Vehicle Excise Acts and the Wireless Telegraphy Acts. Such forms are intended to reduce police time spent preparing reports and to ensure that there is uniformity both among individual police offices and between different police forces in Scotland . . . Fiscals disagree on the general legitimacy of using pro formas, but it is clear that some regard such devices as appropriate in certain statutory offences. This is particularly evident in relation to cases which they define as equivalent to petty misdemeanours where no moral blame can be imputed to the accused: 'statutory ones do not involve much moral blame'; 'a lot of the road traffic stuff, it's called criminal. I just don't think it is criminal, speeding . . . you do it, I do it . . .'; 'it's the kind of thing that you or I could do or someone who is otherwise a respectable citizen.' They are prepared to accept a standard, brief presentation of the facts from the police in such cases since a conviction for such *minor* infringements of the law does not carry with it the same public condemnation as *serious* crime.

They are less happy about the use of the pro forma in Common Law offences and perceive a tendency on the part of the police to present the minimum amount of information when writing reports generally. Theoretically, the fiscal can ask the police to investigate the case further or obtain full statements from witnesses before he decides to prosecute. If there is some glaring evidential flaw or very obvious mistake in police procedure the fiscal will look behind the report and request further information. In our Census this occurred in 6 per cent of all reports and not surprisingly these were generally cited cases which were not reported on pro formas. Fiscals admit that informed decision-making may be hampered where the report is very brief: 'it's very dangerous . . . take, for example, a shoplifting reported on a pro forma. None of the real details are explained to me. A policeman can produce to me on a pro forma something that looks so simple and straightforward—straighforward shoplifting—and it may turn out to be nothing like that'; 'my problem is not having sufficient knowledge of the facts. You can say that the fiscal's discretion is often, maybe too often, exercised in an ill-informed way through no fault of his own. A Reporter to the Children's Hearings gets a social background report before he decides whether to proceed or not. Why shouldn't I? Because if I have the full information, with my experience and my general views on the preservation of life and property, I really feel that I am hardly likely to make the wrong decision.'

The submission of a report by the police inevitably involves a strong presumption in favour of prosecution since fiscals regard it as unlikely that the matter would otherwise be reported to them. Scottish prosecutors generally hold the police in high regard: 'I have always been pro police. They have got a damned difficult job to do and while I don't think it's desirable for the fiscal to regard himself as a jumped up policeman, I think it's bad to consider oneself as so neutral that one is always against the police.' Nevertheless fiscals note that the reporting officer may screen out information which a prosecutor might consider important: 'the police can withhold information . . . they don't usually do it deliberately, but they can do it because they think the fiscal doesn't want to know that or doesn't need to know that'. In this way the police may, albeit inadvertently, undermine the fiscal's position as independent prosecutor: 'we have to rely on the police doing more and more . . . we're giving up our true constitutional function of investigating crime and are almost acting as a rubber stamp for police officers'."

NOTE

Although the prosecutor may in the majority of cases simply endorse what is in effect a police decision to proceed this does not affect the crucial feature of the relationship between the prosecutor and the police, namely that the prosecutor remains independent of the police and cannot be instructed to proceed or not to proceed.

The Royal Commission on Criminal Procedure (Cmnd. 8092) reached similar conclusions to those outlined above with regard to the relationship between the fiscal and the police (Cmnd. 8092-1, Vol.1, paras 6.32 *et seq.*).

(iii)   Renouncing the right to prosecute

The discretion to prosecute may be exercised either way, and the bulk of this book is concerned with the procedures which follow on a decision to prosecute. In the vast majority of cases a decision not to proceed will put an end to matters in a given case, at least so far as a public prosecution is concerned. Particular problems may arise, however, where the prosecutor wishes to recall a decision not to proceed.

1.   **Thom v. H.M. Advocate**

1976 J.C. 49

On 15 May 1975 the applicant appeared on petition before the sheriff at Forfar, charged with embezzlement. Having been fully committed he was liberated on bail. On 18 July 1975 the applicant's solicitor received from the procurator fiscal at Forfar a letter, dated 17 July 1975. The letter was in the following terms:

"Since we last met I have been making a thorough inquiry into the circumstances of this case which of course required obtaining statements from witnesses in other areas and which occasioned a certain delay.

Although I am left in the end of the day with a strong suspicion that Mr Thom is responsible for the defalcations in question, I have come to the conclusion, having considered the whole matter, that the case is not good enough to put before a jury, nor for that matter do I think that I could persuade my sheriff to convict on a summary prosecution—because of the number of loose ends that appear to exist in the evidence relating to what occurred in Mr Thom's former office.

As a result, therefore, I am taking no further steps in this matter and your client, accordingly, may uplift his bail."

The procurator fiscal then made a statement to the press, which was published in the *Dundee Courier* and *The Scotsman* to the effect that no proceedings were to be taken against Mr Thom in respect of this charge.

On 29 November 1975 an indictment was served on the applicant containing the same charge which had been libelled in the petition.

At the first diet the applicant submitted a plea in bar of trial on the ground that the prosecutor had "disclaimed the process" on 17 July 1975. This plea was repelled. The applicant was subsequently found guilty of the charge. He appealed to the High Court.

THE COURT (FULL BENCH): ". . . For the applicant the main submission was that where the Lord Advocate has publicly and unequivocally relinquished or discharged his right of prosecution of a particular individual upon a particular charge he may not thereafter serve upon that individual a competent indictment libelling that charge. A motion by a prosecutor, be he a Procurator-fiscal or an Advocate-depute, to desert the diet *simpliciter* is construed as a thorough relinquishment or discharge of the prosecutor's right of prosecution, with the result that no fresh proceedings may competently be brought against the accused on the same charge. (See Hume on Crimes, vol. ii, p. 277.) The letter dated 17th July 1975 by itself, and the terms of the public announcement in the Press, can be construed only as just such a public relinquishment or discharge of the right to prosecute the applicant on the charge on which he appeared on petition. In the result the indictment served on 29th November 1975 was incompetent and the conviction should be quashed.

In his reply for the Crown, the Solicitor-General conceded that where the Lord Advocate has publicly relinquished or discharged his right of prosecution in the case of a particular charge against a particular individual—or has made a public announcement which falls to be construed as such a relinquishment or discharge—no prosecution on that charge may competently follow. This concession was made, however, subject to the proviso that the public relinquishment or discharge of the right to prosecute, or the public announcement of the kind to which we have referred, must be made in open court. In any event, so ran the argument for the Crown, the letter of 17th July 1975 and the public announcement ought to be construed as no more than a statement of present intention.

From the foregoing narrative of the competing arguments it will be seen that the gap between the applicant and the Crown is a narrow one. In particular these arguments leave only two questions to be resolved. The first is whether the terms of the letter of 17th July 1975 or the terms of the Press announcement, or both, fall to be construed as an unequivocal public declaration by the Procurator-fiscal that the right to prosecute the applicant upon the charge on which he had appeared on petition had been relinquished or discharged. If they are, then it is accepted that this will bind the Lord Advocate. The second, which will arise if the first is answered in favour of the applicant, is whether the only public declaration by or on behalf of the Lord Advocate which will render subsequent proceedings on the same charge incompetent is one made in open court.

As to the first question, we have no doubt that the letter by itself cannot be read as a mere statement of the intention of the Crown for the time being. Properly construed it constitutes an unequivocal and unqualified announcement on behalf of the Lord Advocate that no further steps are to be taken in respect of the charge on which the applicant appeared on petition, or, putting the matter in another way, that the Lord Advocate has decided not to exercise his right of prosecution in the applicant's case. Such an announcement in our opinion can, like a motion to desert *simpliciter*, only be regarded as a declaration of relinquishment or discharge of the right to prosecute upon the relevant charge. The announcement to the Press thereafter merely reinforces the construction which we are compelled to put upon the letter.

There remains the second question. The Lord Advocate is undoubtedly a prosecutor in the public interest and, in general, his right to prosecute cannot be challenged in a particular case unless it has been surrendered by his own act, or by the act of a prosecutor on his behalf. In these circumstances it is right that the act of surrender should be a public act. Is it however necessary, before the public act shall fetter the Crown in the matter of future proceedings on the same charge, that it shall have taken place in open court? This is the question presented by the proviso to the concession of the learned Solicitor-General, and in moving us to answer it in his favour he was unable to cite any authority. Since we are not constrained by authority we ask ourselves whether there is any justification in principle or good sense for restricting the forum in which, or the means by which, an unequivocal relinquishment or discharge of the right to prosecute will be effective to render subsequent proceedings on the same charge incompetent. In our opinion there is none and in the result we hold that the indictment on which the applicant went to trial was incompetent, and that the conviction must be quashed. We have only to say that the letter was written and the Press announcement was made without reference to the Crown Office. It will no doubt be for consideration by the Lord Advocate whether authority to write such a letter or to make such an announcement, without reference to the Crown Office, should in future be confided to a Procurator fiscal.

In light of our decision upon the principal submission for the applicant it is unnecessary for us to express any opinion upon his subsidiary submission that the right to prosecute the applicant had been exercised so oppressively, to his prejudice, that the court should have intervened to stop the proceedings."

The court allowed the appeal and quashed the conviction.

2. H.M. Advocate v. Waddell and Another
1976 S.L.T. (Notes) 61

In August 1976 the accused were charged, *inter alia*, with the murder of a woman. By way of a preliminary plea Waddell contended that the Crown had unequivocally renounced its right to prosecute him for this crime. The alleged renunciation was contained in a number of public statements by the Crown, and in

particular in a statement by the Lord Advocate in a written answer
to a parliamentary question in November 1975, to the effect that
prosecution of Waddell for the crime in question would not be
justified.

LORD ROBERTSON: ". . . Of the preliminary pleas submitted on behalf of
the panel, Waddell, only two were argued videlicet: (1) that the Lord
Advocate or others on his behalf by various public statements had unequivocally discharged his right to prosecute Waddell. This argument was
said to rest on the authority of *Thom* v. *H.M. Advocate*, 1976 S.L.T. 232.
This argument in my opinion is ill-founded. In *Thom* the panel had
appeared on petition in respect of a specific charge, and having been fully
committed for trial on this charge was liberated on bail. Subsequently by an
unequivocal public statement the Crown intimated that this charge was not
to be proceeded with. This public statement was held to be equivalent to
desertion of the charge simpliciter, the consequence of which has long been
held to bar as incompetent further proceedings by the Crown on the same
charge. The decision in *Thom* has no bearing on the present situation where
the panel was not charged and committed on these charges at the time when
the statements were made. This argument therefore fails."

The court repelled
the preliminary plea.

NOTE

For the background to this case see *H.M. Advocate* v. *Waddell*,
supra, p. 20. The second preliminary plea raised by Waddell is
discussed *post*, p. 596.

3. **H.M. Advocate v. Stewart**
1980 J.C. 84

The panel, a former member of Dundee City Council, was charged,
along with two other accused, with offences against the Public
Bodies Corrupt Practices Act 1889, as amended by the Prevention
of Corruption Act 1916. The indictment related to a large number
of incidents alleged to have taken place over a period of 16 years,
between June 1959 and May 1975, while the panel and one of the
other accused were city councillors in Dundee. In respect of certain
of these charges the panel entered a plea in bar of trial on two
grounds: (1) that the Lord Advocate had renounced his right to
prosecute the accused, and (2) that because of the long delay in
bringing the accused to trial, the panel had, or might have, suffered
prejudice in his defence, and that it was oppressive for the Lord
Advocate to pursue the prosecution.

In support of the first ground the panel referred, *inter alia*, to: (1) correspondence in 1965 between the then Lord Advocate and two Members of Parliament concerning the progress of investigations in the case; (2) a statement made at or about that time by the procurator fiscal to the panel's solicitor that no proceedings would be taken against the panel; (3) a statement by the then chief constable of Dundee to the town clerk of Dundee that after investigations no proceedings would be taken against the panel; (4) a statement by the town clerk of Dundee to the Lord Provost that there would be no proceedings against the panel; (5) a statement by a senior C.I.D. officer that papers sent to the Crown Office after investigation were returned marked "No proceedings"; (6) the return of documents seized by the procurator fiscal; (7) widespread press and media reports, following on the above-mentioned statements, to the effect that as a result of investigations by the Crown there would be no criminal proceedings against the panel.

LORD KINCRAIG: "I shall deal with the first accused on the first charge.

The plea in bar of trial to charge 1, under exception of 1 (d) in relation to the contracts numbered 14, 19, 20, 21 and 23 in the Schedule, is taken on two grounds: (1) that the Lord Advocate has renounced his right to prosecute the accused on that charge and his right is thus extinguished; and (2) that the long, unexplained and unjustified delay in bringing him to trial has caused, or may have caused, gross prejudice to him in his defence, due to the death of potentially helpful witnesses, the destruction of important documents and the dimming of the recollection of witnesses, which delay is contrary to normal justice and a violation of the right to a fair trial within a reasonable time.

The first charge alleges, in short, that the accused corruptly solicited and received goods, and other benefits, over a period between March 1960 and February 1965, as inducements to show favour to Crudens in the awarding of specified contracts. As regards the first ground, the accused refers to certain correspondence in 1965 and 1966 between the then Lord Advocate, Mr G. G. Stott, Q.C., and two Members of Parliament, and in particular to a letter dated 10th October 1966 from the Lord Advocate to the Member for South Angus in the following terms—and here I quote from No. 16 of the defence productions as follows: 'I promised to write you as soon as a decision was reached on the allegations concerning the housing committee of Dundee Town Council. These allegations have, as you know, been inquired into, the inquiry being directed in particular into the question of whether there was evidence to justify a charge under the Prevention of Corruption Acts against two members of the Town Council. After investigation by the Procurator-fiscal I have come to the conclusion that the evidence does not warrant criminal proceedings.' This was in response to two letters from the Member of Parliament concerned, the latter of which was dated 7th June 1966, and ended thus: 'I appreciate that enquiries into a matter of this kind are bound to be protracted. But I wonder whether you can give me any indication yet as to how soon you may be in a position to decide whether or not any action is called for by your Department.' The accused also refers in the plea to item 2, which is in the following terms: 'At or about said time the solicitor for the first-named panel, John M. Boath, was advised by the then Procurator-fiscal of Dundee that after investigations there would be no proceedings taken against the first-named accused.' The accused also refers to other circumstances itemised as 3 to 9 in the written plea.

The Advocate-Depute has submitted that all of the matters are irrelevant to the plea in bar. He argued that three features must be present before it can be affirmed that the Lord Advocate has renounced his right to prosecute, namely, (1) the accused has previously been charged with the same offences as appear in the charges in the indictment; (2) the Lord Advocate has intimated in unequivocal terms that he has renounced his right; and (3) such announcement has been made to the public. He found on the case of *Thom* v. *H.M. Advocate*, 1976 J.C. 48 in support of his submissions.

I agree that all of the items in the plea in bar are irrelevant except items 1 and 2. These items are to the effect that by the said letter dated 10th October 1966, after investigations into the activities of the accused in respect of a possible contravention of the Prevention of Corruption Acts 1889 and 1916, the Lord Advocate informed the Member of Parliament for South Angus that there was no evidence to justify proceedings. I have already quoted item 2. It appears that said letter was written by the Lord Advocate in response to a letter from the Member of Parliament concerned in relation to possible criminal proceedings against two members of Dundee Town Council in which the Lord Advocate was asked to inform the Members of Parliament whether he had decided to take any action in relation to these matters.

I have come to the conclusion that, properly construed, this letter is an unequivocal announcement of the decision by the Lord Advocate not to prosecute the two persons referred to in the letter in respect of charges which formed the subject matter of the investigations which had been carried out on his behalf and the results of which he had considered. In my judgment his intimation that there was no evidence to warrant proceedings must be construed in the context of the whole correspondence as a decision not to prosecute, and an abandonment of his right to do so. The letter does not name the persons the right to prosecute whom had been renounced, nor the criminal charges upon which the right to prosecute existed and had been renounced. If, however, the accused can be identified as one of the two persons referred to, and charge 1 in the indictment identified as arising out of and directly relating to matters investigated in 1966 with a view to prosecution, the letter in my judgment constitutes a renunciation of the Lord Advocate's right to prosecute the accused, and a bar to proceeding with charge 1 as restricted. I do not consider it necessary that the accused should have been charged prior to October 1966, with the same offences, if he can be thus identified. I consider therefore that the accused should be allowed to lead evidence to prove such identification.

It was submitted that the decision not to prosecute, not having been made public, cannot amount to a renunciation of the right to prosecute. Support for this proposition was said to be found in the decision of the Court in *Thom*. The passage relied on is as follows: 'The Lord Advocate is undoubtedly a Prosecutor in the public interest and, in general, his right to prosecute cannot be challenged in a particular case unless it has been surrendered by his own act or by the act of a Prosecutor on his behalf. In these circumstances it is right that the act of surrender should be a public act.' In *Thom* the Lord Advocate's decision was in fact announced to the Press and published. It was not argued in that case that it had to be published to constitute a renunciation; it was conceded by the Crown to constitute an effective renunciation if the decision did not have to be announced in open Court. So long as the Lord Advocate's decision is communicated to the accused, to his agent or to one who could be reasonably expected to communicate it to the accused, it does not seem to me to be material that it is not published. It was so communicated, according to the acccused, by the Procurator-fiscal to his solicitor."

The court sustained the first ground of the plea in bar of trial.

NOTE

A number of important and difficult questions arise from these cases. There is, first of all, the question of the method of renunciation. *Stewart* rejects the necessity for a public renunciation, provided that it is communicated to the accused, his agent or to someone who could reasonably be expected to communicate it to the accused. What of a private communication to a third party who might not be expected to communicate it to the accused? Suppose, for example that A, a solicitor, believes that his client, B, has been wrongly convicted of an offence. C has several times publicly confessed to the crime. A writes to the Lord Advocate asking if he will prosecute C. In a private reply to A the Lord Advocate states that he will not prosecute C. Is the Lord Advocate barred from subsequently proceeding against C?

There is also the question of the time of renunciation. At what stage in the proceedings will renunciation present an effective bar to future proceedings? In *Stewart* it was held that the Crown could find itself barred from proceeding against an accused by statements made even before that accused was charged — though it would seem to be difficult to reconcile this with the view expressed by Lord Robertson in *Waddell* where his Lordship distinguished *Waddell* from *Thom* on the ground that Waddell had not even been charged at the time when the Lord Advocate made his alleged renunciation. *Stewart* adopts a very strict line against the Crown, and it is certainly undesirable that the individual should be subjected to the strain of a prosecution which he thought had never really got off the ground. But is it necessarily in the public interest that the prosecutor should find himself irrevocably barred from proceeding against a suspect as a result of a statement made at a very early stage in the proceedings? The moral for prosecutors, no doubt, is "keep mum."

Finally, there is the question of the effect of renunciation. It is clear that an unequivocal renunciation presents a bar to future proceedings at the instance of the Crown. (As to the effect of a Crown renunciation on the rights of other prosecutors see *H*. v. *Sweeney, post*, p. 71.) Again the question arises as to whether the rule that renunciation is an absolute bar is justifiable or necessary in the public interest. Suppose, for example, that a suspect has so well covered his tracks (even to the extent of incapacitating a principal witness) that there seems to be no reasonable prospect of a success-ful prosecution being brought. A decision not to proceed is com-municated to the suspect. At a later date circumstances change so as to permit proceedings to be taken. What interest is served by an absolute bar to those proceedings? It is doubtful if the public interest is served by such a bar. In some cases there would un-doubtedly be a risk of serious prejudice to the accused in allowing a prosecution in such circumstances. It is submitted, however, that the appropriate way to deal with this problem is by application of the developing doctrine that the court will not permit a prosecution to proceed if it is considered to be oppressive (see *post*, p. 304) rather than by an absolute bar to proceedings.

An alternative method of renouncing the right to prosecute is for the fiscal to give the alleged offender a warning either in writing, or orally. The giving of a warning is regarded by the Crown as bar to the Crown (but presumably not a private prosecutor) raising crimin-al proceedings in respect of that case, as the following Crown Office direction makes clear.

C/O Circular No. 1685: Warnings to Accused Persons

"This subject has been much considered both in Parliament and else-where. In the light of that consideration the Lord Advocate considers that a warning is a valuable option available to the Crown and can in appropriate cases be more effective in promoting the aims of the law in a humane and merciful manner than raising proceedings in court.

In a case where the procurator fiscal considers that a warning is the appropriate method of dealing with the alleged offender, *i.e.* where there is in his opinion sufficient evidence that the person concerned has committed a crime known to the law of Scotland but the case is not so trivial as to merit no action, the procurator fiscal will require to give the warning either in writing or in exceptional cases personally. A warning should be an alternative to prosecution and should only be issued in cases in which if the procurator fiscal were not disposed to warn he would prosecute.

In considering whether or not to administer a warning procurators fiscal should have regard to the following:

1. In no circumstances should a warning be administered unless the procurator fiscal has in his possession sufficient evidence which would in his opinion justify him in taking proceedings in court.

2. A warning may be administered whether or not the accused person is alleged to have admitted or denied the offence or made no statement to the police.

3. If the procurator fiscal gives a warning he will be regarded as having decided not to take court proceedings in respect of that case. Accordingly no warning will be administered on the understanding that if it is not accepted, the procurator fiscal will take proceedings in court.

4. Any warning should avoid giving the impression that the procurator fiscal is adjudicating on the guilt or innocence of the person concerned. Although the framing of warning letters is a matter for the discretion of procurators fiscal, the Lord Advocate suggests that it might be said that a report has been submitted to the procurator fiscal alleging a certain offence and that the procurator fiscal considers that there is evidence sufficient in his opinion to justify him in taking proceedings in court against the person concerned, that the procurator fiscal has, however, decided in this case not to take proceedings, but that in the circumstances the procurator fiscal thinks it right to say that should a similar report be submitted against the person in future, the procurator fiscal may well take proceedings in court.

If the procurator fiscal considers that the circumstances require him to deliver a personal warning he will arrange for the person concerned to attend at his office either by writing to him or by such special arrangements as may appear appropriate in the circumstances. For the reason given in 3 above, the invitation to attend at the procurator fiscal's office should be couched in neutral terms and should not in any way amount to a warning. If the person to whom the procurator fiscal desires to deliver a personal warning fails to attend at the procurator fiscal's office after having been given a sufficient opportunity to do so, the procurator fiscal should normally take court proceedings.

Similar considerations will apply to offences reported by public agencies other than the police such as the Investigation Branch of the Department of Health and Social Security and the consumer protection departments of local authorities.

Only the procurator fiscal or the person substituting for him may sign a warning letter. Where the accused's solicitor is known there is no objection to the warning letter being sent to him. Alternatively, the letter may be sent to the accused and a copy sent to the solicitor. A standard style of letter should not be used since each case must be reviewed in the light of its own circumstances although the style in each case may be similar.

It is not possible exhaustively to list the categories of offences which may be dealt with by a warning but examples are: speeding offences, careless driving where no injury has occurred, minor breaches of the peace, shoplifting offences and offences against section 12 of the Children and Young Persons (Scotland) Act 1937 where a normally caring parent has, due to some exceptional circumstances, become the subject of a report. Much will depend on the previous convictions of the accused and what is known of his character.

Once the police have reported a case to the procurator fiscal they are not subject to any directions from him to warn the person concerned in place of criminal proceedings.

Procurators fiscal should maintain a local register of persons whom they have warned. The procurator fiscal must ensure its security in order that its contents do not become known outside his office. Where a second report against a person is received containing evidence of another similar offence sufficient to justify court proceedings, the procurator fiscal should consider the full circumstances of the first report in respect of which the warning was given, including any representations made by or on behalf of the accused in response to the warning, before he decides upon his course of action in respect of the second report."

(iv) Determining the mode of trial

Dunbar v. Johnston
(1904) 7 F. (J.) 40

With the consent of the procurator fiscal, Dunbar brought a summary complaint against Johnston in the sheriff court at Edinburgh, alleging a contravention of section 2 of the Merchandise Marks Act 1887. Section 2(6) of that Act contained the following proviso: "Provided that a person charged with an offence under this section before a Court of Summary Jurisdiction shall on appearing before the Court, and before the charge is gone into, be informed of his right to be tried on indictment, and if he requires be so tried accordingly." The sheriff informed Johnston of his apparent rights under section 2(6), and the latter claimed the right to be tried by a jury. Dunbar then sought to bring a private prosecution on indictment (with the concurrence of the Lord Advocate) in the sheriff court. The sheriff held the indictment to be incompetent, and Dunbar appealed to the High Court by bill of advocation. The High Court held that it was not competent to bring a private prosecution by indictment in the sheriff court. The following observations were made on the alleged right to jury trial:

LORD ADAM: ". . . We may be of the opinion that there is no right in an offender brought up on a summary charge in Scotland to require trial on an indictment. The statute assumes that a right exists, which may exist in England, but certainly does not in Scotland. We were informed that in England there is such a right to demand trial on indictment, when the trial would proceed before a jury, and not summarily before a Judge. I can see, therefore, how the section operates in England, but by no means am I to be held as being of the opinion that there is such a right in Scotland."

LORD MCLAREN: ". . . It may be said that the Merchandise Marks Act assumes a right on the part of an accused person to be tried by indictment, and no doubt an offender can be tried on indictment in Scotland if the Crown thinks that such procedure is appropriate. But I should not wish it to be assumed as entering into my opinion that any such right exists in Scotland as a right to be tried on indictment.

A magistrate may try an offender summarily, or he may commit him for trial, but if he commits him it rests with the Lord Advocate or his depute to decide whether he shall be tried on indictment in the High Court or before the Sheriff and a jury. The question is not a question of form, at least it is a case where form may become substance, and I know of no right on the part of an accused person in Scotland to insist on being tried by indictment.

I do not think that in this view any violence is done to the language of the Merchandise Marks Act, for I have no difficulty in holding that it applies only to cases where the right to be tried on indictment exists, and I cannot help thinking that all this difficulty has arisen out of an attempt to apply to Scotland a provision which was meant to apply only to prosecutions in England."

LORD KINNEAR: "I agree that this indictment was incompetent in the Sheriff court, and as this is enough for the decision of the case, I do not desire to say anything on the other very interesting questions which were argued before us. But I desire, like your Lordships, that it should be understood that we are not deciding that persons prosecuted under the Merchandise Marks Act have a right to be tried on indictment if they demand it. The question is not before us for decision, but since it has been discussed at the bar, I may say that, as at present advised, it seems to me at least arguable that the proviso founded on in subsection (6) of section 2 of the Act does not confer any right, but assumes that there is or may be an existing right to be tried on indictment if the accused so requires. The magistrate is to inform the accused of his right to be tried on indictment. The section applies to both England and Scotland, and enacts that an offender may be prosecuted 'in manner provided by the Summary Jurisdiction Acts.' Now, there are Summary Jurisdiction Acts in England and also in Scotland. Trial in the manner provided by the Summary Jurisdiction Acts means trial in the manner provided by the Summary Jurisdiction Acts in force in either country, according as the trial takes place in the one or the other. Reading the clause therefore upon the ordinary principle of construction, *applicando singula singulis*, it appears to me that trials in England

and Scotland are to be conducted according to the procedure prescribed by the Acts in force in each of these countries respectively. Now, it appears that there is a clause in the English Summary Jurisdiction Act which confers a right to trial on indictment if it is demanded. But it is admitted that no such right is given by any Summary Procedure Act in Scotland. All that the Merchandise Marks Act says is that the magistrate is to inform the accused of his right. The record in this case states that the sheriff informed the accused of his right to be tried on indictment, but we are not told what specific information the sheriff gave him on the subject. But whatever be the true meaning of section 2(6) of the Merchandise Marks Act, it does not affect the question whether this indictment was competent in the Sheriff Court, and I agree with your Lordships that it was not, and that on that ground alone the decision must be upheld."

The court refused the bill.

NOTE

For a discussion of private prosecution, see *post*, pp. 56-78. Advocation is discussed *post* at pp. 493-499.

The discretion of the prosecutor in selecting the mode of trial, though wide, is not absolute. It is limited in the first place by the rules which determine the jurisdiction of the High Court, the sheriff court and the district court. It will be seen from Chap. 3, for example, that the High Court has exclusive jurisdiction in respect of the "pleas of the Crown" and certain statutory offences. Technically this is a reservation of forum rather than a mode of trial (since trial on indictment is of course competent for many crimes in the sheriff court), but since the High Court has no summary trial jurisdiction in effect a right to jury trial is conferred in such cases.

Secondly, there are some suggestions that the High Court has the power to control this aspect of the prosecutor's discretion, at least *ex post facto*. In *Clark and Bendall* v. *Stuart* (1886) 1 White 191, Lord McLaren put forward the following proposition:

"There is no rigorous classification of crimes which the Sheriff may try summarily, and crimes which he may not try without a Jury, and it is not necessary that there should be one, because under our system of public prosecutions, the discretion of determining whether the crimes reported to them should or should not be tried summarily is vested, in the first instance, in the Crown officers. Should a case arise of a crime manifestly unsuited for summary trial being tried by the Sheriff without a Jury, there can be no doubt that the Court of Justiciary has power to give redress by quashing the conviction."

Finally, the prosecutor's discretion may be limited by any specific or general statutory provision determining the mode of trial. See, *e.g.* section 457A of the 1975 Act (inserted by Criminal Justice Act 1982, s. 55).

For a discussion of the factors affecting the prosecutor's choice of court, see Moody and Tombs, *op. cit.*, Chap. IV.

(v) The prosecutor's discretion to accept or reject pleas

Strathern v. Sloan
1937 J.C. 76

The respondent was charged in the sheriff court along with another man with theft of a motor car. The respondent pleaded guilty. The other man pleaded not guilty. The procurator fiscal refused to accept the plea of guilty and moved the court to record a plea of not guilty. The sheriff refused. The procurator fiscal appealed to the High Court by bill of advocation.

LORD JUSTICE-CLERK (AITCHISON): ". . . It is well settled that, in criminal causes triable under solemn procedure, the Crown is not bound to accept a plea of guilty, but may insist upon the indictment proceeding to trial. This was affirmed in the case of *H. M. Advocate* v. *Peter and Smith* [(1840) 2 Swinton 492] . . .

It has never been doubted that the rule of *Peter's* case applies equally to criminal causes triable upon indictment in the Sheriff Court. The question now to be decided for the first time is whether the rule applies to causes that are triable upon summary complaint. The case in which the question was most nearly raised is *Kirkwood* v. *Coalburn District Co-operative Society* [1930 J.C. 38], which was a summary prosecution at the instance of H. M. Inspector of Factories in which alternative charges were libelled in the complaint. The panel tendered a plea of guilty to the minor of the alternative charges. The prosecutor objected to the plea being recorded, but the Sheriff recorded it. It was held on appeal that the prosecutor was entitled to proceed to trial with a view to proving the major charge, upon the ground that a prosecutor is never bound to accept a plea to the minor of two alternative charges so as to be compelled to give up the major alternative. In the course of his judgment the Lord Justice-General (Clyde) stated the wider proposition in these terms (at p. 41): 'I do not think a prosecutor is ever bound to accept a plea, whether the charge be alternative or not, but is always entitled to insist on leading evidence before the jury and obtaining a verdict if he can—Macdonald on Criminal Law, (4th ed.), p. 484, and authorities there collected.' I respectfully agree with this wider proposition, and, as the case Lord Clyde was dealing with arose upon a summary complaint, the observation must be taken as applying to summary complaints in the same way as to charges upon indictment.

This right of the public prosecutor may at first sight appear to be arbitrary, but consideration will point to many good grounds why the right should exist. In serious crime evidence may be necessary to bring out the full enormity of the crime, or perhaps to show mitigating circumstances; or again there may be concern as to whether the proper crime has been libelled, as, for example, where murder is charged, but where there is doubt whether the crime of the panel amounts to more than culpable homicide. Thus, the practice of our Courts in Scotland, and in England also, although not invariably in England, has been for the public prosecutor to refuse to accept a plea of guilty to a murder charge. Again, there may be a question, which can only be fully explored in evidence, as to the mental state of the panel. Or two or more persons may be charged, and the prosecutor may be unable, without inquiry, to assign the proper degree of guilt to each of the panels. There may be other reasons deemed sufficient by the public prosecutor for declining a plea of guilty. It is not necessary that he should assign any reason, the right being one which the law commits to his own judgment and discretion, and which he can exercise whether the proceedings are summary or on indictment.

That being the general law, I desire to add one or two qualifications. (1) The right to refuse a plea of guilty is a right which is vested in the Lord Advocate, or his Deputes, or the Procurator-fiscal, who derives his authority from the Lord Advocate. How far the right extends to other prosecutors, public or private, is a more difficult question, and it may be difficult to differentiate, at any rate as between public prosecutors. (2) Where a plea of guilty is tendered by the panel, and is not accepted by the prosecutor, the formal entry on the record should not be an entry of not guilty, which is contrary to the fact, but should be to the effect that the panel has tendered a plea of guilty, and that the prosecutor has intimated that he declines to accept the plea. The practice of entering a plea of not guilty, contrary to an express and unqualified plea of guilty, is, in my opinion, wrong and should not be continued. In the case of summary complaints the entry of the plea on the record is expressly directed by section 41 of the Summary Jurisdiction Act, 1908. (3) Wherever a plea of guilty is tendered and not accepted by the prosecutor, the plea of guilty must under no circumstances be used against the panel, and, where the trial is on indictment, must not be disclosed to the jury. In all cases, therefore, under solemn procedure, where a plea of guilty is declined at the first diet, the panel should not be called upon to plead at the second diet, unless in the interval the prosecutor has made up his mind to accept the plea if again tendered. If the panel, notwithstanding his plea of guilty, chooses to enter the witness-box, he must have entire freedom to give his evidence, contrary to his plea of guilty which the prosecutor has declined to accept. This does not involve any encouragement of false testimony, as it is not unfamiliar that a panel may offer a plea of guilty, not because he is guilty of the offence charged, but because a public trial might disclose facts more hurtful to his own reputation, or the reputation of others, than the recording of a plea on his own confession. (4) If the prosecutor elects to proceed to trial, and in the course of the trial decides to accept a plea of guilty, he cannot do so unless the panel of new pleads guilty to the offence charged. Whether the panel is willing to do so can always be ascertained by communication with his counsel or agent, and until the panel's mind is known the question should not be put to him in open Court. There may be cases in which, the evidence having disclosed facts prejudicial to the panel, the panel may desire that the trial should proceed notwithstanding his recorded plea, either on the chance of his obtaining an acquittal, or for the purpose of bringing out circumstances that may go to alleviate the offence, if proved against him.

It is unnecessary to add that the right of the public prosecutor to decline a plea of guilty is a right which should be sparingly exercised, and, in my judgment, it should not be exercised where it may result in prejudice to another panel charged under the same indictment or complaint. The governing consideration in every case should be the public interest."

The court passed
the bill.

NOTE

The procedure for the taking and recording of pleas is now largely governed by sections 124 and 336 *et seq.* of the 1975 Act.

Strictly speaking a plea tendered by an accused person is tendered not to the Crown, but to the court: "The question . . . of calling to plead, and of replying to the call, lies between the Court and the panel. It is not a tender addressed to the Crown" (*per* Lord Mackay, *Strathern* v. *Sloan* at p. 82). This has no practical significance, however, other than that the court is obliged to record accurately the accused's plea. In particular, the court has no power to dictate the Crown's reaction to any plea. If, notwithstanding a plea of guilty, the Crown elects to lead evidence against the accused, the court cannot prevent this. Equally, if the Crown elects to accept a plea of guilty to a lesser charge the court cannot insist on the original charge being tried.

The latter point is of particular importance when considering the practice of "plea negotiation." The practice exists in Scotland as in other systems. The important question is how to regulate it in the interests both of the public and the accused. A system which vests in the prosecutor an absolute discretion to accept or reject a plea tendered by the accused puts the practice beyond any external controls. Is it really satisfactory that such issues should be beyond the scrutiny even of the court?

(vi) Control over the imposition of sentence

Noon v. H.M. Advocate
1960 J.C. 52

The applicant was tried on indictment in the sheriff court on a charge of theft. At the end of the trial the jury returned a verdict of guilty. The prosecutor then informed the sheriff of the appellant's age, employment, family circumstances, and also tendered to the court a schedule of previous convictions. These were admitted by the accused, and his solicitor presented a plea in mitigation of sentence. The sheriff then passed sentence. No formal motion for sentence had been made by the prosecutor. Noon applied to the High Court for leave to appeal.

LORD JUSTICE-GENERAL (CLYDE): "The present application is made to this Court upon the ground that, since the prosecutor omitted formally to move for sentence, no sentence could competently be pronounced, and we should consequently quash the sentence leaving the conviction standing.

This objection is a purely procedural one, devoid of any true merits, for, in the circumstances, the sentence pronounced was amply justified. But that, of course, does not absolve us from considering carefully the procedural objection taken and so carefully argued to us by counsel.

It has always been an essential feature of our criminal procedure in Scotland that the prosecutor should remain in charge of the prosecution right up to the time when sentence is actually pronounced. Hence it has always been part of our procedure that, even after the guilt of an accused has been established, the prosecutor should have an opportunity, if he thinks fit, to withdraw the case and allow the accused to go free—see Macdonald on Criminal Law, (5th ed.) p. 348. This, no doubt, dates from the time when, owing to the depth of partisan feelings, juries and even sometimes Judges, might be perverse or unfair, and the right to withdraw a case was thus preserved, to enable an impartial prosecutor to secure that justice was done. But today these partisan feelings in criminal matters at least have faded and perversity on the part of Judges and juries is much more rare. Yet the procedural rule that the prosecutor must still have the opportunity of withdrawing the case, even after a verdict of guilty has been pronounced, is still preserved in the form of his moving for sentence.

If, in the present case, the Sheriff-substitute had proceeded to sentence the applicant without affording an opportunity to the prosecutor to withdraw the case, I should have regarded the sentence as incompetent. But that is not the situation. An opportunity was afforded for this step to be taken. Indeed, the circumstances of the present case are even stronger than that, for the prosecutor proceeded to lay before the Court the previous convictions applicable to the appellant. In terms of section 39 (1) (e) of the Criminal Justice (Scotland) Act, 1949. 'Previous convictions cannot be laid before the Court until the prosecutor moves for sentence.' In the present case, therefore, the prosecutor clearly did not take advantage of his inherent right to withdraw the prosecution after the verdict was pronounced, but, on the contrary, by referring to the previous convictions, he made it clear beyond doubt that he was doing the very reverse.

It is true that he did not formally move for sentence by using those precise words. It would have been much better had he done so and in future, to avoid any possibility of confusion, this course should always be explicitly taken. But, in my opinion, his failure to use these actual words is not fatal, and, provided he is given an opportunity to withdraw the case, and by his conduct he shows clearly that the Court is being asked to pronounce sentence, the law is satisfied. It is nowhere laid down that he must actually use the words: 'I move for sentence' in order to make the sentence competent—see Hume on Crime, vol. ii, p. 471, Alison, Criminal Law, vol. ii, p. 653. In the present case, by dealing with the previous convictions, the prosecutor was in effect asking the Court to deal with the sentence and giving up his right to withdraw the case. In a very real sense, therefore, he was inviting the Court to proceed to sentence the applicant, since it would have been illegal for him to have referred to the previous convictions upon any other basis.

We were referred to the case of *H. M. Advocate* v. *Fraser* [(1852) 1 Irvine 1] in support of the applicant's contention. But I do not regard that case as of assistance in the present connexion. In the case, the prosecutor had moved for sentence in terms, and the issue in the case turned upon the failure of the Circuit Court to continue the case to a specified day and the competency of that Court's order continuing the cause in general terms. This issue does not arise in the present case. I am, therefore, of opinion that the present application fails. I am confirmed in this conclusion by the fact that the Sheriff-substitute obviously regarded the prosecutor as waiving his right to withdraw the case once the jury had reached their conclusion, and, so far from objecting to that course and to the reference to the previous convictions, the applicant's agent admitted them, and addressed the Court in mitigation of sentence. There was, therefore, no dubiety in the minds of parties, or of the Sheriff-substitute, that the Court was being invited to sentence the applicant for the crime of which the jury had found him guilty. I move your Lordships that we refuse the application."

LORD SORN: "In solemn procedure, the prosecutor is in control of the instance and may abandon the prosecution at any stage. Even after the verdict has been returned, he may decline to move for sentence, or may refrain from doing so. In such a situation, the Court cannot, against the will of the prosecutor, proceed to pronounce a sentence. In other words, under our practice, the Judge in solemn procedure only pronounces sentence upon the invitation of the prosecutor. That invitation should be given in formal terms, and a prosecutor should never omit to make a formal motion. But the invitation, in my opinion, does not absolutely require to be made expressly and in formal terms. It is enough if there is an invitation by clear implication.

Turning to the situation here, it seems to me that when, after the verdict, the prosecutor tabled the previous convictions recorded against the accused, and stated certain facts to the Sheriff, which were germane to the question of sentence, he gave an unequivocal invitation to the Court to proceed to the final step. I therefore agree that the application fails."

The court refused
the application.

NOTE

A particular danger in not moving for sentence was highlighted by the case of *Paterson* v. *H.M. Advocate*, 1974 J.C. 35. In that case the appellant, having been found guilty on a charge of murder, and one of attempted murder, appealed against his conviction on the charge of murder. The appeal was successful, and the conviction and sentence quashed. There remained the conviction for attempted murder, but the Crown, in accordance with the normal practice at that time, had not moved for sentence on the lesser charge. The appellant thus escaped without any penalty being imposed. Needless to say, Crown Office policy was appropriately amended.

It should be noted that the public prosecutor has no direct control over the nature of the sentence imposed. However, his control over the choice of court and form of procedure gives him a measure of indirect control in that the selection of the court will in most cases fix the sentencing parameters.

(vii) Controlling the exercise of the prosecutor's discretion

Notwithstanding the extensive nature of the public prosecutor's discretion, it is clear that in the exercise of that discretion the prosecutor is subject to a variety of controls, both judicial and extra-judicial. Thus a decision not to prosecute in a particular case may be challenged by the victim applying to the High Court for permission to bring a private prosecution (*infra*, pp. 56-78). Conversely, a decision to bring a prosecution may be open to challenge, for example, on the ground that the prosecutor has previously renounced the right to prosecute, or that he is acting oppressively in bringing a prosecution (as, for example, where the prosecution is stale or there has been prejudicial pre-trial publicity — see *post*, pp. 304-306). The question of suing the public prosecutor for wrongful prosecution has also been raised, with little success:

Hester v. MacDonald
1961 S.C. 370

Hester brought an action of damages against (1) the procurator fiscal for the Lower Ward of Lanarkshire, (2) the Lord Advocate, and (3) a procurator fiscal depute for Glasgow. The action arose out of the respondent's prosecution and conviction on indictment on a charge of theft. It appeared that due to an administrative error the respondent had never had the indictment served upon him by the Crown, and that, despite protests to this effect during the trial, no attempt was made to verify this fact, and the procurator fiscal conducting the prosecution carried on to the point of conviction and sentence. The action was dismissed *quoad* the first and second defenders, but not the third. On appeal by the third defender:

LORD PRESIDENT (CLYDE): ". . . The first issue raised is the competency of this action of damages by a person tried on indictment before a Sheriff and jury, who sues the Depute Procurator-fiscal who conducted the trial. This question raises a matter of quite fundamental importance in our unique Scottish system relating to indictable offences.

To appreciate its significance, it is necessary, first of all, to consider the position of the Lord Advocate in this system. Under our constitution, the Lord Advocate has a universal and exclusive title to prosecute on indictment (Macdonald, Criminal Law, p. 212). As Baron Hume says (Crimes, vol. ii, p. 155): 'By custom, the process by indictment is the exclusive privilege of the Lord Advocate, or public prosecutor, who alone is possessed of that notorious and public character, which entitles him summarily, and of his own authority, to state himself to the Court as accuser, and call on the Judges for trial of his charge, without any previous licence obtained.' In our system, the Lord Advocate alone possesses the function, in indictable offences, of deciding whether he will prosecute or whether he will withdraw a prosecution, and there is no appeal to any Court against his decision on these matters. No Court or magistrate can compel or direct or recommend to him what he should do. These are matters exclusively for him and exclusively within his province—Alison's Criminal Law, vol. ii, p. 87. His responsibilities and privileges are quite unique, and they depend for their continuance on the confidence of the public in the utter impartiality with which he has always administered his onerous duties regarding crime. From time immemorial it has, therefore, been recognised, as Baron Hume puts it—Crimes, vol. ii, p. 135—that 'a constitutional trust is reposed in that high officer, selected by His Majesty from among the most eminent at the Bar; and it will not be supposed of him, that he can be actuated by unworthy motives in commencing a prosecution, or fall into such irregularities or blunders in conducting his process, as ought properly to make him liable in . . . amends.' As Alison says (vol. ii, p. 93) he is absolutely exempt from penalties and expenses.

It is, therefore, an essential element in the very structure of our criminal administration in Scotland that the Lord Advocate is protected by an absolute privilege in respect of matters in connexion with proceedings brought before a Scottish Criminal Court by way of indictment. (Compare Renton and Brown, Criminal Procedure, (3rd ed.) p. 450.) Never in our history has a Lord Advocate been sued for damages in connexion with such proceedings. On the contrary, our Courts have consistently affirmed the existence of such immunity on his part. For instance, in *Henderson* v. *Robertson* [(1853) 15 D. 292], Lord Justice-Clerk Hope said (at p. 295): 'It is impossible to disguise the great importance of this question, one of the most important that can be raised in reference to the office of public prosecutor. The public prosecutor has by law great and most important protection. As against the Lord Advocate, I do not think that a case of liability to damages could be even stated.' (Compare Lord Young in *M'Murchy* v. *Campbell* [(1887) 14 R. 725], at p. 728.)

It may be that in other departments of his duties and responsibilities a civil action for damages may lie against him, but in connexion with his administration of crime he is in this special position. He is subject, of course, in regard to criminal matters, to the constitutional safeguards of Parliamentary action, but there is no remedy against him by way of action at law.

The position of the Procurator-fiscal is not precisely the same. In the old days he could be liable in damages, if he acted maliciously and without probable cause (Alison's *Criminal Law*, vol. ii, p. 93). But the position of the Procurator-fiscal has altered with the coming into operation of the Criminal Procedure (Scotland) Act, 1887. Many of the decisions on the rights and liabilities of Procurators-fiscal pronounced prior to that Act do not apply thereafter. For the Act resulted in a much closer and more substantial control by the Lord Advocate over the Procurator-fiscal so far as cases tried by jury are concerned. Prior to the Act, prosecution by indictment was confined to the High Court of Justiciary, where the control of the prosecution rested in the Lord Advocate, or was under his authority. The Sheriff's Procurator-fiscal had a certain measure of independence in connexion with the prosecution of crimes in the Sheriff Court, and criminal letters could be taken in his own name there for the purpose of prosecutions before the Sheriff. Under section 2 of the 1887 Act, however, the existing system was materially altered, and thereafter, all prosecutions for the public interest in the Sheriff Court where the Sheriff was sitting with a jury 'shall proceed on indictment in name of Her Majesty's Advocate . . . and shall be signed by Her Majesty's Advocate or one of his deputes, or by a procurator fiscal, and the words "By authority of Her Majesty's Advocate" shall be prefixed to the signature of such procurator fiscal.' By section 1, 'procurator fiscal' includes a 'depute procurator fiscal.'

This change involved a radical alteration. It left summary prosecutions to be conducted by the Procurator-fiscal on his own authority and in his own name. But it required prosecutions for crimes in the Sheriff Court appropriate for trial by jury to be conducted, not on the authority of the Procurator-fiscal, but on the instructions, and under the authority, and in name, of the Lord Advocate, just like indictments in the High Court. It, therefore, assimilated criminal trials by jury in the Sheriff Court on indictment to trials in the High Court of Justiciary. The Lord Advocate was in complete control in both cases.

The criminal trial with which the present case is concerned was a Sheriff and jury trial on indictment. It was approved and authorised by the Lord Advocate, who instructed its prosecution. The Lord Advocate was directly responsible for its conduct, and the immunity from a claim of damages which he enjoyed was, in my opinion, therefore enjoyed also by the Procurator-fiscal and the Depute, who were acting on his authority, and carrying out his instructions, in this criminal trial, as his direct representatives.

The contrast between the situation in a Sheriff and jury case such as that involved in the present instance and a summary case in the Sheriff Court is worth noting. In the latter, the prosecution is at the instance of the Procurator-fiscal (see Sheriff Courts and Legal Officers (Scotland) Act, 1927, sec. 12), and Parliament has expressly recognised the liability of a Procurator-fiscal in such cases to damages, provided, *inter alia*, the person suing for damages shall prove that such Procurator-fiscal did something in the course of the proceedings which was malicious and without probable cause. (Summary Jurisdiction (Scotland) Act, 1954, sec. 75 (1) (*c*)). A similar provision is incorporated in the earlier Summary Procedure (Scotland) Act, 1864, and the Summary Jurisdiction (Scotland) Act, 1908. It has always been a feature of such summary proceedings in Scotland. But Parliament has never made any such provision in regard to solemn procedure by way of indictment where the Procurator-fiscal is not acting on his own authority, but expressly on the authority and instructions and in name of the Lord Advocate. The reason is that, in connexion with proceedings by indictment, our law does not recognise any right to damages against the Lord Advocate or against those acting on his instructions. Moreover, it would be astonishing indeed, if a Procurator-fiscal Depute, when conducting a summary case, should only be liable in damages if malice is proved, but (as the pursuer here claims) that he should be liable in damages, even without proof of malice in a prosecution on indictment where he is acting, not on his own, but on the express instructions of the Lord Advocate.

The result is, therefore, in my opinion, that the pursuer's claim against the third defender in this case is incompetent, and must fail; for, in the proceedings out of which the claim arises, the third defender was acting as the hand of the Lord Advocate. In condescendence 2 the pursuer avers that 'in conducting the prosecution the third-named defender was authorised and instructed by the first-named defender who was responsible for the third-named defender's actions.' This is true, and is fatal to the competency of the pursuer's claim.

It was argued to us that, although the action against the Lord Advocate was incompetent, owing to his immunity from civil claims under the constitution of his office, this did not apply to the third-named defender. But this argument appears to me to be unstateable. If the Lord Advocate, as the responsible criminal prosecutor, is immune, it necessarily must follow that his immunity covers those, such as the third-named defender, who are acting on the instructions and under the responsibility of the Procurator-fiscal who in turn was the hand of the Lord Advocate. It was argued that this result involves a great extension of the immunity from civil claims enjoyed by the Lord Advocate. But it relates to that class of prosecution (indictments in the Sheriff Court) where Parliament has seen fit to put the Lord Advocate expressly in control. It is a tribute to the fairness and efficiency with which the Procurator-fiscal service has performed its work in this class of prosecution that, since 1887, there has never been any suggestion that a Procurator-fiscal is liable in damages for actings in such prosecutions, and it would be a misfortune for our criminal administration if any doubt were to be cast on the immunity which he has hitherto always enjoyed in this regard. The standard of conduct in this service has in the eyes of the public well merited this protection, and the assertion of this protection involves no departure from our well settled practice, but, on the contrary, an affirmation and recognition of it. The Procurator-fiscal's immunity from the consequences of his actings is, of course, not absolute. He may be removed from his office by the Lord Advocate on a report by the Lord President of the Court of Session and the Lord Justice-Clerk (see Sheriff Courts and Legal Officers (Scotland) Act, 1927, section 1.) In these circumstances, in my opinion, it is not open to the pursuer to claim damages in this case against the third-named defender. This is enough to dispose of this present case and would entitle us to hold the action incompetent."

> The court allowed the appeal
> and dismissed the action.

NOTE

The court also held that even if such an action was competent, it would have failed on the merits.

The liability of a prosecutor in summary proceedings, where he is not acting for or on behalf of the Lord Advocate is governed by section 456 of the 1975 Act. In order to succeed in an action against such prosecutor the pursuer must have suffered imprisonment as a result of proceedings, sentence, etc., which has subsequently been quashed, and the person suing must aver and prove malice and want of probable cause on the part of the prosecutor; see also *Graham* v. *Strathern*, 1924 S.C. 699.

Article 13 of the European Convention on Human Rights provides that everyone whose rights and freedoms as set forth in the Convention are violated "shall have an effective remedy before a national authority, notwithstanding that the violation has been committed by persons acting in an official capacity." Does the absolute privilege accorded to the Lord Advocate and his deputies in *Hester* v. *MacDonald* violate article 13?

c. Private prosecution

Due to the dominant position of the public prosecutor in the initiation and conduct of criminal proceedings, private prosecution is very much the exception to the rule. In saying this, however, it is useful to distinguish solemn and summary proceedings. While private prosecution is extremely rare in solemn proceedings, summary private prosecutions are rather more frequent, at least where the title to prosecute is conferred by statute. The following materials discuss private prosecution on indictment.

1. J. & P. Coats Ltd. v. Brown
1909 S.C. (J.) 29

By a contract dated 11 January 1908 the respondent, a coal merchant, agreed to supply the complainers with a quantity of coal described as "Bent Splint Coal." To the respondent's knowledge, only a small proportion of the coal delivered to the complainers conformed to this description. He nevertheless requested, and obtained, payment as if delivery had been made as per the contract. The Lord Advocate refused to prosecute the respondent or to grant his concurrence to a private prosecution at the instance of the complainers. The latter presented to the High Court a bill for criminal letters to prosecute the respondent for fraud.

LORD JUSTICE-CLERK (MACDONALD): "The prosecution of crime in Scotland has for so long a period been practically in the hands of the King's Advocate, and of subordinate public prosecutors acting under his control, and this procedure has been attended with such satisfactory results to the administration of the criminal law, that private prosecution for serious crimes is practically unknown, the public being well satisfied that as a general rule the interests of justice are well guarded by the Lord Advocate's department. The question now arises for the first time for very many years whether a private prosecution shall be allowed to proceed, seeing that the Lord Advocate declines to take up the case or to give his concurrence to a prosecution at the instance of the party who alleges that a criminal wrong has been done to his injury.

A citizen desiring to institute a prosecution at common law for crime requires by law to be in the position — (1) that he has applied to the Lord Advocate to obtain his concurrence to the prosecution, and (2) that the crime alleged be a wrong towards himself. By these rules the accused citizen is safeguarded from malicious or vindictive prosecution by private individuals, the Lord Advocate, or those who represent the public interest under him in the inferior Courts, being responsible for the proper exercise of their office in any question relating to the granting of concurrence to a private prosecutor's action.

But there is not vested in the public prosecutor an absolute right of veto. It is the right of the citizen to complain to the High Court of Justiciary against a refusal by the public prosecutor to grant his concurrence to a private prosecutor where he has declined to take up the prosecution on behalf of the Crown. The Lord Advocate frankly conceded this at the discussion. He must, if called on, shew cause for his declinature, and the Court can consider the question whether the withholding of the concurrence in the circumstances may involve a wrong to the citizen complaining, and a failure of public justice. For the citizen desiring to prosecute is seeking to invoke the law not for reparation to himself, but *ad vindictam publicam*, and this is clearly expressed in the criminal letters granted to him. If he desires personal reparation he must seek that in a civil Court. It is only for the purpose of preventing the right to prosecute being used for vindictive or malicious ends that he must ask for the Lord Advocate's concurrence.

It is in that state of the law that in the present case the complainer presents to this Court a complaint and form of charge by criminal letters, and asks that a private prosecution shall be sanctioned by the Court, either without the concurrence of the Lord Advocate, or by the Court ordaining the Lord Advocate to grant his concurrence. At the debate the Lord Advocate said that if in the end either of these courses commended itself to the Court, he would act as the Court might order.

It seems to me not to be a question of serious importance which of these courses is to be adopted, if the ultimate decision of this case should be that a prosecution is to be allowed. In either case the prosecution would proceed in exactly the same manner. My suggestion to your Lordships would be that the more practical and least embarrassing course would be that the Court should authorise the private party to proceed, rather than that a prosecutor, unwilling in the exercise of his discretion to grant concurrence, should be directed to do so, for its seems to me to be not a good mode of correcting an unsatisfactory exercise of a vested discretion that an official should be forced into the position of saying in words that he concurs, when his non-concurrence is overruled as not being in the circumstances right. Therefore, if your Lordships should be of opinion that this case forms an exception to the rule and requires exceptional treatment, I would suggest that it be rather made an exception by allowing the prosecution without the usual condition of concurrence by the public prosecutor, than that the Lord Advocate should by an order of the Court be made to appear to concur in a prosecution, as to which he has formed an opinion, to which he adheres, that his concurrence ought not to be given . . .

No doubt it may be said that there may be many cases in which such a thing is done where the criminality would be small and perhaps such that the public prosecutor might in his discretion not think it necessary that the act done should be followed by a criminal prosecution. Further, it might be said that explanations might be given which would give a complexion to the case that might justify holding back from public prosecution. But in this case I do not think that there is ground for giving weight to such considerations. The complainers have laid before the Court documents referred to in the proposed criminal letters which, if proved, would tend to shew that the accused endeavoured to support his fraud by the use of · a certificate obtained from a colliery official to the effect that the coal shipped on board in fulfilment of the contract was 'Bent Splint Coal,' and he, knowing the certificate to be false, caused it to be delivered as a true certificate to the complainers. If this were to be proved at a trial, it could not but have a very strong bearing on the question what answer should be made to the charge stated in the criminal letters, unless the defence were able to overcome its weight by evidence which would alter the balance. As regards the magnitude of the fraud, if committed, there can be no doubt, seeing that it related to 500 tons of coal. And as regards possible explanations, these are properly matters of defence, and the Court has nothing before it bearing upon that matter. The Lord Advocate did not in any way suggest that there were such explanations before him as would make the charge untenable if proved. If there are such, they are quite open as matter of defence at the trial. But if it is not thought proper or necessary by the public prosecutor to put such forward as a ground for refusing his concurrence, the Court must deal with the case before it as if there were none, in considering whether a private prosecutor should be permitted to have criminal letters issued.

The Lord Advocate told the Court that if the complainers would proceed to endeavour to obtain reparation by a civil action, he would consider the proceedings in such a case, and if he saw ground for a criminal prosecution in them, would reconsider his determination. I confess I was not able to follow the line of thought indicated by such a statement. If the Lord Advocate has already had the case fully investigated in his department, one would expect that he would know now whether it was permissible to take criminal proceedings. If he has not had such an investigation made, then it is difficult to see how he can be held to be in a proper position to consider whether he should give his concurrence to a prosecution or not. But it seems to me that such a suggestion can hardly be one to influence the Court in the matter. It is quite contrary to the order of procedure in criminal law administration that the whole circumstances of a case should first be thrashed out in a civil Court, with possibly a succession of proceedings of review, ending, it may be, in the House of Lords after a litigation extending over years, and that then the question of criminal prosecution should be finally determined. The case of perjury in civil proceedings was suggested as analogous, but there is plainly no analogy. In such a case the crime does not consist in the past acts which form the subject of the litigation, but in false swearing in the conduct of the case. There is no crime committed before the civil suit, the crime is only committed when perjured evidence is given in that suit. Here it is the very subject-matter of the alleged crime which forms the essence of the civil claim itself. I do not think your Lordships can give any weight to such a suggestion as that it would be proper to postpone consideration of a question of criminal prosecution until civil proceedings had been concluded. Criminal prosecution should follow the crime with all due dispatch, and our law expressly forbids delay in prosecution unless the accused party is allowed to remain at large, which in many cases might be most injurious to the course of justice. And in addition to all this, civil proceedings might be seriously hampered by a defender being able to decline to give evidence which might incriminate him, if he was in the position of knowing that a future criminal prosecution was hanging over his head. Both sides might be hampered by such a course being taken.

My opinion is that in the circumstances as disclosed to us at this stage the private prosecutor has shewn grounds why he should not be shut out from his rights as a citizen to have an alleged crime investigated now, in regard to a matter in which he alleges relevantly that he has been wronged."

LORD MCLAREN: "I understand that your Lordships propose to dispense with the Lord Advocate's concurrence to a private prosecution at the instance of the complainers. I take a different view as to the scope and exercise of the powers of the Court, and as the question is one of public importance, I feel bound to state my reasons for this difference of opinion. The right of private prosecution in Scotland is very rarely exercised. The Lord Advocate in his address to the Court said that he did not think there had been a case during the last century. This is not strictly correct, because there has been at least one case, the trial of Colonel Charteris in 1823, to which I shall afterwards refer. Yet it is the case that the investigation of crime under the Lord Advocate's department has been so efficiently performed, and the confidence which the public has uniformly extended to the administrators of this department of state has been such, that the right of private prosecution has ceased to be of any practical importance in our criminal law.

It is one of the normal conditions of the right of private prosecution that the bill for criminal letters has to be subscribed by the Lord Advocate in token of his concurrence. This concurrence does not commit the Lord Advocate to an opinion on the case; it only means that the matter of the bill is fit for consideration by a Court of criminal jurisdiction. It is therefore, to say the least, extremely unlikely that this concurrence would be refused to a prosecution that had any substance in it.

It is plain enough that an unrestricted right of private prosecution would not be tolerated in any country. That any spiteful or irrational person should have the power to subject his adversary to the indignity of being placed at the bar of a criminal Court, without preliminary inquiry or check of any kind, is a notion too absurd to be seriously entertained.

In England, where we know it is usual to bind over the injured party to prosecute, the necessary check is provided by the preliminary inquiry before a magistrate, who, of course, will not commit the accused person for trial unless the depositions disclose a *prima facie* case of crime or misdemeanour. There is also the further protection of the grand jury, who may dismiss the bill ('ignore,' I think, is the legal word), and thus put a stop to an unconscientious or unsubstantial accusation. I say nothing as to the Attorney-General's right to stay a prosecution by his fiat, because I understand it is rarely, if ever, exercised.

In Scotland we have neither public inquiry before a magistrate nor consideration by a grand jury as a necessary preliminary to a private prosecution, but the object is attained in a different way, by the requirement of the Lord Advocate's concurrence, which will not be given without an inquiry through his department into the facts of the case.

It is, of course, recognised that the Lord Advocate has no arbitrary power, but must exercise the functions of his department impartially and in accordance with sound discretion. The control of the Court in this matter is considered by Hume in a well-known passage in the chapter on 'Prosecutors and their title,' and the author opens the subject by propounding the question, Whether the Lord Advocate, 'by refusing his concourse, may at his pleasure suppress the private instance, and protect the transgressor from the just consequences of his crime?'

To the question as thus put, there can be but one answer, and the author states his opinion that in such a case the Court may either direct the Lord Advocate to give his concurrence, or may dispense with his concurrence, and authorise the issue of criminal letters.

No case was cited by the complainers' counsel, and I know of no case, in which the Court has granted the prayer of a bill for criminal letters without the concurrence of His Majesty's Advocate. But the absence of direct authority does not in any way militate against the power of the Court, which is undoubted. It only proves that this is an extraordinary remedy for an extraordinary and unprecedented occurrence, viz., the undue and arbitrary exercise by an officer of the Crown of a power entrusted to him for public purposes. That I may not be supposed to suggest a doubt as to the powers of the Court, I note that the power has been very distinctly recognised in two modern cases, in one of which I was present as a Judge, but in neither case was the party complainer successful in challenging the Lord Advocate's decision to refuse his concurrence to the desired prosecution.

I will make one other general observation. Hume is a very high authority, but personally I should be disposed to go further than the dictum of Hume. If the Lord Advocate should state as his reason for not giving his concurrence to a bill that the statements contained in the bill did not in his judgment disclose a crime according to the law of Scotland, and if we were of opinion that the bill did disclose a *prima facie* relevant charge of crime, I think we might sustain the bill, leaving the relevancy of the charge to be further considered at the trial. I say this, because I think that in the case of a pure question of law the Supreme Court of criminal jurisdiction may act on its own judgment, and is not bound by the Lord Advocate's opinion. In such a case I do not doubt that the Lord Advocate would give his concurrence, if desired by the Court.

But in the present case the Lord Advocate has withheld his concurrence, because after investigation he came to be of opinion, on the facts of the case, that there was not reasonable ground for a criminal prosecution. In his address to the Court the Lord Advocate said—'The line between the domain of civil and criminal law was sometimes difficult to draw, but in this case the information laid before him disclosed a question which, in his judgment, lay well within the region of the civil law, and plainly outside the region of the criminal law.' On a second consideration of the case, his Lordship continued, 'he satisfied himself that he had information to enable him to form a judgment' and he came without any hesitation to think that there was no reason for altering the judgment at which he had formerly arrived, and that there were no sufficient grounds here for a criminal prosecution.' It is necessary for the purposes of the case that I should say that I am entirely satisfied that the Lord Advocate has made a sufficient inquiry into the facts of the case, and that I have no reason to doubt that the decision neither to prosecute nor to grant concurrence was the result of an attentive and impartial examination into the facts of the case.

In such circumstances I am confronted with the question, how am I to form an independent opinion on the facts as to whether there are or are not grounds for a criminal prosecution? It is one thing to say that we may give redress against an arbitrary refusal of the Lord Advocate's concurrence, or a refusal on legal grounds which are disclosed to us; and it is quite a different proposition that we are to review the Lord Advocate's decision that the facts do not warrant a prosecution. If it were intended by the constitution of the country that this Court should undertake such a review, we should either have the power of calling for the Crown precognitions, or of employing an agent to institute an independent inquiry and to report to us. Nothing of the kind has ever been done, and your Lordships are not proposing to make such an inquiry.

It was argued for the complainers that the charge of fraud depended on documentary evidence, which he said discloses a *prima facie* case.

In my opinion the documents prove nothing. I do not doubt that the defender made use of a colliery certificate that was untrue in fact, but we have only the complainers' statement in the bill for the all-important points that the document was uttered knowing it to be false, and with intent to defraud. Now, I may be altogether wrong, but I must frankly say that on the question whether there is a *prima facie* case for prosecution, I prefer the dispassionate opinion of the Lord Advocate who has studied the case, to the unsupported statements of Messrs Coats, who no doubt honestly believe that they have been defrauded, but who are not the best judges in their own case.

Nor am I much moved by the argument that if the respondent is innocent he will have an opportunity of proving his innocence at the trial of the case. This answer, as I think, entirely fails, because it is an answer that may be made in every case in which the Lord Advocate's decision to concur or not to concur is challenged. I have already observed that I do not find any reported case in which the Court has dispensed with the Lord Advocate's concurrence. The nearest approach to a precedent is in the two cases cited by Hume (*Crimes*, ii, 118) in the paragraph referred to. In the first case, the date of which is 1633, the Court directed the Lord Advocate to give his concurrence to an action of reduction-improbation; but this, as Hume points out, is not a genuine criminal process, and unless a caveat is lodged, I believe the practice has been to grant the concurrence as a matter of course. The second case, which occurred two centuries later, is that of Colonel Charteris, in 1823, where the Lord Advocate withdrew his concurrence at the trial, and the case was allowed to proceed. I may respectfully say that this decision seems to be sound in principle, because the concurrence is only required to the bill for criminal letters, and after the criminal letters are issued the case is out of the Lord Advocate's hands. I may add, with the utmost deference to the opinions of other members of the Court, that personally I should deprecate very strongly the notion that this Court is to be a Court of review of the work of the Lord Advocate's department, a task for which, by its constitution and means of informing itself, the Court is alike unfitted; and my opinion is that the bill should be refused."

LORD JUSTICE-GENERAL (DUNEDIN): ". . . But the chief reason which has influenced my brother Lord M'Laren in his dissent from the majority of your Lordships has been his extreme repugnance of the idea that this Court should sit as a Court of review of the discretion of the Lord Advocate. I do not think there is any difference of opinion upon this bench upon this matter. It is no light matter to interfere with the discretion of the Lord Advocate, and I can conceive very few cases in which we would so interfere.

But we are bound, none the less, to direct our minds to the particular case that has been brought before us, and I agree with the Lord Justice-Clerk in thinking that the actual written documents that are here brought before us go very far to establish the case. Of course I do not wish to say too much upon that matter, because I am not going to prejudice the defence which may be finally brought forward. But when my brother Lord M'Laren went on to say that he thought that the whole matter would turn upon whether it was shewn that the party charged here really knew or did not know that this certificate was false, I am compelled to observe, first of all, that the complainer says so most distinctly, and that, if the Lord Advocate in the exercise of his discretion chooses to maintain a more than usual reticence, I am afraid he must take the consequences of that reticence.

It seems to me nothing would have been easier than for the Lord Advocate to have said—if he could say it—that upon a consideration of the whole circumstances, he had come to the conclusion that the party charged here was under the belief that the certificate was true. If the Lord Advocate had said he was satisfied of that, or even if he had gone so far as this, that he had not had brought before him any evidence which would lead to the conclusion that the party charged knew that the certificate was false, I imagine—at least speaking for myself—that I would not have interfered with the discretion of the Lord Advocate. The Lord Advocate says none of those things, and he leaves us—and that is a matter for him to judge—completely in the dark as to what the form of defence is to be. Under these circumstances the disagreeable necessity—as I think I must call it—is laid upon us of affirming that this is a case where a subject has seemingly been wronged and no real reason has been laid before us why a prosecution should not be allowed."

The court passed
the bill.

NOTE

The respondent was subsequently convicted and admonished (High Court, 26 May 1909).

Lord McLaren was the only member of the court to dissent. His dissent did not concern the complainer's title to prosecute, or the competency of the procedure adopted by the complainer, both of which appear to have been more or less taken for granted by the court. The disagreement related to the extent to which the court was entitled to act as a court of review of the Lord Advocate's discretion. In its narrowest construction the majority opinion seems to have been that if the Lord Advocate failed to provide reasons for his refusal to prosecute, and the complainer established a prima facie case, then the court was entitled to authorise a prosecution. A rather broader view is suggested by the Lord Justice-Clerk whose opinion appears to have been that the court could "consider the question whether the withholding of the concurrence in the circumstances may involve a wrong to the citizen complaining, and a failure of public justice."

Lord McLaren, however, took the view that the granting of criminal letters by the court was an "extraordinary remedy" only available in the event of "the undue and arbitrary exercise by an officer of the Crown of a power entrusted to him for public purposes."

2.   McBain v. Crichton
1961 J.C. 25

LORD JUSTICE-GENERAL (CLYDE): "This bill for criminal letters has been presented to the High Court of Justiciary by Mr A. G. M'Bain, chartered accountant, Glasgow, asking for criminal letters to enable him to initiate a prosecution against a certain bookseller in Glasgow for exposing for sale and selling in his place of business a book called *Lady Chatterley's Lover*, by D. H. Lawrence, which he alleges is lewd, impure, gross and obscene, and contains passages contrived and intended to corrupt the morals of the lieges, and particularly of the youth of both sexes.

Since the Lord Advocate has refused his concurrence to the proposed prosecution, this Court ordered intimation of the bill to be made to the Lord Advocate, as is the custom, and appointed a day for the hearing of the bill. The Lord Advocate has appeared in person at this hearing and has informed the Court that he has fully investigated the matter more than once and, in the exercise of that wide discretion which is invested in the Lord Advocate, he has come to the conclusion that a prosecution would not be justified in connexion with this matter. He has therefore decided not to prosecute at his own instance and not to give his concurrence to the private prosecution which the present complainer desires to raise.

The Lord Advocate is quite entitled to take up this position. In this country he is the recognised prosecutor in the public interest. It is for him, in the exercise of his responsible office, to decide whether he will prosecute in the public interest and at the public expense, and under our constitutional practice this decision is a matter for him, and for him alone. No one can compel him to give his reasons, nor order him to concur in a private prosecution. The basic principle of our system of criminal administration in Scotland is to submit the question of whether there is to be a public prosecution to the impartial and skilled investigation of the Lord Advocate and his department, and the decision whether or not to prosecute is exclusively within his discretion. This system has operated in Scotland for centuries, and—see Alison on Criminal Law, vol. ii, p. 88—the result has completely proved the justice of these principles, for such has become the public confidence in the decision of the Lord Advocate and his deputes on the grounds of prosecution, that private prosecutions have almost gone into disuse. It is utterly inconsistent with such a system that the Courts should examine, as it was suggested it would be proper or competent for us to do, the reasons which have affected the Lord Advocate in deciding how to exercise his discretion, and it would be still more absurd for this Court to proceed to review their soundness. Any *dicta* indicating that such a course is open to any Court are, in my view, quite unsound.

But the lack of the Lord Advocate's concurrence is not necessarily fatal to a private prosecution. Although we cannot review the exercise of the Lord Advocate's discretion nor his reasons for exercising it in the way he did, this Court can permit, and on rare occasions has permitted, a private prosecutor to proceed without the Lord Advocate's concurrence. But to entitle a private prosecutor to do so, he must be able to show some special personal interest in the matter which, notwithstanding the Lord Advocate's decision in the public interest, satisfies us that a private prosecution in respect of this special personal interest may proceed. Hume on Crimes, vol. ii, at p. 119, puts it thus: 'To support his instance the individual complainer must be able therefore to show some substantial and peculiar interest in the issue of the trial; an interest arising out of some injury which he, beyond others, has suffered on the occasion libelled, and at which he is entitled to feel more than the ordinary indignation, with which his fellow citizens will regard it. It is not therefore sufficient, that he has some feeble and remote concern in the issue, or one of a general nature, in common with a whole neighbourhood, or with all of the same order or class of society.' A similar principle is laid down in Alison on Criminal Law, vol. ii, p. 100, where the learned author expresses the matter thus:—'To support his instance or title to carry on such a process (that is to say, a private prosecution) the private party must be able to show some substantial and peculiar interest in the issue of the trial, an interest arising from what he, beyond all others, has suffered on the occasion libelled, and at which he is entitled to feel more than ordinary indignation.' (Compare also Macdonald on Criminal Law, (5th ed.) p. 212; Renton and Brown, Criminal Procedure, (3rd ed.) p. 27 and p. 197.) The same principle is referred to in the opinion of Lord Justice-Clerk Macdonald (with whose opinion Lord Kinnear, Lord Low and Lord Pearson concurred), in the case of *J. & P. Coats, Limited* v. *Brown [supra]* at pp. 33 and 34. This was a case where a private prosecution for fraud was allowed to be instituted without the concurrence of the Lord Advocate. In that case, however, the special personal interest was demonstrable since the complainers were themselves the persons alleged to have been defrauded in the sale of coal to them by a coal merchant. They were, therefore, able to show that, in the words of Alison and of Hume, which I have already quoted, they, 'beyond all others,' had 'suffered on the occasion libelled.'

But, in the present case, the wrong complained of, if it is a wrong (and on that matter, of course, it would be quite improper for us at this stage to express an opinion one way or the other), the wrong, if it exists, is of a quite general and public nature, committed against a whole neighbourhood or perhaps against the whole country, and, in its very nature, devoid of that personal and peculiar interest without which no private prosecution ever has been sustained in Scotland. In the terms of the complainer's bill itself the wrong is not a wrong alleged to have been done to a particular individual, but a wrong to the lieges in general, or, at any rate, to the younger members of the public in general. The wrong alleged is therefore a purely public one.

It was contended before us that there was an element of private interest as well, because of the official position which the complainer held as vice-president of the Glasgow Union of Boys' Clubs. But that interest, even if it had been averred in the bill, is just as much a public interest as the interest which is averred in the bill. It does not partake of that essential quality without which the prosecution could not proceed at the instance of a private party, because it does not show that the complainer personally and beyond all others has suffered owing to the wrong libelled. At the highest it would only invest him with an interest as protector of the morals of a class of persons in the community—namely the younger members of it. This is in its very nature a public and not a private or personal interest.

This distinction is no mere technicality. It involves a clear and definite principle embedded in our law, stated in the institutional writers and referred to again and again in the decisions of this Court. Mr Gow has said all that could be said in favour of this prosecution proceeding at the complainer's instance without the Lord Advocate's concurrence, but I am clearly satisfied that no interest sufficient for that purpose has been made out. In these circumstances, there is no case which would justify this Court in granting the present application.

My motion to your Lordships is that we should refuse it."

The court refused the application.

NOTE

From the point of view of title to prosecute the complainer's case was doomed from the outset. A private prosecutor must satisfy the court that he has suffered a personal wrong through the commission of the alleged offence. On any view of this test the complainer could not establish such an interest—notwithstanding his interest in the moral welfare of the youth of Glasgow. Would it have made any difference if, for example, the complainer had found his own children reading the work in question?

The court's statements on the power to review the Lord Advocate's discretion are not supported by the other authorities. The statement that, "No one can compel him to give his reasons, nor order him to concur in a private prosecution" conflicts, for example, with what was said in *J. & P. Coats Ltd.* v. *Brown*. As regards the first proposition, the majority view was that the Lord Advocate must, if called on, show cause for his declinature. As regards the second, the court in *J. & P. Coats Ltd.* v. *Brown* was of the opinion that the court should not order the Lord Advocate to concur, not because this was incompetent, but because it was inexpedient.

3. Trapp v. M.; Trapp v. Y.
1971 S.L.T. (Notes) 30

The complainer was dismissed from his post as headmaster of an education authority school. A public inquiry was held into the reasons for his dismissal. The complainer alleged that the respondents, who were representatives of the education authority, committed perjury at the inquiry. A succession of Lord Advocates had refused to prosecute the respondents or to concur in a private prosecution. The complainer presented two bills for criminal letters to the High Court.

LORD JUSTICE-GENERAL (CLYDE): "In the present case the crime which the complainer seeks to establish against the two respondents is the crime of perjury in the course of the evidence which each gave at the inquiry before referred to. In Hume, *Crime*, Vol. I, crimes are analysed as falling into two categories, firstly offences to the injury of individuals whether in person, fame or property, and secondly (see Vol. I, p. 366) 'such offences as immediately concern the public as they are hostile to the course of public justice.' Of these the most important is the crime of perjury (see Hume, Vol. I, p. 366). The present two cases are therefore concerned with allegations of a crime which in its nature essentially concerns the public as a whole, and the proper administration of even handed justice in the public interest. These considerations make it all the more difficult for the complainer to qualify a right to prosecute in the case of the crime of perjury. The mere fact that in his two Bills he claims damages against each of the respondents for the wrongs which he alleges were done to him does not advance the matter. Every crime involves in one way or another injury or damage to someone, and a criminal prosecution is not an appropriate process in which to claim damages. As the Lord Justice-Clerk said in *J. & P. Coats Ltd.* v. *Brown*, 1909 S.C. (J.) 29, at p. 34 (1909, 1 S.L.T. 432), 'if he desires personal reparation he must seek that in a civil court.'

Apart from these more general considerations, a scrutiny of the particular allegations in each of the Bills merely confirms how unwarranted the granting of the prayer in either would be. Where the concurrence of the Lord Advocate has been refused the relevancy of the charge made by the complainer must be considered and determined before this court could grant the prayer of a Bill for criminal letters." His Lordship went on to hold that the averments in the Bills could not form a relevant basis for a prosecution for perjury. Reference was also made to *McBain* v. *C.*, 1961 J.C. 25, 1961 S.L.T. 209.

The court refused
the bill.

NOTE

Mr Trapp's contribution to the jurisprudence of private prosecution has been outstanding. He presented a third bill alleging perjury by a Mr G. at the public inquiry. It too was unsuccessful, though the court which rejected the bill based its refusal on an unwillingness to interfere with the Lord Advocate's discretion, rather than the ground that perjury was a "public" and not a private wrong: *Trapp* v. *G.*, 1972 S.L.T. (Notes) 46.

4. Meehan v. Inglis and Others
1974 S.L.T. (Notes) 61

The complainer was convicted of murder in October 1969. The respondents were police officers who had been Crown witnesses at his trial. The complainer alleged that they had committed perjury. Since the Lord Advocate refused to prosecute them, or to concur in a private prosecution at the complainer's instance, a bill was presented for criminal letters.

THE COURT: "Much of the complainer's argument was directed towards establishing that the Lord Advocate was not the *complete* master in deciding whether a prosecution for perjury should be initiated. He sought to persuade the court that in the case of *Trapp*, which is only reported in 1971 S.L.T. (Notes) 30, Lord Justice-General Clyde had implied that in a case of perjury (which was the allegation in *Trapp* (supra)) the Lord Advocate was the complete master of the decision to prosecute or not. This argument concentrated on one passage in Lord Clyde's judgment, where he was quoting from the case of *McBain* v. *C.*, 1961 J.C. 25, at p. 29 (1961 S.L.T. 209), in relation to the exclusive discretion of the Lord Advocate in deciding whether or not there should be a public prosecution. When the judgment is read as a whole (and the court had the benefit of the full judgment in that case and not just the abbreviated version in 1971 S.L.T. (Notes)) it is quite clear that Lord Clyde recognised that the right to decide whether a prosecution should be sanctioned was not a matter for the absolute and sole decision of the Lord Advocate. What he did say was that, for the reasons he gave, private prosecutions in Scotland have steadily grown rarer as time has gone by, and in the last 50 years they have fallen into virtual disuse. The court has the ultimate say on whether a private prosecution should be granted, even when the Lord Advocate has refused his concurrence, but as Lord Clyde pointed out in *Trapp* it would require some very special circumstances indeed to induce the court to make an exception to what has now almost become a settled practice. What Lord Clyde said in *Trapp* was in effect a reiteration of the judicial view of the role of the Lord Advocate as public prosecutor and the stringent conditions which have to be satisfied before a private prosecution will be sanctioned by the court, as enunciated in an anthology of cases of which the most modern examples are *J. & P. Coats Limited* v. *Brown*, 1909 S.C. (J.) 29, 1909 1

S.L.T. 432, *McBain* v. *C.* (supra) and *Trapp* itself. The last reported case where the court granted a bill of criminal letters, and this was a case where the Lord Advocate had refused to give his concurrence to a private prosecution, was *J. & P. Coats Limited* (supra). That, however, was a very special case, and incidentally not a case of perjury, where the interest was much more private than public, and the prima facie case for a prosecution was available from undisputed documents, and was not dependent upon statements from witnesses furnished ex parte.

The complainer in this case seemed to rely on the establishment of three propositions, namely (1) that he, as a private individual, had a right to initiate a criminal prosecution, since the Lord Advocate had not the exclusive right to do so; (2) that he could qualify an interest by showing that he had suffered injury of a substantial, particular, special and peculiarly personal nature beyond all others as a result of the alleged criminal acts of the respondents; and (3) that ex facie of the bill he had made out a prima facie case of the commission of a crime or crimes by the respondents.

There is no doubt that the complainer has the right to initiate a private criminal prosecution, provided always that he receives the sanction of the court to do so. But that sanction will only be granted in very special circumstances. It is true that the complainer has suffered a substantial and personal injury as a result of being sentenced to imprisonment for life if he was wrongly convicted of murder as a result of perjured evidence and a conspiracy to pervert the course of justice. Whether he has stated a relevant charge of conspiracy to pervert the course of justice, and the stating of a relevant charge is a pre-requisite to the consideration of the matter at all, is open to doubt . . . On the third point, he was given a latitude to refer to statements of witnesses whom he said he would adduce in support of his allegations. Whether the court was right in allowing that latitude may be doubted, but it was granted and we shall refer to the position of these statements later.

In the first place we have to consider whether the very special circumstances have been made out by the complainer. This involves the position of the Lord Advocate as public prosecutor, particularly in relation to matters affecting the public interest. The independence of his role in this capacity has long been recognised, and the extent of that independence and its impartiality have been amply demonstrated over the years. As the focal point of our system of public prosecutions, he is here to protect the public interest, to prosecute malefactors in the public interest, and to safeguard individuals against malicious, vindictive and unjustified prosecutions at the hands of interested private parties. Perjury and conspiracy to pervert the course of justice are crimes which strike at the very heart of the proper administration of justice. They are pre-eminently crimes which the Lord Advocate as public prosecutor should investigate and prosecute when the investigation produces evidence to merit such a course. The investigation should be impartial and not ex parte, and the Lord Advocate is the impartial investigator. He has to have regard to all the evidence available to him, and not just the evidence from one source, before arriving at his decision. While, therefore, an individual can say that he has suffered substantial personal injury as a result of perjury and/or conspiracy to pervert the course of justice, if these crimes are established, that is not in itself sufficient to justify the granting of criminal letters since other factors have to be taken into account. If it were sufficient, then any person convicted of a crime and particularly a serious crime such as murder, could allege perjury or conspiracy to pervert the course of justice by witnesses on whose evidence he was convicted and be entitled to criminal letters, despite the fact that the Lord Advocate had investigated the matter fully and had refused to prosecute. This could open the flood-gates of private prosecutions which our system of criminal administration has been devised and developed to prevent, both in the public interest generally and the interests of private citizens. Since such offences strike at the root of the proper and fair administration of justice, the decision whether or not to prosecute them must normally be left to the independent and impartial decision of the public prosecutor. It would require to be a very special case indeed to justify a departure from this general rule, and this broad consideration of public interest and public policy must normally outweigh the private interest which an individual may seek to qualify. This view is reinforced by the other consideration to which we have referred, namely the requirement to have all the evidence investigated before a decision to prosecute is reached and not just the evidence produced by an interested party. In the present case the Lord Advocate in the full sense of his responsibility has informed the court that he has carefully examined the evidence and decided that it neither warrants a public prosecution at his instance nor his concurrence to a private prosecution at the instance of the complainer.

For all these reasons we are of the opinion that the bill should be refused."

The court refused the bill.

NOTE

It seems from the *Trapp* and *Meehan* cases that it is not enough for the private prosecutor to satisfy the court that he or she has suffered a peculiar personal wrong as a result of the alleged offence. These cases suggest that notwithstanding such injury a bill will be refused if the wrong in question falls into an (undefined) category of "public" offences—such as perjury or perverting the course of justice. In *Trapp* the court relied on Hume's classification of crimes into those which injure individuals and those which more immediately concern the public because of their interference with justice. It is clear, however, from the passages in which these views are expressed that Hume is not discussing title to prosecute, and indeed it is also clear from Hume's discussion of title to prosecute that private prosecutions for perjury and subornation of perjury had proceeded before the courts on more than one occasion.

5. H. v. Sweeney and Others
1983 S.L.T. 48

LORD JUSTICE-GENERAL (EMSLIE): "This is a bill for criminal letters by the alleged victim of the crime of rape and of what appears to have been a gruesome and hideous assault in which she was grievously injured and disfigured by repeated slashing cuts of a razor. These events are said to have occurred during the late evening of 31 October 1980 in a disused yard at 10 Davaar Street, Glasgow. What she seeks to do is to bring to trial three youths, the respondents in this bill, upon the following charges: (i) that they did on 31 October or 1 November 1980, in London Road, near Davaar Street, Glasgow, assault the said C.H., strike her on the head with an unknown instrument whereby she became unconscious, drag or carry her to a structure situated in the disused premises at 10 Davaar Street, Glasgow, and there place her on the floor, forcibly remove her clothing, hold her down, lie on top of her and repeatedly rape her; (ii) that they did further at the same place and on the same date, assault the said C.H. by striking her repeatedly upon the head and body with a razor or similar instrument all to her severe injury, permanent disfigurement and to the danger of her life.

In answer to the bill the respondents plead that in the events which have happened the bill at the complainer's instance is incompetent, and that in any event prosecution of the respondents now would be oppressive.

The history of the matter is as follows. The Lord Advocate indicted the three respondents for trial at the May sitting of the High Court, Glasgow. All three pled not guilty to the two charges in that indictment which were in terms identical to those on which the complainer seeks leave to prosecute them now. For two reasons this indictment was not called. The first was that the complainer had moved to an unknown address in England. The second was that the sitting could not proceed anyway because of a strike by sheriff court staff in Glasgow, the result of which was that no jurors were cited for the sitting. The instance accordingly fell and the Lord Advocate then re-indicted the respondents for trial at the next sitting of the High Court, Glasgow, in June 1981. Once again pleas of not guilty to the same two charges were tendered by each respondent and all three were present and available for trial when the sitting began. This second indictment, however, was not called either. The reason for this was that when the complainer presented herself at Justiciary Buildings grave doubt was entertained as to her fitness to give evidence. Arrangements were made to have her examined by a distinguished psychiatrist who gave the following advice in a lengthy and detailed report:

'In my opinion, a court appearance at present would be detrimental to her health, and in fact would be hazardous, which may lead not only to pre-trial suicide attempt, but may disturb her even after the trial, whatever the outcome would be, to the same extent.

I would respectfully suggest to the court that evidence should be taken from her should the court decide to proceed with the case, without the public being present, and with the absolute minimum number of representatives from the legal system. A cross-examination at this stage is only likely to produce a severe block in her communication, which would lead to her retreating in silence.

Finally, it is difficult to foresee an improvement in her state in the next two to four months, as the history reveals that her general mental state and attitude towards the court case has not improved since the incident which occurred in September 1980.

One must never forget that this woman has been very severely physically and psychologically traumatised, and that any further pressure put upon her will only cause more unhappiness, despair and isolation.'

In light of that advice the very proper decision was that the indictment should be allowed to fall. The risk to the complainer's health was so serious as to be quite unacceptable. In September 1981 careful consideration was given to the question whether the proceedings against the three respondents should be kept alive. The decision was that they should not. The background against which this decision was taken was that two of the respondents were under 16 years of age at the time of the alleged crimes and the third was then a young person. They had already been called to answer to two indictments and had presented themselves twice for trials which did not take place. In the particular circumstances of this case there was sufficient evidence to justify prosecution of the respondents on the two charges only if the complainer was available to give evidence herself. The reason for the decision was, as the Lord Advocate has explained to us, that in light of the prognosis contained in the report obtained from the psychiatrist in June 1981 it was concluded that the prospect of material improvement in the complainer's health within the foreseeable future was slight; that accordingly there seemed to be no real likelihood of being able to proceed to the trial of the respondents at a reasonably early date; and that it was therefore thought not to be justifiable to keep the proceedings hanging over the heads of the respondents indefinitely. In these circumstances a letter was sent to each of the respondents dated 15 September 1981 informing them that the Lord Advocate intended to take no further proceedings against them. The effect of that letter was, as the case of *Thom* v. *H.M. Advocate* shows, to deprive the Lord Advocate of his right to prosecute the respondents at any time thereafter on the charges contained in the indictments which had fallen. After 15 September 1981, accordingly, public prosecution of the three respondents ceased to be competent.

In presenting this bill the complainer asserts that in the events which have happened she, as a private individual, has the right with leave of this court, to prosecute the respondents to trial. She qualifies the necessary interest in respect that she is able to show that she has suffered injury of a substantial, particular, special, and peculiarly personal nature beyond all others as the result of the alleged criminal acts of the respondents. Ex facie of the bill, and of the precognitions of necessary witnesses and of the productions lodged in support of the bill, she has made out, she claims, a prima facie case of the commission of the two crimes libelled by the respondents.

Let us first of all test the bill by assuming that it may competently be passed and by ignoring for the moment a special plea by the respondents that to pass it now would be oppressive. There is no doubt that the complainer is well founded in saying that she has the necessary title, and has qualified the necessary interest, to prosecute privately. There is no doubt either that upon the precognitions and productions submitted in support of the bill a prima facie case, sufficient to justify bringing the respondents to trial upon the two charges, is disclosed. The evidential material, indeed, is in all essential respects that upon which the Lord Advocate thought it right to indict the respondents. The Lord Advocate has, however, declined to grant his concurrence and the question for the court thus comes to be whether there are to be found in this case very special circumstances which would justify us in taking the now exceptional step of issuing criminal letters at the request of a private individual. We have no doubt that in this case the circumstances are sufficiently special to require us to pass this bill (a) if it is competent, and (b) if it would not be oppressive to pass it now. The position is that the Lord Advocate, while finding himself disabled from granting his concurrence by reason of his decision in September 1981, has informed us that he does not oppose the passing of the bill on the assumption that the court is satisfied on the material now before it that circumstances have changed materially since September 1981, i.e. that the complainer is now likely to be able to give evidence at a trial of the respondents without exposing herself to the risk of serious injury to her health. As the Lord Advocate explained, the position of the Crown is and always has been since the case was first considered that on the assumption that the complainer was available as a witness there is a sufficient case against the three respondents to justify their prosecution on the two charges. In light of what the Lord Advocate has said to us we have considered the sufficiency of the evidential material available. In our opinion, in the particular circumstances of this case, sufficiency appears to depend essentially (a) upon the complainer herself giving evidence, and (b) depending on circumstances, perhaps also upon a young man who might fall to be regarded as a socius criminis, being willing to testify against the respondents. The learned Dean of Faculty accepted, at once, the correctness of this view upon the question of sufficiency of evidence and we therefore have to ask ourselves (first) whether we have been satisfied that the health of the complainer is now such that she can be expected to present herself as a crucial witness without serious risk and (second) whether the young man can reasonably be expected to testify without incriminating himself. As to the second question, there is, we think, no difficulty, for the complainer, through the Dean of Faculty, has declared an intention to grant him immunity from prosecution at her instance and the Lord Advocate for his interest has intimated to us that the young man will have immunity from suit at the instance of the Crown. As to the first question there is we think enough material before us to warrant the conclusion that the complainer is probably now fit to give evidence. That material is in the form of two recent reports by a consultant forensic psychiatrist and, subject only to the necessity for a last-minute precautionary check on the complainer's health very shortly before any trial, we are informed that her condition has now so much improved that she appears to be capable of giving evidence in court. It is clear, therefore, that in this case the necessary very special circumstances are present. They consist essentially of the marked change which has taken place in the complainer's health and, in light of that change, the Lord Advocate's indication to us that he does not oppose the passing of the bill.

From what I have said so far this is one of those very rare instances in which, unless the bill is incompetent for the reasons advanced by the respondents, or it is demonstrated that to require the respondents to stand trial now would be oppressive, this court would, in my opinion, be prepared to pass the bill and order the issue of criminal letters.

In these circumstances I come now to the important question of the competency of the bill. In support of the plea that it is now incompetent the respondents presented two submissions.

The first was that although the right of a private individual to seek leave to prosecute privately exists in circumstances in which the Lord Advocate declines to prosecute, that is to say refuses to take any steps towards the prosecution of an alleged offender, it is extinguished at once and for all time when the Lord Advocate has taken the step of raising an indictment against him. The mere raising of the indictment, regardless of its fate has, it was said, this dramatic effect. For this somewhat startling proposition the first respondent's counsel, who presented the argument on competency for all three respondents with clarity and skill, relied essentially upon short passages in the opinions of Lord Mackenzie and Lord Justice-Clerk Boyle in the bill of advocation in the case of *Wilson* v. *Hare* in 1829. The most reliable record of the opinions delivered in that case is, I believe, to be found in the supplement to the *Trial of William Burke and Helen McDougal* and from that report I quote the particular passages with which counsel's submission was concerned. Lord Mackenzie at p. 107 said this: 'It is true, that by the law of Scotland, there is a right of private, as well as public prosecution for crimes, and that not for reparation only, but for punishment—a right of which I rather think the Information for Hare speaks too lightly. But then it is just equally true, that unless the private party, having title to prosecute, come forward in time to prevent it, the King's Advocate, raising an indictment in his own name alone, comes to have full power of accusation vested in him . . . Accordingly, it seems that, in general, those ways by which a party obtains protection from punishment by the act of the Lord Advocate, do avail against the private prosecutor, who has not previously come forward.' At p. 138 the Lord Justice-Clerk who had been discussing certain clear abridgements of the rights of private parties to prosecute certain persons criminally, said this: 'They are, however, made to bend, in other respects, to the same interests, as the public prosecutor has the undoubted right of restricting any indictment, at any stage of the proceedings, previous to pronouncing sentence—a privilege that has arisen from usage alone. If, again, he has taken the lead, and raised an indictment, in which he happens to fail from the most purely accidental mistake or blunder, no subsequent trial for the same offence or criminal act, though attempted to be shaped as a different charge, can ever be instituted by the private party.' These passages, said counsel for the first respondent, demonstrate conclusively that the true scope of the right of private prosecution is accurately defined by Alison where, at p. xi of the introduction to vol. 2 of his work on the *Criminal Law of Scotland*, he expressed the fourth of the four principles upon which the criminal institutions of Scotland are founded, in these terms: 'That if the public authorities decline to prosecute at the public expense, an opportunity should still be afforded to the injured party, of himself conducting the prosecution on his own responsibility.' It is not at all surprising to find therefore that in the 153 years which have passed since 1829 the only recorded attempts to initiate private prosecution were in cases in which the Lord Advocate had declined to take any steps at all to prosecute alleged offenders.

I have no hesitation in rejecting this first submission on behalf of the respondents. The rights of a private prosecutor in our system of criminal jurisprudence have grown up alongside those of the Lord Advocate and indeed, historically, bulked larger in earlier times than those of the King's Advocate. These rights still exist and there seems to be no good reason in principle for saying that they should not be available in any case in which the Lord Advocate has, for any reason, declined to prosecute an offender to a conclusion. The passages relied upon by the first respondent's counsel in the opinions of Lord Mackenzie and the Lord Justice-Clerk in *Wilson* v. *Hare* were clearly obiter. The case before the court was concerned merely with the question as to the extent of the immunity from all prosecution of a socius criminis who had given evidence for the prosecution in a criminal trial, and the decision did not turn at all upon the issue which is now before us. In any event, when these passages are read in their context it is impossible to conclude that the judges intended to convey that the mere act of serving an indictment extinguishes for all time the right of a private individual to seek leave to prosecute privately. Lord Mackenzie, indeed, immediately after the two passages quoted from p. 107, explains perfectly clearly that what he had in mind was the effect upon the right of private prosecution of the Act of 1701 and of the comparable effect of a public prosecution which has reached its conclusion in the verdict of a jury. This is what he says: 'Thus, if the King's Advocate is dilatory, or inaccurate in proceedings, after apprehension of the criminal, who thereby obtains final liberation on the act 1701, that criminal is as safe from private, as from public prosecution—though the private prosecutor may be absolutely blameless,—may be absent, abroad, on a sick-bed, *non compos*, or a pupil. The intimation ordered by that statute is, to—"His Majesty's Advocate, or procurator-fiscal, and party appearing by the warrant to be concerned, *if any be within the kingdom.*" So that it is manifest, that in many cases prosecuted by the Lord Advocate, there can be no information to any private *party*, particularly in cases of murder. Yet, the act provides,—"that if the Lord Advocate failzie, the process shall be deserted *simpliciter*, the party imprisoned to be for ever free from all question or process for the foresaid crime or offence:" So, if the Lord Advocate draw the indictment erroneously, in respect of time, place, or circumstance,—or if he omit necessary witnesses (as, for instance, by not calling necessary *socii criminis*), or cite them erroneously, or examine them insufficiently, or allow them to be present in Court, or suffer them to be disqualified by improper communications, or in any other way fail in his prosecution, and the criminal is acquitted,—it cannot be denied that his acquittal is as valid against the private party, who might have prosecuted, as against the King's Advocate: So, if the Lord Advocate restrict the indictment to an arbitrary punishment, or depart from part of it, this avails the criminal equally against the private prosecutor: So, if the King's Advocate decline to move for judgment after conviction.' The quoted passage from the opinion of Lord Justice-Clerk Boyle at p. 138 is, when it is properly understood, concerned with the same set of circumstances and, in particular, with the effect upon the right of private prosecution of a public prosecution which has proceeded to a conclusion and has failed. In the result, I am persuaded that the passages relied upon by the first respondent's counsel do not lend any support for a proposition which seems to accord ill with principle.

The second submission for the respondents on the alleged incompetency of the bill was that in any event the right of private prosecution which the complainer once had was forever extinguished when the Lord Advocate, on 15 September 1981, publicly relinquished his right to prosecute the respondents further on the charges contained in the two indictments which had been allowed to fall. The proposition was that whatever avails against the public prosecutor avails against all the world, and it took as its starting-point those passages from the opinions of Lord Mackenzie and the Lord Justice-Clerk which I have already quoted in their relevant context. In this case, said counsel for the first respondent, the effect of the letters of 15 September 1981 was the same as that of desertion simpliciter on the prosecutor's motion. It made all further proceedings at the Lord Advocate's instance incompetent and this was expressly decided in the case of *Thom* v. *H.M. Advocate*. In order to find out what effect the sending of these letters had upon the complainer's right to seek to prosecute the respondents privately, all that one has to do is to ask what is the effect upon the right of private prosecution of desertion simpliciter on the motion of the public prosecutor. The answer to that question is that it makes *all* further prosecution incompetent, and that includes prosecution at the instance of a private individual. In the *Commentaries* (3rd ed.), ii, 277 Baron Hume said this: 'But if the prosecutor, being present, shall himself move the Court to desert the diet *simpliciter*, and thus neither allude to any dilatory cause for dropping his present libel, nor intimate any purpose to raise a new one; such a measure cannot well be construed any otherwise than as a thorough relinquishment or discharge of his right to prosecution.' That this discharge of the public prosecutor's right of prosecution discharges all right of prosecution was made clear in the case of *H.M. Advocate* v. *Hall*. In that case, in an opinion in which Lord Justice-Clerk Moncreiff, and Lords Deas, Mure, Craighill and Adam concurred, the Lord Justice-General (Inglis), after quoting the same passage from Hume with approval, added: 'Now, it appears to me that that expounds the law on this matter quite consistently, and very clearly, to be that the desertion of a diet *simpliciter* on the motion of the prosecutor is an end of all proceedings against the panel for the offence libelled against him.' It cannot be supposed, so ran the argument, that the Lord Justice-General did not mean precisely what he said, and giving to his opinion all the force it commands, the respondents' plea to competency in this case must be sustained.

I have no hesitation, either, in rejecting this second submission on behalf of the respondents. In the case of *Hall*, which was concerned with the effect upon the Crown's right to prosecute further when there had been desertion of a diet simpliciter by the court, ex proprio motu, the court was considering only the right of the public prosecutor. No question as to private prosecution was in mind at all and I cannot accept that the Lord Justice-General's observation on which the first respondent's counsel relied was intended to do more than echo the words of Hume which he had just quoted. Properly understood in its context in the case of *Hall* the Lord Justice-General's reference to 'all proceedings' against the panel can only have been intended to relate to proceedings at the instance of the prosecutor concerned. The proposition for which the first respondent's counsel contended requires us to accept that desertion of a diet simpliciter on the motion of the public prosecutor is equivalent to acquittal or absolvitor of the accused on the charges upon which he answered at his trial. The opinions in *Hall* and in the earlier case of *Tabram*, which was concerned with a similar narrow question, lend no support for this, and it is of material significance to observe that although in the first edition of the *Commentaries*, ii, 30-31, Baron Hume concluded the passage quoted from the 3rd edition (ii, 277) with the words: 'and equal to a judicial consent on his part, to the passing of *absolvitor* in favour of the pannel,' these words were deliberately excised in all subsequent editions, including the second and third for which the author was himself responsible.

Why these words were deliberately struck out is not known with any certainty. What is important, however, is that they were deliberately struck out by that great authority upon our criminal law. In my opinion the passage which I have quoted from Hume's *Commentaries* (3rd ed., ii, 277) discloses that the only effect of desertion of a diet simpliciter on the prosecutor's motion is to disable that prosecutor from taking fresh proceedings against the accused upon the same charge or charges.

Upon the whole issue of competency of this bill, therefore, I am not persuaded that there are any good reasons, in principle or authority, for holding that in the events which have happened this bill must be rejected as incompetent. In so saying I am content to record that the Lord Advocate, in addressing us, said that he was satisfied that the bill was competent and that had he entertained any doubt upon the question he would have felt it his duty so to inform this court."

The court passed the bill.

NOTE

This was the first successful application for a bill for criminal letters since the case of *J. & P. Coats Ltd.* v. *Brown*. The first respondent was subsequently convicted of rape and assault; the other respondents were convicted of indecent assault (High Court,

28 May 1982). The terms of the criminal letters issued by the court may be found at 1982 S.C.C.R. at pp. 178-180.

It is worth remembering that this case stems very largely from the rule in *Thom* v. *H.M. Advocate* (*supra*, p. 35). The outcome of the application for criminal letters was hardly unexpected. There was a clear title to prosecute, there was a relevant charge (and this question seems to have been assumed as an appropriate question for the court considering the application) and the Lord Advocate did not oppose the application. And it is also clear that the court was concerned for the public's confidence in the administration of criminal justice in Scotland. The court could hardly be seen to be condoning a situation in which allegations of a serious crime could not be tested in court.

d. Prosecution in the public interest

Prior to the Summary Jurisdiction (Scotland) Act 1908 only two kinds of prosecutor were recognised—public and private. The definition of "prosecutor" in that Act (now contained in section 462(1) of the 1975 Act) appears to have created a third category, that of "prosecutor in the public interest." This is curious since the central premise of the system of prosecution in Scotland is that the public prosecutor prosecutes in the public interest.

Templeton v. King
1933 J.C. 58

The respondent was charged on a summary complaint with having failed, without reasonable excuse, to comply with a school attendance order pronounced in respect of his daughter. The complaint was at the instance of the county clerk of Dumbarton, and was signed by a solicitor as agent for the complainer. Objections to the competency of the complaint were upheld by the sheriff, who stated a case for appeal to the High Court. The grounds for the sheriff's decision appear from the opinion of the Lord Justice-General. The question for the opinion of the court was whether the sheriff was right in dismissing the complaint as incompetent.

LORD JUSTICE-GENERAL (CLYDE): "Objections were taken to the competency of this complaint; and the Sheriff-substitute before whom the complaint depended sustained these objections and dismissed the complaint as incompetent. His grounds were (1) that the complainer, not being the 'public prosecutor of a Court' was, within the meaning of section 18 of the Summary Jurisdiction (Scotland) Act, 1908, a 'private prosecutor'; (2)

that, being a private prosecutor, he could not prosecute in Dumbarton Sheriff Court without the concurrence of the public prosecutor of that Court, the complaint being one in which imprisonment without the option of a fine was competent; (3) that, although, by section 4 of the Day Industrial Schools (Scotland) Act of 1893, and the Local Government (Scotland) Act, 1929, the County Council has power to institute such a complaint as the present, and is (by section 14 of the Education (Scotland) Act of 1883 and the Local Government (Scotland) Act of 1929) authorised to appoint any person 'to appear before the Court and conduct the prosecution,' yet—notwithstanding—the County Council has no power to delegate its power to institute such a complaint as the present.

Some explanation is necessary. There are two ways in which school attendance can be enforced. There is the method which was initiated by section 70 of the Act of 1872, according to which a school board, having ascertained the facts and done what it could by remonstrance and otherwise, hands over the papers to the procurator-fiscal 'or other person appointed by the school board,' and the procurator-fiscal or such other person then raises proceedings by way of prosecution. There is another method, originally introduced by section 9 of the Act of 1883 (subsequently repealed), and definitely established by section 8 of the Act of 1908, according to which the school board in the first place pronounces an attendance order of its own, and then prosecutes—if necessary—in order to enforce it. By section 14 of the Act of 1883 (which has not been repealed) it was enacted that, in any prosecution under the Education Acts (including the Act of 1870), 'any person appointed by the school board . . . may appear before the Court and conduct the prosecution.' The complaint is described in said section 14 as the complaint of the school board. But (as has been seen), in section 70 of the Act of 1872 the prosecutor is named as the procurator-fiscal 'or other person appointed by the school board'; and by section 14 of the Act of 1883, the 'person appointed by the school board' is authorised to 'appear before the Court and conduct the prosecution.' Accordingly, neither under the Act of 1872, nor under that of 1883, is there any *express* authority to appoint a person for any purpose connected with prosecution. The power to appoint is left to implication from the fact that a person so appointed is referred to; but there is no express authority to appoint. It would plainly be a mistake to confuse the functions of a 'person appointed'—that is, a person *appointed to prosecute*—with those of a person (who may, or may not, be the prosecutor himself) who is authorised to *appear in Court and conduct the prosecution*. If the procurator-fiscal is prosecutor, then, not only must the complaint run in his name, but he (or the procurator-fiscal-depute) must appear in Court and conduct the prosecution. He cannot employ a law agent to represent him. But 'a person appointed' to prosecute within the meaning of the Acts may have no legal qualifications; and, if—prior to the Act of 1883—he had no such qualifications, he necessarily employed a law agent to appear in Court on his behalf, and to conduct the prosecution raised in his name. All that the Act of 1883 did was to authorise 'a person appointed'—although without legal qualification—to appear in Court and conduct the prosecution. If this is right, the third ground of the Sheriff-substitute's objections cannot be sustained. The power to delegate the capacity to prosecute is one thing, and the County Council plainly has it by implication. The power of the delegate to appear in Court and conduct the prosecution is another, and—while the delegate is authorised to do this—there is nothing in the statutes to prevent him from employing a law agent to appear in Court on his behalf and conduct the prosecution.

The only other statutory enactment which bears upon the question is the Summary Jurisdiction (Scotland) Act, 1908. Under section 18 of that statute all proceedings under the Act for the trial of offences and the recovery of penalties are to be instituted by complaint in the form contained in Schedule C. That itself is significant, because it is a form which bears to run in the name of the prosecutor but may be signed in the name of a solicitor acting for him. But, passing that by, the section goes on to enact that 'such complaint shall be signed by the prosecutor or by any law agent on behalf of a prosecutor other than the public prosecutor of a Court, and any law agent may appear for and conduct any prosecution on behalf of a prosecutor other than the public prosecutor of a Court.' Now, in the present case, the complaint is signed by a law agent on behalf of the prosecutor, that is, the person appointed to prosecute; and it is clear that the person so appointed is not the public prosecutor of the Dumbarton Sheriff Court. He is simply prosecutor appointed by the County Council for a particular purpose. If so, it would seem that any law agent may appear for him and conduct the prosecution.

This may be enough to remove the Sheriff-substitute's second ground of objection, but the matter cannot be disposed of without taking into account, at the same time, his first ground, namely, that the person appointed in the present case is a private prosecutor. Prior to the Act of 1908 a great many questions of this kind occurred (under various statutes) in which the prosecutor was not the procurator-fiscal. Not being the procurator-fiscal, could he be anything but a private prosecutor? How the matter might have stood in the present case if the Act of 1908 had not been passed I do not need to inquire. But when I turn to the Act of 1908 I find that section 2 introduces the following definitions:—'Prosecutor shall include procurator-fiscal, assistant procurator-fiscal, burgh prosecutor, and any other persons prosecuting in the public interest, private prosecutor, and complainer.' Here we have a classification of 'prosecutors.' To which class does the 'person appointed' in the present case belong? I think the answer must be that he belongs to the class of prosecutors 'prosecuting in the public interest.' Therefore he cannot be a 'private prosecutor', and, therefore, he does not require the concurrence of the Procurator-fiscal. As it is impossible to call him the public prosecutor of Dumbarton Sheriff Court, both the first and second grounds of the Sheriff-substitute's objection fail. If that is right, I think the question put to us should be answered in the negative."

The court answered the question in the negative.

NOTE

So a "prosecutor in the public interest" appears to straddle the distinction between public and private prosecutor. Like a private prosecutor he need not appear personally, but may employ a solicitor or counsel to appear for him: 1975 Act, s. 311(3). On the other hand, unlike the private prosecutor, he does not require the concurrence of the public prosecutor of the court in which such complaint is brought: 1975 Act, s. 311(4). Given his "hybrid" quality, what rules should govern his liability for malicious prosecution? Section 456(1) of the 1975 Act (*supra*, p. 56) refers to "prosecutor(s) in the public interest." This cannot be read literally as only referring to this intermediate category, since it would exclude "public prosecutors." But it clearly includes this intermediate category.

CHAPTER 3

JURISDICTION

Apart from courts of special jurisdiction (such as courts-martial) three courts exercise criminal jurisdiction in Scotland: the High Court of Justiciary, the sheriff court, and the district court. Trials before the High Court are conducted according to the rules of solemn procedure before a judge (one of the "Lords Commissioners of Justiciary") and a jury of 15. The sheriff court exercises solemn and summary jurisdiction (the only criminal court to do so). In solemn proceedings the sheriff sits with a jury of 15, and the rules of procedure are identical to those governing procedure in the High Court. In summary proceedings the sheriff sits alone. Proceedings in the district court, presided over by one or more lay justices or stipendiary magistrate, are always summary.

In determining which, if any, of these courts has jurisdiction to try a criminal matter, two questions must be considered. There is first of all the question of geography. Does the matter come within the territorial limits of the court's jurisdiction? Secondly it should be noted that the various criminal courts do not necessarily have authority to try every offence which occurs within their territorial jurisdiction. A sheriff, for example, cannot try a case of murder even if he is satisfied that it was committed within his sheriffdom, since murder falls within the exclusive competence of the High Court. It is necessary, therefore, to consider what limits, if any, there are to the competency of a court within its territorial jurisdiction.

a. Territorial jurisdiction

The jurisdiction of the High Court is general, extending to the whole of Scotland and the territorial waters round Scotland. The jurisdiction of the sheriff and district courts is more limited. Subject to certain exceptions noted below, the sheriff cannot take cognisance of any matter occurring outwith the limits of his sheriffdom. The jurisdiction of the district court is based on the "commission area" (*i.e.* a district or islands area within the meaning of the Local

Government (Scotland) Act 1973) and the authority of that court is limited, subject to certain exceptions, to the relevant commission area.

(i) The rule of territoriality

1. H.M. Advocate v. Hall
(1881) 4 Couper 438

LORD YOUNG: ". . . The general rule is that criminal law is strictly territorial—so that a man is subject only to the criminal law of the country where he is, and that his conduct there, whether acting, speaking, or writing, shall be judged of as criminal or not by that law and no other. The law of allegiance affords an exception in cases of treason; and there are also . . . some other exceptions, as, for example, in the case of a British subject murdering another abroad; but the rule is as I have stated."

2. Lewis v. Blair
(1858) 3 Irvine 16

The suspender, a citizen of the United States, was convicted of a serious assault committed on board a United States ship lying in the Clyde near Greenock. A bill of suspension was presented to the High Court in which it was objected:

"That the Sheriff had no jurisdiction to try him, in respect that as the offence charged was said to have been committed by him, a foreigner, on board a foreign vessel, and upon seamen engaged in that vessel, it must be held to have been committed within the territory of the country to which the vessel belonged; and that the mere circumstance of the vessel being within the Sheriff's jurisdiction (assuming it to have been so), did not render foreigners employed in that vessel subjects to her Majesty, and, as such, subject to the magistrate's jurisdiction."

"The Court was unanimously of opinion that this ground of suspension was untenable."

NOTE

There are, then, two aspects to the rule that criminal law is territorial. The jurisdiction of the various courts will not normally extend beyond their territorial limits. At the same time criminal jurisdiction will normally encompass everyone within those limits, irrespective of their origins. The exceptions to this rule are discussed *post*, p. 90. For a discussion of the factors behind the rule, see Williams, "Venue and the Ambit of Criminal Law" [1965] 81 L.Q.R. 276; 395; 518.

(ii) Determining the place of the offence

1. H.M. Advocate v. Witherington
(1881) 4 Couper 475

Witherington sent letters from England to several traders in Scotland containing false representations, by means of which he induced them to send goods to him in England. He did not pay for these goods, and had no intention of doing so. He was arrested in England and brought to Scotland for trial on a charge of falsehood, fraud and wilful imposition. It was objected on his behalf, *inter alia*, that the High Court had no jurisdiction, the alleged offence having been committed in England.

LORD JUSTICE-GENERAL (INGLIS): ". . . The objection to the jurisdiction of this Court to try the panel for this crime raises a question of much greater interest and importance. But this question has, I apprehend, been settled in the sense adverse to the panel's contention by two decisions of this Court—the case of *Bradbury* in 1872, and the case of *Allan* in 1873, both to be found in the second volume of Couper's Reports.

Under ordinary circumstances I should have thought it enough to refer to these authorities as a sufficient ground for repelling the objection; but some doubts having been suggested as to the soundness of these judgments, and a full Court having been summoned to dispose of the objections to this indictment, it would be hardly satisfactory if the Judges now present did not expound the principle of law on which these prior judgments are founded.

The objection is rested on these considerations; that the panel is an Englishman; that the only fraud or criminal act alleged against him was committed in England; that he never was in Scotland, and is not subject to the criminal law or to the jurisdiction of the criminal Courts of Scotland; that criminal jurisdiction does not extend *extra territorium*, and that the true foundation of ordinary criminal jurisdiction is the *locus delicti.*.

The argument is certainly plausible, and there is, at first sight, something startling and paradoxical in the proposition that a man may commit a crime in a place in which he was never personally present. The proposition is nevertheless not only technically or constructively, but actually true; and if this is so, then the Court of the territory where the crime was committed, and where the panel was never personally present, has jurisdiction *ratione loci delicti*, and the whole argument of the objector falls.

The best and most conclusive example, to my mind, in support of the truth of the above proposition, is the case of a murder by poisoning, which takes place in Edinburgh, while the murderer is domiciled and resident in London, and never was in Scotland. The manner in which the murderer accomplishes his purpose is to send by post, or otherwise, to his victim in Edinburgh, a packet of deadly poison, recommending it to him (knowingly and maliciously for the purpose of accomplishing the death) as a salutary medicine fitted to cure a disease under which he is labouring. If the victim acts on the suggestion and swallows the poison it is not doubtful that a murder has been committed in Edinburgh, and that the murderer was in London all the while. The *species facti* may be varied by supposing that the murderer employs an innocent agent to take the poison to the victim in Edinburgh, and persuade him to swallow it as a useful and potent medicine. The result is the same—the crime is committed in Edinburgh by a man who was never there. Baron Hume, in treating of criminal jurisdiction, after stating that this Court can never sustain its own jurisdiction against a Scotchman, *ratione domicilii*, for a murder or other crime committed beyond the limits of Scotland, proceeds to say—'It does not, however, follow that the law shall apply to those offences which have a continuance of time and succession of acts whereof part may happen here and part abroad. If one compose and print a libel in England and circulate it here, of if one forge a deed abroad and utter it here, certainly the proper Courts for the trial of such a case are those of this country, since it is here that the main act is done which completes the crime, . . . nay, more, it may be plausibly argued that he shall be subjected to the same course of trial who shall write an incendiary letter in England, and put it into a course of conveyance, thence by means of which it is received by the person to whom it is addressed in Scotland.' In support of this latter statement the learned author cites a case which actually occurred in 1818.

Mr Alison, in his Practice of the Criminal Law, following the earlier authority, says—'The principle applies to one who writes an incendiary letter in England and sends it down, whether by post or otherwise, to this country. He stands in the same position with one, who standing on the English side of the border, discharges a gun at a man on the Scotch side, and no reasonable doubt can be entertained of the competence of trying him in this country, where his crime has taken its destined effect.'

To shew that this doctrine is not peculiar to the law of Scotland it may be worth while to advert to a very good example in support of the general proposition which I have advanced, stated by Mr Justice Story (Conflict of Laws, sec. 625, *b*), as having occurred in the Supreme Court of New York. A citizen of Ohio had written what is called a fraudulent paper addressed to citizens of New York, which made him liable to punishment as for a criminal offence. He sent the paper to New York by an innocent agent, and it was there published and the offence there completed. 'The defendant being afterwards indicted in New York for the offence, pleaded that he was a natural-born citizen of Ohio, and owed allegiance to that state; that he had never been within the state of New York, and that the fraudulent paper was executed in Ohio. It was determined that this was no answer to the indictment.'

In all the examples which I have adduced the commencement of the criminal action is in one country and the completion of it in another. But in most of these cases the perpetrator's success in his criminal object is necessary to complete the crime. In the case of poisoners there would have been no murder if the victim had not swallowed the poison, and in the case of incendiary letters there would have been no completed crime if they had not been received by the persons to whom they were addressed. There might, no doubt, have been in either case an attempt to commit a crime, which might have been criminally punishable, but the crime intended would not have been effected.

There are crimes of a different description which may be fully committed without the criminal succeeding in the object for which he commits the crime. The most obvious of these are forging and uttering. If a man forges a bill of exchange or a bank cheque, and sends it by post or by messenger to a correspondent for the purpose of its being used and acted on as genuine, the crime is completed as soon as the document passes out of his own possession or control, although the forger may be immediately afterwards detected, and no one is injured. A good example of this occurs in the case of *Smith*, Couper, vol. ii., p. 1.

Now, the question of jurisdiction here seems to me to depend on whether the offence charged in this indictment belongs to the former or the latter of these descriptions of crime. The false and fraudulent representations are contained in a letter written in Blackburn. But the writing of that letter was not in itself a criminal act. The sending of the letter to Muirhead and its receipt by him would still fall short of constituting the crime charged. It is the success of the scheme which is necessary to complete the crime, and without such success in imposing upon Muirhead and inducing him to send the goods ordered there would be no ground for this indictment. While, therefore, the initiatory act of writing and posting the letter takes place in Blackburn, every other step in the action which is necessary to the constitution of the crime takes place in Edinburgh. It is here that Muirhead is imposed on and induced to believe the false and fraudulent representations of the panel; it is here that he acts on the belief so fraudulently created and delivers the goods in Scotland to a public carrier, who is thereby constituted the innocent agent of the panel in carrying out the fraudulent scheme to its completion. When the goods were delivered to the carrier they passed beyond the control of Muirhead, and the imposition was successful and complete. The poison contained in the Blackburn letter had done its work. For these reasons, I am of opinion that Edinburgh is the *locus delicti* in the present case, just as much as if the panel had sent either an accomplice or an innocent agent to carry out his fraudulent scheme to completion in Edinburgh."

LORD JUSTICE-CLERK (MONCREIFF): ". . .As a question of international jurisprudence this point is ruled by the most elementary rules. Two elements are requisite to complete the jurisdiction of any criminal Court, and these must coincide. The crime must be committed within the territory; and the Court must have power over the person of the criminal. But if these do coincide, no further question remains.

As to the first, every State has the right to punish offences committed within its territory, whatever may be the nationality or residence of the offender. This is, of course, the fundamental principle of civil government, and is of universal application. On the second, it may, no doubt, be that the culprit resides beyond the territory, and so beyond the executive power of the Court; but if the executive authority of the country where he resides thinks fit, by treaty or by legislation, to come in aid of the authorities in the *locus delicti*, that difficulty disappears, and if so, no further question can arise.

Now, here, in my opinion, the crime is sufficiently alleged in the indictment to have been committed in Scotland. It is said that the trader who was defrauded was a Scottish trader; he resided in Scotland; his goods of which he was defrauded were in Scotland, and he parted with them in Scotland in consequence of the fraudulent representations of the accused. It can make no difference that the letters which led to the fraud were written in England. They were intended to take effect, and did take effect in Scotland, and I know of no privilege which an Englishman has to commit offences in Scotland which a Scotchman could not plead.

As to the power of this Court over the person of the accused there is no question. The accused sits at our bar. He is not said to be there illegally, but, on the contrary, he is there through the intervention of an Act of Parliament. Both elements of jurisdiction therefore in this case concur."

The court repelled the objection to jurisdiction.

NOTES

For a general discussion of this case and related issues see Gordon, *The Criminal Law of Scotland* (2nd ed.), pp. 93 *et seq.*

In *Lipsey* v. *Mackintosh*, 1913 S.C. (J.) 104, the Lord Justice-General (Dunedin), with whom the other members of the court agreed, stated: "In all these cases, where something is going on by the medium of the post, the offence is really committed . . . at both ends of the transmission by the post office." His Lordship was relying on the so-called "Long-firm cases" of which *Witherington* is the leading example. This may be so in the case of "continuing" or "conduct" crimes. But the court in *Witherington* was clearly of the opinion that where the offence required proof of some particular result, there was no offence until that result was brought about, and that jurisdiction lay where the representations of the accused were intended to, and actually did, take effect.

The question of jurisdiction in the converse situation to *Witherington*, *i.e.* where acts done within the jurisdiction take effect elsewhere, is unsettled. Macdonald's view (*A Practical Treatise on the Criminal Law of Scotland*, p. 191) was that the Scottish courts would have jurisdiction if the "main act" was committed in Scotland. Quite apart from the difficulties in deciding what the "main act" might be in any given offence, problems arise, for example, where that "main act" is not criminal in Scotland, but gives rise to a consequence which is criminal elsewhere. Gordon's view (*op. cit.*,

p. 97) is that "on principle the better view is . . . that the crime is committed where it takes effect, and only there."

2. Gracie v. Stuart
(1884) 5 Couper 379

Gracie was charged in the sheriff court at Edinburgh with the reset of three silver watches "at some place in the city or county of Edinburgh to the complainer unknown." He was convicted and presented a bill of suspension to the High Court in which he stated that he had bought the watches in his own shop in Glasgow and brought them to Edinburgh and that consequently the sheriff at Edinburgh had no jurisdiction to try the offence.

LORD JUSTICE-CLERK (MONCREIFF): "In the first place, it is contended that the Sheriff of Midlothian has no jurisdiction in this case, as it was not proved that the complainer got possession of the stolen property while within that jurisdiction. . . . Now, upon the first objection I have no doubt whatever, and I am surprised that [counsel for the suspender] should have consumed so much time in arguing a proposition so self-evidently untenable. The crime of reset is committed wherever any person detains from its rightful owner any article which he knows has been stolen. . . . It is beyond dispute that the resetter is committing a continuous crime during the whole time that the stolen article is in his possession, and although he may have passed through a great many places he is answerable to the Courts of each of these places if he went to them with the stolen articles in his possession."

The court refused to pass the bill.

NOTE

The principle applies to other offences of possession, such as possession of a controlled drug contrary to section 28 of the Misuse of Drugs Act 1971, and other continuing offences.

3. Smith v. Inglis
1983 S.L.T. 160

OPINION OF THE COURT: "The respondents were charged with a contravention of s. 1(7) of the Companies Act 1976 in a complaint initiated in the sheriff court at Edinburgh. The complaint was in the following terms: 'you David Anderson Inglis, Margaret Inglis, Russell McKay and Nancy McKay being directors of Abercraggan Exports Limited, a company registered under the Companies Act 1948 to 1980, and having its registered office at 110 Coupar Angus Road, Birkhill, by Dundee, did fail to comply with a requirement of section 1(7) of the aftermentioned Act in that you did between 1 April 1978 and 1 February 1979 being the last day allowed for laying and delivering the documents aftermentioned computed in terms of section 6(1) and (2) of the aftermentioned Act, both dates inclusive, fail to deliver to the Registrar of Companies at 102 George Street, Edinburgh, a copy of every document required to be comprised in the accounts of the company in respect of the accounting reference period of said company ending 31 March 1978 whereby you David Anderson Inglis, Margaret Inglis, Russel McKay and Nancy McKay are guilty of an offence: Contrary to sections 1(7) and 4(1) of the Companies Act 1976.'

Under reference to s. 1(1) of the said Act which lays a duty on the directors of a company to prepare, lay and deliver accounts by reference to accounting reference periods which are specified in the succeeding subsections, s. 1(7)(*a*) provides 'Subject to subsection (8) below [which has no application here], in respect of each accounting reference period of a company the directors of the company—(*a*) shall deliver to the registrar of companies a copy of every document required to be comprised in the accounts of the company in respect of that period.'

It is a matter of agreement that the registered office of the company of which the respondents are directors is in Dundee, as are the residences of the respondents. It is further agreed that the office of the registrar of companies is in Edinburgh.

When the case called before the sheriff the respondents took a plea to the competency of the complaint on the ground that the alleged omission to comply with the requirements of s. 1(7) aforesaid must be deemed to have taken place in Dundee, and there was no jurisdiction in the Sheriff court in Edinburgh to entertain a complaint which libelled an offence committed in Dundee. The sheriff had previously decided this point in a manner favourable to the respondents in the case of *P.F. (Edinburgh)* v. *Jamieson* but as the Crown had failed to mark an appeal timeously in that case, he treated the instant case as a test case with a view to his decision in *Jamieson* being reviewed by this court. Towards that end he annexed to his report in the instant case his written judgment in the *Jamieson* case. He noted with understandable apprehension the volume of work which would accrue to the sheriff court in Edinburgh if all prosecutions under subsection 1(7) were to be funnelled into that court as a matter of Crown policy, as, he was informed, was the intention. Following his decision in *Jamieson* he sustained the plea to the competency in this case and dismissed the complaint.

In his judgment in *Jamieson* the sheriff made a detailed examination of the law in regard to the situation where an offence was committed partly in one jurisdiction and partly in another, and considered whether, in circumstances such as were there (and here) present, the offence was wholly committed at the point of time and place when the documents were dispatched. Coming to the conclusion that the latter point had be answered in the affirmative he found that the Edinburgh sheriff court had no jurisdiction to enterain such a complaint when it did not otherwise have the jurisdiction to do so.

We do not find it necessary to analyse and express any views upon the general law as canvassed by the sheriff, since the short answer here is to be found in the wording of s. 1(7) itself. The requirement therein is for the directors of the company to *deliver* to the registrar of companies a copy of every document. (The emphasis is ours). Irrespective of where the documents are compiled, the omission which constitutes the offence is failure to deliver them to the registrar of companies whose office is in Edinburgh. The offence accordingly takes place in Edinburgh and the sheriff court there has jurisdiction to entertain a complaint libelling such an offence. Whatever further jurisdiction may have been introduced by statute, *e.g.* by s. 49(2) of the Companies Act 1976 or s. 287(2) of the Criminal Procedure (Scotland) Act 1975, that basic jurisdiction stands.

If it be suggested that this places an undue burden on company directors in that they might find it difficult to establish that the documents in question had in fact been delivered after they had been despatched, the answer is to be found in s. 4(2) of the Companies Act 1976 which makes it a defence for a director to prove that he took all reasonable steps for securing that the requirements of s. 1(7) would be complied with before the end of the prescribed periods for returns being made.

We are accordingly of the opinion that *Jamieson* was wrongly decided and that the sheriff's decision in the instant case was wrong. We allow the appeal, recall the decision of the sheriff sustaining the plea to the competency of the complaint and dismissing the complaint, and remit the case back to him to proceed as accords."

Appeal allowed.

NOTE

Previous cases in this section have been concerned with determining the place of criminal acts or conduct. *Smith* v. *Inglis* is concerned with the place of an omission. The view adopted by the court appears to have been that the place of the omission was the place where the duty to deliver should have been carried out: *cf.* Gordon, *op.cit.*, p. 98, *H.M. Advocate* v. *McKay* (1866) 5 Irvine 329 and *Waugh* v. *Mentiplay*, 1938 J.C. 117. The duty in this case could only be performed in one place. Where the performance of a duty may be required in more than one place and is not performed in any of them presumably the courts in each of those places have jurisdiction.

(iii) Exceptions and modifications to the territoriality rule

Certain exceptions and modifications to the territoriality rule are recognised, both at common law and under statute. These may be divided into three broad categories:

(A) Cases where extra-territorial jurisdiction is conferred; '
(B) Cases where offences committed in Scotland are removed from the jurisdiction of the Scottish courts;
(C) Special provisions permitting the sheriff and district courts to deal with matters not occurring within, or wholly within, their respective areas.

Only the more significant examples are included here. For further discussion see Renton and Brown, para. 1-08 *et seq.*

(A) EXTRA-TERRITORIAL JURISDICTION

Murder and culpable homicide:
Criminal Procedure (Scotland) Act 1975

"6.—(1) Any British subject who in a country outside the United Kingdom does any act or makes any omission which if done or made in Scotland would constitute the crime of murder or of culpable homicide shall be guilty of the same crime and subject to the same punishment as if the act or omission had been done or made in Scotland. . . .

(3) A person may be proceeded against, indicted, tried and punished for an offence under this section in any sheriff court district in Scotland in which he is apprehended or is in custody as if the offence had been committed in that district, and the offence shall, for all purposes incidental to or consequential on the trial or punishment thereof, be deemed to have been committed in that district."

NOTE

For a discussion of the common law on this question see Hume, ii, 50-51. The crime of treason, being based on allegiance to the Crown, may be committed outwith the realm, and the Scottish courts have jurisdiction no matter where the offence is committed: Hume, iii, 49.

Theft and reset:
Criminal Procedure (Scotland) Act 1975

"7.—Any person who has in his possession in Scotland property which he has stolen in any other part of the United Kingdom may be dealt with, indicted, tried and punished in Scotland in like manner as if he had stolen it in Scotland.

(2) Any person who in Scotland receives property stolen in any other part of the United Kingdom may be dealt with, indicted, tried and punished in Scotland in like manner as if it had been stolen in Scotland."

NOTE

Identical provisions may be found in section 292 of the 1975 Act with regard to summary proceedings. Section 7(1) may in fact reproduce a common law rule: *H.M. Advocate* v. *Taylor* (1767) Maclaurin's Criminal Cases No. 76, Hume, ii, 53. The Scottish courts may, therefore, have jurisdiction to try a person for a theft committed in, say, the Republic of Ireland, if he is found in possession of the stolen goods in Scotland. See Gordon, *op. cit.,* p. 102, and the unsatisfactory cases of *Hay* (1877) 3 Couper 491 and *Stevenson* (1853) 1 Irvine 341.

Offences on ships:
Merchant Shipping Act 1894
"**684.** For the purpose of giving jurisdiction under this Act, every offence shall be deemed to have been committed and every cause of complaint to have arisen either in the place in which the same actually was committed or arose, or in any place in which the offender or person complained against may be.

685.—(1) Where any district within which any court, justice of the peace, or other magistrate, has jurisdiction either under this Act or under any other Act or at common law for any purpose whatever is situate on the coast of any sea, or abutting on or projecting into any bay, channel, lake, river, or other navigable water, every such court, justice, or magistrate shall have jurisdiction over any vessel being on, or lying or passing off, that coast, or being in or near that bay, channel, lake, river, or navigable water, and over all persons on board that vessel or for the time being belonging thereto, in the same manner as if the vessel or persons were within the limits of the original jurisdiction of the court, justice, or magistrate.

(2) The jurisdiction under this section shall be in addition to and not in derogation of any jurisdiction or power of a court under the Summary Jurisdiction Acts.

686.—(1) Where any person, being a British subject, is charged with having committed any offence on board any British ship on the high seas or in any foreign port or harbour or on board any foreign ship to which he does not belong, or, not being a British subject, is charged with having committed any offence on board any British ship on the high seas, and that person is found within the jurisdiction of any court in Her Majesty's dominions, which would have had cognizance of the offence if it had been committed on board a British ship within the limits of its ordinary jurisdiction, that court shall have jurisdiction to try the offence as if it had been so committed."

NOTE
The crime of piracy may at common law be tried by the Scottish courts irrespective of where the offence is committed, or of the nationality of the offenders or the ship: *Cameron and Others* v. *H.M. Advocate,* 1971 S.L.T. 333. Section 4 of the Tokyo Convention Act 1967 confirms a similar jurisdiction in respect of piracy against an aircraft. Extra-territorial jurisdiction in respect of other offences committed on board British-controlled aircraft is conferred by section 1 of the same Act.

See also section 3(2) of the 1975 Act with regard to the sheriff's jurisdiction in offences committed at sea.

Offshore installations:
Continental Shelf Act 1964

"**3.**—(1) Any act or omission which—

(a) takes place on, under or above an installation in a designated area or any waters within five hundred metres of such an installation; and

(b) would, if taking place in any part of the United Kingdom, constitute an offence under the law in force in that part,

shall be treated for the purpose of that law as taking place in that part . . .

11. (1) Proceedings for any offence under this Act (including . . . anything that is an offence by virtue of section 3(1) of this Act) may be taken, and the offence may for all incidental purposes be treated as having been committed, in any place in the United Kingdom."

NOTE

See also the Continental Shelf (Jurisdiction) Order 1980 (S.I. 1980 No. 84) and the Mineral Workings (Offshore Installations) Act 1971.

(B) EXCLUSION OF LOCAL JURISDICTION

Visiting Forces:
Visiting Forces Act 1952

"**3.**—(1) Subject to the provisions of this section, a person charged with an offence against United Kingdom law shall not be liable to be tried for that offence by a United Kingdom court if at the time when the offence is alleged to have been committed he was a member of a visiting force or a member of a civilian component of such a force and —

(a) the alleged offence, if committed by him, arose out of and in the course of his duty as a member of that force or component, as the case may be; or

(b) the alleged offence is an offence against the person, and the person or, if more than one, each of the persons in relation to whom it is alleged to have been committed had at the time thereof a relevant association either with that force or with another visiting force of the same country; or

(c) the alleged offence is an offence against property, and the whole of the property in relation to which it is alleged to have been committed (or, in a case where different parts of that property were differently owned, each part of the property) was at the time thereof the property either of the sending country or of an authority of that country or of a person having such an association as aforesaid; or (*d*) the alleged offence is the offence of hijacking on board a military aircraft in the service of that force or consists of inducing or assisting, in relation to such an aircraft, the commission of any such act as is mentioned in section 1(4)*(b)* of the Hijacking Act 1971; or (*e*) the alleged offence is an offence under section 1 or section 2 of the Protection of Aircraft Act 1973, or consists of inducing or assisting the commission of any such act as is mentioned in section 3(1) of that Act, where (in either case) one or more such aircraft was or were the only aircraft alleged to have been, or to have been likely to be, thereby destroyed or damaged or whose safety is alleged to have been, or to have been likely to be, thereby endangered:

Provided that this subsection shall not apply if at the time when the offence is alleged to have been committed the alleged offender was a person not subject to the jurisdiction of the service courts of the country in question in accordance with the last foregoing section.

(2) In relation to the trial of a person who was a member of a civilian component of a visiting force at the time when the offence is alleged to have been committed, the last foregoing subsection shall not have effect unless it is shown that the case can be dealt with under the law of the sending country.

(3) Nothing in subsection (1) of this section—

(*a*) shall prevent a person from being tried by a United Kingdom court in a case where the Director of Public Prosecutions (in the case of a court in England or Wales), the Lord Advocate (in the case of a court in Scotland) or the Attorney-General for Northern Ireland (in the case of a court in Northern Ireland) certifies, either before or in the course of the trial, that the appropriate authority of the sending country has notified him that it is not proposed to deal with the case under the law of that country; or

(*b*) shall affect anything done or omitted in the course of a trial unless in the course thereof objection has already been made that by reason of that subsection the court is not competent to deal with the case; or

(*c*) shall, after the conclusion of a trial, be treated as having affected the validity thereof if no such objection was made in the proceedings at any stage before the conclusion of the trial . . .

4.—(1) Without prejudice to the last foregoing section, where a person has been tried by a service court of a country to which this section applies in the exercise of the powers referred to in subsection (1) of section two of this Act, he shall not be tried for the same crime by a United Kingdom court.

(2) Where a person who has been convicted by a service court of such a country in the exercise of the said powers is convicted by a United Kingdom court for a different crime, but it appears to that court that the conviction by the service court was wholly or partly in respect of acts or omissions in respect of which he is convicted by the United Kingdom court, that court shall have regard to the sentence of the service court."

NOTE

The Act applies to the forces of the states listed in section 1 of the Act (as amended) and to those of any other country designated by Order in Council. The list of countries presently includes the Commonwealth countries, the United States, France, etc.

(C) SPECIAL PROVISIONS IN RESPECT OF THE SHERIFF AND DISTRICT COURTS

Criminal Procedure (Scotland) Act 1975

"3.—(1) Subject to the provisions of this section, the jurisdiction of the sheriffs, within their respective sheriffdoms shall extend to and include all navigable rivers, ports, harbours, creeks, shores and anchoring grounds in or adjoining such sheriffdoms and shall include all criminal maritime causes and proceedings (including such as may apply to persons furth of Scotland) provided the accused shall upon any legal ground of jurisdiction be subject to the jurisdiction of the sheriff before whom such cause or proceedings may be raised.

(2) It shall not be competent to the sheriff to try any crime committed on the seas which it would not be competent for him to try if the crime had been committed on land.

(3) Where sheriffdoms are separated by a river, firth or estuary, the sheriffs on either side shall have concurrent jurisdiction over the intervening space occupied by water.

4.—(1) Where an offence is committed in any harbour, river, arm of the sea or other water (tidal or otherwise) which runs between or forms the boundary of the jurisdiction of two or more courts, such offence may be tried by any one of such courts.

(2) Where an offence is committed on the boundary of the jurisdiction of two or more courts, or within the distance of 500 yards of any such boundary, or partly within the jurisdiction of one court and partly within the jurisdiction of another court or courts such offence may be tried by any one of such courts.

(3) Where an offence is committed on any person or in respect of any property on or upon any carriage, cart or vehicle employed in a

journey by road or railway, or on board any vessel employed in a river, lake, canal or inland navigation, such offence may be tried by any court through whose jurisdiction such carriage, cart, vehicle or vessel passed in the course of the journey or voyage during which the offence was committed, and, where the side, bank, or centre or other part of the road, railway, river, lake, canal or inland navigation along which the carriage, cart, vehicle or vessel passed in the course of such journey or voyage is the boundary of the jurisdiction of two or more courts, such offence may be tried by any one of such courts.

(4) Where several offences, which if committed in one sheriff court district could be tried under one indictment, are alleged to have been committed by any person in different sheriff court districts, the accused may be tried for all or any of those offences under one indictment before the sheriff of any one of such sheriff court districts.

(5) Where an offence is authorised by this section to be tried by any court, it may be dealt with, heard, tried, determined, adjudged and punished as if the offence had been committed wholly within the jurisdiction of such court.

5.—(1) Where a person is alleged to have committed in more than one sheriff court district a crime or crimes to which subsection (2) of this section applies, he may be indicted to a court to be held in such one of such sheriff court districts as shall be determined by the Lord Advocate, whether that court is the High Court or the sheriff court.

(2) This subsection applies to —

(a) a crime committed partly in one sheriff court district and partly in another;

(b) crimes connected with each other but committed in different sheriff court districts;

(c) crimes committed in different sheriff court districts in succession which, if they had been committed in one such district, could have been tried under one indictment.

(3) Where, in accordance with the provisions of this section, a case is tried in the sheriff court of any sheriff court district, the procurator fiscal of that district shall have power to prosecute in that case and the sheriff of that district shall have power to try the case and to pronounce sentence on conviction even if the crime in question has in whole or in part been committed in a different district.

(4) The sheriff and procurator fiscal referred to in subsection (3) of this section shall have the like powers in relation to the case in question, whether before, during or after the trial, as they respec-

tively have in relation to a case arising out of a crime or crimes committed wholly within their own district."

NOTE

For the purposes of summary proceedings, section 288 reproduces the provisions of section 3, with the addition of the following subsection:

"(4) The sheriff shall have a concurrent jurisdiction with every other court within his sheriffdom in relation to all offences competent for trial in such courts."

Section 4 is reproduced in section 287 in respect of summary proceedings.

Section 60 of the 1975 Act provides (*inter alia*) that under an indictment for theft the accused may be convicted of reset. Subsection (4) of that section provides that the power to convict a person of an offence other than that with which he is charged is exercisable by the sheriff before such person is tried notwithstanding that that other offence was committed outside the jurisdiction of that sheriff. In *Roy* v. *H.M. Advocate*, 1963 S.L.T. 369 the appellant was originally charged with theft of property in Scotland. It appeared that he had nothing to do with the theft, but that he had received the stolen goods from the thief in England. It was held that since all the elements alleged to constitute the crime of reset took place in England, the above provisions could not be relied upon to obtain a conviction for reset.

Section 3(4) of the District Courts (Scotland) Act 1975 contains, for the district court, provisions similar to those contained in section 4(4) (and section 287(4)) of the 1975 Act.

b. *Specification of the locus of the offence*

The place of the alleged offence must be specified with precision in the complaint or indictment. There are two reasons for this. The first is that the accused is entitled to fair notice of the charge which he is to answer, and this includes details of where it is alleged to have been committed. The second is that it is necessary to show that the court has jurisdiction.

1. **Stevenson v. McLevy and Others**
(1879) 6 R. 33

The respondents were charged on a summary complaint with an offence contrary to section 21 of the Salmon Fisheries Act 1868.

They objected to the competency of the proceedings on the ground
that the complaint did not specify the *locus* at which the offence was
allegedly committed. After the evidence had been led, but before
judgment, the sheriff on the motion of the prosecutor allowed the
complaint to be amended so as to specify the *locus*. The respondents
having been acquitted, the procurator fiscal appealed by stated
case. The first question for the High Court was : "Whether the
amendment . . . was competently made after the proof had been led
but before judgment?"

LORD YOUNG: "There are two questions submitted to us here.
The first raises an important point, and certainly a novel one, under the
Summary Procedure Act of 1864, an Act which is of vast importance in all
summary prosecutions. The question is, whether a complaint under the Act
charging an accused with an offence is competent without a *locus;* or
whether, if there be no *locus,* one may be added during or at the end of the
trial, to suit the facts which have come out in evidence. It was admitted for
the appellant that the omission of the *locus* was a blunder. Such things do
happen occasionally, but the prosecutor must take the consequences,
though the ends of justice may sometimes be defeated by such an oversight.
It is one of the fundamental rules of our law that any complaint charging an
offence shall state the *locus* where the offence was committed. I know of no
exception to this rule, even where the complaint is a statutory complaint. In
a complaint before an inferior Judge, such as a Sheriff, the *locus* is more
necessary to shew that the Judge has jurisdiction, and he cannot proceed at
all unless the fact that he has jurisdiction appears on the face of the
complaint. I think that may be fairly stated as a universal proposition. It is a
rule of our law, and it is also a rule of the law of England, and the reason and
good sense of it must commend itself to every one.
In addition to this, it is necessary to give this information that the accused
may have an opportunity of defending himself. The accused must have
reasonable information of the charge against him, of which the *locus* is first
and foremost, for the purposes of his defence. I know, as I have said, of no
authority for the proposition that a prosecutor may omit the *locus* and then
fill it in at his convenience to suit the evidence led. There would be the
greatest possible danger in sanctioning or countenancing such a course, and
it would be giving a most unfair advantage to the prosecution. I think,
therefore, that the Sheriff went wrong in allowing this amendment, and this
is sufficient to dispose of the case; and I understood the counsel for the
appellant to assent to this, for it would be an idle proceeding in us to send
the case back to the Sheriff when no conviction could, in our opinion,
follow upon it."

Appeal dismissed.

2. McMillan v. Grant
1924 J.C. 13

McMillan, the manager of a firm in Rothesay, was charged with fraudulently altering the registration of a motor vehicle, contrary to section 13(4) of the Roads Act 1920. The *locus* of the alleged offence was not specified and objection was taken to the competency of the complaint. That objection was repelled. McMillan was convicted and presented a bill of suspension to the High Court.

LORD JUSTICE-GENERAL (CLYDE): " . . . A separate point was taken with reference to the second of the three bills, namely, that no specification of *locus*, even of the widest kind, is given in the complaint. The charge is against the managing director of a firm (whose address is given), as the person who was in charge of the firm's business at the date of the offence, and the offence is stated as having been committed 'between Saturday, 31st March, and Monday, 2nd April'; but, so far as the statement in the complaint is concerned, the alleged alteration of the identification mark may have been made at any place to which the motor carriage could have gone between these dates. Specification of *locus* is essential not merely for the reasons given in Hume, but because the jurisdiction of the Court before which the complaint is brought depends upon it. It might have been enough, if the place of the offence was unknown to the prosecutor, to avail himself of the latitude of the sheriffdom. It was suggested that as Rothesay is in Bute, and as Bute is an island, it was unnecessary to give any further specification of *locus* than is implied in the address of the managing director's firm. But so important a matter as the *locus delicti* cannot be left to inference in that way; and, in any case, we cannot know anything of the possibilities of transit to the mainland. I think the entire absence of any specification of *locus,* such at least as to determine the jurisdiction of the Sheriff, amounts to a case of incompetency within the meaning of section 75 of the Summary Jurisdiction (Scotland) Act, 1908, and that—however little the accused may have been actually misled or prejudiced—the conviction which followed on a complaint so deficient as this is ought to be quashed."

The court passed
the bill.

NOTE

See also *Macintosh* v. *Metcalfe and Others* (*post*, p. 404) and *Herron* v. *Gemmell*, 1975 S.L.T. (Notes) 93.

In *Craig* v. *Keane*, 1981 S.C.C.R. 166 the prosecutor sought leave to amend a complaint to add an additional *locus*. The case was distinguished from *Stevenson* v. *McLevy* on the ground that that case was concerned with the situation where the original complaint specified no *locus* whatsoever. The jurisdictional problems were not considered by the High Court.

c. Limits to competency

(i) The High Court
The jurisdiction of the High Court to try crimes committed within
Scotland is almost universal. It may be excluded where jurisdiction
is reserved by statute to some other court, but this must be done
expressly or by necessary implication: *Rowet* (1843) 1 Broun 540,
Duncan (1864) 4 Irvine 474.

The High Court exercises exclusive jurisdiction in cases of
treason, murder, rape, deforcement of messengers, breach of duty
by magistrates and in any case where exclusive jurisdiction is
conferred by statute. The crimes of robbery and wilful fire-raising
which, along with rape and murder, constituted the "pleas of the
Crown" and thus fell within the exclusive jurisdiction of the High
Court, may now be tried summarily or on indictment in the sheriff
court (1975 Act, ss 8 and 291, as amended by section 38 of the 1980
Act).

(ii) The sheriff court

McPherson v. Boyd
1907 S.C. (J.) 42
McPherson was charged in the police court at Ayr on a summary
complaint with driving a motor car at a speed in excess of 20 m.p.h.,
contrary to section 9 of the Motor Car Act 1903. A preliminary
objection that the magistrate in a police court had no jurisdiction to
try the complaint was repelled. He was convicted, and presented a
bill of suspension to the High Court.

LORD JUSTICE-GENERAL (DUNEDIN): "The question before your Lordships
is a very plain one. It is whether under the Motor Car Act of 1903
jurisdiction is given to the Magistrates of burghs, and although it is not of
course raised in this case, the determination will practically also decide
whether it is given to Justices of the Peace. Now, the scheme of the Motor
Car Act is first of all to declare that certain things shall not be done, and,
next, to declare that, if they are done, the doers of them shall be guilty of
offences under this Act. One of the things which is not to be done under the
Act is to drive a motor car on the public highway at a speed exceeding
twenty miles per hour. The section that deals with penalties says that a
person guilty of an offence under this Act will be liable to summary
prosecution and a fine not exceeding £20, and in the case of a second
conviction to a fine not exceeding £50, or, in the discretion of the Court, to
imprisonment not exceeding three months. There is also a set of provisions
which I need not read, by which persons are not allowed to drive motor cars
without licences, and provision is made for the Court which investigates the

offence taking away the licence of the driver or suspending him from driving for a certain period.

Now, the jurisdiction is admittedly not conferred *per expressum* upon either the Magistrates of the burgh or the Justices of Peace of the county. I confess that, as far as I am concerned, that is enough. It is the fact that in numerous statutes, too numerous to recite, which have created in modern times statutory offences, and imposed penalties for those offences, in all cases where it has been intended to confer jurisdiction upon the Magistrates' Courts or Justices of the Peace Courts, it is said in so many words that the offence shall be punishable before the Magistrates or the Justices of the Peace of the counties, or two Justices of the Peace, as the case may be; and the learned counsel who argued the case for the respondent, and who has said everything for the conviction that could be said, has not been able to point to any exception to that rule beyond citing the case of *M'Tavish* v. *Neilson* [(1903) 4 Adam 303], which I shall examine afterwards. That, to my mind, is sufficient. I have always understood it to be the law of Scotland that, in the case of statutory offences, which are not offences at all until they are created so by statute, the jurisdiction must be specially conferred on any Courts which have not universal jurisdiction, and the only Courts which have universal jurisdiction are the Sheriff Court and this Court. I am talking, of course, of criminal matters. When I say universal jurisdiction I mean an inherent universal jurisdiction, which may, however, be curtailed in many ways. But there is an underlying universal jurisdiction in both the Sheriff Court and this Court, and it seems to me, therefore, to be quite settled by long practice that where Parliament is going to give jurisdiction to Courts other than the Sheriff Court or the Court of Justiciary it must say so."

The court passed the bill
and suspended the conviction.

NOTE

The court was also influenced by the fact that the Act gave a right of appeal, in certain circumstances, to the "sheriff-depute." This would have been a quite novel form of appeal from a police court: "It is an attribute of the jurisdiction of County and Burgh magistrates that their judgments are only liable to be reviewed by this Court, and I should be slow to infer that this state of the constitutional law of the country regulating the co-ordination of the courts was intended to be taken away by Parliament by mere implication from a section dealing with other matters" (*per* Lord McLaren).

The police courts, along with other "inferior courts" were abolished by the District Courts (Scotland) Act 1975. 1. The jurisdiction and powers of those courts were, however, inherited by the district court (*ibid.*, s. 3). That jurisdiction has now been amplified by section 7 of the 1980 Act (as to which, see below). Subject to that modification, the High Court and sheriff court remain the only courts of universal jurisdiction.

The jurisdiction of the sheriff may, as the Lord Justice-General pointed out, be "curtailed" as, for example, in the case of offences reserved to the High Court. It may also be limited by the sheriff's powers of punishment. Where the minimum statutory penalty for an offence exceeded the sheriff's powers it was held that he had no jurisdiction to try the offence: *Gallagher* v. *H.M. Advocate,* 1937 J.C. 27.

(iii) The district court

The district court was established by the District Courts (Scotland) Act 1975 and replaced the existing inferior courts (justice of the peace courts, burgh courts, police courts, etc.). The composition and jurisdiction of the district court is governed by the District Courts (Scotland) Act 1975 and the 1975 Act. Part II of the 1975 Act regulates procedures before the district court.

1.   Criminal Justice (Scotland) Act 1980

"**7.**—(1) Except in so far as any enactment (including this Act or an enactment passed after this Act) otherwise provides, the statutory offences which it shall be competent for a district court to try shall be those in respect of which the maximum penalty which may be imposed does not exceed 60 days imprisonment or a fine of £200 or both.

(2) Nothing in subsection (1) above shall empower a district court to try an offence specified in Schedule 4 to the Road Traffic Act 1972 in respect of which disqualification from driving or endorsement of a driving licence is either obligatory or discretionary following conviction."

NOTE

The offence in *McPherson* v. *Boyd* was punishable "on summary conviction" and this term was not sufficient to confer jurisdiction on an inferior court. In *Hall* v. *Macpherson* (1913) 7 Adam 173, however, it was held that where a statute imposed a penalty where a person was convicted before "a court of summary jurisdiction" the word "a" meant "any," and that inferior courts thus had jurisdiction. When the district court inherited the jurisdiction of the inferior courts it inherited this anomaly. The anomaly is now removed by section 7 above, so that the district court will have a general jurisdiction to try summary statutory offences, subject to the powers of sentence prescribed therein, and subject to any express exclusion, or extension of that jurisdiction.

2. Criminal Procedure (Scotland) Act 1975

"**285.** A court of summary jurisdiction other than the sheriff court shall have jurisdiction to try or to pronounce sentence in, but shall, to the extent and in the manner mentioned in the next following section, be entitled to take cognizance of the case of any person—

(*a*) found within the jurisdiction of such court, and brought before it accused or suspected of having committed at any place beyond the jurisdiction of such court any offence, or

(*b*) brought before such court accused or suspected of having committed within the jurisdiction thereof any of the following offences:—

(i) murder, culpable homicide, robbery, rape, wilful fire-raising, or attempt at wilful fire-raising:

(ii) stouthrief, theft by housebreaking, or housebreaking with intent to steal:

(iii) theft or reset of theft, falsehood fraud or wilful imposition, breach of trust or embezzlement, all to an amount exceeding £200:

(v) assault whereby any limb has been fractured, or assault with intent to ravish, or assault to the danger of life, or assault by stabbing:

(vi) uttering forged documents or uttering forged bank or banker's notes, or offences under the Acts relating to coinage . . .

286. If either in the preliminary investigation or in the course of the trial of any offence it shall appear that the offence is one which cannot competently be tried in the court before which an accused is brought, or is one which, in the opinion of the court in view of the circumstances of the case, should be dealt with by a higher court, it shall be lawful for the court to commit the accused to prison for examination for any period not exceeding four days, and the prosecutor shall forthwith give notice of such committal to the procurator fiscal of the district within which such offence was committed, or to such other official as may be entitled to take cognizance thereof, in order that the accused may be dealt with according to law."

NOTE

Section 285 was amended by section 7 of the 1980 Act. The sum mentioned in section 285(*b*)(iii) was formerly £25. Under the former provisions of the 1975 Act, the district court only had jurisdiction in relation to the matters in section 285(*b*)(iii) where the offender had a previous conviction for any offence inferring dishonest appropriation of property. For these purposes a person who had been admonished, or who had been put on probation and in respect of whom there had been no subsequent sentence of imprisonment was deemed not to have been convicted.

The sum mentioned in subsection (*b*)(iii) is subject to alteration by order of the Secretary of State (1975 Act, s. 289D (3A) (*k*)).

CHAPTER 4

ARREST AND DETENTION

a. General distinctions

At common law there existed no power on the part of the police
(or anyone else) to apprehend or detain a person short of arrest. "A
person is either arrested or he is not; there is no half-way house"
(*Swankie* v. *Milne,* 1973 J.C. 1 *per* Lord Cameron, *infra,* p. 123).
Certain statutes did confer on the police more or less limited powers
of detention in particular circumstances (see, for example, the
Misuse of Drugs Act 1971, s. 23, the Edinburgh Corporation Order
Confirmation Act 1967, s. 493, the Prevention of Terrorism
(Emergency Provisions) Act 1976, s. 12). The Criminal Justice
(Scotland) Act 1980 has brought about a radical departure from the
common law position by introducing certain general police powers
to detain suspected persons without arresting them. The justification for the introduction of these powers, and the conditions
governing their use form the bulk of the discussion of detention in
this chapter. It may be useful at this point to note certain general
distinctions between power of arrest and powers of detention.

The power to arrest, with or without warrant, is recognised both
at common law and under an increasing number of statutory
provisions. Since, however, the common law does not recognise a
power to detain, all powers of detention are statutory. One practical
consequence of this is that the circumstances in which it is lawful to
detain are, generally, more precisely defined than the circumstances in which arrest, or at least arrest without warrant, is lawful.

Warrants to arrest are granted, usually by a sheriff, on the
application of the procurator fiscal, and are executed by the police.
The police may, however, arrest without warrant as (in theory at
least) may judges, sheriffs and even private citizens in certain
circumstances. Powers of detention, in contrast, are in general only
exercisable by the police.

Arrest may be employed for a variety of purposes. As an initial
step in criminal procedure it is used to secure the attendance of a
suspect or accused person before a court. Similarly it may be used to
ensure the attendance of persons required as witnesses. Post-trial

104

arrest may be necessary to secure compliance with the order or judgment of the court. But so far as the police are concerned the power of arrest is not limited to such investigatory or administrative functions. The police have a responsibility for the preservation of order (see the Police (Scotland) Act 1967, s. 17) and in the discharge of this duty a constable may arrest without warrant any person committing or threatening to commit a breach of the peace. Detention powers, it is submitted, are in broad terms an addition to the investigatory powers of the police, and this should be borne in mind when considering the exercise of these powers. It would seem, for example, that an attempt to use the powers of detention contained in section 2 of the 1980 Act (*post*, p. 137) for non-investigatory purposes (such as the indiscriminate detention of a large group of persons for the purposes of preserving public order) would be unlawful. There are powers of arrest available in such cases and where they are not available detention should not be employed (*cf.* Thomson Committee, 2nd Report, para. 3.21).

Finally it should be noted that although this chapter is primarily concerned with powers of arrest and detention in the criminal process, a section has been included on arrest and detention in respect of matrimonial interdicts under the Matrimonial Homes (Family Protection) (Scotland) Act 1981. Given the quasi-criminal nature of the procedures involved it seems appropriate that they should be included here.

b. Arrest

(i) Under a warrant

Any judge, sheriff or justice of the peace may issue a warrant for arrest, but in practice application is usually made by the fiscal to the sheriff. In solemn procedure this is done by way of petition, setting out the particulars of the accused (name, address, etc.) and the charge against him. A warrant to arrest may also be granted in summary procedure, though it is naturally less common and is usually granted because the whereabouts of the accused are unknown. The Thomson Committee (2nd Report, para. 4.10) recommended that in summary proceedings the fiscal should not ask for a warrant to arrest unless the whole circumstances of the case justified this.

Once granted, the warrant authorises officers of law to apprehend the accused. A warrant granted by a sheriff may be executed anywhere in Scotland (1975 Act, s. 15) and may be

executed in England by an English constable (1975 Act, s. 17). A
warrant to arrest is usually accompanied by a warrant to search the
person, dwelling-place and repositories of the accused. (Powers of
entry to effect a warrant are discussed below, p. 190.)

According to Hume (ii, 79) a person arrested is entitled to see the
warrant, at least where the officer executing it "is not generally
known for such, or is acting out of his ordinary bounds." This issue
arose, albeit obliquely, in *Stirton* v. *McPhail*, 1983 S.L.T. 34.
Warrants were granted for the arrest of the appellant's husband for
non-payment of fines. Two police officers were instructed by a
superior officer to arrest him. The appellant, who had been informed of the existence of the warrants, tried to prevent the officers
arresting her husband, and was convicted of obstructing and hinder-
ing the officers in the execution of their duty, contrary to section 41
of the Police (Scotland) Act 1967. At no time did the police officers
have the warrants in their possession. The central issue was whether
they were acting in the execution of their duty, and an argument was
presented that in the absence of direct evidence of these warrants
the court could not be satisfied that the officers were so engaged.
The High Court held that the validity of the warrants, so far as the
arrest of the appellant's husband was concerned, was not a relevant
consideration. The officers were acting in the execution of their
duty because they were carrying out the orders of a superior officer.
The Lord Justice-Clerk did state, however, that: "The fact that it
was not proved that such warrants were in existence, that they did
not have these warrants in their possession at the time, and that
their knowledge of them rested only on hearsay might be relevant
when considering a complaint by the appellant's husband that he
had been illegally arrested". Lord Hunter expressly reserved his
opinion as to whether it was in the circumstances necessary for the
arresting officers to have the warrants in their possession at the time
of arrest. While there may be administrative difficulties in ensuring
such personal possession, and the production of a warrant cannot
guarantee a trouble-free arrest, the added authority of a warrant
may be of help in some cases. In any event, since an arrested person
is entitled to be informed of the grounds of his arrest (*cf.* Hume, ii,
79) the availibility of the warrant makes clear sense. For the legality
of detention pending the production of the warrant, see *Farquharson* v. *Whyte* (1886) 1 White 26.

(ii)   Arrest without warrant

Here it is necessary to distinguish between common law and
statutory powers of arrest.

(A) COMMON LAW POWERS

Peggie v. Clark
(1868) 7 M. 89

LORD PRESIDENT INGLIS: "This is an action of damages against the superintendent of police of the county of Kinross, founded on the allegation that, on the 3d of February 1867, being Sunday, he entered the dwelling-house of the pursuer in search of him, and that he apprehended him on the following day, and detained him in custody for two hours, acting on both occasion without warrant, and therefore illegally and oppressively. The Sheriff-substitute found for the pursuer, assessing the damages at £6. The Sheriff altered that interlocutor, and assoilzied the defender. The Lord Ordinary returned to the Sheriff-substitute's interlocutor, and the question between these conflicting judgments is one of some nicety.

The pursuer is a carrier, and occupies, or did occupy, a dwelling-house in Kinross. He had also a horse and cart, and was employed by Gordon, a flesher in Milnathort, to deliver some meat in Burntisland, on Thursday, 31st January 1867, and to receive the price, which he engaged to pay over to Gordon on the following day. He failed to pay the money to Gordon in the course of Friday. He returned to Kinross on the Thursday evening, and was at home all next day till the afternoon in Kinross, which is only two miles from Milnathort. At 4 p.m. on Friday he went by train to the Bridge of Earn, where he remained till the following Monday. In the meantime Gordon, having heard nothing about his money, became alarmed, and, under the impression that the pursuer had absconded, he put himself in communication with the police. Being himself laid up, he sent his wife, who stated the circumstances to the superintendent, and thereafter the proceedings were adopted in respect of which the pursuer seeks reparation.

It appears to me that, if the superintendent had reasonable grounds for believing that the pursuer intended to appropriate the money, and for that purpose had absconded, it was right that he should take prompt measures for his apprehension; and the question therefore comes to be, whether he had reasonable grounds? Now, the event certainly goes far to justify him; for when the pursuer was apprehended on his return home, it appeared that he had spent a part of the money on his own account. Looking to all the circumstances, though it is a narrow case, I am inclined to agree with the Sheriff that the defender had a good ground for believing that the pursuer had committed a criminal breach of trust, and had thereupon absconded. What the defender did was first to go to the pursuer's own house and search for him. He could not get a warrant on Sunday, and I think he was justified in going without it. The pursuer's wife was at home and could give no account of him, except that he had gone to the Bridge of Earn to a marriage; and on the defender's expressing incredulity, she said, 'If you do not believe my word you can go yourself and look for him.' and he did so, without any harshness or rudeness, so far as I see. On the Monday the pursuer was apprehended, and he makes it part of his complaint that he was kept for two or three hours in custody. But that was a good deal owing to his own proceedings, for he wished Gordon to be sent for that he might satisfy him, and this appears to have caused delay. But Gordon came at his request to the police-office, and in the end he was liberated, Gordon having been satisfied about his money. Whether that was a strictly correct proceeding is not here the question . . .

The ground on which the Sheriff puts his judgment is somewhat delicate and hazardous. He rests almost entirely on the 12th section of the County Police Act . . . I am not satisfied that that enactment introduced any new law, or extended the powers of police officers to apprehend without warrant. But I am of opinion that, under special circumstances, a police-officer is entitled to apprehend without a warrant, and it will always be a question whether the circumstances justify the apprehension. There are some cases about which there can be no doubt—thus, when a man is accused of murder, it would be a gross breach of duty on the part of a police-officer if, having an opportunity, he failed to apprehend the accused at once, and without a warrant. This is a different case, but, looking to the circumstances, I think they did justify the defender in proceeding without a warrant."

LORD DEAS: "It would be a strong thing to suppose that a discretionary power was meant to be given to inferior officers, under all circumstances, to apprehend any person they chose, and for offences of whatever kind, on their own suspicion, without a warrant. There are many exceptional cases in which police-officers or constables are entitled to apprehend without a written warrant, and for such cases no statute was required. If a policeman or constable sees a crime committed, it is his duty to apprehend the criminal at once; or if the criminal is pointed out to him running off from the spot, the same rule would apply. If, again, the criminal is in hiding, or the officer is credibly informed, or has good reason to believe, that he is about to abscond, the officer may *de plano* apprehend him, to prevent justice from being defeated. The same thing would hold if the crime believed to have been committed was murder or the like, the very nature of the punishment of which would render absconding the probable and natural result of the crime itself. Still further, if a suspected individual belongs to a class of persons reputed to live by crime, or who have no fixed residence or known means of honest livelihood, in all such cases a police-officer or constable has large powers of apprehending without a warrant. But I agree with your Lordship that the officer is not entitled to overstep the necessity or reasonable requirements of the particular case; and there ought, moreover, in no case, to be undue delay in the following out of such summary apprehension, by obtaining the appropriate formal warrant for the offender's detention. If an individual, even although expressly charged with crime by an aggrieved party, be a well-known householder — a person of respectability — what, in our justiciary practice, we call a 'law abiding party', and where there are no reasonable grounds for supposing that he means to abscond or flee from justice, I find nothing . . . in the common law, to justify a police-officer or constable in apprehending him without a warrant."

The court assoilzied the defender.

NOTE

It is thus impossible to state with any precision either the offences in respect of which arrest without warrant is lawful, or the circumstances in which such arrest may be made. The police may arrest without warrant in the case of common law offences and, though the limits of this power have never been authoritatively determined, in the case of statutory offences as well. But that does not take one very far, and it is clear that regard must be had to all the circumstances surrounding the arrest. Clearly the seriousness of the offence is a primary consideration: "arrest is more easily justified the more serious the offence" (Renton and Brown, para. 5-18), and in some cases the seriousness of the offence will of itself justify arrest. But in other cases regard must be had to the presence or absence of circumstances which would point to immediate arrest as opposed to some other procedure. Is the accused likely to abscond, or destroy evidence or tamper with witnesses? Is he or she likely to repeat the offence or commit further offences? And in weighing up these considerations it is relevant (though not conclusive of the matter) to have regard to the lapse of time between the commission of the offence and the arrest: *Leask* v. *Burt* (1893) 21 R. 32.

In England many of these problems are met by allowing arrest without warrant in respect of "arrestable offences" (Criminal Law Act 1967, s. 2). For these purposes an arrestable offence is one for which the sentence is fixed by law or for which a person on first conviction may by statute be sentenced to a term of imprisonment of five years. A constable may, under section 2 of the 1967 Act arrest, *inter alia,* any person in the act of committing an arrestable offence, any person who has committed or whom the constable with reasonable cause suspects has committed, an arrestable offence, or any person who is about to commit such an offence.

A similar solution for Scotland was rejected by the Thomson Committee (2nd Report, para. 3.04): "As there are no fixed maximum penalties for Scottish law crimes, and as most crimes are based on common law, it is not possible to make any distinction similar to that created by the five year period in England and Wales". So far as concerns the categories of offences for which arrest without warrant is possible, the Committee favoured the status quo, with the clarifying recommendation that the power to arrest without warrant in respect of statutory crimes be restricted to those offences which are punishable by imprisonment without the option of a fine (para. 3.29). As for the circumstances in which such a power may be exercised, the Committee made the following recommendation:

"In the first place we think that arrest should be competent only where the arresting officer has reasonable grounds for believing that he is entitled to charge the arrestee, i.e., that there is a *prima facie* case against him. In the second place we think that a police officer should not be entitled to arrest without a warrant unless in all the circumstances he has reasonable grounds for believing that the interests of justice require arrest at that time. Lapse of time since the commission of the offence should not in itself be a bar to arrest without warrant."

No effect has been given to this recommendation. Quite in whose interests the current vagueness of the law operates is hard to discern. No doubt the system functions as it does because the legality of arrest without warrant is so rarely challenged (*cf*. Renton and Brown, para. 5-18).

A private citizen may arrest without warrant, but such powers are limited to "serious crimes" witnessed by the individual. A private citizen may lawfully assist another who is carrying out a lawful arrest (*cf. Leask* v. *Burt, supra*). The purpose of such "private" arrest is limited to handing the person arrested over to the police, and this must be done as soon as possible.

At common law it is unclear whether arrest without warrant on "mere suspicion" is permissible. Suppose, for example, a constable comes upon a broken shop window. Goods have been removed from the window, and there is blood on the broken glass. Nearby he apprehends X, who has a badly cut hand, but he is not in possession of the goods removed from the window. Is there a power of arrest here? The case does not fall into any of the categories expressly referred to in *Peggie* v. *Clark* or in earlier authorities (see, *e.g.* Hume, ii, 75). The Thomson Committee were unsure (see paras. 3.06 and 3.30). In practical terms today this is not likely to present a problem for the constable who may rely upon his powers of detention in section 1 (and even section 2) of the 1980 Act.

(B) STATUTORY POWERS

One of the most significant developments in criminal law and procedure, especially in past 15 to 20 years, has been the proliferation of statutory powers of arrest without warrant. It would not be possible to include here anything other than a small sample of such powers, but certain broad groups of powers may be identified. The Royal Commission on Criminal Procedure (Vol. 2, Cmnd. 8092-1) identified three main groups (*ibid.*, appendix 9): powers of arrest exercisable only where a person is found, or seen, committing the offence specified; powers exercisable where there is reasonable suspicion that a person has committed or is committing the offence specified; powers exercisable where the name and address of the person cannot be ascertained and/or he is likely to abscond, etc. The following extract contains an example of the first type of power.

1. Civic Government (Scotland) Act 1982
"Powers of constables etc.

59.—(1) Subject to subsection (2) below, a constable may, where it is necessary in the interests of justice to do so, arrest without warrant a person whom he finds committing an offence to which this section applies or a person who is delivered into his custody in pursuance of subsection (3) below.

(2) A constable who is not in uniform shall produce his identification if required to do so by any person whom he is arresting under subsection (1) above.

(3) The owner, tenant or occupier of any property in, upon, or in respect of, which an offence to which this section applies is being committed or any person authorised by him may apprehend any person whom the owner or, as the case may be, the tenant, occupier or authorised person finds committing that offence and detain the apprehended person until he can be delivered into the custody of a constable.

In this subsection 'property' means heritable or moveable property.

(4) This section applies to offences under sections 50, 57, and 58 of this Act.

(5) This section shall not prejudice any power of arrest conferred by law apart from this section."

NOTE

The offences to which this section applies are; offences involving drunkenness in a public place (section 50), being in or on a building or other premises in circumstances inferring intent to steal (section 57), and being a convicted person found in possession or recent possession of equipment for theft (section 58). This provision comes into force on a date to be appointed by the Secretary of State (section 137(2)). A commencement order under section 137(2) "shall of itself have the effect of repealing (*a*) any provision of the Burgh Police (Scotland) Acts 1892 to 1911; (*b*) any local statutory provision . . . to the extent that the provision provides for any matter which is also provided for (whether consistently or not) by or under any provision of this Act commenced by that order."

2. McLeod v. Shaw
1981 S.L.T. (Notes) 93; 1981 S.C.C.R. 54

OPINION OF THE COURT: "[An accused person was charged with a contravention of s. 6 (2) of the Road Traffic Act 1972]. It was established that the respondent was arrested while in charge of a motor vehicle and that the arrest had been made in purported exercise of the powers given to constables by s. 5(5) of the Act. It was established further that upon the faith of that arrest the procedure prescribed by s. 9 (1) of that Act was carried out and that, in terms of an analyst's certificate to which s. 10 (1) applied, the proportion of alcohol in his blood exceeded the prescribed limit. The submission made at the hearing on evidence at the end of the trial was that the arrest of the respondent had not been a lawful arrest under s. 5 (5) with the result that the prosecutor could not rely on any of the subsequent procedure upon which the Crown case depended. The sheriff upheld that submission and acquitted the respondent. In this appeal the procurator fiscal has moved us to hold that the sheriff erred in so doing, and it is common ground that if this contention is well founded the case must be remitted to the sheriff with a direction to convict the respondent.

According to the stated case the circumstances in which the purported arrest of the respondent took place were these. An experienced woman police sergeant, accompanied by a male special constable, observed a motor car standing in the roadway about four feet out from the kerb. The time was 0040 hours on Saturday, 8 December 1979. They approached the car and found the respondent in the driving seat. There were two other persons in the car, both in the rear passenger seat. The sergeant went to the driver's door and had a brief conversation with the respondent who opened his window. Her evidence about this and what followed is recorded by the sheriff thus: 'Because of the position of the vehicle—my main thing—I decided to ask him to come out because we were standing right in the middle of the road. He came out and stood in front of the car. His eyes were glazed. As he came out I felt he put out his hand to steady himself. His speech was very precise. I felt there was slur in his speech. I didn't talk to him for long. I felt he shouldn't be driving. I formed the opinion he had been drinking and his ability was impaired. I told him he was under arrest and cautioned and charged him with s.5 (2) of the Road Traffic Act 1972. In 19 years' experience, I've dealt with drunks—not so many as others. I decided s. 5 (2) as opposed to s. 6 (5) because there had been no accident or anything.' Cross-examined: 'He was co-operative at all stages I conversed with him while he was seated—very little was said—for a moment or two. When he spoke to me in the car he spoke very precisely, but it was slurred. I decided I wasn't happy about the situation and asked him to come out of the car.'

It was in these circumstances that the sergeant formed the honest belief that the respondent was apparently committing an offence described in s. 5 (2) of the Act, namely, the offence of being 'in charge of a motor vehicle which is on a road . . . [while] unfit to drive through drink'. As the sheriff has found, she, the woman police sergeant, then arrested the respondent, taking the view that she was authorised to do so by s. 5 (5) which is in these terms: 'A constable may arrest without warrant a person committing an offence under this section.' For the sake of completeness we should add that when the respondent was examined at the police station at 0120 hours, the examining doctor who noted the smell of drink and certain other matters certified that he was not then unfit to drive through drink.

It was not and could not be in dispute that under s. 5 (5) a constable may arrest a person 'apparently' committing an offence under s. 5 and upon that understanding of the subsection the sheriff proceeded to consider the legality of the arrest of the respondent. After examining the authorities to which he refers in his note he decided that the question he must ask himself was this: 'whether on their own observations the police officers were justified in concluding that the respondent was probably guilty of s. 5 (2)—being in charge of a motor vehicle when unfit to drive through drink and in arresting him without a warrant.'

He then proceeded to look not only at the evidence of the police sergeant, the arresting officer, but at the evidence of the special constable as well. Having done so he decided that it had not been proved that unsteadiness on the part of the respondent had been a factor in the decision to arrest him and that the only factors had been that there was 'some slurring in the respondent's speech which was precise and some glazing in his eyes'. He then reached his own conclusion that these two factors did not justify the belief that the respondent was probably unfit to drive through drink and the result was the respondent's acquittal.

We have no doubt that in reaching his decision to acquit the respondent the learned sheriff misdirected himself. He asked himself the wrong question and having done so made the mistake of attempting to reconcile the evidence of the two police officers present with the result that he excluded from his consideration one of the facts as they appeared to be to the arresting officer, the police sergeant—one of the several grounds upon which she formed the honest belief that the respondent was apparently committing the s. 5 (2) offence. The question which the sheriff should have asked himself can, in this case, be put in this way: 'Am I satisfied that the experienced arresting officer, the police sergeant, had no reasonable grounds for her admittedly honest belief that the respondent was apparently committing the s. 5 (2) offence which she had in mind?' That this was the proper question emerges from a consideration of the cases of *Wiltshire* v. *Barrett* [1966] 1 Q.B.312; *Woodage* v. *Jones* (*No. 2*) [1975] R.T.R. 119; *Seaton* v. *Allan*, 1974 S.L.T. 234; 1973 J.C. 24; and *Breen* v. *Pirie*, 1976 S.L.T. 136; 1976 J.C. 60. It was the state of mind and knowledge of the arresting officer and of no other which is here in issue.

It is not surprising, therefore, that counsel for the respondent agreed that this was so. What the sheriff should have done, accordingly, was to ask himself that question with reference only to the facts as they appeared to the arresting officer, the police sergeant—the facts upon which her admittedly honest belief was founded. Had he done so he could not have held that she had no reasonable grounds for that honest belief. We are certainly not prepared so to hold.

In the result we conclude that the sheriff erred in law in acquitting the respondent for the reason which he gives, and that the prosecutor's appeal must be allowed."

Appeal allowed. Case
remitted to the sheriff
with a direction to convict.

NOTES

Although the decision is one on the construction of particular statutory provisions, the formulation of the issue in terms of whether the officer had reasonable grounds for believing an offence was being committed, means that the case is relevant to other statutory powers of arrest (and indeed detention) formulated in those terms. The decision effectively means that the arresting officer selects the "reasonable grounds" and provided that he reaches an honest conclusion on those grounds that an offence is being committed, the arrest is not open to challenge on the basis of other grounds which would render his honestly held belief unreasonable. (Such other grounds might, of course, affect the *honesty* of the officer's belief.) *Cf. Wills* v. *Bowley* [1982] 2 All E.R. 654 (H.L.).

Where does the onus lie in respect of the reasonable grounds? Must the prosecution show that the officer honestly believed that he was entitled to arrest, and that he had reasonable grounds (as defined above) for that belief? Or is it for the accused to demonstrate the absence of such reasonable grounds? General principle suggests the former, but in *Shields* v. *Shearer,* 1914 S.C. (H.L.) 33 the latter view was adopted. That was, however, a civil action for wrongful arrest where the onus would in any event have lain on the pursuer. See the commentary at 1981 S.C.C.R. 59.

3. Binnie v. Donnelly
1981 S.L.T. 24

The appellant was involved in a motor accident in Scotland. A short while later he drove into England, where he was involved in another accident. Two officers of Lothians and Borders police administered a breath test to him, in England. The proper procedures were followed, the test proved positive, and the appellant was arrested and taken back to Scotland. He was convicted before the sheriff court at Jedburgh of a contravention of section 6 (1) of the Road Traffic Act 1972. On appeal by stated case:

LORD CAMERON: " . . . It was maintained for the appellant before the sheriff that the officers had no jurisdiction to require a breath test or make an arrest without warrant in England. After hearing submissions the sheriff applied his mind to the statutory provisions and, having concluded that the police officers were acting within their powers, proceeded to convict the appellant. Against that decision the appellant has appealed and maintains that the sheriff misdirected himself in law and that, as the police officers had no warrants granted in Scotland by a Scottish magistrate, they had no power to exercise any jurisdiction under their statutes on the English side of the border.

Counsel for the appellant submitted that a court had to be satisfied that the officer making the requirements and proceeding to arrest must be a 'constable' within the meaning of the Act at the material time. To say that at the material time the constables were given power for a particular purpose or purposes in terms of s. 17 (8) of the Police (Scotland) Act 1967 was to beg the question. The question was whether the officers were 'constables' at that place and time: the Road Traffic Act required that the constable be not only a constable but a constable in uniform at the place and time where and when the requirement was or could be made. Counsel recalled the development of the jurisdiction of a constable in Scotland from his status and jurisdiction limited to his burgh to the nationwide jurisdiction exercisable by virtue of s. 17 (4) of the 1967 Act. But this was a limited jurisdiction, its boundaries set at the border. Were it otherwise there would be no need for the very limited extension afforded to officers of border forces provided by s. 18 of the Act. The provisions of that section were a repetition of those which appeared in s. 11 of the Police (Scotland) Act of 1857, and the definition of a 'constable' contained in s. 51 (1) of the 1967 Act showed that he was a constable of a Scottish police force not just a 'constable' which is the word used in s. 8 of the Road Traffic Act of 1972. The language of s. 17 (8) was to be interpreted as referable to the power for particular purposes exercisable by a constable of a Scottish police force, but exercisable within the limits of his statutory jurisdiction, i.e. throughout Scotland.

For the respondent it was submitted that the sheriff's analysis of the statutory provisions led to a correct conclusion. The Road Traffic Act applied throughout the United Kingdom and the powers of this Act were exercisable by a constable. There was nothing in the Act which suggested or supported the proposition that the power for the particular purpose of the enactment could not be exercised where, although the accident had happened in Scotland, the request by the constable seized of the event had been made in England. Such a construction could defeat the purpose of the Act, while there was nothing in the Act to suggest that any such incidental or accidental limit was to be placed upon the jurisdiction of constables in uniform engaged in operating the statutory procedure. Parliament must be assumed to have been aware of the existence of the border between England and Scotland, but no distinction was drawn between officers on either side of the border or any exception made as to the exercise of their powers in a trans-border situation as here. If the appellant's arguments were correct the object of the legislature and the intention of Parliament could in many cases be defeated, but such a result could be avoided by giving the words 'a constable' their ordinary and natural meaning—any constable whether Scottish or English. If that were correct then the officer possessed the necessary jurisdiction to carry out his duty in pursuance of this particular purpose, whether or not it involved his passage of the border to do so. The question should be answered accordingly.

In my opinion the solution to the problem of jurisdiction presented by this case is to be found in an examination of the language of the relevant statutory provisions which define and govern the powers and jurisdiction of police constables in Scotland and by reference to the precise wording of s. 8 (2) of the Road Traffic Act 1972. The governing statute is the Police (Scotland) Act 1967 and in s. 17 it defines the general functions and jurisdiction of constables. By s. 51 (1) of that Act 'functions' are defined to include 'powers and duties'. By s. 17 (4) the geographical boundaries of a constable's jurisdiction are defined in these words: '(4) Any constable of a police force shall have all the powers and privileges of a constable throughout Scotland.' Subsection (5) provides: 'This section shall be without prejudice to s. 18 of this Act and to any other enactment conferring powers on a constable for particular purposes.' 'Enactment' also and necessarily includes Acts of Parliament, as is made clear by s. 82 of and Sched. 4 to the Act. Section 18, which repeats a provision of the earlier Act of 1857, provides a limited extension of the jurisdiction of constables of border counties of England or Scotland as respects the execution of warrants in such border counties. The language of s. 8 (2) of the Road Traffic Act 1972 repeats precisely that of s. 2 of the Road Safety Act 1967 and provides: 'If an accident occurs owing to the presence of a motor vehicle on a road or other public place, a constable in uniform may require any person who he has a reasonable cause to believe was driving . . . the vehicle at the time of the accident to provide a specimen of breath for a breath test' and goes on in subss. (4) and (5) to give the constable power to arrest without warrant if the result of the test is positive or there is a failure to provide the requisite specimen of breath. Now the provisions of the statute are applicable to the whole United Kingdom and there is no limitative definition of 'a constable'. All that the statute prescribes in order to clothe the constable with the requisite power to require a breath test or without warrant to arrest is that he be in uniform. The police officers in the present case were constables and were in uniform and they had reasonable cause to believe that the appellant was the driver of the vehicle concerned in an accident on a road, and on a road in Scotland. The statute makes no reference to the border between England and Scotland or distinction between a Scottish or an English constable, though it is to be assumed that Parliament was fully aware of this fact in enacting legislation to be effectual throughout the United Kingdom. Now the powers conferred on a constable in uniform are powers conferred on him for a particular purpose, to operate the scheme of control over drivers of motor vehicles contained in the provisions of the Road Traffic Act 1972. It is also the case that s. 8 of the Act of 1972 repeats precisely the language of s. 2 of the Road Safety Act 1967, which received the Royal Assent prior to the passage of the Police (Scotland) Act of that year, so that the enactment of this particular extension of jurisdiction was on the statute book at the time the police legislation was before Parliament. Clearly, therefore, it was such an enactment as is covered by the language of s. 17 (8) of the Police Act. The concept of trans-border jurisdiction was familiar to the legislature, as the provisions of s. 18 of the 1967 Act were a re-enactment of a provision which had been on the statute book since 1857. In my opinion the natural meaning to be given to the language of s. 8 (2) is that no distinction is made between a constable according to whether he belongs to a police force raised and administered on one side of the border or the other, and that this conclusion is reinforced by consideration of the express wording of s. 17 (8) of the 1967 Police Act where it clearly refers to an enactment which may for a particular purpose or particular purposes extend the jurisdiction and powers of a police officer beyond those normally possessed and exercisable by him. In my opinion the jurisdiction and power claimed in this case by the police officer are just such as the statute contemplates and the Road Traffic Act confers. For these reasons the learned sheriff in my view reached the right conclusion and his decision should be affirmed and the question in the case answered in the affirmative."

Appeal dismissed.

NOTE

What are the limits of this decision? Clearly it refers only to powers conferred on a constable by legislation "effectual throughout the United Kingdom." It could be argued that the decision is limited to the taking of steps by the police in relation to offences committed in Scotland. But the dicta in the case are much wider. Does it mean that the police constable may exercise his statutory powers anywhere in the United Kingdom at any time? If a Scottish constable exercises in England a power of arrest conferred by a U.K. statute, is the lawfulness of the arrest determined by Scots or English law? Suppose, for example, that the officers had entered the appellant's land as trespassers and there administered the breath test and arrested him. Under English law they would have been acting unlawfully, so that neither the request for the breath test, nor the subsequent arrest would have been lawful: *Morris* v. *Beardmore* [1980] 2 All E.R. 753; *Finnigan* v. *Sandiford* [1981] 2 All E.R. 267. It is by no means clear, however, that the same view of the proceedings would be adopted in Scotland (see below, p. 119). If there is a problem here, then Parliament's decision not to harmonise the powers of arrest in the new breath test provisions (Road Traffic Act 1972, s. 7 (6) and (7) as substituted by the Transport Act 1981) may give cause for regret.

(iii)   Powers of entry to effect arrest

(A)   COMMON LAW OFFENCES

Hume, Crimes, ii

"No officer shall in any case be justified for breaking open doors, to execute his warrant [to arrest] unless he have notified his errand to those within, and demand entrance. But, under that condition, he has a right by our law, though it may be otherwise in England, to break open the doors of a house, to take the person mentioned in his warrant; and this, whether he is certainly known to be the guilty person, or is charged only on probable suspicion; and equally in his own house, or at that of another person, where he is, or is on probable suspicion believed to be, at the time. For the officer is not obliged to trust the word of every one, perhaps the friend or associate of the felon, in that matter; and why should anyone refuse liberty to an officer of the law, to search his house, which is no injury to him, whether the person sought for be there at the time, or not? . . . If the officer duly observe these several precautions, he certainly is not answerable, though in truth the person accused be innocent of the charge, or even though no such felony have been committed" (p.80).

"In cases of breach of the peace, or violent threats of immediate mischief as also in cases of felony which he has seen committed, or has information from others who are sure of the facts, the like power of arresting belongs to a constable, or other officer of the law, proper to the execution of criminal warrants . . . As to the breaking open of doors on such occasions, I have not found any authority, to warrant a constable doing so, in his pursuit of one who flies after committing a breach of the peace; but rather a direction to him, in the act 1717, c.8. to take notice of the master of the house, that he may be afterwords challenged for his contempt, in refusing admission. But it is not to be imagined, that a constable shall be subject to the like restraint in cases of murder, house-breaking, robbery or the like, committed in his presence, or known to him by complaints of others who were present, or have been the sufferers on such occasions . . . It is always to be remembered, that to justify the officer in making a violent entry into any house, (and this is true, though he be the bearer even of a written warrant), he must first demand and be refused admission, and must notify who he is, and the purpose of his coming" (p.76).

NOTE

In summary procedure, section 321 (1) of the 1975 Act provides that "any warrant of apprehension or search shall, where it is necessary for its execution, imply warrant to officers of law to break open shut and lockfast places."

(B) STATUTORY OFFENCES

Whether a statutory power of arrest without warrant infers a power of entry to effect the arrest is not clear. Some statutes confer both powers expressly, from which one may infer that the power to enter does not necessarily follow from the power to arrest. The majority of statutes, however, are silent on this point. There appears to be no recent Scottish authority in which the matter is fully discussed, but it was raised in the following English case:

Finnigan v. Sandiford
[1981] 2 All E.R. 267

The respondent was charged with an offence contrary to section 6 (1) of the Road Traffic Act 1972. Police officers had attended at his home and required him to undergo a breath test, under section 8 (1) of the 1972 Act. At the time the request was made the police officers were, quite lawfully, standing outside the respondent's front door. The respondent was inside. He declined to take the test, and retreated into the house. The officers, without permission, entered the house and arrested the respondent, in accordance with the power of arrest conferred by section 8 (5) of the 1972 Act. The respondent subsequently provided a specimen of blood which proved positive. The information on which he was charged was dismissed by the magistrates. The prosecutor appealed unsuccessfully to the divisional court, and from that court to the House of Lords.

LORD KEITH OF KINKEL: " . . . [T]he only issue which your Lordships have to decide turns on the proper construction of s 8(5) of the 1972 Act, which provides:
'If a person required by a constable under subsection (1) or (2) above to provide a specimen of breath for a breath test fails to do so and the constable has reasonable cause to suspect him of having alcohol in his body, the constable may arrest him without warrant except while he is at hospital as a patient.'
The procedures prescribed by s 9 of the Act as regards the making of a requirement to provide a specimen of blood or urine for laboratory test, which, on compliance, may lead to a charge under s 6(1) or, on non-compliance, to a charge under s 9(3), are applicable only to a person who has been arrested under s 8 (or possibly under s 5(5), relating to driving when unfit to drive through drink or drugs). It follows that, if a person has not been lawfully arrested under the relevant enactment, the s 9 procedures cannot validly be applied to him and the result of the purported application are inept to form the basis of any conviction. Counsel for the appellants, quite rightly, made no attempt to argue the contrary. The question accor-

dingly comes to be whether the power to arrest without warrant conferred by s 8(5) carries with it the power lawfully to enter, by force if need be, the dwelling house of the person whom it is intended to arrest, for the purpose of carrying out that intention.

It may confidently be stated as a matter of general principle that the mere conferment by statute of a power to arrest without warrant in given circumstances does not carry with it any power to enter private premises without permission of the occupier, forcibly or otherwise. Section 2 of the Criminal Law Act 1967 creates a category of 'arrestable offences' in respect of which the power of arrest without warrant may be exercised. Such offences are extremely serious, being those punishable by five years' imprisonment on first conviction, and attempts thereat. Subsection (6) specifically provides:

'For the purpose of arresting a person under any power conferred by this section a constable may enter (if need be, by force) and search any place where that person is or where the constable, with reasonable cause, suspects him to be.'

Apart from the category of arrestable offences, there are a considerable number of instances where a specific power of arrest without warrant is conferred in relation to particular statutory offences. In some instances power of entry is also conferred, for example by s 50(2) of the Firearms Act 1968. In a great many others, no power of entry is conferred. The proper inference, in my opinion, is that, where Parliament considers it appropriate that a power of arrest without warrant should be reinforced by a power to enter private premises, it is in the habit of saying so specifically, and that the omission of any such specific power is deliberate. It would rarely, if ever, be possible to conclude that the power had been conferred by implication. Counsel for the appellants maintained that in the present case such an implication was properly to be drawn from the circumstance that the penalty under s 8(3) for failing to provide a specimen of breath was a minor one compared with that under s 9(3) for failing to provide a specimen of blood or urine, or under s 6(1) in the event of the specimen proving positive. It was therefore to be inferred, so it was argued, that Parliament did not contemplate the possibility of any interruption in the sequence of events from the making of a lawful requirement for a breath test to the formulation of charges under s 6(1) or s 9(3). But that consideration does not offer any sufficient foundation for the implication claimed to be necessary. There can be no question of the legislative scheme being unworkable in its absence. It is also to be observed that, as noticed above, s 9 is tied in with s 5(5) as well as with s 8(5). It would be strange if the latter were held to confer power to enter for the purpose of effecting an arrest, but not the former. The proper conclusion, in my opinion, is that Parliament did not confer such power in either case.

This conclusion is consistent with the principle on which the decision in *Morris* v. *Beardmore* [[1980] 2 All E.R. 753] proceeded, namely that in this particular piece of legislation Parliament cannot be taken to have authorised any further inroads on the rights of individual citizens than it specifically enacted. The conclusion does, however, have a wider significance, in respect that it must be of general application in cases where a statute has conferred a power of arrest without warrant, but no specific power of entry on private premises for the purpose of effecting the arrest.

My Lords, for these reasons I would deal with each of these appeals by answering the certified question in the negative and dismissing the appeal."

LORD SCARMAN: "My Lords, I have had the advantage of reading in draft the speech delivered by my noble and learned friend Lord Keith. I agree with it, and would dismiss each appeal.

I also agree with his comment that the House's conclusion has a wider significance than the mere interpretation of s 8(5) of the Road Traffic Act 1972. It is that, as a general rule, the courts will not construe an enactment conferring a power of arrest without warrant as impliedly authorising a power of entry into private premises for the purpose of effecting the arrest. If it be Parliament's intention to confer a power of entry, the draftsman must ensure that the power is expressly conferred. Parliament is to not be presumed, in the absence of express words, so to intend, unless the implication is irresistible, which would be rare indeed."

Appeal dismissed.

NOTE

Although the views of the House of Lords on a general point of statutory interpretation ought to be persuasive, the following considerations should be borne in mind when viewing Lord Keith's remarks in a Scottish light. (i) Generally, the powers of arrest and search enjoyed by the English constable are more closely circumscribed than those of his Scottish counterpart. (ii) In particular, a very strict line is adopted on the trespassing police officer: see e.g. Morris v. Beardmore (supra), Davis v. Lisle [1936] 2 K.B. 434, McArdle v. Wallace [1964] Crim.L.R. 467, and compare these cases with Smith v. Hawkes, High Court, November 1980, unreported, C.O.C. A32/80.

There are dicta in the case of Shepherd v. Menzies (1900) 2 F. 443 to effect that a power of arrest without warrant conferred upon a constable by section 6 of the Cruelty to Animals (Scotland) Act 1850 entitled the constable to enter upon private premises for the purposes of making that arrest. (See Lord Kyllachy at p.446, affirmed by the Second Division at p.447.) However, it appears that their Lordships were relying on the special wording of the Act in question, coupled with common law powers of entry, rather than any general principle relating to statutory powers. In any event, these remarks must be considered obiter, since the constable did not in fact make an arrest in that case but proceeded by reporting the offence for prosecution by summary complaint.

The position probably is that the courts would have regard to the wording and purpose of the particular Act in question, and the circumstances of the case (*cf.* Lord Moncreiff in *Shepherd* v. *Menzies,* at p.447). It would appear that in some cases the police are accepted as having the power presently under discussion. The revised breath test provisions, inserted into the Road Traffic Act 1972 by the Transport Act 1981, contain a qualified right of entry in connection with breath tests (new section 7(6)) but these provisions extend only to England: section 7(7) (where they are necessary to deal with the *Morris* v. *Beardmore/Finnigan* v. *Sandiford* problem). Section 7(7) provides that "nothing in [section 7(6)] shall affect any rule of law in Scotland concerning the right of a constable to enter premises for any purpose." The clear implication of this provision is that Parliament was advised that in Scotland the constable's powers of entry were at least equal to those conferred by section 7(6) on his English counterpart.

(iv) What constitutes arrest?

The Scottish courts have not been very successful in explaining the criteria by which one might determine whether or not a person has been arrested. This was inconvenient when the only distinction to be drawn was between arrest or liberty. But the introduction of powers of detention has made it necessary to draw the further distinction between these two forms of custody (see *Wither* v. *Reid, post*). It is probably only a matter of time until the courts are called upon to determine whether, in a given case, a suspect was arrested, or merely detained under the 1980 Act. One cannot be wholly confident of the assistance they will receive from the following line of authorities.

1. Muir v. Provost, Magistrates and Councillors of Hamilton
1910 1 S.L.T. 164

The pursuer raised an action against the provost, magistrates and councillors of the burgh of Hamilton, as being vicariously liable for an allegedly wrongful arrest carried out against him by a sergeant in the burgh police force. The Lord Ordinary (Salvesen) held that the defenders were not vicariously liable for the actions of the officer, but then went on to consider the merits of the action:

LORD SALVESEN: " . . . The only complaint against Sergeant Smith is that, having a suspicion that the pursuer had obtained exciseable liquor at the County Hotel, Hamilton, on the Sunday, by falsely representing himself to be a *bona fide* traveller, he 'insisted' that the pursuer should go with him to the hotel, in order to see whether the barmaid would identify him with a person of the same name who had written his name in the hotel book. The pursuer avers that, having protested his innocence, and having offered to meet the police at the hotel in the evening, Sergeant Smith refused to acquiesce in his proposal; and that the pursuer was thereupon marched off through the crowded streets, to Glenlee Street, where he and a constable took a tramway car. There is no suggestion that any force was used, or that anything happened but that the pursuer went in the company of the police to the hotel. It is not said that the sergeant acted maliciously; and, on the pursuer's own statement, he appears to have had probable cause. The only possible ground for action is that Sergeant Smith had no warrant for the alleged apprehension.

In my opinion these facts do not disclose a case of apprehension at all. Had the pursuer refused to comply with Sergeant Smith's request, and had then been handcuffed and forcibly taken to the hotel for purposes of identification, the pursuer's case would have been stronger. All that happened, however, was that the sergeant asked the pursuer to accompany him to the County Hotel, and that the pursuer—fearing that if he did not comply with the request worse might happen—agreed to go. The pursuer being, in fact, innocent, I should have thought it in his interest to get himself cleared of suspicion by at once going down to the hotel. This makes it unnecessary to consider whether the bare fact that the sergeant had no warrant would have been a good ground of action, whether with or without an averment of malice and want of probable cause."

The court assoilzied
the defenders.

NOTE

To use an overworked media expression, Muir was merely "Helping the police with their inquiries." Lord Salvesen's opinion suggests that the pursuer's agreement to accompany the police officer was the key factor in determining whether or not he had been arrested, but how does that "agreement" stand up in the face of the officer's "insistence"? In what sense does a person agree to do X when he has no choice, or believes he has none? In any case, is it not possible to be arrested even though one is quite willing to comply with the police officer's directions? "It's a fair cop guv?"

2. Swankie v. Milne
1973 J.C. 1

While driving his car on a public road the appellant was stopped by two plain-clothes police officers whose car he had overtaken in a dangerous manner. They formed the view that he had been drinking, but since they were not in uniform they could not administer a breath test. They summoned uniformed officers who arrived within five or ten minutes. The sheriff found as a fact that if the appellant had attempted to leave during this time he would have been prevented, and indeed one of the officers took possession of the appellant's car keys. He gave a sample of breath which was positive and was then formally arrested, and taken to a police station where the remainder of the statutory procedure was carried out. He was convicted of driving with more than the permitted level of alcohol in his blood, and appealed. On appeal it was argued that since he had been arrested by the plain-clothes police officers, the breath test was not lawfully administered to a person driving or attempting to drive as required by section 2(1) of the Road Safety Act 1967.

LORD CAMERON: " . . . If there was no arrest then Mr Macaulay's first contention necessarily falls to the ground. Had the plain clothes officers in fact arrested or purported to arrest the appellant, then I can appreciate that a very difficult situation might arise with very difficult legal arguments. In such a situation it could be argued with force that once arrested a person is in the custody of the police and it would or might be difficult to maintain that he could at the same time be in the category of a person 'driving or attempting to drive a motor vehicle.' An arrest is something which in law differs from a detention by the police at their invitation or suggestion. In the latter case a person detained or invited to accompany police officers is, at that stage, under no legal compulsion to accept the detention or invitation. It may well be that in a particular case refusal to comply could lead to formal arrest, but until that stage is reached there is theoretical freedom to exercise a right to refuse to accept detention at the hands of police officers who are not armed with a warrant. I think it is important always to keep clear the distinction between arrest, which is a legal act taken by officers of the law duly authorised to do so and while acting in the course of their duty, carrying with it certain important legal consequences, and the mere detention of a person by a police officer such as is referred to in findings 3 and 4. Once arrested not only is the freedom of action of the person arrested circumscribed but he is also placed in the protection of the law in respect, e.g. of questioning by a police officer. None of these consequences flows from a mere 'detention' for inquiry or to enable the officers or their colleagues to pursue investigation or put forward (as in this case) certain statutory requests. And a person is either arrested or he is not; there is no half-way house. In my opinion it is plain that there was no arrest of the appellant by the plain clothes officers who stopped his van. No charge was preferred by them against the appellant nor is there any finding to establish or even suggest that at the stage when the officers stopped the van they had any intention of preferring the charge ultimately made or a charge under any other statute concerned with the driving of vehicles. If there was no arrest of the appellant by these constables then Mr Macaulay's first contention necessarily fails."

Appeal dismissed.

NOTE

The Lord Justice-General's opinion was that "the appellant was a man who, when driving, had merely been stopped by the police and who, under no lawful restraint, was awaiting the arrival of the uniformed officers". If this was a case of "detention" and the appellant was under no lawful restraint, then presumablly any attempt physically to prevent him leaving would have been a criminal assault.

Lord Cameron comes close to putting the cart before the horse by enlisting the *consequences* of arrest as a means for distinguishing it from detention. Surely these consequences only become relevant once one has effected a lawful arrest. They cannot be employed to define what constitutes that procedure.

The following propositions are all consistent with the decision in *Swankie* v. *Milne*. Are they consistent with one another: the appellant was not arrested; the appellant was free to leave; the appellant would have been stopped if he had tried to leave; there is no half-way house between arrest and freedom?

The court did not consider whether the officers in question had a lawful power to stop the appellant's vehicle. Section 159 of the Transport Act 1972 (formerly section 43 of the Road Traffic Act 1962) confers such a power, but only on a constable in uniform. Nor did the application of section 228 of the Road Traffic Act 1960 (now section 164 of the 1972 Act) receive any attention. It has been held (*Squires* v. *Botwright* [1972] R.T.R. 462) that the power to demand identification of a person alleged to have committed any of the offences referred to in that section infers a power to detain.

3. Wither v. Reid
1979 S.L.T. 192

Section 24 of the Misuse of Drugs Act 1971 authorises a constable, in certain circumstances, to arrest without warrant a person suspected of committing an offence under the 1971 Act. Under section 23 of the Act a constable may, if he has reasonable grounds to suspect that a person is in unlawful possession of a controlled drug, search that person and detain him for the purpose of that search.

The respondent and a companion were suspected by the police of being in possession of drugs. They were approached by police officers who told them that they were arresting them on suspicion of being in possession of a controlled drug, and that they would be searched. They were taken to a police station where the search was carried out. The respondent violently resisted this search and was subsequently charged with assaulting a police officer in the execution of her duty. The sheriff acquitted her and the prosecutor appealed to the High Court:

LORD JUSTICE-CLERK (WHEATLEY) (dissenting): " . . . The sheriff succinctly stated the issue which is the kernel of this appeal when he said in his note: 'If the search carried out by the two female police officers was lawful, there is in my view no question but that the accused is guilty of the offence charged; if, on the other hand, the search was unlawful, the accused in my view was entitled to use all necessary force — short of cruel excess — to resist the removal of her clothing and the indignity and humiliation of a body search.' . . . The Crown case was that on the findings-in-fact the police officers were lawfully acting under the authority of s. 23 (2) (a) (subject to the question of reasonable ground for suspicion), despite the fact that Detective Sergeant Souden undoubtedly informed the respondent that he was arresting her and not just detaining her, because it was clear from the findings as a whole that he was purporting to act under s. 23 (2) (a) procedure. Counsel for the respondent submitted that the fact that Detective Sergeant Souden unequivocally and undisputedly informed the respondent that he was arresting her established that she was in fact arrested at the railway station without any legal authority and that accordingly anything which followed thereafter at the hands of the police was illegal, and that this included the search of the respondent at the police station. This latter view was the one which commended itself to the sheriff and was the basis of his acquittal of the respondent.

Before turning to consider the competing arguments it is perhaps convenient to note a number of points. Counsel for the respondent accepted that if in the circumstances narrated the police were entitled to search the respondent the nature of the search was such as to justify the removal of the respondent to the police station for that purpose, since the railway station was manifestly unsuitable for it. Counsel for the appellant did not suggest that esto the search of the respondent was illegal the actions taken by the respondent amounted to cruel excess. And to crown this unfortunate incident the very thorough search of the respondent's clothing and person disclosed no presence of any drug whatsoever. In these circumstances it is easy to understand the respondent's annoyance, in the light of her personal knowledge that she was not in possession of any drugs, at being subjected to what she considered was humiliation and indignity, but if the police had reasonable grounds for suspecting that she was in possession of a controlled drug, then assuming that the police acted legally in taking her to the police station for the purpose of conducting a search, and it was explained to her that it was, it was her legal duty to submit to and not resist such search even although she knew in her own mind that there was no justification for it. . . . There is, in my opinion, no doubt that Detective Sergeant Souden thought that he was acting under the s. 23 (2) (a) procedure which provides the only statutory authority for a personal search. This, in my view, is borne out by the following facts. Detective Sergeant Souden informed the respondent (and her companion) at the railway station that they were being apprehended under the Misuse of Drugs Act 1971 on suspicion of being in possession of a controlled drug. Although he made it clear to the two suspects that they were under arrest, he informed them that they would be taken to Elgin police office and there searched for drugs, but that they would not be kept there any longer than necessary. In further explanation he informed the respondent that when the police had received information of a suspected drug offence they were bound to take suspects to a police station and search them for drugs and that she would be liberated as soon as possible. This explanation was repeated on at least two occasions in the police office. There was nothing in the evidence which would justify the invocation of s. 24 (1) which authorises arrest. On the other hand the whole procedure followed the pattern of s. 23 (2) (a) apart from the fact that Detective Sergeant Souden told the respondent that she was under arrest and not just being detained. Looking to the explanations referred to above, they seem to me to be much more consistent with being given to a person who is being detained for the purpose of a search than to a person who was being arrested. It would be passing strange if a person who had been arrested was informed that he or she would be liberated as soon as possible. But such an explanation is perfectly intelligible in relation to a person who is detained for the purpose of search. Does the fact that Detective Sergeant Souden used the word 'arrest' when he should have used the word 'detention' vitiate the Crown case, albeit he and his colleagues followed the procedure relevant to detention under s. 23 (2) (a)? No definition of 'detention' in terms of that subsection was cited to us and it was said that there was none. Reference was made to what was said by Lord Cameron in *Swankie* v. *Milne,* 1973 S.L.T. (Notes) at p. 29, but what his Lordship was there considering was 'detention' when there was no legal authorisation for it. Here, however, there is statutory authority for detention under s. 23 (2) (a), and the citation has no relevance to this case. The issue may be put this way. Is the criterion what was said or what was done? Each case will have to be considered on its own facts, and in this case I have come to the conclusion that what was done had full statutory authority and was not vitiated by the fact that Detective Sergeant Souden informed the respondent that she was being arrested and taken to the police station to be searched for drugs when she should have been told that she was being detained and taken to the police station for that purpose. As she could have been detained and taken to the police station for that purpose under statutory authority I do not consider that the fact that Detective Sergeant Souden used the wrong word vitiates the procedure which was otherwise unimpeachable. I accept that a penal statute must be construed in favour of the subject when a doubt arises, but I do not consider this error in terminology should vitiate a conviction. The power of detention given under s. 23 (2) (a) connotes that the subject can in the given circumstances be taken to the police station even against his or her will, just as a power of arrest does. If the conditions of s. 23 (2) (a) are satisfied and the procedure thereunder is followed, and the error in the use of the word did not result in the respondent being taken, even against her will, to the police station when if the correct word had been used she would have been, I regard it as overstraining logic to say that such an error vitiated all that followed in this case. I have accordingly reached the conclusion that the sheriff erred in holding that it did."

LORD KISSEN: " . . . Whatever may have been in the mind of the detective sergeant, he did tell the respondent that she was under arrest. He purported to arrest her. I cannot see how the later explanation to the respondent, apparently based on s. 23 (2) (a), can alter what he specifically said he was doing. His apparent confusion about his powers cannot, in my opinion, mean that he was not putting her under 'arrest', as he himself clearly thought he was doing despite the explanation. The actions which followed the 'arrest' and the events which occurred at Elgin police station are as consistent with a purported arrest as they are with search and detention under said s. 23 (2) (a). If one looks at the actions which followed the events at the Elgin railway station, as counsel for the appellant suggested should be done in order to ascertain whether there was an 'arrest', these actions did not show that she was not·'under arrest'. What the detective sergeant did was to arrest the respondent unlawfully prior to the search despite an explanation by him which indicated a limited statutory detention. The search which followed was referable to the purported arrest and was, therefore, in my opinion, unlawful. It follows accordingly that the sheriff was correct in the view which he reached."

LORD ROBERTSON: " . . . According to the sheriff, the police officers gave clear and unequivocal evidence that the respondent was arrested at the railway station under the Misuse of Drugs Act 1971.

If this is so, then the arrest in my opinion was unlawful. It was not an arrest under s. 24, but was a purported action under s. 23 (2) (a). But that section does not give authority to arrest, only to 'detain' for a limited purpose. There is a vital distinction between 'arrest' and 'detention' (*Swankie* v. *Milne*, 1973 S.L.T. (Notes), Lord Cameron at p. 29). It is true that under s. 23 (2) (a) of the 1971 Act the police are entitled to detain the person suspected for the purpose of searching him, and for this purpose may be entitled to take him to a place where the search may take place. This place might conveniently be the nearest police station. But a penal statute must be construed strictly. In my opinion, in deference to the rights of the citizen, it must be made perfectly clear to the person against whom action is being taken under s. 23 (2) (a) that that is what is being done and that he is not being arrested. If, as apparently happened in this case, the respondent was arrested and told that she was to be taken to the police station under arrest, then in my opinion that was an unlawful arrest. It will not do, in my opinion, to say that she was bound to know the law and so was bound to realise that, although the police officers used the word 'arrest', they really meant 'detain', and were proceeding under s. 23 (2) (a). The police also should know the law and if they were proceeding under s. 23 they should have done so explicitly."

Appeal dismissed.

NOTE

It is submitted that the correct decision was reached in this case. If the issue had simply been one of "arrest or no arrest" then reliance on the use of that term could be considered highly technical, even artificial. In such a case what is crucial is that the constable brings home to the suspect the fact that he or she is no longer a free person (*cf. Alderson* v. *Booth* [1969] 2 Q.B. 216, *R.* v. *Inwood* [1973] 2 All E.R. 645, Thomson Committee, 2nd Report, para. 3.12, *infra*, p. 000). But this case is concerned with a rather different question from that considered in *Muir* and *Swankie*. There was no doubt in *Wither* v. *Reid* that the respondent was under compulsion. The question was whether that compulsion was arrest or detention. Given that the consequences of arrest and detention differ, it seems right in principle that the police should be put on their mettle to distinguish the two forms of compulsion, and explain unequivocally to the person apprehended which procedure is being adopted.

It may legitimately be asked, however, if the respondent suffered any injustice in this case by being told that she was being "arrested." Would her position have been any different if the constable had said "detained," or even used some neutral expression such as "I am taking you to the police station," provided that the respondent was informed of the officer's authority to do so, and the purposes for which this was being done?

4. Christie v. Leachinsky
[1947] A.C. 573

Leachinsky, who ran a rag-merchant's business in Liverpool, was arrested at his warehouse. The police officers who arrested him told him that he was being arrested for "unlawful possession" of certain bales of cloth. The power of arrest which the constables purported to exercise was contained in the Liverpool Corporation Act 1921, but under that Act it could only be exercised if the name and address of the suspect were unknown — circumstances which did not apply in this case. Leachinsky was tried for larceny of the bales, and acquitted. He raised an action for false arrest and imprisonment against the police. In defence to this action it was argued that since the officers suspected him of having stolen or feloniously received the cloth, the arrest was lawful by virtue of the officers' common law power to arrest for felony.

VISCOUNT SIMON: " . . . The question to be determined is therefore whether, when a policeman arrests X. without a warrant, on reasonable suspicion that he has committed a given felony, but gives X. no notice that he is arrested on suspicion of such felony, he is acting within the law. . . . If a policeman arrests without warrant when he entertains a reasonable suspicion of felony, is he under a duty to inform the suspect of the nature of the charge, and if he does not do so, is the detention a false imprisonment? In the Court of Appeal Scott L.J. strongly insisted that it was a false imprisonment. Arrest, he pointed out (1), was the first step in a criminal proceeding against a suspected person on a charge which was intended to be judicially investigated. If the arrest was authorized by magisterial warrant, or if proceedings were instituted by the issue of a summons, it is clear law that the warrant or summons must specify the offence. This rule is now embodied in s. 32 of the Criminal Justice Act, 1925, but it is a principle involved in our ancient jurisprudence. Moreover, the warrant must be founded on information in writing and on oath and, except where a particular statute provides otherwise, the information and the warrant must particularize the offence charged. The famous case of *Entick* v. *Carrington* [(1765) 19 St. Tr. 1029] dealing with the illegality of 'general warrants' is an illustration of the principle. Again, when an arrest is made on warrant, the warrant in normal cases has to be read to the person arrested. All this is for the obvious purpose of securing that a citizen who is prima facie entitled to personal freedom should know why for the time being his personal freedom is interfered with. Scott L.J. (2) argued that if the law circumscribed the issue of warrants for arrest in this way it could hardly be that a policeman acting without a warrant was entitled to make an arrest without stating the charge on which the arrest was made . . .

When the appeal came before your Lordships' House the arguments which had prevailed before the Court of Appeal were repeated, but it was not apparently realized by counsel on either side that there is direct authority, both in text books of acknowledged weight and in cases actually decided, that in normal circumstances an arrest without warrant either by a policeman or by a private person can be justified only if it is an arrest on a charge made known to the person arrested . . .

[His Lordship reviewed certain authorities, and continued:]

The above citations, and others . . . seem to me to establish the following propositions. (1.) If a policeman arrests without warrant upon reasonable suspicion of felony, or of other crime of a sort which does not require a warrant, he must in ordinary circumstances inform the person arrested of the true ground of arrest. He is not entitled to keep the reason to himself or to give a reason which is not the true reason. In other words a citizen is entitled to know on what charge or on suspicion of what crime he is seized. (2.) If the citizen is not so informed but is nevertheless seized, the policeman, apart from certain exceptions, is liable for false imprisonment. (3.) The requirement that the person arrested should be informed of the reason why he is seized naturally does not exist if the circumstances are such that he must know the general nature of the alleged offence for which he is detained. (4.) The requirement that he should be so informed does not mean that technical or precise language need be used. The matter is a matter of substance, and turns on the elementary proposition that in this country a person is, prima facie, entitled to his freedom and is only required to submit to restraints on his freedom if he knows in substance the reason why it is claimed that this restraint should be imposed. (5.) The person arrested cannot complain that he has not been supplied with the above information as and when he should be, if he himself produces the situation which makes it practically impossible to inform him, e.g., by immediate counter-attack or by running away. There may well be other exceptions to the general rule in addition to those I have indicated, and the above propositions are not intended to constitute a formal or complete code, but to indicate the general principles of our law on a very important matter. These principles equally apply to a private person who arrests on suspicion. If a policeman who entertained a reasonable suspicion that X. has committed a felony were at liberty to arrest him and march him off to a police station without giving any explanation of why he was doing this, the prima facie right of personal liberty would be gravely infringed."

Appeal dismissed.

NOTE

There does not appear to be a reported decision in which the Scottish courts have discussed the issues raised by *Christie* v. *Leachinsky.* That a constable when arresting with warrant "should briefly acquaint the party with the substance of his warrant" (Hume, ii, 79) was recognised at common law. The principle is recognised in practice.

For some conflicting decisions on how specific the arresting officer need be as to the grounds of arrest, see *R.* v. *Kulyncz* [1971] 1 Q.B. 367, *R.* v. *Gelberg* [1961] 1 All E.R. 291. For the application of *Christie* v. *Leachinsky* to detention cases, see *Pedro* v. *Diss* (1981) 72 Cr. App. R. 193.

c. *Detention*

The simple distinction between arrest and detention tends to suggest that there is only one form of detention. In fact statute has conferred upon the police a variety of powers of detention. There are, first of all, what might be termed "street detentions" which confer the power to detain for questioning, search, production of documents, etc., but which do not confer any power to take the person detained into custody. (See, for example, section 1 of the 1980 Act, *infra,* section 164 of the Road Traffic Act 1972, discussed *supra,* p. 125.) It appears to be accepted that the power to detain for search may, in some cases, extend to taking the suspect into custody to carry out the search — see the Misuse of Drugs Act 1971, s. 23 and *Wither* v. *Reid, supra.* Secondly, there is the power to detain analogous to the power to arrest, as contained in section 2 of the

1980 Act. Finally, there is the power to detain without charge, but subsequent to arrest, as, *e.g.* in section 12 of the Prevention of Terrorism (Temporary Provisions) Act 1976. The first two types of detention depart from the common law rules in permitting interference with the liberty of the subject short of arrest. The third form derogates from the common law rule that arrest must be accompanied by a charge.

1.   Thomson Committee, Second Report

"The stage of arrest and charge
3.07   At present the rule is that (apart from certain statutory exceptions) an arrest must be accompanied by a charge, (*Chalmers* v. *HM Advocate,* 1954 J.C. 66, 78), and that therefore a person may be arrested only when there is sufficient evidence to charge him. Evidence sufficient to charge means evidence sufficient to report to the procurator fiscal. The accused will be charged in court on a writ at the instance of the procurator fiscal and not on the police 'charge', but this latter does represent a vital step in pretrial procedure. A person can, of course, be 'charged' by the police without being arrested, but the converse is not true.

Detention before arrest and charge
3.13   The policeman's real difficulty arises in investigations where he wants to interview a suspect or prevent him from interfering with evidence such as stolen property. At present the police are powerless to act without the consent of the very person who is likely to have most interest in refusing to give that consent. Clearly the police should not be entitled to arrest anyone they want to interview but it seems plainly wrong, for example, that a suspected violent criminal with significant evidence on his clothing has to be left at large while the police seek other evidence of his guilt sufficient to entitle them to charge.

3.14   We *recommend* that the practice of inviting persons to the police station should be regularised. We are convinced that it will continue if the law remains unchanged and that it can be controlled only by being recognised and made subject to clearly defined limits. We accept that certain people do and will continue to attend at police stations truly voluntarily, such as those who prefer to see the police there rather than have the police be seen to visit them, or those who call to confess to crime, but these are exceptional cases. Our recommendations will also cover the situation where the police stop in the street people who are suspected of committing or having recently committed an offence. At present, except where they act under Police Acts, which relate for the most part to stolen property, or under any other special statute such as the Road Traffic Act 1972, the police have no power to detain and question anyone in the street unless they are in a position to arrest him.

3.15   We *recommend*, therefore, a form of limited, or temporary arrest—

arrest on suspicion. Since the rules governing this 'arrest' will differ from those governing arrest at the moment, we give it a separate name— detention. Detention will include power to take to and keep in a police station, but its duration will be limited by the following general rules:

a. it should not last longer than is necessary in the interests of justice;

b. it should be succeeded as soon as is reasonable by either release or arrest; and

c. it should not in any event exceed a fixed period of time at the end of which the detainee must be either released or arrested and charged.

Grounds for detention

3.16 We *recommend* that this power of detention should be exercisable only where the detaining constable has reasonable cause to suspect the detainee of having committed an offence for which there is power to arrest without warrant (see paragraph 3.29). This, we would point out, is the criterion for arrest without warrant in England and Wales (Criminal Law Act 1967, section 2(4)), and also complies with the provisions of the European Convention of Human Rights, article 5(1)(*c*) of which provides for 'the lawful arrest or detention of a person effected for the purpose of bringing him before the competent legal authority on reasonable suspicion of having committed an offence.' This power of detention should of course not be exercised in every case in which the police have reasonable cause for suspicion but only when the police consider it necessary to detain the suspect for the purpose of their investigations.

Detention in places other than police stations

3.18 The power of the police to detain on suspicion will cover the preliminary detention of a suspect for a short period of time before he is taken to the police station, as well as power to take to a police station and detain him there for a longer period. The person detained must be told immediately the reason for the detention. We considered placing a time limit on this preliminary period of detention. . . . We decided, however, that a rigid time-limit was not desirable where such short periods of time were concerned, and that it would be sufficient to provide that no person should be detained elsewhere than in a police station for longer than is necessary for the following purposes:

a. asking for an explanation of suspicious behaviour;

b. taking name and address of detainee and, where it can be done rapidly, for example, by radio, verifying these;

c. searching outer clothing or baggage for stolen goods, tools of crime, or weapons.

We *recommend* accordingly.

3.19 We are aware that one of the problems relating to a power to detain on suspicion, and particularly a power to search for weapons, is a fear that this will lead to police harassment of young persons, particularly where such persons have a police record. Some may think that such harassment would be a small price to pay for any reduction in the number of assaults

with weapons committed by young persons but apart from anything else
there is a grave risk that any harassment would be counter-productive in the
long run, since it would lead to increased antagonism to the police. We are
anxious that 'reasonable cause to suspect' should be so interpreted by the
police as to avoid this danger. . . .
3.20   Again . . . we wish to stress that mere physical appearance or dress,
or presence or residence in a particular area, should not be sufficient to
justify detention. We think, too, that it is important to stress that the mere
appearance on the street of a person with a police record does not justify the
police in detaining, questioning or searching him.

Detention in police station
3.22   On arrival at a police station the detainee's position should be
considered by the officer in charge for the time being of the station. It
should be for him to decide whether to authorise the detainee's continued
detention. He should do so only where such detention is in his view
justified. The detainee should again be told the reason for his detention and
this, as well as the time of his arrival in the police station, should be
recorded. If there is sufficient evidence to justify the arrest of the detainee,
he should be arrested and charged. If neither arrest nor continued detention is justifiable, the detainee should be released. The time of release or
charge should also be recorded. We so *recommend*.

3.23   Under the present law an arrested person is entitled to have information of his arrest sent to his solicitor, but his only right to see his solicitor is
to see him before his appearance in court. We *recommend* that the detainee
should have the same right to have his solicitor informed as has the arrestee,
and we think that both, too, should have a right to have information sent to
a friend or relative. In addition we are recommending (paragraph 3.24*b*.
and *c*.) that in certain circumstances the detainee should have a right to
legal advice.

The purpose of detention
3.24   We *recommend* that detention in a police station should be for the
following purposes:
a.   To enable the police to isolate the detainee while they continue their
enquiries elsewhere, interview witnesses, search for weapons, goods etc.
b.   To enable the police to obtain the detainee's fingerprints and to search
him without his consent. This involves giving the police power to do things
which generally at present they can do only after arrest. We do not think
that the detainee should have a general right to legal advice, but the
question whether he should be entitled to the presence and advice of a
solicitor before being searched is a more difficult one. The arrested person
has no such right at present. We think that the invasion of person involved
in fingerprinting or in the search of luggage and clothing is so slight as to be
outweighed by the usefulness of the information provided by such a search,
and that the police should have power to carry out these activities without
the intervention of the detainee's solicitor. Such searches can, in any event,

be carried out prior to arrest at present where they are necessary to prevent the destruction of evidence, and this criterion, the criterion of 'urgency', is very widely interpreted by the court (see for example *Bell v Hogg* 1967 JC 49; *Hay v HM Advocate* 1968 JC 40). But where any form of medical examination or search of body cavities or removal of any portion of the body, for example, hair, nail clippings, etc, is sought by the police they must obtain the consent of the detainee, and he must therefore have the opportunity of consulting a solicitor before deciding whether or not to consent. This is without prejudice to any specific statutory provisions such as those of the Road Traffic Act 1972, section 8, and without prejudice to the right of the procurator fiscal to seek a warrant for such examination, etc. . . .

c. To enable the police to secure evidence of identification, it is the practice to have a solicitor present at an identification parade when the suspect so requests, and in view of the type of parade we propose . . . we think it important that a detainee or arrestee should always have the opportunity of having a solicitor present at such a parade. His consent to be placed on parade is inevitably necessary, since an identification parade could not be properly conducted with a protesting accused. On the other hand, where he does refuse to go on a parade he can hardly complain if witnesses are brought to look at him in the station, although the value of such evidence will vary according to the circumstances.

d. To enable the police to ask the detainee questions; . . .

The duration of detention

3.25 Various views were expressed to us on the maximum permissible period of detention in a police station. Some considered that it should be as long as twenty-four hours and there was a strong body of opinion in favour of twelve hours, but we have come to the conclusion that the period ought not exceed six hours and we so *recommend.* This was the minimum period favoured by the police witnesses who considered that generally it would be adequate for their purposes. We are reinforced in this view by the evidence of the representatives of the Scottish Council for Civil Liberties who, although averse to the principle of detention, did not feel that, if such detention was necessary, six hours would be too long. We stress that this is the maximum period of detention and that we expect that in the vast majority of cases the actual detention will be for a shorter period. As soon as the purpose of the detention is served, the police will have a clear duty. They must either liberate the detainee or arrest him. In any event he must be released within six hours of his arrival at the station, unless he is arrested and charged.

3.26 Once he has been charged, the detainee becomes an arrestee with the same rights and liabilities as a person who has been arrested without prior detention."

NOTE
    These passages set out fully the thinking of the Committee on the

use of pre-arrest detention. The Committee's concern for safeguards should be noted, since they were clearly aware of the potential for abuse which their proposals contained. Parliament took much of this to heart when enacting the detention provisions of the 1980 Act (*infra*). It remains to be seen how the courts will react. So far there seems to have been a mixed response; compare, for example, the general attitude disclosed in *Cummings* v. *H.M.Advocate* (*infra*, p. 139) with that expressed in *Tonge and Others* v. *H.M. Advocate* (*post*, p. 177).

It was the Committee's intention that their proposed form of detention should replace, and bring to an end, the practice of inviting persons to the police station to "help with inquiries" (para. 3.14). It is clear, however, that the following provisions of the 1980 Act have not had that effect. The only effect the 1980 Act provisions has had on the pre-existing law is to overrule those dicta which state that there is no "half-way house" between arrest and liberty (*cf. Swankie* v. *Milne, supra.*) Between June 1981 and 31 May 1982, 21,435 persons were detained under the new provisions. At the same time, 8,178 persons signed declarations that they had attended voluntarily at police stations. How many of these were subsequently charged with, or convicted of, an offence we do not yet know. (Figures supplied by the Secretary of State in a written Commons answer, 24 June 1982; Parl. Debs. H.C. (W.A.), cols. 159-60.) The new powers are being fully employed. But old practices have not outlived their usefulness.

2. Criminal Justice (Scotland) Act 1980
"POLICE POWERS
Suspect or potential witness may be required by constable to identify himself
   1.—(1) Where a constable has reasonable grounds for suspecting that a person has committed or is committing an offence at any place, he may require—
(*a*) that person, if the constable finds him at that place or at any place where the constable is entitled to be, to give his name and address and may ask him for an explanation of the circumstances which have given rise to the constable's suspicion;
(*b*) any other person whom the constable finds at that place or at any place where the constable is entitled to be and who the constable believes has information relating to the offence, to give his name and address.
   (2) The constable may require the person mentioned in paragraph (*a*) of subsection (1) above to remain with him while he (either or both)—
(*a*) verifies any name and address given by the person:
Provided that the constable shall exercise his power under this paragraph only where it appears to him that such verification can be obtained quickly;
(*b*) notes any explanation proffered by the person.

(3) A constable may use reasonable force to ensure that the person mentioned in paragraph (*a*) of subsection (1) above remains with him.

(4) A constable shall inform a person, when making a requirement of that person under—

(*a*) paragraph (*a*) of subsection (1) above, of his suspicion and of the general nature of the offence which he suspects that the person has committed or is committing;

(*b*) paragraph (*b*) of subsection (1) above, of his suspicion, of the general nature of the offence which he suspects has been or is being committed and that the reason for the requirement is that he believes the person has information relating to the offence;

(*c*) subsection (2) above, of why the person is being required to remain with him;

(*d*) either of the said subsections, that failure to comply with the requirement may constitute an offence.

(5) A person mentioned in—

(*a*) paragraph (*a*) of subsection (1) above who having been required—

(i) under that subsection to give his name and address; or

(ii) under subsection (2) above to remain with a constable,

fails, without reasonable excuse, to do so, shall be guilty of an offence and liable on summary conviction to a fine not exceeding £200;

(*b*) paragraph (*b*) of the said subsection (1) who having been required under that subsection to give his name and address fails, without reasonable excuse, to do so shall be guilty of an offence and liable on summary conviction to a fine not exceeding £50.

(6) A constable may arrest without warrant any person who he has reasonable grounds for suspecting has committed an offence under subsection (5) above.

Detention and questioning at police station

2.—(1) Where a constable has reasonable grounds for suspecting that a person has committed or is committing an offence punishable by imprisonment, the constable may, for the purpose of facilitating the carrying out of investigations—

(*a*) into the offence; and

(*b*) as to whether criminal proceedings should be instigated against the person,

detain that person and take him as quickly as is reasonably practicable to a police station or other premises and, subject to the following provisions of this section, the detention may continue there.

(2) Detention under subsection (1) above shall be terminated not more than six hours after it begins or (if earlier)—

(*a*) when the person is arrested; or

(*b*) where there are no longer such grounds as are mentioned in the said subsection (1);

and when a person has been detained under subsection (1) above for a period of six hours, he shall be informed immediately upon expiry of this period that his detention has been terminated.

(3) Where a person has been released at the termination of a period of detention under subsection (1) above he shall not thereafter be detained, under that subsection, on the same grounds or on any grounds arising out of the same circumstances.

(4) At the time when a constable detains a person under subsection (1) above, he shall inform the person of his suspicion, of the general nature of the offence which he suspects has been or is being committed and of the reason for the detention; and there shall be recorded—

(a) The place where detention begins and the police station or other premises to which the person is taken;

(b) the general nature of the suspected offence;

(c) the time when detention under subsection (1) above begins and the time of the person's arrival at the police station or other premises;

(d) the time when the person is informed of his rights in terms of subsection (7) below and of subsection (1)(b) of section 3 of this Act and the identity of the constable so informing him;

(e) where the person requests such intimation to be sent as is specified in section 3(1)(b) of this Act, the time when such request is—

(i) made;

(ii) complied with; and

(f) the time of the person's departure from the police station or other premises or, where instead of being released he is arrested in respect of the alleged offence, the time of such arrest."

NOTES

Section 1. The requirement under section 1(1)(a) and (b), and the requirement to remain with a constable under section 1(2) are backed up by criminal sanctions, which are in their turn enforceable by arrest without warrant under section 1(5). Is it really in the interests of police-community relations that a potential witness should be subject to this sort of procedure?

A suspect may only be "asked" for an explanation of the circumstances which have given rise to the constable's suspicion. He cannot be required to do so. Section 1 makes no mention of cautions or warning before such questions are asked. A suspect might well make a self-incriminating statement, and presumably the admissibility of that statement depends on the common law test of "fairness." Given the strict approach adopted by the High Court in relation to questioning while under section 2 detention (see *Tonge* v. *H.M. Advocate, post,* p. 177) the proper approach, it is submitted, is for the constable to administer a caution. This view is reinforced by section 1(4) which requires a constable, when making a requirement under section 1(1) or 1(2) to inform the person in question "that failure to comply with the requirement may constitute an offence." Although this only relates to a "requirement" (which is limited to identification or remaining with the constable) this sort of distinction may well be lost on a suspect, and the general presence of such a threat might well suggest that failure to answer *any* question could be visited with criminal sanctions.

Section 2. This section follows the Thomson Committee in limiting detention to six hours. How is this period to be determined when the Act contains no indication of when detention commences? Section 2(4) makes provision for the recording of the time at which it begins, but that is only the police version. What happens when there is a dispute? Surely the point at which the police state that a person was detained cannot be conclusive of the matter.

What happens when the period of detention comes to an end? The detainee is informed of this fact section 2(2). Is he told that he is free to go (if not arrested or otherwise detained)? Should he be asked to remain, is he to be told that he is free to go?

Section 2(3) prevents re-detention under subsection 2(1). It does not, however, prevent re-detention on the same grounds or grounds arising out of the same circumstances under any other power of detention. Note also, that the whole section appears to be premised on a detention which begins at a place other than the police station. Can detention begin when a person is already at the police station, whether voluntarily or while detained under some other power (such as that conferred by section 23 of the Misuse of Drugs Act 1971)?

3. Cummings v. H.M.Advocate
1982 S.L.T. 487

The appellant was detained under section 2 of the 1980 Act. During that detention he made a number of statements to the police which later became central to the Crown's case against him. When he was detained he was given a full "common law" caution, and on his arrival at the police station he was warned, in terms of section 2(7) of the 1980 Act that he was under no obligation to answer any question other than to give his name and address. At his trial he objected, unsuccessfully, that the statements made in detention were inadmissible because there was no official record of the detention procedures, and in particular there was no such record that the requirements of section 2(4) had been complied with. The police notebooks contained such a record, and these were referred to at the trial. On appeal from conviction:

LORD JUSTICE-CLERK (WHEATLEY): " . . . It is stated in the written grounds of appeal that: 'no record in terms of section 2(4) was on the list of Crown labels or productions and it was not produced at the trial. The sheriff erred in law in allowing the case to go to the jury and in particular in allowing evidence of what the applicant was alleged to have said during his detention when the provisions of section 2 had not been fully complied with, in particular section 2(4)'. This was further developed by the appellant's counsel in argument. It was said that the statement was necessary to provide sufficient evidence in law to warrant a conviction. The procedure under s. 2 constituted an encroachment on personal liberty and accordingly it should be strictly construed and complied with. There should have been an official form in which the details called for by subs. (4) were recorded and this should have been spoken to by appropriate evidence. The failure to observe this requirement vitiated the police powers under the section which had thereby ceased to be operable, and accordingly the statement made by the appellant in purported pursuance of the powers conferred by the section was inadmissible in evidence. It was accepted that at the trial two police officers gave evidence that the requirements of subs. (4) were recorded in their notebooks and the notebooks were there and then produced and the entries therein spoken to. It was argued that as the notebooks had not been listed as productions, which meant that the defence had not had any prior opportunity to examine the entries therein, that evidence should not be regarded as satisfying the requirements of s. 2(4). Counsel took his argument to the extreme by submitting that even if there was failure to record one of the required entries that would be sufficient to vitiate the procedure under s. 2, including most particularly any statement purported to have been taken under the provisions thereof.

There are two matters to be considered arising out of the appellant's submissions, namely (1) the broad general question of the effect of non-compliance with the provisions of subs. (4) in whole or in part, and (2) the question whether there has been any failure to comply with these requirements in the instant case.

We propose to deal with the second of these matters first since in our view the reply to it provides a complete answer to the appellant's complaint. Subsection (4) calls for certain facts to be recorded. It does not specify in what manner or in what form they should be recorded. Therefore, even on the basis that it was necessary in order to sustain the conviction in this case to prove that the required facts were recorded, there was the evidence that they were recorded in the respective notebooks of the police officers, and the relative entries therein were given in evidence. These were presumably the original records from which any 'official' form would in due course be compiled. While these notebooks had not been lodged as productions, the police officers were allowed to refer to their notebooks without objection, and accordingly the requirements in relation to proof of recorded facts in an appropriate manner in terms of subs. (4) were satisfied. On that short ground alone we refuse the appeal.

Lest it be thought that in taking this short approach to the decision we were accepting that there was substance in the submission of the appellant's counsel in regard to the general effect of non-compliance with the provisions of subs. (4) in whole or in part, we wish to make it clear that no such subsumption should be made. We consider that any views which we have on it should be reserved for an occasion when the answer is necessary for the proper determination of the case."

Appeal dismissed.

NOTE

The general principle governing the use of notebooks used in this way is that unless they are lodged as productions, the notes contained therein are not of themselves evidence, but become part of the witness's oral testimony (Walker and Walker, *Law of Evidence in Scotland,* para. 341(b); Macphail, *Law of Evidence in Scotland* (Scottish Law Commission Research Paper), para. 8.47). If, therefore, police notebooks are to be relied upon as a "record" for the purposes of section 2(4) (which in itself would seem to be less than desirable) they should, it is submitted, be lodged as productions.

So far as concerns the question left open by the court, the question would presumably be whether non-compliance with the provisions of subsection (4) so prejudiced the suspect as to amount to unfairness.

The power of detention is exercisable by a "constable". For these purposes this means a constable within the meaning of the Police (Scotland) Act 1967 (1980 Act, s.81). This includes a British Transport Police officer: *Smith* v. *Dudgeon,* 1983 S.L.T. 324.

d. The incidents of arrest and detention

This section deals with that which follows upon, or which may be expected to follow upon, arrest and/or detention. Some of these matters, such as the appearance of the arrestee before a court, are required by law for the protection of the individual. Others, such as search and fingerprinting, arise from the exercise by the police of their investigatory powers. Two matters which are in this sense incidents of arrest or detention—interrogation and bail—are dealt with in separate chapters. (See *post,* Chaps. 5 and 6 respectively.)

(i) Appearance before a court

It is the duty of every constable, in discharging his duty to bring offenders to justice, "to take every precaution to ensure that any person charged with an offence is not unreasonably and unnecessarily detained in custody" (Police (Scotland) Act 1967, s.17(1)).

In solemn proceedings an arrested person must be brought before a court as soon as possible, for the purpose of judicial examination (as to which, see *post,* p. 228). Section 19(3) permits the sheriff to delay such examination for a period not exceeding 48 hours from and after the time of arrest, but only in order to allow time for attendance by the accused's solicitor. Where the accused is brought before the court for further examination, that examination may be delayed for 24 hours to allow time for the attendance of the accused's solicitor.

In summary proceedings, section 321(3) of the 1975 Act provides: "A person apprehended under any such warrant as aforesaid or by virtue of the powers possessed at common law, or conferred by statute, shall wherever practicable be brought before a court competent to deal with the case either by way of trial or by way of remit to another court not later than in the course of the first lawful day after such person shall be taken into custody, such day not being a public or local holiday."

It should be remembered that the right to be brought before a court without delay is only granted to persons arrested. It is for this reason that the safeguards surrounding detention procedures should be scrupulously adhered to.

(ii) Intimation of arrest or detention and access to legal advice

1.   Criminal Procedure (Scotland) Act 1975

"**19.**—(1) Where any person has been arrested on any criminal charge, such person shall be entitled immediately upon arrest:

(*a*) to have intimation sent to a solicitor that his professional assistance is required by such person, and informing him of the place to which such person is to be taken for examination;

(*b*) to be told what rights there are under paragraph (*a*) above and subsections (2) and (3) below.

(2) Such solicitor shall be entitled to have a private interview with the person accused before he is examined on declaration, and to be present at such examination.

(3) [Noted *supra.*]"

NOTE

Section 305 of the 1975 Act provides that in summary proceedings the accused is entitled, immediately upon apprehension, to have intimation sent to a solicitor and to have a private interview with such solicitor prior to being brought before the court. There is no obligation under section 305 to inform an arrested person of his rights.

2.   Criminal Justice (Scotland) Act 1980

"**3.**—(1) Without prejudice to section 19 or 305 of the 1975 Act (intimation to solicitor following arrest), a person who, not being a person in respect of whose custody or detention subsection (3) below applies—

(a) has been arrested and is in custody in a police station or other premises, shall be entitled to have intimation of his custody and of the place where he is being held sent, to a person reasonably named by him;

(b) is being detained under section 2 of this Act in a police station or other premises, shall be entitled to have intimation of his detention and of the place where he is being detained sent, to a solicitor and to one other person reasonably named by him,

without delay or, where some delay is necessary in the interest of the investigation or the prevention of crime or the apprehension of offenders, with no more delay than is so necessary; and the person shall be informed of such entitlement—

(i) on arrival at the police station or other premises; or

(ii) where he is not arrested, or as the case may be detained, until after such arrival, on such arrest or detention.

(2) Where the person mentioned in paragraph (a) of subsection (1) above requests such intimation to be sent as is specified in that paragraph there shall be recorded the time when such request is—

(i) made;

(ii) complied with.

(3) Without prejudice to the said section 19 or 305, a constable shall, where a person who has been arrested and is in such custody as is mentioned in paragraph (a) of subsection (1) above or who is being detained as is mentioned in paragraph (b) of that subsection appears to him to be a child, send without delay such intimation as is mentioned in the said paragraph (a), or as the case may be paragraph (b), to that person's parent if known; and the parent—

(a) in a case where there is reasonable cause to suspect that he has been involved in the alleged offence in respect of which the person has been arrested or detained, may; and

(b) in any other case shall,

be permitted access to the person.

(4) The nature and extent of any access permitted under subsection (3) above shall be subject to any restriction essential for the furtherance of the investigation or the well-being of the person.

(5) In subsection (3) above—

(a) 'child' means a person under 16 years of age; and

(b) 'parent' includes guardian."

NOTES

None of the above provisions guarantees immediate access to a solicitor. The fact of arrest may be immediately intimated, but access is only guaranteed prior to appearance before a court. In the case of detention, intimation may be delayed, as may intimation to a "person reasonably named" whether the suspect is arrested or detained.

No indication is given as to who might be a "person reasonably named." This should comprise any person who may reasonably be expected to take an interest in the suspect's welfare such as a parent, spouse, social worker, etc. A legal adviser would also be such a person and section 3 makes it clear that naming a solicitor does not exhaust this right. *Cf.* Home Office Circular No. 74/1978.

No sanction is attached to failure to grant these rights of intimation (either under the 1975 Act or the 1980 Act). Presumably this would be a factor affecting the fairness issue if a question arose respecting the admissibility of statements made while under arrest or detention. *cf. Cheyne* v. *McGregor*, 1941 J.C. 17.

(iii) Search

Jackson v. Stevenson
(1897) 2 Adam 255

While he was fishing Jackson was seen by two water bailiffs who suspected that he was fishing illegally. They searched him to discover if he was in possession of implements for illegal fishing. He resisted this search and was convicted of resisting the bailiffs in the execution of their duties, contrary to section 39 of the Tweed Fisheries Act 1857. It was not clearly established whether the search took place before or after Jackson was apprehended. His appeal against conviction was upheld on the ground that the complaint was defective in form, but the court also considered the legality of the search.

LORD JUSTICE-GENERAL (ROBERTSON): " . . . The Sheriff's statement of the facts does not make it quite clear whether the appellant had been apprehended before the bailiffs searched his person, or only after. As I read the case, they did not apprehend him, and had not resolved to apprehend him, until the result of their search confirmed their previous suspicions. If this were so, then I do not think that they were within their powers, and therefore I could not hold them to have been in the execution of the Acts when the appellant resisted them.

The right of the bailiffs, be it observed, is to exercise the powers and authorities of constables in the same manner as if the statutory offences were breaches of the peace. Now, a constable is entitled to arrest, without a warrant, any person seen by him committing a breach of the peace, and he may arrest on the direct information of eye witnesses. Having arrested him, I make no doubt that the constable could search him. But it is a totally different matter to search a man in order to find evidence to determine whether you will apprehend him or not. If the search succeeds (such is the condition of the argument), you will apprehend him; but if the search does not succeed, you will not apprehend him. Now, I have only to say that I know no authority for ascribing to constables the right to make such tentative searches, and they seem contrary to constitutional principle. If the constable requires to make such a search, it can only be because without it he is not justified in apprehending; and, without a warrant, to search a person not liable to apprehension seems palpably illegal. A constable or bailiff must make up his mind on what he sees (or hears on credible information) whether to arrest or not; and, if he does arrest in good faith, the law will protect him, whether his opinion at the time of the guilt of the person arrested prove accurate or not."

Appeal allowed.

NOTE

Section 2(5) of the 1980 Act provides that where a person is detained under section 2(1) of that Act a constable may "exercise the same powers of search as are available following an arrest". He may use reasonable force in exercising these powers (section 2(6)).

It should be remembered that statute may permit search in order to justify arrest. See, for example, the breath test provisions of the Road Traffic Act 1972. It should also be noted that a warrant may be granted to search the person of a suspect who has not been arrested (*Hay* v. *H.M.Advocate,* 1968 J.C. 40, *post,* p. 202) and that in cases of urgency such a search may be carried out without warrant (*Bell* v. *Hogg,* 1967 J.C. 49, *post,* p. 207). Powers to search premises are discussed *post,* Chap. 5.

(iv) Fingerprinting and analogous procedures

1. Adair v. McGarry
1933 S.L.T. 482

McGarry was arrested and charged with theft by housebreaking. His fingerprints were taken without a warrant and without his consent having been obtained. His fingerprints were found to correspond with prints found on one of the items of stolen property. Objection was taken at his trial to the admissibility of the evidence relating to the fingerprints, on the ground that it had been illegally obtained. The sheriff upheld his objection and acquitted McGarry. The prosecutor appealed. (Another case, *Byrne* v. *H.M.Advocate,* which raised the same issue, was heard at the same time.)

LORD JUSTICE-CLERK (ALNESS): "The question for decision in this case is whether the police are entitled to take finger-prints of persons who are detained by them as suspects though these persons have not yet been committed to prison. To that question the Crown answers—yea; The respondent replies—nay.

Manifestly the question before us is of importance, not only to the individual, but also to the public. On the one hand, the individual must be protected against any undue invasion of his rights; on the other hand, it is evident that the affirmation of the right claimed by the Crown may facilitate the investigation and detection of crime, and that the denial of that right may impede, if not frustrate, that process.

At the outset it is essential to bear in mind the distinction between the position of a person detained on suspicion of having committed a crime and the position of a person who has been committed to prison on a charge of crime. The rights of the police are wider in the former case than they are in the latter case. The police may arrest a suspect and may interrogate him; but that person may only be committed if a *prima facie* case against him is made out, and no interrogation is, after committal, permitted. Accordingly, the suggestion that finger-prints may be taken, once committal takes place, is far from meeting the demands of the situation.

I propose, first, to survey the problem apart from authority, and then to enquire whether the conclusion at which I arrive, on that survey, is rendered inadmissible by the state of the authorities.

Viewed apart from authority, then, the problem presents itself to my mind thus—the police must be armed with all adequate and reasonable powers for the investigation and detection of crime. Is finger-printing a reasonable incident in that process, not forbidden by the common law, and not unduly invading the rights of the accused?

I say 'not forbidden by the common law' because I think that phrase more correctly expounds the situation than the phrase 'authorised by the common law.' Let me explain what I mean by this. The system of detection of crime by means of finger-prints is a modern scientific discovery, later in date than any of the statutes to which reference was made in the course of the debate, and it would not therefore be reasonable to look for or to expect to find institutional or common law authority for its practice.

As regards undue invasion of the personal rights of the accused, one must have a sense of proportion. Certain it is that in practice, hitherto unchallenged, a person who is suspected of crime may be brought—with reasonable violence in the event of his resistance—to the police station, that he may be paraded for purposes of identification, that he may be stripped, and that he may be searched for any incriminating natural or artificial mark upon his person. That mark may include a birth mark or natural deformity, a tattoo mark, or bloodstains, or the like. All these things are done with a view to establishing the identity of the suspect. And yet it is argued that the comparatively innocuous process of taking a mould of the suspect's thumb is excluded from the rights of the police. I enquire—Why? To that question I have heard no adequate answer. The analogy of straining at a gnat and swallowing a camel suggests itself as apposite to the argument in question.

The suggestion seems to be that the existence of a warrant . . . removes all objection to finger-printing. If I could see that any substantial protection is afforded to the accused by the existence of such a warrant I could understand that view. But nothing is more certain than that such a warrant is a pure formality, is granted for the asking, is, so I am informed, never refused, and, moreover, is granted by a person who may know less about the matter than the police know. The suggested protection by way of warrant is quite illusory.

If the accused is innocent, no harm is done by finger-printing. He has not been subjected to so great 'humiliation'—to use counsel's words—as he may admittedly be subjected to in accordance with time-honoured and unchallengeable practice. If, on the other hand, he is guilty, the process renders it more likely that his guilt may be established. That is, I apprehend, desirable.

Bearing all these considerations in mind, I should have no difficulty in reaching the conclusion, authority apart, that the Crown possess the right which is claimed by them.

[His Lordship then examined the authorities, and concluded:]

I reach the conclusion that I am unimpeded by authority from giving effect to the view which, apart from it, I should, as already stated, have entertained. To sum up then, I consider that the power claimed by the police is a reasonable and proper power, necessary for the investigation of crime and for the detection of the criminal and that it involves no undue invasion of the rights of the individual. To balance the claims of public interest on the one hand and the claims of private interest on the other is often not an easy task; but in this case I do not think it is difficult. There is, as the Lord Advocate said, no suggestion that the police, who have in the past claimed and exercised the powers which in this case are challenged, have abused these powers; there is no public outcry against the system; and, as the right claimed by the Crown is not withheld by the common law, and would in my opinion, if denied, hamper the police in the investigation and detection of crime, I am for sanctioning the right which the Crown claims, and I am for rejecting the argument which would negative its existence."

Appeal allowed.

NOTE

Lord Hunter entered a vigorous dissent: "It was suggested that the taking of fingerprint impressions was useful in enabling the police to detect crimes which might otherwise go undetected. That may explain why the police are anxious to possess the right; it affords no excuse for their doing what is not warranted at common law. It was no doubt upon similar grounds that physical torture was in the Middle Ages employed to extract confessions from persons suspected of crimes. At the present time third degree methods adopted by the police in some countries in questioning suspected persons might equally well be justified, but the common law of Scotland has never sanctioned such procedure" (p.490).

In *Adamson* v. *Martin*, 1916 S.C. 319 the police photographed and took the fingerprints of a suspect (a 17-year-old boy) whom they had not arrested (although a warrant to apprehend him had been granted). He later raised an action for the delivery or destruction of the photographs, negatives, fingerprint impressions, etc. The court held that the police action had been "unwarrantable and illegal" and ordered the fingerprints and photographs to be destroyed. The result would have been otherwise had the police arrested the boy before taking the action they did. This case was distinguished by the majority in *Adair* v. *McGarry*.

It is clear that in cases such as these much will depend upon the nature of the invasion of the suspect's person. Minor invasions are likely to be permitted, especially when the evidence obtained is of a reliable nature (as in *Adair* v. *McGarry*, and see also *Forrester* v. *H.M.Advocate*, 1952 J.C. 28—examination of a wound on the suspect's hand for comparison with a damaged glove found near the scene of the crime). Where, however, the invasion of the suspect's person is likely to be substantial, or the evidence inconclusive, the court should be reluctant to sanction examination without warrant. *cf. H.M.Advocate* v. *Milford*, 1973 S.L.T. 12.

2. Criminal Justice (Scotland) Act 1980

"**2.**—(5) Where a person is detained under subsection (1) above, a constable may . . .

(a) take fingerprints, palmprints and such other prints and impressions as the constable may, having regard to the circumstances of the suspected offence, reasonably consider appropriate:

Provided that the record of the prints and impressions so taken shall be destroyed immediately following a decision not to institute criminal proceedings against the person or on the conclusion of such proceedings otherwise than with a conviction or an order under section 182 or 383 (absolute discharge) or 183(1) or 384(1) (probation) of the 1975 Act."

NOTE

A constable may use reasonable force in exercising this power (section 2(6)). *Cf. Hay* v. *H.M.Advocate*, 1968 J.C. 40, *post*, Chap. 5.

(v) Participation in identification parade

A person arrested may be placed on an identification parade (*Adair* v. *McGarry, supra*). Although he is not entitled to do so, a suspect may refuse to take part. Since the use of force in such a case would defeat the object of the procedure he may thus effectively thwart the use of an identification parade. By doing so, however, he runs the risk of being viewed in circumstances less favourable than a full parade.

The Thomson Committee (2nd Report, para. 3.24, *supra*, p. 134) recommended that one of the purposes of detention should be identification of the detainee. The 1980 Act does not expressly confer a power to place a detainee on a parade. However, section 2(5)(*b*) of the 1980 Act authorises a constable to "exercise the same powers of search" with regard to a detainee "as are available following an arrest". The right to parade a suspect is sometimes treated as an extension of the right to search (*cf.* Renton and Brown, para. 5-30 and *Adair* v. *McGarry*). It is submitted, however, that this would be too great an extension of the statutory provision. The taking of fingerprints, for which express provision is made with respect to detainees, is likewise regarded as an extension of the power of search on arrest. It may be inferred, therefore, that "search" is not intended to include the parading of a detainee. It is further submitted that the considerations which apply to an arrestee who refuses to be paraded do not apply in the case of a detainee, so that the police would not be justified in allowing witnesses to view a detainee outwith a parade.

A suspect, whether detained or at liberty may, of course, volunteer to take part in an identification parade. In what circumstances can a suspect *demand* a parade?

1. Criminal Justice (Scotland) Act 1980

"**10.**—(1) Subject to subsection (2) below, the sheriff may, on an application by an accused at any time after the accused has been charged with an offence, order that, in relation to the alleged offence, the prosecutor shall hold an identification parade in which the accused shall be one of those constituting the parade.

(2) The sheriff shall make an order in accordance with subsection (1) above only after giving the prosecutor an opportunity to be heard and only if—

(*a*) an identification parade, such as is mentioned in subsection (1) above, has not been held at the instance of the prosecutor;

(*b*) after a request by the accused, the prosecutor has refused to hold, or has unreasonably delayed holding, such an identification parade; and

(*c*) the sheriff considers the application under subsection (1) above to be reasonable."

NOTE

For a discussion of identification procedures, and identification parades, see, generally, *Report of the Working Group on Identification Procedure under Scottish Criminal Law* (Bryden Committee), Cmnd. 7096, (1978), Thomson Committee, 2nd Report, ch.12, and *Report to the Secretary of State for the Home Department of the Departmental Committee on Evidence of Identification in Criminal Cases* (Devlin Committee), House of Commons, (1976).

Section 10 of the 1980 Act extends the provisions of the Legal Aid (Scotland) Act 1967 to make provision for the granting of legal aid for representation by a solicitor at any identification parade held by or on behalf of the prosecutor in connection with or in contemplation of criminal proceedings against the person represented. There is no inquiry into means. Where a duty solicitor is available legal aid will not be granted to employ another solicitor for the purposes of representation at an identificatio̅n parade.

Legal representation at a parade was seen by the Thomson Committee (2nd Report, ch.12) and the Bryden Committee (para. 414) as being desirable in the interests of the suspect. With the use of one-way vision screens, it was seen by the latter as being essential (Bryden, para. 4.36; *cf.* Thomson, para. 12.08), since the identification (or non-identification) is made outwith the sight of the suspect.

2. Scottish Home and Health Department Identification Parade Rules

"1. . . .

2.   Every precaution should be taken to see that identification parades are fairly conducted and, in particular, to exclude any suspicion of unfairness or risk of erroneous identification through the attention of the witness being directed specially to the suspected person instead of equally to all the persons paraded. It is desirable in the interests both of the police and of the person on parade that he be legally represented.

Decision to hold an Identification Parade
3.   Subject to the requirements of the Procurator Fiscal, the decision to hold an identification parade would normally rest with the officer in charge of a case or his superior officer. In all cases where identification may be an issue the police should normally hold an identification parade. If a suspect or an accused or his solicitor requests an identification parade, and the police are in doubt about granting it, the request should be referred to the Procurator Fiscal for his instructions. . . .

Rights of Suspect or Arrested Person
7.   When a suspect is not in custody and evidence is not sufficient to justify an apprehension, the suspect should be asked if he is willing to take part in an identification parade, the purpose of which should be clearly explained to him. Such a person's attendance is entirely voluntary, and there should be no question of pressure being exercised on him, or of any inducement to encourage his participation.

8.   An arrested person is not entitled to refuse to take part in an identification parade but any compulsion which results in his becoming particularly conspicuous is obviously undesirable. Where an arrested person declines to

be paraded it may be possible for the police to let the witness see the accused, preferably along with others but in the last resort on his own, in the place where he is detained.

9.   A suspect or arrested person should be informed by a police officer reading the appropriate part of the parade form that an identification parade is to take place, the purpose of the parade, that he has the right to object to the composition of the parade, and that he may have his solicitor and/or the solicitor's assistant present if he so desires. . . .

Any reasonable request which the suspect or arrested person or his solicitor or his assistant may make beforehand should be granted. He should also be informed that he may take up any position in the parade and that he can change position after each witness has viewed the parade and before the next witness enters. The arrested person/suspect or legal representative must not interfere with the conduct of the parade.

Composition of the Parade
10.   The suspect or arrested person should be placed beside persons of similar age, height, dress and general appearance. It is more important that the stand-ins should resemble the suspect or arrested person than that they should be like any descriptions given by witnesses. Similarly it is important that an identification should not be influenced by clothing—for example, if the witness has said that the suspect was wearing a red pullover it would be wrong if the suspect were the only person on the parade wearing a red pullover although the fact that he possesses such a pullover or that he was wearing one when invited to attend the parade would constitute a separate piece of evidence which should be recorded.

11.   . . . The minimum number in any parade should be five (in addition to the suspect or arrested person) but where more persons, up to a maximum of eight (in addition to the suspect or arrested person) are available the larger number is to be preferred.

12.   It is undesirable that witnesses called to attend a parade should discuss either the case in question or the person whom they are being asked to identify. While it is recognised that the police have no power to prevent such a discussion, it is considered that the witnesses should be segregated before the parade if practicable and having regard to the needs of the case (i.e. where the witnesses are thought to be unknown to each other or not to have had an opportunity to communicate with each other about the case prior to coming to view the parade). Alternatively a police officer should be present in the assembly room with a view to inhibiting any discussion of this nature. . . .

19.   The suspect or arrested person or his legal representative, if present, should be asked if he has any objection to make regarding the other persons forming the parade or the arrangements made for the parade. If the objection is to an individual he should be replaced. If the objection is to the

arrangement and is reasonable, it should be met. Any objection made should be noted.

20.   The persons forming the parade should be lined up, preferably with their backs to a wall, and should be numbered consecutively, the position of each person being denoted by a number clearly displayed.

21.   The suspect or arrested person should be invited to choose his own position in the line, prior to the first witness being asked to view the parade. After each witness and before the next witness enters, the suspect or arrested person should be given the opportunity to change position. The position taken up on each occasion should be noted.

22.   One-way vision screens should generally be used in the conduct of parades. . . . While it is highly desirable that a suspect or arrested person be legally represented when a one-way vision screen is used the fact that a suspect or arrested person has elected not to be legally represented at the parade in the knowledge that it is intended to use such a screen, shall not preclude the use of the screen. Where a one-way vision screen is employed it is essential that the suspect or arrested person, who will be unable to observe what is happening beyond the screen, should be able to hear all that is said on the other side by the officer conducting the parade. Where a legal representative and/or his assistant is present it is important that he should be able to observe the whole proceedings on both sides of the screen and hear all that is said.

23.   It is essential that the witnesses who are to view the parade should have no opportunity of seeing the suspect or arrested person, or the other members of the parade within the precincts of the place where the parade is to be held. It is equally essential that witnesses who have viewed the parade should have no opportunity of contact with those still to be called.

24.   Only one witness should be admitted at a time. . .
When a witness identifies a person on the parade by number, the officer conducting the parade should ask that person his name and note the name that is given. The officer conducting the parade should repeat that name to the witness within the hearing of the person identified. If the witness is unable to make a positive identification, he should be asked a second question: 'Is there anyone on the parade who resembles the person?' [His response, if any, should be noted.] Additional questions designed to clarify the witness's evidence as to identification may be put to the witness and these and any answers given should be noted. The witness should then be conducted to the dismissal room and should have no opportunity of communicating in any way with any witness still to view the parade. A witness should not be allowed to view the parade again after he has left the parade room."

NOTE
   These rules have no statutory status and are purely administrative

guidelines. A failure to observe these procedures will not of itself render inadmissible any evidence obtained, even where the reliability of the evidence is called into question through departure from the procedure. Such departure is, however, something which may properly be left to the jury in assessing the reliability of the evidence: *Morley* v. *H.M. Advocate*, 1981 S.C.C.R. 250.

e. Arrest and detention in connection with matrimonial interdicts

The Matrimonial Homes (Family Protection) (Scotland) Act 1981 creates a form of matrimonial order known as an "exclusion order." By means of such an order one spouse (which term includes persons living together as husband and wife) may obtain an order suspending the occupancy rights of the other spouse in the matrimonial home (1981 Act, s.4(1)). The object of such orders is the protection of the applicant or any child of the family from injury at the hand of the party excluded (section 4(2)).

In making an exclusion order the court has the power to grant interdict prohibiting the excluded spouse from entering the matrimonial home, removing furnishings and plenishings, etc., or approaching the matrimonial home (section 4(3)). Interdict may also be granted independently of an exclusion order under section 14, restraining conduct of one spouse towards the other or towards a child of the family, or prohibiting a spouse from approaching the matrimonial home.

A power of arrest may be attached to either form of matrimonial interdict. The procedures governing the granting and exercise of this power, and procedures following on such arrest are set out in the following materials.

Matrimonial Homes (Family Protection) (Scotland) Act 1981
Attachment of powers of arrest to matrimonial interdicts
    15.—(1) The court shall, on the application of the applicant spouse, attach a power of arrest—
    (*a*) to any matrimonial interdict which is ancillary to an exclusion order, including an interim order under section 4 (6) of this Act;
    (*b*) to any other matrimonial interdict where the non-applicant spouse has had the opportunity of being heard or represented before the court, unless it appears to the court that in all the circumstances of the case such a power is unnecessary.
    (2) A power of arrest attached to an interdict by virtue of sub-section (1) above shall not have effect until such interdict is served on the non-applicant spouse, and such a power of arrest shall, unless previously recalled, cease to have effect upon the termination of the marriage.

(3) If, by virtue of subsection (1) above, a power of arrest is attached to an interdict, a constable may arrest without warrant the non-applicant spouse if he has reasonable cause for suspecting that spouse of being in breach of the interdict.

Police powers after arrest

16.—(1) Where a person has been arrested under section 15 (3) of this Act, the officer in charge of a police station may—

(a) if satisfied that there is no likelihood of violence to the applicant spouse or any child of the family, liberate that person unconditionally; or

(b) refuse to liberate that person; and such refusal and the detention of that person until his or her appearance in court by virtue of—

(i) section 17 (2) of this Act; or

(ii) any provision of the Criminal Procedure (Scotland) Act 1975, shall not subject the officer to any claim whatsoever.

(2) Where a person arrested under section 15 (3) of this Act is liberated under subsection (1) above, the facts and circumstances which gave rise to the arrest shall be reported forthwith to the procurator fiscal who, if he decides to take no criminal proceedings in respect of those facts and circumstances, shall at the earliest opportunity take all reasonable steps to intimate his decision to the persons mentioned in paragraphs (a) and (b) of section 17 (4) of this Act.

Procedure after arrest

17.—(1) The provisions of this section shall apply only where—

(a) the non-applicant spouse has not been liberated under section 16 (1) of this Act; and

(b) the procurator fiscal decides that no criminal proceedings are to be taken in respect of the facts and circumstances which gave rise to the arrest.

(2) The non-applicant spouse who has been arrested under section 15 (3) of this Act shall wherever practicable be brought before the sheriff sitting as a court of summary criminal jurisdiction for the district in which he or she was arrested not later than in the course of the first day after arrest, such day not being a Saturday, a Sunday or a court holiday prescribed for that court under section 10 of the Bail etc. (Scotland) Act 1980:

Provided that nothing in this subsection shall prevent the non-applicant spouse from being brought before the sheriff on a Saturday, a Sunday or such a court holiday where the sheriff is in pursuance of the said section 10 sitting on such a day for the disposal of criminal business.

(3) Subsections (1) and (2) of section 3 of the Criminal Justice (Scotland) Act 1980 (intimation to a named person) shall apply to a non-applicant spouse who has been arrested under section 15 (3) of this Act as they apply to a person who has been arrested in respect of any offence.

(4) The procurator fiscal shall at the earliest opportunity, and in any event prior to the non-applicant spouse being brought before the sheriff under subsection (2) above, take all reasonable steps to intimate—

(a) to the applicant spouse; and

(b) to the solicitor who acted for that spouse when the interdict was granted or to any other solicitor who the procurator fiscal has reason to believe acts for the time being for that spouse,

that the criminal proceedings referred to in subsection (1) above will not be taken.

(5)   On the non-applicant spouse being brought before the sheriff under subsection (2) above, the following procedure shall apply—

(a) the procurator fiscal shall present to the court a petition containing—

(i)   a statement of the particulars of the non-applicant spouse;

(ii) a statement of the facts and circumstances which gave rise to the arrest; and

(iii) a request that the non-applicant spouse be detained for a further period not exceeding 2 days;

(b)   if it appears to the sheriff that—

(i)   the statement referred to in paragraph (a) (ii) above discloses a *prima facie* breach of interdict by the non-applicant spouse;

(ii) proceedings for breach of interdict will be taken; and

(iii) there is a substantial risk of violence by the non-applicant spouse against the applicant spouse or any child of the family,

he may order the non-applicant spouse to be detained for a further period not exceeding 2 days;

(c)   in any case to which paragraph (b) above does not apply, the non-applicant spouse shall, unless in custody in respect of any other matter, be released from custody;

and in computing the period of two days referred to in paragraphs (a) and (b) above, no account shall be taken of a Saturday or Sunday or of any holiday in the court in which the proceedings for breach of interdict will require to be raised."

NOTE

Section 15 also makes provision for service of notice of the granting of a matrimonial interdict to which a power of arrest has been attached, or of its recall, to the chief constable of the area in which the matrimonial home is situated, and where the applicant spouse resides in a different police area, to the chief constable of that area.

These elaborate provisions are necessary to safeguard the position both of the spouse threatened with, or indeed suffering, violence, and also the position of the spouse who is the subject of the matrimonial interdict. As regards the former it remains to be seen how effective the new procedures will be, given that they depend largely on the willingness of the police to exercise their powers of arrest.

As regards the position of the arrested spouse it is worth noting that in some cases a considerable period of time may be spent in custody without any criminal charge being brought. Suppose, for example the case of a spouse arrested on a Friday evening. He (since these procedures are generally directed towards the problem of battering men) is not released under section 16(1). The fiscal decides to take no criminal proceedings (section 17(1)(*b*)) (and there is evidence of reluctance on the part of the some fiscals to take criminal proceedings in matrimonial cases: see Moodie and Tombs, *Prosecution in the Public Interest*, pp. 67 *et seq.*). No court is available until the following Monday. On appearance before the sheriff the conditions specified in section 17(5)(*b*) are found to be satisfied, and detention for 48 hours is ordered. Thus over 96 hours' detention are possible under these provisions.

This should be contrasted with the situation where the arrested spouse is charged with an offence. The provisions of section 17 do not apply, and the normal procedures governing an arrested person come into force. The effect of this may well be that the arrestee charged with an offence is liberated more swiftly than the arrestee against whom no proceedings are to be taken.

CHAPTER 5

QUESTIONING AND SEARCH

It will be seen from the materials in chapter 4 that the practical responsibility for the investigation of crime is devolved upon the police (subject to any instructions or guidance issued to them by the public prosecutor). In conducting their investigations the police are frequently required to question suspects and to search for and seize items of real evidence. In consequence, this chapter is effectively concerned with the powers of the police to question and to search. The judicial examination of suspects is dealt with in Chap. 7.

The questioning of suspects, and the search for real evidence raise similar issues. Both procedures may be essential for the detection and investigation of crime. But at the same time, if not contained within proper limits, they may constitute a serious infringement of the liberty of the individual. This much is recognised by most democratic systems, which by and large adopt similar devices to control potential abuses. Such devices may be direct or indirect.

Direct controls may consist in the taking of proceedings (civil, criminal or disciplinary as appropriate) against those who have acted unlawfully or irregularly in the questioning of suspects or the gathering of evidence. But such direct measures of control are rarely seen as being sufficient in themselves. A person aggrieved by the conduct of the police may be unable or unwilling to institute civil proceedings, and may encounter official antipathy to criminal proceedings (where the institution of such proceedings is an available option at all). Similarly, internal disciplinary procedures may not command sufficient public confidence to commend them as an appropriate check on the abuse of powers.

Consequently, recourse has been made to the indirect regulation of questioning and search by means of what is commonly called the "exclusionary rule." By means of this device a court may rule that evidence "illegally" or "irregularly" or "unfairly" (depending on local terminology) obtained is inadmissible against the accused. Legal systems do, however, vary widely in their attitude to this device, some applying it more or less strictly than others. In

157

England, the view has recently been expressed (*R.* v. *Sang* [1979] 2 All E.R. 1222, *per* Lord Diplock at p. 1230) that: "It is no part of a judge's function to exercise disciplinary powers over the police or prosecution as respects the way in which evidence to be used at the trial is obtained by them. If it was obtained illegally there will be a remedy in civil law; if it was obtained legally but in breach of the rules of conduct for the police, this is a matter for the appropriate disciplinary authority to deal with."

Even within a system which operates an exclusionary rule the conditions for invoking that rule may vary from time to time, even to the extent that it may decline to residual status, to be invoked only in "extreme" cases. (Compare, for example, the approach of the High Court in *Chalmers* v. *H.M. Advocate*, 1954 J.C. 66 with the approach of the court in *Hartley* v. *H.M. Advocate*, 1979 S.L.T. 26.) Similarly, the exclusionary rule may be applied more rigorously in some areas than others. Generally speaking, the exclusionary rule tends to be more strictly applied to evidence of extra-judicial statements or confessions than it is to real evidence. (So, for example, Lord Diplock's statement in *Sang, supra*, does not apply to statements obtained in breach of the Judges' Rules (*ibid.*).) This is usually justified on the ground that while a confession extracted by unlawful or unfair means suffers from the additional drawback that it may be unreliable, the probative value of real evidence—such as a murder weapon with the accused's fingerprints on it—is not diminished by the fact that it was obtained without a warrant or otherwise irregularly obtained.

a. Questioning

(i) The "right to silence"

The starting point for a consideration of the police powers of interrogation is the so-called "right to silence." This is a convenient, if misleading shorthand for a number of well-established propositions.

At common law there is no duty on any person to answer questions put to them by the police: *cf. Twycross* v. *Farrell*, 1973 S.L.T. (Notes) 85. Although giving false information in response to police questions does not constitute obstruction of a police officer in the execution of his duty (*Curlett* v. *McKechnie*, 1938 J.C. 176) it may amount to an attempt to pervert the course of justice: *Dean* v. *Stewart*, 1980 S.L.T. (Notes) 85. (Deliberately and maliciously to set in motion an investigation by means of an invented story is an offence: *Kerr* v. *Hill*, 1936 J.C. 71.) The right to silence also encompasses the rule that no one is under a duty to answer questions which might incriminate that person.

1. H.M. Advocate v. Von
1979 S.L.T. (Notes) 62

Von was charged, along with 10 others, with conspiracy to further the aims of the Ulster Volunteer Force by criminal means, including contraventions of section 10 of the Prevention of Terrorism (Temporary Provisions) Act 1976 which prohibits, *inter alia*, soliciting or receiving money or property for use in acts of terrorism. During the trial objection was taken by the defence to the admissibility of a statement made by Von to the police while detained under section 12 of the 1976 Act.

LORD ROSS: ". . .The objection which has been taken is as far as I am aware novel since it turns upon the provisions of s. 11 of the Prevention of Terrorism (Temporary Provisions) Act 1976. . . .

Evidence shows that the accused was interviewed by the police on Saturday, 24 February, and again on the following day. On the Saturday the interviewing officers advised him that it was an offence to withhold information about acts of terrorism under s. 11 of the Act of 1976. That section provides as follows: 'If a person who has information which he knows or believes might be of material assistance— (*a*) in preventing an act of terrorism to which this section applies, or (*b*) in securing the apprehension, prosecution or conviction of any person for an offence involving the commission, preparation or instigation of an act of terrorism to which this section applies, fails without reasonable excuse to disclose that information as soon as reasonably practicable— (1) in England and Wales, to a constable, or (2) in Scotland, to a constable or the procurator fiscal, or, (3) in Northern Ireland, to a constable or a member of Her Majesty's forces, he shall be guilty of an offence'.

On the Saturday the accused apparently made a statement which did not incriminate himself or anyone else. On the Sunday he was seen by police officers on two occasions. On the first occasion he was apparently upset and asked to have some time to himself and added that he would then see the officers again.

After an interval of time the officers saw him for the second occasion when he stated that he wished to make a statement and to tell of his own involvement but that he would not name anyone. At this stage police officers, realising that he was about to make a statement implicating himself, advised him that what he said could be used in evidence.

Counsel for the accused objected to the admissibility of the statement which followed that warning on the ground that the accused in the circumstances had been forced to incriminate himself, being compelled after the provisions of the Act had been drawn to his attention, to make a statement against himself. He contended that the officers ought when they advised the accused of the terms of the section, to have drawn his attention to the fact that the offence was committed if there was failure without reasonable excuse to disclose the information, and he submitted that one could reasonably be excused from not disclosing information if the information would be self-incriminating.

In the circumstances here, if the statement which is now being objected to had been made on the Saturday then it would in my opinion be clear that the statement had been made in response to his being told of his obligations under s. 11 of the Act. As the Crown point out, however, there was an interval of time in this case and the statement objected to was not apparently made until the Sunday around 12.50 p.m., and the question which arises is whether that statement on the Sunday could be said to have been the result of his being told on the Saturday that he had an obligation to disclose the information. . . .

The accused in the present case was apparently detained under the provisions of s. 12 of the Act of 1976, and he was undoubtedly a suspect, as the search warrant which was issued to search his premises indicates. That being so, it seems to me that the question which really arises regarding the admissibility of the statement is the familiar one of fairness.

If on the Sunday the accused had been given the usual full caution or had been informed that he was not obliged to give information which would incriminate himself and he had then made a statement, I would have thought that that statement would have been admissible as being a statement which had been fairly obtained and was not a statement made in response to pressure or inducement or as a result of other unfair means. In the event, however, the statement on Sunday was made by the accused after he had been told on the previous day of his obligations under s. 11 and without his ever having been told that he need not incriminate himself. That being so, I am satisfied that the statement here is not admissible.

So far as the evidence goes, the accused was left in total ignorance of the fact that he was not obliged to incriminate himself. Almost 150 years ago in the case of *Livingstone* v. *Murray* (1830) 9 Shaw 161, Lord Gillies said: 'It is a sacred and inviolable principle that no man is bound to incriminate himself'. I do not consider that a statement can be regarded as being fairly obtained if the accused was never advised of the fact that under our law no person is required to incriminate himself.

In enacting the provisions of the Act of 1976, if Parliament had intended to make statements of suspects admissible against them in the event of their being subsequently charged I would have expected Parliament to have made that clear. I cannot believe that Parliament intended to alter the well-established principle of our law that no man can be compelled to incriminate himself. If Parliament had intended so to do I would have expected it to be made clear.

As I have indicated, if a full caution had been given or clear advice given to the suspect that he need not incriminate himself, the statement might well have been admissible: but the only warning here given was that what he said could be used in evidence, and I do not regard that as a sufficient warning to the accused that he was not obliged to incriminate himself."

The court sustained
the objection.

NOTES

1. *Cf.* the Thomson Committee (2nd Report, para. 7.02):
"Scots law on this matter has proceeded not so much on any
fundamental constitutional or philosophic basis, such as the privilege against self-incrimination, as on a conception of fairness and
a determination by the courts to control police activity in the
interests of fairness."

2. For a full consideration of the "fairness" issue, see *infra*. For
a further discussion of the relevance of the caution to the fairness
issue see *Tonge* v. *H.M. Advocate, infra.*

2. Criminal Justice (Scotland) Act 1980

"2.—. . . (7) A person detained under subsection (1) above shall be under
no obligation to answer any question other than to give his name and
address, and a constable shall so inform him both on so detaining him and
on arrival at the police station or other premises."

NOTES

1. The warning contained in subsection (7) is, by comparison
with a "common law caution," only a partial warning. It does not,
for example, make it clear that any answers given may be taken
down and used in evidence. For the effect of such a partial caution
on the admissibility of any such answer, see *Tonge* v. *H.M. Advocate, infra.*

2. The "right to silence" is not limited to the stage of pre-trial
investigations by the police. It exists at the trial stage also, in the
sense that the accused cannot be compelled to give evidence at his
own trial: 1975 Act, s. 141(*a*) and s. 346(*a*). This is reinforced by the
rule that the prosecutor may not comment upon the failure of the
accused to give evidence: 1975 Act, s. 141(*b*) and 346(*b*). The judge
may, however, comment upon such failure: *Knowles* v. *H.M.
Advocate*, 1975 J.C. 6. The Thomson Committee (2nd Report, ch.
50) considered this aspect of the right to silence and concluded:
"It should in our view be appropriate for the prosecutor, as well
as the judge, to comment on the fact that the accused has failed to
give evidence to counter the *prima facie* case against him. We
accordingly recommend that in every case in which the Crown has
established a *prima facie* case against the accused, it should be
competent for the prosecution to comment on the failure of the

accused to attempt to refute the case against him by giving evidence, and further that, in cases where the judge or jury may have some doubt as to whether or not they should accept the evidence for the Crown, they may draw an inference adverse to the accused from his failure to attempt to refute the evidence for the Crown." (Para. 50.16.)

The Committee rejected the suggestion made by the Criminal Law Revision Committee (11th Report, para. 111) that failure to testify could be taken as corroboration of the prosecution case. Nevertheless, it is worth noting that what the Thomson Committee is recommending is a situation where some kind of onus should be placed upon the accused to refute the prosecution case. The suggestion appears to have the support of the Scottish Law Commission: Memorandum No. 46 (Law of Evidence), para. E.08.

3.   For the impact of the revived procedure of judicial examination on the right to silence, see *post*, Chap. 7.

(ii)   Police questioning and the fairness rule

1.   **Chalmers v. H.M. Advocate**
1954 J.C. 66

The appellant, a youth of 16, was convicted of murder and robbery. During their investigations the police interviewed the appellant on several occasions. On the third occasion he was taken to a police station where he was cautioned and "cross-examined" for about five minutes until he burst into tears and made a "highly incriminating" statement. (This statement was not tendered in evidence by the Crown.) He then took the police to a field where, under his guidance, they obtained certain real evidence relating to the crimes. Over two hours later the appellant's father arrived. The appellant broke down again, and at this point was cautioned and formally charged. He is alleged to have stated: "I did it. He struck me." At the trial, objection was taken, unsuccessfully, to the admissibility of the evidence relating to the visit to the field and the final statement attributed to the appellant.

LORD JUSTICE-GENERAL (COOPER): ". . .I have sympathy with the police in the difficult position in which they are often placed. We have no power to give instructions to the police, but we have the power and the duty to exclude from the cognisance of a jury evidence which, according to our practice and decisions, is inadmissible; and the police have an interest to know why such decisions are taken. Were it possible to do so, I should like to be able to lay down comprehensive rules for the guidance of the police in all the situations which may arise in practice, but I am satisfied that this is impossible because in the border-line case so much turns upon the exact circumstances.

This, however, it is possible to say with regard to Scots law. It is not the function of the police when investigating a crime to direct their endeavours to obtaining a confession from the suspect to be used as evidence against him at the trial. In some legal systems the inquisitorial method of investigation is allowed in different degrees and subject to various safeguards; but by our law self-incriminating statements, when tendered in evidence at a criminal trial, are always jealously examined from the standpoint of being assured as to their spontaneity; and if, on a review of all the proved circumstances, that test is not satisfied, evidence of such statements will usually be excluded altogether. The theory of our law is that at the stage of initial investigation the police may question anyone with a view to acquiring information which may lead to the detection of the criminal; but that, when the stage has been reached at which suspicion, or more than suspicion, has in their view centred upon some person as the likely perpetrator of the crime, further interrogation of that person becomes very dangerous, and, if carried too far, *e.g.* to the point of extracting a confession by what amounts to cross-examination, the evidence of that confession will almost certainly be excluded. Once the accused has been apprehended and charged he has the statutory right to a private interview with a solicitor and to be brought before a magistrate with all convenient speed so that he may, if so advised, emit a declaration in presence of his solicitor under conditions which safeguard him against prejudice. The practice of emitting declarations has very largely fallen into disuse since the Evidence Act of 1898, but the underlying principle survives, and it may be applicable to situations which arise before apprehension and charge. Much reference was made to a person 'detained under suspicion,' an expression which has been used ambiguously in many of our decisions, but the emphasis is on the suspicion and not on the detention. Putting aside the case of proper apprehension without a warrant of persons caught more or less redhanded, no person can be lawfully detained except after a charge has been made against him, and it is for this reason that I view with some uneasiness the situation disclosed in this case, and illustrated by the recent cases of *Rigg* [1946 J.C. 1] and *Short* [30 May 1950 unreported] in which a suspect is neither apprehended nor charged but is simply 'asked' to accompany two police officers to a police office to be there questioned. In former times such questioning, if undertaken, would be conducted by police officers visiting the house or place of business of the suspect and there questioning him, probably in the presence of a relation or friend. However convenient the modern practice may be, it must normally create a situation very unfavourable to the suspect. In the eyes of every ordinary citizen the venue is a sinister one. When he stands alone in such a place confronted by several police officers, usually some of high rank, the dice are loaded against him, especially as he knows that there is no one to corroborate him as to what exactly occurred during the interrogation, how it was conducted, and how long it lasted. If under such circumstances cross-examination is pursued with the result, though perhaps not with the deliberate object, of causing him to break down and to condemn himself out of his own mouth, the impropriety of the proceedings cannot be cured by the giving of any number of formal cautions or by the introduction of some officer other than the questioner to record the ultimate statement. In the ordinary case, as many decisions now demonstrate, that statement, if tendered in evidence at the trial, will not be treated as possessing that quality of spontaneity on which our law insists, and its rejection, when tendered in evidence, may, and sometimes does, wreck the prosecution. The practice exemplified by this and other recent cases in substance puts the suspect in much the same position as if he had been arrested, while depriving him of the privileges and safeguards which are extended by the statute and the decisions to an accused person who has been apprehended. The police have, of course, the right and the duty to produce all the incriminating evidence they can lay their hands on, from whatever source they legitimately derive the clue which leads to its discovery, so long as any admission or confession by the accused is not elicited before the jury as an element in proof of guilt. The matter may be put in another way. The accused cannot be compelled to give evidence at his trial and to submit to cross-examination. If it were competent for the police at their own hand to subject the accused to interrogation and cross-examination and to adduce evidence of what he said, the prosecution would in effect be making the accused a compellable witness, and laying before the jury, at *second hand*, evidence which could not be adduced at first hand, even subject to all the precautions which are available for the protection of the accused at a criminal trial."

LORD JUSTICE-CLERK (THOMSON): " . . . On the first of these topics the difficulty arises from the necessity of reconciling two principles:—(1) that no accused person is bound to incriminate himself, and (2) that what an accused says—apart from what properly falls within the doctrine of *res gestae*—provided he says it freely and voluntarily, is admissible evidence against him. It is when the police, in the course of their duty as investigators of crime, interview someone in relation to some specific crime that the problem arises for decision whether something which has been said by an accused is admissible as evidence against him. Extreme cases are easy. At the one extreme, once the investigation has gone to the extent that somebody is specifically cautioned and charged, thereafter nothing short of a voluntary statement is admissible against him. At the other extreme is the ordinary routine investigation of the police into the circumstances of the crime. In the course of such an investigation the man ultimately accused may be interviewed. It would unduly hamper the investigation of crime if the threat of inadmissibility were to tie the hands of the police in asking questions. It would help to defeat the ends of justice if what the person so questioned said in answer to ordinary and legitimate questions were not admissible in evidence against him. I am assuming throughout that the questioning is not tainted by bullying, pressure, third degree methods and so forth. Evidence obtained by such methods can never be admissible in our Courts, whatever stage the investigation has reached. But there comes a point of time in ordinary police investigation when the law intervenes to render inadmissible as evidence answers even to questions which are not tainted by such methods. After the point is reached, further interrogation is incompatible with the answers being regarded as a voluntary statement, and the law intervenes to safeguard the party questioned from possible self-incrimination. Just when that point of time is reached is in any particular case extremely difficult to define—or even for an experienced police official to realise its arrival. There does come a time, however, when a police officer, carrying out his duty honestly and conscientiously, ought to be in a position to appreciate that the man whom he is in process of questioning is under serious consideration as the perpetrator of the crime. Once that stage of suspicion is reached, the suspect is in the position that thereafter the only evidence admissible against him is his own voluntary statement. A voluntary statement is one which is given freely, not in response to pressure and inducement, and not elicited by cross-examination. This does not mean that, if a person elects to give a statement, it becomes inadmissible because he is asked some questions to clear up his account of the matter, but such questions as he is asked must not go beyond elucidation. It is important to keep in mind also that the point of time at which the axe falls is not necessarily related to the person being in custody or detention of some sort. The fact that he is detained may point to his being under suspicion but he may come under suspicion without having been detained."

The court allowed
the appeal.

NOTES

1. This "hardy perennial" (*per* Lord Avonside in *Hartley* v. *H.M. Advocate, infra*) is included here principally by way of historical background to what follows. Insofar as this case states that admissibility of statements depends upon the stage of the investigation at which they were elicited, it no longer represents the law. It should be noted, however, that the stage of the investigation was more important for the Lord Justice-Clerk than for the Lord Justice-General, whose opinion may be read as concentrating on the *manner* of the interrogation. In this respect his Lordship's judgment differs little from the modern line of authority. *Chalmers* has not yet been overruled, "But if it cannot yet be declared dead, it has become so senile that it can be safely said to have faded away". (Gordon, "The Admissibility of Answers to Police Questioning in Scotland," in *Reshaping the Criminal Law,* ed. Glazebrook, at p. 332.)

2. Chalmers may be a "disembodied ghost" (Gordon, *loc. cit.*) but its spirit still walks abroad. It is regularly cited to the courts, and crops up in virtually every case on the admissibility of statements to

the police. The "stage theory" may in fact have become an element of the fairness test. In *H.M. Advocate* v. *Mair,* 1982 S.L.T. 471 objection was taken to the admissibility of a statement made by a person who had "clearly become in the eyes of the police not only a suspect but the prime and only suspect" (*ibid.,* p. 472). In upholding the objection, Lord Hunter stated (p. 473):

"There is ample authority for the proposition that a statement or confession extracted from an accused person at such a stage and in such circumstances by interrogation, cross-examination, leading questions and pressure will be rendered inadmissible".

2. Hartley v. H.M. Advocate
1979 S.L.T. 26

The appellant, a 17-year-old youth described as suffering from a "disordered personality" was convicted of the murder of a five-year-old boy by drowning him in a burn. He appealed against conviction on the ground, *inter alia,* that a confession allegedly made by him to the police had been improperly admitted in evidence. The appellant had been interviewed by the police on two occasions. During the first interview he gave certain information which disclosed that on the day of the murder he had been working near the spot where the body was found. He denied ever having seen the victim. An appointment was made for him to meet with the police the following day, which he failed to keep. He was found by the police and showed them where he had been working on the day of the murder. He then went voluntarily to a police office where, at about 2.40 p.m., he gave a detailed statement of his whereabouts at the material time.

The appellant remained, voluntarily, at the police station until 2.30 a.m. the following day when, after some general questioning under caution, he became agitated, broke down, and confessed to the killing.

LORD AVONSIDE: " . . . Detective Superintendent Samson, who was in charge of the case, and a constable, Turner, saw the appellant at 2.30 a.m. on Thursday morning. His purpose was to go over the statement of the appellant in detail. He cautioned the appellant. He considered him a suspect. The caution was in the usual proper form. The appellant said: 'It's okay, it wasn't me'. The officer went over the statement down to the part where the appellant was at the burn, and then showed him a photograph of the dead child and asked him, when he had been down there, had he seen this boy at the burn or in the vicinity of the swing park. The appellant answered: 'No'.

At this point senior counsel for the appellant intervened.

Firstly, it was objected that the stage had now been reached when it was plain that the police were going to interrogate or cross-examine a suspect. Not only was that objectionable in itself, but it was rendered all the worse in the particular circumstances. The appellant had been in police custody for 12 hours. He was young. The nature of his confinement must have, and, it would be shown, did demoralise him, and render him particularly open to breakdown under prolonged cross-examination. The evidence about to be given should not be put before the jury.

Counsel first relied on the hardy perennial case of *Chalmers* v. *H.M. Advocate*, and particularly what was said by Lord Justice-General Cooper. Now I accept, and must accept, that once suspicion of crime has centred upon a person, that person is in some respects clearly under the protection of the law. At 1954 S.L.T., p. 184, his Lordship said: 'The theory of our law is that at the stage of initial investigation the police may question anyone with a view to acquiring information which may lead to the detection of the criminal; but that, when the stage has been reached at which suspicion, or more than suspicion, has in their view centred upon some person as the likely perpetrator of the crime, further interrogation of that person becomes very dangerous, and if carried too far, e.g. to the point of extracting a confession by what amounts to cross-examination, the evidence of that confession will almost certainly be excluded'. His Lordship adds that when a person stands alone in a police station confronted by several police officers: 'If under such circumstances cross-examination is pursued with the result . . . of causing him to break down and to condemn himself out of his own mouth, the impropriety of the proceedings cannot be cured by the giving of any number of formal cautions or by the introduction of some officer other than the questioner to record the ultimate statement'.

I make two observations on these dicta. Firstly, police officers may question a suspect so long as they do not stray into the field of interrogation. Secondly, and most importantly, cross-examination is just what it means. It consists in questioning an adverse witness in an effort ot break down his evidence, to weaken or prejudice his evidence, or to elicit statements damaging to him and aiding the case of the cross-examiner.

Brown v. *H.M. Advocate* was also quoted. I should have thought that case unhelpful to counsel for the accused. I refer to what was said by Lord Justice-General Clyde at p. 107. He speaks of questioning and interrogation and concludes his remarks by saying: 'But the test in all of them is the simple and intelligible test which has worked well in practice—has what has taken place been fair or not?'

I pause to interject that that, in my understanding, is today in law the basic test and only test. There has been a steady move towards liberalisation so that justice must, of course, be done to the criminal, but equally justice must be done to the interest of the public and law and order. There have in recent years been many cases in which this has been stated, the last reported one being *Balloch* v. *H.M. Advocate (infra)*.

Counsel for the accused then raised his second objection. That was that, in order to obtain a statement, the appellant had been subjected to physical assault, the grossest of threats and bullying, and inducements that a confession would avoid a murder charge. This led to the lamentable process, so often now condemned, of a trial within a trial. Suffice it to say that the jury were left to be the judges, as they should be. The verdict showed that these allegations were disbelieved, at least by the majority. Very rightly, counsel for the accused did not again raise this matter.

Samson in due course resumed his evidence, explaining that a Detective Constable Turner took notes, and correct notes, of what the appellant said. The appellant was asked general questions as to whether he had seen the dead boy or any other person at the locus, or whether he had heard any cry or shout. The answers were negative. He was asked if he was sure. The appellant became agitated and said: 'I did see something. The wee boy was there and somebody else. He said he knew me. He said, "Don't you say a word." He was one of them from Job Creation. I think he'll come after me and get me too. I saw the wee boy. The guy had him over the edge. He was half in and half out of the burn, you know what I mean. The wee boy was squealing. I watched for about 10 minutes, then ran away frightened'. At this the appellant, after a pause, said: 'It was me'.

The appellant was then cautioned again. He made a clear confession which I will not repeat but which may be found in the notes of evidence.

Samson tried to comfort the appellant, who had now broken down. The appellant said: 'I want to tell you everything'. Samson, very properly, said that if he, the appellant, wanted to make a further statement, an officer unconnected with the inquiry would have to be called in. The appellant said: 'No, the only person I'll tell is the fat policeman. I want to see him'; and: 'Get him, I want to see him'.

This policeman was Detective Sergeant Hyslop, who had to be located and came to the station about 4 a.m. Hyslop reminded the appellant that he was still under caution and not obliged to say anything. The appellant said: 'I'm sorry. I wanted to tell you, but I told the other officers. I don't know why I did it. He was only a wee boy, but I was frightened. I pushed him in. I take these turns and I get violent, and I try not to remember about them. I'm sorry. What will happen now?' He was told he would be charged, and then said: 'Don't think bad of me, I wasn't myself'.

In due course Samson charged the appellant with the murder, to which he replied: 'I am not saying any more'.

In my opinion, the appellant made the clearest admission of murdering the boy McAllister."

LORD GRIEVE: " . . . Counsel referred to the case of *H.M. Advocate* v. *Rigg* [1946 J.C. 1] and maintained that the circumstances of this case were *a fortiori* of that case. There is some similarity in the facts of the two cases, in so far as both the accused in *Rigg's* case and the appellant in this case were 17 years of age and were detained in a police station for a prolonged period before making an incriminating statement. The statement in *Rigg*, however which the Lord Justice-Clerk held to be inadmissible, was in substance a detailed precognition of some 700 words which by the nature of its contents could not have been given spontaneously. The Lord Justice-Clerk clearly considered the statement could only have been obtained by prolonged interrogation of a kind which vitiated its spontaneity. The evidence in this case disclosed no indication of that kind of interrogation. The nearest Samson got to interrogating the appellant, in the sense of cross-examining him, was to ask him if he was sure of the correctness of the answers he had given to the few questions which he had been asked. In no way could that be described as cross-examination, the main purpose of which is to destroy the basis, or content, of the evidence of a witness. An advocate who limited his cross-examination of witnesses to the question: 'Are you sure of what you have just said?', would achieve little forensic success. It has been repeated over several years, with increasing emphasis (the most recent examples of which are *Jones* v. *Milne* and *Balloch* v. *H.M. Advocate*) that the ultimate test is one of fairness—fairness not only to the accused but fairness also to those who investigate crime on behalf of the public. Statements made in answer to fair questions, such as: 'Are you sure?' could seldom be said to have been extracted by unfair means, placing 'cross-examination, pressure and deception in close company'. Even when the person concerned is a suspect, it is not illegitimate to ask him questions. What is illegitimate is to use means to extract from a potential accused extra-judicial admissions which could not have been extracted from such a person in judicial proceedings against him, an accused person not being a compellable witness. In my opinion, the trial judge acted correctly in rejecting counsel's motion to have the confession held to be inadmissible in evidence, and rightly left the question of its spontaneity to the jury, against the background of the very careful directions which he gave them on the matter."

LORD DUNPARK: " . . . Counsel for the accused submitted that there were five factors which, taken together, branded the accused's confession as 'improperly obtained', viz.: (1) the age of the accused—17 years; (2) he had been to a special school (although it was not proved that the police knew this); (3) he had been in custody for 12 hours; (4) he had not slept; and (5) he had had neither legal nor parental advice. These circumstances were said to be sufficient to render inadmissible any incriminating answers which the accused might give to police questioning. They were also said to render the inadmissibility of this confession even more obvious than the statement which the Lord Justice-Clerk (Cooper) held to be inadmissible in *H.M. Advocate* v. *Rigg*; but, in my opinion, this case is not in the same realm as *Rigg*. In *Rigg* (at p. 4) the Lord Justice-Clerk ruled the accused's confession to be inadmissible because it was: 'in substance a detailed precognition of the accused, extending upwards of 700 words, and giving a coherent and elaborate account of his movements and of the relevant facts of the preceding day and the day in question, with numerous references to persons, places and hours', and therefore could not be 'a truly spontaneous and voluntary statement in the sense in which that expression has been used in the decisions, or without such interrogation as would in common experience be indispensable to the taking of such a detailed precognition'. . . . The police are entitled to question suspects about parts of their previous statements which appear not to fit into the jigsaw puzzle which the police are endeavouring to construct, and a self-incriminating response to the question 'Are you sure?' is not necessarily inadmissible as evidence against that suspect at his trial. The case of *Balloch* v. *H.M. Advocate* is the most recent one which vouches this proposition.

Such questions as Inspector Samson asked of this accused were, in my opinion, perfectly proper questions, which arose from statements made by the accused himself and, further, were fairly put after caution. Interrogation there certainly was, but no leading or repetitive questions or any unfair pressure which could reasonably be classified as cross-examination and thus render the answers inadmissible as evidence against the accused. Indeed, this confession emerged, not in answer to a question, but as a correction of his immediately preceding statement that he had seen the deed done by someone else. It has all the hallmarks of a truly spontaneous confession, and, in my opinion, the five background factors founded on by counsel for the accused cannot convert this voluntary confession into one improperly obtained."

The court dismissed the appeal.

NOTES

1.   *Hartley* is the culmination of a line of cases withdrawing from the strict exclusionary stance represented by *Chalmers.* For earlier cases in this line, see: *Miln* v. *Cullen*, 1967 J.C. 21, *Jones* v. *Milne*, 1975 S.L.T. 2, *Murphy* v. *H.M. Advocate*, 1975 S.L.T. (Notes) 17, and *Balloch* v. *H.M. Advocate*, 1977 S.L.T. (Notes) 29 (*infra*).

2.   In *Friel* v. *H.M. Advocate*, 1977 S.L.T. (Notes) 21 the High Court applied the fairness test to interrogations conducted by officers of the Customs and Excise.

3.   *Hartley* confirms the supremacy of the fairness test, but does not make any attempt to define what is meant by it. As to the test for unfairness, see *Balloch* and *Boyne, infra,* and *Murphy* v. *H.M. Advocate*, 1975 S.L.T. (Notes) 17.

4.   One should not allow the adoption of a new test of admissibility to obscure the fact that there has been a marked change in the attitude of the courts towards police interrogation of suspects. The courts today take a much more generous view of the practice than formerly. This may be tested by applying the current standards of fairness to the facts of *Chalmers,* or, conversely, applying the *Chalmers* approach to the facts of *Hartley.*

3.   **Balloch v. H.M. Advocate**
1977 S.L.T. (Notes) 29

Balloch was convicted of murder and presented an application for leave to appeal against conviction on the ground that the trial judge had erred in allowing evidence of a statement made by the applicant to police officers. The applicant contended that the statement had been unfairly obtained.

LORD JUSTICE-CLERK (WHEATLEY): " . . . The applicant had been in the police station being interviewed by police officers from 8.30 p.m. He was upset and distressed when he arrived. He was subjected to more or less continuous questioning from at least 10 p.m. until midnight. Certainly from 11 p.m. (if not before) onwards he was under suspicion by the police officers. During this period he was shown or confronted with certain belongings of the deceased, in the words of the police officer who was interviewing him, 'to see what his reaction was to this', and this was a form of bringing pressure to bear on him. Before the incriminating statement was made, the interviewing officer had formed the view that there were inconsistencies in the applicant's statements which aroused his suspicions, and he reported this to his superior, whereupon his superior, about midnight, without administering any caution asked the applicant if he was sure that he was telling the truth. The applicant thereupon broke down, put his hands over his face and said: 'I did it for Marion's sake'. Marion was the wife of the murdered man, and since the previous interviewing had led the police officers to suspect that there was an illicit association between the applicant and the murdered man's wife, this statement was highly significant and incriminatory. Thereafter the applicant was cautioned and charged and made a full confession . . .

The advocate-depute, however, put a different picture on the facts, based on the record of what took place during the interviewing of the applicant, as contained in the interviewing officer's notebook which was a production in the case. The applicant had been asked to come to the police station not as a suspected person, but as a witness who might be able to provide information to the police to enable them to get on to the track of the culprit.

It was he who had telephoned the police to say that the deceased was missing from his home. He lived in the house with the deceased and his wife, and so they were obviously witnesses who had to be interviewed. The body of the murdered man had been badly burned, and it was necessary to get identification of his belongings from the applicant and the wife with a view to establishing his identity. It was not surprising that in these circumstances the applicant and the wife would be upset and distressed, as one would expect innocent persons to be. It was obviously desirable for the police to try to elicit from such witnesses as much information as possible about the murdered man and his movements. The interviews thus began as inquiries involving ordinary witnesses, which by their nature would take some time. The record showed that only a small part of the interview dealt with the incriminatory period. There was nothing to suggest that there was anything unfair in the questioning. What did happen was that the interviewing officer began to find some of the applicant's answers were unsatisfactory about a number of things, such as the relationship between the applicant and the murdered man's wife. When the interviewing officer reported the situation to his superior at midnight nothing had been said by the applicant that would have justified a charge being preferred against him, but the inconsistencies in his account had given rise to some suspicion about him. There was nothing to suggest that the interviewing officer had in any way sought to pressurise the applicant into making a statement. When the superior officer went into the room and asked the applicant if he was sure that he was telling the truth there had been sufficient inconsistencies to warrant that question, but that was not pressurising the applicant to make a confession to the murder or extracting such a confession from him . . .

The law on this subject has been canvassed in many cases, and we find it unnecessary to rehearse the trend of these authorities. Suffice to say, a judge who has heard the evidence regarding the manner in which a challenged statement was made will normally only be justified in withholding the evidence from the jury if he is satisfied on the undisputed relevant evidence that no reasonable jury could hold that the statement had been voluntarily made and had not been extracted by unfair or improper means. Applying that test to the instant case, we are of the opinion that, to say the least, the question was so open that the trial judge acted perfectly correctly in allowing the issue to go to the jury for their determination. That having been done, it is not suggested that proper directions thereanent were not given to the jury by the judge. In point of fact the judge's directions to the jury on this point were wholly in consistence with the law that has been laid down.

Counsel for the applicant made the somewhat startling proposition that in any event a judge should be reluctant to remit such a question to the jury because of the difficulty of a jury understanding what is involved in unfairness. That proposition not only flies in the face of the test which the judge has to apply in deciding whether the evidence should be admitted to or excluded from the jury, but also would appear to desiderate that the judge should usurp the function of the jury in what ex hypothesi has become a question of fact.

On the whole matter, therefore, we are of the opinion that the application for leave to appeal against conviction should be refused."

> The court refused
> the appeal.

NOTES

1.   It is clear from *Balloch* and other authorities cited above that there are two types of unfairness. There is unfairness which is so grave that, as a matter of law, it must be removed from the jury. The test to be applied here is the "no reasonable jury" test. (In *H.M.Advocate* v. *Whitelaw,* 1980 S.L.T. 25, at p. 26, Lord Cameron stated that evidence of statements should go to the jury "unless it is abundantly clear that the rule of fairness and fair dealing have been flagrantly transgressed.") On the other hand, there is unfairness

which is not so flagrant. This is left to the jury to consider, as a matter of fact, along with all the other evidence.

2. Where two possible interpretations can properly be put on the situation, one of which falls into the category of unfairness, and the other into the category of fairness, the judge should leave the determination of the category to the jury: *Murphy* v. *H.M. Advocate*, 1975 S.L.T. (Notes) 17, *per* the Lord Justice-Clerk (Wheatley) at p. 18.

3. The question of fact for the jury in such cases is whether or not there has been "unfairness." If the jury decides that there has been "unfairness" they should then reject the evidence, since fairness is the criterion for admissibility. But how are we to know what the jury decide on this point? And what if the jury think that the evidence was unfairly obtained, but is nonetheless reliable?

4. In effect the jury is being asked to determine the acceptable limits of police practice in relation to the questioning of suspects. Is this properly a task for the jury?

4. **Boyne v. H.M. Advocate**
1980 S.L.T. 56

Boyne was found art and part guilty of murder. The principal evidence against him consisted of certain statements allegedly made by him to the police. At the trial it was argued that in the circumstances of the case the statements had been unfairly obtained. The trial judge, however, directed the jury that there was no evidence from which they could infer that the statements were unfairly obtained. Boyne appealed on the ground, *inter alia*, of misdirection.

LORD JUSTICE-CLERK (WHEATLEY): " . . . In considering the submissions made in support of the various grounds of appeal we consider it appropriate to deal in the first place with the argument that the trial judge misdirected the jury in the case of Boyne in that he excluded from their consideration the question whether the statements made by Boyne to the police had been unfairly obtained. No argument was advanced in the case of Brown that any unfairness was attached to the taking of statements from him, so the point did not arise in his case. The importance of this point in Boyne's case is that the advocate-depute frankly admitted that without these statements no convictions would be warranted against Boyne on charges 4, 6 and 10.

The passage in the judge's charge to the jury which was the basis of this complaint was in these terms: 'There is accordingly, ladies and gentlemen, in this case against Boyne no evidence before you from which you could hold that these statements had been extracted unfairly in the legal sense from Boyne, and I so direct you.'

This passage was interpreted by counsel for Boyne as meaning that the judge was directing the jury as a matter of law that they were not entitled to consider the question of unfairness in the manner in which the statements were obtained or made in determining what evidential value if any, should be attached to them. This, said counsel for Boyne, was a clear misdirection in law. He prayed in aid the final passage in the judgment of Lord Justice-Clerk Thomson in *Chalmers* v. *H.M. Advocate,* 1954 S.L.T. p. 186, where his Lordship said: 'It is impossible to ask a jury to accept as an item of evidence a statement made by an accused while preventing it from considering the circumstances under which it was made . . . The jury's problem is to find out the truth; in their search for the truth a statement made freely by the accused may be of immense signification, but the degree of the significance must depend for the jury on their view of its spontaneity.' We in no way differ from what the Lord Justice-Clerk there said, but we cannot accept the wide interpretation which counsel for Boyne put on it. He submitted that once the judge had admitted the evidence about the taking of a statement it had to be left to the jury, under proper direction, in every case to decide on their view of the spontaneity of the statement whether the statement had been fairly obtained. In our opinion that passage should be regarded against the background of dispute as to the circumstances in which the statement was made or had been obtained. It should not be read as depriving the judge of the power to direct the jury as a matter of law that there was no evidence on which they could find that the rules of fairness had been infringed. Counsel for Boyne argued that it was not competent for a judge to make this decision where there was evidence of unfairness. Where there is evidence on which a jury, properly directed, could hold that there was unfairness, this is so. Where, however, there is no such evidence, the judge is entitled to direct the jury accordingly as a matter of law. That will turn on the circumstances of the particular case.

We now turn to consider the circumstances in which the judge's words which were the subject of complaint were uttered. The judge clearly was of the view that counsel for Boyne had represented to the jury that it was sufficient to establish unfairness that there was evidence to show that the statements made by Boyne resulted from questioning by the police and that this in itself rendered the statements inadmissible in evidence. Counsel's recollection was that this was not the submission which he made. We do not have the extended notes of what counsel said to the jury, but we are always prepared to take into consideration what responsible counsel who conducted the case at the trial recollects was said. We accordingly deal with the matter on the basis that the judge may have misunderstood what counsel's submission to the jury was. What the judge did, however, was to give the jury the law on the subject of when questioning of a suspect (as Boyne then was) is permissible and when it is not, in conformity with a line of recent decisions . . .

Having given these general directions in law, which were in no way criticised as being wrong in any respect, he went on to consider the facts of the instant case. He told the jury: 'in the case of Boyne in this case no objection was taken to any line of questioning by the police of Boyne, no evidence was led which showed that the police officers had strayed into the realm of cross-examination or interrogation or illegal methods.

It would have been perfectly possible for the accused to give evidence on this matter, but he did not do so, and he did not say that there was anything unfair about the giving of these statements or that anything unfair had been done'. It was at that point that he said: 'There is accordingly in this case against Boyne no evidence before you from which you could hold that these statements had been extracted unfairly in the legal sense from Boyne, and I so direct you'. He followed this up immediately with the following direction: 'The advocate-depute was quite right in referring to these statements which in his case are simply part of the evidence in the case, and are to be treated by you as any other piece of evidence. You would of course be quite entitled to consider all the circumstances in which they were taken, his youth and the length of time and all that sort of thing, but these criticisms in the circumstances would go to the quality of the evidence in the statements and not to their competence'.

The points taken by counsel for the appellant to support his claim of unfairness were founded not on any direct evidence but on inferences to be drawn from the youth of the appellant (he was 16 years old at the time), the length of the questioning and the hours at which the questioning took place. There was, however, no evidence, least of all from the appellant, that these factors had any effect on him in giving the statements or influenced him in any way. As we have already said, each case turns on its own special circumstances, and in the instant case we are of the opinion that, having regard to the factors alluded to by him above and the points taken by counsel and our observations thereon, the judge was entitled to hold that there was no evidence on which a reasonable jury could find that the statements had been extracted unfairly from Boyne in the legal sense."

The court refused this ground of appeal. Appeal allowed on other grounds.

NOTES

1. This case suggests that unfairness cannot be inferred merely from the circumstances in which the questioning took place or the statements were made. There must be evidence that these factors influenced the accused or had some effect on him.

2. The case is an illustration of the tendency to suggest that it is for the accused to show unfairness. It is submitted that this is quite contrary to principle. If a party wishes to rely on evidence the onus is on that party to establish that it is admissible evidence. There is no onus on the other party to demonstrate that it is inadmissible. The onus is on the Crown to lead evidence that the confession was freely and voluntarily given. (*Thompson* v. *H.M. Advocate,* 1968 J.C. 61, *per* the Lord Justice-General at p. 66.)

(iii)   The trial within a trial

The "trial-within-a-trial" procedure was adopted into Scots law by the High Court in *Chalmers (supra)*. The Lord Justice-General outlined the procedure as follows:

"When objection is taken to a line of evidence upon the alleged unfairness of the methods used in eliciting it, the jury ought to be excluded, and the evidence bearing upon the attendant circumstances should be heard by the Judge in the absence of the jury, including, if so advised, the evidence of the accused himself. If, in the light of such evidence and argument, the Judge sustains the objection, the jury should be told nothing about the matter. If on the other hand the Judge repels the objection, the case will proceed in the presence and hearing of the jury, and, if either prosecution or defence chose to do so, the evidence bearing upon the attendant circumstances can be made the subject of examination and cross-examination a second time. In the end of the day it will be for the Judge to direct the jury that, in considering the weight and value of the evidence to which objection has been taken and repelled, it is for the jury to have regard to the attendant circumstances as proved before them, and, in so far as they may consider that the evidence objected to is not to be relied upon by reason of the circumstances in which it arose, to discount it or exclude it from their deliberations."

The procedure has, however, met with increasing hostility. In *Thompson (supra)* the Lord Justice-General suggested that the procedure laid down in *Chalmers* might have to be reconsidered. This has not happened, but a series of recent decisions suggests that it will only exceptionally be employed. In *H.M. Advocate v. Mair*, 1982 S.L.T. 471 Lord Hunter stated (at p. 473):

"In my view the procedure of a trial within a trial has a number of unsatisfactory and rather dangerous features and may conflict with the normal practice in our criminal procedure that the whole evidence should be led in the presence of the jury. Making the assumption for this purpose that the procedure may in appropriate circumstances survive as a competent procedure, I am disposed to think that the procedure . . . is one which at best should only be used sparingly and in very special circumstances."

Lord Cameron in *H.M.Advocate v. Whitelaw*, 1980 S.L.T. (Notes) 25 suggested a rather more precise formula for determining the appropriateness of the trial within a trial procedure (at p. 26):

"I have never been in favour of any extension of the practice of a trial within a trial unless . . . the circumstances already established or admitted are such as to be prima facie indicative of unfairness towards an accused who is in the hands of the police and of transgression of the fundamental rules of fairness which lie at the root of our criminal procedure."

In that case the grounds of objection to the alleged confession were "(1) the age of the accused [16]; (2) the presence of more than one senior police officer; (3) having indicated that he did not wish the presence of his father the accused was not at that stage informed he was entitled to the presence of a solicitor; and (4) he was not given a second caution after the police officer had informed him that he had reason to believe he was responsible for the offence." His Lordship held that these circumstances did not warrant the use of a trial within a trial (*i.e.* that they did not amount to a prima facie case of unfairness).

(iv) Statements while in detention under the 1980 Act

Criminal Justice (Scotland) Act 1980

"2.—. . . (5) Where a person is detained under subsection (1) above, a constable may—

(*a*) put questions to him in relation to the suspected offence:

Provided that this paragraph shall be without prejudice to any existing rule of law as regards the admissibility in evidence of any answer given."

NOTE

The relationship between section 2(5), the warning under section 2(7) and the common law rules regarding admissibility of statements is discussed in *Tonge* v. *H.M. Advocate, infra.*

(v) The significance of the caution

Tonge and Others v. H.M. Advocate
1982 S.L.T. 506; 1982 S.C.C.R. 313

During the investigation of an alleged rape the appellants were interviewed by the police. Tonge and Gray were interviewed while detained under section 2 of the 1980 Act, and Jack when he attended voluntarily at a police office. During the course of these interviews all three appellants made self-incriminating statements. Immediately prior to making these statements Tonge and Gray had received warnings in terms of section 2(7) of the 1980 Act (*supra,* p. 161), but neither received a full common law caution at that time. It was disputed whether Jack had received a caution at all, and if he received one, whether it was a common law caution or a warning under section 2(7). Consequent upon these statements the appellants were cautioned and charged with rape.

At the trial objections to these statements were taken on behalf of all three appellants, but all were repelled. Tonge and Jack denied making the statements. Gray did not deny his statement but disputed the police version of how it was made. In his charge to the jury the presiding judge (Lord Ross) directed them that if they were satisfied that the statements were made, and were freely made, and that they had been accurately recorded, they would be entitled to accept them. He also stated that there was "no hard and fast rule about giving of a caution" before a suspect was charged and that whether a caution should be given depends upon whether, in all circumstances, fairness required that a caution should be given, either at the outset or after the individual had begun to incriminate himself. So far as Jack was concerned, Lord Ross referred to a conflict between the police evidence that a caution was given and Jack's statement that no caution was given. He did not, however, refer to the confusion as to whether a full caution was given or only a section 2(7) warning. On appeal against conviction:

LORD JUSTICE-GENERAL (EMSLIE): " . . . For the appellants Tonge and Gray their appeal against conviction is presented upon the ground that the trial judge erred in repelling the objections to the admissibility of their alleged voluntary statements. In light of the evidence before him as to the circumstances in which these alleged statements were made it was plain that they had been unfairly obtained, and the trial judge should have held them to be inadmissible on that account.

[His Lordship outlined the evidence relating to the offences and continued:]

As it turned out the only persons who found themselves in the dock charged with the alleged rape of the complainer with others unknown were those who, it was said, had made voluntary statements to the police. It is perfectly clear in the case of all three appellants that their alleged voluntary statements were of critical importance. Without these statements there was insufficient evidence against each to support conviction.

I come now to the circumstances in which the statements allegedly made by Tonge and Gray were obtained. It will be remembered that objection was taken on behalf of each to the admissibility of the alleged statements, the contents of which were self-incriminating, and that after a trial within a trial in each case the trial judge repelled the objection and allowed evidence of the alleged statements to go to the jury, leaving it to the jury to decide whether or not they had been fairly obtained.

The first chapter in the circumstances leading up to the emission of the alleged incriminating statement by Gray began when he was detained by two police officers who called at his home. According to these officers the first thing they did was to caution him at common law—a caution which not only advised him of his right to silence but warned him that anything he chose to say would be taken down and might be used in evidence. The detention was, however, in purported exercise of the entirely new powers of detention and inquiry conferred upon the police by s. 2 of the Criminal Justice (Scotland) Act 1980, and the evidence was that the requirements of that section were then fulfilled by the detaining officers. For the purpose of this appeal the provisions of s. 2(7) are of particular importance: 'A person detained under subsection (1) above shall be under no obligation to answer any question other than to give his name and address, and a constable shall so inform him both on so detaining him and on arrival at the police station or other premises.' It will be observed at once that while this subsection requires the giving of a warning to the detainee at each of the two separate stages of detention it does not in terms direct the constable to inform the detainee that anything he may choose to say in answer to questions or otherwise may be taken down and used in evidence. It is to be observed also that while subs. (5) authorises the constable to question a person who has been detained in relation to the suspected offence and, by necessary implication, to his own part in it, that subsection contains this very important proviso: 'Provided that this paragraph shall be without prejudice to any existing rule of law as regards the admissibility in evidence of any answer given.' The position is, accordingly, that the admissibility in evidence of anything said by a detainee falls to be determined by the common law and where the common law and proper practice would require, in the interests of fairness and fair dealing, that a full common law caution be given, the omission to give it before questioning a suspect who has received no more than the limited warning prescribed by s. 2(7), will, at the very least, on that account alone, place the admissibility of any evidence elicited from the suspect in peril. The giving of the statutory warning does not, accordingly, relieve any constable who intends to exercise the power to question, either at the time of detention or at any time while it is in force, from the obligation to observe the ordinary rules of law and proper practice which are designed to secure fairness to the suspect. In this case, as I have said, it appears that at the time Gray was detained he was at that stage given a caution in common law terms.

The second chapter began when Gray reached the police station at about 6.20 p.m. He was then given the statutory warning required by s. 2(7) and the s. 2 procedure was again carried out. He was searched and placed in a cell.

I now come to the third and crucial chapter of events relating to Gray. At about 6.40 p.m. two police officers, Detective Sergeant McMorran, accompanied by Constable Jenkins, the investigating officer, entered the cell. Until that moment they had not seen Gray at all. Their purpose was to question him. Detective Sergeant McMorran did not think that there was enough evidence against him to charge him and frankly admitted that it was in his interest to get some more evidence from Gray himself in order to be able to do so. What happened was this. They introduced themselves, explained that they were making inquiries into the alleged offence for which he had been detained, and asked him for his name and address. Gray was then, according to Constable Jenkins, 'fairly nervous'. Constable Jenkins then accused him of complicity in the crime. What he actually said was that they 'had reason to believe he was responsible, along with others, for the crime'. Gray then started to speak, beginning with the words: 'I'd like to get it all cleared up.' He then went on to make a fairly long statement of a self-incriminating character without, it was said, any interruptions by either officer and, according to their evidence, he was asked no questions. There were, however, they admitted, pauses from time to time while Gray gathered his thoughts. The important feature in the whole transaction was that although the police officers freely conceded that in dealing with a suspect in Gray's position before s. 2 of the Act of 1980 came into force, they would first have administered a full common law caution and would certainly have administered such a caution to a suspect as soon as he indicated that he wished to make a statement, they did not caution Gray at all before accusing him of the crime, immediately after he declared that he would like to get it all cleared up, or at any stage during the making of the relatively long statement when it was evident that he was almost certainly going to incriminate himself. Their reason for not cautioning Gray was that they assumed that he had received a full common law caution when he was detained in terms of s. 2.

The events leading up to the taking of the alleged voluntary statement by Tonge began when he was detained under the powers conferred by s. 2 of the Act of 1980 and taken to the police station where he remained in statutory detention. By this time the police had obtained the alleged statement by Gray. In Tonge's case there is no question of his having received a common law caution at any time in connection with his detention. All that he received at the two separate stages of detention was the limited information provided for in s. 2(7). He was, in short, merely informed that he was under no obligation to answer any questions other than to give his name and address.

In due course Detective Sergeant McMorran and Constable Jenkins went to see Tonge. Their only purpose, they said, was to charge him with the alleged crime of rape. They identified themselves as officers investigating the crime for which he was being detained and asked him for his name and address. They then asked him if he understood that he was being detained in connection with an alleged rape of a 22-year-old female in a field which they described. Instead of proceeding there and then to caution him and to charge him in formal terms—for that was their only purpose, they said,—what they did instead, without cautioning him at all, was to accuse him of the crime which had been described to him. The formula used by Constable Jenkins was: 'I believe you are responsible along with others for doing this', and he agreed that he would not normally say anything of the kind to a person he was about to caution and charge. The evidence of the two police officers was that this provoked an immediate response, for Tonge at once said, 'Aye, wait a minute, boys. You've got it all wrong', and proceeded, without interruption or questioning, to make a relatively long explanation which was self-incriminating. Tonge's first sentence which I have quoted indicated to the officers that Tonge was about to make a statement. They agreed that if this had happened in the case of a suspect in Tonge's position the practice would have been to have the statement which he obviously intended to make taken by officers unconnected with the investigation. Whether or not that practice was followed, a full caution would always be given and Detective Sergeant McMorran agreed that in such circumstances a full caution was essential. In the case of Tonge, however, they did not caution him after he had uttered his first sentence and they did not caution him at any stage thereafter even when it appeared that he was likely to incriminate himself. There was ample opportunity for the giving of a full caution at any of these stages. Why was no caution given? It was not given, they say, at any time while the officers were with Tonge because they assumed, wrongly as it turned out, that he had been fully cautioned in common law terms when he was detained under s. 2 of the Act. All that I need add is that when Detective Sergeant McMorran was asked why, after introducing themselves to Tonge, they did not immediately do what they had come to do—charge Tonge—his answer was that they were not given a chance.

For the appellants Gray and Tonge the short, sharp submission was that upon the undisputed relevant evidence which I have just set out the trial judge should have sustained the objections to the admissibility of the alleged statements. In the particular circumstances the failure of Detective Sergeant McMorran and Constable Jenkins to give to Gray and Tonge a full common law caution was fatal to the admissibility of their alleged statements in evidence. The long list of cases beginning with *Chalmers* v. *H.M. Advocate* shows that in questions of admissibility of such statements each case will depend upon its own facts and circumstances and that the decision must turn upon whether or not there has been unfairness on the part of the police. Self-incriminating statements which are induced from prime suspects by unfair actions on the part of police officers can be regarded as neither spontaneous nor voluntary and are thus inadmissible. In most cases it will be necessary for a trial judge to allow the alleged statements, and the evidence as to the circumstances in which they were made to go before the jury, so that they may, under proper directions, resolve the issue of fairness or unfairness. There are circumstances, however, in which the trial judge himself ought to withhold such evidence from a jury.

[His Lordship referred to the opinion of the Lord Justice-Clerk in *Balloch* v. *H.M. Advocate* (*supra*) and the opinion of Lord Cameron in *H.M. Advocate* v. *Whitelaw* (*supra*) and continued:]

In the present case it is plain that on the relevant undisputed evidence no reasonable jury could have held the alleged statements of Gray and Tonge had been voluntary and had not been extracted by unfair or improper means. It was, . . . abundantly clear that the rules of fairness and fair dealing had been transgressed. A wholly new chapter began when Detective Sergeant McMorran and Constable Jenkins approached these two appellants in detention. They had little or no evidence that the alleged crime had been committed or that either Gray or Tonge had been among its perpetrators. They hoped to get such evidence from Gray himself and it is an inescapable inference from the evidence that they hoped for the same response from Tonge. What they did was to accuse Gray and Tonge of participation in the alleged crime without first cautioning either. This was

clearly calculated to provoke a response and the opening words of the
response which the accusation elicited from each demonstrated that each
was about to make a statement, possibly self-incriminating. Even then they
did not caution either man and they did not caution either thereafter when
it clearly began to appear that he was, in fact, about to incriminate himself.
In these circumstances the unfairness of the police officers was manifest and
it is clear from their own evidence that proper practice, prior to 1980,
demanded the giving of a caution at least once to persons in the position of
Gray and Tonge. Without their alleged statements there was not sufficient
evidence to warrant their conviction and since the verdicts proceeded upon
evidence which was inadmissible there has been a miscarriage of justice.

For the Crown the learned advocate-depute reminded us of the common
law caution and the s. 2 warning given to Gray at the separate stages of his
detention and of the s. 2 warning which had been given to Tonge. The
existence or absence of a caution at common law when each was interviewed later by the Detective Sergeant and Constable Jenkins was, he
argued, merely one of the circumstances which it would be proper to take
into account in judging the question of fairness. The trial judge was
perfectly correct when he decided that it should be left to the jury to judge
that question and to determine under his directions whether each statement
was truly spontaneous and voluntary. This in short was not one of the
exceptional cases of the kind mentioned in *Balloch* and in *Whitelaw*.

The problem faced by the trial judge was an extremely difficult one. The
circumstances which he had to consider were complicated, if not actively
bedevilled, by what was done to these two appellants in purported exercise
of the powers newly conferred by s. 2—a section which, inexplicably, does
not require the detainee to be warned not only that he is not obliged to say
anything, in answer to questions or otherwise, but that if he does so, what
he chooses to say will be taken down and may be used in evidence. In the
case of one of them a full caution appears to have been given when he was
first detained and yet when he reached the police station he was merely
given the limited information prescribed by s. 2(7). In the case of the other,
he was told only what s. 2(7) says he must be told. It is, I think, easy to
understand why the trial judge, in the urgency of the trial, considered that it
might be going too far, too fast, to give effect to the defence submission that
he should take the bold and irreversible course of ruling that the alleged
statements were inadmissible in evidence. We, however, have had the
advantage, which he could not enjoy, of reading closely, and rereading, in
the extended notes precisely what was the course of events before the
alleged statements were made, and of examining the questions of admissibility in light of a very full and excellent argument on both sides of the bar.
Making full use of that special advantage, I have come to be of the opinion
that the alleged statements of Gray and Tonge were clearly inadmissible
and should have been withheld from the jury. This was, in my opinion, one
of those exceptional cases in which, upon the undisputed relevant evidence,
it can be said that no reasonable jury could have held that the statements
had been voluntary and had not been induced by unfair or improper means
(vide *Balloch* v. *H.M. Advocate*). In my judgment upon a close scrutiny of

the notes of evidence it is abundantly clear that the rules of fairness and fair dealing were flagrantly transgressed (vide *H.M. Advocate* v. *Whitelaw*). I do not say that in no circumstances will a statement by a detainee (a suspect within the meaning of s. 2(1) be inadmissible merely because, when it was made, he had not received a full caution. What I do say is that the failure of the investigating officers to caution Gray and Tonge in the special circumstances of this case is fatal to the contention that the rules of fair dealing and fairness were properly observed.

In Gray's case the hope of the two officers was that when they saw him he would provide what was conspicuously lacking, namely, self-incriminating evidence. He was already impressed with the character of a suspect within the meaning of s. 2(1) and they undoubtedly approached him with that hope in their hearts, and with the intention of questioning him if necessary. It is of critical importance to notice what they did. They accused him of participation in the crime. Now, as is pointed out in Walkers' *Law of Evidence in Scotland*, p. 39, para. 45: 'It is proper practice that, when a person is charged with a crime, the caution should be given, since, without it, the reading of the charge may be interpreted by the accused as a question, or as an invitation to reply, in which case any statement then made is not spontaneous and voluntary.' I go further and say that the proper practice is now so long and so well entrenched that it may be taken that a full caution before a charge is made is a requirement of the law itself. The reading of a charge is calculated to provoke a response from the accused and it is quite essential that he should know, in advance, of his right of silence, and of the use which may be made of any response which he chooses to make. To charge an accused person without cautioning him is to put pressure upon him which may induce a response and I have no doubt that by accusing Gray, although not in the formal language of a charge, the accusation was clearly calculated, as a formal charge is calculated, to induce a response from the person accused. The accusation placed pressure upon Gray and I am persuaded that since no caution was administered before it was made, it is impossible to regard the statement made in response to it as spontaneous and voluntary. It was plainly induced by the accusation and in the circumstances was induced by unfair means. It cannot be left out of account either that no caution was administered when the first sentence uttered by Gray made it plain that he intended to make a statement, and that no caution was administered when it became obvious that he was about to incriminate himself. As the evidence of the police officers demonstrated, it would have been proper practice to caution a suspect in Gray's position before he was allowed to proceed with a statement and, in my opinion, nothing in s. 2 of the Act of 1980 excuses compliance with that practice.

In Tonge's case I reach the same conclusion. Tonge, who had not received at any stage of the detention procedure a full caution in common law terms, was seen by the investigating officers with the single purpose of charging him. Had they carried out that purpose, they would have required to caution him. They did not do so. What they did, without cautioning him, was to accuse him of the crime, just as they had accused Gray of the crime. This, as Constable Jenkins agreed, was not a usual thing to do where the sole purpose of the encounter was to charge the suspect. Be that as it may the accusation was made without caution, no caution was administered when the first sentence of Tonge's response demonstrated that he was about to make a statement, and no caution was administered at any point while the alleged statement was being made. It is impossible to accept that the officers did not 'get a chance' to charge Tonge and the excuse for not cautioning him was the unfounded assumption that he had already received a full caution when he was detained under s. 2. For all the reasons which led me to hold that the alleged statement by Gray was inadmissible I also hold that the alleged statement by Tonge was inadmissible and should not have been left for consideration by the jury.

In light of what I have said I would allow the appeals of Gray and Tonge and quash their conviction. . . .

. . . . Before leaving this case, which has illustrated the problems and confusion created by the provisions of s. 2 of the Act of 1980, I would strongly urge police officers throughout Scotland who proceed to accuse a detainee or to question him or to take from him a voluntary statement, to rely not at all upon the efficacy of the warning described in s. 2(7), and to appreciate that if any use is to be made in evidence of anything said by a detainee in these circumstances the ordinary rules of fairness and fair dealing which have been developed by the common law should be strictly observed. The wise course will be, inter alia, to administer to the detainee in the events which I have mentioned a full caution in common law terms. The omission to give such a caution will, by itself, at the very least place the admissibility of anything said by the detainee in peril and the appeals by Gray and Tonge demonstrate circumstances in which the omission of the interviewing officer to caution these men in such terms was fatal."

LORD CAMERON: ". . . In expressing my concurrence with your Lordship in the chair I would only venture to add certain observations of my own on the provisions and operation of s. 2 of the Act of 1980. It is not a happily drafted section, and in particular it is not easy to understand the reasons which induced the legislature to enact subs. (7). The section, by subs. (1), confers new powers on the police of detention for a limited period of a person suspected on reasonable grounds of having committed or of committing an offence punishable by imprisonment and, during that period, to interrogate a suspect, search, and take fingerprints and other impressions, 'for the purpose of facilitating the carrying out of investigations—(a) into the offence; and (b) as to whether criminal proceedings should be instigated against the person'. The right to interrogate a suspect is contained in subs. (5) which provides that a constable 'may—(a) put questions to him in relation to the suspected offence'. The exercise of this power however is conditioned by the provisions of subs. (7) which provides that a person detained under s subs. (1): 'shall be under no obligation to answer any questions other than to give his name and address, and a constable shall so inform him both on so detaining him and on arrival at the police station or other premises'—to which he is to be taken 'as quickly as is reasonably practicable'. Now whatever else subs. (7) may mean what it provides is neither an alternative to nor a substitute for the giving of a caution in the well-recognised and regular form in circumstances where the law and proper practice demands or requires. It is not indeed immediately apparent what useful purpose this innovative and possibly confusing provision is designed to serve, as the proviso to s. 5(a) states that 'this paragraph [sic] shall be without prejudice to any existing rule of law as regards the admissibility in evidence of any answer given'. This, in my opinion, means and can only mean that nothing in s. 2 alters the pre-existing rules of law or of safe and proper practice in the matters of cautioning persons who may be questioned in the course of police investigations of crimes or suspected crimes or at the time when a person is being charged with a crime or offence. It is of course well established that police officers are entitled to question a suspect as to his possible complicity in a crime which they are investigating, and that his replies will be admissible in evidence if they have not been extracted or compelled by unfair or improper means including threats, intimidations, offers of inducements, or cross-examination designed or intended to extract incriminating replies, but it is equally well recognised that in the case of one on whom suspicion of responsibility or complicity has centred, in order that his replies should be admissible in evidence, it is proper practice that any further questioning should be preceded by a caution in the common form. The proviso to subs. (5) is of such wide generality that it leaves no doubt in my opinion that the warning specified in such limited terms which is required to be given in compliance with the provisions of subs. (7), is not and cannot be in substitution for the cautions which the law and practice require to be given as a condition precedent to the admissibility of evidence obtained from questioning of a suspect or the replies to a charge made by an accused, but is of an entirely independent character which does not in any way determine the admissibility of evidence obtained by the questioning which the provisions of s. 2 permits.

It would appear to me to follow from this that in the case of a suspect of the kind figured in subs. (1) it would be wise and proper practice that he should receive a caution in recognised form before questions are put to him, in order that no conflict may arise as to the admissibility in evidence of any replies given by him in the course of such questioning. This conclusion appears to me all the more necessary when it is kept in view that the whole basis on which the right to detain or to question rests on the very definite character of the police officers' suspicion as set out in subs. (1).

Apart however from the question as to what is required to make admissible in evidence any replies made by a suspect detained under the powers given by s. 2 to questions by a police officer in course of his authorised investigation, there are two other matters to which I would refer in relation to the actions of the police officers concerned in the investigations in this case. The first is as to the regular and well-known practice of police officers in taking a voluntary statement from one either suspected or actually charged with a crime, and the second is the rule of law which requires a caution to be given to an accused when a formal charge is made if his reply to the charge is to be admissible in evidence—either for or against him. The regular and proper practice when an accused or suspect indicates or intimates he wishes to make a voluntary statement is that the statement should be taken by officers unconnected with the particular investigation, and authenticated by the signatures of the officers concerned and the maker of the statement himself. In the case of the appellants, although the detailed and incriminating statements ascribed to them are recorded in police notebooks, no attempt was made to have them given to or taken by independent officers or even to have what is recorded in the officers' notebooks signed by the appellants themselves. The investigating officers in this case were fully aware of this proper practice and of the reasons for it, so that it cannot be argued that what is recorded in their notebooks and testified to in evidence were at the time regarded as 'voluntary statements' of the kind I have referred to.

As to the second, in my opinion it is a requirement, which goes beyond one of proper practice and is now a requirement of law, that when preferring a charge against an accused, police officers should caution him as to the possible use to be made of any reply made to that charge. Now the circumstances and manner in which the investigating officers proceeded in the case of all the appellants have already been fully set out by your Lordship, and I have no doubt that not only had the officers determined to prefer charges of rape even before they proceeded to interview the appellants, but also that their immediate intimation of their purpose and intention was in a form which, while lacking the precise formality of a charge, was no more and no less than the levelling, in words which were indistinguishable from those of the formal charge which immediately followed the 'voluntary statement', of a detailed accusation of rape—but one which in the case of the detainees Gray and Tonge was admittedly not preceded by a caution. At that stage of the inquiry there were at the least serious grounds for doubt as to whether the police had sufficient evidence on which to justify making a charge, and it was thus a matter of the highest importance that the appellants should be induced to make some statements of an incriminatory character. In offering the explanation for their presence and the subject and purpose of their investigations the police officers concerned did so in a manner which was accusatorial in form and substance and, whether by design or inadvertence it matters not, would be likely to evoke from the person addressed some form of immediate response, explanatory or exculpatory or incriminating. That being so I am clearly of opinion that in the case of Gray and Tonge their statements, in the absence of a precedent caution, were inadmissible in evidence."

Appeals allowed.

NOTES

1.   A proper caution should inform the suspect that he or she is not obliged to say anything (*cf. Von* v. *H.M. Advocate, supra*) but that anything he or she says will be taken down and may be given in evidence (*Tonge*). It has been held in England that it is improper to tell the suspect that anything taken down may be given in evidence

against him, since this might discourage a suspect from making any statement, including one consistent with innocence.

2. The decision in *Tonge* affects the use of the caution at two distinct "stages"—suspicion and charge. So far as the latter is concerned it is now a "requirement of the law itself" that before a formal charge is made the police must caution the suspect. Failure to observe this requirement (presumably) renders inadmissible any statement made in response to a charge.

So far as the stage of suspicion prior to charge is concerned, the practical effect of *Tonge* will be (a) to ensure that the police administer a full caution to suspects before questioning them, and (b) to make section 2(7) of the 1980 Act redundant, except to the extent that a *detainee* should be warned that he or she is required to give a (genuine) name and address.

3. Certain possible qualifications to *Tonge* should be noted:

 (a) The court did not say that a failure to caution a suspect will render any statement inadmissible, but merely that such statements will normally be imperilled. Prior to *Tonge* the view has been that the absence of a caution was merely a factor to be taken into account in determining the fairness issue: *Miln* v. *Cullen*, 1967 J.C. 21, *per* Lord Strachan at p. 27. The difference between *Tonge* and *Miln* v. *Cullen* is, therefore, rather one of degree than of principle.

 (b) Technically, the decision could be restricted to the admissibility of statements made in response to accusation of guilt rather than questioning. (Such accusations are, of course, encouraged by the provisions of section 2(4) of the 1980 Act.) However, the general tone of their Lordships' opinions makes it clear that any form of approach by the police to a suspect—whether by accusation or questioning—should, as a matter of fairness, be preceded by a caution.

 (c) It could be argued that much of what is said applies only to detainees (which was the status of Tonge and Gray, but not Jack). However, since detainees under section 2 of the 1980 Act are only a particular form of suspect (*cf.* the Lord Justice-General, *supra* p. 183) this seems unlikely. In any case, there would have been little relevance to the misdirection in Jack's case if a distinction were to be drawn between detainees and other suspects.

4. Lord Cameron alludes to the "proper practice" of statements being taken by police officers unconnected with the investigation. It is not clear what sanction is attached to breach of this practice, though it may well be a matter to be weighed in the balance of fairness.

5. Since it will now normally be necessary for the police to caution suspects, it once again becomes necessary to ascertain who fall into this category. Detainees necessarily do so, but clearly they do not exhaust the category. As to this, see Lord Justice-Clerk Thomson in *Chalmers, supra.*

6. Of course much of what is said in *Tonge* (and *Von* for that matter) depends on the assumption that a suspect's response to police questioning might be conditioned by his being informed of his rights. This is a very difficult matter to assess, but research carried out for the Royal Commission on Criminal Procedure in England suggests that in only a minority of cases does the caution have the effect of encouraging the suspect to adhere to his right of silence: Royal Commission on Criminal Procedure, Research Study No. 4, "Police Interrogation—An Observational Study in Four Police Stations" (Softley, *et al.*), p. 74. (The actual figures were 2 out of 106 suspects, or less than 2 per cent.)

7. Jack's appeal was allowed on the ground that the presiding judge's failure to remind the jury that there was a dispute as to whether Jack had received a caution or a section 2(7) warning, constituted a misdirection which amounted to a miscarriage of justice.

(vi) Tape recording police questioning

Thomson Committee (Second Report)

"**7.13** We *recommend* that it should be competent for the Crown to lead evidence of statements made by a suspect before arrest in answer to police questioning. We further *recommend* that the admissibility of such evidence should be subject to the following qualifications:

c. Interrogation of suspects in police stations must be recorded on tape. Tapes cannot easily be provided for questioning which occurs outside a police station. Our object is to provide a safeguard for persons being interrogated in the privacy of a police station and also to protect the police against unjustified allegations. We therefore do not suggest that interrogations conducted elsewhere need be recorded on tape.

7.21. . .

b. Answers made to police questions by a suspect
In paragraph 7.13c. we recommend that interrogation of suspects in police stations must be recorded on tape. We carried out a practical experiment with simulated interrogation of a suspect by police officers and found the result to be technically satisfactory. While we accept that there will of course always be difficulties with inarticulate suspects or with those who use unfamiliar dialects, the quality of reproduction was sufficiently good to satisfy us that it is practicable to obtain on tape an adequate record of

interrogations. Furthermore we confidently expect that the availability of more sophisticated equipment will improve the standard of reproduction and that with training the technique of interrogation by police officers will also improve, so that vague or ill-expressed statements are not allowed to go unexplained. The cost of tape recording is not prohibitive. . .

The presence of a tape recorder may upset some persons, but on balance we consider that the vast majority of persons will be reassured by knowing that anything that is said will be accurately recorded. The fact that the police know that the interview is being recorded on tape will tend to reduce the chances of interrogation being conducted with any impropriety. We think that tampering is unlikely but to reduce that possibility we *recommend* that the tape be sealed and placed in the custody of the procurator fiscal as soon as possible after the conclusion of the interrogation. If the interrogation does not take place within a police station, and a tape recorder is not used, a police officer will require to rely on his notebook.

7.23 It is appreciated that our proposals rely to a large extent on the effectiveness of tape recorders. We realise that all or part of a police interrogation may not be recorded through failure of a tape recorder. The question arises whether or not an account of any unrecorded interrogation given by a police officer from memory and notes made at the time or immediately afterwards, should be admissible in evidence. We consider that it should not be admissible, as we feel strongly that particularly accurate recording of interrogation in a police station is essential as a safeguard to all the persons concerned. The same considerations do not apply to a voluntary statement which, although recorded on tape, will also be recorded in a written document authenticated by the accused. Such a statement should be admissible in evidence, even though the tape recorder has failed. We accordingly so *recommend.*"

NOTES

1. The provision of an objective record of what took place during an interview with a suspect was seen by the Thomson Committee as an essential safeguard for those questioned while in detention (and, for that matter, for the police conducting that interrogation). The government, however, have refused to implement this recommendation in statutory form, but have since 1 May 1980 been running an experiment in various police stations throughout Scotland in the use of tape recorders. There can be little doubt that the repeated extensions of the experiment are due to the government dragging its feet in response to police opposition, rather than to any technical problems encountered.

2. The admissibility of such tape recordings has been discussed by the High Court on two occasions: *H.M. Advocate* v. *McFadden*, High Court, Perth, 12 August 1980, unreported (see (1981) 56 SCOLAG Bul. 260) and *H.M. Advocate* v. *Anderson*, High Court,

Stirling, 17 March 1981, unreported. For a discussion of these cases, and the general problems surrounding the admissibility of such recordings, see Gane, "Tape Recording Police Interrogations" (1981) 57 SCOLAG Bul. 272 and 59 SCOLAG Bul. 304. For an examination of the practical problems involved, see *Report of the Departmental Committee on the Feasibility of an Experiment in Tape-Recording of Police Interrogations*, Cmnd. 6630 (1976) and Royal Commission on Criminal Procedure, Research Study No. 8, *Police Interrogation: Tape Recording*.

b. Search

The powers of the police to search the person of an arrestee or detainee were discussed in Chap. 4. This section discusses the remaining powers of the police to search persons and premises with or without a warrant.

(i) Search under warrant

(A) THE SCOPE OF THE WARRANT
General and unspecific warrants are said to be illegal. But this must be read subject to (1) the qualification that they are illegal only if there is no safeguard against oppression in their execution, and (2) the tendency of the courts to allow specific warrants to be used as general warrants.

1. Bell v. Black and Morrison
(1865) 5 Irv. 57

During the investigation of an alleged criminal conspiracy involving a man called Pringle the respondents, joint procurators fiscal for the county of Fife, obtained information suggesting that other persons, including Bell, were involved in the conspiracy. The respondents presented a petition for a search warrant in which they stated: "That the petitioners are informed, and have reason to believe, that written documents and other articles referring to, and connected with, said conspiracy and threatening letters are in the possession of the said John Bell, ... and as it is necessary, for the purpose of said precognition, to recover and take possession of the same, the present application for warrant to search becomes necessary."

The prayer of the petition was "to grant warrant to officers of Court . . . to search the dwelling-house, repositories, and premises . . . occupied by the said John Bell . . . for the said written documents, and all other articles tending to establish guilt, or participation in said crimes, and to take possession thereof".

The warrant having been granted and executed, Bell brought a bill for its suspension.

LORD JUSTICE-CLERK (INGLIS): "There are some marked and important peculiarities in this petition and warrant (for the warrant, as we read it, is granted simply in terms of the prayer of the petition). In the first place, the warrant is granted against five different persons, none of whom is under a charge for any crime. It is stated in the petition that the persons against whom the warrant is asked are shown, by documents recovered in the course of the precognition against Pringle, to have been engaged in the same conspiracy, and in writing and sending threatening letters. But as no charge has yet been made against any of these five persons, this amounts to no more than a statement of suspicion or belief of the Procurators-fiscal that they are implicated in the same crimes as Pringle. In the second place, the leading object of the warrant is to obtain possession of the papers of the parties against whom it is directed, without any limitation as to the kind of papers, for by the term 'written documents' nothing else can be meant than all writings of every description. The only limitation is to be found in the words which follow—'tending to establish guilt or participation in said crimes,' and in the words in the body of the petition—'referring to and connected with said conspiracy and threatening letters.' But these words, while they may be supposed in one sense to have a limiting effect, are in another view capable of a very elastic interpretation: for it is not proposed to limit the seizure of papers in each person's house to those which inculpate himself; but, on the contrary, the words of the warrant would justify the seizure of papers tending to inculpate anybody in the crimes charged against Pringle, or at least, and in the most favourable sense, would justify the seizure of all papers in the possession of the complainer Bell which would tend to inculpate any of the other four parties against whom the warrant is directed, in addition, of course, to Pringle, and so in regard to the papers of each of the four other persons against whom the warrant is issued. In the third place, the execution of the warrant is entrusted absolutely and without control to ordinary sheriff-officers and their assistants, who are thereby commanded, whether in the presence or absence of the parties, who are under no criminal charge, and who have no notice of the application for or granting of the warrant, to seize their whole papers *per aversionem*, and themselves to read and examine all these papers for the purpose of finding traces or proofs of guilt either against the owners and possessors of the papers, or against some other person or persons.

The question which is thus raised for our decision has been represented to us by the learned counsel as one of great importance, and no one can doubt that it is so. It involves considerations of such high constitutional principle, that if we had felt any hesitation as to the judgment we should pronounce, we should have asked the assistance and advice of the other Judges of this Court. But entertaining no doubt at all, we consider it our duty at once to pronounce this warrant to be illegal. The seizure of papers, as distinguished from their recovery as articles of evidence, and also as distinguished from the seizure of other articles which are invested with no character of confidentiality or secrecy, is, under all circumstance, a matter of extreme delicacy. But the seizure of papers made in the circumstances with which we have to deal, is a proceeding quite unknown to the law of Scotland. Something was said of practice, though no example of such a seizure as this was mentioned. We think it right to say that no mere official practice would, in our eyes, justify such a warrant. Nothing short of an Act of Parliament, or a rule of the common law founded on usage known to and recognised by the Court, would at all affect our judgment on this question. If any such practice really exists, which we do not believe, the sooner it is put an end to the better. The Court are therefore of opinion that the warrant must be suspended. They attach no importance to the objection stated for the respondents, that the warrant has been executed, and therefore the suspension is too late. The warrant, according to its letter, is not exhausted, and might be enforced again. But further, we hold that even if it were exhausted, the complainer would have a good title to apply to this Court to suspend the warrant, on the ground of illegality."

Warrant suspended.

2. Nelson v. Black and Morrison
(1866) 4 M. 328

For the background to this case see *Bell* v. *Black and Morrison, supra*. Nelson was amongst those suspected by the respondents and a warrant, similar in terms to that granted in the above case, was granted for the search of his home, repositories, etc. The warrant was not executed in view of the successful suspension in the above case. Nelson brought an action for slander in respect of the allegations contained in the petition for the warrant. The respondents argued, *inter alia*, that without an averment of malice and want of probable cause the pursuer's action was irrelevant. The pursuer argued that since the warrant was illegal such averment was not necessary.

LORD PRESIDENT (MCNEILL): ". . . That may lead to a question of great nicety, viz., how far a procurator-fiscal puts himself outwith that protection that he would otherwise have, by asking something which he is not entitled to have; and that again may depend upon the nature of the illegality involved. If it is out of all law and reason that a man's repositories should be searched, that is one form of illegality. If, on the other hand, the objection is merely that the premises ought not to have been searched in this particular form, that is another matter. The one relates to the substance of the proceedings; the other to the want of formality, or the want of caution in carrying them out. In regard to illegality of the first kind, I think the pursuer would be entitled to have an issue without malice and want of probable cause. In regard to the other, I am of a different opinion.

It appears to me that this case falls under the latter class. I think it was competent for the Sheriff, under this application, to grant a perfectly legal warrant. For example if he had limited the search to particular documents, or appointed it to be carried out at the sight of the Sheriff himself, I cannot say that there would have been any illegality in such a warrant. That has not been done. But it does not follow that the defenders' application was out and out, and in substance, contrary to law."

LORD ARDMILLAN: ". . . I . . . am of opinion that the warrant as taken and executed in the case of Bell was illegal. It was a wide and indefinite warrant to search for written documents tending to establish guilt, or participation in guilt, of a serious crime. . . . a general warrant for a sweeping and indefinite search in the dwelling-house of a person not put under a charge, for written documents, in regard to which there is this peculiarity that they must be read before it can be seen what they instruct, is a very strong and startling procedure; and if granted at all, such a warrant should have been accompanied by some security against oppression, and against the violation of private confidence. The most secret and sacred writings were, or might be, exposed to the perusal of a Sheriff-officer and his concurrents; and the personal attendance of the Sheriff, or some person of discretion and authority, to superintend the search, and to inspect and select the documents, was, in my opinion, necessary to secure the fair execution of the warrant, and to prevent its having oppressive consequencess. The illegality of the warrant lay in the absence of such securities.

I am not prepared to say that a general search warrant for articles of evidence, and, among other articles, for written documents tending to instruct an occult conspiracy, could not, in any case, be granted to the public prosecutor against parties named in the petition, if accompanied by proper securities against oppressive execution. I agree with your Lordship that such a warrant might have been legally granted."

NOTES

The responsibility of the sheriff for the investigation of offences has passed to the fiscal, and from thence in practice to the police. Does the presence of a police officer at the execution of a search warrant secure the attendance of a person "of discretion and authority"? This may well depend upon the rank of the officer concerned. Presumably the attendance of the fiscal at such a search would provide a sufficient safeguard.

3. H.M. Advocate v. Turnbull
1951 J.C. 96

The accused, an accountant, was suspected of making fraudulent income tax returns on behalf of certain of his clients. A search warrant was obtained in relation to returns made on behalf of one client. During the execution of that warrant the police seized and removed a large number of documents relating to the affairs of other clients. All of these papers were contained in files clearly marked with the client's name. The information contained in these papers subsequently provided a foundation for further charges against the accused. Six months after the search a warrant was obtained retrospectively authorising the seizure of these documents. At the trial, objection was taken to the admissibility in evidence of these documents, on the ground that they had been unlawfully obtained:

LORD GUTHRIE: ". . . On these admitted facts counsel for the defence submitted, first, that possession of the documents other than those relating to charges 1 (a) and 1 (b) had been illegally obtained, and, second, that in the circumstances they were not admissible in evidence. . . .

The basis of the first submission was that the warrant granted on the first petition did not include the other documents, so that their retention and examination was without authority. They were the private papers of the accused and their unwarranted use for the purpose of obtaining evidence to enable further charges to be made against him was an infringement of the rights of the citizen. The files and the documents contained therein showed *ex facie* that they did not refer to the affairs of the client named in the first petition. When this was ascertained they should have been returned to the accused. Their continued retention and examination of their contents were deliberate and inexcusable. The irregularity of their seizure and use could not be validated *ex post facto* by the warrant granted on the second petition. In these circumstances the documents so irregularly obtained should not be admitted in evidence.

The Advocate-depute argued in reply that, as the documents had been obtained under the first warrant, the police were entitled, when examination of them showed that other charges might lie, to retain and use them to assist inquiry into these charges. The objection was purely technical, he maintained, since a warrant was ultimately obtained under which these documents could have been secured. The evidence had not been obtained by an unfair trick and in these circumstances it was admissible. . . .

The first matter argued, as to whether the retention and use of the documents was illegal, can be disposed of briefly. The general rule is that the search of private repositories by police officers is illegal unless a warrant has been obtained from a magistrate. Further, "a wide and indefinite warrant to search for written documents" is illegal—*Nelson* v. *Black and Morrison* (supra), referred to in *Stewart* v. *Roach* (1950 S.C. 318). Accordingly, as is shown by the form of warrant ordinarily craved and granted, a warrant must be specific as to the purpose and limitations of the search. The warrant used in practice authorises the securing "for the purpose of precognition and evidence, all writs tending to establish guilt or participation in the crime (or crimes) foresaid." In the present case the warrant of

20th May 1949 was specifically limited to the recovery of writs relating to the crime specified in that petition. It contained no authorisation of a search for or seizure and retention of any other writs. Consequently the retention of files and their contents which obviously did not bear upon the affairs of the person mentioned in the first charge was not authorised by the warrant and was illegal. The initial illegality was not cured by the granting of the second warrant six months later after the contents of the writs had been examined and used to enable the subsequent charges to be brought. Possession and use of the documents was not obtained under that second warrant. It was not retroactive. It authorised future and not past actions of officers of law. The argument of the Advocate-depute that the objection taken by the defence is technical is without substance. To hold that the second warrant nullified the complaint of misuse of the first would be to utilise the results achieved by an illegal act to wipe out the illegality. Accordingly I am of opinion that the warrant of 20th May 1949 only authorised the police officers to examine the documents in order to ascertain whether they fell within the scope of that warrant, and that the retention and examination of them in order to obtain evidence of other crimes was unauthorised and illegal. To reach the opposite conclusion would largely destroy the protection which the law affords to the citizen against invasion of his liberties by its requirement of the specific warrant of a magistrate for interference with these liberties.

I have found the second submission for the defence as to the admissibility of evidence so obtained a matter of greater difficulty.

[His Lordship then considered the principles governing the admissibility of evidence unlawfully seized, referring to *Lawrie* v. *Muir, infra*, p. 212; *H.M. Advocate* v. *McGuigan, infra*, p. 206; *McGovern* v. *H.M. Advocate*, 1950 J.C. 33 and *Fairley* v. *Fishmongers of London*, 1951 J.C. 14, and continued:]

In the present case there were, firstly, no circumstances of urgency. Secondly, the retention and use over a period of six months of the documents bearing to relate to other matters than that mentioned in the petition show that the actions complained of were deliberate. The police officers did not accidentally stumble upon evidence of a plainly incriminating character in the course of a search for a different purpose. If the documents are incriminating, their incriminating character is only exposed by careful consideration of their contents. Thirdly, if information was in the hands of the criminal authorities implicating the accused in other crimes, these could have been mentioned in the petition containing the warrant under which the search was authorised. If they had no such information, the examination of private papers in the hope of finding incriminating material was interference with the rights of a citizen. Therefore to hold that evidence so obtained was admissible would, as I have said, tend to nullify the protection afforded to a citizen by the requirement of a magistrate's warrant, and would offer a positive inducement to the authorities to proceed by irregular methods. Fourthly, when I consider the matter in the light of the principle of fairness to the accused, it appears to me that the evidence so irregularly and deliberately obtained is intended to be the basis of a comparison between the figures actually submitted to the inspector of taxes and the information in the possession of the accused. If such important evidence upon a number of charges is tainted by the method by which it was deliberately secured, I am of opinion that a fair trial upon these charges is rendered impossible.

Accordingly, when I apply the principles to be derived from the authorities to the facts of this case, I am driven to the conclusion that the objection taken to the admissibility of the documents is well founded. I shall therefore sustain the objection."

The court sustained
the objection.

4. H.M. Advocate v. Hepper
1958 J.C. 39

The accused was charged with the theft of a quantity of whisky and an attaché case. At the trial objection was taken to the admissibility in evidence of the discovery of the attaché case in the accused's possession. The circumstances are set out in the opinion of Lord Guthrie:

LORD GUTHRIE: "On 19th November 1957 police officers called at the residence of the accused on business not connected with the present charge. The accused was at home and consented to the police searching his house. In the course of his examination in the witness-box, the detective superintendent who called at the accused's house was asked whether he had taken possession of anything, and objection was taken to the line of evidence. Counsel for the panel stated that the consent to search was restricted to the business upon which the police had called at the accused's residence, and that, if the police in the course of that search discovered and removed an article which it was proposed to prove in evidence as relating to the present charge, such evidence should be excluded on the ground that it had been improperly obtained. Reference was made to *H. M. Advocate* v. *Turnbull* [*supra*, p. 193] and *Jackson* v. *Stevenson* [*supra*, p. 144]. In such cases, as the Lord Justice-Clerk, Lord Thomson, has repeatedly pointed out in recent years, the problem is always to reconcile the interest of society in the detection of crime with the requirement of fairness to an accused person. In the present case I am of opinion that the evidence is admissible. The police, in the course of their duty, when searching the accused's house with his consent in connexion with another matter, came upon the article which they removed. In *Turnbull* I distinguished that case, in which I excluded evidence as to documents taken possession of by police officers searching the accused's premises under a search warrant which clearly did not cover these documents, from a case in which police officers accidentally stumbled upon evidence of a plainly incriminating character in the course of a search for a different purpose. That distinction was based upon earlier authorities to which I was referred in *Turnbull's* case. It may be that the article which the police officers stumbled upon in their search of the accused's house was not an article of a plainly incriminating character, but it was at least an article of a very suspicious character, since it was an attaché case which contained within it the name and address of another person. In the circumstances, I do not think that the police officers acted in any way improperly in taking away that article in order to make further inquiries about it. If they had not done so, it might have disappeared. It appears to me that in the circumstances it was their duty, being officers charged with the protection of the public, to have acted as they did. But even if it cannot be put so highly, and if it be thought that their action was irregular, I am still of opinion that the evidence, even if irregularly obtained, is admissible in view of the interest of society in the detection of crime. I do not think that this is a case in which the evidence ought to be excluded because of a breach of the principle of fairness to the accused. I therefore hold that the evidence is admissible."

The court repelled
the objection.

NOTES

1. The police in this case were not acting in the execution of a warrant, but with the consent of the accused. The situations are, however, analogous in that consent and a warrant both authorise the search. They differ, however, in that while the authority conferred by a warrant is determined by its terms, the authority conferred by consent depends not only on the limits of the consent, but on the power of the person granting it to do so. Could, for example, the 16-year-old daughter of a suspect grant authority to the police to search her parent's house? And see *Leckie* v. *Miln, infra.*

2. The effect of *Turnbull* and *Hepper* is that the police, while searching under a warrant or with consent, cannot actively search for evidence beyond the limits of the warrant or consent. If, however, they happen upon evidence of a suspicious character, they may seize that evidence. There need be no connection between the "extra" items seized and the offence originally under investigation, nor need the police even suspect such a connection.

5. Leckie v. Miln
1982 S.L.T. 177; 1981 S.C.C.R. 261

The appellant was arrested on petition on a charge of theft from a dentist's surgery. The petition craved warrants in the usual terms, including warrant to search "the person repositories and domicile" of the accused for articles related to the charge. Warrant for search was granted as craved. Two police officers were informed that the accused had been arrested and were instructed to search the house occupied by Leckie and a Miss D. At no time did these officers have in their possession, or see, the petition, nor did they know the nature of the charge on which the accused had been arrested. On arrival at the house they informed Miss D that the appellant had been arrested on a petition warrant, and received her permission to search the house. During this search certain items were found which were later alleged to have been stolen from an office and a school. He was subsequently convicted of these thefts and appealed by stated case on the ground that the evidence of these thefts was wrongly admitted by the sheriff.

OPINION OF THE COURT: " . . . The findings-in-fact which describe the search are findings 8, 9 and 10. According to finding 8 two police officers learned from their inspector that the appellant had been arrested on petition at Perth on a charge of sneak theft. That was all they were told. They were then instructed by the inspector to go to the appellant's house and search it. This they proceeded to do. But finding 8 tells us that the officers in question never saw the petition upon which the appellant had been arrested; that they were completely unaware of the nature of any charge in that petition except to the extent that it was a charge of theft of the sneak theft variety; that they did not know at all what articles had been stolen during that theft and did not, of course, in the circumstances, have the petition in their possession, containing the warrant to search, when they went to the appellant's house. On arrival at the house they met a lady called Miss Dailly (known as Mrs Leckie) and they informed her that they were police officers and that the appellant had been arrested by the police at Perth on a petition warrant. Having said that they informed Miss Dailly that they wished to search the house. No objection to the proposed search was made. Finding 10 then describes the search which took place and the discovery, in the course of that search, of the business cards to which we have referred in the top drawer of a chest of drawers in the only bedroom of the house, a top drawer which contained the clothing of Miss Dailly, and the discovery of the library ticket and the receipt which we have already mentioned inside a jacket hanging in the wardrobe of that bedroom. For the appellant the submission was that the search which was carried out in all the circumstances disclosed in findings 8, 9 and 10 was quite unlawful in respect that it was neither authorised by the warrant to search in the petition on which the appellant had been arrested in Perth nor was it authorised by any implied consent given by Miss Dailly. If that submission is sound, as counsel for the appellant urged us to accept, then it followed, according to counsel, that the evidence given by the police officers about their findings was inadmissible. This is not a case in which officers carrying out an active search within the scope of a lawful warrant came across articles unrelated to the particular crime with which they were concerned. In such a case the finding of other articles indicating guilt of other crimes may be perfectly admissible in evidence. The fundamental proposition here was that neither upon the warrant nor upon any implied consent was the active unlimited search carried out by the officers justified in law. The Crown position was simply this. There existed, no doubt, authority for a search of the appellant's premises and that authority was the warrant granted upon the petition on which the appellant had appeared in Perth. It is the case that the officers admittedly did not carry out an active search within the limitations of that warrant to search for they were wholly ignorant of the contents of the petition and the scope of the warrant to search granted upon its presentation. But given the authority for a lawful search of the premises, the search which was carried out was carried out by the officers in the manner in which they carried it out with the full consent given by Miss Dailly by plain implication. The question in the case therefore comes to be whether Miss Dailly did give consent for the unlimited search carried out by the officers . . . . We are of opinion that by no stretch of the imagination can it be said that the consent given by Miss Dailly was consent for an active unlimited search regardless of the limitations in the warrant which admittedly existed. Finding 9 tells us that before Miss Dailly was informed that the officers wished to search the premises they told Miss Dailly that they were police officers and that the appellant had been arrested by the police at Perth on a petition warrant. It follows from that that any consent given by Miss Dailly must be assumed to have been given upon the footing that the officers intended to carry out a search within the authority contained in the warrant to which they referred, and that authority was, it is perfectly plain, an authority of a limited character. The search was nothing of the kind for, as we have already pointed out, the officers had no knowledge of the contents of the petition and what they did was to carry out a random search of the appellant's house in the hope of finding something which might conceivably have been the proceeds of a sneak theft anywhere. In these circumstances we are satisfied that the evidence of the finding of labels 2 and 4 should not have been admitted and if that is right then it follows that the conviction cannot stand for the evidence aliunde was insufficient to warrant the conviction of the appellant."

Convictions quashed.

NOTES

1.   Objectively speaking, the warrant authorised a fairly extensive search, and had the police officers known of the terms of that warrant the seizure of items relating to different thefts would have been justified under the *Hepper* principle. But where the police are ignorant of the terms of a warrant any search carried out must be random and therefore unlawful.

2.   The court held that since the police referred to the warrant when obtaining Miss D's consent, her consent was limited to a

search of the nature authorised by the warrant. Would this follow if (a) it was shown that Miss D had no idea of the limited authority conferred by the warrant, or mistakenly thought it conferred a much wider authority; (b) the police had not mentioned the warrant at all but merely asked to search the house?

3. For a full discussion of this case see Finnie, "Police Powers of Search in the light of *Leckie* v. *Miln*," 1982 S.L.T. 289.

(B) SEARCH WITHOUT PRIOR ARREST

It is no objection to the competency of a search warrant that the person whose premises are named therein has not been arrested or charged with an offence.

Stewart v. Roach
1950 S.C. 318

The pursuers brought an action of damages in the sheriff court against a police officer on the ground that he had wrongfully carried out a search (under a warrant) of their house at a time when they had been neither arrested nor charged. The sheriff found for the pursuers, and awarded them £30 damages each. The defender appealed to the Court of Session, where the case was heard by the First Division and three consulted judges of the Second Division.

LORD PRESIDENT (COOPER) (delivering the opinion of the consulted judges, with whom the members of the First Division concurred): "This case was sent to seven Judges on the question 'whether it is illegal to grant and execute a warrant to search for stolen goods the premises of a person who has not been apprehended nor charged with an offence.'

The sole point taken is that the searches were wrongous because the pursuers were neither charged nor apprehended before the warrants were applied for and obtained. Prior charge or apprehension is said to be an essential prerequisite. Otherwise, the warrants are admitted to be sufficiently specific and the procedure regular.

It is difficult to see on principle why the lesser invasion of the pursuers' rights involved in a search of their houses for stolen goods should be objectionable simply because the more extreme step of charging or apprehending them had not been taken. However that may be, it was argued to us that the matter was concluded by authority, and particularly by a decision of the High Court of Justiciary—*M'Lauchlan* v. *Renton* [(1910) 6 Adam 378]."

[The circumstances of that case were outlined, and the following observations of Lord Salvesen quoted:

"There can be no doubt, at common law, it is illegal to grant a warrant to search the premises of any citizen who has not been charged with an offence, however much the Crown authorities may have reason for suspicion against him."]

"Lord Salvesen gives no authority for this pronouncement, but it is clear from the argument presented that the supposed basis of the doctrine is *Bell* v. *Black and Morrison* . . .

The opinion of the Court [in that case] was delivered by the Lord Justice-Clerk. Three grounds for the decision are stated:—'In the first place, the warrant is granted against five different persons, none of whom is under a charge for any crime. It is stated in the petition that the persons against whom the warrant is asked are shown, by documents recovered in the course of the precognition against Pringle, to have been engaged in the same conspiracy, and in writing and sending threatening letters. But as no charge has yet been made against any of these five persons, this amounts to no more than a statement of the suspicion or belief of the Procurators-fiscal that they are implicated in the same crimes as Pringle.'"

[The remaining grounds were here outlined.]

"It will be observed that the first of these grounds is relevant to the present topic and indeed, as it turns out, is the only basis on which the argument for the pursuers rests. Had the Court regarded a charge as an essential prerequisite, we think that the opinion would have said so in terms and, indeed, that would have been decisive without further elaboration. It seems to us clear not only from the way in which the first ground is worded but also from the incidental reference to the absence of a criminal charge in the course of the formulation of the third ground, that they regarded the absence of charge as only one element for consideration in conjunction with the other circumstances of the case. The substance of the opinion is that, in the whole circumstances disclosed, what was sought was far too wide and not fenced with sufficient safeguards, especially having in view that no charge had been preferred. That this is the true emphasis of the opinion appears from this later passage:—'The seizure of papers, as distinguished from their recovery as articles of evidence, and also as distinguished from the seizure of other articles which are invested with no character of confidentiality or secrecy, is, under all circumstances, a matter of extreme delicacy. But the seizure of papers made in the circumstances with which we have to deal, is a proceeding quite unknown to the law of Scotland.'

That this is the true view of this case is borne out by what was said by the Judges who took part in two subsequent cases in the Court of Session arising out of the same matter."

[The court referred to the opinions in *Bell* v. *Black and Morrison* (1865) 5 Irvine 57 and *Nelson* v. *Black and Morrison* (1866) 4 M. 328, *supra,* and continued:]

"It is apparent that the First Division with both the previous cases before them give no countenance to the view that charge or apprehension is a prerequisite. Indeed, the opinion of Lord Deas goes far to negative it, while the opinion of Lord Ardmillan shows that he did not understand the opinion of the Court in the suspension as turning on that point.

In these circumstances we come without hesitation to the conclusion that charge or apprehension is not an essential prerequisite to the granting of a search warrant and that the proposition in *M'Lauchlan* v. *Renton* is too broadly stated. Special circumstances productive of exceptional hardship may make the granting of a search warrant illegal, and in such cases the absence of charge or apprehension may be a relevant consideration but will not *per se* render the warrant illegal. That is a very different thing from stating as a proposition of general application that 'it is illegal to grant a warrant to search the premises of any citizen who has not been charged with an offence, however much the Crown authorities may have reason for suspicion against him.'"

The court allowed the appeal and assoilzied the defender.

NOTE

The ratio of this case is not confined to searches of premises. The decision was followed in *Hay* v. *H.M. Advocate*, 1968 S.L.T. 334 (*infra*) which concerned a warrant to search the person of a suspect.

(C)   PERSONAL SEARCH UNDER WARRANT

It is competent to obtain a warrant to search the person of a suspect who has not been arrested.

Hay v. H.M. Advocate
1968 S.L.T. 334

OPINION OF THE COURT (Five judges): "The appellant . . . was found guilty . . . on a charge of murdering L.P. When her body was found there were marks on her right breast of a human bite which had been inflicted at or about the time of her death. The precise shape and configurations of this bite formed an important element in the identification at the trial of the appellant as the murderer. Evidence was led from witnesses called on behalf of the Crown to show that the peculiarities of the tooth structure in the appellant's mouth exactly fitted the marks of the bite on the girl's breast. It was not in dispute that if that evidence was properly admitted there was ample evidence, if the jury accepted it, of identification of the appellant as the person who caused them.

At the trial a question arose as to the competency of the course adopted on behalf of the Crown to secure evidence of the configuration of the appellant's teeth. In view of the importance of the matter the presiding judge heard argument upon it along with two other judges. The presiding judge held that the course adopted on behalf of the Crown was competent and intimated that the two other judges concurred in this view. He therefore allowed the evidence. After the appellant had been convicted he appealed and a special sitting of five judges has therefore been convened to hear the appeal.

The appellant at the time of the offence was an inmate of Loaningdale Approved School which is situated not far from the scene of the crime. In an endeavour to identify the person who made the marks, and to eliminate the innocent, impressions of the teeth of some 29 inmates of the school (including the appellant) and of the staff there were obtained with their consent. As a result all 29 were eliminated with the exception of the appellant. The Crown's advisers then expressed a desire for a more elaborate and scientific examination of the appellant's teeth in order to enable them to express a confident opinion one way or the other. An application was accordingly presented by the procurator-fiscal to a sheriff-substitute for a warrant to the police to convey the appellant to the Glasgow Dental Hospital, and to grant warrant to two named medical men there to take such further dental impressions, photographs and measurements of the teeth of the appellant as they might consider reasonably necessary for the furtherance of the comparisons of his teeth with the marks on the murdered girl. The sheriff-substitute considered the petition and granted the warrant as craved. The appellant was not present nor represented at the hearing before the sheriff-substitute. When the warrant was obtained the appellant had not yet been apprehended, although he was obviously under considerable suspicion . . .

As regards the first and main issue in the appeal — namely the legality of the warrant — it has been observed in more than one of the cases (e.g., *Adair* v. *McGarry*, 1933 J.C. 72) that two conflicting considerations arise. On the one hand, there is the need from the point of view of public interest for promptitude and facility in the identification of accused persons and the discovery on their persons or on their premises of indicia either of guilt or innocence. On the other hand, the liberty of the subject must be protected against any undue or unnecessary invasion of it.

In an endeavour as fairly as possible to hold the balance between these two considerations three general principles have been recognised and established by the Court. In the first place, once an accused has been apprehended, and therefore deprived of his liberty, the police have the right to search and examine him. In the second place, before the police have reached a stage in their investigations when they feel warranted in apprehending him they have in general no right by the common law of Scotland to search or examine him or his premises without his consent. There may be circumstances, such as urgency or risk of evidence being lost, which would justify an immediate search or examination, but in the general case they cannot take this step at their own hand. But in the third place, even before the apprehension of the accused they may be entitled to carry out a search of his premises or an examination of his person without his consent if they apply to a magistrate for a warrant for this purpose. Although the accused is not present nor legally represented at the hearing where the magistrate grants the warrant to examine or to search, the interposition of an independent judicial officer holds the basis for a fair reconciliation of the interests of the public in the suppression of crime and of the individual who is entitled not to have the liberty of his person or his premises unduly jeopardised. A warrant of this limited kind will only, however, be granted in special circumstances. The hearing before the magistrate is by no means a formality, and he must be satisfied that the circumstances justify the taking of this unusual course, and that the warrant asked for is not too wide or oppressive. For he is the safeguard against the grant of too general a warrant.

We were referred to a series of cases which appear to us to confirm the propositions above set forth. In *Jackson* v. *Stevenson* (1897) 24 R. (J.) 38, (4 S.L.T. 277), the Lord Justice-Clerk, at p. 41, said: 'I know of no authority for ascribing to constables the right to make such tentative searches (i.e., before apprehension) and they seem contrary to constitutional principle. If a constable requires to make such a search it can only be because without it he is not justified in apprehending: and without a warrant, to search a person not liable to apprehension seems palpably illegal.' (Compare Lord Kinnear, at p. 42). In *Adamson* v. *Martin*, 1916, 1 S.L.T. 53, 1916 S.C. 319, it was held that the taking of photographs and fingerprint impressions by the police of an accused who had not been apprehended was illegal at common law and under the statute. As Lord Guthrie said at p. 331: 'The pursuer not having been in custody, and the police not having obtained a warrant, the photographs and fingerprints were unwarrantably obtained.'

This case was distinguished in *Adair* v. *McGarry* (supra), where fingerprints were held to have been lawfully taken. But the reason was that in this latter case the accused had been apprehended. In the opinions of the judges there are references to a magistrates' warrant which, in the view of the Court, would legalise the taking of fingerprints from a man who has not yet been apprehended (see Lord Justice-General, at p. 78). It was argued to us that as this was a fingerprint case the warrant in question was a warrant obtained under the regulations made in virtue of the Penal Servitude Act 1891. But this contention is unsound. The Court was dealing with common law warrants and the statute and regulations were held not to affect the issue. The observations of the judges are therefore inconsistent with the present appellant's contention.

The case of *Stewart* v. *Roach*, 1950 S.C. 318, 1950 S.L.T. 245, decided that it was competent to grant and execute warrants to search the houses of suspected persons prior to apprehension: If the safeguard of obtaining a warrant for this purpose makes it lawful in the case of a man not yet apprehended it seems difficult to appreciate why a similar safeguard in the case of such an accused should not equally legalise an examination of his person after a warrant for that purpose has been obtained.

Lastly, we were referred to *McGovern* v. *H.M. Advocate*, 1950 J.C. 33, 1950 S.L.T. 133. In that case scrapings from the finger nails of an accused person were taken without his consent and before his apprehension. The evidence so obtained was held to be incompetent. The distinction between that case and the present is that in that case the evidence was obtained without any warrant from a magistrate.

In the circumstances of the present case the obtaining of the warrant prior to the examination in question in our opinion rendered the examination quite legal, and the evidence which resulted from it was therefore competent."

The court refused
the appeal.

NOTES

1. The court went on to hold that even if it had found that the warrant was illegal they would nonetheless have upheld the admissibility of the evidence, either on the ground of "urgency" (as to which see *infra*, p. 206) or in the exercise of the court's discretion to overlook irregularities in the obtaining of evidence (as to which, see *infra*, p. 212).

2. Without a warrant the police may not search the person of a suspect (or any other person) prior to arrest unless this is permitted by statute or justified on the grounds of urgency (*infra*).

(ii) Search without warrant

(A) UNDER STATUTE

A variety of statutes permit search without warrant, as they do arrest without warrant. The following is simply one example:

Civic Government (Scotland) Act 1980

"**60.**—(1) Subject to subsections (2) and (3) below, if a constable has reasonable grounds to suspect that a person is in possession of any stolen property, the constable may without warrant—

(*a*) search that person or anything in his possession, and detain him for as long as is necessary for the purpose of that search;

(*b*) enter and search any vehicle or vessel in which the constable suspects that that thing may be found, and for that purpose require the person in control of the vehicle to stop it and keep it stopped."

NOTE

For other commonly encountered examples of a statutory power of search, see the Criminal Justice (Scotland) Act 1980, s. 4(1) (search for offensive weapons) and the Misuse of Drugs Act 1971, s. 23 (search for controlled drugs). The powers of the police to search detainees under section 2 of the 1980 Act have already been noted (*supra*, p. 144).

(B) AT COMMON LAW

It has already been noted (Chap. 4) that the police may search arrested persons (and that power is extended by section 2 of the

1980 Act to the case of detained persons). The following cases discuss the powers of the police to search without warrant in cases of "urgency." It will be seen that these powers may be employed whether or not the suspect has been arrested.

1.   H.M.Advocate v. McGuigan
1936 J.C. 16

The accused was charged with murder, rape and theft. At the trial counsel for McGuigan objected to the admissibility of certain evidence taken without warrant by the police from the tent in which the accused lived. The circumstances in which the evidence was seized are outlined in the Lord Justice-Clerk's opinion:

LORD JUSTICE-CLERK (AITCHISON): " . . . The ground of the objection is that this search was carried out, and I take it certain articles seized, without the warrant of a magistrate; and it is said, accordingly, that the search and the seizure of the articles were both illegal. Now, the facts are these: On the evening of 28th August the accused had been identified—or was alleged to have been identified—by Marjory Fenwick, and immediately thereafter he was apprehended and charged. The charges made against him were three in number. First, murder; second, rape; third, theft of a pocket book; the apprehension and charge took place about eight o'clock at night. Thereafter the accused was searched. Both the apprehension and the search of the accused were carried out without warrant. I have no doubt that, in the circumstances, this was quite regular. The police were amply justified in acting at their own hand. Between 9 and 10 o'clock the same night Inspector Davidson went to the accused's tent. He found the tent occupied by the accused's mother and the accused's stepfather. He disclosed who he was, and what his purpose was. No objection was raised, as was natural enough. On the other hand, no consent was asked for, and the search proceeded. Now it must be obvious that, the accused having been arrested on so grave a charge as murder, it might be of the first importance to the ends of public justice that a search of the tent in which the accused had been living should be made forthwith. The police acted at their own hand, just as they acted at their own hand in apprehending and searching the person of the accused. In the circumstances, the matter being in the view of Inspector Davidson one of urgency, the police were entitled, in my view, to act without delay and without having obtained a warrant from a magistrate."

The court repelled
the objection.

NOTES
1.   The Lord Justice-Clerk went on to hold that even if he had concluded that the search was unlawful, the evidence would not necessarily have been inadmissible.

2. *Cf. McLorie* v. *Oxford* [1982] 3 All E.R. 480; *Jeffrey* v. *Black* [1978] Q.B. 490 and the much more restrictive view of police powers in such a situation adopted by the English courts.

2. **Bell v. Hogg**
1967 J.C. 49

While investigating the disappearance of a quantity of copper telegraph wire from a railway line, the police intercepted the appellants in a van. They informed them of the nature of their inquiries, cautioned them, and asked to see their hands. The police observed on the hands of the appellants a substance which could have been verdigris. The appellants were then taken to a police station (not under arrest) where, in response to an invitation from a police officer each gave a rubbing from his hands. They were not expressly told that they were entitled to refuse. The substance proved to be verdigris, and this evidence was crucial to their subsequent conviction for theft of the wire. They appealed against conviction on the ground that this evidence had been wrongly admitted, it having been unlawfully obtained.

LORD JUSTICE-GENERAL (CLYDE): " . . . In these circumstances, in my opinion, the sergeant took a perfectly proper and legitimate step in securing a record of what was on the appellants' hands before it was eliminated by washing or otherwise. The urgency of the matter is its justification, as was held by Lord Justice-Clerk Aitchison in *H. M. Advocate* v. *M'Guigan* [*supra*] where he held that in a case of urgency, in order to preserve evidence which might otherwise be lost, the police were entitled to search an accused person's tent without a warrant. This decision was quoted with approval in the Whole Court case of *Lawrie* v. *Muir* [*infra*]. In the course of the argument in the present case the decision in *M'Govern* v. *H. M. Advocate* [1950 J.C. 33] was also referred to. In that case, which the Lord Justice-General described as 'distinctly unusual', the accused had not yet been charged nor apprehended in connection with a safe-blowing, but had been kept in the police station for some six hours, when 'as a further precaution' the police obtained the contents of his finger nails by scraping them with a view to subsequent chemical analysis of the scrapings. After carrying out this operation the police then 'deemed it advisable' to charge him. This incident was treated by the Court on the concessions of the Crown as an irregular proceeding on the part of the police. There was no question of urgency and no knowledge by the police as to whether the scrapings would yield any evidence of the suspect's connection with the offence. This all makes it a highly special decision. In the present case there was on the contrary obvious urgency involved in the obtaining of the impressions; and the analysis of these impressions was necessary, not in the hope of connecting the appellants with the offences but in order to secure a reliable analysis of the gray-green marks on their hands which had been seen by the light of the torch at the railway station shortly beforehand, in order to confirm whether they were made by verdigris or not. The test of the admissibility of the evidence of the analysis is whether what was done was done fairly. In this case there was no compulsion about what the police did. There is no trace or any suggestion of bullying or trickery on the part of the police, still less any element of third-degree treatment. I do not regard it as unfair that the accused were not specifically told that they need not consent to the impressions being taken. It might have been better if this had been said, but the absence of such a warning is not in the circumstances fatal, particularly as the appellants had already been cautioned. After all, the analysis might well have been favourable to the appellants and, if they had not been parties to the offences, it could have done them no harm. In these circumstances the actings of the police are not shown to be in any way unfair, and, if so, the evidence arising out of these steps was properly admitted by the Sheriff-substitute."

LORD MIGDALE: " . . . In my opinion the Sheriff-substitute was right in accepting this evidence. I think, however, he could have held that Sergeant Muirhead acted within his rights as a police officer who acted in an emergency. The Sheriff-substitute has held that the taking of the rubbings was a justifiable infringement of the rights enjoyed by the appellants as citizens. I find authority for this view in the case of *H. M. Advocate* v. *M'Guigan.*

If the evidence could be recovered at a later stage after apprehension, as in the case of *M'Govern* v. *H. M. Advocate,* the balance would be in favour of the suspect, but if, as in the present case, the evidence is likely to be lost if not recorded immediately, I think the police are entitled to act at once. Urgency itself justifies the action and this falls under the first part of the ruling given by the Lord Justice-Clerk. It is part of the function of the police to preserve evidence which is likely to be useful in proving the guilt of a suspected criminal just as it is part of their function to prevent a crime being committed. For these reasons I think that the police acted properly.

Even if this is wrong, then in this case the action of Sergeant Muirhead was justified under the second part of the Lord Justice-Clerk's ruling and the principle laid down by Lord Cooper in *Lawrie* v. *Muir.* The balance of interest in the present case is clearly in favour of the action taken by the police."

LORD CAMERON: " . . . In the present case I have no doubt that the police officers were entitled to question the appellants and that any answers obtained by them were admissible in evidence. In these circumstances I should have thought that the use in evidence of a material substance handed over to the police at their request—a request related to the transaction which the police were investigating—would be equally admissible. But there was an additional circumstance which in my opinion justified the action of the police and made the use in evidence of the substance obtained competent and admissible. The problem which faced the police was whether they were to lose permanently evidence which was evanescent and once gone could not be recovered. It was thus from a practical point of view urgent that this evidence should be recovered for examination and identification. It is also to be noted that at the time it could not be determined whether the substance was wholly innocent—a factor in the appellants' favour—or whether its presence and nature might point towards their guilt. This could not appear until expert examination had taken place. To wait might have meant the loss of possibly vital evidence and, as it turned out, evidence which in this case was in fact of critical importance. The ultimate determination of whether the situation is truly one of urgency is, I think, for the Court to decide upon the whole facts and not for subjective decision. In my opinion the situation which was presented to the police at the time in question was one of urgency. If the material was to be of value, either criminative or exculpatory, its instant recovery and preservation in the hands of the authorities was imperative. It would obviously not have been practicable to obtain a search warrant there and then to permit a search of the appellants or a checking of their finger-prints; the use of force would have involved an assault and would certainly have led to the rejection of evidence so obtained. In these circumstances I should not have thought that there was any impropriety or unfairness to the appellants in asking them, particularly after they had already been cautioned and put on guard as to their rights at least in the matter of questioning, to make available for examination what was on their hands . . . the principle of urgency as a justification for acts which would in less compelling circumstances require the authority of a warrant is settled beyond doubt. It is only where there has been irregularity, that is, lack of legal justification, in obtaining evidence that its admissibility may depend on whether the irregularity can be excused . . . There is nothing in the present case to suggest that the appellants were unfairly induced or tricked into providing the material or that they were subjected to any kind of pressure. I therefore think that, apart from any other considerations to which I have referred and upon the single issue of urgency in the circumstances, as I think there was, the evidence which was obtained is admissible in law and that consequently the questions should be answered as proposed by your Lordship in the chair."

The court refused
the appeal.

NOTES

1. The police action in this case seems to have been entirely reasonable. The appellants were found in suspicious circumstances with what appeared to be prima facie evidence of connection with the offence on their hands. The public as a whole would have been entitled to be highly critical of police officers who stood idly by and allowed the destruction of such evidence. But the limits of the power under discussion should be closely confined to cases of genuine emergency, where no other lawful means of preserving evidence is available. Cf. *McHugh* v. *H.M. Advocate, infra.*

2. The use of the caution in such cases raises a difficult issue. It is submitted that a standard caution, directed towards the making of statements, is not appropriate where the police are seeking to obtain real evidence. The caution should be so phrased as to direct the suspect's attention towards what is being asked of him and his right to refuse that request.

3. See also *Walsh* v. *McPhail*, 1978 S.L.T. (Notes) 29.

A further question arises as to whether the statements in *Bell* v. *Hogg* concerning the absence of a specific warning of the right to refuse to give the samples are affected by the decision in *Tonge* v. *H.M. Advocate* (*supra*). It should be recalled that *Bell* v. *Hogg* was decided within three months of *Miln* v. *Cullen*, and follows that decision's approach to the caution very closely. Could it now be argued that the police in a case such as *Bell* v. *Hogg* ought to give a specific caution? Or would the urgency of the situation excuse a failure to do so?

3. McHugh v. H.M. Advocate
1978 J.C. 12

McHugh and another man were suspected of an assault and robbery in which a sum of money consisting of identifiable bank-notes was stolen from a shop. In the early hours of the morning following the robbery the police went, without a search warrant or a warrant for arrest, to the house of McHugh's suspected accomplice. According to the police evidence (which was disputed by the accused) McHugh was then cautioned, charged and arrested. He was then searched, and some of the stolen notes were found in his possession. McHugh was convicted of assault and robbery and appealed on the ground, *inter alia*, that evidence relating to the finding of the banknotes in his possession should not have been admitted at the trial, as it had been illegally obtained.

LORD JUSTICE-GENERAL (EMSLIE): " . . . The second submission was that the trial Judge misdirected the jury by admitting for their consideration the evidence of police officers of finding stolen notes, which were productions in the case, on the person of the appellant. As we understood the argument, counsel began by saying that this was a case in which the search was conducted without warrant. Although police who have lawfully arrested a person may quite properly search the arrested man without a warrant, it was not certain that an arrest had taken place in this case, or that if it had taken place, it had taken place legally. The only other circumstance in which a search of a citizen may be justified is where, although there is no warrant and no lawful arrest, the need to search is demanded as a matter of urgency to prevent the possible loss or destruction of important evidence. In this case, said Mr Taylor, it was by no means clear that the police were telling the truth when they said they arrested M'Hugh before they searched him. In any event, said Mr Taylor, it is by no means clear either that they had reasonable grounds for arresting M'Hugh, or that there were any considerations of urgency which could have justified the search which revealed the stolen property. In short the submission for the appellant seemed to be this:—Where the admission in evidence of the fruits of a search is challenged on the ground that they have been improperly obtained and the question of the credibility of the searchers on the matter of the propriety of the search is raised by the defence, the trial Judge should leave that question to the jury to resolve and direct the jury to consider the evidence as to the fruits of search only if the question of credibility is resolved in the searcher's favour. To this somewhat curious submission there is a short answer. It was for the Judge to dispose of the objection to the admissibility of the disputed evidence for that is a question of law. He has disposed of that objection and in our opinion his decision cannot be faulted. The evidence bearing upon the circumstances of the search was all one way and remained unshaken in cross-examination. It was to the effect that the officers had set out with the primary purpose of arresting M'Hugh, for that was their alloted task. They carried out that task and the search was a sequel to the arrest. They did not arrest without reasonable cause, and in particular merely to provide an excuse for a search. In any event it is perfectly clear that the search of M'Hugh, a prime suspect, was, according to the evidence, essential as a matter of urgency, to avoid any risk that any of the numbered notes which he might have in his possession would be lost, hidden or destroyed. In this state of matters and particularly having regard to the sufficient evidence of the urgent need to search, the criticism of the direction given by the trial Judge is without real substance."

> The court refused
> the appeal.

NOTES

1. Strictly speaking the remarks about urgency in this case are *obiter* since the court found that the accused had been arrested prior to search, and the search can thus be justified on ordinary principles (see *supra*, Chap. 4).

2. The court's reliance on urgency is unfortunate. It comes very close to permitting search without warrant to justify arrest, in conflict with the principle laid down in *Jackson* v. *Stevenson* (*supra*, Chap. 4). In any case, was there really a matter of urgency in the search of McHugh? What could he have done to dispose of the evidence with the police standing there? Perhaps he might have eaten it.

3. Compare the approach of the court in McHugh with *Leckie* v. *Miln, supra*. Why did the court not rely upon the notion of urgency in that case?

(iii) Illegality and admissibility

The rules governing the legality of search and seizure are in principle distinguishable from the rules governing the admissibility of evidence obtained by these means. Thus it is quite possible for a court to hold that the evidence was obtained by unlawful means (which may give rise to civil or other sanctions) and yet simultaneously hold that the evidence is admissible. (Compare this with the position with regard to statements and confessions where both these aspects are effectively merged in the fairness rule.)

Lawrie v. Muir
1950 J.C. 19

The appellant was convicted of an offence contrary to the Milk (Control and Maximum Prices) (Great Britain) Order 1947 in that she used for the sale of milk certain milk bottles belonging to other milk suppliers without their consent or other lawful authority. The evidence relating to the use of these bottles was obtained by two inspectors who had unlawfully, but in good faith, conducted a search of her premises. On appeal by stated case:

LORD JUSTICE-GENERAL (COOPER) (delivering the opinion of the Full Bench): "From the standpoint of principle it seems to me that the law must strive to reconcile two highly important interests which are liable to come into conflict—(a) the interest of the citizen to be protected from illegal or irregular invasions of his liberties by the authorities, and (b) the interest of the State to secure that evidence bearing upon the commission of crime and necessary to enable justice to be done shall not be withheld from Courts of law on any merely formal or technical ground. Neither of these objects can be insisted upon to the uttermost. The protection of the citizen is primarily protection for the innocent citizen against unwarranted, wrongful and perhaps high-handed interference, and the common sanction is an action of damages. The protection is not intended as a protection for the guilty citizen against the efforts of the public prosecutor to vindicate the law. On the other hand, the interest of the State cannot be magnified to the point of causing all the safeguards for the protection of the citizen to vanish, and of offering a positive inducement to the authorities to proceed by irregular methods. It is obvious that excessively rigid rules as to the exclusion of evidence bearing upon the commission of a crime might conceivably operate to the detriment and not the advantage of the accused, and might even lead to the conviction of the innocent; and extreme cases can easily be figured in which the exclusion of a vital piece of evidence from the knowledge of a jury because of some technical flaw in the conduct of the police would be an outrage upon common sense and a defiance of elementary justice. For these reasons, and in view of the expressions of judicial opinion to which I have referred, I find it quite impossible to affirm the appellant's extreme proposition. On the contrary, I adopt as a first approximation to the true rule the statement of Lord Justice-Clerk Aitchison [H.M.Adv. v. McGuigan, *supra*] that 'an irregularity in the obtaining of evidence does not *necessarily* make that evidence inadmissible.'

It remains to consider the implications of the word 'necessarily' which I have italicised. By using this word and by proceeding to the sentence which follows, Lord Aitchison seems to me to have indicated that there was, in his view, no absolute rule and that the question was one of circumstances. I respectfully agree. It would greatly facilitate the task of Judges were it possible to imprison the principle within the framework of a simple and unqualified maxim, but I do not think that it is feasible to do so.

Irregularities require to be excused, and infringements of the formalities of the law in relation to these matters are not lightly to be condoned. Whether any given irregularity ought to be excused depends upon the nature of the irregularity and the circumstances under which it was committed. In particular, the case may bring into play the discretionary principle of fairness to the accused which had been developed so fully in our law in relation to the admission in evidence of confessions or admissions by a person suspected or charged with crime. That principle would obviously require consideration in any case in which the departure from the strict procedure had been adopted deliberately with a view to securing the admission of evidence obtained by an unfair trick. Again, there are many statutory offences in relation to which Parliament has prescribed in detail in the interests of fairness a special procedure to be followed in obtaining evidence; and in such cases (of which the Sale of Food and Drugs Acts provide one example) it is very easy to see why a departure from the strict rules has often been held to be fatal to the prosecution's case. On the other hand, to take an extreme instance figured in argument, it would usually be wrong to exclude some highly incriminating production in a murder trial merely because it was found by a police officer in the course of a search authorised for a different purpose or before a proper warrant had been obtained."

The court quashed
the conviction.

NOTE

The Lord Justice-General went on to hold that in the circumstances of the case, and in particular the fact that the inspectors were not police officers enjoying "a large residuum of common law powers" but persons who "ought to know the precise limits of their authority," the balance ought to be held in favour of the appellant.

CHAPTER 6

BAIL

The law on bail in Scotland was radically altered by the Bail etc.
(Scotland) Act 1980, a statute which incorporated most of the
reforms suggested in Chapter 11 of the Second Report of the
Thomson Committee (1975 Cmnd. 6218). Formerly, the deposit of
money was an essential precondition of release if a bail application
was granted, but the Act now provides for release on a series of
conditions, breach of any of which is itself an offence (see, *e.g.*
Aitchison v. *Tudhope*, 1981 S.L.T. 231, *infra*, p. 282).
    The court or the Lord Advocate may only impose a condition as
to the deposit of money bail where such a condition is appropriate to
the special circumstances of the case: s. 1(3).
    But the Act did not alter the fundamental principles which must
be considered by a court when confronted with a bail application by
an accused person in custody. For this reason, the body of pre-1980
case law in which those principles were developed is still of relevance today.

a. Should bail be granted?

1. Mackintosh v. McGlinchy
1921 J.C. 75

An accused person was charged with firearms offences and was
granted bail by the sheriff. The procurator fiscal appealed to the
High Court.

LORD JUSTICE-GENERAL (CLYDE): "In one form or another bail was
always, or at any rate from very remote antiquity, a part of our criminal law.
Prior to the statute of 1701 the practice of exacting sureties from persons
accused of even the gravest capital offences for their appearance to answer
the charge was known and observed according to Baron Hume (Crimes,
vol. ii., p. 87). But the advantages of this practice were not available to
accused persons as matter of right. On the contrary, bail was allowed or
refused according to the discretion of the Court. 'Though such an indulgence may have been given in particular cases,' says Baron Hume (p. 88),
'yet still it is difficult to believe that any police could ever be maintained
under a system, which uniformly allowed so great a latitude of dismissing
the highest and most notorious offenders, on so insecure a footing. And in
truth, on the whole, the just construction of the foregoing statutes rather

seems to be, that they marked out a course of proceeding to the magistrate, and bestowed a discretion on him, which he might use if he saw cause, or could not easily attach the criminal's person; than that they intended to create an absolute privilege of bail in favour of the delinquent, which he might insist on after imprisonment, as a matter of right.' There is little ground for thinking that, as the law was administered prior to the Act of 1701, the Court was in the habit of exercising this discretion with any excess of leniency.

The main defect in the criminal law and practice which led to the passage of the Act of 1701 was that persons who were under accusation of crime, and had been apprehended accordingly, had no efficient protection against prolonged incarceration before their case was brought to trial. The problem of bail and the problem of protecting accused persons against lengthy imprisonment without trial are closely related, and the statute of 1701 dealt with both. First with regard to bail, the statute divided offences into what it called bailable and non-bailable offences. With regard to the latter class, namely, non-bailable offences, the law and practice as existing prior to the Act was left unchanged. That is to say, the Court could be asked to exercise the discretion naturally belonging to it, after the Act of 1701 just as before, in the case of a non-bailable offence. But in the case of bailable offences, the statute provided certain hard-and-fast maximum measures of caution (applicable to persons of various degrees), which, if tendered to the Court, entitled those persons as a matter of right to bail. The value of this right must be measured in light of the fact that non-bailable offences included the whole range of offences to which at that time a capital sentence was applicable in accordance with the letter of the law—almost the whole field of crime, petty offences excluded. In Hume, vol. ii., page 89, and in Sheriff Alison's Criminal Law, vol. ii., page 162, there are included among non-bailable offences cases of deforcements of the officers of the revenue; assaults with loaded firearms, or sharp instruments; thefts by one habit and repute, or repeatedly convicted—or of articles of considerable value, as above £100—or of any thing, however small, by housebreaking, or of a horse, or ox, or more than one sheep; all cases of robbery or stouthrief, how small soever the value of the article taken; and all cases of forging notes, or uttering forged notes, or forging bills or instruments for payment of money. Further the Act of 1701 provided means by which a person who was not admitted to bail but remained in prison could take steps to hasten the trial of his cause. The machinery was cumbrous, and, judged by more modern standards, not over-effective.

The law with regard to these matters—subject to a variety of minor modifications—continued to rest upon the principles of the Act of 1701 until the passing of the Criminal Procedure Act, 1887, and the Bail Act of 1888. Both these Acts deal with the allowance of bail in words which admit of no doubt or ambiguity. Both of them say that, except in cases of murder and treason, bail can be granted in the discretion of the Court before whom the accused person is brought. The argument which has been presented to-day—in its major proposition—challenged the existence and reality of that discretion, and—in its minor proposition—sought to establish some limitation or restriction (it was not clear what) upon its exercise. So far as it related to bail, the Act of 1701 was completely repealed by the Act of 1888, and it follows that, if any ground exists for importing any particular limitation or qualification of the discretion expressly given to the Court by the Acts of 1887 and 1888, that ground must be found, not in the repealed provisions of 1701, but in the substituted enactments of 1887 and 1888. We have had our attention fully directed to the terms of those statutes. There is nothing whatever, either direct or indirect, express or implied, in the provisions of either of those statutes which would justify giving to the word 'discretion' any other meaning than that which it naturally bears. That answers the major proposition, and it really disposes of the minor proposition also. In considering generally what is the nature of that discretion of which the statutes of 1887 and 1888 speak, one cannot do better than have regard to the judicial description of the discretion which the Court undoubtedly possessed—prior to the passage of those Acts—in the case of the non-bailable offences under the Act of 1701. In 1878, in connexion with the trial of the Directors of the City of Glasgow Bank (who were indicted for an offence which was non-bailable, at least in one view of the *species facti*), Lord President Inglis said this 'The petitioners further appeal to the discretion of the Court to liberate them on such bail as may be sufficient to ensure their appearance hereafter to answer the charges made against them. That we possess such discretionary power cannot be disputed. But in prosecutions conducted by the public prosecutor the discretion is vested, in the first instance at least, in the Lord Advocate; and unless it can be alleged that the Lord Advocate has refused bail, not for the purpose of securing the ends of justice, but for some other and therefore illegitimate purpose, I think the Court ought not to interfere, because such interference would be nothing less than relieving the Lord Advocate of the responsibility attaching to his high office. He is subject to this responsibility, and vested with the corresponding discretion, because he has means and appliances for obtaining information and forming a judgment which are not within the reach of any other official, and are not possessed by this Court. But it has not been suggested that the Lord Advocate is not discharging his important and responsible duties with fairness and impartiality, and with a sole view to the public interest, and to secure the ends of justice.' In this passage the weight which the Court is entitled to attach to the view of the Lord Advocate in such matters—one of the incidental advantages of the system of public prosecution—is emphasised. But the principle laid down applies to the exercise of its discretion by the Court as much as to the discharge by the Lord Advocate of his duties. The discretion must be used with a sole view to the public interest and to secure the ends of justice. The Acts of 1887 and 1888 took away nothing from the discretion which was thus exercised prior to their coming into force. Accordingly, my opinion on the statutes is that the Court has in this matter of bail a discretion, and that the broad consideration which rules its exercise is a single regard to the public interest and the ends of justice, and that, in considering any appeal to that discretion, a statement made to the Court on the high responsibility of the Lord Advocate is entitled to great weight.

The particular ground on which the public prosecutor most commonly opposes bail, and on which the Court most frequently exercises its discretion by refusal of it, is that it is apprehended that bail will be ineffectual to secure that the accused will appear to answer the charge. That was the particular ground alleged by the Lord Advocate in the City of Glasgow Bank case, in which the general principles applying to the matter were expounded by the judgment just quoted. But it was said on behalf of the appellants here that this was the only consideration with reference to which the Court can exercise its discretion. In support of this contention reference was made to a passage in the judgment of Lord Dunedin in the case of *A B* v. *Dickson* [1907 S.C. (J.) 111]; and we were told that this passage had been thought in some quarters to imply a restriction of the breadth previously attributed to the discretion of the Court in this matter. The report of the case negatives the idea that any general question with regard to the discretion of the Court was raised or debated. The case was one of rape, and followed on a previous case for the same offence in which some expressions had been used which might be read as implying that bail ought to be refused in all rape cases. The propriety of any such general rule was the subject of discussion, but (as I have said) no general question with regard to the conditions under which bail should be allowed was raised or argued. In giving judgment Lord Dunedin said (at p. 112), 'That the Court has power to grant liberation on bail I do not think can be doubted. If the Lord Advocate assures the Court that in his view the effect of that will in all likelihood be to defeat the ends of justice by the prisoner absconding, as the Lord Advocate's only object must be to secure his presence at the trial, the Court will no doubt give weight to that statement. If it is thought that that is not likely to happen, there is no reason why liberation should not be granted.' In this passage Lord Dunedin cites, as an example of the grounds on which the Court refuses bail, the particular ground which most frequently recurs. It was the only ground with which the discussion was concerned, as against the supposed rule excluding bail altogether in rape cases. But I cannot read the passage as one intended to contain an exhaustive exposition of the whole law on the subject, or as restricting the discretion of the Court as theretofore practised. Lord McLaren makes the true meaning of the judgment clear when he says (at p. 112): 'I think it is in accordance with good sense and justice that great weight should be given to the representations of the procurator-fiscal on this question, if, for example, he states that he has good reason to fear that the accused will go away and forfeit his bail.' In short the probability that the accused will abuse his liberation by absconding is one, but only one, of a number of ways in which the ends of justice may be defeated by the indiscriminate allowance of bail, and which the refusal of bail can and ought to be used to prevent. The practice of the Court since 1888 — at any rate as I have known it — has not conformed to the narrow view of the discretionary power of the Court which is contended for by the accused; and, if I thought that the passage from Lord Dunedin's judgment to which I have referred really supported that narrow view, I should be compelled respectfully but emphatically to dissent from it.

A good deal was said in the argument before us about the classes of case in which the discretion of the Court is appropriately exercised by refusing bail. It is neither possible nor expedient to categorise them; for, when appeal is made to a discretionary power, the only safe rule is that each case must be considered on its own merits, with the sole view to the public interest and to securing the ends of justice. As illustrations, cases have been mentioned in which the Lord Advocate has reason to apprehend that an accused person intends to defeat the ends of justice, if liberated, by tampering with the evidence. Again, there are cases such as incest or brutal domestic assault, where the gravest consequences will ensue from the return of the accused to his home pending trial. An important class of case also was referred to, where the person accused is not acting alone, but in association with others who may not themselves be the objects of criminal proceedings, and where liberation would leave the accused free to continue in association and co-operation with these people for the very same criminal objects participation in which has brought him to justice. Many other examples can be cited in which it might be proper to submit the facts to the Court, and to ask the Court to exercise its discretion with a sole view to the public interest, and to secure the ends of justice.

It is perhaps right to make in conclusion, the self-evident observation that, when an accused person asks for bail or appeals for bail, bail he must get, unless a sufficient ground is brought forward requiring the Court to exercise its discretion by refusing it. A good deal was said about the presumption of innocence. I prefer not to treat the matter as a question of presumption. The accused person has the right to ask for bail; he has the right to have his application considered; and, unless the Court has before it some good reason why bail should not be granted, bail ought to be allowed."

The court refused bail after hearing that the Crown believed that the accused was likely to abscond.

NOTE

The stress placed by the Lord Justice-General on the discretionary function of the court considering a bail application is equally apt today. As in this case, the Crown's attitude to bail is very important, as is also the gravity of the offence and the record of the accused. Under the provisions of the 1980 Act, an accused who is granted bail is usually released on the "standard conditions" listed in section 1(2) of the Act, but it is open to the court or the Crown to insist on additional conditions, such as surrender of passport, as the case requires. In practice, conditions as to money bail under section 1(3) have been rare in practice.

2.   McLaren v. H.M. Advocate
1967 S.L.T. (Notes) 43

An accused person was charged with murder. Under section 2 of the Bail (Scotland) Act 1888 it was provided that all crimes and offences, except murder and treason, were bailable, although section 8 of the Act specifically reserved the right of the Lord Advocate or the High Court to admit to bail any person charged with any crime or offence. The accused applied for bail by petition to the High Court.

LORD JUSTICE-GENERAL (CLYDE): "As the crime charged here is murder the bail provisions in the 1888 Act are consequently not available, hence the present application is made direct to the High Court of Justiciary not under the Act but at common law, in an appeal to the discretionary powers of this Court which lie behind any statutory provision in an Act of Parliament. Indeed, the existence of these discretionary powers is expressly preserved in s. 8 of the 1888 Act. The fact that there are these discretionary powers in the Court is recognised by our standard writers on Criminal Law (see Hume on *Crimes*, II, p. 90), and they are only exercised when the Court sees reasons for such an indulgence in the whole circumstances of the case. The ambit of this discretionary power is similar to that exercisable under the statutes and is described in these terms by the Lord Justice-General in the full Bench case of *Mackintosh* v. *McGlinchy* (supra), at p. 80:— 'The Court has in this matter of bail a discretion and the broad consideration which rules its exercise is a single regard to the public interest and the ends of justice and, in considering any appeal to that discretion, a statement made to the Court on the high responsibility of the Lord Advocate is entitled to great weight'

In the present case the charge is one of murder. Moreover, the Lord Advocate in the exercise of a discretion which is vested in him is opposing the granting of bail in the light of the circumstances as known to him. This is a factor of very great importance in any consideration of the matter by this Court, for he has means of obtaining information and forming a judgment on the matter which are not possessed by us. It was suggested that the abolition of the death penalty has changed the situation and made murder a less important crime than it was in the past. But although Parliament has seen fit to abolish the death penalty for murder and to substitute a period of imprisonment, in the eyes of a court of law murder is still murder whatever the punishment for it may be and we cannot disregard the fact that the charge in the present case is murder.

In the light of these facts, a very strong argument would be necessary to entitle us in the exercise of our discretion to differ from the conclusion to which the Lord Advocate came. Notwithstanding the careful and clear argument presented to us by counsel for the petitioner, we see no reason for reaching any different conclusion from that at which the Lord Advocate himself arrived.

In these circumstances the prayer of the present petition will not be granted."

Bail refused.

NOTE

Sections 2 and 8 of the Bail (Scotland) Act 1888 are now sections 26(1) and 35 of the 1975 Act. In *H.M. Advocate* v. *McTavish*, 1974 S.L.T. 246 an accused charged with the murder was released pending trial after a Crown application to extend the 110-day period was refused. No bail was fixed, the accused being simply ordained to appear. See *infra*, p. 259

3. Young v. H.M. Advocate
1946 J.C. 5

A convicted prisoner appealed against conviction and applied for interim liberation pending his appeal. A single judge refused this application, and the accused then appealed to a Bench of the High Court.

LORD JUSTICE-CLERK (COOPER): ". . .Under section 9 of the Criminal Appeal (Scotland) Act, 1926, it is provided that the Court may, if it seems fit, on the application of an appellant, admit the appellant to bail pending the determination of his appeal. In such a case it appears to me that the considerations by reference to which bail should be granted or refused are not those which are properly applicable to the case of an application for bail by an untried prisoner. In the case of the untried prisoner the presumption of innocence involves, as the well-known case of *Mackintosh* v. *M'Glinchy* indicated, that, unless good reasons can be shown to the contrary, the applicant has a right to be released on bail, if the crime with which he is charged is a bailable crime. But once the prisoner has been convicted, the presumption of innocence is displaced, and the *onus demonstrandi* is on the applicant thereafter to show cause why, pending any appeal which he may take, he should be released from the prison confinement to which he was sentenced following upon the conviction. I note that, in applying a provision in identical terms, the English Court of Criminal Appeal have consistently taken the line that bail pending determination of the appeal is to be granted only in exceptional and unusual circumstances (cases cited in Archbold, Criminal Practice, (31st ed.) p. 285); and while we are not bound by decisions of the Court of Criminal Appeal, still I must state my own view that that rule impresses me as salutary and appropriate.

But in this case the facts are distinctly unusual. The applicant was convicted on 25th April and sentenced to three years' penal servitude on various charges of large scale theft and housebreaking. This is the 9th of October, nearly six months after the imposition of the sentence. The applicant has been granted an extension of the time within which to appeal, and an appeal has been lodged, and will be disposed of by other Judges of this Court within the next two weeks. The case thus comes before us in the extraordinary situation that the applicant, having remained in prison serving his sentence for the greater part of six months, now desires to be released for the final two weeks or thereby which remain before his appeal will be finally determined.

The only ground Mr Taylor put forward in support of this unusual plea is that a co-accused charged under the same indictment, against whom the evidence may or may not have been the same, has in the interval appealed to the High Court of Justiciary and the conviction against him has been quashed. On that ground Mr Taylor maintained that there was, as he put it, 'at least a possibility' of success in the present appellant's appeal. I should hope that the same could be said in the case of every appellant who appeals to the High Court, but such a circumstance seems to me to fall very far short of the exceptional ground which, in my judgment, ought to be advanced in a special case like this for releasing the prisoner and granting bail for the short period which has still to expire before his case is disposed of. I may add that it is to my mind a material consideration that the present applicant has nine previous convictions, and has served quite a number of long terms of imprisonment, the dates of which sufficiently indicate that on more than one occasion he cannot have long been released from prison on one offence before he had committed another. In these circumstances I have no hesitation in advising your Lordships that this application, which is in substance an appeal to us against a decision by the Lord Justice-General refusing bail, should be dismissed."

Bail refused.

NOTE
While it is no doubt true that the presumption of innocence is displaced by the conviction of the accused, Lord Cooper's view that bail pending an appeal should only be granted in exceptional and unusual circumstances may not be of such force today.

Under the 1980 Act, the sanctions for non-compliance with the bail conditions may prove to be more onerous that the forfeiture of any money bail which was required prior to the Act, and in practice, since then, interim liberation on the standard conditions pending appeal against conviction has not been at all uncommon. This point, along with others arising from the operation of the 1980 Act was taken up by Lord Justice-Clerk Wheatley in the following case.

4. Smith v. M.
1982 S.L.T. 421; 1982 S.C.C.R. 115

An accused person was granted bail by the sheriff, even although he had a number of previous convictions, was on probation and had three other cases pending, for one of which he was already on bail. The procurator fiscal appealed to the High Court against the grant for bail.

LORD JUSTICE-CLERK (WHEATLEY): "The reasons for the Crown's opposition to bail were these. At the time when the alleged offence was committed the respondent was in the following position. (1) He was undergoing a probation order for one year which had been imposed on 2nd November 1981 on conviction of a charge of theft. (2) He had three cases outstanding against him in respect of two charges of theft on 28th April 1981 and 6th May 1981 and one charge of fraud on 20th June 1981. For the last of these he was made the subject of a bail order on 2nd February 1982. (3) He had a long list of previous convictions from 1970 onwards showing a regularity of offending. This record consisted of 31 court appearances involving 38 offences. In 1981 alone he had five convictions for theft, including one on indictment. In these circumstances I find it difficult to understand how the sheriff found it appropriate to grant bail to this man. Of course, no report is available from the sheriff under this procedure to explain the reasons for his decision and there might be a perfectly good one. None, however, is apparent to me, and the only one which counsel for the respondent could think of was that the respondent was undergoing out-patient treatment at the Andrew Duncan Clinic for a drink problem which, it was said, should not be interrupted. That certainly does not appear to me to be a legitimate reason for granting bail in view of the circumstances to which I have alluded. I accordingly grant the appeal.

In the light of a fairly extensive experience of the Bail, etc. (Scotland) Act 1980 I consider it desirable to set down certain guidelines in relation to the allowance or refusal of bail in the present state of the law. This is a field in which no absolute classifications can be made, as each case has to be dealt with on its own facts. But it seems to me that there are certain considerations which should generally regulate the decision on allowance of bail, and adherence to such general considerations while having regard to the facts of the individual case could, I am sure, save a lot of needless appeals, thus saving a great deal of judicial time and public expense.

Regard should be given not only to the letter but to the spirit of the Bail, etc. (Scotland) Act 1980. There is, however, the consideration of the public interest. An accused should be granted a bail order unless it can be shown that there are good grounds for not granting it. A complete catalogue of such grounds cannot be compiled. Generally, however, they can fall into two broad categories: (1) the protection of the public and (2) the administration of justice. Previous convictions per se should not be regarded as an automatic reason for refusal of bail, but if there is a significance in the record and the nature of the charge(s) then being preferred against an accused, the consideration of the protection of the public arises. Thus, to take an extreme case, if an accused who has had a persistent record of crime over the years, particularly in relation to one form of crime such as theft by house-breaking, had just recently been discharged from prison for such an offence or offences, it would be reasonable to infer that it was in the public interest that he should not be at large pending his trial. In such cases bail can appropriately be refused. Before turning to consider other considerations, I shall deal with the submission that the presumption of innocence should in logic and equity result in a person charged being released on bail. If this was a good argument in the sense that it should automatically apply, then no bail would be refused except in those cases where no bail is allowed. The presumption of innocence is no doubt a factor, but it does not exclude competing factors which may be more formidable in the circumstances of the case.

One of the factors which in my view is of importance is the allegation that at the time when the alleged offence (or offences) was (or were) committed the accused was in a position of trust to behave as a good citizen and not to breach the law. That can arise in a number of ways and the list which follows is merely illustrative of the more common examples and not exhaustive. I tabulate them as follows: (1) When the accused was already on bail in respect of another offence or offences. (2) When though not on bail he was in an equivalent position, namely, had been ordained to appear at a subsequent court diet for trial on another offence. (3) When he was on probation or undergoing a community service order. (4) When he was on licence or parole. (5) When he was on deferred sentence. In such circumstances I take the view that unless there are cogent reasons for deciding otherwise bail should be refused. Other circumstances which warrant refusal of bail are the nature of the offence in very special circumstances, alleged intimidation of witnesses by assaults or threats, absence of a fixed abode, or reasonable grounds for suspecting that the accused will not turn up for his trial. On the other side of the coin, I do not regard it as good ground for refusing bail that after full committal bail is opposed by the Crown on a vague or unspecified ground that the police are making further enquiries. If the Crown can show it is in the public interest or in the interest of the administration of justice that an accused should be further detained while further enquiries are being made, that is a different matter.

There is another situation with which I am called upon to deal on appeal, namely when after conviction an accused is remanded in custody for reports. As a result of enquiries made I have been informed that the tests which are made to determine the accused's fitness for borstal or a detention centre require his continued detention in a appropriate institution for a period of time. Refusal of bail in such circumstances is understandable. On the other hand, detention in custody is not normally required for a social enquiry report, and there seems no reason why an accused should not be released on bail pending the obtaining of such a report unless there are good reasons for keeping him in detention.

Finally, I am regularly asked to grant interim liberation pending appeals.

If the appeal is against sentence alone, no technical problem arises. If the appeal is against conviction the appellant has first of all to lodge a note of intention to appeal and later on a note of appeal which contains the grounds of appeal. An application for interim liberation can only be properly considered when the grounds of appeal have been lodged, and it is at that point that such an application should be made. As I have already indicated, there may be other considerations one way or another in these various situations, but I have felt constrained to set out these guidelines in view of the divergent attitudes to bail in the lower courts which appeals have disclosed."

Crown appeal allowed; bail refused.

b. *Rights of appeal and review*

Detailed provisions are to be found in sections 30-33 and 299 and 300 of the 1975 Act, but there has been some case law on the circumstances in which review of a decision on bail is competent.

1. **H.M. Advocate v. Jones**
1964 S.L.T. (Sh.Ct.) 50

An accused person was refused bail by the sheriff, appealed against that decision and had his appeal refused by the High Court. Subsequently he applied to the sheriff to have the earlier decision reviewed.

SHERIFF C.H. JOHNSTON, Q.C.: "This is an application made today for review of the decision of this court purporting to be made under section 37 of the Criminal Justice (Scotland) Act, 1963. It is contended by the Crown that the application is incompetent. The material facts are these. The applicant originally applied in this court for bail in respect of the charges at present laid against him on 29th April 1964. The Crown opposed the granting of bail upon two grounds: (a) that the offences of which the applicant is now accused were said to have been committed while he was on bail in respect of other matters, and (b) that the applicant has a substantial record of convictions. This court refused the application for bail and this decision was appealed to the High Court of Justiciary and was upheld by that court. Yesterday, 9th June 1964, the applicant was acquitted by a jury of the charges in respect of which bail had earlier been granted. The applicant is now simply an untried prisoner awaiting trial. In that situation, his solicitor maintains that this court has power in terms of section 37(2) of the 1963 Act to review its earlier decision of 29th April 1964, albeit that decision has been upheld by the High Court on appeal. The Crown contends that the determination of the High Court of an appeal from a decision of this court is in itself a 'decision' within the meaning of section 37, and that all applications for review made thereafter must be made direct to the High Court of Justiciary, whether of the present type or as to the amount of bail fixed, if bail is fixed. I was informed by both parties that section 37 has not been the subject of any authoritative decision binding on me, and also that section 37 contains the whole of the provisions relating to review as distinct from appeal. In my view, the Crown's contention is well founded. There can be no doubt that the determination of the High Court on an appeal from a decision of this court is a decision in the general sense. The question is whether it is a decision within the meaning of this section. Such applications can be made only at the instance of an accused person. It is open to such a person to make repeated applications for review either of a decision to admit to bail or of a decision as to the bail fixed, and in fact many applications of the latter type come before this court. If the Crown's contention is sound, in every case in which the High Court on an appeal from an inferior court grants bail, or upholds the decision of the judge of first instance to grant bail, these repeated applications for review would require to be made to the High Court.

The result may be to encumber the High Court with an ever-increasing number of applications for review, but I do not find warrant in this section for the view that a judge in an inferior court has power to review either the amount of bail fixed by the Supreme Court, or, as in this case where a material change of circumstances has taken place, the ultimate determination as to the allowance or refusal of bail. Such a course would offend against all established practice, and could be pursued only upon the clearest legislative warrant. This is absent. This application is incompetent, and ought to have been made to the High Court of Justiciary. I think it right to add that I have been greatly assisted in my consideration of this technical but not unimportant point of procedure by the clear arguments of the procurator-fiscal depute and the solicitor for the applicant."

Application refused.

NOTE

Section 37 of the Criminal Justice (Scotland) Act 1963 is now sections 30 and 299 of the 1975 Act. The references to "bail" and "amounts of bail" found in those and other pre-1980 enactments have now to be construed in terms of section 1(4) of the Bail etc. (Scotland) Act 1980.

In practice *H.M. Advocate* v. *Jones* is often thought of as authority for the proposition that once the matter of bail has been considered in the High Court, any reconsideration of the matter must also take place there. But this is not quite accurate, as the next case shows.

2. **Ward v. H.M. Advocate**
1972 S.L.T. (Notes) 22

An accused person was allowed bail by the sheriff. The Crown appealed against the grant of bail, but the High Court refused the

Crown appeal. The accused then presented a note to the High Court craving review of the amount of bail fixed by the sheriff.

LORD CAMERON: "When an appeal is taken by the prosecutor against allowance of bail and the appeal is refused, then further procedure depends upon the terms of the relevant statute, which in this case is the Criminal Justice (Scotland) Act 1963. Section 37(2) of that Act gives a court the power to review its decision as to granting or refusing bail, or, in particular, as to the amount of bail, if bail is allowed. In my opinion the court referred to in s. 37(2) is the same court as is referred to in s. 37(1) and therefore, when the question is one of reduction of the amount of bail already fixed, it is prima facie for the court which has in the first instance fixed the amount of bail to deal with that issue on a review. In the present case, as it is now admitted (contrary to what was said in the note of appeal) (1) the only appeal to the High Court was by the prosecutor against the allowance of bail and (2) the amount of bail to be found if the prosecutor's appeal failed, as it did, was not in issue; in these circumstances the question of the amount of bail to be found is still within the purview of the court which initially fixed the amount of the bail and whose decision in that respect has not so far been subjected to review. As the High Court dealt only with one particular point then, the case stands thus: The appellant was admitted to bail by the competent court: its decision in so doing was upheld on appeal and the initial statutory power of review of the amount of bail fixed by that court was not affected, as no determination on that point was made by the High Court. It therefore appears to me that it is still open to the court which originally fixed the amount of bail to exercise the power of review in that regard which is specifically provided for by s. 37(2) of the Act of 1963 and consequently that this appeal is incompetent as being premature.

My attention has been drawn to the case of *H.M. Advocate* v. *Jones*, 1964 S.L.T. (Sh.Ct.) 50. That was a somewhat unusual case and differed substantially in its circumstances from the present. In that case, far from the sheriff being invited to review his own decision in terms of the statute, he was being invited to review a decision of the High Court. All that s. 37 says is this — 'A court shall . ∴ . have power to review its decision.' The Act does not say a court which has allowed, refused or fixed the amount of bail shall have power to review the decision of another and a superior court in any of these matters. The issue in the case of *Jones* (supra) was in effect whether the sheriff-substitute had power to reverse a decision of the High Court on an appeal from the sheriff-substitute. In holding that such a review was incompetent, I think the sheriff-substitute was correct, but that is not this case. Where a High Court decision has been given on an appeal on whether or not bail should be allowed, but the issue of amount of bail, if allowed, is not raised, then I am of the opinion that review of the amount of bail is still within the competence of the court which originally allowed bail and fixed the amount of it. In these circumstances the present appeal will be refused."

                                                        Note refused.

NOTE

This decision would appear to be unaffected by the Bail etc. (Scotland) Act 1980. For example, a sheriff might impose as a condition of bail that the accused surrender his passport. If that issue were not subsequently canvassed in the High Court on a Crown appeal against the grant of bail, then that condition could competently be reviewed by the sheriff on the motion of the accused.

CHAPTER 7

FIRST STEPS IN SOLEMN PROCEDURE

a. Judicial examination and committal

Once an accused person has been charged by the police and the procurator fiscal decides to proceed by petition rather than summary complaint, the accused will normally be brought before the sheriff next day for judicial examination. The sheriff court is not required to sit on Saturdays, Sundays or court holidays, but may sit on any day for the disposal of criminal business: Bail etc. (Scotland) Act 1980, s. 10 (1). Prior to the first appearance of the accused in court the accused has a statutory right under section 19 of the 1975 Act to have intimation sent to a solicitor that legal assistance is sought, and to a private interview with the solicitor. No practical difficulties usually arise, as accused persons who have not availed themselves of this right are automatically offered the services of the duty solicitor acting under the Criminal Legal Aid Scheme.

Judicial examination as reconstituted under section 6 of the 1980 Act is still somewhat of a novelty. For an excellent description of the procedure to be followed, see Sheriff I.D. Macphail, "Judicial Examination" (1982) 27 J.L.S. (Workshop) 296.

As at the time of writing, only two cases have come before the High Court wherein the procedures followed under the new sections 20A and 20B of the 1975 Act have been made the subject of challenge.

1. Carmichael v. Armitage
1983 S.L.T. 216

An accused person emitted a declaration at judicial examination. The fiscal objected to the declaration being read to the jury. The sheriff overruled the Crown objection and the fiscal appealed to the High Court.

OPINION OF THE COURT: "This appeal raises for the first time an important point in relation to the manner in which a declaration can be emitted by an accused during a judicial examination in terms of the Criminal Procedure (Scotland) Act 1975 as amended. The declaration was made on 15 March

228

1982 and at a preliminary diet on 20 September 1982 the appellant moved the sheriff not to allow the declaration to be read to the jury at the trial on 18 October 1982. The ground for the motion was that the declaration by the respondent was not an account by the respondent himself of the events described in his statement, since the statement had been written out by his solicitor, Mr Devlin. There was another ground submitted by the appellant to the sheriff, namely that the declaration was not spontaneous, being read by the respondent from a previously prepared statement, but this ground was not argued in this court, it being accepted that a previously prepared statement could be used by an accused provided it was truly his own, and prepared and written out by himself. The sheriff refused the appellant's motion, and against that decision this appeal has been taken.

The ground of appeal stated by the appellant in his note of appeal is in these terms: 'The said statement was written and edited by Gerald A. Devlin, solicitor, on behalf of his client said Andrew Armitage, and accordingly when said statement was read out by said Andrew Armitage at his judicial examination he was not giving an account in his own words of what happened but reading from a statement prepared by his solicitor. Said statement is accordingly not a true declaration by said Andrew Armitage and should not be allowed to be read to the jury'. In his report to this court the sheriff draws our attention to the fact that the appellant did not imply any question of impropriety on the part of the solicitor Mr Devlin, and this we unreservedly accept. The report goes on to provide the following facts. Mr Devlin agreed that the declaration at the judicial examination was read from a prepared script which was in his handwriting. He said, however, that what was written was prepared on the respondent's instructions, and that while the whole tenor, sense and meaning of the declaration were those of the respondent, there were some words in the declaration imported by himself to give cohesion to the declaration. He was unable to state from recollection which particular words fell into that category. At a later stage in the hearing Mr Devlin clarified his concession regarding the composition of the declaration by saying that it was virtually verbatim of the respondent but was *structured* to make it reasonable. (The emphasis is ours.) He pointed out to the sheriff that an accused is fully entitled to be advised before emitting a declaration and that such advice must include advice as to how best to express the meaning of his account of the matter. Without such advice, many inarticulate, weak and flustered accused could be deprived of the benefit of a declaration which is, and always has been, for the ascertainment of the truth of the matter and not for the benefit of one side or the other.

The sheriff in refusing the appellant's motion stated that he could find nothing in the agreed facts of the case which indicated that the declaration was not what the respondent deliberately said himself freely and voluntarily, when in his sound mind and sober senses, or that his solicitor did other than advise before the examination. Having so expressed himself, he gave leave to appeal.

The current statutory provisions regarding the judicial examination of an accused are in ss. 19, 20, 20A and 20B of the 1975 Act aforesaid. Subsection

(2) of s. 19 provides: 'Such solicitor shall be entitled to have a private interview with the person accused before he is examined on declaration, and to be present at such examination.' Section 19 is in almost similar terms to s. 17 of the Criminal Procedure (Scotland) Act 1887. The only differences are: (1) the lay-out of the provisions, and (2) subs. (2) of s. 19 of the 1975 Act does not contain the suffix 'which shall be conducted according to the existing practice' which appeared in s. 17 of the 1887 Act. The only additional provisions which affect the position of the solicitor for the accused at the examination given by the 1975 Act are to be found in subss. (3) and (4) of s. 20A. The former provides that if the accused is represented by a solicitor at the examination the sheriff has to tell the accused that he may consult that solicitor before answering any question. The latter provides that, with the permission of the sheriff, the solicitor may ask the accused any question the purpose of which is to clear up any ambiguity in an answer given by the accused to the procurator fiscal at the examination, or to give the accused an opportunity to answer any question which he has previously refused to answer.

The learned advocate-depute submitted that the reason for the omission of the words 'which shall be conducted according to the existing practice' from s. 19(2) was that the existing practice was being innovated upon by the introduction of the rights to the accused and his solicitor conferred by subss. (3) and (4) of s. 20A. In this he was right in our opinion. The advocate-depute then submitted that the existing procedure provided no authority for the respondent's argument and the sheriff's decision, and that subss. (3) and (4) aforesaid in no way altered that submission. The basis of his argument was this. The procedure envisages that at the examination the accused will be asked certain questions. If he elects to answer these questions the answers must be his own. To allow him to read out a statement prepared by his solicitor, even if it purported to be what he himself said to his solicitor, was not the equivalent of his own answers. The advocate-depute accepted that if an accused prepared and wrote out a statement himself it would be admissible, treating it as an aide-memoire, because it was entirely his own composition, but once everything beyond that was allowed it could give rise to all kinds of questions of authorship of and responsibility for the contents. While it was not suggested that the statement here had been in any way affected other than as frankly admitted by Mr Devlin, once the principle that only the accused's own and unassisted statement was admissible was breached the door was being opened to innumerable problems. Neither statute nor authorities lent countenance to the sheriff's view, which seemed to run contrary to the whole concept of the procedure. In support of his contention the advocate-depute referred us to certain authorities which dealt with the earlier procedure, and counsel for the respondent accepted that these fully and properly represented the law on the purposes for which they were cited. Hume on *Crimes*, vol. 2 at p. 328 says: 'Fully to establish the credit of a declaration, the witnesses must have been present while it was emitted, and be able to swear, that it was the pannel's own free and advised act, done by him in his sound mind, and sober senses'. This, in effect, is repeated in Alison's *Criminal Law*, vol. 2 at

p. 557. In Anderson's *Criminal Law of Scotland* (2nd ed.) it is stated that the agent is not allowed to interfere during the examination of the prisoner. It is further stated that 'strictly speaking a prisoner's declaration is not evidence, and it may be used by either party merely as an explanation of actual evidence'. In the article on Crime—Solemn Procedure by Mr J. Robertson Christie, Q.C., then Clerk of Justiciary, in vol. 5 of the *Encyclopaedia of the Laws of Scotland* (1928) at p. 210, para. 518, the author states: 'But where, failing declinature, the examination proceeds, the function of the law agent becomes merely advisory, and it would seem that he is not entitled to intervene in the examination, as the Act of 1887 provides that this is to be conducted according to the practice previously existing.' These authorities, it was maintained, neither sanctioned nor envisaged the procedure which the sheriff had accepted as permissible. On the contrary, they ran contrary to it, and there was nothing in the statutory provisions which either authorised or countenanced it.

Counsel for the respondent argued that each case involving this procedure has to be decided on its own facts. The passage in Hume supra talks of the pannel's own free and advised act. This clearly indicates that an accused is entitled to have full advice from his solicitor concerning his declaration and this must include advice on how it should be stated. There was no practical difference between the solicitor discussing with the accused beforehand what he would say in his declaration and writing down what his client says in that regard to enable the client to use the written statement properly to facilitate the presentation of his declaration. The fact that in the instant case the solicitor had 'structured' the statement to make it reasonable did not invalidate it, since it was accepted that the solicitor had done nothing more than he had frankly admitted doing. The basic question is—was the statement the respondent's own declaration or did the solicitor's help change the character of the document? That question should be answered in the respondent's favour and the sheriff's decision should be upheld.

In our opinion the Crown's contention is well founded and the appeal must be granted. The whole concept of the procedure is that it is the accused and the accused alone who must make the declaration, whatever prior advice he may have had from his solicitor. While the declaration may not be strictly evidence the basic rules of evidence must attach to it. What the respondent and his advisers seem to regard as permissible procedure in the taking of the statement from the accused which the solicitor reduces to writing seems not to differ from the taking of a precognition, and a precognition cannot be used in evidence. The dangers envisaged by the Crown in the procedure sought to be sanctioned are very real indeed. Even in cases like the present one when no impropriety of any kind is imputed to the solicitor, well-intentioned solicitors in 'structuring' the statement may, even unconsciously, affect its nature. Terminology different from that used by the accused may be used and that can affect the content of the statement. A reason why a precognition cannot be used in evidence is that it is not the document of the witness but the document of the person taking the precognition. By parity of reasoning the statement is not that of the accused when reduced to writing by his solicitor. We agree with the Crown that such a substitution for the oral evidence of an accused can play no part in the procedure, and that the sheriff here came to the wrong decision. We shall accordingly sustain the appeal and order that the record of the declaration made by the respondent at the judicial examination should not be read to the jury."

Crown appeal allowed.

NOTE

This case is a perfect example of eighteenth- and nineteenth-century institutional authority still influencing the development of modern law. None of the new statutory provisions deal with the unique problem thrown up, so the High Court went back two centuries to try to find an answer by reference to first principles. So well-intentioned solicitors must not "structure" a declaration, any more than well-intentioned policemen must not "structure" a statement by a suspect or accused.

2. MacKenzie v. H.M. Advocate
1983 S.L.T. 304

An accused person allegedly made a "confession" to the police. This was put to him at judicial examination, where the prosecutor asked him whether he made the statement alleged. The defence objected to the question, but the sheriff allowed it. At the preliminary diet the decision was upheld and the accused appealed to the High Court.

LORD ROBERTSON: "This is a note of appeal in a case from the sheriff court in Glasgow where a preliminary diet was held in the case of Her Majesty's Advocate against Lewis Wylie MacKenzie. The diet for trial is fixed for 29 November 1982. The question posed in the note of appeal is the competency of a question put by the procurator fiscal at the judicial examination of the said Lewis Wylie MacKenzie on 25 February 1982 in the sheriff court. The matter arose in the course of the questioning of the panel by the procurator fiscal. The matter arose in this way. The procurator fiscal, in the course of his examination posed the following question: 'Can I direct your attention to the sheet of paper which was attached to the copy petition which contains an alleged confession made by you? The sheet of paper contains a written record of an extra-judicial confession allegedly made by you at Rutherglen Police Office on 24 February 1982 or in the hearing of Detective Constable Philip MacDonald and Douglas Brown and reads "just my luck, I knew I'd be picked out" '. "The question then was: 'Did you make that statement to the police officers?" Apparently at this point the solicitor for the panel took exception to the question on the basis that the purported extra-judicial confession was not a confession as such and asked the learned sheriff to rule on the matter. It was submitted to the learned sheriff that the words did not constitute a confession and in particular they were not of an incriminating character and relevant to the charge and in the circumstances the question should not have been allowed and as a consequence thereof the further remarks appearing in the transcript of the proceedings should be struck out because they were incompetently received in the course of the judicial examination. The sheriff rejected the submission and allowed the question. On appeal it was submitted by counsel for the appellant that the sheriff had not taken the proper course in terms of the procedure laid down in the statute. Section 20A of the 1975 Act as amended lays down that an accused on being brought before the sheriff for examination on a charge may be questioned by the prosecutor in so far as such questioning is directed towards eliciting any denial, explanation, justification or comment which the accused may have as regards (a) matters referred to in the charge or rather matters averred in the charge and (b) the alleged making by the accused to or in the hearing of an officer of police of an extra-judicial confession whether or not a full admission, relevant to the charge, provided that questions under this paragraph may only be put if the accused has, before the examination received from the prosecutor, or from an officer of police, a written record of the confession allegedly made.' The argument put was that the statement allegedly made by the panel was not or did not come within the clear category of an extra-judicial confession and accordingly that questioning under s. 20A(1)(b) was not legitimate. The wording of this particular section does not appear to be as clear as it might have been. There is no definition of 'confession' in the statute and it is accordingly doubtful as to exactly what is intended. The wording 'extra-judicial confession (whether or not a full admission) relevant to the charge' suggests that the confession referred to is something less than a full admission and must be susceptible of interpretation provided the statement is relevant to the charge. In the context it seems to me that the definition of 'confession' must be that the statement is clearly susceptible of being regarded as an incriminating statement. I did not understand counsel for the appellant to differ from that. In the present case the statement allegedly made is perhaps not a full admission but in my view it cannot be said that the statement was not or cannot be susceptible of being regarded as an incriminating statement. In my view the margins of what can be properly regarded as coming under the definition of 'confession' in the section may not be entirely clear but in the present case (and that is all that we are considering here) I do not think it can be properly said that this statement is not susceptible of being so interpreted. Taking that view I do not think that the sheriff has been shown to have been wrong in making the decision he made with regard to the statement. The matter remains for fuller consideration at the trial. It, as I understand, was accepted, that it will be open to the panel to challenge the admission of this statement at a later stage. This court at the present moment is only considering the matter in terms of s. 76 of the Act, 76(1)(c) of which in setting out the court's jurisdiction, says that there must be some point which could be resolved with advantage before the trial. It is upon that section that the appeal is based. I am not able at present to see how it can be said that the matter can be resolved with advantage before the trial. On the narrow basis that each case must be decided upon its own facts I consider that this matter would be better left for future consideration. I do not accept that the panel will suffer any prejudice if that course is taken. I accordingly move your Lordships to reject the note of appeal."

Appeal refused.

NOTE
    This seems a very narrow decision and Lord Robertson appears to concede as much. While it is no doubt true that the admissibility of the statement can be challenged at the trial, it should always be made the subject of objection at judicial examination, lest silence on the part of the accused is made the subject of comment later.
    But was the court right in its view that the phrase "Just my luck, I knew I'd be picked out" is susceptible of being interpreted as a confession? Surely it is not an admission of a crime, only of bad luck!
    Once the examination is complete, the next step is committal, either for further examination or "until liberated in due course of law," known as "full committal." Until comparatively recently, there was some doubt as to the length of time for which an accused might be committed for further examination.

3.   **Herron v. A,B,C and D**
1977 S.L.T. (Sh. Ct.) 24

Four accused persons appeared on petition on 14 April 1976. They were committed for further examination. On 23 April 1976 warrants for full committal were placed before the sheriff. He refused to grant the warrants.

SHERIFF MACPHAIL: "At 2 p.m. this afternoon [23 April 1976], before the commencement of the business of the summary court, the procurator fiscal depute appeared before me in chambers and moved me to commit accused persons for trial in a number of cases. In each case the pro forma warrant of committal was, as usual, printed on the same sheet as the petition, warrant for apprehension and search, and warrant of committal for further examination. When looking over these documents I observed that in three of the cases—the cases of A, who is charged with housebreaking with intent to steal, B, who is charged with assault, and C and D, who are charged with housebreaking—the warrant of committal for further examination had been signed by Sheriff Stone on 14 April 1976. I am informed that these accused persons had appeared before Sheriff Stone at 2 p.m. on that date, and it is recorded in each warrant that no declaration was emitted and the sheriff committed the accused for further examination. In each of these cases the pro forma warrant of committal for trial which was laid before me today had been date-stamped '22 April 1976'. But today's date is 23 April 1976. I was informed that the warrants should have been placed before me yesterday, but that had not been done, through some administrative oversight, the details of which I shall consider later in this judgment. In view of the fact that eight clear days had elapsed between the signature of the warrants for committal for further examination on 14 April and the placing of the warrants of full committal before me today, I was in some doubt as to the competency of granting warrants of full committal in these cases, and asked the procurator fiscal depute to address me on the matter after the disposal of the business of the summary court. That hearing took place in chambers at 4.30 p.m. Neither the accused persons nor their solicitors were present at any part of these proceedings today: that is another matter about which I will have something to say later. At the conclusion of the hearing I announced my decision, which was to refuse to grant the warrants for full committal. Since it is highly unusual, if not unique, in modern practice for a sheriff to refuse to commit an accused person for trial, I have decided to issue a written statement of the reasons for my decision.

It appears that in modern times two different views are entertained as to the present law relating to the length of time which may elapse between committal for further examination and committal for trial. The first is that the length of time is not absolutely fixed, but as a general rule does not exceed eight days. The second is that the length of time is absolutely fixed at no longer than eight days by the Criminal Procedure Act 1701. If the first view of the law is correct, I must consider whether any good reason has been stated for departing from the general rule. If the second view is correct, it is impossible for me to grant a warrant because the limit of time fixed by the Act of 1701 has been exceeded.

Because of the pressure of other judicial duties as summary sheriff and the desirability of issuing as soon as possible a written explanation of my decision for the consideration of the Crown authorities and the legal advisers of the accused, it is impossible to examine the law as fully as the importance of the subject deserves. From a cursory review of the sources available to me, it appears that the first view is derived from Hume, ii, 81-82, and the authorities there cited: *Andrew* v. *Murdoch* (1806) 13 F.C. 569, *Mor. App.* s.v. 'Wrongous Imprisonment' No. 3, and (1814) 2 Dow's App. 401; and *Arbuckle* v. *Taylor* (1815) 3 Dow's App. 160. Hume, having explained that a prisoner who has been committed for further examination is not entitled to bail, continues: 'Yet certainly, on the other hand, in this as in all other things, the magistrate must observe good faith and fair dealing with the prisoner: For if he unreasonably delays to proceed with his precognition, or make use of false and affected pretences of further inquiries, on purpose to lengthen the man's confinement; this, without a doubt, is a malversation, and an act of oppression, for which the magistrate shall be answerable at common law'. Hume's footnote to that passage is in the following terms: 'In this opinion, the author has been confirmed by that of the Lord Chancellor, given on occasion of remitting the case of *Arbuckle and Taylor*: "At the same time, what I said in the case of *Andrew* v. *Murdoch*, I repeat in this: A commitment for further examination must not be made use of, as a commitment for custody in order to trial, and, therefore, the law has properly limited it: the law has said that it shall be a commitment for further examination, to take place within a reasonable time. What is a reasonable time, may be difficult to say; whether one, two, three, four or five days; for what may be a reasonable time in one case, may not be so in another; but a Magistrate is bound to terminate his commitment for farther examination within a reasonable time. And I cannot entertain a doubt, that an action might be maintained against a Magistrate for committing for further examination, if his view and purpose in so doing were, to put the party under the same hardship and oppression as would belong to a commitment for custody in order to trial." See Dow's Reports of Appeal Cases, vol. iii., p. 184.'

The second view is based on the Criminal Procedure Act 1701, which was originally entitled, 'Act for preventing wrongous Imprisonments and against undue delayes in Tryals.' In its original form, the Act provided: 'And his Majestie with advice and consent forsaid Extends this Act for preventing of wrongous imprisonment to the case of all confinements not either consented to by the party or inflicted after tryal by sentence And farder Discharges all closs imprisonments beyond the space of Eight dayes from the commitment under the pains of wrongous imprisonment above set down' (A.P.S., x, 272 at pp. 274-275). Much of that passage was repealed by the Statute Law Revision (Scotland) Act 1964, Sched. 1, so that the only remaining clause is, 'And farder Discharges all closs imprisonments beyond the space of Eight dayes from the commitment.' The Act of 1701, so far as unrepealed by the Statute Law Revision (Scotland) Acts of 1908 and 1964, is conveniently set out in the volume of the *Acts of the Parliaments of Scotland, 1424-1707*, second revised edition, printed by authority in 1966, at pp. 162-163. The first part of the Act, from 'Our Sovereign Lord' to 'shall be void and null' was repealed by the Criminal Procedure (Scotland) Act 1975, Sched. 10, Pt. I, but it would appear that otherwise the Act of 1701, to the extent printed by authority in 1966, remains in force.

As to the passage which I have quoted, Hume observes in ch. IV of his second volume, 'The statute concludes with forbidding, under the same pains, all *close* imprisonment, or, as I understand it, solitary and inaccessible imprisonment, for more than eight days from the time of commitment' (Hume, ii, 117). He does not, however, suggest in ch. II that the statute limits to eight days the period for which the prisoner may be imprisoned between the two diets of committal.

Alison, in his chapter on 'Arrest and Precognition', stated that the Act of 1701 has no application to committal for further examination. He writes: 'A prisoner committed under a warrant for farther examination, is entitled to have that temporary state of confinement brought to a conclusion within a reasonable time, as applied to the circumstances and nature of the case; but he is not entitled, as a matter of right, to bail, nor does his incarceration fall under the Act of 1701' (Alison, ii, 135). He goes on to say that the provisions of the Act apply only to a 'custody in order to trial' and not 'that temporary detention, while as yet it is undetermined whether there shall be any custody in order to trial or not.' It is true that the earlier provisions of the Act are concerned with 'custody in order to trial', but the latter part of the Act, in which the clause discharging 'closs imprisonment' occurs, begins, in its original form, with a statement that the Act 'for preventing of wrongous imprisonment' is extended to the case of *all* confinements not either consented to by the party or inflicted after trial by sentence. The authorities cited by Alison (*Fife* v. *Ogilvie* (1762) Mor. 11750; *Andrew*, supra; *Arbuckle*, supra) are primarily concerned with the question whether a prisoner committed for further examination is entitled to apply for bail, and it may be that any opinions therein to the effect that the Act does not apply to commitments for further examination are to be understood secundum materiam subjectam. Indeed, elsewhere, when discussing the clause of the Act which discharges 'closs imprisonment', Alison writes: 'By close confinement, here mentioned, is to be understood solitary and inaccessible confinement; and, therefore, it is worthy of consideration, whether it is safe to prolong the solitary confinement, in which prisoners are usually kept in the interval between their being committed for further examination, and committed till liberated in due course of law, beyond that period. Indeed, in the general case, it is not expedient to continue the confinement on this hazardous warrant for a longer time than eight days, and it will require special circumstances to render any longer continuance not a matter of risk at common law' (Alison, ii, 209-210).

Alison's work was published in 1833. In the first edition of Macdonald's *Criminal Law* (1867), the law was stated thus: 'When the prisoner has been examined, he may then be committed, either for trial or for further examination—if the latter, he is not entitled to bail, and therefore such confinement must only be for a reasonable time. No exact time can be fixed, as the reasonableness of a delay may depend very much on circumstances. But whatever be the time during which the accused is detained under commitment for examination, it is not lawful to keep him in close confinement for more than eight days from the first commitment' (p. 297). The authorities cited are Hume, ii, 81-82; Alison, ii, 134-135; *Fife*, supra; *Andrew*, supra; *Arbuckle*, supra; and the Act of 1701. That passage was preserved, substantially unaltered, in the second edition (1877), p. 263. By the time of the succeeding edition, s. 18 of the Criminal Procedure (Scotland) Act 1887 had been passed, enabling the accused to apply for bail at any time after being brought before a magistrate for examination. The last sentence of the passage quoted was dropped, and the third edition (1894) read: 'When the accused has been examined, he may be committed to prison until liberation "in due course of law", or for further examination—if the latter, it must be for a reasonable time. . . . What may be a reasonable time depends on circumstances. But as the accused can now apply for bail after he has been brought before a magistrate, for examination, the duration of commitment for further examination is of little consequence' (p. 272). The same sentences appeared in the fourth edition

(1929), pp. 303-304, and a passage to the same effect appears in Green's *Encyclopaedia of the Laws of Scotland*, vol. 5 (1928 ed.), para. 523. But in the current (5th) edition of Macdonald (1948), the paragraph is entirely rewritten, and includes the following passage: 'The object of a commitment for further examination is to enable the prosecutor to complete his enquiry, *e.g.* by precognition of persons who may be cited to attend for that purpose under the warrant granted on the petition to apprehend. This commitment ought not to exceed a reasonable time (Hume, ii, 81-82; Alison, ii, 134-135), which in practice means eight days' (pp. 203-204). No reference is there made to the Act of 1701.

In Anderson's *Criminal Law of Scotland* (2nd ed., 1904), p. 240, the law is stated thus: 'In the case of commitment for further examination the commitment must be for a reasonable time (*Fife; Andrew; Arbuckle*). In no case can close confinement be ordered for more than eight days from the first commitment (Act 1701, cap. 6).'

Successive editions of Renton and Brown's *Criminal Procedure* have included the following passage (at p. 46 in the current edition): 'The length of time which may intervene between committal for further examination and committal for trial is not absolutely fixed, but as a general rule does not exceed eight days. This must be particularly observed in those cases where bail cannot be insisted upon till after committal until liberation in due course of law.' The learned editor of the current (4th) edition (1972) has added at the end of the first sentence a footnote reference to the speech of Lord Eldon, L.C., in *Arbuckle* supra at p. 184; but no reference is made to the Act of 1701.

The most recent statement of the law is contained in the Second Report of the Departmental Committee on *Criminal Procedure in Scotland* (Chairman: The Hon. Lord Thomson) (1975, Cmnd. 6218). In ch. 10, on committal procedure, the committee state: 'Eight days is laid down by the Criminal Procedure Act 1701 as being the limit of the time which an accused may spend in prison between the two diets of committal' (para. 10.05; see also para. 10.01). Against that view must be set the statement by Professor J. D. B. Mitchell that the Act of 1701 'does not of itself deal with the period between arrest and committal for trial' (*Constitutional Law* (2nd ed.), p. 339). Professor T. B. Smith appears to share that view because he suggests 'that express provision by statute should be made limiting the lawful period of detention for "further examination" without commitment for trial' ('Bail before Trial: Reflections of a Scottish Lawyer' (1960) 108 Univ. of Pennsylvania L.R. 305, reprinted in *Studies Critical and Comparative*, p. 252, at p. 264).

It is clear from the foregoing survey of the sources and literature which are available to me that two views are held in modern times. On the one hand, according to the current editions of Macdonald and of Renton and Brown, the length of time which may intervene between the two diets of committal is not absolutely fixed, but 'ought not to exceed a reasonable time, which in practice means eight days' (Macdonald), or 'as a general rule does not exceed eight days' (Renton and Brown). According to the Thomson Committee, on the other hand, the Act of 1701 has absolutely fixed eight days as the limit. It is obviously difficult to make a quick decision on this matter, but I have formed the opinion that the latter view is to be preferred. The clause of the Act which discharges 'all closs imprisonments beyond the space of Eight dayes from the commitment' appears in a different part of the Act from that which is concerned with persons 'imprisoned for custody in order to tryal.' The clause was understood by Alison, Macdonald (who was himself responsible for the first and second editions of his work) and Anderson to refer to persons who had been committed for further examination. Parliament must be assumed to have been aware of the law and practice as enunciated by these writers when it took care to preserve that clause, while repealing other clauses of the Act, by the Statute Law Revision (Scotland) Acts of 1906 and 1964 and the Criminal Procedure (Scotland) Act 1975. I have already noted that the Act of 1964 repealed the surrounding clauses while leaving the clause under discussion standing. It must therefore still have an effective meaning today. In my opinion its only possible application is to imprisonment upon a warrant of commitment for further examination. The rights of those who are imprisoned upon a warrant of commitment for trial are fully dealt with elsewhere in the Act of 1701 and in the modern rules in s. 101 of the 1975 Act (formerly s. 43 of the Criminal Procedure (Scotland) Act 1887). If the expression 'closs imprisonment' means no more than solitary confinement, it would have been unnecessary to preserve the clause in 1964, because by that date it was not competent for a judge to order imprisonment with solitary confinement. The expression must therefore mean no more than the condition of detention appropriate to a person committed for further examination.

If the clause is so understood, it follows that in the cases presently before me it is now impossible to commit the accused for trial. The warrants of committal for further examination are now spent, and all procedure on the present petitions has come to an end.

I shall, however, also consider the matter upon the basis that, contrary to the opinion which I have expressed, the Act of 1701 is inapplicable, and there is nothing more than a general rule of practice that the length of time between the diets of committal should not exceed eight days. Such a rule must nevertheless be a rule of considerable importance in relation to the due administration of justice and the interests of the accused in particular. It is of importance that his full committal should not be delayed any longer than necessary, because thereafter he will be in a more advantageous position when applying for bail and will be entitled to appeal against a refusal of his application, and the 110-day rule and the other rules provided by s. 101 of the 1975 Act will come into operation. In the present cases, the explanation which I have been given of the delay in applying for full committal is as follows. When an accused person is committed for further examination, the petition relating to him is retained by the sheriff clerk's department, and when the procurator fiscal desires to have the accused fully committed, an officer of his department so informs the sheriff clerk's department. On the day when full committal is desired, the petition is date-stamped and brought before the sheriff by an officer of the sheriff clerk's department in the presence of a procurator fiscal depute, who moves the sheriff for a warrant for full committal. In daily practice a number of accused persons are fully committed in this court by the summary sheriff, so that a number of petitions are placed before him each day at 2 p.m. If the officer of the sheriff clerk's department has neglected to place before the sheriff any of the petitions desired by the procurator fiscal, that fact is likely to escape the notice of the procurator fiscal's department until the following day, when the latter department receives from the sheriff clerk's department a list of those accused persons who have been fully committed. As I understand the explanation tendered to me, the procurator fiscal's department desired that these cases should come before me yesterday, but, in accordance with the administrative arrangement which I have described, no check to see whether in fact that had been done was made until today. The original failure is to be attributed to the sheriff clerk's department, and the failure by the procurator fiscal's department to discover that mistake until today should be attributed to the working of the administrative arrangement. But it appears to me that such failures cannot be excused, having regard to the importance of full committal as a step in criminal procedure. The procurator fiscal depute suggested in argument that the delay in the present cases was not oppressive, but that is not an assumption which I would be prepared to make. It seems clear from Hume, ii, 81-82, that any unreasonable delay is per se oppressive; and I cannot characterise as reasonable a delay caused by a failure, however understandable in the context of the prevailing administrative arrangements, to ascertain timeously whether the persons sought to be fully committed had in fact been fully committed. Accordingly, upon this alternative view of the law, I would also be prepared to hold that it is incompetent to commit these accused persons for trial.

That is sufficient to explain my refusal of the present applications for full committal, but I think I should add that my consideration of the matter has been somewhat hampered by the absence of any contradictor of the arguments advanced on behalf of the procurator fiscal. I have already mentioned that neither the accused nor their solicitors were present today, or at the time of the hearing later in the afternoon. It appears to be the established practice of this court that neither the accused nor his solicitor is present at the diet of committal for trial. I am unaware of the origin of the practice, but I would observe that in a situation such as the present, where a question of difficulty or importance arises, it is less than convenient. The whole responsibility for protecting the interests of the accused is thrown upon the sheriff. This afternoon, when I appointed the hearing, I instructed the sheriff clerk to try to arrange for the attendance of the accused persons' duty solicitors. Understandably enough, one of them could not be found, and the other was unable to be present. After the hearing, I instructed the sheriff clerk to inform the duty solicitors of the result. It is, of course, the responsibility of these solicitors to represent the accused until they are admitted to bail or liberated in due course of law, under para. 8 of the Legal Aid (Scotland) (Criminal Proceedings) Scheme 1975.

It is unnecessary for me to express any view as to the competency of the practice to which I have referred. It is, however, interesting to consider whether, if the accused had been present today, they would have been at once entitled to be set at liberty as soon as I had announced my decision. In addition, it may be observed that the practice does not assist the accused to make an application for bail immediately upon being fully committed, as he would be entitled to do if he were present. His solicitor may be able to ascertain in advance from the procurator fiscal's department the date when it is proposed that he should be fully committed, and make an application for bail on that date to the diet court sheriff immediately after full committal by the summary sheriff. But otherwise the accused may have to await intimation of the warrant for imprisonment under s. 22 (3) of the Act of 1975, and only then, once he knows that he has been fully committed, may he be aware of his right to apply for bail and instruct an application. All this may take time, so that he may be in custody quite unnecessarily between the time when he is fully committed and the time when the sheriff considers his application for bail. His situation may be compared with Hume's account of the provisions of the Act of 1701 which, he says, 'leave no room for eluding the beneficient intention of the law. The statute has positively allowed (which might otherwise have been doubtful) that the application may equally be made before as after imprisonment; so as to obtain from the Judge a discharge of his warrant of commitment, if not yet carried into execution, and thus save the accused from the hardship and disgrace of being carried to a gaol' (Hume, ii, 93). It may also be observed that the practice deprives the accused of the opportunity of submitting to the sheriff reasons why he should not be fully committed. Occasions when valid reasons exist must be rare, but the present cases illustrate sufficiently that such occasions may occur. I should be happy to think that consideration might be given to the question whether it would be proper to allow the practice to continue."

Warrants refused.

NOTE

The peculiar Glasgow practice illustrated in this case has now ceased and all accused are now produced in court for full committal. It should be noted that neither committal for further examination nor full committal bear any similarities whatever to English committal proceedings. The primary importance of full committal in Scotland is in relation to bail (see *infra* Chap. 6) and in relation to the 110-day rule, *infra* p. 253 *et seq*.

b. Precognition

Following full committal, the Crown moves to the stage of precognition, so that the case may be reported to the Crown Office for directions on how to proceed. Crown precognitions are confidential to the Crown, although where the defence have difficulty in obtaining their own precognition from a Crown witness, the Crown will sometimes disclose the contents of its precognition to the defence.

1. Arthur v. Lindsay
(1894) 1 Adam 582

In a civil action for slander, the pursuer claimed that the defender, a procurator fiscal, had inserted false and calumnious statements about the pursuer in various Crown precognitions, and had shown these precognitions to persons not entitled to see them. The pursuer sought diligence to recover the precognitions and certain communications between the fiscal and the Crown Office.

LORD PRESIDENT (ROBERTSON): "The Lord Advocate has appeared by Counsel to object to the diligence asked by the pursuer being granted, and we have to attend to the responsible statement made by his representative. His Lordship objects to allow the precognitions to be produced, on the ground that to do so would be an infringement of that confidentiality which enables the effectual prosecution of crime in this country. I readily grant that, in the present case, the precognitions are relevant to the issues to be tried. They are even of a high materiality, and it may be that the want of them will be prejudicial or even fatal to the pursuer's claim. But it is undoubted that private rights must sometimes yield to the requirements of general public policy, and it seems to me that the essential confidentiality of communications passing between a Procurator-Fiscal and the head of the Criminal Department in Scotland is a paramount consideration. I do not say that there would be anything illegal in the production of such documents, because the Lord Advocate, as head of the department, might, in the exercise of his discretion, conceive that the general administration of public justice might, in some highly exceptional circumstances, not be prejudiced by the production. The Lord Advocate is the judge of that. But, in the present case, the Lord Advocate comes forward to object on the ground of this general rule and principle founded on the public interest, and I see nothing to shew that in the present case that rule should give way. It has been said that in a statement made for the Crown in the case of *Donald v. Hart*, 6 D. 1255, it was admitted that the general rule might yield to some 'great and overwhelming necessity.' These are very large and general words, and I do not think that an ordinary action of damages for defamation of character in which a Procurator-Fiscal is defender is such a case as is there described. I have shewn, I hope, that I realise the evil which is done to the pursuer's case by the enforcement of the general rule and the consequent loss to him of the precognitions; but, at the same time, I think that this is just one of those instances in which private rights have to yield to the general rule upon which the successful prosecution of crime so largely depends. I am for sustaining the objection made by the Lord Advocate and refusing the diligence."

LORD MCLAREN: "Two points in this case seem to me to be settled beyond dispute. The first is, that according to the present law and practice in the official investigations of crime, precognitions taken under the authority of the Lord Advocate, and reported to him or his depute, are confidential, and, unless under very exceptional circumstances, cannot be obtained for the purposes of evidence in a cause. The second point is that the confidentiality is personal to the head of the Criminal Department; his consent would remove any difficulty, and therefore it cannot be said that in such cases there would be a wrong without a remedy. It may be presumed that the Lord Advocate has obtained all the necessary information to enable him to judge whether this is a case in which it is proper for him to give up these precognitions to a pursuer in a civil action. He has before him information which the Court cannot get, for we have only the statements made by Counsel at the bar in accordance with their instructions. No doubt the Court has always maintained its right to make such an order in cases of emergency, some of which duly figured in the judicial opinions referred to at the debate, but this is qualified by the fact that no authority has been found where the jurisdiction was in fact exercised, and it is most unlikely that, while criminal administration remains as at present, the Court ever will exercise this supplemental power.

In the circumstances there is no reason for doubting that the objection of the Crown Office is well founded, and if it were to be got over by the mere averment of malice against a procurator-fiscal, any one wishing to harass the Crown officials might get access to these confidential documents simply by averring malice, and this would certainly be prejudicial to the public interest."

Diligence refused.

NOTE

Normally, witnesses are simply summoned to attend at the office of the procurator fiscal for precognition and in the vast majority of cases will do so. If however the Crown has reason to fear that the witness might subsequently go back on his precognition later by giving different evidence in court, the fiscal may precognosce that witness on oath.

2. Coll, Petitioner
1977 J.C. 29

A witness was precognosced on oath before the sheriff. He read over and signed his precognition. He was then cited to give evidence in a trial, but presented a petition to the *nobile officium* of the High Court craving the production and destruction of his precognition.

LORD JUSTICE-CLERK (WHEATLEY): "Counsel for the petitioner submitted that, before giving evidence at the trial of a case in respect of which he had been precognosced, a witness is entitled to have destroyed a precognition which was taken on oath. Support for that submission was sought from Hume's Commentaries (1844 edition), vol. 2, pp. 81, 82 and 381; Alison's Criminal Law, vol. 2, pp. 504 and 534; Dickson's Law of Evidence, vol. 2, para. 1591; Macdonald's Criminal Law, 5th edition, p. 298; Renton and Brown's Criminal Procedure, 4th edition, pp. 55 and 398; and the *obiter dictum* (for which no authority was given) of Lord Justice-Clerk Macdonald, with whom his brethren concurred, in *Cook* v. *McNeill*, 5 Adam 47: 'And it is also competent for a witness to ask that his precognition be delivered up to him to be destroyed before he can be called upon to give evidence.'

Prima facie this would appear to be a formidable body of support for the petitioner's claim. An examination of the texts of these writers discloses that Alison based his proposition on Hume and the later writers based their views on Hume and Alison. It is accordingly necessary to consider whether the circumstances which prevailed in the days of Hume and Alison, which no doubt had a bearing on the opinions expressed by them, are those which exist at the present time, or whether there have been changes in the interval which affect the applicability of their *dicta* to modern requirements. In particular, consideration has to be given to whether the different forms which a 'precognition' can take has a bearing on the issue in the instant case. In those earlier days there were many more private prosecutions than there are today, when virtually all prosecutions are public prosecutions and private prosecutions are so circumscribed that (statutory exception apart) they are now an extreme rarity. The procedure initiating prosecutions in those days was much different from our present-day procedure. None the less, what was said by those earlier writers was applicable to a 'precognition,' whether it was a statement made on oath on judicial examination or a statement taken *ex parte* and not on oath by a person preparing the case for one side or the other. The reason given by Hume and Alison why a witness should be given the right to have his precognition delivered up to him and destroyed before he could be called upon to give evidence was that unless this was done a witness might feel trammelled by his previous statement and would try to make his evidence agree with it instead of speaking freely from his recollection at the trial. The view was taken that a person could not be tried for perjury because at the trial he had given evidence on oath which contradicted the evidence he had given in his declaration—cf. the case of *Patrick Maccurly* in 1777, referred to in Hume *supra*, vol. 2 at p. 381 Note 4 and also in Vol. 1 at p. 369 (Note). All this, however, was before the passing of the Evidence (Scotland) Act 1852. Section 3 of that Act provides: 'It shall be competent to examine any witness who may be adduced in any action or any proceeding as to whether he has on any specified occasion made a statement on any matter pertinent to the issue different from the evidence given by him in such action or proceeding; and it shall be competent in the course of such action or proceeding to adduce evidence to prove that such witness has made such different statement on the occasion specified.'

This was undoubtedly enacted to secure in the interests of the administration of justice that a person who was giving evidence on oath in an action or proceeding could have the veracity or reliability of that evidence tested by what he had said thereanent on a previous occasion. That statutory enactment supersedes any previous common law rule of law that conflicts with it. The Hume and Alison concept of the law that a person should not be constrained by his previous statement from giving his evidence freely when on oath in an action or proceeding is obviously affected by it. How then is a precognition affected? Is it a statement within the meaning of section 3? There are several ways in which a statement can be made. One is by a person engaged in preparing the case for one of the parties in an action or proceeding taking a statement from a potential witness. This is what is now commonly called a precognition. Another is, for example, a statement taken from a potential witness by a police officer who is investigating a crime. A third is a judicial declaration taken on oath *ex parte* from a potential witness in an action or proceeding.

Whatever latitude may have been given to allow a precognition in the first of these categories to be used for the purposes of section 3 aforesaid in the period following the passing of the 1852 Act, it is quite clear from the cases of *McNeilie* v. *H. M. Advocate* 1929 J.C. 50 and *Kerr* v. *H. M. Advocate* 1958 J.C. 14 that it cannot be so used. The reason for this was succinctly given by Lord Justice-Clerk Thomson in *Kerr* when he said: 'In a precognition you cannot be sure you are getting what the potential witness has to say in a pure and undefiled form. It is filtered through the mind of another, whose job it is to put what he thinks the witness means into a form suitable for use in judicial proceedings. This process tends to colour the result. Precognoscers as a rule appear to be gifted with a measure of optimism which no amount of disillusionment can damp.'

It will always be a question of circumstances whether a statement is a precognition or not. Even a statement made to a police officer may fall into the category of a precognition if it is taken at a time when the stage of preliminary investigation has passed and the police officer is in fact taking a 'precognition'—see *McNeilie* and *Kerr, supra*.

What then is the position of a statement made in the form of a judicial declaration on oath? While it is a statement obtained *ex parte* it is obtained subject to safeguards which are calculated to avoid the possible defects and unfairness which Lord Justice-Clerk Thomson had in contemplation. The presence of the judge who has control of the proceedings should ensure that words are not being put into the witness's mouth. The official record should ensure that what is recorded is what the witness has said, not what a precognoscer wishfully thought he had said. The statement when recorded is read over and signed by the witness. Added to all this is the fact that the statement was made on oath. It is difficult to conceive a situation more apposite for the invocation of the section 3 procedure. While, therefore, each case has to be determined on its own facts, in our opinion such a declaration would normally be competent as a basis for challenging under that section the evidence of a witness. It would only be when it is alleged that the safeguards of the procedure had not been observed that a challenge to its use for that purpose could be made.

If, then, the statement which a witness has made under that procedure may competently be used to challenge the accuracy of the evidence he has given in the action or proceeding, what justification is there for a rule of law which entitles him to have the written record of his statement, which he has signed, destroyed? In our opinion there is none. That signed statement might be the best evidence on the point. On his averments as to how the statement was obtained we are of the opinion that the petitioner is not entitled to recover it and have it destroyed before he is called upon to give evidence. We shall accordingly refuse the petition.

In arriving at this decision we find comfort in the thought that the clarification of the legal position on this point gives legal sanction to a procedure which can be invoked to counter one of the deadly blows which is being struck at the administration of justice at the present time, namely, witnesses going back on their earlier statements when giving evidence in criminal trials."

Petition refused.

NOTE

As Lord Wheatley infers, precognition on oath is becoming increasingly necessary. From the Crown's point of view, it strengthens its position from the viewpoint of proceedings for perjury, where the problem often arises of proving exactly what was said on the previous occasion. But since section 9 of the 1980 Act came into force, precognition on oath by the defence has become possible, simply as a means to overcome the reluctance of some Crown witnesses to speak to the defence. However it may be that section 9 will only be invoked in exceptional circumstances.

3. Low v. MacNeill
1981 S.C.C.R. 243

A defence solicitor tried to obtain a precognition from a crucial Crown witness, who refused to co-operate. The procurator fiscal gave the solicitor general information about what the witness might be expected to say, but the solicitor petitioned the court under section 9 seeking a precognition on oath. The fiscal indicated he would make the Crown precognition of the witness available to the defence.

SHERIFF SCOTT: ". . . Section 9(1) of the 1980 Act provides: 'The sheriff may, on the application of an accused, grant warrant to cite any person (other than the co-accused), who is alleged to be a witness in relation to any offence of which the accused has been charged, to appear before the sheriff in chambers at such time or place as shall be specified in the citation, for precognition on oath by the accused or his solicitor in relation to that offence, if the court is satisfied that it is reasonable to require such precognition on oath in the circumstances.' The cardinal points of the provision are (1) that the precognition is to be *on oath*, and (2) that the procedure is only to be permitted if the court is satisfied that it is reasonable in the circumstances to require it.

Provision is made for the procedure to be followed under section 9 in the Act of Adjournal (Procedures under Criminal Justice (Scotland) Act 1980 No. 1) 1981 (S.I. 1981/22). The procedure envisaged by section 9 and by paragraph 2 of the Act of Adjournal is to my mind likely to prove cumbersome and expensive. The petition has to be prepared in the form set out in the Schedule to the Act of Adjournal. The sheriff has to order intimation and fix a diet. If the prayer of the petition is granted he must order the precognition to be taken, fix a diet and grant warrant to cite the witness or witnesses. There has to be personal service. Where the witness appears the proceedings have to be recorded by an official shorthand writer. The notes have to be extended and lodged. Yet another diet has to be fixed for the witness to sign the precognition. The shorthand writer has to be paid and the witness is entitled, if he wishes, to have his expenses paid in advance.

It is the legal aid fund, for the most part, which defrays the cost of persons tried on indictment. If the procedure made possible by section 9 is frequently used the cost to the public purse, through criminal legal aid, may be considerable.

If this application proves typical of others under section 9 such applications will almost inevitably be made at a late stage, when the trial is imminent. Solicitors often say that they cannot set about precognoscing Crown witnesses until they have had the list of witnesses annexed to the indictment and are unlikely, if this is so, to find that a witness will not make himself available for precognition until the date for trial is almost upon them. The pressure on sheriff court diaries is well known. In this court, certainly, it is extremely difficult to find space in the diary at short notice for any kind of urgent business. When such space has to be found it frequently means that other business has to be put off.

It is well known that it is by no means rare for the defence to be unable to obtain precognitions from *Crown* witnesses. There are many reasons for this. One of them, and it may be the reason in this case, is that letters from the accused's solicitor never reach the witnesses. If all Crown witnesses who do not respond to a defence request for precognition had to be precognosced on oath the work of the sheriff courts would be thrown into confusion.

It is more than likely that there will be cases where a reluctant witness, having been cited for precognition on oath, will fail to attend. Although a warrant may then be issued for his arrest the chances of his being arrested and brought before the sheriff for precognition before the trial diet may be small. If he cannot be found in time, the question may well arise whether the trial should be adjourned. If a sheriff has decided that it is reasonable for the accused to be allowed to precognosce a witness on oath it may be difficult for the court to insist on the trial proceeding when the witness has not been precognosced.

There is no inexhaustible supply of official shorthand writers and the difficulty of arranging diets for proof or jury trial in the confidence that a shorthand writer will be available is also well known.

All of these considerations lead me to the conclusion that, on practical grounds, the power conferred on the sheriff by section 9 is one to be exercised with caution. Nevertheless, I recognise that each application must be examined on its own merits and the overriding consideration must be to ensure so far as possible that the accused person is in the end of the day fairly tried.

The practice of precognoscing witnesses on oath dates back to the days when precognitions in criminal cases were compiled by the examining judge or magistrate before whom a person arrested was brought. After taking the prisoner's declaration the judge or magistrate had to satisfy himself that there were grounds for detaining the prisoner and, if there were, the particulars thereof, in order that they might be transmitted to the prosecutor. The prisoner would ordinarily be committed to prison for further examination and, when the precognition was completed, until liberated in due course of law. The examining judge or magistrate then submitted the precognition to Crown counsel who would decide whether to raise an indictment.

It was a matter for the examining judge or magistrate to decide which witnesses to precognosce. Witnesses could be cited for precognition on his own motion or that of the prosecutor. The prisoner had no right to cite witnesses for precognition but in practice the examining judge or magistrate would examine witnesses, of his own authority, where it was suggested by the prisoner that their evidence might be material to the defence.

It appears that sometimes, but by no means always, the examining judge or magistrate might precognosce a witness on oath. If he chose to do so it was in order that by means thereof he might extract the truth from witnesses, (Alison's Criminal Practice, 138); or if the truth could not be otherwise ascertained (Hume on Crimes, ii, 82). In other words, the purpose in putting witnesses on oath was to obtain evidence thereby which could not otherwise be ascertained.

It was only the examining judge or magistrate who could put witnesses on oath. The prosecutor was not permitted to precognosce on oath privately (Alison's Criminal Practice, 504).

In time the role of the examining judge or magistrate in ascertaining whether or not there was evidence to justify a prisoner's committal became vestigial. Subject to provisions for prevention of delay in trials, and the right of a prisoner to ask for bail, prisoners came to be committed to prison, either for further examination or until liberated in due course of law, on the ex parte statement of the prosecutor that he had credible information that a crime had been committed. The procurator fiscal took over the function of preparing the precognition and submitting it to Crown counsel. Precognition on oath became a rarity (Renton & Brown's Criminal Procedure, 4th edn, para. 5-69). The procurator fiscal as a matter of course obtains warrant to cite witnesses for precognition and exceptionally he may request the court to supervise the taking of a precognition on oath. The modern practice, so far as it goes, is for certain 'suspect or reluctant' witnesses to be precognosced on oath, not so much with the object of eliciting evidence which cannot otherwise be obtained as with a view to ensuring that evidence given on precognition is not departed from at a trial: see *Coll, Petnr*, 1977 J.C. 29.

It is against this background that section 9 was enacted. The defence never had the right to precognosce witnesses on oath. Now they have, subject to the court being satisfied that it is reasonable in particular circumstances to allow it. Prima facie, Parliament's intention in enacting section 9 was to give the defence the same facility as the Crown to take precognitions *on oath*. If so, it is my opinion that the circumstances in which it should be allowed must be circumstances which are analogous to circumstances in which, in modern practice, the Crown precognosces *on oath*.

Section 9 does not give the defence the right to seek a warrant to cite witnesses for precognition privately. This is puzzling at first glance, because one would imagine that in many cases the granting of such a warrant would be enough to serve the purpose of enabling the defence to obtain a precognition. Only if a citation to attend for private precognition was ignored might it become necessary to have a witness cited to appear before the sheriff. Perhaps it was feared that there would be a danger of a power of compulsion granted to defence solicitors being overworked, although it is difficult to see how this could happen if the court was given a discretion to grant or refuse warrant to cite witnesses for private precognition. In my view, the reason for the omission to give the defence a right to seek warrant to cite witnesses for private precognition must be that such a right is in general unnecessary. There is a duty on Crown witnesses to give information to the defence and the Crown if need be reminds its witnesses of this duty. Often, as in this case, the Crown will oblige defence solicitors by making information available to them. The court may adjourn a diet of trial in order that witnesses who have refused to be precognosced may be seen by the defence. If witnesses are in custody, say, the Crown will make arrangements for them to be seen in prison by the defence. It may still be competent, in exceptional cases, for an accused to present to the court a petition stating that a witness is in custody or otherwise inaccessible, whereupon the court will give such remedy as the justice of the case requires (Alison's Criminal Practice, 535).

Accordingly, in my opinion, the situation where it is a case simply of finding out what a Crown witness is going to say is adequately catered for by existing law and practice. Section 9 is not, in my opinion, designed to deal with the everyday situation where the defence has difficulty in getting hold of some Crown witnesses in order to obtain an indication of the evidence they are to give. Rather it is intended to deal with unusual and exceptional circumstances, analogous to those in which the Crown seeks to precognosce *on oath*. The circumstances must be such that it is reasonable that a precognition should be given *on oath*, not merely such that it is reasonable that a witness should be required to give a precognition.

In my opinion, the kind of circumstances referred to in section 9 must in general be those where evidence cannot be obtained other than by putting a potential witness on oath or where it is necessary to put a potential witness on oath lest he depart from his precognition at a trial. There may be other categories of circumstances where a petition under section 9 should be granted, but they cannot, in my opinion, extend to circumstances where it is immaterial whether the desired precognition be on oath or not.

I can appreciate Mr Monro's desire to take all proper steps on his client's behalf. He has shown responsibility in confining his application to the cases of the crucial Crown witnesses and not those whose evidence is to be uncontroversial. Clearly Mr Monro has to take all steps reasonably open to him to ascertain the line of the Crown evidence. In this case, though, I am satisfied that he has done so. Once he has in his hands the Crown precognitions of the witnesses named in the petition he will be in as good a position as the Crown to know what the evidence of these witnesses is likely to be. The situation would be quite different if, say, he was seeking to have precognosced witnesses whom he had reason to believe had information favourable to the defence which they had declared they were unwilling to give in court. I do not think that it is a proper consideration to take into account that if Mr Monro saw these witnesses a plea of guilty would be more likely to be forthcoming. If he knows as much as the Crown does about the likely evidence of these witnesses he should already be in a position to give appropriate advice to his clients.

For these reasons I refused the prayer of each petition."

Petition refused.

NOTE

While the reasoning of Sheriff Scott in this case seems clear enough, the defence in a criminal case are perhaps less likely than the Crown to know if a witness is likely to perjure himself at the trial. Information can always be obtained relatively easily about potential witnesses by the procurator fiscal from the police, but the defence do not have quite the same resources at ready disposal.

A witness may be detained in custody to ensure his attendance at trial, as the next case shows.

4.   Stallworth v. H.M. Advocate
1978 S.L.T. 93

OPINION OF THE COURT: "This petition to the nobile officium of the court is presented in the following circumstances. A man named Archibald Collict has been charged with a contravention of the Misuse of Drugs Act 1971, s. 4, and is due to appear for trial on 19 May 1977 in the Dunoon sheriff court. On 22 April 1977 the procurator fiscal presented a petition to the sheriff at the Dunoon sheriff court seeking a warrant for the apprehension of the petitioner and his detention in prison until the trial of the said Archibald Collict, or until the petitioner found sufficient caution for his compearance as a witness at the said trial. The reason stated by the procurator fiscal was that the petitioner had absconded from the United States ship on which he was serving, and which was stationed in the Holy Loch, without leaving any information as to the place at which he might be found, and he had good reason to believe that the petitioner's purpose in doing so was to avoid giving evidence at the trial. The sheriff, after hearing evidence and the submissions of parties, on 23 April 1977 granted the warrant, but refused to make any order regarding caution. The warrant was executed and the petitioner has been detained in Barlinnie Prison since then. He presented a bail appeal to the High Court of Justiciary, but this was dismissed as incompetent, since the bail procedure does not apply in such a case. The present petition was submitted on the view that in the circumstances it was only by petitioning the High Court of Justiciary to exercise its nobile officium that the order of the sheriff could be suspended. He accordingly seeks such a suspension and warrant for his liberation on finding such caution as the court may order. The facts presented to this court by his counsel were these. Collict had been refused bail on the submission by the procurator fiscal that he was liable to interfere with witnesses. The petitioner had been interviewed by the police and the procurator fiscal, and he was required as a principal witness for the prosecution. He had been in the United States Navy for 18 months, and while serving in his ship in the Holy Loch he resided in a house on the mainland with his wife. The latter, however, had returned to the United States as she was going to have a baby. He, however, continued to live in the house with a friend. On Sunday, 19 April, when he was off duty in Dunoon, he was assaulted by other sailors. He associated this with the fact that there was a considerable misuse of drugs in the service, and regarded it as an attempt to dissuade him from giving evidence at Collict's trial. This was confirmed when on the Sunday night the windows of his house were smashed and threats were made about what would happen to him if he attended the trial. He believed that if he avoided his sailor colleagues there was less likelihood of a repetition of the attack. He did not return to his ship on Monday, 20 April, as he was due to do, but on that Monday, and on the following Tuesday, Wednesday and Friday he reported to the US Naval Investigative Service. He was in due course arrested by the police on the Friday under the warrant granted by the sheriff, and has been detained in Barlinnie Prison since then. There he has been kept in a cell by himself, and, not being a convicted prisoner or a person on remand, he has not been allowed to mix with other prisoners. Counsel stated that the petitioner was willing to give an undertaking to appear at the court for the trial, and submitted that it would be very difficult, if not impossible for him to leave Scotland. In all these circumstances, it was said, justice required that he should be liberated.

The learned advocate-depute informed the court that before absconding the petitioner had said that there was a severe risk of him being interfered with by persons connected with Collict. He also intimated that he had been credibly informed that the US Naval authorities could not give an assurance that if the petitioner returned to his ship he would or could be restrained from again absconding. Counsel for the petitioner did not submit that it was not competent for the sheriff to grant the warrant without giving him the opportunity of finding caution. In our opinion he was well advised in not making such a submission, since manifestly there may be circumstances where it is so clear that there is a real danger of a witness taking steps to avoid appearing at a trial even at the sacrifice of caution (and caution should be related to the witness's means and not fixed at an impossible sum) that the only sure way of securing his attendance at the trial is by keeping him in detention. Accordingly, while it is normal procedure to apply for a warrant seeking detention of a witness until caution is found, and this is reflected both in Alison's *Criminal Law*, vol. 2, at p. 398 and Burnett's *Criminal Law*, at p. 469, we are of the opinion that it is always open to the court to order detention without giving the witness the opportunity of finding caution, if the circumstances satisfy the court that such a procedure is required to secure the proper administration of justice. Having accepted that it became a matter for the court's discretion to decide whether the witness should be kept in detention pending the trial, counsel maintained that the test of whether the discretion should be exercised in favour of detention was whether the court had grounds for believing that it was probable that the witness would not turn up for the trial. In support of this contention, counsel referred to a passage in Burnett's *Criminal Law*, at p. 469. The use of the word 'probable' there has to be read in the context of that passage as a whole. It begins by considering the need to provide a method of securing the attendance of witnesses against whom a suspicion arises that they will absent themselves and not attend the trial. It goes on to state that when a party, whether prosecutor or prisoner, suspects that a witness may abscond he may apply for a warrant until caution be found. It then contrasts the position where in the case of private parties applying for such a warrant their oath is sometimes required that the witness's evidence is material and they have reason to suspect he will abscond and the position where the application is by the Lord Advocate or where the witnesses are of such description and so connected with the party as to render it probable that they will abscond and forfeit any security, when warrant is granted de plano, and without any oath, to imprison them until further orders. This may be largely a matter of semantics, but in our view the test can more properly be stated in the form that the court may grant the warrant for detention without adjecting a requirement for caution which, if satisfied, will result in liberation if, on the information before it, it has reasonable grounds for apprehending that there is a real risk of a material witness not obeying his citation to appear in court for the trial. This proposition is vouched by the passage in Alison's *Criminal Law*, vol. 2, at p. 399. Applying that test to the circumstances of the present case, we have reached the conclusion that the sheriff adopted both a competent and a correct course. The facts that, on his own showing, the petitioner had been subjected to violence and threats by ill-disposed fellow sailors who were seeking to dissuade him from giving evidence at the trial, that there was a serious risk of further interference by persons connected with the accused Collict, and that in these circumstances he did not turn up for duty on his ship for five days subsequent to the violence and threats, clearly establish that there was a real risk of him not turning up at the trial. We find reassurance in our conclusion in the consideration that if the petitioner is in peril of further attacks and intimidation (and it was said that it was to avoid such a possibility that he sought to avoid his naval colleagues by not reporting for duty) then it is in his own interests that he should be placed out of harm's way. The method which the sheriff adopted to secure that the administration of justice is not put in jeopardy is—maybe paradoxically—the best means of securing the petitioner's own safety during the nine days until the trial. We shall accordingly refuse the petition."

Petition refused.

NOTE

This was an extremely exceptional case: very few witnesses are locked up *before* the trial, although of course this happens frequently during trials where there is prevarication or perjury.

c. Time-limits for trial

The date of full committal is vitally important from the viewpoint of the time-limit for proceeding to trial. Before the 1980 Act, there was no outside time-limit beyond which an accused on bail could not be tried, and many such trials took place many months after the initial appearance of the accused on petition. The 110-day rule (as then constituted) provided protection for accused in custody whose trials normally had to be concluded within 110 days of full committal. Now, under section 101 of the 1975 Act (as amended by section 14 of the 1980 Act) bail cases must normally be commenced within 12 months of the first appearance of the accused on petition in respect of that offence, but custody cases are governed by section 101 (2), which provides that an accused who is fully committed in custody cannot be detained "by virtue of that committal for a total period of more than . . . 110 days, unless the trial of the case is *commenced* within that period." So periods of custody not referable to *that* committal are left out of account. The following case was decided before section 101 was re-written in 1980, but shows that the re-written section has not changed the law in this regard.

1. Wallace v. H.M. Advocate
1959 J.C. 71

An accused appeared on petition in August 1958 and was allowed bail. Subsequently he was charged with a further offence on which he was fully committed in custody on 31 October 1958. In November 1958 he was sentenced to two years' imprisonment on the charge relating to August of that year. He appeared for sentence on the subsequent offence on 3 March 1959, when he objected to the competency of proceeding further on the ground that more than 110 days had elapsed since his committal. This objection was repelled and the accused appealed against the sentence then imposed. At the appeal hearing it was argued that the proviso to section 43 of the 1887 Act (the forerunner of section 101, *supra*) applied to him.

LORD JUSTICE-GENERAL (CLYDE): ". . . The section makes provision for the service of an indictment not being unduly delayed where a prisoner 'is in prison on a commitment until liberated in due course of law.' No question arises in the present case in regard to that aspect of the matter. The section then goes on to provide—and this is the provision which falls to be construed by us in the present appeal—'Provided always, that where a person accused has been incarcerated for eighty days, and an indictment is served upon him, and he is detained in custody after the expiry of such eighty days, then, unless he is brought to trial and the trial concluded within one hundred and ten days of the date of his being committed till liberated in due course of law, he shall be forthwith set at liberty, and declared for ever free from all question or process for the crime with which he is charged.' The appellant's contention is that this proviso applies to him, and that, as the one hundred and ten days from the date of his committal until liberated in due course of law (namely 31st October 1958) expired before the conclusion of his trial on 2nd March 1959, the sentence pronounced on him on 3rd March 1959 is incompetent.

But, in my opinion, this proviso cannot be invoked by the present appellant, for it does not apply to him. The proviso applies to an accused who is incarcerated and held because of a committal warrant or warrants. The present appellant was not such an accused. Since 19th November 1958 he was held in prison in virtue of a sentence pronounced on 19th November of two years' imprisonment in respect of the first charge of which he had been found guilty. On 19th November 1958 that sentence superseded, at any rate during its currency, the committal on the other charge. He cannot therefore, in my view, invoke the proviso, since it does not relate to his case at all.

I have reached this conclusion in view of the language of the proviso itself. It relates to a person accused, not to a person convicted and held in prison because of that conviction. Moreover, my conclusion seems to be put beyond doubt by the consequences enacted in the section in the event of the proviso being applicable. These consequences include that 'he shall be forthwith set at liberty,' a consequence quite inappropriate and inapplicable to the situation of a convicted person already in course of serving a sentence for another crime, who can obviously not be set at liberty forthwith.

The ostensible purpose of the section is to prevent delay in bringing accused persons to trial, but the real underlying object is to prevent the lieges being deprived of the liberty to which they are entitled if they are not guilty of the pending charge. But this has no bearing upon the person who has during the currency of the one hundred and ten days been convicted on a different charge, and who at the end of the one hundred and ten days is in course of serving a sentence of imprisonment in respect of it, for such person cannot be set at liberty unless the sentence on which he has been convicted has expired. That is the appellant's position.

We were referred to certain cases in the matter, but these shed no real light on the question in this appeal. In *H. M. Advocate* v. *Dickson* there were two warrants for commitment until liberation in due course of law in respect of two separate charges, and there was no question of the accused in that case being imprisoned during the one hundred and ten days in respect of a sentence following upon a conviction. The *species facti* is therefore quite different from that in the present case. In *H. M. Advocate* v. *Bickerstaff* there was also two commitments, but they were both in respect of the same offences, the diet on the first indictment having been deserted *pro loco et tempore*, as the accused had been found unfit to plead. Consequently a further indictment had been served when he was released from the asylum. Here again, there was no prison sentence running during the one hundred and ten days as in the present case. On the whole matter, therefore, in my opinion, the trial Judge arrived at the correct conclusion on the interpretation of section 43 and was right in treating it as not covering the present case."

Appeal refused.

NOTE

In this case the sentence imposed in November 1958 interrupted the 110 days which started to run on the other committal warrant of 31 October 1958. In *H.M. Advocate* v. *Park*, 1967 J.C. 70, the case of *Wallace* was applied to cover the situation where an accused who was serving imprisonment committed a further offence while in jail. It was held that in his case the 110 days commenced on the expiry of his sentence. See also *H.M. Advocate* v. *Boyle*, 1972 S.L.T. (Notes) 16. "Commencement" of a trial is the point when the oath is administered to the jury: 1975 Act, s. 101 (6).

The Crown does however have a remedy where the delay in proceeding to trial is not of its own making (such as the inability to add up to 110—see *H. M. Advocate* v. *Seery and Steele*, Glasgow High Court, June 1972, unreported). This is the power to seek from the court an extension of the 110 days, now contained in section 101 (4) of the Act (formerly embodied in section 43 of the Criminal Procedure (Scotland) Act 1887 and then as section 101 of the 1975 Act before its amendment in 1980). Where the delay in proceeding is due to *inter alia* "any other sufficient cause which is not attributable to any fault on the part of the prosecutor" the High Court may extend the 110 days.

2. H.M. Advocate v. Bickerstaff
1926 J.C. 65

An accused person was detained in custody after full committal. At the trial diet he was found insane and unfit to plead and was thereupon detained in an asylum. He recovered, was discharged and then re-arrested and re-indicted. At the trial diet a motion was made for his immediate release. This was referred to a Full Bench of the High Court. At the hearing, the Lord Advocate moved the court to extend the 110 days, if the court held that the 110 days had been exceeded.

LORD JUSTICE-GENERAL (CLYDE): ". . . It is true in a very broad sense that any question which concerns the right of an accused person to be set at liberty, either after trial or (as in the present case) without ever having been tried, raises what may be called a constitutional question. The subject of delay between commitment and a completed trial was the matter of reference in the Claim of Right, and has been the subject of legislation at least twice since. But the area of constitutional right in this department is now so fully covered by definite statutory provisions that such a point as that which we now have to determine rises hardly, if at all, above the position of a question of statutory construction. Even so, I think Mr Aitchison, whose advocacy of the accused's case lost nothing by the moderation and restraint with which it was presented, was right in saying that the flavour of constitutional right which still adheres to the topic should influence the Court to construe the statutory provisions to which I have referred benignly, and in favour of liberty rather than against it. But whether either the necessity or the opportunity of applying a general consideration of that kind does or does not occur must, of course, depend upon the particular circumstances and character of the question raised.

In the first place, I think it is made out in the present case that the accused had been detained in prison for more than 110 days prior to the date when he was brought up for trial at Stirling. The circumstances are no doubt special; but leaving out of account the period of the accused's temporary unsoundness of mind (while he was under the care of the authorities in lunacy), and adding together the period of detention in prison prior to his being found insane and the period subsequent to his re-arrest upon recovery, the total period of detention prior to his appearance the other day at Stirling appears to have amounted to 140 days or thereby. Some argument was presented to us on behalf of the prosecution with regard to the effect of section 52 of the 1887 Act (which keeps the original commitment in force notwithstanding a desertion of the diet *pro loco et tempore*) on the provisions of section 43. But I do not think that argument touches the present question, and I do not find it necessary to discuss it further. I think we must take it that—within the meaning of section 43—the 110 days had been exceeded in the present case.

The crux of the matter depends upon whether counsel for the accused is well founded in contending that the provisions of the section (to the effect that when the 110 days have expired without a completed trial the prisoner is entitled to be released and declared immune from further question) are absolute, peremptory, and unqualified, or whether, on the contrary, the section does not itself contain a qualification of them. I say that question lies at the root of the case, because, if the contention for the accused is sound, there is an end of the matter. The earlier part of the section is directed to prevent any undue delay in serving a prisoner with the indictment on which he is to be tried, and is not in question here. But the later part is directed to secure that there shall be no undue delay in bringing the entire proceedings against a prisoner to the final conclusion of a completed trial, and enacts that—whether an accused person has been continuously detained in prison, or whether the period of his imprisonment has been interrupted by a liberation—he shall not be detained in prison more than 110 days in all, and that, unless his trial is concluded within such 110 days, 'he shall be forthwith set at liberty and declared for ever free from all question or process for the crime with which he was charged,' or 'for which he was committed' (both of these expressions are used in the later part of the section). The case for the accused is founded entirely on this enactment; and, if the section ended there, his right to go free would be abundantly clear. But the section does not end there. On the contrary, it immediately thereafter proceeds as follows: 'But it shall be competent for the High Court of Justiciary in any case brought before it under this section, upon its being shown to the satisfaction of the Court, that the trial of a person accused ought to be suffered to proceed after the lapse of 110 days as aforesaid, when the delay in prosecuting to verdict is owing to the illness of the accused, or the absence or illness of any necessary witness, or the illness of a judge or juror, or any other sufficient cause for which the prosecutor is not responsible, to order the person accused, notwithstanding the expiry of the said period of 110 days, to be kept in custody, with a view to trial, for such further period or periods as to the said Court may seem just.' Now, it appears to me plain that this clause contains a very material qualification of the provisions which immediately precede it. If the contention of counsel for the accused were to be accepted to its full extent, it seems to me that this clause would have to be read out of the statute altogether. But this would be obviously inadmissible. There is no method of expression more familiar in draftsmanship, and in the draftsmanship of statutes in particular, than that of beginning with a general proposition stated in absolute terms, and then proceeding to expound it by means of qualifications or exceptions; and in all such cases the meaning of the Legislature can only be arrived at by reading the qualifications or exceptions along with the general proposition (however absolutely stated) which they explain and control.

The Lord Advocate has submitted that, in the circumstances of this case, the Court should use the discretion conferred upon it by the clause to which I have just drawn attention. But before we can determine upon our duty in that matter, it is necessary to consider a second line of defence relied on by counsel for the accused. Assuming—contrary to their primary contention—that the right of the accused to be liberated after confinement in prison for 110 days in all is not absolute, but, on the contrary, is subject, in a proper case, to possible qualification in the discretion of the Court, counsel for the accused contended that, on a sound construction of the clause, appeal to such discretion could only be made *before* expiry of the 110 days, and not (as in the present case) *after* it. Now, the clause applies, in terms, to '*any* case brought before the Court under this section'; and there is certainly no express limitation of the Court's power to cases brought before it prior to the expiry of the 110 days. The present is none the less a 'case brought before the Court under the section,' although it is so brought after the 110 days have elapsed. Again, the power given to the Court is 'to order the person accused, *notwithstanding* the expiry of the said period of 110 days, to be kept in custody with a view to trial.' A natural reading of these words leads to the result that the order can be made although the prisoner has already been in confinement for 110 days; and I have not been able to find anything in the section as a whole, or in that part of it which is the immediate subject of discussion, pointing to an intention to exclude the exercise of the power in such a case. The conclusion indicated by these considerations seems to me to be reinforced by the *species facti* on which the Court's discretion is to be exercised. The first ground mentioned in the clause is 'the illness of the accused'—say, a physical ailment which overtakes him during his confinement in prison. The duration of such an ailment may be impossible to foretell, and so also may be the after effects it will have in making it impossible—consistently with the dictates of justice and humanity—to put the prisoner in the dock and complete his trial within the 110 days. I think it would be unreasonable, in the absence of any positive provision to that effect, to construe the section to mean that, in such a case as I have just figured, the discretion given to the Court must be exercised (if at all) before the expiry of the 110 days. How, in such a case, could the Court fix (in advance) a period during which the accused should be kept in custody with a view to trial? It may be that your Lordships would be less disposed to exercise the discretion conferred by the statute, the longer the delay (from whatsoever cause arising) in appealing to it. But I do not think it is possible to affirm the contention of counsel for the accused that the appeal cannot competently be made after the 110 days have expired.

The question thus comes to be whether the circumstances of the present case require the exercise of the discretion conferred by the section. The fact that the accused's temporary unsoundness of mind is the origin of the difficulty in prosecuting the case to a verdict cannot be left out of account. That temporary unsoundness was established on the ninety-eighth day of the accused's confinement in prison, and he was then (on being brought up for trial) handed over to the authorities in lunacy, the trial diet being deserted *pro loco et tempore*. The authorities in lunacy dismissed him, as recovered, after some six or seven months' treatment, on 22nd October 1925. It was not maintained on behalf of the accused—I do not suggest that it could have been—that this period of treatment should be imputed to the 110 days of confinement in prison. He was re-arrested on the day on which the authorities in lunacy dismissed him, and was re-committed five days thereafter, and re-indicted without avoidable delay on 19th November 1925. But, before service of the re-indictment, the total period of his confinement in prison had exceeded 110 days, that period having expired on 7th November 1925. The statutory time-table was thereafter strictly observed, and he was brought up for trial at the second diet at Stirling on 7th December 1925, when the questions we are now considering were raised by his counsel. It is impossible in these circumstances to say that the delay which has occurred in prosecuting the case to a verdict is due to any cause for which the prosecutor is responsible. On the contrary, the case is one which appears to me to call for the exercise of the discretion which the statute confers upon us. My opinion, therefore, is that—notwithstanding that the 110 days have expired—the case is one in which the accused should be kept in custody with a view to his trial, but only for such period as to the Court may seem just, and we will hear what the parties have to say with regard to that matter."

The court extended the 110 days for just over a month.

NOTE

Although this case was decided in the days when the 110 days ran to the end of the trial, there is no reason to suppose that the reasoning today would be any different. In 1979 and 1981 when industrial action by civil servants disrupted the Scottish courts, the High Court frequently granted extensions of 40 days to the Crown, holding that court strikes fell within the exceptions listed in section 101 (4). This was in spite of arguments that the Lord Advocate (as public prosecutor) was through his ministerial role as a Law Officer of the government somehow responsible for the situation which had arisen. Considerable disquiet was felt on all sides that the constitutional protections to accused persons in custody were being insidiously eroded.

3. H.M. Advocate v. McTavish
1974 S.L.T. 246

An accused person was charged with murder and detained in custody. The Crown discovered that due to complexities in the preparation of their case, it would not be possible to conclude the trial within the 110 days. The Crown sought an extension.

LORD JUSTICE-CLERK (WHEATLEY): ". . . The primary ground on which the petition is founded is that certain tests are being carried out at the present time and that some time of necessity must elapse before the results of these tests are known. These tests might disclose that there would be evidence to justify a more serious charge being brought against Miss McTavish than the charge on which she has been committed. Various arguments of a preliminary nature were debated before us, but I think it is unnecessary to deal with these in this case. Assuming in favour of the

Crown that what has been referred to as the ejusdem generis rule does not apply to the circumstances under which such a petition can be brought by the Crown authorities, and assuming in the Crown's favour that, in any event, such a petition is not confined to delays occasioned by procedural matters but can be founded on any ground reasonably stated for which the prosecutor is not responsible, I am of the opinion that the Crown has failed to satisfy the court that there are good reasons in this case to justify the court exercising the power conferred on it by s. 43 of the 1887 Act. That section was designed to give protection to the lieges, to ensure that they were not held in custody for an undue period of time before the case was finally disposed of. That is a very important right, and it can only be departed from when sufficient cause is shown to the court to justify that departure. Whatever the other conditions may be, it is certainly a positive condition that the delay in respect of which the case is said not to be able to go on within 110 days is not a delay for which the prosecutor is himself responsible. We are told, however, that in the present case it would be possible to bring to trial within 110 days the charge on which Miss McTavish has been committed, and that the purpose of the extension so far as the Crown is concerned is to see whether these further tests might disclose the possibility of a more serious charge being preferred against Miss McTavish. On the face of it, that seems to me to be a wholly unjustifiable ground for the court granting the extension. In any event, I am not satisfied that the Crown has shown that despite all due expedition it has not been possible to get the results of these tests to enable the prosecution to proceed to its conclusion within the requisite 110 days period. In these circumstances I am of the opinion that the petition should be refused.

I wish, however, to make reference to another argument which was advanced by the learned advocate-depute. It was that the mental health of Miss McTavish was such that it would be desirable in her own interests to have her detained in custody for this extended period, rather than have her liberated if the petition were not granted. In his view, rightly or wrongly, proceedings could not be taken under the Mental Health (Scotland) Act of 1960 to have Miss McTavish detained for what might be deemed to be the requisite treatment in an appropriate place, and it was argued that if the extension was granted and bail was refused then she would be detained in prison, but that would be in her own interests. In my view this is not a reason in itself for depriving the accused of her statutory rights in terms of s. 43 of the 1887 Act. We have been assured by her counsel that appropriate safeguards would be taken if she was released from prison.

I would only add in conclusion that the learned advocate-depute explained that this petition was brought because it was thought desirable in the interest of justice that it should be brought, and that the point relating to accused's mental health had been taken, so that it should not be thought that the Crown had been unaware of the possibilities flowing from the possible release of the accused and wanted it to be made public that the Crown were alive to these possibilities and were taking all steps in their power to see that they had discharged their duty not only to the accused but to the public. I appreciate this, but it is not a reason for granting the prayer of the petition. I would accordingly move your Lordships to refuse the petition."

Petition refused.

NOTE

Following Lord Wheatley's decision the accused was released without bail and simply ordained to appear for trial. She was eventually indicted many months later and duly appeared.

For a comparative view of the problem of "stale" prosecutions, see R. v. Grays Justices, ex p. Graham [1982] 3 All E.R. 653.

4. Gildea v. H.M. Advocate
1983 S.L.T. 458

An accused person appealed to the High Court against an order by Lord Murray extending the 110-day period by 30 days. The extension had been sought and granted on the basis that administrative difficulties, time-tabling and pressure had rendered it impossible for the Crown to proceed timeously.

OPINION OF THE COURT: "The appellant was, on 29 November 1982, committed until liberated in due course of law upon serious charges of contravention of ss. 1(1) and 4(1) of the Firearms Act 1968, and of assault. He was thereafter detained in custody and the period of 110 days provided for in s. 101(2)(b) of the Criminal Procedure (Scotland) Act 1975 was due to expire on 18 March 1983. An indictment was served upon him on or about 4 February 1983 for trial at the circuit in Glasgow commencing on 7 March 1983. The trial of the appellant and the co-accused was the fourth in the list of trials set down to be held in the south court and it was contemplated that it would be begun on or about 15 March 1983. By that date it had become clear that for various reasons it was unlikely that the trial could be commenced on or before 18 March 1983, and on 15 March 1983 the Crown applied to the judge of the High Court, sitting in the south court in Glasgow, to extend the period of 110 days, and the judge, acting under s. 101(4) of the Act granted the application by extending the period by a further 30 days. It was and is contemplated that the trial of the appellant will commence on 25 March 1983. This appeal is brought under s. 101(5) to challenge the grant of the extension sought by the Crown.

It is accepted that the extension was granted because the judge was satisfied that the inability of the Crown to commence the trial of the appellant on or before 18 March 1983 was, under reference to the words of s. 101(4), due to a sufficient cause which was not attributable to the fault of the prosecutor. The submission for the appellant was that the judge erred in be so satisfied.

In approaching the question for our decision which is, we think, whether the judge was entitled to be so satisfied, it must be remembered that it was for the Crown to demonstrate that there was a sufficient cause for the difficulty in which they found themselves which was not attributable to any fault on the part of the Crown. As the Lord Justice-Clerk (Wheatley) pointed out in *H.M. Advocate* v. *McTavish*, 1974 S.L.T. 246; 1974 J.C. 19 (a case concerned with s. 43 of the Criminal Procedure (Scotland) Act 1887): 'That section was designed to give protection to the lieges, to ensure that they were not held in custody for an undue period of time before the case was finally disposed of. That is a very important right, and it can only be departed from when sufficient cause is shown to the court to justify that departure.'

These observations apply with full force to the provisions of s. 101 of the Act of 1975 which in its present form, was introduced by the Criminal Justice (Scotland) Act 1980. Equally apt are the words of the Lord Justice-Clerk (Macdonald), speaking again of s. 43 of the Act of 1887, in *H.M. Advocate* v. *Macaulay* (1892) 3 White 131 at p. 135: 'I remark first that this exception is framed to meet such difficulties as might happen without any failure in diligence upon the part of anyone at all. viz:— the illness or absence of a necessary witness or of a judge or juror. The words "or any other sufficient cause" must, therefore, relate to some other cause of a similar nature to those mentioned. But in addition to that, it must also be the fact that the prosecutor shall not be responsible for the failure.'

In this case the Crown sought to justify the grant of their application for extension in the following submission. It cannot be contended that in serving the indictment upon the appellant on 4 February 1983 there was any failure of due diligence, for it was then within reasonable contemplation that having regard to the business set down for disposal in Glasgow on the March circuit, the trial of the appellant would commence before 18 March 1983. The probabilities fall to be tested by consideration of the business set down for disposal in the south court for it was known that the first trial for disposal on that circuit in the north court was quite unlikely to end before 18 March 1983. The first case for trial in the south court involved charges of injury and the danger of life, murder and contravention of s. 3(1)(b) of the Bail (Scotland) Act 1980. The accused was in custody and the 110-day period in his case was due to elapse on 20 March 1983. The wholly reasonable expectation that this trial would be concluded within two days was borne out in the result because it ended on 9 March. The second trial for south court disposal also involved an accused in custody and in his case the 110-day period was due to expire on 18 March 1983. This trial was reasonably estimated to require no more than two days to complete. In the event no trial took place because when the diet was called the accused pled guilty. The third trial was of a single accused charged with rape and there were only 23 witnesses on the Crown list. The entirely reasonable expectation was that this trial would be completed within two days and at worst on the third day. The fourth trial, that of the appellant, was accordingly expected to begin not later than 15 March and since it could not reasonably be expected to last more than two days it was confidently expected that the fifth trial of five accused, in the case of three of whom the 110-day period was due to expire on 18 March 1983, was likely to begin before that date. What in fact happened was unforeseen and was not reasonably foreseeable. The third trial on the south court list, contrary to all reasonable expectation, and for reasons difficult to understand, consumed not two days, not three days but five days of the time of the court. It was not suggested that this expenditure of time was due to any cause for which the Crown was or could be held responsible. In this situation the Crown had a difficult decision to make. The decision was to proceed at once with the fifth case on the list involving the five accused and to apply in the case of the appellant for the extension of time granted by the judge on 15 March 1983.

For the appellant the submission was that this explanation by the Crown did not satisfy the test which was prescribed by s. 101(4)(c). By delaying service of the indictment until 4 February 1983 the Crown failed to exercise due diligence and it was evident upon the explanation given by the advocate-depute that from that moment on they were at grave risk. Even if it be accepted that the forecasts of the time likely to be consumed by the first three south court trials were those mentioned by the advocate-depute the Crown was allowing to itself a safety margin of only two days, at the most, if it were to be able to commence both the trial of the appellant and the fifth trial in the list before 18 March 1983. It is, it was said, notoriously difficult to predict the length of a trial on a charge of rape and it cannot be said that because the third trial in the list took five days to complete instead of two or three days this was not reasonably to be foreseen. The risk courted by the Crown was quite unacceptable, and by neglecting to requisition a special sitting for the disposal of the indictment against the appellant, or to release him from custody, the Crown cannot be held to have demonstrated that there was sufficient cause for which the Crown was not responsible, for their failure to be in a position to commence the trial of the appellant before 18 March 1983.

We do not pretend that the problem presented by this appeal is easy to resolve. With some hesitation, however, we have decided that the appeal should be refused. The Crown undoubtedly took a calculated risk in relation to the commencement of 110-day cases for disposal on the March circuit in the south court. The question is whether the decision to take that risk was unreasonable and whether the judge who heard the application and was himself the presiding judge in the south court was entitled to decide it was not. In our opinion he was so entitled and his decision was correct. The critical factor was the expected duration of the single accused rape trial, number three in the list. In our judgment it was wholly reasonable to predict, for that trial, a disposal time of one-and-a-half days to two days, and at the very worst three days. That it should take five days to complete, is, we think, almost impossible to understand, and it was not from what we know of the case reasonably to be anticipated. In the foregoing circumstances we are persuaded that the Crown was suddenly faced with such a difficulty as might happen without want of due diligence on the Crown's part, and that the judge who granted the extension sought, who, incidentally was the trial judge in the disposal of the single accused rape case which grossly overran its reasonably anticipated span, was well entitled to be satisfied that the Crown had established what required to be established in support of their application in terms of s. 101(4)(c) of the Act of 1975."

Appeal refused.

NOTE

In the view of the present authors, this is one of the most unconvincing decisions to be made by the High Court in recent memory. The court (consisting of the Lord Justice-General (Emslie), Lords Cameron and Avonside) heard argument in this case on the morning of 22 March 1983 and, after a short consultation on the bench, announced that the appeal would be refused, with written reasons to follow later. It is respectfully submitted that their Lordships would have done Scots law a greater service by taking the case to *avizandum*, perhaps only overnight, and considering in depth the implications each way for the future, before jettisoning in such an unsatisfactory fashion the principles and authority carefully built up over two centuries. Without being in any way melodramatic, *Gildea* gives the impression that the 110-day rule, the existence of which has been the proud boast of Scots lawyers at home and abroad for so long, and which more than meets the minimum standards laid down by the European Convention on Human Rights, is now almost worthless. Consider the following flaws:

(1) The *ratio* of the decision appears to be that where delay in proceeding is not reasonably to be foreseen by the Crown, then an extension can be justified. But the 110-day rule is not, and never has been, about what is, or may be foreseeable, either subjectively or objectively assessed. The rule is couched in peremptory terms, with no room for considerations of this sort.

(2) It appears that the appeal would have been allowed if the court had been convinced that the Crown's decision to take its calculated risk about the 110-day cases was unreasonable. But it has always been thought that extensions are only justified *inter alia* where the prosecutor is not at fault, which presupposes a situation *outwith his control*. But "calculating risks" is within a prosecutor's control, and if he miscalculates the risk (or simply miscalculates, as in *H.M. Advocate v. Seery and Steele, supra*) he pays the penalty. In *McTavish*, the Crown sought an extension so that further tests might be carried out. They *calculated* that they could not proceed in time. The extension was refused, the clear implication being that calculations, whether correct or not, do not enter into the problem.

(3) It may be true that no-one could foresee that an apparently short rape trial would overrun. But who is responsible for precognoscing cases, serving indictments, requisitioning a High Court sitting and deciding the running order of cases?

(4) What protection does an accused now have against other Crown miscalculations? Here they miscalculated the running time of the previous case, an admittedly patent miscalculation. But what about all the miscalculations which may be latent, such as the time taken to interview witnesses, or draft the indictment? The accused cannot know what goes on in the Crown Office, only what he can observe or what his advisers can find out. It was primarily to *protect* the accused against such latent happenings that the 110-day rule was enacted in 1701.

(5) The appeal court has apparently given the stamp of approval of the Crown practice of persistently sailing close to the wind at High Court circuits, particularly in Glasgow. Everyone knows that the court is congested, but the way to solve the problem is to provide more resources, not to extend the 110 days whenever the seams burst. Presumably the Crown can now be expected to apply for extensions at every other sitting.

A final ironic twist to the case. The accused's trial duly proceeded on 25 March 1983. He was acquitted of all charges.

CHAPTER 8

THE PROBLEMS OF RELEVANCY AND COMPETENCY

a. Framing the indictment — relevancy

Following the completion of the Crown precognition, the procurator fiscal sends all the papers to the Crown Office for directions on further procedure. The next step is usually the drafting of the indictment in the Crown Office, its revisal by the fiscal and service on the accused. Styles of indictment are to be found in Schedule A to the 1887 Act as amended by the Criminal Justice (Scotland) Act 1949, s. 39 (1) and Sched. 12. Indictments run in the name of the Lord Advocate, or the Solicitor-General if there is no Lord Advocate in office. A defect in the instance may lead to a fundamental nullity.

H.M. Advocate v. Hanna
1975 S.L.T. (Sh. Ct.) 24

"Archie Murray Hanna was charged on indictment with offences under the Firearms Act 1968 and the Prevention of Crime Act 1953. The indictment was 'at the instance of The Right Honourable William Ian Stewart, Her Majesty's Advocate,' and was signed 'By Authority of Her Majesty's Advocate "J. L. MacLeod" Procurator Fiscal . . .' Before the jury was balloted it was argued for the panel that there was no effective indictment. Mr Stewart had held the office of Solicitor General for Scotland and in the period following the former Lord Advocate's appointment as a Senator of the College of Justice he continued in office as Solicitor General for Scotland but was never Lord Advocate. Reference was made to Renton and Brown, *Criminal Procedure According to the Law of Scotland*, 4th edition, at pp. 23-24 (paras. 4-02 and 4-03). The Criminal Procedure (Scotland) Act 1887, s. 3, and the Law Officers Act 1944, s. 2, detailed the provision for public prosecution in Scotland where the office of Lord Advocate was vacant. The general rule was that the Lord Advocate did not demit office until his successor was appointed, albeit that he had resigned. In circumstances where the Lord Advocate died in office or was removed from office there was provision that indictments should be brought in the name of the Solicitor General for Scotland until a new Lord Advocate was appointed. Following the decision in *The Solicitor General for Scotland* v. *Lavelle*, 1914 J.C. 15, 1913 2 S.L.T. 427, it was the case that when a Lord Advocate was appointed to judicial office he was deemed to be removed from the office of Lord Advocate. In such circumstances public prosecutions should be brought in the name of and by the authority of the Solicitor General. In the circumstances the present indictment was fundamentally null and any trial would be a nullity. Faced with this argument the procurator fiscal moved to desert the diet of trial pro loco et tempore and the sheriff granted the motion."

Diet deserted.

NOTE

It has been argued that the indictment was not in fact fundamentally null, since all that was wrong was a misdescription of the designation of Mr Stewart, the Solicitor-General, who had actually authority to raise indictments: see G.H. Gordon, "Fundamental Nullity and the Power of Amendment," 1974 S.L.T. (News) 154. If the sheriff had allowed the fiscal to amend the indictment, the accused would not have suffered any prejudice. It is this question of prejudice which looms large when challenges are made to the terms of indictments. To avoid such a challenge, the Crown must frame a *relevant* indictment; relevancy has three aspects in that the indictment must set forth with sufficient specification: (1) the time of the alleged crime; (2) the place where it occurred; and (3) the *modus* by which it was committed.

(i) Specification of time

At common law the general rule was that a latitude of three months was allowed in stating the time of the offence. By sections 50 and 312 (f) of the 1975 Act this is now implied in all charges, except where an exact time is of the essence of the charge. But in some cases an exceptional latitude as to time is allowed.

1.   H.M. Advocate v. MacKenzies
(1913) 7 Adam 189

An accused person was charged that "between 3rd July 1907 and 2nd April 1913 . . . you . . . did steal a book". A preliminary plea to the relevancy of the charge was stated on the ground that too great a latitude of time had been taken.

LORD JUSTICE-CLERK (MACDONALD): "The first charge in this indictment is a charge of theft against the male prisoner. It sets forth a very great latitude in respect of time, ranging over nearly six years. The justification of the latitude taken, which is unprecedented so far as I am aware, is made in argument on the ground that the book said to have been stolen was a book of recipes, and that it was taken in order to obtain copies of these recipes, and that the prosecutor does not know when the actual taking occurred. I should myself have expected that a prosecutor proposing to take such a latitude would have set forth facts to indicate his difficulty in being more precise, as, for example, that the accused was in the employment of the owners of the book during the period given, and thus had the opportunities of taking possession of it without his having done so becoming known to the owners. And certainly if the case were allowed to go to trial, the prosecutor would have to show by his evidence that the latitude taken was not unfairly taken; and if he failed to do so, his failure might lead to his not being able to obtain a verdict. While I refrain from expressing an opinion as to whether the extreme latitude of time taken should not be fatal to the charge, for lack of justifying statement, I may say that as I understand no trial is to proceed on the present indictment without a new service, the advisers of the Crown may well consider whether, if they are to proceed further with the case, they will not frame an indictment which may be more satisfactory in this respect. I am not prepared to cast the indictment on this point, but it certainly would be more satisfactory in a case so peculiar for the prosecutor to express in the indictment the cause justifying a latitude so extreme."

Objection repelled.

NOTE

Under sections 50 (3) and 312 (f) of the 1975 Act, there is no obligation on a prosecutor who takes an exceptional latitude as to time to set out in the charge the facts and circumstances which he alleges justify the exception. But in *Mackenzies* it was clear that the court felt great unease about the Crown's position in the absence of such statements.

2.   H.M. Advocate v. A.E.
1937 J.C. 96

An accused was charged with incest on various occasions with his two daughters. The first charge spanned the periods between 1 April 1927 and 5 July 1933, and 28 November 1933 and 14 January 1937. The second charge covered the periods 1 February 1931 and 5 July 1933, and 28 November 1933 and 3 June 1936. He objected to the relevancy of the indictment.

LORD JUSTICE-CLERK (AITCHISON): "I have some doubt as to the relevancy of this indictment owing to the very exceptional latitude taken by the Crown. The panel is called upon to meet two separate charges, the first extending over a period of nine years and six months and the second extending over a period of five years. I am not aware of any case in which so great a latitude has been taken by the Crown, but, having regard to the nature of the charges, and to the statement of the learned Advocate-Depute that what he is going to seek to prove is not an isolated instance or isolated instances but a course of criminal conduct over a period of time, I think it would be wrong to exclude inquiry. I am influenced in this by the fact that in the case of the first of the two girls named in the indictment, the alleged improper conduct began when she was only about eight years of age. In the case of the second of the two girls named, the alleged improper conduct began when she was only ten years of age. That being the position, it may not be possible for the Crown to give very much in the way of specification, at any rate as regards the earlier periods, but I wish to point out that there will rest a heavy onus on the Crown owing to the latitude of time they have thought right to take, and it may be necessary to give a direction to the jury that they must be satisfied that the panel has suffered no prejudice owing to the latitude taken. That, however, is a matter that does not arise now. I repel the objection to the relevancy, and the case must proceed to trial."

                                                              Objection repelled.

NOTE

Thus an exceptional latitude will be allowed where the Crown seeks to prove a course of conduct by the accused, but not where the offences have merely taken place on various unspecified occasions between particular dates.

3.   Ogg v. H.M. Advocate
1938 J.C. 152

An accused was charged with committing acts of gross indecency "on various occasions between 1st January 1930 and 1st June 1937, the particular dates being to the prosecutor unknown." An objection to the relevancy of the charge was taken.

LORD RUSSELL: "Objection is taken by counsel for the panel to the relevancy of charge (1) in respect that the latitude in the time over which the offences charged are alleged to have taken place is so unusual and exceptional that it renders the charge irrelevant from lack of specification. In this charge the accused is charged with committing on various occasions between 1st January 1930 and 1st June 1937 certain acts, at a locus described, with another male person described. The particular dates are said to be unknown to the prosecutor. Now, on the face of this charge it is clear that the intention of the Crown is not to prove a continuous course of conduct during which the offences charged were committed by the accused with the person named. The indictment clearly specifies various occasions, the particular dates of which are unknown. I think that the principle by which the time latitude—which in the normal case extends to three months and which in exceptional cases may be extended—is usually regulated is well given in one of the passages cited from Alison, where the learned author says this: 'In general, however, it is true of all those cases where an extraordinary latitude in point of time is allowed, that the law allows it unwillingly, and from necessity only; and therefore, that it will not sustain such a latitude where, by due diligence, a more accurate and specific detail could have been given, or where there is nothing appears, either from what is set forth on the face of the libel, or from the nature of the facts charged, to warrant such a departure from the ordinary rule.' Now, I am prepared to assume that in this case by due diligence a more accurate and specific detail could not have been given, but even on that assumption, apart from the fact that the offence charged is one of an occult nature, there is nothing set forth *in gremio* of the charge itself which seems to me to warrant such a departure from the ordinary rule as to justify a period of seven years and five months as a tract of time during which various offences on various occasions in that time are said to have occurred. I am impressed by what was said by Lord Justice-Clerk Macdonald in the case of *H. M. Advocate* v. *Mackenzie,* where, with reference to a latitude of time taken in an indictment charging the accused with stealing a book by making copies of various recipes contained in the book, and where the latitude in time extended over nearly six years, the learned judge said this: 'I should myself have expected that a prosecutor proposing to take such a latitude would have set forth facts to indicate his difficulty in being more precise, as, for example, that the accused was in the employment of the owners of the book during the period given, and thus had opportunities of taking possession of it without his having done so becoming known to the owners. And certainly if the case were allowed to go to trial, the prosecutor would have to show by his evidence that the latitude taken was not unfairly taken; and if he failed to do so, his failure might lead to his not being able to obtain a verdict. While I refrain from expressing an opinion as to whether the extreme latitude of time taken should not be fatal to the charge for lack of a justifying statement, I may say that, as I understood no trial is to proceed on the present indictment without a new service, the advisers of the Crown may well consider whether, if they are to proceed further with the case, they will not frame an indictment which may be more satisfactory in this respect.' Now, it is true that that was an *obiter dictum*, but it was an *obiter dictum* of a judge whose pronouncements are entitled to the greatest weight in the criminal courts. I keep in view that the offences here charged are of an occult nature. I also keep in view that the conduct libelled is not libelled as a continuous course of conduct, but is one of conduct which is said to have taken place on various unspecified occasions, the particular dates being unknown. In that situation I am satisfied that no precedent has been quoted which would justify me in holding that exceptional latitude is justified by the circumstances in this case. The case cited of *H. M. Advocate* v. *A.E.*, a case of incest, was obviously a case where the circumstances were very special, and very peculiar, and I am satisfied that the course that was taken by the Lord Justice-Clerk in that case was right and proper. In the present case, however, the situation is quite different, and I am of opinion that the wide latitude in time taken here, without any justification therefor appearing *ex facie* of the indictment, is unreasonable; and that, if it were to remain unaltered, the charge to which it relates could not be allowed to go to trial."

Objection sustained.

NOTE

Exceptional latitudes are thus in the main confined to exceptional cases. Nor will the statutory implied latitude which replaced the common law in section 10 of the Criminal Procedure (Scotland) Act 1887 (now sections 50 and 312 (f) of the 1975 Act) necessarily avail a prosecutor who perils his case on stating a specific date or dates between which the crime is alleged to have been committed.

4. Creighton v. H.M. Advocate
(1904) 4 Adam 356

A man was charged with having unlawful carnal knowledge of a 15-year-old girl "between 14th January and 6th February 1904 (the particular date being to the prosecutor unknown)". The evidence disclosed that the offence definitely did not occur between these dates, but pointed to a date sometime in December 1903. The sheriff charged the jury that they could convict, provided they found that the crime occurred subsequent to 11 December 1903, that being within three months of service of the indictment. The accused was convicted and sought to have the conviction suspended by the High Court.

LORD STORMONTH-DARLING: "This indictment charged the complainer with having committed an offence under the Criminal Law Amendment Act, 1885, 'between 14th January and 6th February 1904 (the particular date being to the prosecutor unknown)'; and the leading question is, whether under such an indictment the prosecutor was entitled to avail himself of the provision in section 10 of the Criminal Procedure (Scotland) Act, 1887, to the effect that 'the latitude now in use to be taken in stating time in indictments at the instance of Her Majesty's Advocate shall be implied in all statements of time where an exact time is not of the essence of the charge,' so as to warrant a conviction for an act done in December 1903. It is admitted by the prosecutor that at the trial he failed to prove the commission of the offence within the period expressly libelled, and therefore that, in order to obtain a conviction, it was necessary for him to resort to the latitude implied by the statute, if he could competently do so.

Now, what the statute declares to be implied is 'the latitude now in use to be taken in indictments'; and this refers us to the practice in existence before the 15th October 1887. The first thing to be noted with reference to that practice is that the latitude was always express. Sometimes in crimes of an occult or continuing character it extended to a period of months or even years. In the ordinary case where the information in possession of the prosecutor enabled him to condescend on the actual day of the month it was usual to guard against any slip of memory on the part of his witnesses by stating, as an alternative, one or other of the days of that month or of the month immediately preceding or of the month immediately following. Sometimes this common mode of libelling time was varied by the prosecutor confining himself to the month of the crime and the month immediately preceding, as, for example, where the accused had been taken into custody shortly after its commission, and the succeeding month was therefore impossible. This limitation to two months frequently occurred when the crime was said to have been committed in the night beginning with the last day of one month and ending with the first day of another. But it would, I think, be correct to say that the most common latitude was three months, and that this was never exceeded unless in special cases and for the reasons of which the Court was judge, and which were expressed in the libel, unless it was obvious that the nature of the crime made specification difficult, as, for example, in the case of reset. In any event, the latitude being always carefully expressed, the accused person could have no difficulty in knowing the precise length of time over which the evidence for the prosecution might extend, and he could take objection before the case went to trial, if so advised.

Under the existing law it is still quite competent for the prosecutor to express the latitude which he intends to take. The 10th section of the Act of 1887 nowhere forbids that. It merely abolishes the necessity of setting out at length words which had come to be words of style, where to imply them could raise no ambiguity and cause no prejudice to the accused. It is in conformity with the whole scope and tenor of the Act of 1887 that criminal writs shall be shortened by leaving out mere alternatives, which, under the old practice, were set forth always in the same manner. But the Act is equally careful to provide that indictments shall tell accused persons everything which is material for them to know in order to meet the case against them. While, therefore, the framer of an indictment is quite right to avail himself of the latitude implied by section 10 wherever it is quite simple to ascertain the limits of time by implication, it is in my judgment a misuse of the section to trust to the implied latitude in any case where to do so may create an ambiguity. In all such cases the proper course is to express the latitude which the prosecutor desires to take.

The present case is a fair illustration of the ambiguity resulting from this mode of libelling. Crown counsel were unable to define the latitude for which they contended. Was it the whole months of January and February 1904, with the addition of December 1903, or of March 1904, or of both these months, or was it a period of three months, calculated from the middle of the express period, and so beginning 25th December 1903 and ending 25th March 1904? As it happens, the section of the Criminal Law Amendment Act requiring that no prosecution shall be commenced for the offence more than three months after its commission made it specially material for the accused person to know what the prosecutor's case was to be, for as he was apprehended and charged on 11th March 1904, he could not lawfully be prosecuted for any offences committed prior to 11th December 1903. We are told that the Sheriff so directed the jury (in my opinion rightly), and we must assume that the jury obeyed the direction. But if one of the definitions which I have suggested as a possible definition of the latitude claimed by the Crown had been expressed the indictment would have been seen to be incompetent on the face of it. I mention this as an illustration of the practical inconvenience of the mode of libelling here adopted; but I desire to rest my judgment on the broad ground that the latitude implied by section 10 of the Act of 1887 ought never to be resorted to except in cases where no ambiguity can arise as to its commencing and concluding dates, and where, therefore, it is impossible for the accused to be misled."

Conviction quashed.

NOTE

As will have been observed from all the foregoing cases, the undercurrent running through each is that the accused is entitled to fair notice of the case which he has to meet. For example, he might be able to plead a defence of alibi in relation to particular dates. Fair notice is at the heart of all disputes as to relevancy. In *R.L.* v. *H.M. Advocate*, 1969 J.C. 40, where there were three charges each alleging that on one occasion between 1 August 1966 and 17 June 1968 the accused used indecent practices towards a child, an appeal against conviction was successful on the ground that too great a latitude had been taken by the Crown. Another practical difficulty arises now since judicial examination under section 6 of the 1980 Act has been introduced. At this stage a petition is the only notice which the accused has of the charge against him. While hitherto it has been quite common for the terms and dates specifying the crime contained in any subsequent indictment to be somewhat different from those in the petition, due to the fact that the case has by then been precognosced properly by the Crown, there would now seem to be a greater necessity for the petition to be as accurate as possible if the Crown is going to examine the accused immediately. This may even require the Crown to state the actual time of day at which it alleges the commission of the crime, if it wishes to preclude the accused from concocting an alibi at a later stage.

(ii) Specification of place

This is important from the viewpoint of jurisdiction, on which generally see ch. 3, *supra*. Considerable latitude will be allowed in cases of embezzlement, theft and reset.

Gold v. Neilson

(1907) 5 Adam 423

An accused person was convicted of reset at four separate places "all in Glasgow, or at one or other of said places, or elsewhere in Glasgow." He objected to the relevancy of the charge, both before the magistrate and subsequently after conviction, to the High Court.

LORD JUSTICE-CLERK (MACDONALD): ". . . But it is said here that the prosecutor took too great a latitude. The place of the crime is stated as, *inter alia*, 'or elsewhere in Glasgow to the prosecutor unknown.' I should like to say that prosecutors ought always to avail themselves of the simpler forms of stating place and time which are authorised by the statute, which makes a great deal that is often found in complaints like this, such as this statement of 'elsewhere to prosecutor unknown,' quite superfluous. But as regards the latitude here taken, such latitude has been long ago decided to be legitimate in cases of reset. There are two cases in Bell's 'Notes' which clearly show this. In the first of these cases, *M'Intosh*, 4th January 1831, Bell's 'Notes to Hume on Crimes,' p. 213, the place libelled was 'within your house in King Street, Leith, or in some other part within the town or in the vicinity of Leith to the prosecutor unknown.' In the second case, *Wilkinson*, 30th September 1835, Bell's 'Notes to Hume on Crimes,' p. 213, the place libelled was 'some place in the county of Perth to the prosecutor unknown.' Such latitude is necessary in cases of reset. It is a continuing crime. The person accused may originally have got the goods honestly, but if he afterwards finds that he got them from a thief, the moment he knows this he is guilty of reset, unless he takes steps at once by informing the police to show that he has no guilty intention with regard to the goods."

Appeal refused.

NOTE

Such a latitude is often necessary because of the circumstances of the crime of reset itself. But where the *locus* of the crime is capable of precise description, it should always be specified, from the viewpoint of fairness to the accused. Mere misdescription, as opposed to non-description, will be capable of amendment: see *Herron* v. *Gemmell*, 1975 S.L.T. (Notes) 93.

(iii) Specification of mode

The essential element here is that the indictment or complaint must set forth facts and circumstances such as to constitute a crime known to the law of Scotland. No *nomen juris* is necessary.

1. H.M. Advocate v. Anderson
1928 J.C. 1

An accused woman was charged with attempted abortion. The defence objected to the relevancy of the indictment.

LORD ANDERSON: "The charge against the panel is that she 'did insert pieces of slippery elm bark or other substance into the private parts of Agnes M'Kain in the belief that she was then pregnant, and for the purpose of causing her to abort and did attempt to cause her to abort.' An objection to the relevancy of this charge has been stated in the following terms: 'That the indictment does not set forth that Agnes M'Kain was in fact pregnant at the time of the alleged crime, and that no facts are set forth from which facts, if proved, the crime of attempting to procure abortion could be inferred.'

The question for decision is whether or not this objection to the relevancy is well founded. If I had any serious doubts as to how this question ought to be decided, or if the point taken raised any matter of general importance, I should have thought it my duty, in order that an authoritative judgment should be pronounced, to report the case for consideration of the High Court in Edinburgh. But I have formed a clear impression that the objection to the relevancy is well founded, and it does not appear to me that any point of general importance is involved in the decision. The objection is concerned with the particular facts of this case, facts which are so special, and indeed unique, that it is barely conceivable that they will ever recur. I therefore propose to decide the question here and now.

The Crown, according to the libel, offers to prove three things, (1) that the accused inserted pieces of bark or other substances into the private parts of Agnes M'Kain, and I assume, as I am bound to do, that this part of the libel can be proved; (2) that the accused was in the belief that Agnes M'Kain was then pregnant, and I again assume, although this assumption is more difficult to make, that the Crown is able to prove what was in the mind of the accused; and (3) that the purpose of the accused was to cause Agnes M'Kain to abort. On these three allegations being established by evidence, the view of the Crown is that the jury would be bound to hold that the crime libelled had been proved, and that the accused had thereby attempted to cause Agnes M'Kain to abort.

There is, however, a noteworthy omission from the libel, which, in my judgment, is fatal to its relevancy. It is not alleged that Agnes M'Kain was, in point of fact, pregnant. I am bound to assume that she was not pregnant, for if she had been, this fact, which I hold to be essential to the relevancy of the charge, would have been libelled by the prosecutor. An allegation of pregnancy is, in my opinion, an essential part of a charge of procuring or attempting to procure abortion. To insert deleterious substances into the private parts of a non-pregnant female, with her consent, may or may not give rise to a criminal charge. If death results, the charge of culpable homicide would probably lie. If injury short of death were the consequence, it is doubtful whether any criminal offence has been committed. At all events, I am satisfied that this present charge would not lie. Again, it does not appear to me to be material that the accused believed there was pregnancy, if in point of fact there was none, or that the purpose of the act was to cause abortion, if there was nothing to abort. In short, in the absence of an allegation of pregnancy, I consider that I am bound to treat this charge as if the libel had been that the accused had inserted injurious substances into the private parts of a virgin in order to effect an abortion. Had the indictment been so framed, it would manifestly have postulated a contradiction in terms, and have charged the accused with the commission of what was a physical impossibility. To attempt to do what is physically impossible can never, in my opinion, be a crime.

The ground of my judgment is that, in a charge of procuring or attempting to procure abortion, which is a charge of an attempt to commit a well-known crime, the prosecutor must libel, and, to secure a conviction, must prove, that the patient was pregnant. This proposition seems to be made good by consideration of what is involved in the crime, and by having regard to the presumptive reasons whereby the acts resulting in abortion are regarded as criminal. Abortion, in the sense of the criminal law, is held to be criminal because its successful accomplishment results in the destruction of potential human life. That is the main consideration. I agree with the Advocate-depute that, incidentally, but only incidentally, regard is also had to the possible injury to the prospective mother. If, however, there is no pregnancy, none of these considerations are applicable.

All that I have said seems to be warranted by what is found in the text books and in the statements of institutional writers. At the time when Hume wrote, the crime was not recognised under its now well-known *nomen juris*, because Hume only refers incidentally to the matter in his first volume at page 187, and he alludes to the case, commented upon in Alison, of Catherine Robertson and George Bachelor. Hume points out that the libel in that case was found relevant to infer an arbitrary punishment, the crime being 'wilful causing or procuring a pregnant woman to abort, or to part in an untimely manner with the *fœtus* or child in her womb'; and Alison refers to the same case in a chapter in which he is dealing with innominate offences. He states in section 4: 'Administering drugs to procure abortion is an offence at common law, punishable with an arbitrary pain, and that equally whether the desired effects be produced or not,' and then he goes on to refer to the case of Catherine Robertson and George Bachelor alluded to in Hume. When the late Lord Justice-Clerk Macdonald came to write, the crime had been fully recognised and had been described by the well-known *nomen juris* of 'procuring abortion,' and the learned author deals with it at page 382 of his Treatise on Criminal Law, where he suggests the appropriate charge to make in a case when this particular offence is meant to be libelled. He puts the matter in this way:—'A charge of procuring the abortion of a pregnant woman, after a narrative of a certain woman having become pregnant, states—"You did" (a certain act described) "for the purpose of causing her to abort, and did cause her to abort."' The Act of 1887 does not, if I remember aright, contain in its Schedule a form applicable to abortion, but what I have quoted is the suggestion of Lord Justice-Clerk Macdonald as to the proper form of indictment, and, according to him, an essential part must be a narrative that the woman operated upon had become pregnant.

It may, at first sight, appear to be a narrow construction to which I am subjecting this indictment. The accused, according to the charge, acted just as she would have done had M'Kain been pregnant, and she owes her escape from trial to the fortuitous circumstance that there was no pregnancy. But, in the realm of criminal law, an accused person is entitled to have the charge construed with the utmost strictness, and to take advantage of any chance which enables a conviction to be avoided. The Advocate-depute submitted two points in support of the libel. He said, and I have already dealt with this point, that it is an element in the crime of abortion that the woman operated upon may be injured, and he submitted that, as that element was present in this case, whether there was pregnancy or not, the crime might be committed. I doubt whether any crime, in such circumstances, would have been committed; but it is enough to destroy his first contention that the crime of attempting to procure abortion could not have been committed. His other point is based upon a well-known doctrine in criminal law, which is referred to in Hume, vol. i., p. 12, and by Macdonald at p. 252, to the effect that the High Court of Justiciary is entitled to stamp with the mark of criminality any new offence which presents criminal features. There is no doubt about that, but this is not a libel of a new offence. This is a libel of an old and well-known offence, and in my opinion, it is a bad libel. The same answer falls to be made to the argument of the Advocate-depute which was based upon the terms of section 5 of the Criminal Procedure (Scotland) Act, 1887. That section provides that 'It shall not be necessary in any indictment to specify by any *nomen juris* the crime which is charged, but it shall be sufficient that the indictment sets forth the facts relevant and sufficient to constitute an indictable crime.' Now, this indictment does specify the crime charged by a *nomen juris*. The *nomen juris* is 'attempt to cause abortion.' Accordingly, this is not a novel form of crime, but a recognised form of crime; and, it being such, and having a known *nomen juris*, I reach the conclusion, without difficulty, that the objection to the relevancy is well founded and falls to be sustained. I accordingly sustain the objection to relevancy."

Objection sustained.

NOTE

For a discussion of the declaratory power of the High Court referred to by the Crown in argument in this case, see Gordon, *The Criminal Law of Scotland* (2nd ed. 1978) paras. 1-15 *et seq*.

2. H.M. Advocate v. Grainger and Rae
1932 J.C. 40

Two accused were charged that they had carnal knowledge of and did ravish a woman named "while she was in a state of insensibility or unconsciousness from the effects of intoxicating liquor". They claimed the indictment was irrelevant in respect that it did not disclose the crime of rape according to the law of Scotland.

LORD ANDERSON: ". . . Rape (save in the exceptional cases of pupils and idiots) is the carnal knowledge of a woman forcibly and against her will—Macdonald's Criminal Law, (4th ed.) p. 175; Hume on Crimes, vol. i., pp. 301-302; Alison's Criminal Law, vol. i., p. 209. Accordingly, it was urged by the accused, the crime cannot be committed unless a woman is in a condition physically and mentally, to exercise her will power and offer resistance. In the present case the libel sets forth that the woman was in a condition when she was incapacitated, by reason of intoxication, from offering any resistance to her assailants or from exercising her will power in the way of giving or refusing consent. The offence charged, accordingly, it was said, does not amount to rape. This contention seems to me to be well founded. It is not alleged that the accused supplied the woman with the liquor with which she became intoxicated. Had this allegation been made, the charge of rape might have been sustained, as it has been decided that it is rape to have connexion with a woman whose resistance has been overcome by drugging her—Macdonald's Criminal Law, (4th ed.) p. 176; Hume on Crimes, vol. i., p. 303; Alison's Criminal Law, vol. i., p. 212; *Fraser* [(1847) Ark. 280]; *Sweenie* [(1858) 3 Irv. 109]. It might be suggested that the present case falls to be assimilated to that of an idiot female; but this does not seem to me to be a true analogy. The idiot has, in law and in fact, no will; in the present case the woman assaulted had a will, the activity of which was but temporarily suspended by her intoxication. The true analogy seems to me to be the case of the woman who is taken advantage of while asleep. Such an offence is not rape—Macdonald's Criminal Law, p. 175; *Sweenie*. Just as a sleeping woman is temporarily in a state of unconsciousness wherein she is incapable of exercising her will power, so here it seems to me that the woman was in the same temporary condition of unconsciousness by reason of intoxication.

The objection to relevancy must therefore be sustained."

                                                        Objection sustained.

NOTE

Lord Anderson went on to indicate that in his view the actings of the accused amounted to another separate criminal offence: that of inflicting clandestine injury on a woman, which goes to show the flexibility of the law, provided the prosecutor libels conduct which *is* criminal.

3.   H.M. Advocate v. Smith
1934 J.C. 66

An accused person was charged with perjury during the trial of two persons, Turner and Ord. He stated two objections to the relevancy of the indictment, the second of which is dealt with in the following extract:

LORD JUSTICE-CLERK (AITCHISON): ". . . The second objection to the relevancy of this indictment is much more formidable. It is maintained by Mr Duffes that the evidence of the accused Smith, which is alleged by the Crown to have been knowingly false, was incompetent evidence, and accordingly that perjury cannot attach to it. Now, the first question, accordingly, that arises is whether the evidence of the accused Smith in relation to the matters to which I have referred was or was not competent evidence. I have no doubt at all that that evidence was incompetent. Statements made by Mr Graham, Mr Wilson, and Mr M'Lellan to the accused Smith outwith the presence of Turner and Ord could not be evidence against Turner and Ord. Similarly, the evidence that Graham, Wilson, and M'Lellan had called at the accused Smith's house and reported that Turner and Ord had solicited bribes could not be evidence against Turner and Ord. It appears to me to be equally clear that any statement by the accused Smith, whether by way of admission or denial, when he was a witness in the previous trial, that Graham, Wilson, and McLellan had called and had made statements to him could not be evidence against Turner and Ord, and similarly any statement made by Smith at the alleged interview, or his admission or denial of any statement, could not competently be received in evidence.

It must be kept in view that Mr Wilson and Mr Graham were really in the position of complainers in the former trial. It is so well settled that no authority is required to vouch it, that statements made by complainers outwith the presence of the party accused are never evidence against that party, except in certain very exceptional cases. A fortiori, statements made to complainers outwith the presence of the party accused can never be evidence. In cases of assault committed on women or on children, where complaint is made de recenti, the Court will allow such complaint to be received in evidence, but that is the exception to the rule. So also if the statements made by Graham, Wilson, and M'Lellan had been made at the time of the alleged offence, so as to form part of the res gestae of the crime alleged, it may be that they would have been admissible in evidence, and any statement made by the accused Smith at the time of the alleged offence might, if part of the res gestae, have been admissible in evidence. But the statements here upon which the indictment for perjury is based are statements alleged to have been made on the 11th of April 1933, whereas the crime libelled in the former trial occurred, as I have pointed out, on the 9th of April 1933.

It was maintained on behalf of the Crown that the questions put to the accused Smith and the answers given by him were competent as bearing upon the credibility of Smith as a witness. I am quite unable to assent to this view. Great latitude is allowed in cross-examination of a witness in order to test the credibility of the witness, but the latitude can never be extended so far as to admit evidence that is incompetent evidence, and that may be prejudicial evidence against the prisoner who is being tried. I therefore have no doubt that, if objection had been taken at the trial of Turner and Ord to the admissibility of the evidence of the accused Smith upon the matters set forth in this indictment, the learned judge at the trial would have had no alternative but to disallow the evidence, upon the ground that it was incompetent and could not be regarded as either relevant or pertinent to the issue. No objection was in fact taken to the admission of the evidence, but that circumstance will not make incompetent evidence competent.

If, accordingly, the evidence was incompetent, the only remaining question is whether perjury can attach to it. Now, that matter appears to me to be concluded beyond all doubt against the Crown upon authority which I am bound to follow. The most authoritative statement of the law is the statement contained in Hume in his Commentaries on the Criminal Law. Baron Hume says this: 'The oath, in that part of it which is challenged as false, must be pertinent to the point at issue: It must relate to some of those substantial facts, which may have an influence in the decision of the interest that is at stake, in the proceeding where the oath is made.' It is not possible to get a more authoritative statement of the law than that. Exactly the same doctrine is laid down by Burnett in his Criminal Law, by Alison, and by Lord Justice-Clerk Macdonald, than whom there is no greater authority. I will not occupy time in reading what they say, because what they say is simply what Hume said in the passage I have read.

I accordingly in this case, without difficulty, reach the conclusion that the second objection to the relevancy of the indictment is well founded and must be sustained. I desire to add this observation. The rule that perjury cannot attach to incompetent evidence is not a technical rule; it is a rule of substance. The foundation of the rule is that incompetent evidence is so prejudicial to the administration of justice that the Courts will not assign to it the character of perjury and will treat it as if it had not been given. That rule has been laid down by lawyers of great distinction with a proper appreciation of what justice requires, and in my view it is a rule that should be rigidly adhered to. The result is that I sustain the second objection to the relevancy of this indictment, and direct that the accused be liberated."

Objection sustained.

NOTE

This is an unusual case, but perjury is of its essence a crime which involves the libelling of the alleged false statement previously given in a judicial proceeding. Presumably the perjury indictment would never have been raised if the original evidence had been struck out as inadmissible. See also *Angus* v. *H.M. Advocate*, 1935 J.C. 1.

4.   **Campbell v. McLennan**
(1888) 1 White 604

An accused person was charged that "having on 14th November 1887, within the inn of Dunvegan, found in money one pound, you did deny having found the same and did appropriate and thus steal same." He challenged the relevancy of the indictment.

LORD MCLAREN: ". . . Now, in my opinion, that is not a relevant charge of theft, because everything set out might be true, and yet the accused might not be guilty of theft. I am not prepared to affirm that the mere finding of a £1 note, coupled with a denial of having found it, is tantamount to felonious appropriation. One would like to know who the owner of the note was, and whether the person to whom the accused is said to have denied having found it, had a right to ask the question. The circumstances set out are only these two: that the accused found a £1 note, and that he denied having found it. Now it may be morally wrong to deny having found a £1 note; on the other hand, such a denial, if addressed to a person who had no business to put the question, does not raise a presumption of theft.

In the result, my opinion is that the Procurator-Fiscal having undertaken, by the form of the charge, to set out such particulars as would amount to charge of theft, has failed to do so. He has in the terms of the charge given an argumentative statement of circumstances which he considers amount to theft, but which are also consistent with a possible case of innocence."

Charge irrelevant.

NOTE

Nowadays charges of theft by finding simply proceed on a narrative that on a particular date at a particular place the accused "did find [article], dishonestly appropriate the same to his own use and did thus steal the same."

5. **Strathern v. Seaforth**

1926 J.C. 100

An accused person was charged with clandestinely taking possession of a motor car belonging to another, well knowing that he had not received permission from the owner and that he would not have obtained permission to his so doing, and with driving and using the car. He challenged the relevancy of the charge on the ground that the *species facti* did not infer any crime known to the law of Scotland. The sheriff sustained the objection and the Crown appealed to the High Court.

LORD JUSTICE-CLERK (ALNESS): ". . . Counsel for the Crown say that that complaint discloses a crime which the Court was bound to investigate, and that that crime consists in taking and using something clandestinely, without the permission of the owner having been given. It appears to me that the proposition for which the Crown contends is supported by the authorities which were cited. But, speaking for myself, I should not have required any authority to convince me that the circumstances set out in this complaint are sufficient, if proved and unexplained, to constitute an offence against the law of Scotland.

The matter may be tested by considering what the contention for the respondent involves. It plainly involves that a motor car, or for that matter any other article, may be taken from its owner, and may be retained for an indefinite time by the person who abstracts it and who may make profit out of the adventure, but that, if he intends ultimately to return it, no offence against the law of Scotland has been committed. I venture to think that, if that were so, in these days when one is familiar with the circumstances in which motor cars are openly parked in the public street, the result would be not only lamentable but absurd. I am satisfied that our common law is not so powerless as to be unable to afford a remedy in circumstances such as these."

NOTE

Nowadays, such an accused would be charged under section 175 (1) of the Road Traffic Act 1972. But the case clearly confirms that the test of relevancy is met if the charge sets forth sufficient facts from which criminal liability can be inferred, even if the crime is not named. See, *e.g. H.M. Advocate* v. *Parker and Barrie* (1888) 2 White 79 and, more recently, *W.* v. *H.M. Advocate*, 1982 S.L.T. 420. See also *Tudhope* v. *Usher*, 1976 S.L.T. (Notes) 49.

b.   Are the proceedings competent?

Preliminary pleas to the competency should not have anything to do with the adequacy or otherwise of the facts laid out in the indictment. Such a plea is directed to the essential validity of the proceedings themselves, for example lack of jurisdiction, want of proper citation and the like. The following cases illustrate the nature of the plea.

1. **Aitchison v. Tudhope**
1981 S.L.T. 231

An accused person was charged with driving while disqualified and, on the same complaint, a contravention of the Bail etc (Scotland) Act 1980. He was convicted and appealed by stated case.

LORD JUSTICE-CLERK (WHEATLEY): "The appellant was charged on a summary complaint at the instance of the respondent which set forth that: 'You did on 12 June 1980, at the premises at 41 Netherton Road, Wishaw, District of Motherwell, having been liberated from Hamilton Sheriff Court on 14 May 1980 on a Bail Order issued under the Criminal Procedure (Scotland) Act 1975 and the Bail (Scotland) Act 1980, and being subject to the conditions therein, break the said conditions of the Bail Order by contravening the Vagrancy Act 1824, section 4: Contrary to the Bail (Scotland) Act 1980, section 3 (1).'

Section 3 (1) aforesaid is in the following terms: 'Subject to subsection (3) below, an accused who having been granted bail fails without reasonable excuse — (*b*) to comply with any other condition imposed on bail, shall be guilty of an offence'. One of the conditions in the bail order was: 'That the accused does not commit an offence while on bail'. There is express warrant for such a condition being imposed in s. 1 (2) (*b*) of the Bail etc. (Scotland) Act.

The major issue in the appeal raised a question of general importance. To obtain a conviction on the charge libelled in the complaint the Crown had to establish that the appellant had committed an offence while on bail. The question is — can the Crown prove that fact within the ambit of the trial of the alleged contravention of s. 3 (1) or must the Crown establish it in a prosecution on a separate complaint libelling the offence?

In the instant case the former procedure was followed without objection. There is no mention of any such objection having been taken either in the minutes of procedure or in the sheriff's note appended to his findings-in-fact. The Crown adduced two police witnesses to establish that the appellant had contravened s. 4 of the Vagrancy Act 1824. The relevant part of that very long section is in these terms: 'Every person being found in or upon any dwelling house, warehouse, coach-house, stable, or outhouse, or in any inclosed yard, garden, or area, for any unlawful purpose' shall be guilty of an offence. No evidence was led for the defence, and the sheriff held that the offence had been proved. His finding on this matter was not challenged in the appeal.

The submission by the appellant's counsel was that even if no objection was taken to this procedure, it was funditus null and the conviction should accordingly be quashed. There could not be a conviction under s. 3 (1) unless the appellant had been convicted of a contravention of s. 4 of the Vagrancy Act. He had not been convicted and was entitled to the presumption of innocence until he was convicted. There were two separate offences involved here. One was a contravention of s. 3 (1) and the other a contravention of s. 4 of the Vagrancy Act. Each could be charged separately, but it was wrong to libel the latter within the framework of the former, and in effect get a finding of guilt in respect of the latter when it could not be recorded as a conviction in the complaint before the court. It was necessary for the Crown to obtain a conviction of the offence alleged to be a breach of a condition of the bail order before a contravention of s. 3 (1) could be established, and such a conviction could only be obtained on a separate complaint. The advocate-depute on the other hand maintained that the procedure followed was quite competent. It was not the policy of the Crown in cases of this nature to charge a person both with a contravention of s. 3 (1) and with the offence which was a breach of the bail order. It was a matter for the Crown to decide which of the two offences would be charged. It was accordingly competent for the Crown to prove within a s. 3 (1) complaint the manner in which the condition of the bail order had been breached in order to constitute the offence libelled.

What has to be decided is the competency of the procedure followed here, not whether another procedure would be more desirable. We are not concerned with Crown policy about not charging an accused with two separate offences. The charging of offences in our criminal law (with very limited exceptions) is entirely a matter for the Crown. That does not necessarily mean that because of that policy it would be competent here to libel two separate charges. In my opinion, however, the contention of the

Crown that the procedure followed here was competent is well founded. The condition of the bail order said to have been breached was that the appellant should not commit another offence. It does not say that the appellant has been convicted of another offence. What the Crown has to prove is that the accused has committed an offence during the currency of the bail order. The manner in which that is done may vary according to circumstances. If, leaving aside the current Crown policy, an accused had already been convicted of another offence, an extract conviction of that offence could suffice. If the accused had not been already convicted of that offence I see no reason why the Crown should not prove that the accused was guilty of a contravention of s. 3 (1) by leading evidence to establish that he had committed the libelled offence which was of the essence of the complaint. The fact that this would not result in a conviction on that offence is not in my view material. A person charged with fraud may be faced with a libel that in pursuance of that fraud he uttered forged documents to enable the fraud to be perpetrated. It is not necessary to charge him with a separate charge of uttering, and if found guilty, he would only be guilty of fraud, not of uttering and fraud. If the other offence was the modus whereby the charge libelled was committed, then, provided fair notice of the nature of that other offence is given in the libel, it must surely be competent to lead evidence about the modus. And I reiterate, what had to be established here was that the applicant had committed the specified offence in breach of the condition of the bail order, not that he had been convicted of that offence, and that was the modus whereby the contravention of s. 3 (1) took place.

Two other points were taken by counsel for the appellant. The first, which was also taken before the sheriff but rejected by him, was that the Crown had failed to prove that at the time of the libelled contravention of s. 4 of the Vagrancy Act the bail order was still in operation. There is certainly no finding-in-fact that it was. The advocate-depute, however, submitted that it was not necessary to do so because of the provisions of s. 312 (x) of the Criminal Procedure (Scotland) Act 1975 which is in the following terms: 'where an offence is alleged to be committed in any special capacity, as by the holder of a licence, master of a vessel, occupier of a house or the like, the fact that the accused possesses the qualification necessary to the commission of the offence shall, unless challenged by preliminary objection before his plea is recorded, be held as admitted'. The libel here narrates that 'having been liberated — on a Bail Order — and being subject to the conditions therein [you did] break the said conditions of the Bail Order by contravening the Vagrancy Act 1824, section 4: contrary to the Bail (Scotland) Act 1980, section 3 (1).' In my opinion that libel brought the appellant within the provisions of s. 312 (x) aforesaid and no preliminary objection was taken. He had been granted what in effect was a licence to be at liberty pending his trial, but that was on certain conditions, and it was only such a person who had the qualification necessary for the commission of the offence libelled under s. 3 (1). I accordingly reject the submission by the appellant's counsel.

The second point taken was that the alleged contravention of s. 4 of the Vagrancy Act was lacking in specification. As I have already indicated, if the Crown seeks within the trial of the charge under s. 3 (1) to establish that another offence has been committed in violation of a condition of the bail order fair notice should be given of what the Crown seeks to prove. Normally that involves notice of when, where and how that offence took place. In the present complaint notice is given of where and when but not how. Even if this was a material deficiency it was one which could have been rectified by amendment. However, no objection was taken to the relevancy of the complaint for lack of specification either at the pleading diet or the trial diet. Having regard to the provisions of s. 454 (1) of the Criminal Procedure (Scotland) Act 1975 that point is not now open to the appellant."

Appeal dismissed.

NOTE

It appears that in this case the defence were confusing the question of specifying the *modus* (a problem of relevancy) with that arising from the revelation in the charge that a previous crime had been committed, (a problem of competency.) Commonly, where an accused is charged with driving while disqualified and other road traffic offences, those other offences are usually embodied in a separate complaint. Both complaints will be *prima facie* relevant and no problem of competency should arise. As to the timing of a plea to the competency (or relevancy) in solemn proceedings, the accused should apply for a preliminary diet under section 76 of the 1975 Act (as inserted by the 1980 Act, Sched. 4, para. 5). In summary procedure the matter is regulated by section 334 (1) of the 1975 Act.

<h3 align="center">2. Sugden v. H.M. Advocate</h3>
1934 J.C. 103

An accused person was in 1934 charged with bigamy, allegedly committed in 1909. He presented a preliminary plea to the competency of the proceedings, claiming that the crime had prescribed and the prosecutor had no title to proceed. This plea was repelled and the accused was convicted after trial. He appealed to the High Court.

LORD JUSTICE-CLERK (AITCHISON): ". . . If this question can be regarded as an open one, for myself I have little difficulty in reaching the conclusion that there is no prescription of crime by the law of Scotland. I would agree in that matter with the view of Lord Justice-Clerk Macdonald in his Criminal Law (4th ed., at p. 312), that 'there is no rule of law establishing a prescription of crime.' But the real difficulty arises upon the case of *H. M. Advocate* v. *Macgregor* [(1773) Mor. 11146]. In that case, in the year 1773, a full bench of the High Court of Justiciary, consisting of five Lords Commissioners, was invited by the Crown, on a plea stated by the panel *in limine*, to decide this very question. Whether the Court did so is, I confess, left in some obscurity. It is accordingly necessary to examine the case carefully in order to see what it did decide, and, if it did lay down a rule, what the rule was, and whether it was absolute or subject to limitation.

The panel Malcolm or Callum Macgregor, *alias* John Grant, was charged on indictment that, on the evening of Christmas Day, 1747, he did attack and barbarously murder one John Stewart, tenant in Abergairn, in the Parish of Glengairn and Shire of Aberdeen, and the libel proceeds that the panel did immediately abscond and flee from that part of the country, and was never again seen there, except to some few persons by stealth and in the night time, and further that a justiciary warrant was thereupon issued for apprehending and incarcerating him, which warrant bears date 21st January 1748. The Books of Adjournal record that the indictment was read over in open Court and thereafter 'Mr Alexander Lockhart, as counsel for the pannell, represented that no proceedings could be had upon this indictment exhibited against the pannell in respect the crime therein charged is said to have been committed so far back as the year 1747, and therefore is prescribed by the elapse of more than twenty years.' The record proceeds: 'Partys procurators were then heard at great length thereupon,' and informations were ordered. The informations are set out at length, and then under date 9th August 1773, there is this interlocutor: 'The Lords Justice-Clerk and Commissioners of Justiciary having considered the Information given in for His Majesty's Advocate, for His Majesty's interest, and the said Malcolm or Callum Macgregor, *alias* John Grant pannell, and before recorded, and in respect it does not appear, that any sentence of fugitation passed against the pannell, they therefore sustain the defence and dismiss the Indictment and the pannell from the barr.'

Prima facie there can, I think, be no doubt that this judgment did sustain a prescription of twenty years as a competent defence to an indictment for crime by the law of Scotland. Such a decision may seem surprising and indeed anomalous. Each of the civil prescriptions in the law of Scotland is statutory; here there is no statute. Nor is there uniform and unvarying usage. According to Baron Hume (Commentaries respecting Crimes, vol. ii., p. 136), the equitable rule of the Roman law 'which gives the accused his *quietus* at the end of twenty years,' although sustained in this case, was not established in our older practice. Sir George Mackenzie, who published his Laws and Customs in matters Criminal in the year 1678, 'inclined' to the opinion, based on some analogy drawn from the law of Saxony, that there was a vicennial prescription of crime. But, notwithstanding, he writes, 'It may be doubted with us, if prescription has place at all.' And again, 'There being *jus quaesitum* to the King, by the committing of the crime, both *quoad vindictam et bona fisco applicanda*, that right cannot be taken away from him, but by a publick law, or his own privat remission'; and he adds, 'There is no instance in all our practicks, where prescription hath been sustained, but on the contrary, crimes of an old date, even after forty years, have been punished.' Instances of the contrary practice to which Sir George Mackenzie refers are to be found in the case of *James Wilson*, tried on 20th

December 1649 for incest and adultery committed by him thirty-five years before, and also the cases of *Jean Weir, William Dodds*, and *George Turnbull* referred to by Hume and the older authorities. The case of *William Dodds* was a trial on 2nd October 1663 for the murder of one Andrew Hardie, committed in November 1640. Thus there was not only no statute and no unvarying custom, but there were instances of a contrary custom. And also, prior to 1773, the Roman law in this matter had not been received into the law of Scotland. The Lord Justice-Clerk (Sir Thomas Miller of Barskimming) referred to the question as 'quite entire.'

When the matter is examined in the light of these considerations, and when regard is had to the recorded opinions of the judges, to which I shall afterwards refer, I think the sounder view is that the rule of a twenty years' limitation of the Advocate's title was really laid down as a rule of practice based on justice and expediency, and not as a prescription in the absolute sense. The judgment in the case of *Macgregor* is explained as a striking illustration of the exercise by the High Court of Justiciary of the inherent right the Justiciary had always claimed to formulate and declare rules in all matters criminal. This inherent power, so far as the declaring of new crimes is concerned, is stated by Hume (Com., vol. i. 12) in these words: 'Our Supreme Criminal Court have an inherent power as such competently to punish (with the exception of life and limb) every act which is obviously of a criminal nature; though it be such which in time past has never been the subject of prosecution.' This fundamental assertion of right was judicially affirmed by a Full Bench in 1838 in the case of *Greenhuff* [(1838) 2 Swin. 236]. A modern example of its exercise is to be found in the case of *Strathern* v. *Seaforth* [1926 J.C. 100]. The power so claimed and asserted is not a usurpation of the powers of the Legislature, it is a prerogative of the Justiciary derived from its history, and coming down from the days of the Justiciar, to do what it deems to be just in all matters criminal, and affecting on the one hand the rights of the Crown, and on the other hand the liberties of the subject. The exercise of this power was seen not only in the declaring of new crimes—that is, crimes not before known to the law of Scotland—but also in the abrogation of old defences, and an illustration of this is furnished in the very matter of prescription itself.

Under the old law of Scotland there existed certain customary limitations of the prosecutor's title or prescriptions of crime. They are referred to by Hume. There was, for instance, a customary prescription of rape. The title of the complainer to proceed with a libel was extinguished under the older law if she delayed to make a complaint to the magistrates of the vicinity of the crime beyond a single night. This at one time was admitted as a plea *in limine* as a bar to prosecution. A relic of this old rule survives in our modern rule that the complaint of the assaulted woman must be made *de recenti*, but under the older law the objection went to the title of the prosecutor and not merely to the weight of the complaint. Again, in the case of hamesucken, no man could be heard to accuse another if he delayed to make his accusation 'by the space of ane nicht and wha maks nae fresh and recent pursuit.' According to Hume (Com., vol. i., p. 322), 'The prosecution for hamesucken, like that for robbery or murder, is said to have been subject of old to a very strict limitation in respect of time (Reg. Maj., C. 4. c. 10). But this rule, if observed of old, has now, for more than a century, been so entirely laid aside, that in the case of Keith of Lentush, action was sustained at the distance of more than three years. In the case of Richard Hamilton, in July 1807, the lapse of ten years even was found to be no bar to the prosecution.' A similar limitation at one time applied in the case of assault or real injury.

The point to be noticed is, that these customary prescriptions (there may be dispute as to whether they were not all statutory), which went to the title of the prosecutor, and were not pleadable merely to set up a defence of prejudice before the assize, were all abrogated by decision of the Court of Justiciary. They were treated as rules of practice, and as matters within the competency of the Court to discard. This abrogation I regard as of great importance as pointing to the inherent power of the Justiciary to modify the practice of the Courts where circumstances no longer require the imposition of restraints. If the rule of *Macgregor* is to be read as truly a rule of practice, then it is within the authority of this Court, in the exercise of its inherent power, as a Court to admit such exceptions to the rule as considerations of justice may require, or to abrogate the rule itself. And this is specially to be insisted in when the rule was laid down in times that are far removed from our own, as regards both the instance of prosecutions and the motives by which they are inspired.

I read the decision in *Macgregor* as having introduced into our practice and laid down that in the ordinary case the expiry of twenty years from the date of the crime will extinguish the right of the prosecutor to proceed with a libel. But the rule was not absolute. I reach this conclusion upon the following grounds. In the first place, the judgment itself introduced a limitation. It was not put on the lapse of time *simpliciter*; it was put *per expressum* in respect that it did not appear that any sentence of fugitation had passed against the panel. No warrant had been executed against the panel although one had been taken out, a precognition had not been taken, nor had any libel been raised although the panel was all the while within the kingdom and not absconding. The libel, indeed, sets forth that the panel had absconded and fled from justice, but it appears from the information for the panel that he had had his constant residence in Scotland, and for a great part of that time in the county of Aberdeen not far distant from the place where the supposed crime was alleged to have been committed, and that he had carried on business as a dealer in different parts of the country and at various fairs and markets. I think the interlocutor proceeds upon the view that the prosecutor had been in a position to proceed with a libel and had refrained from doing so. In the second place, it is, I think, quite impossible to read the opinions of the judges—we have not the full text, but I see no reason to think the record inaccurate—without seeing that the judges treated the matter as one rather of bar than of prescription in the absolute legal sense. This construction of the judgment is strongly supported by these passages which I quote from Maclaurin (Decisions, p. 603)—Auchinleck: 'Do not consider this as a prescription, but as a rule of justice . . . clear that prosecutions ought not to last for ever: the question—

How long?' Kames: 'Do not say that a prescription is here fixed, but take this case as it stands.' Pitfour: 'I am now reconciled to this prescription, though at first had some difficulty . . . prosecution extinguished no matter whether the word *prescription* be used or not.' Coalston: 'Had the panel absconded or been fugitated'—showing very clearly that the Court did not accept the allegation in the libel that the panel had absconded—'he could not have pleaded this defence. But the question is, Whether can a man that has appeared publicly for fifteen years be prosecuted . . . taciturnity a strong plea in law . . . independent of statute and listened to in questions as to bills. Claim for the *jus relictae* at the instance of the widow's executors, repelled at the distance of twenty years.' These passages all confirm that what the judges had in mind was bar based upon *mora*, and not prescription. Again Kennet: 'Highly expedient there should be a limitation . . . Prosecutor may always stop the prescription.' This I think clearly implies that the prosecutor is aware of the crime and of the person who committed it. Finally, the Lord Justice-Clerk said this: 'Law pays great attention to the just defence of pannels. If such prosecution competent to the public, it must be equally so to the nearest-in-kin of the deceased. The private prosecutor may be supposed to have watched his opportunity.' This last observation is significant, because it must not be forgotten that, in 1773, the right of prosecution was not vested, as now, solely in the public prosecutor, with certain limited exceptions, but the right of the private individual to prosecute for an injury done to himself or his kin still existed alongside the title of the Advocate for the public interest. There were obviously strong and compelling reasons for a limitation. Political rancour, clan antagonisms, and civil tumult, with their legacy of hatred, and bigotry, and the lust for vengeance, all enforced the argument from expediency. The Lord Justice-Clerk goes on, after referring to the Roman law, 'Why then not sustain a defence for the prisoner founded on that law or on expediency?' Coalston added: 'Interlocutor ought to be guarded. Fugitation — effect of it would have lasted till the party accused surrendered himself to justice.'

I think it is a fair and reasonable reading of these recorded opinions that what the Court did in the case of *Macgregor* was to introduce a rule of practice that the title of the prosecutor is subject to a limitation of twenty years to be reckoned from the date of the crime. The rule, however, was qualified by exception in any case in which the panel had absconded and sentence of fugitation had been passed upon him. I am unable to read the decision as laying down that the rule would not have been subject to exception in any case in which twenty years had expired without discovery of the crime or of the person by whom the crime was committed. The decision did not, in my view, introduce into the law of Scotland, or declare as our law, the vicennial prescription of the Roman law. If the contrary view were to be affirmed, the result would be to introduce into our law what would be essentially a one-sided prescription. In the civil prescriptions the right of the person against whom the prescription runs is a right that continues throughout the whole prescriptive period. But I think cases can be figured in which the Court might sustain a plea of bar on a lapse of time far short of twenty years, where it appeared to the Court *in limine*, on facts admitted by the Crown, that grave prejudice to the accused might result if the trial were allowed to proceed. The correct doctrine in this matter is, I think, stated by Mr Burnett in his Criminal Law (at p. 309) in this passage: 'As His Majesty's Advocate . . . cannot be compelled to give his *instance*, so this officer cannot be controlled as to the way and manner in which he is to give it, or as to the *time* when he is to exercise his right, except in as far as he has been restrained by express enactment as to the form of trial and the period within which it must be brought, or by the interference of the Court of Law upon any case of hardship or oppression towards the party accused, by undue delay or otherwise, in conducting the trial.'

As I have already pointed out, the rule laid down in *Macgregor's* case was laid down in times that are far distant from our own, and under social and political conditions affecting the purity of prosecutions, that have long since passed away. I cannot regard a rule so laid down 160 years ago as fixed and unalterable, and so sacrosanct that it is beyond the power of this Court to declare that the rule no longer exists. I think it should be so declared.

This appears to me to be in accordance with justice and expediency. Twenty years may be a long time when men look forward, but it is a short time when men look back. It requires no effort of the imagination to figure a notorious crime committed twenty years ago, in which, were the criminal allowed to walk abroad with impunity merely because twenty years had run, such a liberty would be against the public conscience, and contrary to the community sense of what is just, upon which the law and respect for the law must ultimately be based. I am glad that we are not compelled to acquiesce in any such situation. I accordingly think that the learned Sheriff was right in repelling the plea of prescription, and that the appeal should be refused."

Appeal dismissed.

NOTE

This case was in fact decided by a majority of a Full Bench of 12 judges. The Lord Justice-General was apparently the only absent judge. The case also illustrates the power of one Full Bench to overrule another Full Bench comprising a lesser number of judges.

For cases on jurisdiction, see Chap. 3, *supra*.

CHAPTER 9

PRE-TRIAL PROCEDURE

Once the indictment has been framed under reference to the problems discussed in the last chapter, it is served on the accused, either at his domicile of citation or on him at any prison or other institution in which he may have been detained. Until the 1980 Act, accused persons were cited to attend both a pleading diet and a trial diet, but under section 12 of the 1980 Act the mandatory first diet has been abolished. If however some preliminary point needs to be raised prior to trial, any party may apply for a preliminary diet to deal with such a matter, all in accordance with the new section 76 of the 1975 Act, as inserted by the 1980 Act, Sched. 4, para. 5. In particular, if the accused wishes to take a plea to the competency or relevancy of the indictment, this procedure must be used. This chapter deals with other pre-trial problems which may arise.

a. Separation of charges

An accused who is charged with more than one offence on the same indictment may seek that the charges be separated. If the accused wishes to move for separation, he should seek a preliminary diet, as explained above.

1. H.M. Advocate v. Bickerstaff
1926 J.C. 65

An accused person was charged with (1) indecent assault on one complainer, and (2) indecent assault, including a charge of murder, involving another complainer. The offences were alleged to have happened on the same day. He moved for separation of charges.

LORD JUSTICE-GENERAL (CLYDE): ". . . There was, as I have explained above, a further question raised, viz., whether there should be a separation of the charges. The question is not one of the separation of trials (a question not so uncommon), but as to the separation of charges (a point which is less common). The two charges here are (*first*) an indecent assault on one little girl, and (*second*) an indecent assault amounting to murder on another little

291

girl, occurring on the same day and in the same place, by which is meant the town of Stirling. It is familiar that more offences than one should be charged under the same indictment. The submission made on behalf of the prisoner is that some prejudice may be suffered by him if the two charges are taken and tried together. I think it would be extremely difficult—and I have no intention of attempting the task—to define the circumstances in which the combination of more charges than one in the same indictment is legitimate and fair to the accused. But it is familiar that there are many instances of criminal conduct which are divisible into successive stages, and in which each stage is distinguished by the commission of some particular act which (regarded in isolation) would in itself be a crime. It has never been the practice of the Court to insist, in such a case as that, that there should be a separation of charges. On the contrary, there exists in such a case a connexion of time, of circumstances, of character (one, or more, or all) between the acts charged which makes it both fair and legitimate to put them all in one indictment and to lead evidence in respect of all of them together. It was suggested that this principle has no application to a case in which (as in the present case) the persons assaulted or attacked were different persons. I am unable to follow the grounds upon which that suggestion can be made good. A man may assault more than one person in turn against whom he is moved by a common and equal sentiment of anger or revenge; so, a man may commit a continuous series of crimes of the class to which the present indictment relates against one little girl after another, moved by the same criminal impulses or desires. Without attempting to dogmatise upon the matter, it seems to me that the present case presents an illustration of offences, in themselves capable of being treated as separate crimes, which are so closely connected in time, circumstance, and character as to make it fair and legitimate to try them together. I realise that in all such cases—I mean in all cases where more than one charge is tried under one indictment—there may arise in the course of the trial questions of more or less difficulty with regard to what shall be regarded as competent and relevant evidence, depending on the closeness of the relation—in time, circumstance, and character—between the charges included in the same indictment. Questions of that class inevitably arise, and it is the function of the Judge to allow or disallow evidence, and to guide and direct the jury with regard to what evidence they are entitled to consider in relation to the various parts of the case they have to decide. But that is an incident common, more or less, to all criminal trials. What we are asked to do is *ab ante* to decide that the two charges in the indictment against the accused should be tried separately. I do not think there are any good grounds for so deciding in the present case."

Motion for separation refused.

NOTE

It is thus apparent that no fixed rule exists on this question: whether to separate charges is purely discretionary. The onus is clearly on the accused to demonstrate prejudice.

2. H.M. Advocate v. McGuinness
1937 J.C. 37

An accused was charged with two charges of assault allegedly committed on 3 October 1936, a charge of murder allegedly committed on 24 or 25 October 1936, and a further charge of assault allegedly committed on the latter day or days. He moved for separation of charges.

LORD JUSTICE-CLERK (AITCHISON): "Counsel for the panel Richard M'Guinness has moved for a separation of charges in this indictment to the effect that charges 1 and 2, which affect his client only, should be tried separately from charges 3 and 4, which affect four and five persons respectively, including the panel M'Guinness. Charge 3 in the indictment is a charge of murder. Now, the law as to separation of charges was laid down by a Court of five judges in the case of *Bickerstaff*, and I do not think there is any doubt as to what that law is. Separation of charges is a matter in the discretion of the Court, and the test to be applied in every case is whether it is fair to the person or persons accused to put a particular accumulation of charges in one indictment. The crimes charged may be separated by an interval of time, and yet may be so inter-related by circumstances, or by similarity of character, or by the relevancy of one to proof of another, that the charges cannot reasonably be separated. Now, in the present case the learned Advocate-Depute has very fairly and properly admitted that he is unable to say that the evidence to be led in charges 1 and 2, which are charges of assault, is relevant to charge 3, which is a charge of murder, and to charge 4, which is a charge of assault. The date libelled in charges 1 and 2 is the 3rd of October 1936. The date libelled in charges 3 and 4 is 24th or 25th October 1936, and charge 3, as I have already said, is a charge of murder. Wherever murder is charged I am quite clear that it is the duty of the Court to prevent any risk of prejudice which might arise to the panel if the whole of the charges in the indictment were tried together. If there is any risk of prejudice, it is the clear duty of the Court to separate the charges. I propose, therefore, to give effect to the motion which Mr Thomson has made on behalf of his client, and to direct that charges 1 and 2 be tried separately, which means by a different jury from charges 3 and 4."

Motion granted.

NOTE

With the abolition of the death penalty, the reasoning of the Lord Justice-Clerk may have slightly less force. It has become not unusual to find indictments against one accused containing other charges additional to the murder charge. The only link in such cases is that it is the same accused who is charged: see Hume, ii, 172.

3. Pollock v. H.M. Advocate
1974 S.L.T. (Notes) 8

Two accused were jointly charged with four charges. While all the alleged offences took place in Clydebank, it was conceded that only the third and fourth charges had any interconnection in time and place and circumstances. The accused moved for separation of charges, which motion was refused by the trial judge. The accused were convicted and appealed.

OPINION OF THE COURT: "Counsel for the applicants submitted that the judge's refusal to separate the charges as proposed constituted an error in law or amounted to oppression. It was not clear to us which of these two horses he was riding. These are applications for leave to appeal under the Criminal Appeal (Scotland) Act 1926, and in the circumstances advanced in the grounds of appeal the only reasons for granting an appeal would be for a wrong decision on a point of law or on the ground of a miscarriage of justice. It could only be said that the trial judge made a wrong decision on a point of law if he failed to give legal effect to something which in law he was bound to do. If he was not bound in law to order a separation of the charges, his refusal to do so cannot be said to be an error in law. All that can be argued then is that in the exercise of his discretion (not his 'purported' discretion as counsel described it) he gave a ruling which in the circumstances of the case caused such prejudice to the applicants as to be oppressive and to constitute a miscarriage of justice.

But is even this argument open to the applicants? We can visualise circumstances in which it could be said that in relation to such a motion the trial judge had acted oppressively, as for instance if he refused to listen to the arguments in support of it. That, however, did not happen in this case, and that is not what we have to consider.

When a motion such as this is made at the outset of a trial, the trial judge has to make his decision on the basis of the charges in the indictment and the statements and representations made by counsel. At that stage he has no knowledge of what the evidence is to be. From very early days it has been recognised that matters such as the separation of charges or separation of trials are matters for the discretion of the trial judge. This is to be found in the writings of Sir George Mackenzie and Hume. A motion for the separation of charges was considered in *H.M. Advocate* v. *Bickerstaff* (supra). In that case the trial judge certified the question inter alia to the High Court of Justiciary for determination, and the case was dealt with by a full bench when it was still at that initial stage. The motion for separation of charges was refused. The legal position is succinctly put by Lord Hunter, at p. 127. His Lordship said: 'As regards the matter of separation of the charges, that is entirely within the discretion of the court. In the first instance, of course, the Lord Advocate is entitled to bring what charges he likes against an accused person; but the court, if on the face of the indictment it appears that there might be a prejudice to the accused, has the right to separate the charges.' That simply echoes what had been said frequently before, but it puts the position in a nutshell. The court has the right to order a separation of charges, but is in no way under a legal obligation to do so on a motion to that effect being made. Each case has to be considered on its own facts, and the decision is left to the discretion of the court. That decision cannot be impugned or appealed against unless it is alleged that the court has in some way transgressed the principles of natural justice in such a manner as to constitute a miscarriage of justice. No appeal lies on what we would term the merits of the motion. There is, accordingly, no substance in the grounds stated in support of the present applications, which we accordingly dismiss."

Appeals refused.

NOTE

This case was of course decided before the 1980 Act came into force. Now, under section 76A of the 1975 Act (inserted by the 1980 Act, Sched. 4, para. 5) provision is made for appeals against a decision made at a preliminary diet. Such an appeal requires leave of the court of first instance, and must be taken not later than two days after such a decision: section 76A(1).

See also *Davidson & Anr* v. *H.M. Advocate*, 1981 S.C.C.R. 371, where it is suggested that an appellate court should not interfere with a trial judge's discretion unless there has been a "palpable failure of justice." In this case there was also an appeal against sentence, on which see *infra*, p. 549.

b. Separation of trials

Where several accused are indicted together, they may apply to be tried separately, and such an application should again be made at a preliminary diet convened for this purpose.

Sangster and Others v. H.M. Advocate
(1896) 2 Adam 182

Five persons were indicted before sheriff and jury on a total of eight charges, each charge being against two or three accused. Each accused applied for separate trials, so that the evidence of each on a charge in which he was not implicated should be available to the others, but only one such motion was granted. After three others had been convicted they appealed to the High Court.

LORD MONCREIFF: "This bill of suspension is presented by three parties, Andrew Sangster, Thomas Henderson, and John Roger. In the indictment two other parties, John Craib and William Roger, were charged, but we have nothing to do with them. At the first diet a motion was made for separation of the trials of the various prisoners, and the Sheriff-Substitute, after consideration, sustained the motion with regard to John Craib, whose name appears only in the fifth charge, and the diet against him was deserted *pro loco et tempore*. The result of the trial of the other parties was that William Roger was acquittted, and therefore we have only to deal with the cases of Andrew Sangster, Thomas Henderson, and John Roger, who were convicted.

Now the first ground of suspension, which has been very fully argued, is that the conduct of the Sheriff in refusing to allow a separation of the trials was oppressive. A motion for separation of trial is very frequently made, but very seldom granted. Still more seldom does this Court quash a conviction on the ground that it has been refused. There may be other cases, but at present I know of no other except *Kerr* v. *Phyn* (21st March 1893, 3 White 480, 20 R. (J.C.) 60). The reason is that the question is one for the discretion of the presiding Judge, and unless it can be made out conclusively that he was wrong in the exercise of that discretion, we will not interfere. Now in the present case it would seem that the Sheriff has carefully applied his mind to the question, with the result that he has allowed a separate trial in the case of John Craib, and refused it in the case of the other prisoners. All the accused were represented by competent procurators. There is therefore *primâ facie* no sign of oppressive conduct, but we are bound to look at the indictment to see whether the case is one in which any real injustice would be done by refusal to separate the trials. The case is undoubtedly a peculiar one. There are three bankruptcies, those of William Henderson, John Roger, and William Roger, and there are five prisoners; but then we find that all the acts charged are of the same kind, and amount to a charge of fraudulent bankruptcy by putting away and concealing the bankrupt's effects from the creditors. We find also that all the offences were committed about the same time. What is still more peculiar is that Andrew Sangster, Thomas Henderson and John Roger were all more or less involved in all the acts alleged. Thus in the first two charges relating to the bankruptcy of William Henderson, Andrew Sangster and Thomas Henderson are charged. Turning to the bankruptcy of John Roger, we find that Andrew Sangster, Thomas Henderson, and John Roger are all implicated in the charges connected therewith; and in the bankruptcy of William Roger we find Thomas Henderson and Andrew Sangster again involved. That being the case as appearing on the face of the indictment, it indicates a close connection and contingency between the various charges. That in itself is a reason for a single trial stronger than we find in most cases where prisoners are charged together. The passage quoted from Hume seems to me to apply directly to the present case. He says (vol. ii., p. 177), 'For although, as I have said, our practice does disown this sort of cumulation in ordinary cases, and in respect to crimes and persons nowise connected with each other; yet in numerous instances the prosecutor has been allowed to accumulate his charges on account of an affinity among the panels or their crimes, much less intimate than in the case of these two riots. And indeed wherever there was any natural contingency of the matters charged, as when the several crimes arose out of each other, or were directed towards the same object, or when the several panels appeared to be in a society for committing crimes of a certain sort—nay, in some instances where the offences were only of the same class and were not the result of any such confederacy; or where all the panels were charged with some of the articles in the libel though not with others—in any of these cases it seems to have been nowise unusual to allow the cumulated action.' It seems to me that on the face of this indictment there is disclosed a confederacy among the prisoners to assist in concealing the effects of those of them who were or pretended to be bankrupt from their creditors. We have not the evidence before us, neither had the Sheriff, but I think that, looking to the indictment, the Sheriff acted quite properly in refusing separation of the trials."

Appeal on this ground refused.

NOTE

Once again, it is oppressive conduct only on the part of the trial judge which will give rise to an appeal against his decision not to separate the trials. But on the particular point thrown up in this case of one accused wishing to call another, the law has recently been re-written: see section 28 of the 1980 Act, which re-casts sections 141 and 346 of the 1975 Act. However, it is highly doubtful whether the change in the law makes separation of trials easier to obtain. That one accused desired the evidence of another was held in *Morrison* v. *Adair*, 1943 J.C. 25 *per se* not to be a sufficient reason for separation of trials; see also *Gemmell and McFadyen* v. *H.M. Advocate*, 1928 J.C. 5 *per* the Lord Justice-General at p 8 For the converse situation in which conjunction of trials may be appropriate, see *H.M. Advocate* v. *Clark and Others*, 1935 J.C. 51.

c.   *Pleas in bar of trial: generally*

The accepted pleas in bar of trial are: non-age, insanity in bar of trial, *res judicata*, and where the accused has immunity from prosecution: see Renton and Brown, paras. 9-23 to 9-36. In addition, prejudicial pre-trial publicity may give rise to a plea in bar of trial. If the accused seeks to raise such an issue, he should seek a preliminary diet under section 76 of the 1975 Act (as amended by the 1980 Act, Sched. 4, para. 5). The following cases deal with the plea of "tholed assize" and pre-trial publicity. The question of immunity is more evidential than procedural, on which the see Full Bench decision in *O'Neill* v. *Wilson* (High Court, June 1983, as yet unreported).

(i) Tholed assize

1. Hilson v. Easson
(1914) 7 Adam 390

An accused person was charged on summary complaint and pleaded in bar of trial that he had tholed his assize. The sheriff upheld the plea and the Crown appealed to the High Court.

LORD JUSTICE-GENERAL (STRATHCLYDE): "The procedure in this case appears to me to be hopelessly deranged, and can only be put in gear again by a commencement being made *de novo*.

The accused was charged in the Sheriff Court at Jedburgh, at the instance of the procurator-fiscal of Roxburghshire, with the crime of obtaining goods of the value of some £31 by false pretences from a certain firm of wood merchants in Jedburgh. It is not disputed that the complaint is relevant and that the Sheriff Court at Jedburgh was a Court of competent jurisdiction; but, when the complaint was called in Court on 5th January 1914, as the minutes of procedure bear, the accused objected to the relevancy of the complaint in respect that he had already tholed an assize, and the Sheriff-substitute adjourned the case to the 8th of January for the production of evidence thereupon. That plea was palpable nonsense; but nevertheless, the Sheriff-substitute heard evidence in support of it on 8th January. The sister of the accused and his solicitor from England were examined, and certain productions were given in. The evidence discloses that, on 13th October 1913, the accused had been charged before a Court of Quarter Sessions, at Wakefield, with the crime of obtaining goods under false pretences from English people on 5th April 1913. After trial, he was found guilty by the jury, and was sentenced to three months' imprisonment with hard labour by the Court of Quarter Sessions. But a note appended to the extract conviction bears that, before sentence, the prisoner admitted committing an offence at Jedburgh for which a warrant had been issued, and the Court took this further offence into consideration in fixing his punishment. How all that came about is very clearly disclosed in a conversation which is set out in the appendix to the case, and of which I will read a portion: [His Lordship read the extract from the shorthand-writer's report].

It is difficult to take this procedure seriously. A more complete travesty of justice and orderly procedure I have never seen. But upon the evidence of what transpired at Wakefield, the learned Sheriff-substitute expresses the opinion that the course taken was equivalent to a formal trial for the Jedburgh offence, and that it must consequently be held that the accused had been duly tried for the offence, even although the warrant proceeded from a Court in Scotland instead of from an English Court. I am exactly of the contrary opinion. How it could be said that what took place before the Court of Quarter Sessions at Wakefield is equivalent to a formal trial at Jedburgh of the offence charged in the complaint in the Sheriff Court at Jedburgh at the instance of the procurator-fiscal it is very difficult to see.

There was no trial at Wakefield, and there could be no trial at Wakefield, for there was no prosecutor at Wakefield, there was no accused at Wakefield, there was no complaint at Wakefield, and there was no Court of competent jurisdiction at Wakefield. There could, therefore, be no plea either of guilty or of not guilty. The procedure might just as well have taken place before the Town Council or the Chamber of Commerce for that matter. And, therefore, to speak of this man having 'tholed an assize' was nothing more or less, in my opinion, than downright nonsense.

Accordingly, I am very clearly of opinion that all the interlocutors which have been pronounced in the Sheriff Court must be recalled, for it is nothing to the purpose to say that no objections could have been taken if this man had been properly charged with this offence, as he might have been, at Newcastle-on-Tyne, and if the complaint preferred against him at Newcastle-on-Tyne had been before the Court at Wakefield, and if the prosecutor at Newcastle-on-Tyne had given his consent to the prisoner's offence at Newcastle-on-Tyne being considered at Wakefield in pronouncing sentence there; for none of these things happened. Accordingly, this case must go back to the Sheriff Court and be commenced anew. When the prisoner is brought before the Sheriff Court and, for the first time, pleads guilty to the complaint preferred against him, it will be for the Sheriff-substitute to hear both the accused and the procurator-fiscal upon the question of the appropriate punishment to be pronounced, and the Sheriff-substitute will then give such weight as he thinks proper to what happened before the Court of Quarter Sessions at Wakefield and modify the punishment or, possibly, inflict no punishment at all, according as he in his discretion thinks proper, for he is master, and he alone, of all procedure in his own Court.

I am of opinion, therefore, that we ought to answer the question put to us in the negative, and remit the case to the Sheriff Court."

Crown appeal upheld.

NOTE

This judgment makes the true nature of the plea very clear indeed, but in spite of the outrage expressed by the High Court and the almost intemperate language used, misconceptions did not completely vanish, as the next case shows.

2. H.M. Advocate v. Cairns
1967 J.C. 37

An accused person gave exculpatory evidence at his trial for murder and was acquitted. He subsequently confessed his guilt to *The Daily Express*. He was charged with having committed perjury at the murder trial and pleaded that he had tholed his assize.

LORD JUSTICE-CLERK (GRANT): "The plea in bar of trial and the objections to competency and relevancy are three different facets of what is basically the same point. The question raised in each case is whether, if an accused person is acquitted at his trial, having given evidence on oath denying the crime charged, the Crown is entitled thereafter to charge him with perjury in respect of that evidence. In seeking to persuade us to answer that question in the negative Mr Bennett based his argument on the maxim that no man can be made to thole an assize twice for the same matter (Hume, vol. ii, pp. 465-467) and on considerations of practice and natural justice.

As Hume points out (at p. 466), the prosecutor cannot evade the maxim by altering the shape of the former charge and laying the second libel 'for the same facts, under a new denomination of the crime,' *e.g.* by charging fraud instead of theft or falsehood instead of forgery. On the other hand, for the maxim to apply, the previous trial 'must have been for the same crime, depending upon the same evidence, and not for what is truly another crime.' [Macdonald on the *Criminal Law of Scotland* (5th ed.), p. 272.] Thus it is well settled that a person who has been tried and acquitted, or tried and convicted, on a charge of assault may subsequently be tried on a charge of murder if, after the first trial, the victim dies (*Cobb or Fairweather* [(1836) 1 Swin. 354]; *Stewart* [(1866) 5 Irv. 310]). That is so notwithstanding the fact that the Crown will seek to establish at the second trial the assault which was the sole *de quo* at the first. The supervening event changes the character of the offence and the second charge is one which could not possibly have been made at the earlier trial.

In the present case the Crown are, in my opinion, in an even stronger position than in the cases to which I have just referred. The perjury charged in the present indictment is alleged to have occurred in the course of the earlier trial. Not only could it not have been the subject of a charge at that trial, but it is a crime wholly different in nature from that of which the panel was acquitted and it is libelled as having taken place at a different place and on a different date. In *Fraser* [(1852) 1 Irv. 66] Lord Justice-General M'Neill points out (at p. 73) that a person may be tried if he has never been in jeopardy *for the offence with which he is charged*; and in *Dorward* v. *Mackay* [(1870) 1 Coup. 392] Lord Neaves refers (at p. 397) to the 'plain identity' of charges which is needed if the maxim is to apply. The panel here has never been in jeopardy for any offence libelled as having been committed in the High Court at Glasgow on 1st March 1966 and I can find no identity between the present charge and the charge of murder of which he was acquitted. Evidence will no doubt be led tending to show that, as is set out in the indictment, he did in fact assault and stab Malcolmson, but that seems to me to be of no more avail to the panel than it was in *Cobb or Fairweather* and *Stewart*. It is identity of the charges and not of the evidence that is the crucial factor. In my opinion, the plea that the panel has tholed his assize clearly fails.

Nor do I think that the panel can succeed on the basis of practice or natural justice. Practice is a matter for the Lord Advocate of the day and the decision whether to prosecute or not must in each case rest with him as master of the instance. He is not bound by any practice which may have been followed by his predecessors nor is it for us to lay down what practice should or should not be adopted by him. Furthermore, in order to succeed on the 'natural justice' argument the panel would have to show that, even though he does not come under the rule in regard to tholing an assize, there is something so inherently inequitable in prosecuting a person for giving false evidence at his trial denying his guilt that the giving of such evidence does not amount to perjury under the law of Scotland. Mr Bennett founded on a passage in Sir George Mackenzie's Criminal Law (1678 ed., at p. 298) as giving some support to this view, although the question could not, as I understand it, have become a live one until the panel became a competent witness on his own behalf under the Criminal Evidence Act, 1898. In my opinion, the right given to the panel by that Act to give evidence on his own behalf does not carry with it a licence to tell falsehoods upon oath. In principle and in logic I can see no good reason for making any distinction, so far as the law of perjury is concerned, between an accused person who falsely denies his guilt on oath and a witness who equally falsely supports him. The exception to the normal law of perjury which the panel seeks to establish here is not, in my opinion, justified by authority and is indeed contrary to principle.

For these reasons the plea in bar and objections must, in my view, be repelled."

Plea repelled.

NOTE

Cairns was never tried on the perjury indictment: he committed suicide before the trial.

3. H.M. Advocate v. Dunlop and Marklow
1974 S.L.T. 242

Two accused were charged on indictment and pleaded that they had tholed their assize. This plea was repelled by Lord Cameron, and the accused appealed.

OPINION OF THE COURT: "In this case the appellants were charged on indictment with a series of offences arising out of an incident which occurred on 29th October 1973. In particular both accused were charged with attempted extortion of money from two named persons under threats of violence while they were passengers in a motor car on a certain roadway and also in a car park in Stirling University. This forms the first charge in the indictment. The second charge also involved both accused and was one of theft at the same locus. In the third charge the accused Dunlop was charged alone with assaulting the female complainer in the first charge by driving at her the motor car referred to in that charge.

The remaining charges also relate to the accused Dunlop alone and consisted of alleged breaches of s. 6 of the Road Traffic Act 1972 and of certain statutory regulations.

To all charges the appellants pled not guilty and in limine pleaded in bar of trial in the High Court that they had tholed their assize. The trial judge, Lord Cameron, repelled the plea of 'tholed assize'. The appellants then tendered certain pleas of guilty to parts of the indictment which were accepted by the Crown, and they were duly sentenced.

In this appeal before us, the appellants contend that the trial judge erred in repelling their pleas in bar of trial and renewed their argument that, in the circumstances to which we now allude, the plea of 'tholed assize' should be sustained.

Both accused were indicted in the sheriff court on charges identical in form and substance to those on which they were indicted in the High Court.

In the sheriff court both accused pled not guilty to the major charges and adhered to their pleas at the second diet on 21st January. At the pleading diet the appellant Dunlop tendered a plea of guilty to the three minor statutory charges. A jury was empanelled and sworn and thus the appellants were formally 'remitted to the knowledge of an assize'. After a certain amount of evidence had been led for the prosecutor the appellants offered to change their pleas. The appellant Dunlop then tendered a modified plea to the first charge, a plea of not guilty to the second and guilty to the third. The appellant Marklow tendered a plea of guilty to the first charge and of not guilty to the second. These modified pleas were accepted by the procurator-fiscal and duly recorded. Thereafter the prosecutor moved for sentence and the sheriff proceeded to hear pleas in mitigation of sentence and thereafter remitted both appellants to the High Court for sentence. The jury was then discharged without having returned a verdict on any of the charges against either appellant. An attempt was made to reconvene the jury but only 14 jurors could be found, who then, under direction of the sheriff, returned what purported to be a verdict reflecting the pleas tendered and accepted. The result was that a purported conviction was recorded which had not proceeded upon the verdict of a jury. Thereafter the sheriff again remitted the appellants to the High Court for sentence. We need say nothing of the subsequent events save this: when the appellants appeared in the High Court upon this pretended remit it was recognised that, in respect that there had been no conviction, it was inept. No sentence was passed upon the appellants, and the diet was deserted pro loco et tempore.

For the appellants before us counsel presented his argument with skill and commendable brevity. It may be summarised thus: it is undoubtedly the law that a plea of 'tholed assize' will lie if an accused person, having been charged with identical offences in an earlier indictment and having pled not guilty, was remitted to the knowledge of an assize which returned a competent verdict of guilt or innocence. The essential foundation of the plea in such a case is that an accused has undergone a properly conducted trial culminating in a determination of his guilt or innocence. In this case the issue of guilt or innocence was determined as soon as the appellants' pleas of guilty were tendered and accepted, and it was not essential to the plea in bar that the jury should have returned any verdict.

In our opinion, this argument is unsound. Lord Cameron, in our view, reached the correct decision upon a proper appreciation of the effect of the authorities which he reviewed with care. Where a plea of 'tholed assize' is tabled by a person who has, upon a plea of not guilty, proceeded to trial before an empanelled jury, it must be demonstrated, if the plea is to succeed, that the trial, properly conducted, has concluded in a determination of the issue of guilt or innocence. This we deduce from the authorities examined by Lord Cameron and in particular the cases of *Hilson* v. *Easson*, 1914 S.C. (J.) 99, 1914 1 S.L.T. 275 and *H.M. Advocate* v. *Fraser* (1852) 1 Irv. 66. It is clear, too, that in such circumstances there can be no determination of the issue of guilt or innocence until the assize, the jury, has done its duty by returning a competent verdict. So far as we are aware, there is no authority for the proposition that the tendering of a plea of guilty by an accused person (accepted by the prosecutor) after he has gone to trial before a jury, may be regarded as the equivalent of a jury's verdict and counsel frankly accepted that there was none. Where such a plea is tendered in such circumstances, it amounts to no more than a judicial confession and there can be no valid conviction on which a valid sentence can proceed until the jury, under direction of the presiding judge, returns a verdict of guilty in respect of that confession. The validity of sentence upon an accused person who has been remitted to the knowledge of an assize depends essentially upon a competent verdict by that assize and, that being so, it cannot be maintained, and it has never been held, that the issue of guilt or innocence can be competently determined at any stage prior to the return of a competent verdict. It matters not that sentence may not have been pronounced after a verdict of guilty has been returned and recorded, but there must, in the circumstances we have been considering, be at least a verdict. In short, before the plea of 'tholed assize' will lie the person accused for the second time must show that the assize on the first occasion has done its duty, and that duty is only done by the return of a competent verdict.

We have only to add that in repelling the pleas in bar of trial of the appellants Lord Cameron's second reason for doing so was that when the appellants appeared for sentence at the High Court on the inept remit by the sheriff the diet was deserted pro loco et tempore, and no challenge of the competency of the High Court's interlocutor was made. Before us the Crown did not seek to support this second reason. As a result we heard no argument upon it. We accordingly express no opinion of our own thereon and we say nothing of the effect, for the purposes of a plea of 'tholed assize', of desertion of the diet simpliciter by the prosecutor in course of a trial upon indictment.

In the whole matter we are of the opinion that the appeals must be refused."

Appeal refused.

NOTE

So if the whole jury had been asked to give a verdict (directed by the sheriff), then the plea of tholed assize on the subsequent indictment would have succeeded. The general rule that in indictment cases a case which has been "remitted to the knowledge of an assize" can only be terminated by the jury's verdict (whether under direction or not) is only subject to one exception: where a submission of "no case to answer" has been successful. Section 140A (3) of the 1975 Act (as inserted by section 19 of the 1980 Act) requires "the judge" to acquit the accused after a successful submission.

(ii) Pre-trial publicity

The landmark decision in *Hall* v. *Associated Newspapers Ltd.*, 1979 J.C. 1 and the Contempt of Court Act 1981 (as to which, see *supra*, Chap. 1) have had the combined effect of giving the press and media relatively clear indications as to the point at which pre-trial publicity may become contemptuous. The other side of this problem is of course whether court proceedings may become fatally tainted by publicity.

Stuurman v. H.M. Advocate
1980 J.C. 111

Four accused persons were arrested on drugs charges. The following day a radio station broadcast a detailed account of the circumstances and the next day further similar publicity was given to the case by a Scottish national newspaper. The material published was highly prejudicial to the accused and was made the subject of contempt proceedings. Several months later each accused tabled pleas in bar of trial, alleging that, in consequence of the publicity, they could not expect to receive a fair trial. These pleas were repelled by the trial judge, after argument before him and two other consulted judges, and the accused were convicted. They appealed on the ground that their pleas in bar of trial should not have been rejected.

LORD JUSTICE-GENERAL (EMSLIE): ". . . The only question for us is whether, as the applicants contend, the Court of three Judges erred in allowing the trial to proceed in the circumstances which we have already mentioned.

The test which fell to be applied and which was applied in disposing of the plea in bar is not in doubt. As the authorities show, the High Court of Justiciary has power to intervene to prevent the Lord Advocate from proceeding upon a particular indictment but this power will be exercised only in special circumstances which are likely to be rare. The special circumstances must indeed be such as to satisfy the Court that, having regard to the principles of substantial justice and of fair trial, to require an accused to face trial would be oppressive. Each case will depend on its own merits, and where the alleged oppression is said to arise from events alleged to be prejudicial to the prospects of fair trial the question for the Court is whether the risk of prejudice is so grave that no direction of the trial Judge, however careful, could reasonably be expected to remove it. [See the opinion of the Court delivered in the case of *Stewart* v. *H. M. Advocate*, 1980 J.C. 103.]

In presenting his submissions the single proposition advanced by counsel for Stuurman was that the Court which repelled the pleas in bar of trial erred in their application of the correct test to the special circumstances of this case. The contents of the publications which were the subject of contempt proceedings were highly prejudicial. In the case of the radio broadcasts in particular the offending news item was repeatedly transmitted on 1st October 1979 in the very area from which the jurors for the trial of the applicants were drawn. Other newspapers of varying kinds and quality, circulating throughout Scotland, contained articles of the same character as the one published in the Glasgow Herald on 2nd October 1979. All of this prejudicial material was, accordingly, the subject of the widest dissemination in Scotland, and the Edinburgh area in particular, in the period 1st to 3rd October 1979. In these particular and special circumstances the risk of prejudice to the fair trial of the applicants was so grave that no direction by the trial Judge, however careful, could reasonably be expected to remove it. The Court which repelled the pleas in bar erred in failing to recognise this. The trial should not have been allowed to take place, and, having taken place, a miscarriage of justice has occurred, and the convictions of the applicants should be quashed.

The submissions of counsel for Ruiter and Merks were upon similar lines. In the case of the applicant Ruiter, counsel conceded that his client's position was virtually indistinguishable from that of Stuurman. He therefore contented himself by adopting the argument presented by Mr Daiches for Stuurman, and by inviting us to take into account, in addition, the possibility that the minds of the witnesses at the trial might also have been prejudiced by reading or hearing the offending news items. The point, it was said, was important, for the defence of Ruiter and Merks was that they were unaware of what others might have been doing. The contents of these publications may have encouraged witnesses to associate Ruiter and Stuurman in their minds. Counsel for Merks urged us to accept that the publication of the offending material was even more gravely prejudicial to his client than it was in the case of Stuurman and Ruiter. He was present in the place or places in which Stuurman was said to be producing drugs only for relatively short periods, and his defence was that he came merely to deliver some equipment which had been ordered and once to buy a car. The case against him entirely depended upon the inference to be drawn from his proved presence from time to time. In these circumstances there was a grave risk that in considering what inference to draw the jury might take into account something that had been said in one of the prejudicial news items. These news items contained many statements damaging to Merks which were wholly untrue. These mis-statements of 'fact,' it was contended, made it quite impossible for the trial Judge to give any direction which would be adequate to secure for Merks at least a fair trial at the hands of the jury.

Upon considering all the submissions for the applicants and the reply by the Lord Advocate, we have reached the conclusion that the Court did not err on 25th January 1980 in repelling the pleas in bar of trial. We are not impressed by the supposed risk that the evidence of witnesses would or might be tainted by anything they had read or heard in the period 1st to 3rd October 1979 for the basis upon which any witness's evidence or opinion was given or expressed was open to the test of cross-examination. We are not impressed either by the contention that a distinction falls to be made between representations in the offending publications which were unfounded in fact and those which were true. What matters is that the contents of these publications, true or false, were such as might prejudice the prospects of fair trial of the persons described therein and the question for us is whether on 25th January 1980 the risk of prejudice as the result of these publications was then so grave that even the careful directions of the trial Judge could not reasonably be expected to remove it. In our opinion that question falls to be answered in the negative. The publications occurred almost four months before the trial diet was called. In considering the effect of these publications at the date of trial the Court was well entitled to bear in mind that the public memory of newspaper articles and news broadcasts and of their detailed contents is notoriously short and, that being so, that the residual risk of prejudice to the prospects of fair trial for the applicants could reasonably be expected to be removed by careful directions such as those which were in the event given by the trial Judge.

Upon the whole matter we are satisfied that the pleas in bar of trial were correctly repelled for the right reasons and that all three applications for leave to appeal against conviction must be refused."

Appeal refused.

NOTE

So such a plea in bar will only succeed if it would be oppressive to proceed. This is a very high test indeed, as was shown in relation to the "Glasgow rape case", now reported *sub nom. H.* v. *Sweeney*, 1983 S.L.T. 48 and *X.* v. *Sweeney and Others*, 1982 S.C.C.R. 161, *post*, p. 335. The granting of criminal letters in this case is discussed *supra*, Chap. 2. The report of the case deals only with the limited question of whether criminal letters should have been issued, but one of the principal arguments advanced against such a proceeding was that a fair trial was impossible, and, under reference to *Stuurman*, that it would be oppressive to proceed. After the issue of criminal letters, pleas in bar were in fact tabled and rejected, and the trial proceeded. It seems therefore that only in the clearest case, such as pre-trial publicity immediately preceding the trial diet, could the test of oppression be met: see *Atkins* v. *London Weekend Television Ltd.*, 1978 J.C. 48, a shocking case of contempt of court. However in *Stuurman*, Lord Avonside, one of the judges consulted by the trial judge, cast doubt on whether a plea in bar, had it been tabled in *Atkins*, would have succeeded: see 1978 J.C. 111 at p. 117.

d. Special defences

The four accepted special defences in Scotland are alibi, self-defence, incrimination (sometimes called impeachment) and insanity: but see Renton and Brown, paras. 7-20, 7-21, where the possibilities of the existence of other special defences are canvassed. For time-limits for lodging a special defence, see section 82 (1) of the 1975 Act, as amended by section 13 of the 1980 Act. With the exception of the special defence of insanity, a special defence does not have to be proved to any particular standard and therefore the only purpose in lodging a special defence is to give the Crown fair notice.

Lambie v. H.M. Advocate
1973 S.L.T. 219

An accused person was convicted of theft. He appealed against conviction on the ground that the sheriff had misdirected the jury to the effect that there was an onus on the accused to establish that defence. The appeal was heard by a Full Bench.

OPINION OF THE COURT: ". . . The relevant passage in the sheriff's charge is in the following terms: 'Reverting now, ladies and gentlemen, to the accused Lambie, and the charge upon which he faces you, he has given evidence himself. Now, if you believe what he says and if what he says is consistent with innocence, then, of course, you will acquit him. He has put forward a special defence of impeachment—this means that he is saying it was not he who committed the crime, but that it was some others. In order that he may succeed in this he must produce evidence and corroborated evidence. Now, it seems to me that he certainly has not done the second thing, and it is doubtful if he has done the first thing. There is no corroborated evidence which would entitle you to come to a decision on the special defence of impeachment put in by the first accused. Therefore you will not consider that special defence. Now, in saying that I am not in any way saying that you have not to consider the allegations—because that is really what his evidence amounted to—with regard to other people being involved. All I am saying is that there is insufficient evidence to entitle you to find the accused not guilty on the basis that he has made out a special defence of impeachment. The other evidence, and the inference which Mr McSherry invited you to draw from the evidence relating to some other people having been involved, is still before you, and if that evidence produced in your minds a reasonable doubt then, of course, you will acquit the accused because, as I say, it is for the Crown to prove beyond reasonable doubt that the accused person is guilty.'

As will be seen from the quoted passage the direction plainly asserts (i) that there is an onus on the accused to prove his special defence; (ii) that the onus can only be discharged by corroborated evidence; and (iii) that there is no corroboration of the accused's evidence incriminating any of the persons named in the special defence. For the applicant it was conceded that the third of these propositions was accurate. It was conceded further, for the purposes of the argument, that in presenting the first two of these propositions to the jury the sheriff was merely following a widespread practice among trial judges which appears to have developed since the cases of *H.M. Advocate* v. *Lennie*, 1946 J.C. 79, 1946 S.L.T. 212 and *H.M. Advocate* v. *Owens*, 1946 J.C. 119, 1946 S.L.T. 227. Against the background of these concessions the submission was that a proper charge required the sheriff to proceed to tell the jury that although they could not hold the special defence to have been affirmatively proved, they must still consider the appellant's uncorroborated evidence on incrimination and if they believed him or if, while not wholly believing him, found that his evidence created a reasonable doubt as to his guilt of the crime charged, they must acquit him. In this case, however, the sheriff followed up his first three directions by saying: 'Therefore you will not consider that special defence.' Now, it was not disputed by the Crown that, had the charge stopped there, there would have been a plain and grave misdirection by the sheriff, and the question at the end of the day came to be whether the sufficiency of the charge was saved by reading the quoted sentence in the context of the whole passage dealing with the special defence and, in particular, in conjunction with the sentences which immediately follow it. Upon this question we have come to be of opinion, albeit with some hesitation, that, standing the practice to which we have referred, the charge on the special defence read as a whole would sufficiently inform an intelligent lay jury, in spite of the quoted sentence which might otherwise have misled them, that they *were* to consider the applicant's evidence of incrimination and to acquit if it produced in their minds a reasonable doubt of his guilt. In these circumstances we would not have been disposed to sustain the appeal on the second ground.

The matter cannot, however, be allowed to rest there since in course of the argument the soundness of the practice to which we have referred, and the soundness of the observations in *Lennie* (supra) and *Owens* (supra) on which it was based, were seriously questioned. Suffice it to say that the criticisms made were such that it is desirable to look afresh at the whole matter of the proper charge which should be given where there has been lodged by an accused person a special defence of alibi, self-defence or incrimination.

It must be accepted that it has been the practice of many judges since the cases of *Lennie* and *Owens* to direct juries, where any of these special defences is in issue, (i) that there is an onus upon the accused to prove it by evidence sufficient in law on a balance of the probabilities, but (ii) that even if the special defence is not established, the jury must, nevertheless, consider even the evidence of a single witness speaking to alibi, self-defence or incrimination, and if they believe that witness, or find that his evidence creates in their minds a reasonable doubt of the guilt of the accused, they must acquit him, since the burden of proof of guilt is on the Crown throughout. The critical question is whether it is at all appropriate to introduce into a criminal trial, where such a special defence has been lodged, any suggestion that there is at any time any onus on an accused person.

In searching for the answer to this question we begin by noticing what was said in *Lennie* and *Owens*. In *Lennie*, which was a case involving alibi, the Lord Justice-General (Normand) in delivering the opinion of the court said this:

'As regards the question of onus, there is no doubt that the onus is throughout on the Crown to prove its case. But it is also true that the onus of proving the alibi was on the appellant. That that has been from the earliest times our law is made clear by the passages in Hume on *Crimes* upon the proving of alibi in olden days. I refer particularly to Vol. II, p. 298 et seq., and pp. 410 et seq., and these passages also show that it was not uncommon in olden times to take the proof of alibi separately and before remitting the libel to assize. To lay on the Crown the onus of disproving the alibi of which the defence has given notice would be a complete inversion of the rules for the conduct of proofs or trials of which one of the most fundamental and most rational is semper praesumitur pro negante. But, if the jury deals first with the defence of alibi and decides not to sustain it, so that they must then address themselves to the Crown evidence, they must not treat the onus as transferred or affected by the failure of the defence of alibi. The question whether the jury are entitled to reconsider the evidence for the alibi in connection with the evidence for the Crown and in rebuttal of it does not admit of a simple answer yea or nay.'

In *Owens* where self-defence was in issue the same Lord Justice-General in giving the opinion of the court said this:

'When we speak of the onus being on the panel to set up self-defence we merely mean that the accused must take the sting out of his own admission that he delivered the fatal blow. If he does this by proving that he was attacked and put in danger of his life (or had reasonable apprehension of danger to his life), he has set up his defence so that he must be acquitted. But, although he may choose to undertake complete legal proof as the best line of defence in the circumstances of his case, he is not bound to lead such evidence as would amount to a discharge of proof. He can rely on his own sworn statement that he was acting in self-defence and rely on his own credibility to outweigh any colourable case the Crown has laid before the jury; and the jury, if satisfied on a review of the whole evidence in the case of his credibility, is entitled to accept the panel's single sworn explanation and to reject evidence which would probably, without the explanation, have been sufficient for a conviction . . . It may therefore be necessary for the presiding judge, not only to ask the jury to consider whether the special defence has been made out but to ask them also to consider whether it has not had the effect of so shaking reliance on the Crown evidence as to warrant an acquittal from the charge.'

In our opinion there can be no doubt that in *Lennie* and less explicitly in *Owens* the court did subscribe to the proposition that the onus of proving not only alibi but self-defence affirmatively rests on the accused although the judgments at the same time emphasise that the onus of proof of guilt remains on the Crown throughout and that even if proof of the special defence fails for want of corroboration the jury must still consider, in the context of the evidence as a whole, the evidence of even a single witness speaking to alibi or self-defence; and if the evidence of that witness creates in their minds a reasonable doubt of guilt, must acquit. We must accordingly consider whether there was, in law, any warrant for these references to an onus upon the defence, since it is from these references that the charging practice to which we have referred has been derived. What, then, was the state of the law with regard to special defences before 1946? In posing this question we ignore the special defence of insanity at the time since it is quite clear that there is in such a case an onus upon the defence to establish it, since proof of insanity is required before the presumption of sanity can be displaced.

Special defences in our law derive from the requirements of the law in earlier centuries for written defences in answer to a criminal libel when accused persons were limited in their defence to evidence in support of these defences, the relevancy of which had to be affirmed by a court before the matter was remitted to an assize. The 'special defence' of today is the vestigial survivor in modern criminal practice of the written defences of our earlier criminal procedures.

An examination of the earlier authorities discloses no trace of a rule that couples putting forward of a 'special defence' with the necessary acceptance by an accused of an onus of proof of that defence by sufficient, i.e. corroborated evidence, far less of any statement that, should he fail to discharge that onus, the defence as such must fail. It is not to be found in Hume in the passages dealing with 'special defences' (see Hume, Vol. II, pp. 283 and 301) nor in Burnett's *Criminal Law* (published 1811) p. 596, Alison, Vol. II, pp. 369 and 624 nor Macdonald's *Criminal Law* in any edition, nor is it to be found in Anderson's *Criminal Law of Scotland*, p. 274. It is to be observed also that in summary proceedings no notice of such special defences as self-defence or incrimination is required of an accused. In the most recent editions of Renton and Brown, *Criminal Procedure*, the matter is put thus — 'The burden of proof that the accused committed the crime libelled against him rests upon the prosecutor throughout the trial. The standard required is proof beyond reasonable doubt. This onus is not transferred or affected by any common law defence pleas other than insanity or diminished responsibility.' The only current statutory requirement relative to the presentation of a special defence in solemn procedure is contained in s. 36 of the Criminal Procedure Act 1887.

By the time Hume was writing, the function of a special defence was limited to giving fair notice to the prosecutor of the line which an accused's defence might take and the requirement of the law was that due notice should be given to the prosecution of such an intention. As put by Hume (Vol. II, p. 301) it was (and is) because 'to let him maintain silence in that respect, till the proof in support of the libel has been closed, would be downright injustice to the prosecutor, who might thus lose the fair means of meeting the defences and strengthening his own case with evidence, in the relative and proper parts'.

It is of course true, as is pointed out in the judgment of the court in *Lennie*, that in earlier times, for reasons which are set out in the passages from Hume cited in that judgment, when in his written defences an accused pleaded alibi, a preliminary proof on the separate issue of alibi was frequently held and if the plea succeeded the libel fell and was not proceeded with. This practice, however, had, at least by the time Hume was writing, fallen into desuetude.

In the case of *H.M. Advocate* v. *Hillan*, 1937 J.C. 53, 1937 S.L.T. 396 one of the grounds of appeal was that the presiding sheriff in a charge of assault had misdirected the jury in respect that he directed the jury on a plea of self-defence to this effect—'that defence (self-defence) is entirely shouldered and must be discharged by the panel . . . He must have corroborative evidence before you can accept it as established that he did this in self-defence'. The appeal on this point succeeded and Lord Justice-Clerk Aitchison said this at p. 398: 'I think that this direction was unsound. Many cases occur in which from their very circumstances a plea of self-defence must depend upon the evidence of the panel himself. . . . It is no doubt true that a plea of self-defence cannot be affirmatively established upon the evidence of the panel himself, but great injustice might arise if the jury were left with a direction that the plea must fail from want of corroboration. Wherever a plea of self-defence is put forward and supported by evidence, the jury should be explicitly directed that the special defence must be weighed by them in light of the whole proved facts in the case.'

This option was before the court in the subsequent cases of *Lennie* and *Owens* and no doubt was cast upon the accuracy of Lord Justice-Clerk Aitchison's statement of the law or of the decision at which the court arrived.

In light of this review of the law and practice before 1946 we have come to be of opinion that the references in *Lennie* and *Owens* to there being an onus upon the defence were unsound. It follows that the passage in Walkers' *Law of Evidence*, § 83 (b) to the effect that 'when a special defence is stated by the accused, the onus of proving it is upon him' can now be regarded as an accurate statement of the law only in the case of the plea of insanity at the time. Apart from the unsoundness of its source the practice of referring at all to an onus being upon the defence inevitably complicated the directions of the presiding judge to such an extent as to be calculated to confuse most juries.

The only purpose of the special defence is to give fair notice to the Crown and once such notice has been given the only issue for a jury is to decide, upon the whole evidence before them, whether the Crown has established the accused's guilt beyond reasonable doubt. When a special defence is pleaded, whether it be of alibi, self-defence or of incrimination, the jury should be so charged in the appropriate language, and all that requires to be said of the special defence, where any evidence in support of it has been given, either in course of the Crown case or by the accused himself or by any witness led for the defence, is that if that evidence, whether from one or more witnesses, is believed, or creates in the minds of the jury reasonable doubt as to the guilt of the accused in the matters libelled, the Crown case must fail and that they must acquit.

Thus, for example, evidence given of acting in self-defence, as this is defined by law, is in no different position from any other evidence consistent with the innocence of the accused and ought to be considered by the jury in precisely the same way."

Conviction quashed.

NOTE

The comments of the High Court thus relate only to the special defences of self-defence, alibi and incrimination. The special defence of insanity is in a different position: the onus is on the accused to prove on a balance of probabilities that he was insane at the time of the offence: see, *e.g. Brennan* v. *H.M. Advocate*, 1977 S.L.T. 151. For a general discussion of the burden of proof in criminal cases, see Chap. 1, *supra*.

e. Examination of productions

Statutory rules govern the lodging of productions for both Crown and defence: see the 1975 Act, ss. 82-84. So far as examination of the productions by each side is concerned, there is usually no difficulty, but occasionally it may be necessary to crave a specific warrant.

1. **William Turner Davies, Petitioner**
1973 S.L.T. (Notes) 36

An accused was charged on indictment before sheriff and jury. Before the indictment was served, the Crown refused to allow the defence to examine a pair of gloves which were to be a Crown production. The accused applied to the *nobile officium* of the High Court.

OPINION OF THE COURT: "This is a petition to the nobile officium of the court seeking a warrant for the scientific examination by a named scientist of gloves which are labelled as a production in the indictment against the petitioner at the instance of Her Majesty's Advocate, under such conditions as to their delivery and care as the court may direct.

The petitioner avers that for the proper preparation and presentation of the defence it is necessary for the gloves to be subjected to scientific examination under laboratory conditions for specified reasons. On the instructions of the Crown the gloves have been subjected to a scientific examination by two forensic scientists who are listed as Crown witnesses in the indictment.

The history of events is as follows. Before the indictment was served, the solicitor for the petitioner made a request to the procurator-fiscal to make the gloves forthcoming for examination by a named expert. The procurator-fiscal, who already had in his possession a joint report by the two Crown forensic scientists which had disclosed a negative result, did not accede to the request but simply sent the gloves back to the Crown's forensic scientists for a further examination and so informed the petitioner's solicitors. Some nine days later the procurator-fiscal informed the solicitor that he had received the gloves back. By this time the indictment had been served, and at the pleading diet on 12th February 1973 the petitioner's solicitor made a motion to the sheriff in terms similar to those of the prayer of this petition. The sheriff refused the motion, basically on the ground that there was no precedent or authority for it. At the hearing before this court the learned advocate-depute said that the Crown was anxious to get an authoritative ruling on the point, and that if the motion was competent he had no objection to it being granted in the circumstances of this case.

Counsel for the petitioner submitted that the motion was competent. He referred to s. 37 of the Criminal Procedure (Scotland) Act 1887, which is in the following terms: 'A person accused shall be entitled to see the productions according to the existing law and practice in the office of the sheriff clerk of the district in which the court of the second diet is situated, or where the second diet is to be in the High Court of Justiciary in Edinburgh in the Justiciary Office.'

In relation to the then existing law and practice he referred to Hume's *Commentaries* II, p. 388 and, in particular, to the case of *William Muir* in the footnote at pp. 389 and 390, and to *H.M. Advocate* v. *Alexander Humphreys* or *Alexander* (1839) 2 Swin. 356.

I am satisfied from the authority of Hume (supra) and the case of *William Muir*, that an application for a warrant to inspect is competent. It will then be a matter for the court to decide whether in the particular circumstances it should be granted. In the normal case I am of the opinion that provided sufficient safeguards can be attached it should be granted. I see no reason why, generally speaking, the defence should not have the same facilities as the prosecution to make an inspection and examination of a production in a case. In saying this, I realise that there may be special circumstances which make the granting of such a warrant impossible, impracticable or undesirable.

The question of procedure was raised before us, and it is desirable that the procedure should be made clear. Where an indictment is served, the productions referred to therein are lodged with the sheriff clerk who has a duty to retain them in his custody and make them available at the trial. At that stage, the only body with the authority to allow the productions to be inspected and examined is the court, and the proper procedure is to make application to the court thereanent. It is then for the court to decide whether the application should be granted or refused. Before the indictment is served, the productions, which at this stage are only potential productions, are in the possession and control of the procurator-fiscal. He has a responsibility to safeguard such productions so that they can be lodged with the sheriff clerk at the appropriate time. In any given case it would be a matter for his discretion in the first instance whether at that earlier stage productions should be handed over to the defence for inspection and examination. Whether he could be compelled at that stage by an order of court to hand over to the defence productions for inspection and examination is another matter, and is not a point on which I would like to express an opinion until the issue is specifically raised. This is not the issue, however, in this petition, and for the reasons which I have given I am of the opinion that the application was competent and that in the circumstances it should have been granted. I would accordingly grant the prayer of the petition.

I would add, for the benefit of practitioners, that in my opinion an application for a warrant to inspect and examine a production listed in an indictment is competent in the court where the trial is to take place without recourse to the nobile officium of the High Court of Justiciary."

Warrant granted.

NOTE

Section 37 of the 1887 Act is now section 82 of the 1975 Act (as amended in 1980). Only the High Court has a *nobile officium* to deal with unforeseen matters — see Chap. 18, *infra*. The most important procedural rule regarding productions is however that any article referred to in an indictment (or complaint) should be produced in evidence unless there is a practical difficulty in its production.

2.   Maciver v. Mackenzie
1942 J.C. 51

An accused was charged on summary complaint with taking possession of a wreck, contrary to the Merchant Shipping Act 1894, s. 518 (*b*). The various pieces of the wreck were not produced by the Crown. The accused appealed against his conviction.

LORD JUSTICE-GENERAL (NORMAND): ". . . The question in the case depends on the fact that, though none of the wreck was produced in the proceedings before the learned Sheriff-substitute, questions were put to witnesses about marks upon certain of the timber alleged to have been found and kept by the appellant. A witness was asked whether these particular pieces of timber bore small splashes of crude oil, and whether some of it was frayed by the action of the sea. It was said that, when that question was put, it was an endeavour to elicit evidence which was not the best evidence, because the best evidence was the timber itself, and that it might have been brought and examined in Court or, if that was for any reason inconvenient, examined outside the Court.

The learned counsel for the appellant asserted that there was an obligation on the prosecutor to produce any article which was referred to in an indictment or complaint, unless it was beyond his power to do so. There is certainly no such rule. It is, no doubt, the proper practice to produce any article referred to in the indictment or complaint where there is no practical difficulty in doing so. There are, however, many cases where it is inconvenient, though not wholly impossible, to make articles productions in the case because of the size of the article. Live stock cannot conveniently be made productions in all cases. Perishable goods cannot be made productions, and there are other examples. The question in each case is whether the real evidence is essential for proving the case against the accused. In a case of forgery I can conceive it would be very difficult to prove the charge unless the document alleged to be forged was in Court, but even in that case I am not satisfied that the proof would be impossible.

In this case, however, the real question seems to me to be related rather to the competence of questions put to the witnesses than to the alleged duty of the prosecutor to produce the timber referred to in the complaint. When the witness was asked about the marks upon the timber alleged to have been found in the possession of the appellant, the agent for the accused was entitled to object to the question on the ground that that was an attempt to elicit evidence about markings on the wood when the wood itself might have been produced and examined, for the timber itself would have been the best evidence of its condition. What would have happened if that objection had been taken we do not know. There might have been some reasonable explanation which would have shown that it was impracticable to have the timber produced, or the result might have been that the timber would have been instantly produced, or there might have been an adjournment to allow it to be produced. But in the absence of the objection we really do not even know why it was that the timber was not produced.

The case, therefore, falls within the terms of section 75 of the Summary Jurisdiction (Scotland) Act of 1908, which provides that no conviction shall be quashed in respect of any objection to the competency or admission or rejection of evidence at the trial unless such objection shall have been timeously stated at such trial by the law agent for the accused. That applies, of course, when the accused has a law agent representing him at the trial, as was the case here.

In my opinion, therefore, we are bound by the terms of that section to refuse to entertain this representation, and the answer to question 3 is No, and to question 4, Yes."

Appeal dismissed.

NOTE

As will be observed the defence failure to object timeously to what they (later) claimed was inadmissible evidence was fatal. Objection should always be taken at the time. Whether, however, such a timeous objection would have been upheld is another matter.

This area of procedure straddles the so-called "best evidence" rule, the effect of which broadly is that where primary evidence, such as an actual article, is available, secondary evidence of its existence and condition will not be admitted. Such a broad statement is however riddled with qualifications, on which see, *e.g. MacLeod* v. *Woodmuir Miners' Welfare Society Social Club*, 1961 J.C. 5; and particularly the following case:

3.   Anderson v. Laverock
1976 J.C. 9

An accused person was charged with unlawful possession of salmon, contrary to the Salmon and Freshwater Fisheries (Protection) (Scotland) Act 1951, s.7. He had been found by the police in possession of the salmon and taken to the police station where the fish were examined outwith his presence. The fish were destroyed next day. At the trial, the defence objected to the leading of secondary evidence as to the condition of the salmon and also to the fact that they had not be kept long enough for examination on behalf of the accused.

The objections were repelled by the sheriff, who convicted. On appeal to the High Court the sheriff's rejection of the first defence objection was upheld. On the secondary point,

LORD JUSTICE-CLERK (WHEATLEY): ". . . This brings us to the last point which was debated before us, namely, whether the fish should have been retained for inspection by an expert witness on behalf of the appellant before being destroyed. It is incorporated in question 2. This is the one point in the case which has given us concern. On this point the Sheriff in her note says: 'The submission that the fish should have been preserved for examination by an expert witness on behalf of the appellant would have been relevant only if the appellant had indicated to the police when the fish were impounded that he wanted them to be held for such inspection. No such request was made at the time, nor did the appellant ask that he should be allowed to inspect them himself. Of course, since the fish had been in his possession prior to being seized by the police it is clear that he had ample opportunity to examine them had he wished to do so.' The relevant finding is finding 17. The appellant's argument was this. *Esto* it was in order to destroy the fish and subsequently lead secondary evidence about their physical condition at the trial, since witnesses for the prosecution had been afforded (and in fact had taken advantage of) the opportunity to examine the physical condition of the fish for relevant evidence equity demanded that the defence should have been given the same opportunity. This entailed that before the fish were destroyed the appellant should have been informed by the police of the intention to destroy them and if he signified a wish to have them examined by himself or by an expert a reasonable time should have been allowed to elapse to enable such a wish to be fulfilled. The

Sheriff had taken the view that the question of preserving the fish for examination by an expert on behalf of an accused was only relevant if the accused informed the police when the fish were impounded that he wanted them to be preserved for such a purpose. In the instant case the Sheriff had found in fact that no such request was made by the appellant, and she had accordingly rejected the submission that prejudice had been suffered by the appellant. The Sheriff was wrong in law in ruling that the *onus* was on the appellant to inform the authorities of his wish and to ask for a postponement of the disposal of the fish until an examination by him or on his behalf was made. On the contrary, the *onus* was on the authorities who had impounded the fish to inform an accused of the intention to dispose of them and to afford the accused a reasonable time before disposal to allow an examination to be made, if desired. This was a matter which went beyond the instant case and was one of general interest and importance. So ran the argument.

It seems almost unnecessary to propound that in the interests of justice and fair play the defence, whenever possible, should have the same opportunity as the prosecution to examine a material and possibly contentious production. The fact that such opportunity has not been afforded to the defence is not *per se* a ground for quashing a conviction. There may be a variety of reasons, some good some bad, why the opportunity was not provided. The production may have been lost or destroyed before the opportunity reasonably presented itself. It was said by the Advocate-depute that, even if the opportunity was available but was not presented, the only effect of this was possibly to affect the quality of the evidence of the prosecution witnesses who testified to the appearance of the production. In our opinion it goes further than that. It becomes a question whether prejudice was suffered. The questions then arise: 'Was there prejudice?' and 'If so, was it of such materiality as to cause such an injustice that the ensuing conviction falls to be quashed?' The materiality of the production will always be an important factor. It is impossible to lay down hard and fast rules to cover every possible case. Each case will depend on its own facts. In the present case from the Crown point of view the important feature of the production, namely the fish, was to estabish that there were present on the fish or absent from the fish marks which would indicate beyond reasonable doubt that the fish had not been caught by rod and line. The prosecution led evidence, which was eventually fully accepted by the Sheriff, to the effect that there were significant marks present and significant marks absent which led to the conclusion that the fish had not been caught by rod and line. It is clear from the stated case that the police, in whose custody the fish were, offered no opportunity to the appellant to have the fish examined by himself or by an expert on his behalf before they were destroyed on the following day. There is nothing in the stated case to indicate that the appellant was informed by the police that the fish were going to be destroyed.

The Sheriff took the view that the obligation to provide an opportunity to the appellant to inspect the fish or have them inspected on his behalf by an expert would only arise if the appellant asked for it. If she was right, then no prejudice was suffered because the appellant did not ask for it. Provision is made in the Act for forfeiture of any fish seized, and persons seizing the fish are authorised to sell it, the net proceeds of the sale being used in lieu of the fish for forfeiture. The Act specifies the three categories of persons who may seize the fish, but does not say that such persons have to warn the persons from whom the fish has been seized of their intention to sell it, or provide him with an opportunity to inspect it before it leaves their possession for sale. That, however, does not entitle us to ignore the canons of justice and fair play. Where it is reasonably practicable, as it was here, we are of the opinion that a person who has lawfully seized a fish and intends disposing of it one way or another should inform the person from whom it has been seized that the fish is going to be disposed of and that, before it is, he will have the opportunity of examining it or having it examined. Reasonable practicability will depend on the circumstances, which could include such considerations as the delay that would be occasioned by the request and the effect of such delay on the effective disposal of the fish. Here the appellant was provided with no such information or opportunity. The question of reasonable practicability did not therefore arise, but as the fish were going to be destroyed and not sold for consumption there was no obvious extreme urgency. The suggestion by the Advocate-depute that the information given to the appellant that he could have his solicitor present at the police station (an offer which incidentally was not accepted) was an effective substitute is not a tenable one in the circumstances of this case.

We are accordingly of the opinion that the Sheriff applied the wrong test here, and what we conceive to be the correct procedure was not followed. That in itself, however, is not sufficient. It has to be established that the appellant suffered a material prejudice thereby before the conviction is quashed. The Sheriff has stated in her note, though not as a finding in fact, that as the fish had been in the appellant's possession prior to being seized by the police, he had ample opportunity to examine them if he wished to do so. His own story was disbelieved by the Sheriff, and in our view it was so incredible that it would be unsafe to latch on to any part of it that was not established *aliunde* or was not disputed. Twenty-six salmon or sea-trout weighing 10-16 lbs were stacked in the back of his car. He was alone in the car. It is a reasonable inference that he stacked them there or was a party to that operation. He is an expert fisherman. For the past three years he has held the British and World Fly-casting Championships. He is an instructor in the art, and has held classes on it in the Borders. In the course of a normal year he expects to catch between three and four hundred salmon and sea-trout. If he had the opportunity properly to examine the fish, he would have known what to look for since he was an expert. But the whole affair took place at night when it was dark, and while one might suspect that he had the opportunity to examine the fish before they were impounded, that cannot be assumed. In any event, because of his personal involvement he may well have wished to have the services of another expert if he had been certiorated of his right to have one before the fish were destroyed. This he was undoubtedly denied. Since the marks or absence of significant marks on the fish were crucial to establishing the Crown case, and we are informed by the Sheriff that the Crown witnesses who made the inspection were cross-examined at length and in detail about the physical appearance of the fish, we cannot say that the deprivation of the opportunity to have them examined before disposal by or on behalf of the appellant did not result in substantial prejudice to him. It may be that even if such an opportunity had been provided and evidence contradictory of the Crown case had been adduced, even from an independent expert, the Sheriff would have reached the same conclusion, but that is a matter of pure speculation and one which this Court is not entitled to take into account. We are accordingly of the opinion that for the reasons stated this conviction cannot stand and must be quashed. We reach this conclusion with regret because in our view the appellant's conduct that night reeked of suspicion. His exculpation derives not from his actions and evidence but from a mistake in procedure.

Since the evidential procedure went astray in the Court below, we feel that the questions in law can best be answered thus: questions 1 and 3 fall to be answered in the negative, and the matters raised in question 2 can best be answered by reference to the opinion which we have expressed *intus*."

Conviction quashed.

NOTE

The crucial question in this area is therefore: is there material prejudice suffered by the accused in relation to what happens when the productions are taken by the police? This case is somewhat special and turned on its own peculiar facts. For further examples of the correlation of the "best evidence" rule and the production of essential items, see, *e.g. Miln* v. *Maher*, 1979 S.L.T. (Notes) 10, *Darroch* v. *H.M. Advocate*, 1980 S.L.T. 33 and *Hughes* v. *Skeen*, 1980 S.L.T. (Notes) 13.

f. Recovery of documents

Normally all documents which the defence require and which are in the hands of the Crown will be made available to the defence. Sometimes however a commission and diligence for their recovery is necessary, especially where the documents are in the hands of third parties.

1. Downie v. H.M. Advocate
1952 J.C. 37

An accused person was charged before sheriff and jury with embezzlement. She petitioned the High Court for recovery of certain documents.

LORD JUSTICE-GENERAL (COOPER): "We have had presented to us this morning a petition by a person who has been indicted on a charge of embezzlement before a Sheriff of Lanarkshire and a jury at Hamilton. The first diet is to-day, and the trial is fixed for Monday week, the 28th January. There is to be lodged at the first diet to-day a special defence to the effect that 'the panel pleads not guilty and specially and without prejudice to said plea that the sums set out in the indictment' (except one item), 'if embezzled' not by the panel but by another person named, who was at the material times the servant of the panel at the post office at which the alleged embezzlements took place. The purpose of the petition is to obtain recovery of a number of documents set out in an annexed specification.

We were informed that during the present century there have been two precedents in the High Court for an application of this kind, and that its competence is supported by a statement in Hume and a case of a distinctly exceptional character referred to in the note to the passage in Hume. So far as I am aware there is no reported case dealing with such an application, and no record of an application to the High Court in relation to a case appointed to be tried before a Sheriff and jury. The point of practice is obviously of importance in every case and especially in a case such as this in which this rare type of special defence is presented; and, had it been necessary, I should have been in favour either of convening a larger Court to lay down the appropriate practice, or of dealing with the matter by the enactment of an Act of Adjournal. It seems to me, however, that it is possible for us to solve the immediate difficulty upon the following basis.

The second and third items of the specification relate to documents *ex facie* innocuous, the objection to the production of which rests upon the Crown's submission that they have no conceivable relevance either to the prosecution or to the special defence. As we do not have before us the closed record, which is the guide to the Court in dealing with similar applications in a civil case, we have of course no means of knowing whether the documents are required or not. It is well known that, in accordance with the traditions which have prevailed for generations, the Crown is always ready in every prosecution to make available to the defence, and if necessary to make a Crown production in the case, any documents which could reasonably be regarded as likely to be of assistance to the defence and to further the interests of justice; and the Solicitor-General has indicated that, if the petitioner is able to show to him—what so far she has made no endeavour to do so far as this Court is concerned or so far as the Crown Office is concerned—for what purpose and to what end production of the second and third documents is required, he will be prepared to consider that application on its merits and to deal with it in the generous and fair spirit in which such matters have always been dealt with in the Crown Office.

As regards the first item, however, which relates to statements made by the third party to Post Office investigators and put in writing either at the time they were made or subsequently, relative to the affairs of the post office in question, I do not think that it is going beyond our present function to say that I find it very difficult to figure circumstances in which any Court would order the production of such a document. The absolute privilege attaching to Crown precognitions (or to documents such as those in question which are *prima facie* indistinguishable from Crown precognitions in the case of a Post Office embezzlement charge) is undoubted, and its preservation is vital to the system of criminal administration which prevails in this country.

Having said as much I meantime propose to say no more as regards the competency or the form or the merits of this application as addressed to this Court, but simply to continue the petition, upon the footing that, if, in order to investigate the propriety of production of the documents in 2 and 3, it is necessary for some time to be absorbed, the Solicitor-General will, should the necessity arise, desert the diet for the trial on the 28th of this month."

Petition continued.

NOTE

It will be observed that although the trial was to be taken before sheriff and jury, the petition was presented to the High Court. The case illustrates the general attitude of the Crown in dealing with such requests: this attitude still persists today.

2.   Hasson v. H.M. Advocate
1971 S.L.T. 199

An accused person was charged with *inter alia* fraud and embezzlement. He sought a commission and diligence to recover certain documents.

LORD CAMERON: ". . . The real difficulty in dealing with such an application as the present lies not in deciding as to its competency, but as to the relevance and width of the calls which are made and as to the accused's right to recover the particular documents covered by the calls in the specification. As the Lord Justice-General pointed out in *Downie* there is the obvious initial difficulty in considering such a specification that it is not—as in civil procedure—related to adjusted pleadings. Beyond the indictment and (where tendered) the terms of a special defence, there are no written pleadings. Further, in the presentation of a defence, very considerable latitude is necessarily allowed to an accused person and, in practice, it is often difficult, if not impossible, to discern ab ante the relevance of a particular document or piece of evidence. This means that the familiar tests of the legitimacy of a call for production of a document cannot be applied nor, in particular, is it in consequence easy to recognise and reject a particular call as being of the character of a 'fishing' diligence.

The case of *Downie* is subjected to criticism of an adverse nature in Renton and Brown on *Criminal Procedure*, 3rd edition, p. 77, as though it laid down certain principles of universal or at least general application. But consideration of the judgment and arguments in the report of this case show that the observations of the Lord Justice-General to which particular reference is made in Renton and Brown were directed to particular circumstances of a somewhat unusual character in that case, and did not touch the wider issues of the tests to be applied in determining whether to grant or refuse a specification for the recovery of documents. I certainly demur to the suggestion (which appears implicit in the criticism of the particular passage in his judgment referred to in Renton and Brown) that Lord Cooper was in effect taking the decision as to the relevancy of a call in a specification out of the hands of the court and placing it in the hands of the Crown. But there is a further observation I would make on the case of *Downie*. At the date when *Downie* was decided there was no system of legal aid in criminal cases such as obtains today and, therefore, the advisers of accused persons were more under the necessity and the habit of seeking the aid of the Crown to recover documentary productions and even to obtain the evidence of skilled or lay witnesses. It was obviously in light of, and with reference to, this well established and valuable practice that Lord Cooper made the observations which are adversely criticised in Renton and Brown on *Criminal Procedure*, 3rd edition, p. 77. Although the situation has been materially changed by the introduction of criminal legal aid, the problem remains for solution of deciding which documents are or are not recoverable and the limits of such recovery. On this point the late learned editor of the edition expresses the opinion 'That in general a statement by the accused's responsible adviser that the document in question is required for the conduct of the defence should be regarded by the court as sufficient'. As at present advised, I would regard this as too broad and bald a statement of the law and am not prepared to accept it as an adequate or sufficient test of the relevancy of a call for production of documents in the hands of third parties, especially when themselves not on the list of witnesses for the Crown or defence. In light of modern conditions I think this is an issue of very considerable difficulty and one which will at some time require authoritative definition and determination. I think something more than the mere ipse dixit of a responsible adviser is required, even if it be only an indication in general terms of the relation of the call to the charge or charges and the proposed defence to them. There are, as I have briefly indicated, very obvious difficulties in defining the limits within which such specifications may be granted. I do not think that it can be safely assumed that the well-known rules which are applicable to specifications in civil proceedings are necessarily applicable in criminal practice. Thus, for example, the rule which protects a witness against self-incrimination may place certain difficulties in the way of forcing a particular haver to produce incriminating documents, and there are other matters of substance and procedure which will require consideration. Fortunately, however, in this case it is not necessary to enter upon them. Counsel for the accused was able to link his calls to what is contained in the indictment. He was in a position to point to the terms of charges three and four in the indictment as justifying the first call (as amended). The second call (as now amended) was justified by reference to the special defence of incrimination which has been tendered; in addition to which, the person named in that special defence is himself on the Crown list of witnesses and presumably will be called by the Crown. In any event, being placed on the Crown list, he is absolved from the risk of prosecution for any part he may have played in the transactions libelled. These two calls as now amended make plain first, the purpose for which the calls are made in relation to the charges contained in the indictment and to which they specifically refer and also provide sufficiently clear guidance to the Commissioner as to the documents for which recovery is sought and authorised. The right of a haver, however, to take any objections competent to him at the diet (if any) of course reserves itself. No question arose on call three, as I understand that the process in the civil action referred to has already been made available to the defence. No objection in the form or substance of the calls as amended was made by the Crown. In these circumstances I shall, therefore, grant a commission in terms of calls one and two of the specification as amended and refuse call three as unnecessary."

Commission and diligence granted.

NOTE

This case indicates that the responsibility lies with the defence advisers to indicate in general terms the relationship between the call and the charge, with the defence thereto. One can see the court in a sense straining not to import the rigors of the rules in civil proceedings into criminal cases. In practice, applications for recovery of documents in the latter are relatively rare. In *P. Cannon (Garages) Ltd., Appellants*, 1983 S.L.T. (Sh. Ct.) 50, Sheriff Principal Dick refused an appeal by a company against refusal by a sheriff to make an order against the Crown in terms of section 1 of the Administration of Justice (Scotland) Act 1972 requiring the police and the fiscal to release to the company a blood sample and the certificates by the doctor and the analyst under section 10 of the Road Traffic Act 1972. The sample and the certificates had been prepared in connection with potential criminal proceedings but, due to the court strike, the prosecution did not proceed. It was held that the company could not recover the sample and the certificates for use in a civil litigation being pursued by them, as the totality of all reports by the police to procurators fiscal were confidential and that recovery by the appellants would not be in the public interest.

CHAPTER 10

THE TRIAL DIET

Once all preliminary matters have been dealt with the accused will appear for trial either before sheriff and jury or the High Court of Justiciary. This chapter deals with the procedure which is followed.

a. Diet peremptory

The case must be called on the date set down, or within the period during which a sitting of the court is to take place, otherwise the instance falls.

Hull v. H.M. Advocate
1945 J.C. 83

An accused was charged before sheriff and jury. At the pleading diet objections to relevancy were stated, and that diet was twice adjourned to later dates, due to the length of the debate. On 14 September 1944 the court further adjourned until 21 September so that judgment on the objections might be given. Nothing at all happened on 19 September, which was the date set down for trial. A trial was however held in October, at which the accused was convicted. She appealed against conviction.

LORD JUSTICE-CLERK (COOPER): ". . . It is a cardinal rule of our criminal procedure that a criminal diet is, and must be made, peremptory, and that, if the diet is not called or duly adjourned or continued on the date in the citation, the instance falls (Hume, vol. ii, 263, 264; Alison, vol. ii, 343, 344; Macdonald, (4th ed.) 471). The rule has again and again been rigorously enforced, its non-observance being treated as involving a fundamental nullity requiring that any conviction which has followed should be quashed. It was applied to a High Court case in *H. M. Advocate* v. *Fraser* [(1852) 1 Irv. 1], and it was extended to summary procedure even before the Act of 1908, and declared to be equally applicable to 'all cases truly criminal, whether the proceedings are summary or not, or whether in the Sheriff Court or in the High Court' (*M'Lean* v. *Falconer* [(1895) 22 R. (J.) 39, Lord Adam at p. 41]). It was again applied with the result of quashing convictions in *MacArthur* [(1896) 23 R. (J.) 81], *Craig* [(1897) 24 R. (J.) 88], *Jamieson*

[(1901) 3 F. (J.) 90], *Taylor* [(1906) 8 F. (J.) 74], *Corstorphine* [(1910 S. C. (J.) 21], and *Coubrough* v. *Howman*, 6th July 1939 (unreported). In most, if not all, of these cases, the acquiescence of the accused was treated as irrelevant. In face of this impressive array of precedents, it would be impossible for us, even if we were disposed to do so, to treat the rule as a mere technicality. But it is not a mere technicality. As Lord M'Laren said in *M'Lean* (at p. 41), 'although in the particular case the error may have resulted in no tangible injustice to the accused, it is of essential importance that we should enforce the strict observance of rules which are intended as securities for the liberty of the subject. One can easily see that if a dispensing power were permitted to be exercised by the Judge, or if deviations from this proper and regular form of procedure were allowed in one case, it might be that in other cases injustice or oppression might result.' I respectfully accept that statement, believing that the vigilance advocated in 1895 is no less necessary at the present time.

It has further to be kept in view that the trial of criminal causes before the Sheriff and jury is no novelty in our law, and that, except in so far as expressly modified by later statutes, the procedure in the Sheriff Court (as in the High Court) is based on long-established practice. That practice was partially codified in the Act of Adjournal of 17th March 1827 (Alison, vol. ii, 39 *et seq.*), which, as Alison observes, was practically a replica of the then practice in the Court of Justiciary, and which in terms directs that in trials by Sheriff and jury the forms of the Court of Justiciary shall be observed. By the Sheriff Courts (Scotland) Act, 1853 [16 & 17 Vict., c. 80], section 35, the expedient of two diets of compearance, with the requisite procedural machinery, was applied compulsorily to the Sheriff Court. That expedient was only applied optionally to the High Court fifteen years later, but the statute of 1868 [31 & 32 Vict., c. 95] became a dead letter (*Muir* v. *Hart* [1912 S.C. (J.) 41], at p. 47), and the High Court was only brought into line with the Sheriff Court in this respect by the Act of 1887 [50 & 51 Vict. c. 35]. In the Act of 1887 the direction as regards both first and second diets is that the procedure shall be according to the existing law and practice, except in so far as varied by the Act (sections 28 and 40). It follows that the basic principles of procedure enunciated by Hume and Alison and applied in decisions are just as applicable to trial by Sheriff and jury as to trial before the High Court, and indeed that the Sheriff Court has had considerably longer experience of the two diet system than the High Court.

With these considerations in mind I return to this case, putting first the question—What was the effect of the order of 14th September adjourning the Court until 21st September for judgment? This order cannot be read as an adjournment by implication of the second diet fixed for 19th September, for it was not within the power of the Sheriff on 14th September to adjourn by anticipation the peremptory second diet for 19th September. That could only be done on 19th September. The order can therefore be read as an adjournment of the first diet; and as this adjournment carried the first diet to a date two days after the second diet, the statutory procedure was reduced to confusion, for there were then outstanding two contradictory orders against the appellant, one citing her to the second diet on 19th

September and the other citing her to the adjourned first diet on 21st September. The next question is—Was anything done on 19th September to rectify the position? I do not consider that anything could be done; but, in any event, nothing was in fact done, for the general continuation of 'the whole remaining cases' to 20th September cannot be read as a continuation of the second diet in a case the first diet of which had already been made the subject of an express continuation to 21st September. For these reasons, and as the peremptory diet of 19th September was neither called nor otherwise disposed of on that day, it follows that the instance fell at latest at midnight on 19th September, and the position became irretrievable so far as the original indictment was concerned, except possibly by resort to section 42 of the Act, which was never invoked. The Crown's attempt to defend the propriety of the procedure therefore fails."

Conviction quashed.

NOTE

The rule that a criminal diet is peremptory is thus inviolable. It cannot be overcome by the argument that no prejudice has been suffered. At p. 88 of the report, the Lord Justice-Clerk commented further: "Were it once admitted that it was a question of facts and circumstances in each case whether a serious deviation from regular procedure should be ignored, the anchor of the entire system would drag." On the calling of the case therefore, something must happen, whether it be for example an order for an adjournment to another specific day, or a plea of guilty, or a trial itself. But the falling of the instance does not bar the prosecutor from further proceedings *in the case*, only from further procedure on that indictment. See also section 127 of the 1975 Act (as amended by the 1980 Act, Sched. 4, para. 27) which provides *inter alia* by subsection (1): "Where at the trial diet (*a*) the diet has been deserted *pro loco et tempore* for any cause, or (*b*) an indictment is for any cause not brought to trial and no order has been given by the court postponing such trial or appointing it to be held at a subsequent date at some other sitting of the court, it shall be lawful at any time within nine clear days after the date of such trial diet to give notice to the accused on another copy of the indictment to appear to answer such indictment at a further diet".

It is however competent on conviction of an accused in solemn proceedings to interrupt those proceedings by (a) considering a conviction against that person in other proceedings pending before the court for which he has not been sentenced, (b) passing sentence on that person in respect of the conviction in those other proceedings: Act of Adjournal (Sentencing Powers etc.) 1978 (printed at 1978 S.L.T. (News) 60). By paragraph 2 (3) of that Act of Adjournal no such interruption has the effect of causing the instance to fall, a provision effectively overruling the decision in *Law and Nicol* v. *H.M. Advocate*, 1973 S.L.T. (Notes) 14.

A trial must also proceed from day to day till conclusion. Each daily adjournment is minuted. Sometimes, however, a case may have to be put off completely.

b. Adjournment of the trial diet

In certain circumstances it may appear to either Crown or defence that an adjournment of the trial is appropriate. Often the matter can be disposed of by agreement between the parties; but where there is objection by one side to the other's motion, the court will be asked to adjudicate. The following cases illustrate the principles to be applied.

1. Vetters v. H.M. Advocate
1943 J.C. 138

An accused person was served with an indictment. He sought a postponement of his trial on the ground that an essential witness would be unavailable for the trial.

LORD JUSTICE-GENERAL (NORMAND): "This is a petition to the Court praying it to discharge the diet of trial of the petitioner on 22nd June 1943 on the ground of the absence of a witness essential to the defence. The charge against the petitioner is one of culpable homicide, in respect that, while under the influence of intoxicating liquor, he drove a motor omnibus in a culpable and reckless manner and at an excessive speed and failed to keep a sufficient and proper look-out, and that he did cause the said omnibus to mount the grass verge on the side of the road, that he permitted the witness (whose absence is the occasion of this petition), who was then under the influence of drink, to enter and remain in the driver's cabin of the motor omnibus although the cabin was not constructed to hold more than one person, that he did cause the said motor omnibus to collide with a motor car then being driven in the opposite direction, whereby its three occupants were so severely injured that they died there almost immediately thereafter, and that he did kill these three persons.

The witness is a seaman. He is at present absent from this country on a voyage, and it is uncertain whether, or when, he will return to it. He is also a foreigner, and it may be impossible to compel his attendance, if he does not voluntarily return to this country. As the indictment stands, it is obvious that part of the charge could not fairly proceed in his absence, because it is of the essence of that part of the charge that this man himself, while in a state of intoxication, was allowed to enter and remain in the cabin. The Advocate-Depute, however, gave an undertaking that he would delete from the indictment at the appropriate time that part of the indictment which founds upon the alleged permission by the petitioner to the witness to remain in the cabin. Nevertheless, the counsel for the petitioner was not satisfied with that concession, and maintained that, upon the charge as a whole, even with the omission of the particular part of it which refers specifically to the witness, the witness's evidence is essential. I would find it difficult to decline to accept a statement that a witness is essential from a counsel of experience, especially when he states that, after consideration, he puts it forward with all the responsibility which rests upon him. But it is obvious that, as this witness was alongside the driver who was charged with reckless conduct in the driving of the motor omnibus, he must be a witness of the very greatest importance.

The Crown had in its list certain witnesses who are in the armed forces of the Crown, and it succeeded in making arrangements with the naval and military authorities for their attendance at the second diet. These witnesses were certainly no more essential than this seaman who has now gone abroad on a merchant ship, and I think the Crown might have made equal endeavours to retain him. It would be deplorable if the petitioner were to be put on his trial, and possibly convicted, in the absence of a witness who might have given him the most material, and even conclusive, assistance. I think, therefore, that the justice of the case requires that the diet should be discharged, and I say so though fully recognising that the Crown may find considerable difficulty in obtaining the attendance at one time of all the witnesses."

Adjournment granted.

NOTE

The prime question is thus: "Is it in the interests of justice that an adjournment be granted?" The discretionary element in the court's decision cannot be stressed too highly. Many of the authorities turn on their own facts. If the court misuses its discretion on a motion to adjourn, such misuse can be attacked on appeal. Both the following cases deal with summary trials, but illustrate the general principle.

2. Skeen v. McLaren
1976 S.L.T. (Notes) 14

A sheriff refused a Crown motion to adjourn a trial. A Crown witness was on holiday and would not be available, but the sheriff held that this was an insufficient reason. The prosecutor appealed to the High Court by bill of advocation.

OPINION OF THE COURT: ". . . The motion of the prosecutor was made upon the ground that an essential witness was not available. When a motion is made by one party or the other to adjourn a diet of this kind on this ground and no question arises as to whether it is well founded in fact, there are two questions to which the sheriff must address his mind if he is to arrive at a proper decision upon the motion. The first question is whether the granting or refusal of the motion will be prejudicial to the accused and if so what is the probable extent of that prejudice. The second question is whether prejudice to the prosecutor would result from the granting or refusal of the motion and once again the degree of probable prejudice must be estimated. These two questions are the cardinal questions and this can be discovered in the judgments delivered by the court in the case of *Mackellar* v. *Dickson* (1898) 2 Adam 504. To these two questions we would add a possible third, namely, prejudice to the public interest which may arise independently of prejudice to the accused or to the prosecution in the particular case in which the motion is made. It is plain from the reasons which he has given that the sheriff did not address himself either to the two cardinal questions or even to the third which we have suggested. In the result, he has arrived at his decision upon a wrong principle and a decision arrived at upon a wrong principle is per se oppressive. We do not in this case reach the stage of having to consider whether the degree of prejudice to the complainer can itself be called oppressive. That stage would only be reached in a case in which the sheriff has proceeded to his decision upon a balancing of prejudice and where it is sought to show that his decision on that balance is erroneous. In the whole matter, as we have indicated, we shall pass the bill and remit to the sheriff to proceed as accords."

Appeal allowed.

NOTE

The third of the court's possible questions to be considered in dealing with a motion to adjourn is a new suggestion, but one which has come to assume equal importance with the two traditional questions of prejudice to Crown or defence. The next case brings this out clearly.

3. Tudhope v. Lawrie
1979 S.L.T. (Notes) 13

The procurator fiscal at Hamilton moved the sheriff to adjourn a trial diet, due to pressure of business in the court that day. The sheriff refused the motion, but when the fiscal indicated he would lead evidence, the sheriff refused to hear the evidence and left the bench. The fiscal appealed by bill of advocation against the sheriff's refusal of the Crown motion.

OPINION OF THE COURT: "There can of course be no doubt that it lies within the power of a sheriff to refuse to grant an adjournment of a diet with the consequence (as in this case) that an instance may fall and a prosecution be brought to an end. But at the same time this is a power which, in view of the possible consequences of its exercise to parties and to the public interest, must be exercised only after the most careful consideration on weighty grounds and with due and accurate regard to the interests which will be affected or prejudiced by that exercise. And when it appears that the sheriff has either failed to have proper regard to the interests which will suffer or may suffer prejudice by a refusal of an adjournment, whether sought by the prosecutor or on behalf of an accused, or has misdirected himself as to the extent or consequences of the prejudice to be suffered or has erred in his balancing of relative prejudice which will or is likely to arise from such a refusal, then his decision is open to attack and may be set aside. Nor will it suffice that a sheriff has paid lip service to the principles which should guide his decision should it appear that in substance he has failed to pay due and proper regard to them.

The matter came under review in this court in the recent case of *Skeen* v. *McLaren*. There the court laid it clearly down that in considering whether or not to refuse a motion for adjournment the sheriff must have regard to three questions: prejudice to the prosecutor; prejudice to the accused; and prejudice to the public interests in general. In that case it appears from the report that the sheriff had not applied his mind to the issue of actual or possible prejudice and this failure was of course fatal to his decision. In the course of his judgment however the Lord Justice-General said: 'We do not in this case reach the stage of having to consider whether the degree of prejudice to the complainer can itself be called oppressive. That stage would only be reached in a case in which the sheriff has proceeded to his decision on a balancing of prejudice and where it is sought to show that his decision on that balance is erroneous.'

It is the issue of balance which arises in this case and in our opinion when the sheriff's report is examined it is clear that he has failed to give proper weight to the prejudicial consequences which would follow if his decision were sustained. The sheriff 'realised that the Crown was bound to be prejudiced' — as indeed was the fact. The instance fell at midnight and further proceedings on the complaint were brought to an end. The sheriff however added that the 'situations would never have arisen had the trials been organised so as to give this trial precedence'. This can only imply that the Crown had only itself to blame—for which there is not a shred of evidence in the bill or the answers. Indeed it would appear that the Crown, for reasons that do not appear but which are not suggested as the responsibility of the prosecutor, was overtaken by events in respect that the first trial to be taken exceeded its estimated duration causing the prosecutor to seek a 2 o'clock adjournment of four cases including that in question here. In any event, it is the court which fixes diets and puts cases out for trial and not the prosecutor—though doubtless there is some measure of communication between the sheriff clerk and the prosecutor when the roll of cases for trial is prepared and intimated—but the responsibility for the roll is that of the court. On the information contained in the statements in the bill and in the answers and in the sheriff's report there appears no foundation for this implied criticism of the Crown. So far as the respondent was concerned no doubt there would be prejudice if an adjournment were granted, but principally of a pecuniary character, but here the sheriff erred in fact. The respondent was not self-employed: it was his witness, according to the accused, who was in that category. It is not possible to assess what weight the sheriff attached to this point, but obviously it was of some materiality in his balancing of relative prejudices. Further, the sheriff gives no reason for his assertion that an adjourned diet of trial 'would probably have been in July 1978 or later', although he was aware that the case had been set down for trial in March as a 'priority' trial. This question of further delay is obviously one of importance or at least appeared so to the sheriff, yet he deals with it in a manner which verges on the perfunctory.

When the sheriff came to consider the prejudice to the public interest he indicates that no *serious* prejudice was likely to result — on the ground that the charge was 'not a very serious one'. The offence was one which could attract a fine of £100 plus a further £5 for every day the offence continues. The complaint which was served on the respondent on 1 October 1977 libels a contravention between 7 May 1976 and 27 July 1977 and that the contravention continued to the date of the complaint. The offence itself was not one which in light of its circumstances and prolonged duration could, in our opinion, be lightly regarded having regard to the continuing and prolonged risk of injury and damage consequent upon the offence libelled. Here the sheriff failed to give due weight to the circumstances libelled in the complaint and in our opinion plainly misdirected himself as to the true quality of the prejudice to the public interest with his refusal to grant the adjournment sought by the Crown.

Having considered the sheriff's report we are of opinion, for the reasons we have given, that he has materially miscalculated the relative weights to be given to the prejudicial consequences to which his decision would give rise and that this material miscalculation fatally vitiates his decision. In our opinion to refuse the adjournment which the Crown sought was oppressive and the sheriff's interlocutor must be recalled and the case remitted to the sheriff at Hamilton to proceed as accords."

Crown appeal allowed.

NOTE

The problem facing the sheriff had been that the Crown had set down too many summary trials for that day, but the High Court indicated that his method of solving the problem was inappropriate. Overcrowding of the court's calendar has been an increasing problem, particularly in summary cases, but the issue being decided here is whether adjournment in the particular circumstances was justified. On the mechanics of seeking an adjournment in solemn cases, see section 77A of the 1975 Act, inserted by the 1980 Act, Sched. 4, para. 7. See also Renton and Brown, paras. 10-12 to 10-14.

c. *Desertion* simpliciter *and* pro loco et tempore

Where a prosecutor deserts the diet *simpliciter*, he cannot raise a fresh libel; that position also now represents the law where a *court* deserts *simpliciter* either *ex proprio motu* or, perhaps, on the motion of the accused: see section 127 (1A) of the 1975 Act, as inserted by section 18 of the 1980 Act.

If there is a serious difficulty in proceeding to trial, the diet may be deserted *pro loco et tempore*, that is, put off for the time being. The Crown must then serve a fresh indictment or avail itself of section 127 of the 1975 Act if it wishes to proceed. A motion to desert may be made either by the prosecutor, or the court may take this step at its own hand. If the motion is made by the prosecutor, its grant or refusal is entirely discretionary. It may be opposed and indeed refused if there would be injustice to the accused.

1. H.M. Advocate v. Hannah McAtamney or Henry
(1867) 5 Irv. 363

Two accused persons were served with an indictment. One accused objected successfully to its relevancy, and the diet against him was deserted *pro loco et tempore*. So far as the second accused was concerned, the indictment was held relevant, but the prosecutor sought to desert *pro loco* against her. She objected to this.

LORD DEAS: "It would be contrary to the ends of justice to give effect to this motion. The female prisoner though she may have been assisted, was the sole party implicated in the commission of the alleged offence. She has been in prison since December last; and is now present with counsel, agent, and witnesses in attendance. It would therefore be a great hardship for her if this motion were granted. I cannot see how the ends of justice will suffer by the case going to trial now. The public prosecutor has all the witnesses present and he can afterwards, if he thinks proper, bring the other panel to trial. If the counsel for the prisoner had not objected, the motion would have been granted."

Crown motion refused.

NOTE

It is somewhat unusual for the defence to object to a Crown motion to desert *pro loco* except, as here, where an accused is in custody. The question of whether the accused would suffer any prejudice is the core issue.

2. H.M. Advocate v. Brown and Foss
1966 S.L.T. 341

During a trial on indictment of two accused, one became medically unfit to give evidence or to instruct his defence. The defence were given leave to lead evidence to this effect. The High Court pronounced the following interlocutor:

"The Court being satisfied on the evidence adduced that the panel, Andrew Galloway Brown, was unfit by reason of his medical condition to continue to give evidence or to give instructions for his defence in the foreseeable future, *discharged* the jury as regards the trial of both panels, and *deserted* the diet *pro loco et tempore, reserving* to Her Majesty's Advocate the right to raise a new libel against either or both panels."

Diet deserted.

NOTE

In such cases there is clearly a duty on the defence to bring to the attention of the court the difficulty which has arisen. Whether it is at the instance of the prosecutor or the court itself, the essence of desertion *pro loco et tempore* is that the Crown may serve a fresh indictment, if so advised.

d. Jury selection and management

The selection of the members of the jury proceeds by ballot. By section 180 (1) of the 1975 Act (as amended by section 23 of the 1980 Act) each accused may challenge three jurors, as may the prosecutor, without giving any reason. Beyond these peremptory challenges, further challenges may be allowed on cause shown. There is very little authority on what constitutes sufficient cause.

1. H.M. Advocate v. Devine and Another
(1962) 78 Sh. Ct. Rep. 173

In a sheriff and jury trial, the solicitor for two accused used all his peremptory challenges for each, and then sought to challenge a further juror "on cause shown."

SHERIFF-SUBSTITUTE C.H. JOHNSTON, Q.C.: "Objection to a member of the public balloted for service on a jury other than an objection which constitutes a peremptory challenge must be an objection personal to that member of the public. In this case the solicitor for the accused has, on behalf of one of his clients, objected to a jurywoman upon a ground which he states to be a personal one, that by reason of her service on a jury in a case concerned with an incident at or about the same time, at the same locus and on the same date as that with which she is now called upon to serve she may have a view antagonistic to the present accused.

I have heard careful debate upon this matter, both from Mr. Reilly for the accused and from Mr. Smith, who although not holding any particular view on behalf of the Crown was good enough to give me such assistance as he had available. Neither of the procurators before me was able to give me any direct authority, and accordingly I have to consider this matter as it affects this particular case upon first principles.

I am in no doubt that it is within the capacity of a member of the public acting as a juror and properly directed to set aside from her mind the evidence which she may have heard in one case when considering the evidence in another case, which, if perhaps similar, is not identical either in the terms of the indictment or in the particular nature of the case. I accordingly repel the objection."

Objection to juror repelled.

2. M. v. H.M. Advocate
1974 S.L.T. (Notes) 25

An accused person was charged on indictment with contraventions of the Explosive Substances Act 1883. The *locus* of one alleged offence was the Derry Apprentice Boys Club in a district in Glasgow. He was convicted and successfully appealed to the High Court. In the course of his opinion allowing the appeal on other grounds, the Lord Justice-General (Emslie) commented on the method of jury selection adopted at the trial.

LORD JUSTICE-GENERAL (EMSLIE): "Before the jury were balloted, an invitation was made to the judge by counsel for one of the accused to put a question to the persons who had been cited for possible jury service. That question was eventually put, of consent, and the matter arose in this way. Counsel suggested that the case involved matters possibly associated with the current religious and political disturbances in Ulster, and that there might, therefore, be potential jurors who had, for example, lost near relatives in these disturbances, who, as a result, would not be able to give unbiased consideration to the issues involved. As it turned out, no juror declared himself in any difficulty or in any fear of bias and the ballot proceeded in the ordinary way.

We do not approve of the course which was followed, for two reasons. Firstly, there should be no general questioning, either by the judge or on behalf of the prosecutor or the accused, of persons cited for possible jury service to ascertain whether any of them could or should be excused from jury service in a particular trial. Secondly, apart from peremptory challenges, special cause must be shown before a juror can be excused. It is not a sufficient cause for a juror to be excused that he is of a particular race, religion or political belief or occupation, or indeed that the juror might or might not feel prejudice one way or the other towards the crime itself or to the background against which the crime has been committed. A juror can, of course, be excused on limited personal grounds. If he is personally concerned in the facts of the particular case, or closely connected with a party to the proceedings or with a witness, or if he suffers from some physical disability such as deafness or blindness or dumbness, there would be special cause for excluding him. Personal hardship or conscientious objection to jury service by itself may also be a ground for excusing a juror, at the discretion of the trial judge. The essence of the system of trial by jury is that it consists of 15 individuals chosen at random from amongst those who are cited for possible service."

NOTE

It is thus apparent that there is very little room in Scots procedure for challenging jurors. Anything even approaching an American-style *voir dire* is out of the question. Even if there has been considerable pre-trial publicity, any challenge to a prospective jury on this ground is not likely to find favour, in view of the attitude of the High Court in the next case.

3. H. v. Sweeney and Others
1983 S.L.T. 48; 1982 S.C.C.R. 161

Miss H. brought a bill for criminal letters to the High Court seeking authority to raise a private prosecution for rape against three youths. The Crown had previously decided not to prosecute, a decision which caused widespread media comment. One of the objections stated by the respondents to the granting of the bill was that the pre-trial publicity would fatally taint the minds of prospective jurors, and that it would be oppressive to proceed. In repelling this objection the High Court made the following observations:

LORD JUSTICE-GENERAL (EMSLIE): ". . . The remaining question of importance is focused in statement 5 in the answers for each of the respondents. Shortly stated, the submission was that the widespread publicity about this case in the period 13 January to 13 February 1982, in the press, on television, on radio, and in Parliament itself, has made it impossible for the respondents at any time to obtain fair and impartial trial anywhere in Scotland. To put the respondents on trial would, in short, constitute oppression. In presenting this submission on behalf of all three respondents, counsel for the second respondent recognised, under reference to the recent cases of *Stewart* v. *H.M. Advocate* and *Stuurman* v. *H.M. Advocate*, that the question for this court to answer is whether the risk of prejudice to the prospects of fair and impartial trial is so grave that no direction of a trial judge, however careful, could reasonably be expected to remove it. In this case he contended that the answer is emphatically in the affirmative, when the nature and contents of the publicity are considered. The publicity began when there was a public outcry about an apparently inappropriate sentence imposed upon a convicted rapist by a circuit judge in England. The subject of rape and the handling of this crime by the courts became then of immediate concern to the media and to Parliament. In this situation it became known to a reporter of the *Daily Record* newspaper that proceedings against the three respondents on the two charges in the two fallen indictments had been dropped by the Crown on or about 15 September 1981. Having regard to the serious nature of the two alleged crimes and upon the assumption—an erroneous one as it has now been demonstrated—that those who had been accused of these crimes could never be brought to trial, there was sparked off a welter of publicity, informed and ill-informed, designed to find out why the decision to abandon public prosecution of the respondents had been taken. This legitimate public discussion, however, said the second respondent's counsel, got out of hand because it began to focus attention upon the three respondents as a group, without differentiating among them, and upon their alleged guilt of the crimes which had been libelled against them. In no time at all the case became notorious. It acquired the label of 'the Glasgow rape case' and the general effect of the whole saturation coverage which it received was to encourage a wave of public sympathy for the alleged victim, and public animosity against those alleged to be responsible. For almost a month (before and after the Lord Advocate made his now well-known statement in Parliament on 21 January 1982—a statement repeated by the then Solicitor-General in the House of Commons) the complainer, 'her case', and the three respondents, who were not, of course, named, were kept constantly in the public eye. The implication of all that was said and printed was that a mistake may have been made by the Crown Office, and the average reader, it was said, could not fail to draw the inference that the three respondents should have been prosecuted and that the probable result would have been conviction. In the period in question no fewer than 160 articles about the case appeared in daily newspapers circulating in Scotland, 46 of them before the Lord Advocate's statement in the House of Lords on 21 January 1982. The case received similar massive coverage in television and radio programmes in course of some of which there were interviews with the complainer herself and with the solicitor who came to act for her after she was apparently spirited away to the Highlands by a newspaper and her former solicitor had been prevented from getting in touch with her. Further, the publicity included remarks attributed to sources in the police and in the procurator fiscal service expressing disquiet that the proceedings had been abandoned and the idea that a grave mistake had been made was fostered by linking the resignation of the Solicitor-General, quite wrongly, with the decision to abandon proceedings itself. The worst feature of the publicity, however, was in the *Daily Record* of 19 January 1982 (before the possibility of private prosecution was indicated in the Lord Advocate's statement in the House of Lords). In that newspaper, on that day, there were published, inter alia, some of the dramatic contents of an alleged 'confession' by one of the three respondents (who were not identified) and of alleged 'statements' by two of the respondents (also unidentified) and by a fourth youth who was to have been a Crown witness.

Publication of such material and of references to other so-called 'evidence', much of which was picked up and repeated in the media generally, was by itself so damaging to the prospects of the presentation of a defence by any of the three respondents that it destroyed the slightest chance that they could ever be tried fairly by an unprejudiced jury. No matter where and when any trial might take place in Scotland the whole public outcry will be recalled to the minds of those balloted for jury service in a trial of a unique character, and it cannot be said, as was said in *Stuurman*, that the only problem will be a residual risk of prejudice. The risk is large and substantial and will still be large and substantial even if the respondents were to face trial at the earliest practicable date, namely the end of May 1982.

I have considered closely the contents of the selected publicity material placed before us by counsel for the second respondent and, as the learned Dean of Faculty very properly conceded, his proposition is a formidable one which I have examined with more than usually anxious care. It cannot be disputed that the massive publicity, and in particular the matters referred to first in the *Daily Record* of 19 January 1982, have created a risk of injustice in that the respondents might not receive a fair trial from an uninstructed jury. As the cases of *Stewart* and *Stuurman* show the question for us is whether, in a few months' time, the risk of prejudice as the result of the publicity, true or false, the most damaging of which occurred before 21 January 1982, will still be so grave that even careful directions by a trial judge could not reasonably be expected to remove it. In this case this question is of the greatest difficulty and it is only after considerable hesitation that I have been persuaded to answer it in the negative. In considering what the answer should be I have not forgotten that while the public interest in securing fair trial of accused persons is of the highest importance, so too is the public interest in the fair administration of justice and the detection and trial of alleged perpetrators of crime. Great weight must be given to this latter aspect of the public interest in this case, for the crimes alleged are of a particularly serious and horrible nature. In light of this consideration, and my assessment of the probable course which presentation of available evidence at a trial would follow, can I confidently affirm now that fair and impartial trial of the three respondents cannot reasonably be secured? I have come to be of the opinion that I cannot so affirm. Trials in cases which have become notorious are not uncommon, and that this case should be remembered as the notorious 'Glasgow rape case' does not move me to think that fair and impartial trial of those accused by the complainer will be, on that account, impossible. As to the particular allegations made first in the *Daily Record* newspaper on 19 January 1982, it must be borne in mind that public memory of the detailed content of newspaper articles and of broadcasts is notoriously short. Having read all the relevant material for myself I have formed the distinct impression that the burden of its message is that the alleged perpetrators of the alleged crimes ought to have been put on trial, and that what will remain in the minds of potential jurors in a few months' time will be a recollection that the massive publicity between 13 and 21 January 1982 had been directed to express public anxiety that this might not happen. There was then sufficient evidence to justify prosecution of the three respondents, always on the assumption that the complainer herself was fit to testify. The fact that the three respondents were twice indicted so demonstrates. That is still the position today and while, for obvious reasons, I wish to say nothing whatever about the apparent strength or otherwise of possible evidence apparently available against any one of the respondents in relation to one or other or both of the alleged crimes, I am prepared to accept that the particular references to alleged 'evidence' in the *Daily Record* of 19 January 1982 are unlikely to be remembered in any detail by potential jurors, and to have any material influence upon their ability to remain true to their oath, and to accept faithfully and to apply the directions of the trial judge who will, no doubt, in this case, find it necessary to identify precisely for the jury the only evidential material upon which they are entitled to consider whether the guilt of any accused has been established beyond reasonable doubt. The *risk* of prejudice will undoubtedly be present. I find myself unable to hold, however, that a trial judge will be unable, when all the admissible evidence has been led, to secure, by careful directions, that the members of the jury will reach their verdicts upon an unprejudiced consideration of that evidence, and that evidence alone. The risk of prejudice arising in various ways is present inevitably in the course of many trials and our system essentially depends upon the assumption that jurors will behave with propriety and exclude from their deliberations all considerations which have not been presented to them in evidence in court in the course of the trial. In this case I have concluded, although not without some hesitation, that this necessary assumption can still be made."

NOTE

For further discussion of the case, see *supra*, Chap. 2. The factual basis for the assumption made by the court can never be established one way or the other, given the fact that jury deliberations are secret. One is tempted to think this is just as well; the reasons for the decisions of some juries might not stand too close scrutiny.

In Scotland there has been none of the controversy recently seen in England in relation to "jury vetting". No statutory provisions exist nor are any guidelines laid down by the Lord Advocate on the matter. In England the Attorney-General issued guidelines in 1975 permitting jury vetting in very rare cases, such as those involving serious offences where strong political motives were involved. Lord Denning M.R. was highly critical of the practice in *R. v. Crown Court at Sheffield, ex p. Brownlow* [1980] 2 All E.R. 444, describing it as "unconstitutional." However, the practice of supplying prosecuting counsel with information about potential jurors' convictions was held in *R. v. Mason* [1980] 3 All E.R. 777 not to be unlawful, and, following that case, the Attorney-General issued revised guidelines: see [1980] 3 All E.R. 785. Broadly speaking, checks may now be made in England in (a) cases in which national security is involved, and part of the evidence is likely to be heard *in camera*, and (b) terrorist cases.

In view of the remarks of the High Court in *M.* v. *H.M. Advocate* (*supra*), such a practice in Scotland would appear to be utterly inappropriate. Nor have we yet encountered here the problem which faced Nottingham Crown Court in *R.* v. *Danvers* [1982] Crim. L. R. 680, where a West Indian accused challenged the entire jury panel on the ground that not a single member was non-white. He claimed that as such the jury panel could not reflect the ethnic composition of the jury, that an all-white jury could not comprehend the mental and emotional atmosphere in which black families live, and that a black accused could not have unreserved confidence in an all-white jury. The recorder repelled the objection, holding that there existed in English law no requirement that there should be a black member of a jury or a jury panel.

4.   Stewart and Others v. H.M. Advocate
1980 J.C. 103

Mrs Gallo, one of the jurors in a long trial at Edinburgh High Court was approached by a person claiming to be the brother of one of the accused, who attempted to bribe her. She indicated to the presiding judge that she had important information for him, but he told her to discuss the matter with the other jurors before doing anything further. Subsequently the juror made the nature of the information known to the judge, who discharged her. The judge refused a defence motion to desert the diet *pro loco et tempore* and the accused were convicted. They appealed on the ground that the judge should have discharged the whole jury and that what he had done had created a substantial risk of grave prejudice to the accused.

LORD JUSTICE-GENERAL (EMSLIE): "We are here concerned to examine (i) an irregularity consisting of the alleged approach to the juror Mrs Gallo which was brought to the notice of the trial Judge and the other jurors in course of the trial before the jury had retired to consider its verdicts; and (ii) the soundness of the action taken by the trial Judge thereafter. There is no doubt that the question for our decision must be considered in light of two general principles—those of substantial justice and of the requirements of a fair trial (Hume on Crimes, ii, p. 418). The problem facing the trial Judge fell to be resolved in light of these very same principles, and since the submission for the appellants was to the effect that the action taken by the

Judge was the wrong one leading to a miscarriage of justice, we propose to begin by considering the probable effect of the report of the alleged approach upon the minds of the jury, in the absence of any instruction from the trial Judge. That the events which happened created a risk of injustice, in that the appellants might not receive a fair trial from an uninstructed jury, may be accepted at once. The learned trial Judge obviously thought so and this was conceded by the Advocate-Depute. The first question therefore comes to be whether the risk of prejudice was so grave that no direction of the trial Judge, however careful, could reasonably be expected to remove it. In posing this question we have to record that counsel for the appellants very properly did not contend that the mere disclosure of an irregular approach to a juror carrying some risk of prejudice to the fair trial of the accused must result in the discharge of the diet. It was recognised, and correctly recognised, that where an irregularity of this kind is disclosed in course of a trial, the question whether it is one which introduces a degree of prejudice incapable of being removed by proper direction must be a question of circumstances in every case. This being so it is, we think, impossible and undesirable to attempt to lay down any rigid criteria against which the quality and effect of such an irregularity are to be judged. In each case, however, the actual facts of the particular irregularity and the context in which its disclosure occurred will obviously be matters for consideration. In so saying it must not be forgotten that while the public interest in the accused receiving a fair trial is of the highest importance so, too, is the public interest in the fair administration of justice and the detection and punishment of criminals. To seek to apply any rigid rule that any interference or intercourse with a juror in course of a trial must automatically result in bringing a trial to an abortive conclusion would invite mischievous and ultroneous interventions designed solely to have this effect. Equally to permit the same result to follow where the intervention is deliberate on the part of the accused, his associates or friends, would place a weapon ready to the hand of guilty persons. This was noted by Hume in writing of interference with juries or jurors after their inclosure (Hume, ii, 427) and in our judgment the observation applies with equal force to similar activities prior to the jury's inclosure.

In light of these considerations we return to the particular disclosed irregularity with which this submission is concerned. The trial Judge did not, it seems, doubt the veracity of the juror who reported it. It may be accepted, too, that he recognised that the disclosure of Mrs Gallo's report to the other jurors gave rise to a risk of prejudice to the appellants. In some cases it may be desirable for a Judge faced with disclosed intercourse with a juror to go a stage further and attempt to investigate the merits of the reported incident. This was the course followed by Lord Ross in the case of *H. M. Advocate* v. *Dingwall* on 14th July 1977, and there may be other cases in which a similar investigation, or even a Crown investigation during an adjournment, would be appropriate and desirable. In this case, however, the trial Judge cannot be criticised for declining to institute an investigation of the events reported by Mrs Gallo in order to discover, if possible, the identity of the person responsible. Such an investigation in this case was, we think, neither necessary nor likely to be fruitful, and if one had been ordered by the trial Judge it might have led him into very deep waters. The form of the alleged attempt to interfere with Mrs Gallo was itself so bizarre as to suggest very strongly the likelihood that it was a hoax or a piece of singularly reprehensible mischief. The self-identification of Mrs Gallo's visitor was in the highest degree reckless and self-defeating, and the absence of any suggestion as to how the bribe offered was to be paid over in the event of Maxwell's acquittal is again suggestive of mischief or folly rather than of criminal intent in the interests of Maxwell. In these circumstances the trial Judge was entitled to examine the possible effect upon the trial of Mrs Gallo's report, in light of the reasonable assumption that the members of the jury were not unintelligent, and in the knowledge that if the trial proceeded they would receive careful directions and warnings that they must proceed solely upon the evidence which had been led before them and, in particular, must consider the evidence against each accused separately and avoid all speculation. He was entitled to have regard, also, to the fact that the jury had taken the appropriate oath and would be directed specifically as to the matters to which they were entitled to have regard in reaching their verdicts. Finally the trial Judge was entitled to have in mind the presumption upon which our system of trial by jury depends, namely, that jurors will accept and obey implicitly every direction in law given to them by the presiding Judge, including directions such as are given in many trials to put out of their minds certain matters which have been disclosed to them which do not constitute admissible evidence against particular accused. In all these circumstances the trial Judge was, in our judgment, well entitled to conclude that any possible prejudice or risk of injustice which might have been created by the report of the bizarre event by Mrs Gallo could readily be corrected by clear and specific direction on the matter to a reasonably intelligent and sworn jury. He was not, in the circumstances of this case, bound to desert the diet *pro loco et tempore*, and we go further and say that while cases will occur in which such a course will be dictated as the only proper course open to a trial Judge, such cases are likely to be rare. The primary submission for the appellants accordingly fails.

All that remains for consideration on this branch of the appeal is the subordinate contention that the specific directions in fact given by the trial Judge were not adequate in the circumstances of this case to eliminate the risk of a miscarriage of justice. The specific directions, although brief and succinct, were clear and to the point. We cannot and do not agree that they were inadequate. More might have been said, but what was said was quite enough to remove the risk that a miscarriage of justice might otherwise occur.

Before leaving this chapter of the case we wish to say only this. Where alleged interference or other intercourse with a juror is brought to the notice of a Judge in course of a trial it will usually be of assistance to him in deciding on his course of action to inform the prosecutor and those appearing for the defence of the report which has been made to him (if they do not know of it already) and invite discussion of the problem in court in the absence of the jury.

Appeal dismissed.

NOTE

The circumstances of this case are obviously special, but guidance has now been given as to dealing with this sort of problem should it arise in future. For discussion of the earlier proceedings in this case, see *supra*, Chap. 2.

e. *Specialities of the trial itself*

(i) Does the accused understand English?

The trial is conducted in the English language: if the accused (or a witness) does not understand English, an interpreter must be provided.

1. **H.M. Advocate v. Olsson**
1941 J.C. 63

A Swedish sailor was charged with murder. The following direction was given prior to the trial by the judge:

LORD JAMIESON: "The panel is a foreigner and does not understand the English language. It is inherent in the proper administration of justice that a person tried on indictment must be present during the proceedings, in order that he may hear the case against him, and it is obvious that the mere physical presence of the accused in this case will not satisfy the requirements of justice, and that provision must be made for having the evidence led communicated to him through an interpreter. I am informed that such a course was adopted by Lord Mackenzie in the trial of Alexander Kindereso, otherwise Gilbert, for murder in 1913, and that he expressed the hope that it would be followed in similar cases.

The question was fully considered by the Court of Criminal Appeal in England, and the English authorities and practice reviewed, in the case of *Rex* v. *Lee Kun* [[1916] 1 K.B. 337]. The Court there laid it down that, where a foreigner who is ignorant of the English language is on trial on an indictment for a criminal offence and is not defended by counsel, the evidence given at the trial must be translated to him, and that compliance with this rule cannot be waived by the prisoner. The Lord Chief Justice (Reading), who delivered the opinion of the Court, after pointing out that, where such an accused was defended by counsel, the practice had varied, said (at p. 343):—'We have come to the conclusion that the safer, and therefore the wiser, course, when the foreigner accused is defended by counsel, is that the evidence should be interpreted to him, except when he or counsel on his behalf expresses a wish to dispense with the translation and the judge thinks fit to permit the omission.' I propose to follow that course, and the evidence must be translated to the accused, except where his counsel asks that translation be dispensed with; but subject to this comment, that the evidence, the translation of which the Chief Justice appears to have thought might fairly be omitted, was evidence repeating what had been said at the preliminary proceedings before the magistrates under the English procedure. That does not apply to our procedure, and the only evidence which I think counsel for the defence will probably be justified in asking not to be translated will be evidence of a purely formal nature, such as proof of productions and the like. But, even where a request is made to omit translation, if there is any point which in my view it is material that the accused should be informed of, I will see that this is done."

Proceedings translated.

NOTE

A further feature of this case was the refusal by the trial judge to admit evidence of a statement said to have been made by the accused, on the ground that no interpreter was present when the statement was made.

2. Liszewski and Others v. Thomson
1942 J.C. 55

Three Polish soldiers were convicted of breach of the peace. They appealed against conviction.

LORD JUSTICE-GENERAL (NORMAND): "Three Polish soldiers complain in this case of a miscarriage of justice. They were convicted by the magistrate on a charge of breach of the peace. Two of them had no knowledge of the English language. The third knew a little English. A sworn interpreter was not employed at the trial, and in place of such an interpreter the soldier who had some knowledge of the language was allowed to act as an interpreter for the others. . . .

That appears to me to be entirely inconsistent with the due administration of justice. It is clear that the magistrate neglected his judicial duty and failed to take the proper steps to make sure that each one of these men had the fullest opportunity of understanding the charge that had been made against him and the proceedings which were taking place in Court. Two of them were wholly unable to follow the proceedings, and the third man was, so far as I can judge, not competent to follow them accurately and confidently. It was manifestly unfair and improper that he should have been put in the position of acting as interpreter for his two fellow-soldiers, who were accused along with him, and at the same time attending to those aspects of the case which concerned him personally. In my opinion, an interpreter should have been got for these three men, and the failure to get one was inconsistent with the traditional methods of administering justice in this country. The conviction must be quashed."

Conviction quashed.

NOTE

Either Crown or defence should bring any translating difficulties to the notice of the court without delay, so that an interpreter can be engaged as an official of the court. Similar considerations apply where the accused or a witness is deaf and/or dumb. However, a Gaelic speaker whose first language is English is not entitled to have the trial conducted in Gaelic: see *Taylor* v. *Haughney*, 1982 S.C.C.R. 360. See also the European Convention on Human Rights, art. 6(3).

(ii) The leading of evidence

The rules of evidence in criminal cases are outwith the scope of this book, although it is sometimes difficult to ascertain whether any particular rule is truly evidential or procedural. The reader is referred to the standard works on evidence, subject always to the provisions of the 1980 Act which introduce hitherto unheard-of specialities such as evidence on commission in criminal cases, evidence in replication and submissions of "no case to answer".

The order in which the evidence is taken in a criminal trial emphasises the accusatorial nature of the system: the Crown accuses and must prove its case: the accused is presumed innocent until proved guilty. The Thomson Committee on Criminal Procedure commented in 1975 (Cmnd. 6218, para. 1.10): "It became apparent to us early in our deliberations and from the evidence we received from our witnesses that our existing system of criminal procedure was fundamentally sound and that improvement was all that was needed and not radical change. We are of the view that there is no *prima facie* case for abandoning the present accusatorial system in favour of an inquisitorial system of the kind adopted in certain European countries". Thus, the procedural reforms of 1980 have left intact the basic system, although individual rules, such as those on "six hour" detention have been criticised from a libertarian viewpoint.

Since the onus of proof is on the Crown to establish the guilt of the accused beyond reasonable doubt, the Crown leads its evidence first. That evidence must be sufficient in law to support the charge. If the defence feel that at the end of the Crown case there is no case to answer, a submission to this effect may be made to the judge, in the absence of the jury: section 140A of the 1975 Act (as inserted by section 19 of the 1980 Act). By subsection (1) thereof, such a submission may be made both on an offence charged in the indictment and on any other offence of which he could be convicted under the indictment, were the offence charged the only offence so charged. By subsection (3), the effect of a successful submission of no case to answer is the acquittal of the accused for that offence. By subsection (4), if the submission is rejected, the accused may still give evidence and call witnesses.

Even if no submission is made, the accused has the right to lead evidence in exculpation, although there is generally no onus on him at all. By section 142 of the 1975 Act: "Where the only witness to the facts of the case called by the defence is the accused, he shall be called as a witness immediately after the close of the evidence for the prosecution".

Once all the evidence is in, both sides address the jury and thereafter the judge delivers his charge.

(iii)   The judge's charge

Following speeches, the judge charges the jury. Unlike the position in England, where the judge frequently reviews the whole evidence in some detail, in Scotland a judge often does so in far less exhaustive terms. The position was summed up in the following case.

Hamilton and Others v. H.M. Advocate
1938 J.C. 134

A number of accused were convicted of fraud. They appealed to the High Court. Various objections were made at the hearing to aspects of the judge's charge.

LORD JUSTICE-GENERAL (NORMAND): ". . . As your Lordship has pointed out, a number of objections were taken to the charge of the learned Sheriff-substitute. Upon these it is not necessary to pass judgment. I feel, nevertheless, impelled to say that I was far from convinced that any one of these objections was well founded. Some of them appeared to be based on a misconception of the duty of the presiding judge. For example, it was said that he ought to have rehearsed certain evidence and to have pointed out that it might be held to exculpate the panels from one of the less important charges, although it was admitted that counsel for the panels had not put this view of it before the jury in their addresses. I say this not as reflecting on counsel, for I think that there were excellent reasons from the point of view of the defence for concentrating on the main charges. But it is altogether unreasonable to complain, after that course had been taken, that the presiding judge did not make the point for the defence in his charge. The primary duty of the presiding judge is to direct the jury upon the law applicable to the case. In doing so it is usually necessary for him to refer to the facts on which questions of law depend. He may also have to refer to evidence in order to correct any mistakes that may have occurred in the addresses to the jury, and he may have occasion to refer to the evidence where controversy has arisen as to its bearing on a question of fact which the jury has to decide. But it is a matter very much in his discretion whether he can help the jury by resuming the evidence on any particular aspect of the case. I am confident that the anxious willingness of judges to give every help that they can to the jury may be relied on to guide them aright on the extent to which they ought to review the evidence in the case, and I am little disposed to attend with patience to the criticism that more should have been said about the evidence by way of exposition or explanation than the judge thought proper at the time. A Court of appeal is not in a position to review this discretion of the presiding judge on matters which concern the best way of conducting the case before him."

Appeals allowed.

NOTE

These remarks have been reiterated frequently in recent years. Appellants often try by diligent dissection of a judge's charge to find factual errors, misquotes or apparent unfairness to the defence. But the appeal court will look at a charge broadly, not as if it were a conveyancing document. Provided the proper issues have been identified and fairly put in the living context of the trial, then the appeal court will not interfere. This is not to say of course that misdirection is never fatal: it sometimes taints the whole case. For a discussion of the topic, and the extent to which misdirections may give rise to a successful appeal, see Chap. 14, *infra.*

(iv) Essential qualities of a verdict

For a verdict of a jury to be appropriate in law, it must be express, it must be consistent with the indictment and it must be unambiguous: see Renton and Brown, para. 10-60.

1. **MacMillan v. H.M. Advocate**

(1888) 1 White 572

An accused person was charged with embezzlement. The jury found that he had "misappropriated" certain funds and the sheriff sentenced him to three months' imprisonment. He appealed by bill of suspension. The Bill stated:—

"The complainer was, on 23rd December 1887, tried on the said indictment at Cupar before the Sheriff-Substitute and a Jury.

The Jury returned a verdict in the following terms:—'The Jury unanimously find the prisoner guilty to the extent of £276, 10s, 9d. of misappropriation of the Burgh Assessment Fund of Pittenweem; and owing to the loose manner in which the accounts of that burgh were looked after, strongly recommend him to the leniency of the Court.'

The Sheriff-Substitute requested the Jury to substitute the word 'embezzlement' for the word 'misappropriation' but the Jury, after a short consultation among themselves declined to accede to this request. The Sheriff-Substitute then expressly put it to the Jury, 'The charge, gentlemen, is embezzlement; is it your feeling that you don't want to return a verdict of embezzlement?' The Jury, through their Chancellor, replied, 'Yes.' Thereupon the verdict was recorded in the terms above written, as it had been drafted by the Jury.

It was contended for the complainer that this was a verdict of not guilty, and the motion of the Procurator-Fiscal for sentence was opposed. The Sheriff-Substitute, however, in respect of the above verdict, sentenced the complainer to three months' imprisonment. The complainer was removed to the prison of Cupar, where he is undergoing the said sentence of imprisonment.

The complainer is innocent of the said charge, and the said verdict was a verdict of not guilty. He was wrongly sentenced in respect of said verdict, and the conviction should be set aside, and the sentence suspended."

These arguments were supported in the bill by the appropriate pleas-in-law to the effect that the conviction and sentence were inept. When the bill was called in the High Court, the Crown offered no opposition to it being passed and the conviction and sentence were quashed.

NOTE

Embezzlement is of course a notoriously difficult crime to define, let alone establish to the satisfaction of a jury: see Gane and Stoddart, *Casebook on Scottish Criminal Law*, ch. 13, pp. 392 *et seq.*

2.   Young v. H.M. Advocate
1932 J.C. 63

A number of accused were charged on indictment with issuing a company prospectus which they knew to be false in pursuance of a common fraudulent purpose to deceive the public and thus defrauding members of the public of a sum of money. The indictment set forth by certain subheads the particulars in respect of which it was alleged that the scheme was false. Young and another accused Todd were convicted of this charge as libelled, except as regarded a common fraudulent purpose. The verdict made no mention of the various subheads. Both appealed against conviction.

LORD JUSTICE-GENERAL (CLYDE):
"*Reasonableness of verdict in point of form* (*Charge* (1)).

The appellants' first contention was that the verdict was an unreasonable one in relation (as they put it in their notes of appeal) to the law and to the directions given by the trial Court to the jury. This point refers only to charge (1) of the indictment, which is a charge against a number of persons (including the appellants) of concealing material particulars in the prospectus of a new company (to be called Scottish Amalgamated Silks), for the purpose of deceiving those who were invited to apply for shares, in pursuance of a common fraudulent design. The material particulars in respect of which the crime is said to have been committed are separately libelled under six distinct heads (*a*) to (*f*). The verdict on charge (1)—so this Court is informed—was announced by the foreman as a general one of guilty of the charge. But head (*d*) of charge (1) had been withdrawn at some time during the trial; and further, the trial Court, in its summing up to the jury, had directed that there was no evidence of common fraudulent purpose on the part of any of the accused. Accordingly the verdict—as actually recorded with the assent of the jury—excepted head (*d*), and also excepted 'the aggravation of acting in pursuance of a common fraudulent purpose.' Apart from these two exceptions, the verdict remained a general one of guilty of charge (1).

The appellants' contention is that, where—as in the present case—a number of distinct sets of particulars are separately libelled under one general charge, the verdict must disclose which set of particulars the verdict proceeds upon; and that it is an unreasonable verdict if it does not do so. They relate this contention to the Criminal Appeal (Scotland) Act, 1926, on the one hand, and to the directions given to the jury with regard to their verdict on the other hand. They say, *in the first place*, that, now that a convicted person has the right of appeal, it is only reasonable that the verdict should clearly disclose (by way of exception or otherwise) which of the sets of separately libelled particulars it proceeds upon, because it is inconsistent with the right of appeal that a convicted person should be left in any doubt as to the matters in respect of which he has been convicted. In the present case, the particulars separately libelled in heads (*a*) to (*f*) vary greatly from the point of view both of criminality and of facility of attack upon appeal; and it is (they say) unfair to require an appellant to assail the verdict on each and all of the separately libelled particulars, when (for aught he knows) the verdict may really have proceeded only on one or two of the sets of particulars, which may be comparatively trivial, and which (by themselves) might be comparatively easy for him to displace on appeal. *In the second place*, the appellants say that the only direction relevant to this matter which was given by the trial Court to the jury was one to the effect that a verdict under charge (1) could be returned if the jury thought the charge proved with respect to any one or more of the separately libelled sets of particulars; and they contend that this direction should have been accompanied by a further direction to the effect that, if the jury thought the charge was proved with respect only to one or more of the separately libelled sets of particulars, they must disclose in their verdict (by way of exception or otherwise) on which of those sets the verdict truly did proceed. The trial Court gave no such direction; and the appellants contend that the verdict is vitiated accordingly.

At first sight, the point appears a formidable one. So far as mere form goes, it might be formally answered that—as the verdict was recorded with the assent of the jury—the natural, and indeed the necessary, meaning to be attributed to it is that the jury found the appellants guilty under all the heads of charge (1), except (d), and subject to the qualification that the appellants had not acted in pursuance of a common fraudulent purpose; but, in the administration of criminal justice, points of form must not be pressed against the person charged. As, however, the argument on the appeal proceeded, it became evident that the appellants' complaint against the inadequacy of the direction (and against the general form of the verdict which they attributed to that inadequacy) lost the materiality which at first sight it seemed to possess. They attacked the verdict on charge (1) on the merits—with what result will appear in the sequel; but the attack was based on grounds substantially common to all the heads, and, accordingly, the dimensions of their complaint—even on the assumption that the jury did not truly mean to convict on all the heads of charge (1) other than (d)—was reduced to such hardship as was involved in having to attack the verdict on each and every one of the heads; for the jury must (even on the assumption made by the appellants) have convicted on one or more of them. In these circumstances it is in vain to complain that the Court's direction was inadequate; and this ground of appeal must therefore fail.

Nothing that has been said is intended to throw doubt on the need for care on the part of the Court to see that, in any case where separately libelled particulars are comprehended under a general charge, the verdict is returned and recorded in a shape which excludes doubt as to which of the separate particulars forms (or form) the basis of it. The proper way of exercising this care is no doubt by way of direction given to the jury by the Court. Before the Criminal Appeal Act, the only importance of disclosing these particulars was for the purpose of enabling the Court to impose an appropriate sentence; but, since the Act, it is right that the convicted person should have them plainly disclosed to him."

Appeal on this ground refused.

NOTE

The problem for a jury in sorting out verdicts on a general charge with subheads must be enormous. This arises today particularly in relation to charges of conspiracy, where the convoluted forms of indictments now encountered make charging the jury, reaching a verdict and recording it a major problem. See generally, Gordon, *Criminal Law* (2nd ed.), paras. 6-57 to 6-62 and the cases there discussed. See also Gane & Stoddart, *Casebook on Criminal Law*, pp. 84 *et seq*.

3. Hamilton and Others v. H.M. Advocate
1938 J.C. 134

Three accused were charged *inter alia* with fraud. Certain convictions were recorded and the accused appealed.

LORD MONCRIEFF: "The three appellants were tried by jury in the Sheriff Court in Glasgow on charges of having, while acting in concert, formed a fraudulent scheme to defraud the Scottish Milk Marketing Board by means of pretences and with consequences specified; and in pursuance of that scheme, while acting in concert, having by various specified detailed pretences defrauded or attempted to defraud the Board of various sums more particularly set forth in the indictment. There are three separate charges, set forth in detail in the indictment, of fraud or attempted fraud. The indictment contains a fourth charge of having, by exhibiting them to a representative of the Board as part of the machinery of the execution of these acts or attempts, uttered as genuine false and fabricated books. All three of the appellants are indicted upon each of these four charges, and it is a principal feature of each of the offences charged that they were carried through and completed by the three appellants acting in concert in the execution of the single fraudulent scheme previously described in detail.

The fraudulent scheme which is charged as having underlain the particular acts or attempts complained of is set forth in much detail in the indictment, but may be summarised as follows. The three appellants were directors of limited companies each of them dealing in bulk with milk; the milk required for the operation of these companies had to be obtained by them from the Scottish Milk Marketing Board; that Board gives its licensees supplies of milk at different prices according as the licensees are to distribute the milk for liquid consumption or are to use the milk as raw material for the manufacture of butter, cheese or cream; the price of milk fixed by the Board is higher when the milk is supplied for liquid consumption than in cases of supply for purposes of further manufacture. The appellant John Hamilton was a director of Ideal Dairies, Limited, a company which had a large business as distributors of milk for liquid consumption. Had that limited company applied to the Board direct for a supply of milk, it would have required to pay the higher prices charged by the Board for such milk. The appellant William Barr Haddow was a director of the Cardowan Creameries, Limited, and the appellant Walter Brown Kyle was a director of that company and was also a director of the West of Scotland Buttermakers, Limited. These two latter companies did an extensive business in the manufacture of margarine and butter from liquid milk, and held manufacturers' licences from the Board. These licences overlapped, but covered a composite period extending from February 1935 to June 1936. As licensees these limited companies applied for and got deliveries of milk for manufacture. This milk was then transferred to Ideal Dairies, Limited, and distributed by that company for liquid consumption. The appellants are charged with having, in the execution of the fraudulent scheme to defraud the Board which they carried out while acting in concert, and by means of false and fraudulent returns and false and fraudulent books and records, pretended to the Board that the whole milk supplied on the application of the Cardowan Creameries and the West of Scotland Buttermakers for milk at manufacturing prices had been used for the purpose of manufacture; whereas large quantities of the milk so supplied had not been so used, but had been transferred or sold by these companies to Ideal Dairies for liquid consumption. A consequence of the operation of such a scheme would be, of course, as set forth in the indictment, that Ideal Dairies would obtain milk for liquid consumption at the manufacturing rate; and that those responsible for the scheme (as the appellants are charged with having been responsible) would thereby succeed in defrauding the Board of the difference between the manufacturing price which in fact was paid for the milk and the liquid price which ought to have been paid. It is in execution of this scheme, and as acting in concert, that the three appellants are charged in the indictment with having done the acts and made the attempt which are the subject of the first three particular charges. The first of these acts is specified as having been executed by the three appellants in concert by using, as the machinery of the fraud, applications for milk made by the Cardowan Creameries, Limited. The second act and the attempted act which are the subjects of the second and third particular charges, are in like manner said to have been executed by the three appellants in concert by using, as the machinery of the fraud, applications for milk made by the West of Scotland Buttermakers, Limited. The books which are said to have been fabricated in concert by the three appellants are books which record the operations of both these limited companies.

At the conclusion of the trial all the appellants were convicted by the jury, but each of them was not found guilty in similar terms. The appellant John Hamilton alone was found guilty as libelled of all four charges; the appellant William Barr Haddow was found guilty as libelled of the first and fourth charges only; while the appellant Walter Brown Kyle was found guilty as libelled of all four charges except the first. As regards charges 2 and 3, the jury found these charges not proven against Haddow, and in like manner found the first charge not proven against Kyle. Numerous reasons of appeal were intimated on behalf of each of the appellants, and various grounds of appeal were relied on by the counsel who represented them at the hearing of the appeal. As a principal ground of appeal it was maintained on behalf of each of the appellants that the verdict returned by the jury contained findings which were irreconcilable one with the other, that the verdict was self-contradictory as evidenced by its terms, and that such a verdict could not be allowed to stand.

I propose to deal in the first instance and at this stage with this objection. Analysing the verdict, and reading the requisite passages together, it results, as regards the first charge, in a finding of guilty as libelled against Hamilton and Haddow, with a finding of not proven in favour of Kyle. It was maintained that such a verdict was in itself irreconcilable with the terms of the indictment, seeing that the act had been charged against each of the appellants as having been executed by all three of them in concert. It was suggested that a finding of guilty as libelled implied a finding that each of the parties so found guilty had acted in concert with both the other two, and that, therefore, the acquittal of one of the three was inconsistent with the terms of the charge. In my opinion, this suggestion is not well founded. I see no reason why, when concert of three parties is charged in an indictment, such an indictment should not be read as charging concert among these parties or between two of them, and as available to support a verdict against any two of them with acquittal of the third. This view appears, moreover, to receive support from the terms of section 6 of the Criminal Procedure (Scotland) Act 1887. I find little assistance, however, from the cases of *Myers* [1936 J.C. 1] and *Hamilton* [(1844) 2 Broun 313], which were cited as authorities. Seeing that concert was a principal and conditioning element of the charge, a different question would have arisen if two of the three parties to the concert had been acquitted; but it is not necessary in this case to entertain that question.

In like manner the jury, in returning their verdict as regards the second charge, convicted two only of the appellants and acquitted the third. In this case, however, they made a different selection among the three, having acquitted Kyle under charge 1, while in this case acquitting Haddow under charge 2. It was argued that, whereas it might be competent to make a selection of any particular group from among the parties charged with having acted in concert, once such a group had been selected as had been done in this case in the verdict returned on the first charge, that group must be regarded as having been crystallised for all effects in the reading of the indictment, so that a verdict of 'guilty as libelled,' (which was the verdict returned in answer to both charges in this case) could only be supported by proof of concert between the members of that one particular group. Although this argument when first stated appeared to be logical and attractive, on further consideration I do not see my way to sustain it. The flexibility which is introduced by the Act of 1887 seems to make such an indictment open to be read as regards concert in all its possible permutations, and with every such occasional shifting of these permutations as may at any stage be required. Under an indictment which charges A, B and C as having acted in concert, unless indeed a single indivisible concert of three be quite determinately charged, a verdict is, in my opinion, within the indictment and may properly find 'guilty as libelled' any duality of persons selected from the group of three; may so find whether A and B or A and C or B and C be selected; and may affirm 'guilty as libelled' against one or other or more than one of these groups, whether in repetition or in succession. Nevertheless, I am clearly of opinion that, in all such cases of variation, and more especially of repeated dissimilar variation between indictment and verdict, special verdicts, and not verdicts of 'guilty as libelled,' should be adjusted and returned. While I desire to draw attention to this as a point of practice, I am, however, of the opinion that neither of these two arguments can be sustained.

A more formidable challenge against the consistency of the verdict was, however, based upon a contrast between the findings of the jury in answer to the first and second of the charges as above narrated, and the answer given by them to the fourth charge. This argument was stated as follows. In answer to the first and second charges, as already noted, the jury had not only found various selected groups of two among the accused guilty, but had in each case acquitted one of the accused. In so acquitting in succession these two of the accused, the jury had necessarily negatived that there was proof against them of having had part in the fraudulent scheme so far as concerted with reference to these charges. Notwithstanding these verdicts of acquittal, the jury had nevertheless proceeded in answer to the fourth charge to find each of the three appellants guilty as libelled; and so to affirm an active share in the conspiracy from start to finish as against *inter alios* the two appellants who had already been acquitted of participation in the scheme at least in part. It was argued for the appellants, and was eventually not disputed by the learned Solicitor-General, that the answers so given by the jury to the various elements of charge were inconsistent and irreconcilable, and that the verdict as a whole could not stand as so returned. In my opinion, such a concession could not have been withheld. Unless some solution of the difficulty can be found, it is clear, accordingly, that the verdict must be set aside.

Alternative solutions of the difficulty were suggested by counsel for the Crown. In the first of these the Court was invited somewhat half-heartedly to remodel the verdict returned by the jury in answer to the fourth charge, and edit and reconstruct that element of the verdict in the light of the verdicts given in answer to charges 1 and 2. Once remodelled as so suggested the verdict would read as a verdict finding Hamilton and Haddow guilty under the fourth charge during the earlier period detailed in the charge (being the period of the active operations of the Cardowan Creameries, Limited), and finding Hamilton and Kyle guilty during the subsequent period throughout which the West of Scotland Buttermakers, Limited, was the agent of the fraud. It may be conceded that, if this reconstruction should be made, all inconsistency appearing on the face of the verdict would disappear. It would so disappear, however, by the intervention of the Court for the exercise of the functions, and for the redirection of a completed self-misdirection, of the jury. Such an intervention by the Court does not appear to be authorised either by practice or in principle. I have no hesitation in rejecting this first alternative solution. A verdict must be left to reflect the mind of the jury, but may not be made a medium of introducing illumination to it.

The second alternative solution suggested for the Crown, which was that the verdict of the jury in answer to the fourth charge should be deleted as being inconsistent with the earlier part of the verdict, appears to me to invite action by the Court which should be regarded as even less permissible. If a jury have given evidence, in the verdict which they have returned in a criminal case, of complete inconsistency of outlook in their treatment of the questions submitted to them for adjudication, and if this be made apparent by an *ex facie* irreconcilability one with another of the separate elements of that verdict, the right of persons convicted by that verdict is not merely a right to insist on the inconsistencies being eliminated from it, but is a right to challenge *ab initio* the competency of the jury to deal with the question of liberty which had been referred to them for adjudication. It is an inevitable consequence of the answer of the jury to the fourth charge that they must be regarded as having found Kyle and Haddow as having acted in concert in the execution of the single fraudulent scheme. *Per contra* it is a consequence of their answers to the first and second charges in the indictment that they failed to find evidence of any such concert between Kyle and Haddow. The conviction of all three in answer to the fourth charge must, in my opinion, be contrasted, not with the partial conviction of selected groups under charges 1 and 2, but with the acquittal of two among the three conspirators in successive answers to the first and second charges. As so contrasted, one or other branch of the verdict, and it is impossible to tell which branch, is contradictory of the single determination of the jury on the question of concerted guilt, and cannot be reconciled with any single determination of that question as consequential on it. Seeing that, in my opinion, the answer of the jury to the fourth charge can neither be reconstructed nor deleted from the verdict, I am, accordingly, of opinion that a verdict, of which the answer to that charge forms part and falls to be taken along with the answers previously given by the jury to the first and second charges, is one which is vitiated *ex facie* by a vice and a defect which is insusceptible of cure and is fatal to the verdict.

It is, accordingly, not necessary to deal with the particular reasons of appeal which were maintained against the charge of attempting to commit a fraud which follows the first and second charges. These reasons would have deserved particular examination had it not been that, as the verdict must stand or fall together, and as in my opinion for the reasons I have given the verdict cannot stand, no purpose would be served by examining any further reasons of appeal. For the same reason I find it unnecessary to refer to the various other reasons of appeal which were maintained.

I desire to add that I entirely agree with the views to be stated by your Lordship, in an opinion which I already have had the advantage of reading, as to the limits of the duty of a judge, when charging a jury in criminal cases, to make particular reference to matters dealt with in the evidence, yet not made prominent on behalf of the prosecution or of the defence; or by formal repetition to deal afresh with matters which in the opinion of the judge are not controversial and which have been already made entirely clear in the speeches of counsel. It may be that certain judicial observations, or even certain recent decisions, will require to be reconsidered by the Court.

I further desire to add that I have arrived at the conclusion that this verdict cannot stand with quite unusual regret. It was directly admitted by learned counsel who represented the appellants that their clients did not come before this Court of appeal with clean hands; nor did counsel dispute that, had the indictment been more wisely framed or the verdict more intelligently returned, the circumstances surrounding these transactions were such as would have made it salutary that penalties should have been imposed. I regard it as unfortunate in this case that the indictment was so heavily charged in its framework and in its detail. The substance of the complaint is contained in what I have referred to as the first and second charges. Had these two serious charges stood alone, the difficulties which have resulted in the shipwreck of this verdict would not have been introduced into the proceedings, while the accused would have been rendered answerable, in substance if not in logic, for all the criminal conduct which in such cumbrous form has been charged against them."

Convictions quashed.

NOTE

The lessons for the Crown are clear. An indictment should not resemble a closed record: it must be intelligible to a jury.

(v) Motion for sentence

For cases on this topic, see Chap. 2, *supra*.

(vi) Remit for sentence

The provision covering this matter is section 104 of the 1975 Act (as amended by the 1980 Act, Sched. 4, para. 15). The amended provision enjoins the sheriff to remit an accused where he "holds that any competent sentence which he can impose is inadequate so that the question of sentence is appropriate for the High Court".

(A) DO INQUIRIES REQUIRE TO BE MADE INTO THE ACCUSED'S MENTAL OR PHYSICAL CONDITION?

H.M. Advocate v. Clark
1955 J.C. 88

An accused pleaded guilty under section 31 of the 1887 Act (now section 102 of the 1975 Act) to a charge of incest and contravention of section 4(1) of the Criminal Law Amendment Act 1922. The Crown led evidence under section 24(1) of the Criminal Justice (Scotland) Act 1949 before the sheriff as to the mental condition of the accused, which satisfied the sheriff that the accused was mentally defective. The sheriff then remitted the accused to the High Court for sentence.

LORD WHEATLEY: ". . . It might be thought that, since the proceedings to-day are merely a continuation of the proceedings which took place in the Sheriff Court, the evidence of the medical practitioners in the Sheriff Court would have sufficed and that I would have been entitled to adopt that evidence. I take a different view. In my opinion, it is the Court called upon to pass sentence which has to consider what is the appropriate method of dealing with an accused. It is that Court which has to be satisfied as to the mental condition of the accused, and, in my opinion, that Court cannot be satisfied on evidence which it has not heard itself. It is that Court, namely, the Court which has to pass sentence, which has to decide at the date when the sentence is to be imposed what is the appropriate course to follow, having in view the mental condition of the accused and the availability or otherwise at that date of a place in an appropriate institution for mental defectives. For that reason I considered it necessary to hear the evidence again and get an up-to-date report from the medical practitioners. By the same token I conceived it my duty to get an up-to-date report on the availability or otherwise of a place in an appropriate institution which could receive the accused and give him the necessary treatment if such a method of dealing with the accused commended itself. In these circumstances I decided that the case should again come before me at the present sitting of the High Court of Justiciary in Glasgow. I am fortified in having taken that course by the fact that, although it appeared at the time when the case appeared in the Sheriff Court that there was not a place available in an appropriate institution, the more recent report indicates that such a place is now available.

The experience of this case has made me deem it desirable to express my views on the appropriate procedure to be followed in a case such as this. Where a case of this nature and involving these circumstances comes before a Sheriff and it appears to the Sheriff that, by reason of the nature of the offence charged or the circumstances attending the offence, it is a case which is appropriate for remit to the High Court of Justiciary for sentence, then, even when the prosecutor has followed the procedure set out in section 24(1) of the Criminal Justice (Scotland) Act, 1949, he should remit the case in the normal way, leaving it to the latter Court to decide what is the proper method of dealing with the offender in the light of the alternatives to be considered, including, where appropriate, the invocation of the procedure set out in section 24 of the Criminal Justice (Scotland) Act, 1949."

NOTE

Section 24 of the Criminal Justice (Scotland) Act 1949 covers only mental defectives. Although Lord Wheatley limits his opinion to "a case of this nature and involving these circumstances," the principles underlying his view is similar to that which covers cases where the High Court defers sentence for reports. Obviously it is the sentencing, and not the remitting, court which requires the up-to-date information on the accused.

(B) WHAT HAPPENS IF THERE ARE MULTIPLE ACCUSED?

H.M. Advocate v. Duffy
1974 S.L.T. (Notes) 46

Two accused pleaded guilty before the sheriff to various offences. The sheriff remitted one and dealt with the other himself. When the remitted accused appeared in the High Court, the following comments were made:

LORD JUSTICE-CLERK (WHEATLEY): "I have repeatedly said that where two or more accused appear on the same indictment in the sheriff court, and are convicted, then the sheriff, if he decided that one of them should be remitted to the High Court for sentence, should remit both or all of them.

The purpose of this procedure is to allow the same judge to determine the appropriate sentences for all accused, having regard to such relative matters as the number of offences on which each accused has been convicted, previous records, personal circumstances and backgrounds. When accused in such circumstances are dealt with in different courts, disparities which sometimes create embarrassment are liable to creep in.

It is only in exceptional circumstances that the procedure should not be followed. If, for instance, there are two accused, and each is convicted of offences not involving the other, the sheriff would be entitled to deal with one of them himself while remitting the other to the High Court for sentence. But where both are convicted of the same offence or offences, whether or not they are also convicted of other offences not involving the co-accused, then both should be remitted to the High Court.

If the sheriff is of the opinion that in the case of one of the accused there are circumstances present which would justify him imposing a sentence within his competence, he can refer to these circumstances in his report to the High Court.

Since even an experienced and conscientious sheriff like the one involved in this case seems to have misunderstood the directions previously given on this matter, I deem it expedient to repeat and emphasise the procedure which should be followed."

NOTE

The effect of this procedure is of course that the High Court often finds itself passing sentence well within the competence of a sheriff on accused persons who perhaps have relatively short records, compared to a more experienced colleague who is the real reason for the remit. However, uniformity of sentencing practice is doubtless enhanced thereby.

(C) WHAT HAPPENS IF THERE ARE MULTIPLE INDICTMENTS?

H.M. Advocate v. Stern
1974 S.L.T. 2

LORD JUSTICE-CLERK (WHEATLEY): "The accused in this case was charged on two separate indictments. The first was a common law charge of the reset of a motor car. The second was a contravention of s. 99 (c) of the Road Traffic Act 1972 (driving while disqualified). The circumstances of the two offences were inter-connected, and the reason why the charges were in separate indictments and not in a single indictment was apparently the current practice of the Crown not to include in the same indictment two charges, one of which would indicate to a jury that the accused had been previously convicted of an offence. This is an understandable practice, since it is designed to prevent prejudice to an accused, but, as in the present case, it can lead to complications if proper regard is not had to the procedure. Each indictment has to be called and dealt with separately. The accused in the present case pled guilty to both indictments. In view of his long list of previous convictions the sheriff remitted him to the High Court for sentence in terms of s. 2 of the Criminal Procedure (Scotland) Act 1921. This was quite a competent course in relation to the first indictment (the common law charge of reset). Presumably to allow the inter-connected events to be dealt with at the same time by the same court, he also remitted the accused to the High Court for sentence on the second indictment (contravention of s. 99 (c) of the Road Traffic Act 1972). This was quite incompetent. The statutory authority for such a remit is s. 2 aforesaid. It only operates when the sheriff holds that any sentence which he can competently pronounce is inadequate. The maximum sentence on indictment for a contravention of s. 99 (c) is 12 months or a fine of £100 or both. Any sentence which the sheriff could impose for this charge was completely within his competence, and he had accordingly no authority to remit this single charge on that separate indictment to the High Court. That remit is therefore incompetent, and I shall accede to the advocate-depute's motion to desert the diet pro loco et tempore.

This situation has arisen more than once, and despite directions from the High Court about the proper procedure to be followed the practice continues of remitting cases incompetently in circumstances such as were present here. I accordingly deem it desirable to restate the proper procedure in the hope that it will be regularly followed in the future.

If an accused is charged on two or more indictments, each has to be dealt with separately. If the indictments are being dealt with in the sheriff court, the sheriff has to consider what should be done in each separate case. If the circumstances in a case are such that any appropriate sentence which he could competently pronounce would, in his view, be inadequate, he can remit the case to the High Court for sentence. If more than one case falls into that category he can remit all such cases so that they can be disposed of together in the High Court. Where the charges in such indictments are inter-connected that is an obviously desirable course, even although separate sentences have to be passed on the individual indictments. The ability of the court to pass concurrent or consecutive sentences provides the latitude necessary to meet differing conditions. Where, however, the maximum sentence which he can impose is within his competence, then he must dispose of the case himself and not remit it to the High Court. If the offence is inter-connected with another offence which has been remitted to the High Court for disposal, the sentence for that offence can be taken into account by the judge in the High Court when considering the other offence.

It will be appreciated that what I have said only relates to the situation where there are separate indictments. Where a number of charges are contained in the one indictment then if, in relation to one or more charges, the s. 2 procedure is competent and appropriate, there can be a remit of the whole indictment even if it contains a charge (or charges) which, if it stood by itself in an indictment, could not be competently remitted."

NOTE

The situation in this case is really only likely to be encountered where section 99 (*b*) charges are involved. Most other offences can be libelled on the same indictment. The "sheriff" who remits need not be the "sheriff" who took the trial: *Borland* v. *H.M. Advocate*, 1976 S.L.T. (Notes) 12.

CHAPTER 11

THE INITIATION OF SUMMARY PROCEEDINGS

Summary criminal procedure is applied in the sheriff court and district court, being now the only courts of summary jurisdiction: see ch. 3, *supra*. The accused is charged on a summary complaint, usually at the instance of the procurator fiscal. The following two preliminary matters have given rise to a certain amount of case law.

a. Are the proceedings timeous?

As has been observed, common law offences never prescribe: see *Sugden* v. *H.M. Advocate,* 1934 J.C. 103, *supra,* p. 285. Statutory offences prescribe according to any terms of the relative statutes: *e.g. Robertson* v. *Page,* 1943 J.C. 32. Where no time-bar is stated, then section 331 of the 1975 Act applies. By section 331(1) it is provided *inter alia* that in such cases proceedings must be commenced within six months (that is, calendar months) after the contravention occurred; by section 331(4) proceedings are deemed to commence on the date on which a warrant to apprehend or to cite the accused is granted, if such warrant is executed without undue delay. On warrants and citation generally, see section 314 of the 1975 Act (as amended by section 11 of the 1980 Act) and also section 315 thereof.

1. Smith v. Peter Walker & Son (Edinburgh) Ltd.
1978 J.C. 44

A building firm was charged on summary complaint. This complaint was dismissed as incompetent by the sheriff. The Crown appealed by stated case.

LORD JUSTICE-GENERAL (EMSLIE): "The respondents in this Crown appeal were charged with four contraventions of the Construction (Working Places) Regulations 1966. They were, it seems, undertaking the rebuilding of a chimney head at 30 Woodburn Terrace, Edinburgh, and the charges related to the state of a ladder used by their men on 14th December 1976, and to a working platform and suspended gin wheel used on the site

360

on 16th December 1976. The alleged contraventions, accordingly, related to a certain transient state of matters on two separate days only, and were contraventions within the scope of section 331 (1) of the Criminal Procedure (Scotland) Act 1975. In terms of that subsection as it applied in the circumstances of this case, proceedings in respect of these contraventions required to be commenced within six months of 16th December 1976, i.e., not later than 15th June 1977.

The complaint in this case was not served until 30th June 1977. At the first diet on 21st July 1977 an objection that the complaint was out of time was intimated and, after debate on 25th August 1977, the Sheriff upheld the objection and sustained a plea to the competency of the proceedings. His decision involved consideration of section 331 (3) of the Act which is in these terms: 'For the purposes of this section proceedings shall be deemed to be commenced on the date on which a warrant to apprehend or to cite the accused is granted, if such warrant is executed without undue delay.' It was common ground (i) that warrant to cite the respondents was granted on 10th June 1977 (when the diet of 21st July 1977 was assigned by the Court) and, as we have said, (ii) that that warrant was not executed until 30th June 1977. The dispute between the appellant and the respondents involved the single question viz., whether in all the circumstances of this case the warrant to cite had been executed 'without undue delay.' The decision of the Sheriff was that it had not and the question which both parties invited us to answer is this: 'Having regard to the whole circumstances stated, including particularly the dates of raising the complaint, assignation of a diet and postal service of the complaint, was the Sheriff entitled to hold that there had been undue delay in execution of the warrant to cite the respondents within the meaning of section 331 (3) of the Criminal Procedure (Scotland) Act 1975?'

For the Crown the submission was that although there is little guidance to be found in authority on the meaning of 'undue delay' in section 331 (3) it is clear enough that it means 'excessive' delay. If the delay which occurred in this case between the granting of the warrant to cite on 10th June 1977 and the execution thereof on 30th June was not excessive it would follow that the proceedings had been commenced within the time limit prescibed by section 331. Whether a delay is or is not 'excessive' in any case will be a question of degree in the particular circumstances. In this case the interval between the date of the warrant and its execution was only 20 days. Execution was only 15 days later than the expiry of the six-month period. The assigned diet was 21st July 1977 and ample notice of that diet was given to the respondents. Had the warrant been executed before 15th June 1977 the citation would have told the respondents precisely the same as the citation of 30th June, namely, that they were required to appear to answer the complaint at the assigned diet on 21st July. The Sheriff, it was said, had given no good reason for holding the delay which occurred in this case to be excessive, and since the respondents were not prejudiced thereby the appeal should be allowed.

In reply the respondents submitted that the question of whether delay in execution of a warrant to cite an accused person is or is not undue is one of fact, circumstance and degree. In this case the Sheriff adopted the correct approach and in the circumstances of this case was entitled to reach the conclusion that execution of the warrant had been unduly delayed.

In our judgment the submission for the respondent must receive effect. It can no doubt be said that undue delay in the context in which these words appear in section 331 (3) connotes delay which is excessive in the circumstances, but this does not take us very far. The provisions of section 331 (1) are designed for the protection of those accused of statutory contraventions and the clear intention is that no one shall be exposed to prosecution for any such contravention if proceedings have not been commenced before the expiry of the statutory time limit of six months. Where no complaint has been served upon a person accused of a statutory offence until after that time limit has expired, proceedings by the prosecutor will only be saved in the special circumstances set out in section 331 (3). These special circumstances are: (1) that a warrant to cite the accused has been granted before the expiry of the time limit, and (2) that citation of the accused on the authority of that warrant after the expiry of the time limit has been effected without undue delay. It appears to us, accordingly, that if a prosecutor seeks to avail himself of the very limited latitude allowed to him by section 331 (3) it is for him to demonstrate that execution of a warrant to cite after the expiry of the time limit can, in the circumstances of the case, be regarded as justifiable. To delay service of a complaint charging a statutory contravention until after the expiry of the time limit is a circumstance which will always call for explanation and we are clearly of opinion that the expression 'undue delay' in section 331 (3) carries the implication that any delay in service of such a complaint may be regarded as excessive if, in the circumstances of the case, no justification for it can be seen. In the case of *Farquharson* v. *Whyte* 1 White 26, the Court in holding that an admittedly long delay in service of the complaint was fatal to the conviction attached importance to the fact that the delay was entirely unexplained and we see no reason to quarrel with the treatment of 'undue delay' in Renton & Brown's Criminal Procedure, 4th Edn., at p. 187 in a passage in these terms: 'What constitutes undue delay must be a question of fact in each case. It must not be due to any act for which the prosecutor is responsible. The expression 'without undue delay' implies that there has been no slackness on his part and that any delay in execution is due to some circumstance for which he is not responsible, e.g., the conduct of the accused.'

When the expression 'without undue delay' is understood as we have explained it, it cannot be affirmed that the Sheriff was not entitled to reach the conclusion which he did. No explanation for the delay which occurred in this case was offered by the prosecutor. The six-month time limit was almost at an end before warrant to cite the respondents was sought and granted. There is nothing in the stated case to suggest that the respondents in any way contributed to the delay which occurred thereafter before the warrant was executed. The charges contained in the complaint relate to states of fact said to have existed on only two separate days in December 1976 in course of the operation of rebuilding a chimney head. The passage of time is bound to prejudice investigation of charges such as these and, if the prosecutor delays in seeking a warrant to cite an accused to answer such charges as these until almost the eve of the expiry of the statutory time limit, the need to act on the warrant with all speed is clamant. As we read the stated case it cannot be said that the Sheriff reached his conclusion without considering all the relevant circumstances or that he took into account any irrelevant considerations. It follows, accordingly, that his decision on a question which is one of fact, circumstances and degree cannot be disturbed and we shall answer the question in the case, as we have restated it of consent of parties, in the affirmative, and refuse the appeal."

Appeal refused.

NOTE

So it all depends on the circumstances. There is no doubt that pressure of business in many fiscals' offices often leads to several months' delay before non-custody cases are processed, and the lesson for the defence must always be: scrutinise the complaint carefully to ensure (1) that section 331 of the 1975 Act applies; and (2) that it has been complied with. A court strike is not a good excuse for not executing a warrant: see *Tudhope* v. *Mathleson*, 1981 S.C.C.R. 231.

2. **Young v. Smith**

1981 S.L.T. (Notes) 101

An accused person challenged the competency of summary proceedings in respect of a complaint served on him. His plea was repelled and, after conviction, he appealed by stated case.

OPINION OF THE COURT: "The circumstances which led to the appearance of the appellant before the sheriff to challenge the competency of the proceedings were these: (i) The alleged contraventions of the statute were said to have occurred on 22 October 1979; (ii) On Friday, 18 April 1980—four days before the expiry of the period of six months after 22 October 1979—the procurator fiscal applied for and was granted a warrant to apprehend the appellant. He received it in the afternoon just as his office was about to close, and when the clerical staff were leaving; (iii) Monday, 21 April 1980 was a public holiday; (iv) On Wednesday, 23 April the procurator fiscal posted a letter to the appellant informing him of the grant of the warrant to apprehend him 'in respect of the driving incident on 22 October 1979 when you were charged with contraventions of sections 2, 6, 25 and 143 of the Road Traffic Act 1972.' The letter went on to say: 'I write to give you an opportunity of attending the Court voluntarily in respect of those matters and you should therefore attend on Thursday, 1 May at 10 a.m. in Court 1, when the complaint will be served on you. Please note that failure to attend on that date will result in the Warrant being passed to the Police for enforcement.' This letter was probably dictated on Tuesday, 22

April. It was received by the appellant on Thursday, 24 April; (v) On 1 May 1980 the appellant accompanied by his solicitor duly presented himself at court in response to the invitation in the procurator fiscal's letter. The complaint with which this stated case is concerned was then served upon him, and the court adjourned the diet without plea until 15 May 1980 when the plea to competency was tabled. . . .

In this case it is common ground that no complaint was served upon the appellant before the expiry of the statutory time limit of six months. If these proceedings against the appellant are to be saved, accordingly, it must be because, in the particular circumstances of this case, they are saved by s. 331 (3), properly understood.

For the appellant the submission was that in the events which happened there was no 'execution' of the warrant at all within the meaning, and for the purposes, of s. 331 (3), and, in any event, there was no 'execution' thereof without undue delay. Subsection (3) is in effect an escape clause for a prosecutor who has, for one reason or another, failed to satisfy the primary intention of Parliament, namely, to serve a complaint upon statutory charges within the six months' time limit laid down. If, therefore, the prosecutor is to pray it in aid to permit prosecution for alleged statutory offences, otherwise out of time, he must comply strictly with the terms of the escape clause, strictly construed. The language of subs. (3) is clear and unambiguous. If the prosecutor chooses to obtain a warrant to apprehend in the hope of beating the time bar nothing short of execution of that warrant (without undue delay) will satisfy the requirements. Execution means just what it says. In the case of a warrant to apprehend there is and can be no execution unless and until apprehension on the faith of the warrant has been effected. Nothing less will do and the writing of the letter of 23 April and the appellant's appearance in court on 1 May in response to it, do not and cannot demonstrate that the only conditions upon which out of time prosecution may be saved have been satisfied. In any event in respect that the prosecutor could have written and posted his letter to the appellant on 18 April, or at the latest on 23 April, and that there was no sound explanation tendered for his failure to do so, it cannot be said that there was execution of the warrant without undue delay.

The response of the learned advocate-depute was that it cannot be supposed that it was the intention of Parliament that where a prosecutor has obtained the grant of a warrant to apprehend an accused within the six months' period, he must, whatever the circumstances, proceed to the physical arrest of the accused in order to be able to rely upon s. 331 (3). To construe s. 331 (3) in this way offends against common sense and considerations of humanity. The object of obtaining such a warrant is to secure the early attendance at court to receive service of a complaint and there can be no good reason why, if an accused who learns of the existence of the warrant wishes to attend voluntarily, and so achieve the object of the warrant, he should nevertheless be denied that opportunity and be subjected to the humiliation and indignity of arrest and, perhaps, search of his house, merely to enable the prosecutor to satisfy the supposed demands of the subsection. It has for long been the practice for prosecutors, in possession of a warrant to apprehend, in cases such as this, to adopt the procedure followed by the procurator fiscal here. Until this case it has never been contended, far less held, that where an accused has appeared voluntarily in court in response to a letter like the letter of 23 April 1980, the prosecutor may not rely on s. 331 (3) because the warrant to apprehend, which it was not necessary to enforce, was not followed by the arrest of the accused. Upon a proper construction of the subsection in accordance with the demands of common sense steps such as were successfully taken here on the faith of the existence of the warrant to apprehend, constitute sufficient 'execution' of the warrant. Alternatively the question of execution of such a warrant without delay should be seen to arise for the purposes of s. 331 (3) only where, in order to secure the objective of the warrant, it has been necessary to proceed to its execution.

The first question for consideration is whether what happened in this case can possibly be said to amount to 'execution' of the warrant to apprehend. The answer to that question is, emphatically, no. There cannot, in law, be 'execution' of such a warrant until what is authorised is carried out in accordance with its terms. The next question—and the real question in the case—is whether a prosecutor who has obtained, timeously, a warrant to apprehend, and who seeks to rely upon s. 331 (3) must, in order to do so, proceed to the physical arrest of the accused in all circumstances, and even where it is quite unnecessary to do so. We do not consider that it is permissible to presume that Parliament had any such intention. Section 331 of the Act of 1975 repeats and re-enacts the provisions of s. 23 of the Summary Jurisdiction Act of 1954 which, in turn, echo the terms of s. 26 of the corresponding Act of 1908. Section 331 (3) provides that, for the purposes of the section, 'proceedings shall be deemed to be commenced on the date on which a warrant to apprehend . . . is granted, if such warrant is executed without undue delay.' It does not provide that it is an essential prerequisite of the competency of such proceedings that the warrant to apprehend therein mentioned be enforced according to its terms in all circumstances, including the circumstances that enforcement, without undue delay, is rendered quite unnecessary by the voluntary action of the accused concerned. Execution of such a warrant without undue delay on the prosecutor's part may be forestalled by an accused's voluntary surrender of his person to the court when, for example, he has learned of its issue before effective action upon it has been possible. Is it to be supposed that Parliament contemplated that such an act by an accused should have the result of denying to the prosecutor any right to rely on s. 331 (3)? We think not. Such a situation is not covered by the language of the subsection. We are certainly not prepared to accept that an accused who learns of the existence of a warrant to arrest him on statutory charges, and who makes his arrest unnecessary by voluntarily submitting himself to the jurisdiction of the court before it has been enforced without undue delay should be able thereby to nullify subsequent proceedings merely by asserting that he had not been subjected to an unnecessary arrest. Nothing in the language of s. 331 (3) compels us to hold that unnecessary arrest on the faith of a competent and timeously obtained warrant to apprehend is a condition precedent to the prosecutor's right to rely upon it. The reference in the subsection to execution without undue delay must, we think, be understood to deal only with the situation in which a warrant to apprehend for the purposes of s. 331 (3) requires to be enforced and is enforced. It has no application whatever to the situation in which, there having been no undue delay on the prosecutor's part, the necessity for its execution is elided by the voluntary act of the accused concerned which achieves the entire objective of the warrant. That is the situation disclosed by the facts of this case and for this reason, and upon our construction of s. 331 (3), the appeal fails.

We are fortified in the conclusion which we have reached upon a consideration of the practice referred to by the learned advocate-depute and by the sheriff in his note. Counsel for the appellant did not attempt to deny the existence of this practice over many years. As we have said s. 331 (3) is not new. It is, to say the least, surprising if the competence of this practice had been in doubt—a practice which is consistent with good sense—that it should not have been the subject of decision on appeal long since. It has not, as we understand it, hitherto been challenged in the context of s. 331 and its statutory precursors, and it is perhaps instructive to observe that in the recent but unreported case of *Aird* v. *Macnab* [noted at [1971] J.C.L. 114] the appellant was a seafarer whose frequent absences defeated the efforts of the police to arrest him on the faith of a warrant granted within the six months' time limit. In the result he came before the court after a substantial lapse of time and the warrant was never, in fact, executed. The only challenge to the competency of the proceedings was on the ground of alleged 'undue delay' and in affirming the competency of the proceedings the sheriff and this court on appeal were well aware that the arrest of the accused, for long impossible, had in the event proved to be unnecessary.

Upon the whole matter and upon grounds which differ from those on which the sheriff's decision was based we affirm that decision and refuse the appeal by answering the question in the case in the affirmative. In so doing we have not overlooked the question of 'undue delay.' The sheriff held that there was none and we see no ground upon which his decision on that matter—a question of fact, circumstances and degree—could possibly be disturbed (see *Smith* v. *Peter Walker & Son (Edinburgh) Ltd.*, 1978 J.C. 44)."

Appeal refused.

NOTE

This appeal was surely doomed from the start. For a further case on the interpretation of the phrase "without undue delay" see *Farquharson* v. *Whyte* (1886) 1 White 26.

3.   Lockhart v. Bradley
1977 S.L.T. 5

An accused person was charged on summary complaint. He stated a preliminary plea to the competency of the complaint to the effect that the proceedings were time-barred. The sheriff upheld this plea and dismissed the complaint. The procurator fiscal appealed by stated case.

OPINION OF THE COURT: "The respondent was charged with certain contraventions of the Road Traffic Act 1972 arising out of a road traffic incident on 18 September 1975. On 10 March 1976 an assigned diet for the disposal of the case was obtained by the prosecutor under s. 314 (1) (*a*) of the Criminal Procedure (Scotland) Act 1975, hereinafter referred to as 'the Act.' The appellant cited the respondent to attend that assigned diet by a citation sent by recorded delivery post to his dwelling-house, and posted on 18 March 1976. Attempts to effect delivery of the citation were made by the postal authorities on 19, 20 and 22 March, but these were unsuccessful through no fault on the part of the respondent, but in the event he received the citation on 23 March. The short question at issue in the case is whether in terms of s. 331 (1) of the Act the proceedings were commenced within six months after the contraventions occurred.

Section 331 (1) is in the following terms so far as relevant to the present case: 'Proceedings under this Part of this Act in respect of the contravention of any statute or order shall, unless the statute or order under which the proceedings are brought fixes any other period, be commenced within six months after the contravention occurred.' The appropriate period in the instant case was six months. Subsection (3) of the said section enacts: 'For the purpose of this section proceedings shall be deemed to be commenced on the date on which a warrant to apprehend or to cite the accused is granted, if such warrant is executed without undue delay.'

It was submitted by the learned advocate-depute and accepted by counsel for the respondent that if the warrant to cite granted on 10 March 1976 had been executed within six months of 18 September 1975 no question of the validity of the proceedings would arise. The six months expired on 18 March 1976. The debate before the learned sheriff proceeded on the basis that the crucial date was not the date of the posting of the citation but the date on which it was received, which was outwith the six months' period, and the only issue which the sheriff considered and decided was whether in that situation there had been undue delay in executing the citation. With some hesitation he held that there had been undue delay, and accordingly he sustained the plea to the competency of the proceedings which had been tendered by the respondent's solicitor, on the ground that the deeming provisions of s. 331 (3) could not be invoked to fix the commencement of the proceedings as 10 March 1976, and that the proceedings were accordingly time-barred.

In our opinion, however, a preliminary point has to be determined, namely when was the warrant to cite executed? If it was executed on 18 March 1976, when the citation was posted by the prosecutor the proceedings were timeously commenced. Which then is the appropriate date: the date of posting or the date of receipt?

Section 314 (1) (*a*) of the Act provides for the assignment of a fixed diet to which an accused may be cited. Section 315 (1) enacts that the Act itself is sufficient warrant for the citation of an accused to such an assigned diet (inter alia). Section 316 (1) states that the citation of the accused to such a diet shall be effected as provided in that section. Subsection (3) thereof is in these terms: 'It shall be deemed a legal citation of the accused to such a . . . diet . . . if the citation be signed by the prosecutor and sent . . . through the recorded delivery service to the dwelling-house . . . of such accused.' Section 319 is in the following terms: '(1) When the citation of any person other than a witness is effected by post in terms of the foregoing terms of this Act, the induciae shall be reckoned from 24 hours after the time of posting. (2) It shall be sufficient evidence that a citation has been sent by post in terms of any of the foregoing provisions of this Act, if there is produced in court a written execution, signed by the person who signed such citation and in the appropriate form contained in an Act of Adjournal under this Act, or as nearly as may be in such form, together with the Post Office receipt for the relative registered or recorded delivery letter.'

In our opinion, the reading of these sections together, with particular notice of the provisions of s. 316 (3), results in the word 'executed' in s. 331 (3) being interpreted as being the action taken by the prosecutor in effecting the citation, whether by post or by the other methods prescribed by s. 316. That view is confirmed by consideration of the proviso to s. 316 (3) namely, 'Provided that, if the accused shall fail to appear at a diet . . . to which he has been cited in the manner provided by the subsection, paras. (*b*) and (*c*) of s. 338 of this Act shall not apply unless it shall have been proved to the court that he received the citation or that the contents thereof came to his knowledge.' This seems to us further indication that the execution of the citation is the action taken by the prosecutor to serve it and that if there is any need to prove its receipt the provisions of the proviso and of subs. (4) come into operation.

That being so, we are of the opinion that the citation of the respondent here was executed when it was posted on 18 March 1976, and on that basis the proceedings ex concessu were timeously brought.

We shall accordingly answer both questions of law in the negative, and remit the case back to the sheriff to proceed as accords."

Appeal allowed.

NOTE

So posting equals "execution," in the particular circumstances of this subsection. By comparison, posting by the accused of a letter pleading guilty does not appear to be equivalent to a plea of guilty; it only takes effect where the prosecutor produces it to the court, "and the court is satisfied that such written intimation has been made or authorised by the accused." See section 334(3)(*a*) of the 1975 Act.

b. Framing the complaint: relevancy again

The initiating document in summary procedure is a complaint drawn up by the procurator fiscal. The general principles of relevancy discussed *supra* at p. 266 apply equally to summary cases as to those taken in indictment. Forms of complaint, including samples of charges, are to be found in Schedule 2 to the Summary Jurisdiction (Scotland) Act 1954.

(i) Common law charges

Renton and Brown (para. 13-38) say that the safe rule in framing complaints for common law offences is strictly to adhere to the statutory forms. But this can have some odd results.

McLeod v. Mason
1981 S.L.T. (Notes) 109

Three accused were charged that they did "force open a lockfast motor car . . . with intent to steal and did attempt to steal." They were acquitted. The procurator fiscal appealed by stated case.

OPINION OF THE COURT: "The first charge was a charge of opening a lockfast motor car in a particular location with intent to steal and the charge libels that they did attempt to steal. The second charge was a charge that at another locus the three respondents attempted to force open a lockfast motor car with intent to steal and that they did attempt to steal. No objection to the relevancy or specification of the complaint in these terms was tabled at any stage of the proceedings. Evidence was led and concluded and the sheriff ex proprio motu decided to question the specification of the two charges. He appeared to think that because the lockfast places were motor cars it was necessary for the Crown to libel and prove that the intention to steal was directed at the contents of the car or directed at the car itself or both. In the absence of such specification he took the view that it would be wrong to convict the respondents who had had no notice that the Crown might at the end of the day contend that it did not matter that they were unable to show that the intention was to steal the car or the contents or both. In effect, therefore, the sheriff held that the two charges were irrelevant for want of essential specification. In so holding he misdirected himself. As many decided cases show the charges as framed in this complaint were relevant in all essential respects. There was no need for the Crown in order to establish the commission of a completed crime to show that it was the intention of the respondents to steal the car or its contents or both. It is quite sufficient to libel the opening of a lockfast motor car with the criminal intent of theft and in many cases it will be impossible to prove more. Contrary to the sheriff's view we do not consider that a verdict of guilt upon a charge thus libelled presents any real difficulty in the matter of sentencing.

We now turn to the sheriff's second reason for holding the charges not proven. It was not established, he said, whether the illegitimate object of the respondents was theft or merely the statutory offence of contravention of s. 175 of the Road Traffic Act 1972. That is no doubt a perfectly accurate observation, so far as it goes, but in the circumstances of this case it ought to have been presumed, in the absence of evidence that the illegitimate intention was merely contravention of a statute, that the intention was theft.

Upon the whole matter we are satisfied that the sheriff's reasons for holding the charges not proven cannot be supported. Upon the facts found he ought to have convicted as libelled and we shall answer the question in the case in the negative and remit to the sheriff with a direction to convict and to proceed to sentence."

Appeal allowed.

NOTE

Attempted theft and forcing open a lockfast place with intent to steal are individual crimes. In charges of attempted theft, the item which the accused is trying to steal is always specified, while the criminality of opening a lockfast place with intent to steal is clear from the unauthorised effraction of the lockfast article. But coupling the two together, without specifying what is to be stolen, makes this form of charge difficult to defend logically, hence the sheriff's decision. The accused might have had a perfectly adequate defence if the charges had specified the article they were allegedly attempting to steal. The rejection by the High Court of this appeal leads to the conclusion that this peculiar crime consists in "doing something which displays wickedness," which of course is consistent with Humean notions of dole, but inconsistent with modern views of *mens rea*. In England, the difficulties highlighted in this case would not have occurred, for the three accused would have been charged with the statutory offence of vehicle interference: see Criminal Attempts Act 1981, s. 9 whereby: "(1) A person is guilty of of the offence of vehicle interference if he interferes with a motor vehicle or trailer or anything carried in or on a motor vehicle or trailer with the intention that an offence specified in subsection (2) below shall be committed by himself or some other person. (2) The offences mentioned in subsection (1) above are (*a*) theft of the motor vehicle or trailer or part of it; (*b*) theft of anything carried in or on the motor vehicle or trailer; and (*c*) an offence under section 12 (1) of the Theft Act 1968 (taking and driving away without consent); and, if it is shown that a person accused of an offence under this section intended that one of those offences should be committed, it is immaterial that it cannot be shown which it was."

(ii)   Contraventions of statutes

A complaint (or indeed an indictment) including a charge of contravening a statute must aver facts sufficient to constitute the offence and give the accused fair notice. See also the 1975 Act, s. 312 (*p*)-(*r*).

Yeudall v. William Baird & Co.
1925 J.C. 62

An accused company was charged with a contravention of section 29 (1) of the Coal Mines Act 1911. The sheriff dismissed the complaint as irrelevant and the procurator fiscal appealed by stated case.

LORD JUSTICE-GENERAL (CLYDE): "By subsection (1) of section 19 of the Summary Jurisdiction Act, 1908, it is enacted that 'the description of an offence in the words of the statute contravened shall be sufficient.' It follows that, since this alteration of the law, there are many complaints which must be regarded as relevant and sufficient, although they might not have passed muster prior to the Act of 1908. It is therefore in vain to quote cases decided before the 1908 Act, when the requirements of the law in the matter of specification of *modus* were applied rigorously—it may be too rigorously—to summary complaints.

I do not, however, mean to cast any doubt upon the opinions which have been expressed in cases since the Act of 1908, to the effect that, if in the case of a statutory offence some further specification is necessary as a condition of fair notice, the Court has the right to insist on such further specification as a condition of relevancy. But it must be recognised that, since the Act of 1908 became law, the necessity of specifying *modus* has suffered, in the case of summary complaints founded upon statutory enactments, a material modification.

In the present case the accused are charged with having failed to produce an adequate amount of ventilation to dilute and render harmless noxious gases in a particular part of a mine belonging to them. They complain that that is not fair notice of what they are called to meet. I think—having due regard to the nature of the offence—it is fair notice. It is notice that, at the time and place in question, the ventilating system of the pit was defective for its purposes. It is true that the prosecutor does not attempt to trace the defect to its source, and that the true source may be more or less recondite. But the respondents presumably know their own system—they work it and are responsible for it: the prosecutor is not. A system of ventilation is by its own nature an integral whole, and depends for its efficiency on the co-operative relations of all its parts. The complaint gives the respondents fair notice that, time and place mentioned, their system of ventilation was inadequate to perform its statutory function; and, that being so, I do not think they have any good ground for grievance. In my opinion the complaint complies with the Act of 1908, and is not so defective in respect of want of fair notice as to justify the learned Sheriff-substitute in holding it irrelevant."

Appeal allowed.

NOTE

Section 19 (1) of the 1908 Act referred to by Lord Clyde is now section 312 (*p*) of the 1975 Act.

2. Macrorie v. Bird
(1911) 6 Adam 527

An accused person was charged on a summary complaint with a revenue offence in that he did not give full particulars in a statutory declaration required of him under the Revenue Act 1869. The magistrate repelled a preliminary objection to the relevancy of the complaint. The accused was convicted and appealed by stated case.

LORD DUNDAS: "The first question, and indeed in the view I take of it, the only question for consideration here, is whether or not the complaint is relevantly and sufficiently charged. I have come to the conclusion that it is not. The appellant is charged with a contravention of the Revenue Act, 1869, section 22, in respect that, on a certain day he did 'deliver a declaration such as is mentioned in the Revenue Act, 1869, section 22, relating to a motor-car numbered S.D. 148, wherein the particulars required by said Act to be therein set forth were not fully and truly stated,' in a certain respect which is set forth, 'contrary to said section, whereby you are liable to the penalty of twenty pounds.' With regard to that complaint I would make several observations. In the first place, it is libelled wholly and solely upon one Act, and upon one section of that Act, namely, the Revenue Act of 1869, and section 22 thereof. Next, that Act and that section of the Act cannot and do not apply to a motor-car at all. They apply to carriages; and 'carriage,' as defined by the Act of 1869, excludes the idea of motor-car altogether. Accordingly it seems to follow that no 'declaration such as is mentioned in' section 22, and no 'particulars required by said Act,' could or do refer to a motor-car at all. And, lastly, I would point out that the sole section libelled, namely, section 22 of the Revenue Act of 1869, neither creates an offence nor imposes any penalty therefor. At first sight it is rather difficult to see the connection between the section under which the complaint was libelled and this declaration referring to a motor-car, but the Solicitor-General has bridged the gap by making reference to (I think) section 4, sub-section 3, of the Act of 1888 (Customs and Inland Revenue Act), and section 86 of the Finance Act (1909-10), 1910, and the Treasury regulations as to motor-cars. But he admitted, and in my opinion he was quite right to admit, that to maintain the relevancy and sufficiency of this complaint would have been a hopeless task if it had not been for the provision of the Summary Jurisdiction Act, 1908, section 19 (2); and the question comes to be narrowed to this, whether that provision is such as to make proper and relevant this complaint which otherwise would not have been in proper and relevant form. It is enacted by section 19 (2) of the Act of 1908, that 'where the offence is created by more than one section of one or more statutes or orders, it shall only be necessary to specify the leading section or one of the leading sections.' I confess that I am not clear as to the precise scope and intention of that enactment, and I should be sorry to attempt to lay down any definition or pronounce any general opinion on the subject. I think that its scope and application will require to be defined by experience, and I further think that the Court will have to go step by step, and that it will be for the Court in every case to say whether the enactment does or does not apply to the particular case before it. It must always be for the Court to decide whether the sections libelled are or are not 'leading sections' within the meaning of the enactment. If one tries to apply the Act in that spirit I cannot think that this section can be said to be the leading section in the matter. It is difficult to see how a section which admittedly has no reference and could have no reference to a motor-car, could be the 'leading section' in a complaint founded on the failure to give particulars in regard to a motor-car. In my opinion the test in each case for the Court to apply must be whether the complaint on the face of it gives to the person charged fair and reasonable notice of what he is charged with, and what offence he is said to have committed; and I do not think it can be said to be fair notice to select as the sole ground libelled one section of an Act, and to reserve for future introduction and application any number of unlibelled sections, some of which may bear directly on the charge. I have already pointed out that the sole section libelled neither creates an offence nor imposes a penalty; and I think it must be at least a minimum of what is required of the prosecutor, that he should give a definite notice in the complaint of the offence which is said to have been committed and the penalty said to be incurred. For the reasons I have stated it seems to me that this particular case does not come within the scope and application of section 19 (2) of the Act of 1908; and I do not intend to go into the region of what may require to be laid down in future cases.

I therefore suggest that we should answer the first question in the negative; and, so far as we are concerned in the matter, that disposes of the present case."

Appeal allowed.

NOTE

Section 19 (2) of the 1908 Act is now section 312 (*r*) of the 1975 Act. Such mistakes as that made by the prosecution in this case may be curable by amendment, on which see the 1975 Act, s. 335.

3. Marshall v. Clark
1957 J.C. 68

A bus conductress was charged under statutory regulations with failing to take all reasonable precautions to ensure the safety of passengers in, or on, or entering or alighting from her vehicle. Her solicitor objected to the relevancy of the complaint on the ground that the particular regulations did not specify what were reasonable precautions. He also claimed that the regulations were too vague to infer criminal liability. The objection was repelled, the accused was convicted and an appeal by stated case was presented to the High Court.

LORD JUSTICE-CLERK (THOMSON): "By virtue of section 85 of the Road Traffic Act, 1930, the Minister of Transport may make regulations as to the conduct of, *inter alios*, conductors of public service vehicles when acting as such. Subsection (2) of that section provides that, if any person to whom any such regulations apply contravenes or fails to comply with any of the provisions of the regulations, he shall be liable to a fine.

The Public Service Vehicles (Conduct of Drivers, Conductors and Passengers) Regulations, 1936, which were made by the Minister of Transport in virtue of that section and which therefore have the force of an Act of Parliament, provide, *inter alia*, that a conductor, when acting as such, shall take all reasonable precautions to ensure the safety of passengers in or on or entering or alighting from his vehicle. The appellant, a conductress, was charged with failing to comply with this regulation. The objection which she took to the relevancy of the complaint was that it is not possible for a Scots prosecutor to frame a relevant complaint based on that regulation. In other words Parliament has stultified itself and, while appearing to create an offence, has failed to do so, as the offence cannot be translated into a relevant charge.

This proposition is on the face of it somewhat startling and would appear to accuse an omnipotent parliament of legislative ineptitude. The ineptitude lies, according to the argument, in the failure of Parliament to point out a standard against which the negligence of the conductress can be measured. As there is no touchstone, there can be no offence. The foundation of this attack on the relevancy is *Allan* v. *Howman* [1918 J.C. 50] which has been followed, not always with great enthusiasm, in a number of cases. I am entirely in agreement with your Lordship's review of this trend of authority and with your conclusion that it should be overruled. I shall confine myself to a few observations on *Allan* v. *Howman* as being the *fons et origo malorum*.

The attitude of the Court is succinctly put by Lord Johnston (at p. 53): 'It is for the Order which creates the offence to leave no dubiety as to what the offence is and not to leave it to the Judge who tries the case to determine on evidence, and to a large extent according to his opinion, in what the offence consists.' The Lord Justice-General said (at p. 53): 'I seek to throw no blame upon the prosecutor for having laid before the Court an irrelevant complaint. In the circumstances it would have been impossible for him to have done otherwise.' Lord Mackenzie also said (at p. 54): 'There are not, at present, materials from which the Procurator-fiscal could construct a relevant complaint . . . I cannot assent to the proposition that a man can be charged in a criminal Court on a complaint which merely tells him that he did something unreasonable.'

No doubt in 1918 regulations of this kind were something of a novelty but since then a good deal of water—some of it pretty muddy—has flowed under Parliamentary bridges and we are now habituated not only to regulations but to legislative enactments of all sorts couched in similar general terms. For myself—quite apart from the duty which rests on both prosecutors and Courts to do what Parliament tells them—I feel no particular anxiety that the liberty of the subject will be imperilled or fair trial impeded because an enactment made by Parliament or on Parliamentary authority says that a man must take adequate care or reasonable steps and so forth and leaves it to the Judge to determine on evidence in what the offence consists. The theory of *Allan* v. *Howman* is that no measuring rod has been provided in advance. I see no reason why the measuring rod should not emerge at the trial. This is the only practical way to look at the matter. When a man is accused of doing something unreasonable or of failing to take adequate precautions or reasonable steps or the like, the accusation is made in regard to some particular sphere of human activity in which he is engaged and of the ordinary incidents of which he must be well aware. It may be in regard to his family, his factory, his farm, his driving of his motor car or similar activities. In some of these activities the reasonableness or adequacy of his conduct may be easily enough ascertained by the Judge. In others, the situation may be complicated and a good deal of investigation may be necessary. Where there is a complicated background, if the prosecutor does not provide material sufficient to enable the Judge to reach a proper conclusion, the case against the accused will fail. It is all a question of circumstances. But in neither class of case is there any impropriety or injustice in leaving the measuring rod to be sought at the trial. In the varied activities of modern life it would be impracticable to provide it in advance.

Once it is established that the *ratio decidendi* of *Allan* v. *Howman* is unsound and that a statutory enactment does not necessarily lose its force by its failure to provide in advance a standard by which the conduct of the accused is to be measured, this stated case is plain sailing. As your Lordship has observed, there may be enactments so defectively worded that it is impossible to spell a relevant charge out of them. This particular regulation presents no such problem. There is, moreover, very full specification of the *modus* and indeed no question of relevancy in its secondary sense of lack of specification was raised. I wish, however, to reserve my opinion as to whether a complaint following literally the terms of a widely drawn and unspecific enactment might be successfully attacked on the ground of absence of fair notice, either as irrelevant in the strict sense of the word or as lacking in specification. On this aspect issues of some nicety might arise, the solution of which would turn on the precise terms of the enactment and the relative complaint."

Appeal dismissed.

NOTE

On specification in statutory offences, see generally Renton and Brown, paras. 13-43 to 13-47, and also paras. 13-52 to 13-57 for a discussion of the law on exceptions and qualifications in describing statutory offences and the situation where an offence is said to have been committed in a special capacity. See also, *Smith* v. *Elsey*, 1983 S.L.T. (Sh. Ct.) 34.

CHAPTER 12

CITATION AND RECORD

a.   Citation—formalities

Once the complaint is duly prepared, the next usual step is service. Various modes of service are competent, on which see generally the 1975 Act, ss. 315-319. It is essential that, where citation is necessary, the formalities thereof should be properly carried out, otherwise the proceedings may be imperilled.

1.   **Beattie v. McKinnon**
1977 J.C. 64

An accused person was convicted of a statutory offence and appealed by stated case.

LORD JUSTICE-CLERK (WHEATLEY): "The appellant was charged with the statutory offence of a contravention of section 6 (1) of the Road Traffic Act 1972 (cap. 20) on 4th March 1976, and by reason of the provisions of section 331 (1) of the Criminal Procedure (Scotland) Act 1975 (cap. 21) proceedings had to be commenced within six months of that date. By subsection (3) of that section proceedings are deemed to be commenced on the date on which a warrant to apprehend or cite the accused is granted, if such warrant is executed without delay.

On 16th August 1976 a police officer served a copy of the complaint in the appropriate statutory form on the appellant personally. However, apart from the fact that the copy signature of the clerk of court assigning the diet had not been inserted in the copy complaint, the date when the appellant had to appear in court was also omitted. There was a date stamp '31 August 1976' on the front of the copy complaint, but it was not maintained, nor could it be, that this was due notice to or proper citation of the appellant to appear in court on 31st August 1976. On that date, however, the case was called in court and understandably neither the appellant nor anyone on his behalf appeared. The Procurator-fiscal produced an *ex facie* valid execution of citation by a police officer, and on the strength of that the Sheriff granted a warrant to apprehend the appellant under section 338 of the 1975 Act. This warrant was not executed, but in due course the appellant came to hear about it. He consulted his solicitor who contacted the Procurator-fiscal and the latter arranged for the appellant to appear in court in answer to the complaint on Monday 20th September 1976. On that day the appellant and

377

his solicitor arrived at the court only to find the building shut, it being the Autumn holiday in Paisley. They turned up on the following day and the case was called, whereupon the appellant's solicitor submitted a plea to the competency of the proceedings basically on the ground that the citation was inept in respect that no date of a diet was contained therein. The Sheriff repelled this plea for reasons which will be stated later, whereupon a plea of not guilty was tendered on behalf of the appellant and a diet of trial was fixed for 20th December 1976. When the case was called on this date, the plea of not guilty was withdrawn and a plea of guilty tendered. The Sheriff thereupon admonished the appellant and disqualified him from holding or obtaining a driving licence for one year and endorsed his licence. The question stated by the Sheriff for the opinion of the Court is: 'Was I right in repelling the objection to the competency of the proceedings?'

The Sheriff explains that he accepts that the appellant was not properly cited, but states that he can see no reason why that should invalidate the appearance of the appellant to answer the charge on 21st September 1976. He considers that the situation is covered by section 334 (6) of the Act of 1975 which enacts that it shall not be competent for any person appearing to answer a complaint to plead want of due citation or informality therein or in the execution thereof. Moreover, he expresses the view that on the information provided to the Court the warrant to apprehend was properly granted and that the appellant's apprehension (he was never in fact apprehended) and subsequent appearance in Court were entirely lawful; and that any defects in the earlier citation were superseded by the granting of the warrant and the actual appearance in Court of the appellant who had been served with a copy of the complaint.

The alleged offence took place on 4th March 1976 and accordingly proceedings had to be commenced by midnight on 3rd September 1976 (section 331 (1)). Proceedings could be deemed to have commenced on the date on which the warrant to apprehend or the warrant to cite was granted if executed without delay (section 331 (3)). The learned Advocate-depute accepted that the citation was inept by reason of the failure to state a date therein, thereby echoing the view of the Sheriff, and also reflecting the view of this Court. He argued, however, that the defect in the citation could not be pleaded by the appellant because of his appearance in court on 21st September 1976 and the provisions of section 334 (6) of the Act. That being so proceedings in this case must be deemed to have commenced when the copy complaint and the imperfect citation were served on the appellant on 16th August 1976, which was within the statutory period of six months.

In order successfully to invoke the provisions of section 334 (6) the Crown must establish that the omission to state a date in the citation was 'want of due citation or informality therein.' The absence of a date cannot be said to be an informality. It was crucial for the appellant to know when he had to appear in court and he could not possibly know this from the citation served on him. 'Want of due citation' may be a temporal matter— for instance, failure to observe the proper *induciae*, e.g., in relation to sections 315 (2) and 319 (1) of the Act. In our opinion, it cannot be held that failure to state the date on which an accused is to appear in court is simply want of 'due citation.' It is not citation at all. For these reasons we are of opinion that section 334 (6) is not applicable in the circumstances of this case and, that being so, proceedings cannot be deemed to have commenced in this case on 16th August 1976. The Advocate-depute did not argue that even if this were so the proceedings could be deemed to be commenced on 31st August 1976 when the warrant to apprehend was granted, which was still within the six-month statutory period, but as the Sheriff seemed to think that they could, we shall deal with that point too. The warrant to apprehend must presumably have been granted by the Sheriff under section 338 (c) of the Act. That section reads: 'Where the accused on a summary prosecution fails to appear at a diet of which he has received intimation, or to which he has been cited, the following provisions shall apply (c) the Court may grant warrant to apprehend the accused.' The appellant here neither received intimation of the diet nor was cited to attend on 31st August 1976. The prerequisite of the application of the section was accordingly not satisfied. While there was *ex facie* evidence that the appellant had been cited to attend on that date, *de facto* he had not. The section does not say that the Court may grant the warrant to apprehend if satisfied that the accused has received intimation or has been cited to attend at the diet. It says that non-appearance when the accused *has* received intimation or *has been* cited to the diet authorises the granting of a warrant to apprehend. A warrant granted when these conditions have not been fulfilled is not in our opinion a warrant which can be founded on to date the commencement of proceedings in terms of section 331 (3).

We accordingly hold that the proceedings were not commenced within the statutory six-month period and that the objection to the competency was well founded. We therefore answer the question of law in the negative."

Appeal allowed.

NOTE

So the lack of proper citation was fatal to the Crown case. Forms of complaint and citation are now regulated by the Act of Adjournal (Forms of Complaint) 1978. Furthermore, some statutes, such as the Road Traffic Act 1972, make special provision for service of particular documents, such as notices of intended prosecution.

2. McGlynn v. Stewart
1974 S.L.T. 230

An accused person was convicted of careless driving and appealed by stated case.

LORD JUSTICE-CLERK (WHEATLEY): "The answer to the questions raised in this stated case turns on the interpretation of s. 179 (2) of the Road Traffic Act 1972 and its application to the circumstances of the case.

On 11th August 1972 the appellant was the driver of a motor car which was in collision with another motor car on a public road on the Island of Islay. After the accident the appellant was cautioned by the police that he need not make a statement, and that the facts would be reported to the Procurator-fiscal. He was given no other warning by the police. The appellant was at that time taking his annual holiday in Islay, something which he has done for the past nine years. He gave to the police both his home address in Pencaitland in East Lothian and his holiday address in Islay, informing them that he would be at the latter address until 2nd September 1972. He did not have his driving licence with him, and in view of the information that he would be in Islay until 2nd September 1972 a police constable marked the appropriate form H.O./R.T.I. 'to be produced after 2/9/72.' This information was conveyed by the police to the respondent, who is the Procurator-fiscal for the area, with his office at Campbeltown. On 18th August 1972 the respondent sent a notice of intended prosecution addressed to the appellant at his Pencaitland address. The appellant did not receive this notice, which was returned to the respondent marked 'no answer.' As a matter of courtesy the respondent sent a second but out-of-time notice on 1st September 1972. This was the only notice received by the appellant.

When the trial took place it was argued by counsel for the appellant that there could not be a conviction of the charge under s. 3 of the Road Traffic Act 1972, which had been preferred against the appellant, since the provisions of s. 179 (2) of that Act had not been obtempered. Section 179 (2) provides that a person prosecuted for an offence under the section shall not be convicted unless . . . '(c) within . . . fourteen days a notice of the intended prosecution specifying the nature of the alleged offence and the time and place where it is alleged to have been committed, was (ii) . . . served on him or on the person, if any, registered as the keeper of the vehicle at the time of the commission of the offence; and the notice shall be deemed for the purposes of para. (c) above to have been served on any person if it was sent by registered post or recorded delivery service addressed to him at his last known address, notwithstanding that the notice was returned as undelivered or was for any other reason not received by him.'

Section 179 (3) provides that 'the requirement of subs. (2) above shall in every case be deemed to have been complied with unless and until the contrary is proved.'

The sheriff rejected this argument, holding, under reference to the case of *Phipps* v. *McCormick* [1972] R.T.R. 21, that the appellant's address at Pencaitland was the place where the appellant would normally expect to receive correspondence, and that a notice of intended prosecution sent to that address was in the circumstances a fulfilment of the requirement imposed by s. 179 (2). He then proceeded to convict the appellant of the charge under s. 3.

Two questions are submitted for the opinion of this court. The first is whether the notice of intended prosecution sent to the appellant on 18th August 1972 was addressed to him at his last known address in accordance with the provisions of s. 179 (2). The second is whether the sheriff was entitled to find the appellant guilty of a contravention of s. 3 of the 1972 Act.

It was not argued that the sheriff was not entitled to convict under s. 3 on the evidence adduced on the merits, but it was strongly argued that the conviction was bad because the provisions of s. 179 (2) had not been obtempered. Thus, the answer to the first question determines the answer to the second question. In *Phipps* v. *McCormick* (supra), Cook, J., giving the leading judgment, in which Lord Widgery, C.J. and Bean, J. concurred, said in relation to the corresponding provision of s. 241 (2) of the Road Traffic Act 1960 as amended by the Road Traffic Act 1962: 'It seems to me, however, that the purpose of the service provision in the subsection requiring that the notice should be served at the last known address is that the notice should be served at a place where he would normally expect to receive correspondence, an address which, from his point of view, has some degree of permanence.'

The Crown in this appeal, like the sheriff in the court below, founded strongly on this opinion as justifying an effective service on the appellant in this case. In *Phipps* v. *McCormick* the defendant was involved in a motor accident on 20th September 1970, out of which the proceedings arose. Following the accident he was admitted to hospital, a fact of which the prosecutor was aware. On 23rd September 1970 a notice of intended prosecution was sent by recorded delivery addressed to the defendant at his home. At the time when the notice was sent the defendant was still in hospital, but he was in fact discharged therefrom on the following day, 24th September 1970. There is nothing in the report to indicate that the prosecutor knew for how long the defendant would be in hospital. Cooke, J., held that in the circumstances the hospital did not satisfy the requirements of his formula, whereas the defendant's home address did.

In my opinion, the proper approach to the issue is to look at the intendment of the subsection. It is manifestly to provide a prospective accused with notice within a reasonable time of the intention to prosecute. In the interest of fairness this is plainly desirable, because if not only prevents the person involved from being kept unduly long in a state of suspense without knowing whether or not he is going to be prosecuted, but it enables him, if need be, to collect evidence for his defence at a time when the recollection of potential witnesses is fresh. The 'deeming' provisions of s. 179 (2) (c) were introduced originally in the 1962 Act to cover circumstances revealed by cases such as *McLeod* v. *Anderson*, 1961 J.C. 32, 1961 S.L.T. 297 in Scotland, and *R.* v. *London Quarter Sessions, ex p. Rossi* [1956] 1 Q.B. 682 in England. In regard to the latter—cf. Lord Parker, C.J., in *Burt* v. *Kirkcaldy* [1965] 1 All E.R. 741, at p. 743.

It is quite clear from the reported cases that although the intention of the subsection is to certiorate the prospective accused of the proposal to institute appropriate proceedings, the requirements of intimation may be satisfied in certain circumstances even if he has not personally received the notice or has not personally been served with it, e.g., if it has been received on his behalf by an agent. Thus the non-receipt personally of the notice is not in itself any criterion, a fact which is underlined by the final words of the subsection. What then is the construction to be given to the phrase 'his last known address'? It is not necessarily the permanent residence, or for that matter the permanent business address. In my opinion it must also mean an address at which it is reasonably to be expected that the person on whom the notice is served will receive it. Hence the conditions desiderated by Cooke, J., namely (1) that it is a place where a person would normally expect to receive correspondence, and (2) that it is an address which, from the person's point of view, has some degree of permanence. Thus, if a person is absent from home for short periods on business or pleasure, posting of the notice to his home address would normally satisfy the requirements of the sub-section. Manifestly, since the prosecutor cannot be expected to know the person's movements, there ought to be a place where it is reasonable to expect that a posted notice will be received by him. But is the sending of a notice to a person's normal home address sufficient to qualify for the provisions of the subsection in every case, or has each case to be considered on its own facts to see whether some other address is the appropriate one? In my opinion it must be the latter.

If the prosecutor is informed that the person will not be at his home address (at which he would normally receive correspondence) for the currency of the statutory period during which the notice has to be served, but will be at another stated address during that period, then, unless the statute otherwise requires, common sense as well as fairness seems to demand that the notice should be sent to the latter and not the former address. I doubt if Parliament intended that a notice would be good if sent to an address where it was known that it would not be received by the addressee, although there was another address where it was known that it would be received.

In the present case the prosecutor was informed that the appellant would be at the address in Islay during the whole currency of the statutory period. When Cooke, J., referred to the address having some degree of permanence, he was presumably recognising that this was a relative term, depending on circumstances. So far as the prosecutor knew, the appellant was going to be in Islay during the whole of the effective period and beyond, and so during that period there was going to be permanence of address in Islay, relatively speaking. Accordingly, in my view, the address in Islay, (1) was the last address known to the prosecutor for the purpose of this statutory notice, (2) was the place where for the purpose of *this* correspondence (i.e., the notice) the appellant would normally expect to receive it, and (3) had a sufficient degree of permanence, relatively speaking, to make it the effective one for the receipt of the notice as part of his correspondence during this period. I am, therefore, of the opinion that in the circumstances here present the appellant has proved that his home address did not satisfy the provisions of s. 179 (2), whereas the Islay address did. I would add that if, for any reason, the appellant had left Islay for home (or elsewhere) within the statutory period and before the notice was served, without informing the prosecutor, and the notice was thereafter timeously posted to the Islay address, the appellant could not have successfully challenged the validity of the service on the ground that it should have been served at his home address, in view of the provisions of s. 179 (4). I would accordingly answer both questions of law in the negative."

Appeal allowed.

NOTE

This case of course relates only to the specific wording of section 179 of the Road Traffic Act 1972. The phrase "last known address" is not used in section 316 of the 1975 Act. By section 334(6) of that Act, it shall not be competent for any person appearing to answer a complaint, or for a solicitor appearing for the accused in his absence, to plead want of due citation or informality therein or in the execution thereof. But see also *Laird* v. *Anderson* (1895) 2 Adam 18, where it was held that where the mistake renders the proceedings fundamentally null, appearance by the accused does not cure the defect.

Section 311(5) of the 1975 Act requires service of a notice of penalties for a statutory offence along with the complaint. This has caused problems in relation to endorsement of convictions on driving licences (and now endorsement of penalty points). Are such endorsements "penalties" for the purpose of section 311 (5)? For a discussion of this question see *Scott* v. *Annan* 1981 S.L.T. 90 and *Tudhope* v. *Stirrup*, unreported, c/o Circ. A40/82, *post* Chap. 16.

b. Is citation essential?

In normal practice, whether the offence is statutory or at common law, the accused is served with the complaint prior to his being called upon to plead. But this does not appear to be essential.

Kelly v. Rae

1917 J.C. 12

An accused person was convicted of a statutory offence and appealed by bill of suspension.

LORD JUSTICE-CLERK (SCOTT DICKSON): "The complainer's senior counsel ultimately supported the bill of suspension on two only of the grounds set forth in his printed case. Of these grounds the two he has selected, although I do not think them good grounds, are undoubtedly the best.

The first is that no complaint was served upon the complainer. I think the objection is a bad one. I can find no warrant in the Summary Jurisdiction Act of 1908 for the proposition that, until a complaint is formally served upon an accused person, the proceedings against him are not initiated, and that, consequently, everything which is done in the case, unless and until a complaint has been *served*, is null and void. In this case the complainer on Saturday 12th August 1916 was arrested by the police *in flagrante delicto*, and was charged with an offence under the Street Betting Act, 1906, section 1. On the following Monday he was brought before the magistrate, and a charge of committing the offence in question was made against him in his presence. He pled not guilty, and the Court adjourned the diet to the 21st, and (as the minutes of procedure bear) ordained the accused to appear then. Upon that day he appeared in Court, represented by a law-agent, and the complaint was read over to him. In my opinion this complied sufficiently with the statutory requirements anent the initiation of summary criminal proceedings.

Section 18 of the Summary Jurisdiction Act, 1908, provides that all proceedings shall be instituted by complaint in the form contained in Schedule C. That clearly is an imperative requirement, but no reference is there made to citation or service of the complaint. In section 29 it is provided that, where the accused is present at the first calling of the case, the complaint, or the substance thereof, shall be read to him. That seems to me to imply that service is not necessary, because, if service were an essential, there would be no reason for providing that the complaint should be read. What, however, is still more striking, is the provision in section 32 (2), that, in the circumstances there dealt with, 'the prosecutor shall, if desired by the accused, furnish him with a copy of the complaint if he has not already got a copy.' It seems to me that that provision is consistent only with the view that in certain circumstances service of the complaint is not an essential to the institution of the proceedings. I think one of the cases—it may, indeed, be the only case—where such service can be dispensed with is, where the accused is, as in the present case, apprehended *in flagrante delicto*. This seems to be in accordance with what has been an ancient practice in summary proceedings of this kind. I think that practice is founded on good sense and on good law, and that no reason has been stated for our interfering with it. I am, therefore, of opinion that the suspension, so far as founded upon that ground, ought to be refused."

Appeal refused.

NOTE

To a certain extent, this case has been overtaken by section 311(5) of the 1975 Act which *requires* service of a complaint and notice of penalty in relation to a statutory offence, whether the accused is to be cited or in custody. But these statutory provisions apply only to statutory offences. The only other provision which seems to *require* service of a complaint is section 357(1)(a) of the 1975 Act, which relates to the situation where the prosecutor wishes to libel a previous conviction. So, where the accused is a first offender charged at common law, it appears that technically no service of a complaint is necessary. Thankfully for *inter alios* duty solicitors, this situation is never now encountered in practice. Proceeding without a complaint may constitute oppression—see *Carlin* v. *Malloch* (1896) 2 Adam 98.

c. The record of proceedings

In summary cases this is governed by section 359 of the 1975 Act which provides: "Proceedings in a summary prosecution shall be conducted summarily *viva voce* and, except where otherwise provided, no record need be kept of the proceedings other than the complaint, the plea, a note of any documentary evidence produced, and the conviction and sentence or other finding of the court: provided that any objections to the competency or relevancy of the complaint or proceedings, or to the competency of admissibility of evidence, shall, if either party desires it, be entered in the record of the proceedings." The minutes of procedure are kept by the clerk of court.

1. Barr v. Ingram
1977 S.L.T. 173

An accused person appealed by bill of suspension against his conviction, on the ground that the proceedings were fundamentally null. His trial had proceeded in stages on the due date, with various interruptions throughout the day so that the court might deal with other business. None of these interruptions were treated as adjournments nor minuted by the sheriff clerk. When the bill came before the High Court, it was conceded that the interruptions were effectively adjournments.

OPINION OF THE COURT: "Despite the terms of the first plea-in-law for the complainer in the bill, and the averments in support of it, his counsel did not dispute that the sheriff had adjourned the trial on the various occasions referred to or that it was competent for him to do so. The gravamen of his complaint was that these adjournments were not minuted and authenticated on each occasion, as they ought to have been. His argument entailed an assertion from which he did not shrink, that when an adjournment to a later period on the same day, was granted during the course of the day on which an accused had been cited to attend for his trial, not only should the adjournment be minuted, but the time on that day to which the trial was adjourned should also be minuted. If, when that time arrived, the court was not in a position to re-start the trial, the case should nevertheless be called and further adjourned to a later specified time, again to be minuted and authenticated in the minute of proceedings. Incidentally, if at that point another case was in progress, the same procedure would have to be followed for that case.

The learned advocate-depute accepted that if a trial had to be continued from one day to another, the date and time of the adjourned diet should be recorded and authenticated in the minute of proceedings. He submitted, however, that this did not apply to adjournments during the course of the day on which the accused had been cited to attend for trial. An accused is required by his citation to attend court on the date specified therein in the knowledge that his case must be dealt with that day or continued formally to another day when the same considerations would apply. When he attends on the day of citation he can object to any continuation or adjournment proposed, it being for the court to decide whether it should be granted. A citation to attend court on a particular day extends to midnight on that day. The considerations underlying the fixing of a peremptory diet are threefold: (1) to secure fairness to the accused and not prejudice him by not having a fixed date for the hearing of his case; (2) convenience of the public—e.g. witnesses who are under citation to attend the trial; and (3) to avoid delays in the hearing of the case. Accordingly, if the court adjourns the trial at any time to a later hour on that day in order to dispose of other business, the accused is still under citation to be in attendance on that day, and there is no real risk of prejudice or unwarranted delay in the disposal of the case, since the basic underlying considerations referred to are observed. Another consideration, however, was the reasonable expedition of the court's whole business for the day. In the instant case what were described by counsel for the complainer as 'interruptions' but what were in fact unminuted adjournments by the court were for the general convenience, since other people had been brought to the court on the same day, as the history of events narrated by the sheriff principal disclosed. So far as the complainer was concerned there was no loss of certainty about when his case would be heard, namely on that day, and no real inconvenience had been suffered by him. In the circumstances the absence of a recorded entry of the adjournments in the minute of proceedings was not fatal to the convictions and sentences.

We are only concerned here with adjournments during the day on which the complainer was cited to attend the court. In that narrow context, the submission by complainer's counsel was based on the decision in *Corstorphine* [1910 1 S.L.T. 86] and the dicta of Lord Justice-Clerk Macdonald and Lord Low therein, to which reference will be made shortly. The advocate-depute conceded that if the particular passage in the Lord Justice-Clerk's judgment correctly represented the law, there was no answer to the submission made by complainer's counsel, since admittedly the adjournments here had not been minuted. He argued, however, that the passage in question did not properly represent the law and should not be followed.

We accordingly turn to examine the case of *Corstorphine*. In that case an accused was charged with different offences in two separate summary complaints. On the conclusion of the evidence in the first case the sheriff-substitute found the accused guilty but delayed sentence until the conclusion of the evidence in the second case on the same day, whereupon he proceeded to sentence the accused on the first charge. There was no written record of the adjournment in the first case, and the court suspended the conviction and sentence on the ground that this omission was fatal to the proceedings. The passage in the Lord Justice-Clerk's opinion on which counsel for the complainer founded is to be found in 1910 1 S.L.T. at p. 87: 'In my opinion the proceedings in the first case fell, in respect that no means were taken to keep them in life by adjourning them either to a later period of the same day or to a new day. It is quite true that the first case was both tried and finally disposed of on the same day; but that does not seem to me to make any practical difference, because a case must be kept going, either by its being proceeded with or by its being formally adjourned. That was not done, and I am of opinion that the omission is fatal to the proceedings in the first case.'

Lord Ardwell agreed, saying that as far as he knew it was universal practice both in the sheriff court and in the High Court that all adjournments must be minuted. Lord Low accepted that if the adjournment was to a later date it had to be minuted but had obvious doubts on the applicability of that rule to an adjournment to a later time on the same day, regarding that as too technical a point. However, apparently in deference to the longer experience of his colleagues in such matters, he did not dissent from the judgment proposed.

If the decision in *Corstorphine* was correct, and the dictum of the Lord Justice-Clerk therein correctly states the law, then ex concessu the omission to record the adjournments in the minute of proceedings in the instant case was fatal to the proceedings.

Counsel for the complainer maintained that *Corstorphine* was merely illustrative of a cardinal rule which had been enunciated by Hume and endorsed as early as *H.M. Advocate* v. *Fraser*, and had been approved by Lord Justice-Clerk Cooper in *Hull* v. *H.M. Advocate*, 1945 S.L.T. at p. 202. Moreover, *Corstorphine* had stood unchallenged in the 68 years since it was decided, and the Lord Justice-Clerk had stated in his opinion therein that the rule—which was a fixed rule—had always been one which our courts had observed (1910 1 S.L.T. at p. 86). That was still the position in our courts both in principle and in practice. He sought recent support for his contention in the case of *Law* v. *H.M. Advocate*, but the facts in that case were different, and the irregularity which foundered the conviction was an interruption to deal with another case without adjourning the case that was being heard.

While it would appear from Lord Justice-Clerk Macdonald's opinion that he considered that all and every adjournment required to be minuted, counsel was ultimately constrained to admit that, standing the decision in *Tocher* v. *H.M. Advocate* the rule was not universally applicable. When that seemed to weaken his argument, he sought to make a distinction between what he called 'physical interruptions' and 'procedural interruptions'. Whether such a distinction is justified in principle only requires to be considered if the extension of the rule by Lord Justice-Clerk Macdonald was correct.

The question is not what is the rule but how far does it extend? If the adjournment is to another day, it has been clearly established by an anthology of decisions that the adjournment must be minuted. The rule applies whether the procedure is solemn or summary: *McLean* v. *Falconer* (1895) 1 Adam 564, per Lord Adam at p. 567. Does the rule apply to adjournments within the day of citation?

The recording of adjournments is not one of the matters which successive statutes have required to be inserted into the record of proceedings—cf. s. 42 of the Summary Jurisdiction (Scotland) Act 1908; s. 38 of the Summary Jurisdiction (Scotland) Act 1954; and s. 359 of the Criminal Procedure (Scotland) Act 1975. The rule is founded on common law, and it was accepted by both parties here that its inclusion in the matters which had to be recorded fell within the phrase 'except where otherwise provided', in all the forementioned sections. The Lord Justice-Clerk in *Corstorphine* so treated it. The genesis of the rule is said to be found in Hume's *Commentaries*, vol. ii at p. 263. What is said there is: 'the diet of a criminal process is a peremptory diet . . . Unless expressly continued by an act of Court on the day of compearance, the libel must be called therefore on that day, and in some way or other disposed of; otherwise the particular action, or *instance* as we call it, perishes, and can never afterwards be stirred or resumed . . . unless the diet be continued to another day, by an act of Court. But so it may be, by an entry in the Book of Adjournal. . . The reason is obvious why the diet is peremptory in a criminal process . . . [it] requires the personal presence of the accused, whose anxiety and distress must be considered: Not to mention the witnesses and persons of assize, who cannot be kept waiting indefinitely, out of indulgence to the prosecutor, who ought to be finally resolved and fully prepared, before he stir in a matter of such importance'. The rule thus stated clearly relates only to a continuation to another day, and does not relate to a case which is 'disposed of in some way or another' on the day of the peremptory diet, as was the case here. This passage in Hume was the basis of the views expressed in Alison and Macdonald's *Criminal Law*, and in *Hull* itself and in the reported cases cited by Lord Justice-Clerk Cooper therein (1945 S.L.T. at p. 202) (with the exception of *Corstorphine*) the adjournment in question was one to another day. When the rule was being considered, as for example by Lord Justice-General McNeill and Lord Justice-Clerk Hope in *Fraser*, it was in relation to an adjournment to a future date.

It was said by counsel for the complainer that Lord Justice-Clerk Cooper had endorsed the decision in *Corstorphine*, but Lord Cooper was referring to the passage in Hume cited supra and was dealing with the position where the diet is not called or duly adjourned or continued on the date of citation. The Lord Justice-Clerk in *Corstorphine* (with the approval of Lord Ardwall) stands alone in applying the rule to an adjournment or continuation to a later hour on the date of the peremptory diet. The decision in *Corstorphine* was in direct conflict with the decision in the earlier case of *McIntyre* v. *Linton*, where another trial had been interposed during the trial of the accused, but the court held that this in itself was no ground for a suspension. There were no opinions delivered in that case, and it was not referred to either in argument or in the opinions in *Corstorphine*. Nonetheless it was a case to which attention should have been paid, and reasons stated (and if need be expedients adopted) for giving a contradictory decision. Lord Justice-Clerk Macdonald, after examining the rule, simply extended it to adjournments during the date of citation without giving any reasons for doing so, and without examining the considerations which justify the application of the rule to an adjournment to a future date to see whether such considerations require the extension of the rule to adjournments to a later hour on the day of citation. Some of these considerations were examined by Hume and by Lord Justice-Clerk Hope in *Fraser* at p. 16, and these and others were submitted to this court by the advocate-depute as noted supra. In our opinion the dangers and/or the prejudice which the rule was devised to avoid relate only to an adjournment to a later day and do not arise when an adjournment is.simply to a later hour on the date of the citation. The reasons why it was thought necessary to have the adjournment minuted in the former type of case do not arise in the latter one. The fact that the case is either completed on the date of citation or is continued by an adjournment duly minuted to a later date is sufficient to give an accused adequate protection. We are accordingly of opinion that the extension of the rule by *Corstorphine* to adjournments during the date of citation was not justified and must be overruled. Thus the fact that an adjournment on the day of citation is not minuted is not per se a ground of suspension. If the practice of minuting such an adjournment had been one of long standing and universal application there might have been difficulties in altering it. It would seem from the case of *McIntyre*, however, that the practice was not universal in those earlier days, and it is clear from the sheriff principal's report that 'interruptions' or adjournments during the day of citation, such as those complained of, are not minuted in the sheriff court today—a practice which is not outwith our own experience. The operation of the *Corstorphine* rule would have made the work in some of the already over-burdened sheriff courts today an almost intolerable task, but if it had been a rule which the principles of the common law required to be observed only legislation could have altered it. It is with some satisfaction, therefore, that we have been able to find that the *Costorphine* view of the law is not justified.

We accordingly refuse to pass the bill."

Appeal refused.

NOTE

One can almost hear the sighs of relief from sheriff clerks up and down the country. Indeed, the next case again shows the High Court's unwillingness to overrule convictions on excessively technical grounds.

2. Pettigrew v. Ingram
1982 S.L.T. 435; 1982 S.C.C.R. 259

An accused person appealed by bill of suspension against his conviction.

LORD JUSTICE-CLERK (WHEATLEY): "An accused person presented a bill of suspension to the High Court of Justiciary in which he craved suspension of a pretended conviction and sentence recorded against him at Forfar Sheriff Court, on the ground that the sheriff clerk had failed to minute until

18 September 1981 an adjournment of the proceedings ordered on 17
September 1981. The complainer argued that this failure rendered the
whole proceedings fundamentally null. The facts are not in dispute. On 10
September 1981 the complainer appeared in court to answer the complaint
and pled guilty. On that date the sheriff deferred sentence until 17
September and ordained the complainer to appear to produce his licence.
When the case called on 17 September, the complainer was not present and
the sheriff again deferred sentence until 24 September 1981 and ordained
the complainer to appear on that date. On 24 September the complainer
appeared with his solicitor, when the sheriff fined him £50 and disqualified
him from driving for a period of three years. The sheriff clerk did not on 17
September 1981 record in the minute of proceedings the adjournment
ordered by the sheriff on that date, and the explanation given by the
respondent is that, due to pressure of business, the sheriff clerk was unable
to minute this adjournment until the morning of 18 September 1981. It is
not disputed that the adjournment was ordered by the sheriff on 17
September, but the submission by counsel for the complainer was as
previously noted that that order was of no effect unless recorded in the
minute of proceedings before midnight on 17 September.

There is no doubt that the minuting of the adjournment ordered by the
sheriff on 17 September was essential to the validity of these proceedings—
Barr v. Ingram, 1977 S.L.T. 173 at p. 176,; but the question is whether the
failure to minute the adjournment eo die is a fundamental nullity or merely
an irregularity which is not fatal to the validity of the proceedings.

Section 430(1) of the Criminal Procedure (Scotland) Act 1975 (hereinafter referred to as 'the 1975 Act') requires 'any order of a court of summary
jurisdiction . . . [to] be entered in the record of the proceedings in the form,
as nearly as may be, of the appropriate form contained in Part V of
Schedule 2 to the Summary Jurisdiction (Scotland) Act 1954 or in an Act of
Adjournal under this Act, which shall be sufficient warrant for all execution
thereon and for the clerk of court to issue extracts containing such executive
clauses as may be necessary for implement thereof'. The section re-enacts
verbatim s. 56 of the Summary Jurisdiction (Scotland) Act 1954, which
itself was a re-enactment of s. 53 of the Summary Jurisdiction (Scotland)
Act 1908. Any doubt whether the word 'order' in s. 430(1) of the 1975 Act
includes an order adjourning the diet would seem to be removed by
reference to Pt. V of Sched. 2 to the 1954 Act, which includes a form of
entry in 'the minutes of procedure' for adjournment. So, on the basis that s.
430(1) of the 1975 Act requires adjournments of diets to be entered in the
minutes of procedure, neither that subsection nor any other statutory
provision requires that a record of an order of court adjourning a diet must
be made and signed on the day when the order was made. This is
undoubtedly the proper procedure, but it is not required expressly or
impliedly by statute.

The answer to the question whether the adjournment requires to be
minuted on the day on which the court made the order can be found in the
case of Furnheim v. Watson, 1946 S.L.T. 297; 1946 J.C. 99. In that case
there was a delay of 16 days in recording the conviction and sentence of an

accused, owing to the absence of the clerk on holiday, yet the court refused to quash the conviction on the ground of fundamental nullity. The Lord Justice-Clerk (Cooper) said this (1946 S.L.T. at p. 301): 'Now, I am extremely reluctant in this or in any other case to attempt to lay down rigid cast-iron rules to regulate the day-to-day practice of inferior criminal Courts; but, it does appear to me that the Act of 1908, though it nowhere in express terms prescribes after what interval the record or minute of the proceedings may be signed by the clerk or by the Judge, plainly implies that that shall be done as soon as reasonably possible, and, I should think, in almost every case on the day on which the sentence is pronounced or order made. I do not attempt by any generalisation to state the rule more strictly than that. If that is the rule—the rule of good statutory practice—and if in particular it is essential, as I think it is, that the authentication of the record should, in any event, be complete before extract or execution, then the delay which occurred in this case from 4 August until 20 August, a period of 16 days, attributable merely to the fact of the absence of the depute clerk on holiday, was quite unjustifiable, and I do not think that this Court can do otherwise than condemn laxity of the type which this case displays and which in some cases might be fatal to the proceedings. But while that is so, the question which remains for us as the serious question is—what is to be the effect upon the proceedings which have taken place in this case?' Later on his Lordship said: 'Finally, it is, I think, necessary to note that in this instance we are not concerned with a breach of an exact statutory requirement, for, as I have observed, there is no exact statutory requirement prescribing when the record must be authenticated.' He concluded: 'I suggest to your Lordships that this is a case where, while we can certainly hold that the proceedings were irregular and characterise them as such, nevertheless the interests of justice do not require that these proceedings should be set aside. On the contrary, on a fair view of the general obligation imposed on the Court by section 75 of the Act of 1908, it is, in my view, right that we should, while condemning the irregularity, decline to visit it with the extreme penalty.' The general obligation to which the Lord Justice-Clerk referred in the context of *Furnheim* was the penultimate provision of s. 75 of the 1908 Act that no conviction should be quashed unless the High Court was of opinion that the accused had been prejudiced in his defence on the merits and that a miscarriage of justice had resulted thereby. This provision appeared in s. 454(2) of the 1975 Act but was repealed by para. 14 of Sched. 3 to the Criminal Justice (Scotland) Act 1980 and replaced in the context of this bill in more general terms by s. 453A(1), which relates to miscarriage of justice in criminal proceedings. There is, in our opinion, nothing in the summary procedure legislation since 1908 which affects the statement of the law by the Lord Justice-Clerk in *Furnheim*, a statement with which we respectfully agree. We consider that this was a statement of general applicability and was not confined to the circumstances of that particular case. On that view we regard it as apposite to the circumstances of the instant case.

The authorities primarily relied upon by counsel for the complainer related to the peremptory nature of criminal diets and the fact that if a diet is not called or duly adjourned or continued on the date in the citation the instance falls—Lord Justice-Clerk Cooper in *Hull* v. *H.M. Advocate*, 1945 S.L.T. 202; 1945. We do not require to follow counsel through that tract of authority, which is not in dispute. If counsel was right in his submission that the oral intimation in court on 17 September of the adjournment to 24 September was not sufficient to keep the instance alive after midnight on the 17 September because the adjournment had not been minuted by then, he would of course succeed. But in view of the decision which we have reached regarding the minuting of the adjournment, which was executed before the adjournment diet was reached, the diet was duly adjourned on 17 September. That kept the instance alive and the proceedings on 24 September were accordingly valid. On any view there was not, and could not be, any suggestion that this delay had prejudiced the complainer, who had pled guilty, nor could it be said that what was done here had resulted in a miscarriage of justice. We therefore refuse to pass the bill."

Appeal refused.

NOTE

As with many procedural niceties, the crucial question is thus whether the accused has suffered any prejudice. Minuting should of course be done at the time, and errors in the record may be corrected under section 439 of the 1975 Act, as amended by s. 20 of the 1980 Act. Prior to that amendment, such correction could only be done prior to execution of of the finding of the court, a point which caused difficulty in *Kelly* v. *MacLeod*, 1960 J.C. 88, where the accused was sentenced to sixty days imprisonment, his licence was ordered to be endorsed and he was disqualified from driving for 10 years. Only the imprisonment was minuted at the time; some days later (after the accused had started his jail sentence) the additional parts of the sentence were entered in the minutes. On appeal, the High Court suspended the endorsation and disqualification, holding that there had been execution of the finding.

Now, errors after execution may be corrected under the authority of the sentencing court: s. 439(2)(*b*) of the 1975 Act.

3.   Jacobs and Another v. Hart
(1900) 3 Adam 131

An accused person was charged with stealing 600 Italian liras to the value of £24 sterling. Certain Italian and Scots banknotes were produced during the trial, but the record of proceedings did not record that fact. The accused appealed against his conviction.

LORD McLAREN: "The Summary Jurisdiction Acts, while exempting the sheriff or magistrate trying the case from the duty of preserving a note of the evidence, directs him to note the documentary evidence put in at the trial, and that in the form set forth in a schedule annexed to the Act of 1864. Now, although the words used in the schedule are slightly different, I take it that we must interpret the words there used as being identical in meaning with the words used in the enacting section.

In this case the charge was the theft of 600 liras (Italian money), and the objection to the conviction is that certain bank-notes produced in evidence are of the nature of documentary evidence and ought to have been noted on the record. I suppose, although we are not directly informed, that the Italian notes produced were represented to be the money alleged to be stolen, and the question is whether notes alleged to be stolen and produced in proof of the theft, are on a fair construction of the statute, documentary evidence required to be noted.

While I am unable to agree with Lord Adam in the result of his opinion, I think we are at least in agreement on the question of principle, that there may be things stolen and referred to in evidence and yet not required to be noted as documentary evidence. The case of a printed book was referred to, and I may remark that the person whose pocket is picked may be able to identify the book by its binding, or other external marks, without the book being read or even opened. In such a case it would be absurd to say that the book was put in as documentary evidence. In the present case I do not think that the notes produced were documentary evidence any more than a book, or gold or silver coin, or a watch with an inscription on it, because in all those cases the inscription, if read at all, is only read for the purpose of identifying the thing and not for using its contents as evidence.

I venture to suggest as the true criterion for the determination of what is or is not documentary evidence requiring to be noted; the question, 'Is it necessary that the judge should read the contents of the writing produced, or is it only shewn to the witnesses for the purposes of identification?' I cannot see that there is any difference in legal effect between the production of the notes stolen in the case and the production of gold or silver coin in any other case where money is alleged to be stolen. The judge may look at the shilling or sovereign to satisfy himself that it is genuine, or that it corresponds with the description of the articles libelled as stolen. Part of the process of identification may be that he or the witness may have to read the inscription on the coin, not because that is documentary evidence, but because you identify the coin by means of the written and pictorial marks upon it.

A banker or money-changer is doubtless familiar with the external appearance of the notes of all the leading States, and he may be able to distinguish a real note from a counterfeit without being able to read the language in which the obligation is written. Many people who cannot read or write know a bank note and its denomination: to such persons the note is certainly not documentary evidence. It is not necessary that the judge should personally inspect the notes if he is satisfied with the statement of the expert witness that they are Italian notes. But if the notes are documentary evidence, it would be the duty of the judge to read the printed words which are said to be evidence.

What I have said applies equally to the Scotch notes which were given to the accused in exchange for the Italian notes. These, in my opinion, are not documents which the judge is required to note. I think the Note of Suspension should be refused."

Appeal refused.

NOTE

Lord Adam dissented from the view expressed by Lord McLaren and the Lord Justice-General. For a discussion of this case and the nature of the documentary evidence, see Renton and Brown, paras. 14-75, 14-76.

Under section 353(2) of the 1975 Act it is provided that: "any order by any of the departments of state or government or any local authority or public body made under powers conferred by any statute, or a print or copy of such order, shall when produced in a summary prosecution be received in evidence of the due making, confirmation and existence of such order without being sworn to by any witness and without any further or other proof, but without prejudice to any right competent to the accused to challenge any such order as being *ultra vires* of the authority making it or on any other competent ground, and where any such order is referred to in the complaint it shall not be necessary to enter it in the record of proceedings as a documentary production." *Production* of the order is however vital.

4.   **Herkes v. Dickie**
1958 J.C. 51

A licensee was convicted of an offence under a local bye-law. He appealed by stated case.

LORD PATRICK: "The appellant was tried and convicted in the Police Court of the Burgh of Dumfries. The charge against him was that he sold by the hands of his servants three bottles of ale after one P.M. on New Year's day, that being the hour appointed by the licensing authority for the Burgh of Dumfries for the closing of premises licensed to sell exciseable liquor within the burgh, contrary to the terms of his certificate and the Licensing Act, 1921, section 4 (*a*).

Neither the Act nor the certificate prescribes the hour at which licensed premises shall cease to sell liquor on New Year's day. Section 4 forbids the sale of exciseable liquor except during the permitted hours. The certificate has the same effect. For specification of the permitted hours we must look elsewhere. Section 41 of the Licensing (Scotland) Act, 1903, empowers a Licensing Court to make bye-laws for, *inter alia*, closing licensed premises wholly or partially on New Year's day. It is said that the Licensing Court for the Burgh of Dumfries made bye-laws in 1931 and 1941 whereby all licensed premises within the burgh must be closed on New Year's day with the exception of such hours before one P.M. as are permitted hours, provided that exciseable liquor might be sold to any person lodging in the licence-holder's inn or hotel, or during such hours as are permitted on weekdays to travellers.

At the trial of the complaint before the magistrates the prosecutor closed his case without putting in evidence a copy of these alleged bye-laws, but in his address to the magistrates he referred to them in order to establish that a sale of exciseable liquor after one P.M. on New Year's day was a sale outwith the permitted hours, and therefore an offence. Counsel for the accused contended that the bye-laws had not been proved and consequently that no offence had been proved. The magistrates thought there was no need to prove the terms of the bye-laws which were within the knowledge of the Court, the licensing court being the magistrates of the burgh.

We were referred to a number of cases in which the question has been discussed whether bye-laws and orders of bodies other than Parliament must be put in evidence in the course of a criminal prosecution. These were *Todd* v. *Anderson* [(1912) 6 Adam 713], *Brander* v. *Mackenzie* [1915 J.C. 47], and *Macmillan* v. *McConnell* [1917 J.C. 43]. I need not consider these cases in detail, because it is conceded by counsel for the prosecutor that bye-laws made under the authority of the Licensing Acts must be proved by the prosecutor putting a copy of them in evidence before he closes his case, unless there is something in these Acts which can be construed as giving such bye-laws the status of an Act of Parliament, which of course does not require to be proved in any Court. Every one is presumed to know the statute law of the land.

Now, counsel for the prosecutor (Mr Johnston) was unable to point to any provision of the Licensing Act which had that effect. Apart from that fatal defect, subsection 41 (5) of the Licensing (Scotland) Act, 1903, provides that a copy of any bye-laws made under the section signed and certified by the clerk to a Licensing Court to be a true copy and to have been duly confirmed shall be evidence, until the contrary is proved, in all legal proceedings of the due making, confirmation, and existence of such bye-laws, without further or other proof. That plainly implies that the bye-laws have not the status of an Act of Parliament. If they had that status, there would be no need for the subsection.

Mr Johnston then suggested that in this matter of the proof of bye-laws in criminal proceedings we should, as he put it, 'start afresh' by dividing bye-laws into two categories, those in which the penalty was prescribed in the bye-law, in which case the bye-law must be proved, and those in which the penalty was prescribed in the statute empowering the making of the bye-law, in which case there should be no necessity to prove the bye-law. I can see no reason for adopting the presence or absence of a penalty in a bye-law as the test whether the bye-law need be proved. I suspect that the only reason for choosing this test is that it is one which would suit Mr Johnston's case, since the Licensing Acts do in fact prescribe the penalties for breach of the bye-laws made in virtue of them. I should have thought that an accused person was as interested in having it proved that there was a bye-law which created an offence as he was in having it proved that a bye-law prescribed a penalty. In any event there is no warrant in our law for dividing bye-laws into categories by the application of the test suggested.

A further argument for the prosecutor was that if no challenge was made of the relevancy of the complaint there was no necessity to prove the bye-laws. The basis of this argument was section 16 of the Summary Jurisdiction (Scotland) Act, 1954. That section deals with the form of complaints, and subsection (b) provides that the statement that an act was done contrary to a statute or order shall imply a statement that the statute or order applied to the circumstances existing at the time and place of the offence, that the accused was a person bound to observe the same, that any necessary preliminary procedure had been duly gone through, and that all the circumstances necessary to a contravention existed. The argument is wholly misconceived. The subsection is dealing solely with the form of complaints and pruning them of matters it was thought unnecessary to include in them. It does not deal with the proof of matters, and does not render unnecessary the proof of any matter which it would otherwise be necessary to prove.

The last point made by Mr Johnston on this branch of the case was that the magistrates could take judicial notice of the bye-laws in as much as the magistrates made them. Now these bye-laws were made in 1931 and 1941. It does not in the least appear that the magistrate who tries a case of alleged contravention of the bye-laws in 1958 took part in the making of them and has an exact knowledge of their contents. In any event if any matter requires to be proved in a criminal prosecution the want of proof of the matter cannot be mended by the private knowledge of the Judge. In my opinion, the prosecutor should have put a copy of the bye-laws, duly authenticated, in evidence before he closed his case. He did not do so and there was not evidence to warrant a conviction. That is sufficient for the disposal of the stated case. I express no opinion on other grounds of challenge of the conviction which were argued before us.

I suggest to your Lordships that we answer the question in the case in the negative."

Conviction quashed.

NOTE

This case is confined to the situation where the order relied on did not have statutory status. Acts of Parliament and statutory instruments do not of course have to be proved.

CHAPTER 13

PRELIMINARY OBJECTIONS, PLEADING AND TRIAL

a. Preliminary objections and pleading

If there are any preliminary objections to competency or relevancy, these should be dealt with at the first calling of the complaint. Section 334(1) of the 1975 Act provides *inter alia* that no such objections shall be allowed to be stated at any further diet in the case except with the leave of the court, which may be granted only on cause shown. The general principles of competency and relevancy discussed *supra* in ch. 8 apply equally to summary as to solemn procedure.

However an appeal court will take note of the situation where the complaint is fundamentally null, even if no preliminary objection has been stated, and this may lead to quashing of the conviction even although section 454 of the 1975 Act appears to exclude appeals based on alleged irrelevancy where the point has not been taken in the lower court.

1. O'Malley v. Strathern
1920 J.C. 74

An accused person was charged on summary complaint with an offence under the Spirits (Prices and Description) Order 1919. He was convicted and appealed by stated case. In dealing with an argument by the appellant which related to the relevancy of the complaint, the Lord Justice-General (Clyde) made the following preliminary observations on the interpretation of section 75 of the Summary Jurisdiction (Scotland) Act 1908 (the forerunner of section 454 of the 1975 Act).

LORD JUSTICE-GENERAL (CLYDE): ". . .Preliminary to the consideration of whether the Order itself was a lawful order or not, there comes the question of how far that point is open in the present case. For the respondent, reference was made to the Summary Jurisdiction Act of 1908, and particularly to section 75. Section 75 provides that no conviction shall be quashed for want of form; and that no conviction shall be quashed, where the accused was represented by a law-agent, in respect of any objection to the relevancy of the complaint unless such objection shall have been timeously stated. In this case the accused was represented by a law-agent. No objection to relevancy based on the alleged invalidity of the Order was tabled, and it was accordingly maintained that the objection with regard to the validity of the Order comes too late. There can be no doubt at all, I think, that section 75 did make some difference on the law as it was practised prior to 1908. I think that is shown by the fact that the exclusion of objections to relevancy which section 75 enacts is made applicable only to cases in which the accused was represented by a law-agent. And, although in practice, prior to 1908, there may have been some distinction made in cases where a law-agent was employed, so far as I am aware no such hard-and-fast line was drawn in that matter as is drawn by the Act of 1908. I should be very sorry to be compelled to read section 75 as excluding from this Court power to deal with cases, even though no objection to relevancy has been taken, where *ex facie* of the proceedings themselves, and particularly *ex facie* of the complaint, there is what has been called in the course of the debate a fundamental nullity. Such cases do occur; and the justification for doing right in such cases as those, even although no objection has been taken to the relevancy, is that the objection is patent on the face of the complaint or of the proceedings, and the prosecutor is, therefore, not entitled to say that he had no notice of the objection. I do not read section 75 as excluding from the Court power to deal with such cases, and I found on the case of *Rogers* v. *Howman* [1918 J.C. 88], and particularly upon the first paragraph in the opinion of the Lord Justice-General in that case. I found upon that as authority for the proposition that this Court has recognised that, notwithstanding section 75, the power to which I have referred still remains to it. The appeal in *Rogers* was by stated case, and the only question submitted to the Court was similar to the only one submitted here. If the language used by the Lord Justice-General is examined, it will be found that the legitimacy of entertaining an objection to relevancy, not stated in the Court below and not raised by the stated case, but patent on the face of the complaint, is affirmed. His Lordship contrasted the case he was deciding with one in which an irrelevancy is disclosed on the face of the complaint. I think, accordingly, that the Court retains the power of dealing with cases in which, although no objection to the relevancy was taken in the Court below, there is patent, and disclosed on the face of proceedings, an irrelevancy which makes the proceedings fundamentally null."

NOTE

In this case the High Court went on to uphold the conviction on the ground that the alleged irrelevancy did not in fact arise *ex facie* of the proceedings. But some comfort can be derived from Lord Clyde's remarks, which have in fact been followed in a number of cases. The most recent appears to be *Shaw* v. *Smith*, 1979 J.C. 51, in which three people were charged on summary complaint with boarding a train without paying or intending to pay. On appeal, the High Court held that this complaint was irrelevant since it disclosed no crime known to the law of Scotland. The court affirmed that it was competent even at the stage of an appeal to raise a matter constituting a fundamental nullity in the proceedings although it had not previously been raised.

Once any preliminary objections have been dealth with, the accused is called upon to plead guilty or not guilty. In certain cases he may do so in absence, and if he pleads not guilty the case is usually adjourned to a later date for trial. If the accused pleads guilty, he will usually be dealt with there and then.

Normally an accused person who has pleaded guilty on summary complaint, and whose plea has been accepted by the prosecutor, cannot change his mind. The plea must now be taken from the accused personally, if he is present in court: see Act of Adjournal (Sentencing Powers etc.) 1978, para. 3. But where there is genuine misapprehension the court may, in special circumstances, allow withdrawal of the plea.

For a discussion of s. 454 of the 1975 Act see *post*, p. 470.

2. Williams and Another v. Linton
(1878) 6 R. (J.) 12

Two accused were charged with shebeening. They initially pleaded not guilty, but when their case was called for trial, both their counsel and agent were not present in court. They both pleaded guilty and were in the process of being sentenced when their counsel returned to the courtroom. He asked the magistrate to allow the plea to be withdrawn, but this was refused. The accused appealed to the High Court by bill of suspension.

LORD JUSTICE-CLERK (MONCREIFF): "My first impression in reading the evidence in this case was, I am bound to say, that it was not a case for interference, because I thought that the magistrate had acted to the best of his judgment in a matter which was properly for his discretion. But, on maturer reflection, though I still think that the magistrate did act to the best of his judgment, I have come to be of opinion that the conviction ought not to stand.

I do not mean for one moment to say that in all cases a prisoner is entitled to have his trial postponed and postponed indefinitely till professional advice is forthcoming. But this is a very special case. In the first place, the charge is a serious charge, one of the most serious that can come before a police magistrate, and the penalty imposed is about the most severe that a police magistrate can inflict. But, besides this, the magistrate was informed that the prisoners were to be represented by a professional adviser, though he was not informed by whom. A member of the bar had also communicated with the magistrate, and informed him that he was engaged in one of the cases to be tried before him, but was obliged to leave the Court for a short period. In these circumstances, if it did not occur to the magistrate that the case in question was most likely the one to which the counsel referred, at least it would have been proper for him to inquire who the legal adviser of the accused was, before allowing them in his absence, and I may almost say because of his absence, to withdraw a plea of not guilty which they had at first given. When counsel returned to Court he was not at first aware of what had occurred, but, on hearing the magistrate proceed to give sentence he at once interposed to stop the proceedings. The magistrate refused to go back upon what had been done, thinking that it was not competent for him to do so. In this, I think, he was in error. I think, as the sentence had not been taken down and signed, even if it was formally pronounced, which is a matter of doubt, that the magistrate had power to go back upon the proceedings and try the case as requested.

On these grounds I think there has been a departure from substantial justice in this case, and that the conviction should be quashed."

Appeal allowed.

NOTE

So once a sentence has been recorded and signed, a plea of guilty cannot be withdrawn. This case was followed in *Tudhope* v. *Colbert*, 1978 S.L.T. (Notes) 57, where a solicitor who had been delayed by bad weather on the way to the court arrived there to find his client had pleaded guilty in person. But since the conviction and sentence had not been minuted, the court allowed the guilty plea to be withdrawn. The High Court dismissed as incompetent a Crown appeal against this decision. See also the saga of *MacNeill* v. *MacGregor*, 1975 J.C. 55, 1975 S.L.T. (Notes) 46 and *MacGregor* v. *MacNeill*, 1975 J.C. 57, 1975 S.L.T. (Notes) 54, *post* Chap. 15.

b. Statements in mitigation inconsistent with plea

If a plea is accepted by the prosecutor, he will narrate the facts to the court so that the appropriate sentence can be fixed. While the defence are always entitled to address the court in mitigation, care must be taken by both sides not to make factual assertions inconsistent with the plea accepted.

Galloway v. Adair
1947 J.C. 7

An accused person pleaded guilty to driving at an excessive speed on a complaint which libelled reckless driving. He was sentenced to a term of imprisonment and appealed by bill of suspension. In disposing of the bill, Lord Moncrieff made the following observations:

LORD MONCRIEFF: "Before the appellant was sentenced the depute-fiscal had made a statement as to the circumstances attending the commission of the offence. This was in accordance with practice and was, in my opinion, entirely proper. Indeed, without such a statement it would not only be embarrassing, but might scarcely be possible, to pronounce an appropriate sentence in the case of a plea of guilty. If a prisoner pleads guilty to an offence under a charge of assault or a charge of homicide or any charge of an offence in committing which the culpability may vary within wide limits, it is proper and in accordance with practice that an explanation of the circumstances attending the offence should be given to the Court which has the duty of imposing the sentence. At the same time it must be kept in view that by pleading guilty an accused person becomes entitled to the advantage of excluding all sworn evidence as to the circumstances of the offence which he has committed, and therefore that, if the accused denies any of the statements made by the Crown, these are statements which cannot be taken into consideration by the Court; unless indeed it can be demonstrated that such a denial is inconsistent with his plea of guilty, or should be disregarded as being manifestly false when taken along with the circumstances admitted by him. The accused has, of course, a corresponding right, either by himself or by his solicitor or counsel, to make a statement in extenuation, and the same considerations apply to any statement which may be so made by him or on his behalf. If such a statement is not disputed by those representing the Crown, it may be accepted as introducing extenuating circumstances in considering what sentence should be imposed, but if, it be disputed, it also must be left out of consideration.

When the statement was made by the depute-fiscal in the present case, being a statement in considerable detail to which I shall have to refer hereafter, it was not suggested by or on behalf of the accused that that statement was not in accordance with the facts. Accordingly, had the circumstances adverted to in that statement been relevant to illustrate and support the charge, I do not think it would now be competent before this Court of appeal to deny either in whole or in part the truth or accuracy of the statement which was so made; and I therefore do not find myself able to take into consideration the partial denial of the truth of the statement which is made part of the replies of the complainer in this bill of suspension. At the same time it is always the right of the complainer to have any charges contained in such a statement strictly directed towards the supporting of the charge to which he has pleaded guilty and not towards the support of any other and different charge. It is clear that, if that right were not asserted in his favour, it would result in his being sentenced for an offence other than that which was covered by his plea, and accordingly it is necessary to consider first of all what were the limits of the charge in the complaint to which the appellant pleaded guilty, and secondly what was the substance of the statement which was made by the depute-fiscal.

Section 11 of the Road Traffic Act of 1930 deals in all its applications with driving to the danger of the public, but it deals with this under three heads. If a person drives a motor vehicle on a road recklessly to the danger of the public, he commits an offence under the section; secondly, if he drives a motor vehicle at a speed which is dangerous to the public, he commits the statutory offence; and thirdly, if he drives a vehicle in a manner which is dangerous, he again is guilty of an offence under the section. In this complaint the prosecutor ignores all heads of the statutory offence except the second, and charges the appellant only with driving a motor vehicle at a speed which was dangerous to the public. He makes no reference, as he might have done, to reckless driving to the danger of the public or driving in a manner which was dangerous; and accordingly the only offence to which the appellant pleaded guilty was an offence of driving at a speed which was dangerous to the public. Any circumstances illustrating the committing of an offence in respect of speed were thus properly included in the statement which the depute-fiscal thought proper to make; and there are certain details of conduct included in the statement so made by him which are strictly limited and related to this question of dangerous driving in respect of speed. But in the eight particular details referred to in the depute-fiscal's statement there are I think only two which are solely concerned with the offence of driving dangerously in respect of speed. Thus in the first detail where a rather high rate of speed is charged incidentally, the substance of the offence which was narrated by the depute-fiscal was that the appellant had started his car before the green light at a crossing had appeared. That was an act of reckless driving to the danger of the public, but was not an act of driving at a speed dangerous to the public. In the same way in the second detail the charge again is of starting while the yellow and red lights were showing. The third is a charge of starting before the green light permitted a start, and also of thrusting his vehicle between a stationary lorry and a north-bound tramway car with so little warning that the driver of the tramway car had to make a sudden emergency stop to avoid the risk of an accident. That again is not an offence which need have resulted from dangerous speed, but is a definite offence of reckless driving. In the next detail the appellant is said to have ignored a clear hand signal from a moving vehicle about to turn off its course, resulting in a sudden swerve on his own part and his narrowly missing striking a lamp standard. The other offences are again (without going into them in detail) associated only remotely, if at all, with speed, except the last detail which is of a speed of 40 miles per hour and of such speed only.

Now, although there was no denial of the truth of these details before the learned Sheriff, that judge had still a farther duty to consider whether or not he was entitled to take these details into his consideration as relevant to aid him in measuring the sentence to be imposed for an offence of driving only at a speed which was dangerous to the public. In my opinion, these circumstances should not have been taken into consideration in measuring the sentence for that single offence. The appellant had pled guilty to the offence of driving at a dangerous speed, but he did not plead guilty to the various disregards of traffic lights and to the various trespasses upon the rights over the road of other vehicles, which form the substance of the statement; and it is always open to an accused person to say, *esto* the facts stated be accepted as true, these facts are not relevant to support or to measure the only offence to which I have pleaded guilty. In the present case it is, however, only if such irrelevant facts be taken into consideration that the learned Sheriff would have been justified in remarking that the case was among the worst of its kind in his experience. Had the circumstances upon which the learned Sheriff proceeded been relevant, I think that the sentence pronounced by him might have been regarded as an appropriate sentence. If on the other hand the irrelevant circumstances disappear from the case, a wholly different question requires to be determined. It is accordingly necessary to consider in this Court, and to determine as of new, what would be an appropriate sentence for the only offence to which the appellant has pleaded guilty. That plea convicts him of having driven his vehicle at a speed which is dangerous to the public, and that is far from a negligible offence; but beyond the statement of the depute-fiscal that at certain stages he had been driving at a rather high rate of speed and the circumstances that for four-tenths of a mile he maintained a speed of 40 miles an hour until he was stopped by the constables, there appears to be nothing left in the statement which it was proper for the learned Sheriff when measuring the sentence to entertain or have in view.

That being so, the sentence of sixty days' imprisonment with the suspension of the licence for the period of a year may, I think, be properly regarded as oppressive, though, had the circumstances which the learned Sheriff thought he was entitled to take into consideration been properly before him, it would have been difficult to make or to entertain such a suggestion. It is clear therefore that the sentence must be revised, and I would suggest to your Lordships that in place of a sentence of imprisonment a fine should be imposed, and that the fine might be for a sum of £15 with the usual alternative of sixty days' imprisonment. I would farther suggest that we should allow a period of three weeks within which to make payment of the fine."

Appeal allowed.

NOTE

It is thus of paramount importance to keep the narration of facts within relevant bounds. The sheriff here had before him material which he was not entitled to consider, a situation which led to a revisal of the sentence.

c. Procedure on a plea of not guilty

Once a plea of not guilty has been taken and recorded, the diet is adjourned for trial to take place on a later day. On that day, the diet must be called, or the instance falls. Evidence will then be led.

Certain statutes require that certain steps be taken before the trial commences. For example, under section 26(1) and (2) of the 1980 Act, statutory certificates on which the Crown intend to rely

404 PRELIMINARY OBJECTIONS, PLEADING AND TRIAL

must be served 14 days before the trial (section 26(3)); and under section 10(3) of the Road Traffic Act 1972 an analyst's certificate only acquires its evidential value if served seven days before the hearing or trial. This raises the question of when the trial commences, a question not really answered in *Handley* v. *Pirie*, 1977 S.L.T. 30. (For a discussion of this case, see C.N. Stoddart, "When does a summary trial commence?" (1976) 21 J.L.S. 393). However it is clear from *English* v. *Smith*, 1981 S.L.T. (Notes) 113 that so far as section 10(3) of the 1972 Act is concerned, the trial commences on the day to which the diet has been adjourned for trial, although the court still failed to identify the point in the proceedings on that day at which it commenced. Nowhere in the 1980 Act is a general provision made, but section 18(2) thereof inserts a new section 338A in the 1975 Act to the effect that a prosecutor in a summary trial cannot move the court to desert the diet *pro loco et tempore* after the first witness is sworn. The clear implication is therefore that a summary trial commences at that point, and phrases such as "before the trial" must be construed accordingly.

Once the trial has commenced by the leading of evidence, various procedural specialities may arise.

(i) Amendment of the complaint

Section 335 of the 1975 Act provides:

"(1) It shall be competent at any time prior to the determination of a summary prosecution, unless the court sees just cause to the contrary, to amend the complaint or any notice of penalty or previous conviction relative thereto by deletion, alteration or addition so as to cure any error or defect therein, or to meet any objection thereto, or to cure any discrepancy or variance between the complaint or notice and the evidence.

(2) Nothing in this section shall authorise an amendment which changes the character of the offence charged, and if the court shall be of opinion that the accused may in any way be prejudiced in his defence on the merits of the case by any amendment made under this section, the court shall grant such remedy to the accused by adjournment or otherwise as it shall think just."

It will thus be observed that many defects can be cured by amendment under the above section.

1. **Macintosh v. Metcalfe and Others**
(1886) 1 White 218

An accused person was charged on summary complaint with a statutory offence. No *locus* of the offence was specified, but the sheriff allowed the complaint to be amended to specify the *locus*. The accused was convicted and appealed by stated case.

LORD MCLAREN: "Your Lordships have not thought it necessary to call for a reply except upon the want of specification of the *locus*. This is an important point, as it bears upon the jurisdiction of the Sheriff. It is now admitted and it appears *ex facie* of the proceedings, that the complaint did not specify the place or places where the alleged crimes were committed. It does not even say that they were committed within the county of Forfar. But the Sheriff-Substitute allowed an amendment to be made, supplying this defect, and the question is whether that amendment was rightly allowed. The *locus* is a very material point, especially in the case of crimes of the peculiar nature here charged, viz., the attempt to transfer the members of one friendly society to another without their written consent. One sees that very delicate questions of jurisdiction might be raised under a libel of this description, such as whether the crime was committed at the residence of the transference or at the office of the society's agent. Under the Summary Procedure Act, section 5, power is conferred upon the Judge or Magistrate to amend the complaint, and to rectify all mistakes in substance as well as in form. These are very wide words, for 'substance' and 'form' include really everything in the libel. The question here is, I think, partly solved by considering what is meant when an action is dismissed for want of jurisdiction. In that case 'want of jurisdiction' means that the Court has no jurisdiction. Now, to remedy a defect does not mean to transform into a libel what was never a libel. But before the Sheriff can consider the complaint at all he must have a complaint before him which contains the essentials of a criminal charge. In the Stornoway case [*Matheson* v. *Ross*, infra] there was a misdescription; a mistake was made as to the date of the offence charged, and the Court thought that that could be remedied. But I find that in giving the leading opinion, Lord Young said,—'I cannot think that this amendment is otherwise than competent. It differs from an amendment of the *locus*, because that may raise a question of jurisdiction.' It is my opinion that failure to specify the *locus* is the kind of defect which cannot be rectified by amendment."

NOTE   Appeal allowed.

So a complaint which is fundamentally null cannot be cured by amendment. Here there was nothing to amend, or indeed any indication that the sheriff had jurisdiction. *cf. Stevenson* v. *McLevy & Others* (1879) 6 R. 33, *supra*, Chap. 3.

2.   Matheson and Others v. Ross
(1885) 5 Couper 582

An accused was tried on summary complaint. After the Crown case closed, the prosecutor sought to amend the date of the alleged offence. This was allowed and the accused appealed by bill of suspension.

LORD YOUNG: "The appellants here were brought to trial before the Sheriff-substitute of Ross-shire, at Stornoway, for the crime of deforcement and assault, and were convicted and sentenced by him to various periods of imprisonment. The conviction and sentence is complained of, first, upon the ground that the Sheriff allowed the complaint on which it proceeded to be amended in the date in the course of the trial, and, indeed, after the close of the prosecutor's evidence. The date originally stated the complaint as the date of the offence was the 8th of November 1884. On that day, the prosecution alleged the appellants had deforced and assaulted an officer and his assistant in the exercise of his duty in serving summonses, dated the 29th November, or three weeks after the offence was said to have been committed. Although it was plain that the dates were incompatable, and one or both must be wrong, it did not appear on the face of the libel which was wrong, or whether both were wrong. But I assume, for that alone is consistent with the course the case took, that the real date was 8th December, and accordingly that was the date the Sheriff allowed in the course, or rather at a late period, of the trial to be substituted for the original one of 8th November. The question is whether he was lawfully entitled to allow that amendment at that stage. Now one thing is quite clear, assuming December to be right, and not November, that no injustice was done in making the charge, and it is not suggested that any injustice or disadvantage has been suffered. Of course that is subject to the observation that, if the amendment was illegal, the appellants were legally entitled to any unearned advantage out of the prosecutor's error, of which they were deprived by the amendment. But I take it that they suffered no disadvantage and were put to no inconvenience. I mean that they were in no way prejudiced in their defence or put to any greater peril by the amendment than they would have been if the date had been right at first.

Now, taking the case so, was the amendment legal? I think the prosecution would have been competent under the Act 9 George IV., c. 29, Sir Wm. Rae's Act; for I do not agree with Mr Kennedy's argument that a case of deforcement such as this—an assault upon an officer of the law in the execution of his duty—could not be competently tried under that Act. It might be more or less discreet to try it under that Act and there are certainly many cases of deforcement and assault which might with perfect propriety be so tried. But as to the competency of so trying such a case I cannot entertain a doubt for a moment. If it had been so tried, the prayer of the complaint would have limited the punishment on the very face of it. But then the Summary Procedure Act of 1864 applies expressly to all complaints before the Sheriff in the exercise of the summary jurisdiction conferred upon him by the Act 9 George IV., c. 29; that is to say, it applies to all complaints which, before the statute, might competently have been brought under the older Act of Geo. IV. The complaint here bears on the face of it that it is under the Summary Jurisdictions Acts of 1864 and 1881, and the punishment which, under the Act of Geo. IV., is limited by the terms of the complaint, does not require in this prosecution to be limited in the prayer as under the Act of George IV., because in all prosecutions under the Summary Procedure Act the punishment is limited by statute, and the Act of 1881, which is one of the Acts mentioned in the title of the complaint, prohibits for the future any prosecution under 9 Geo. IV., and *requires* that any which previously would have been brought under it should thereafter be brought under the Acts 1864 and 1881. The importance of these provisions is that clause 5 of the Act of 1864 provides that no objection shall be allowed by the Court to any complaint under this Act, or for any alleged defect therein in substance or in form, or for any variance between any such complaint and the evidence adduced on the part of the prosecutor or complainer at the hearing thereof, not changing the character of the offence charged; but if any such objection or variance shall appear to the Court to be such that the respondent has been thereby deceived or misled, it shall be lawful for the Court to adjourn the hearing till some future day, and at the same time, or at any stage of the proceedings, to direct such amendment to be made upon the complaint as may appear to be requisite, not changing the character of the offence; and such amendment shall be authenticated by the signature or initials of the Judge or Clerk of Court. Now I think that in the Sheriff's place it would not have occurred to me that the accused could take any prejudice from the amendment being made upon the spot when the error was pointed out; nevertheless, I think the Sheriff acted with becoming discretion when he offered to the accused or their agent to adjourn the case if they desired it. No such desire was expressed, and the amendment was ordered and authenticated as the statute required. I cannot think that this amendment was other than competent. It differs from an amendment of the *locus*, because that may raise a question of jurisdiction. As it is not of that nature, we have not to determine any such question as was raised in the case of *Stevenson* cited, Couper, vol. iv., p. 495, in which the Appeal Court declined to sanction the insertion of a *locus* for the first time after the conclusion of the evidence, to fit the evidence that had been led. The matter in the present case is one of time, and I assume that the evidence upon which the appellants were convicted, of violent conduct upon the 8th December, applied to that date. In one view, and I think the right view, of clause 5 of the Summary Procedure Act, the Sheriff might have proceeded upon that evidence, and made his conviction apply to the 8th December, disregarding the discrepancy between that date and the 8th November. The magistrate is required to proceed on the truth of the substance of the matter, disregarding any such discrepancy owing to an error; but I think the Sheriff acted properly in correcting the error, and, indeed, that was necessary if a conviction was to be made by reference to the complaint."

Appeal refused.

NOTE

Section 335 of the 1975 Act is founded on the equivalent provision of the 1864 Act under discussion in the instant case. Once again the question of prejudice is paramount. For a discussion of this problem generally, see G.H. Gordon, "Fundamental Nullity and the Power of Amendment," 1974 S.L.T. (News) 154.

(ii) Abandonment of proceedings

The common law relating to desertion of diets, whether *simpliciter* or *pro loco et tempore*, is of course the same in summary proceedings as it is in solemn cases—see *supra* p. 332. See also section 338A of the 1975 Act (as inserted by section 18(2) of the 1980 Act) which provides as follows:

"(1) It shall be competent at the diet of trial, at any time before the first witness is sworn, for the court, on the application of the prosecutor, to desert the diet *pro loco et tempore*.

(2) If, at a diet of trial, the court refuses an application by the prosecutor to adjourn the trial or to desert the diet *pro loco et tempore*, and the prosecutor is unable or unwilling to proceed with the trial, the court shall desert the diet *simpliciter*.

(3) Where the court has deserted a diet *simpliciter* under subsection (2) above (and the court's decision in that regard has not been reversed on appeal), it shall not be competent for the prosecutor to raise a fresh libel."

In *Tudhope* v. *Gough*, 1982 S.C.C.R. 157, Sheriff Kearney held that it was competent to desert *pro loco et tempore* even after refusing an adjournment, but in the particular circumstances of that case, where the prosecutor had omitted (without explanation) to cite an essential witness, he refused a Crown motion to desert *pro loco* and instead deserted the diet *simpliciter*.

Proceedings may also be abandoned by not calling a complaint and, if appropriate, substituting another complaint.

Cochran v. **Walker**

(1900) 3 Adam 165

An accused was convicted after trial on summary complaint, the third which had been called. He appealed by bill of suspension.

LORD JUSTICE-CLERK (MACDONALD): "We have heard a very clear statement of the case from counsel for the suspender, and it is not necessary to call for a reply.

It is said that the suspender was brought up for trial on more than one complaint, and that no copy of any complaint was served on him. What happened was this. The suspender was apprehended on 3rd March on a charge of assault, and pleaded not guilty before the magistrate on 5th March. Some doubt arose as to whether the nature of the injuries inflicted on the person assaulted might not necessitate a graver charge being libelled, and the magistrate remitted the case to the Sheriff. The prosecutor, however, departing from the first complaint brought a second summary complaint, to which the suspender again pleaded not guilty, and the case was adjourned. In all this there was nothing irregular—nothing unfair.

At the adjourned diet on 13th March the prosecutor allowed the previous complaint to drop, and the suspender was asked to plead to a third complaint. All this was quite competent. The same course is followed in all our criminal tribunals from the most summary up to the highest Court in the country. It is always in the power of the public prosecutor to depart from one libel and proceed to charge the accused upon a fresh libel. In the higher Courts the *induciæ* must be allowed to run in each case, but in the case of a summary complaint there are no *induciæ*. But in neither case is any record made of the dropping of the old libel.

In the present case the suspender, having appeared in court on the 13th March, the diet to which the second complaint had been adjourned, was asked then and there to plead to a new complaint. He was informed by the reading over of the charge that it differed from the previous libel in that the prosecutor now added the aggravation of a previous conviction of assault. It is of importance to note that during all these proceedings the suspender was represented by a law-agent and no objection was taken to the legality of the proceedings, nor was any motion made on his behalf for any adjournment. I know of no case where in a Summary Court the accused has been represented by an agent and no objection has been stated at the time in which this Court has afterwards interfered to quash the proceedings on the ground of the alleged illegality by there being no adjournment. But, further, I do not think that it could be held that there was any irregularity in the proceedings here even if objection had been taken earlier. It is not said that an adjournment was asked for and refused. It is said that no copy of the complaint was handed to the accused, but it was not necessary to do so in the circumstances, and it is not said that a copy was asked and refused."

Appeal refused.

NOTE

On abandonment generally, see Renton and Brown, paras. 13-97, 13-98. On adjournment of diets, see *supra*, p. 327.

(iii) Conduct of a summary trial

The rules of evidence relating to the testimony given at a summary trial are outwith the scope of this work, but various cases have arisen in which summary courts (often those presided over by lay justices) have made procedural mistakes. The following points have sometimes given rise to difficulty.

(A) WHOLE CASE TO BE TAKEN IN PRESENCE OF ACCUSED

Aitken v. Wood

1921 J.C. 84

An accused person was convicted in the police court of assault. He appealed by bill of suspension.

LORD JUSTICE-GENERAL (CLYDE): "This bill of suspension is brought against a conviction for assault. It is alleged that the assault was committed on the person of a Mrs M'Niddler, whose arm was seized and compressed by the accused. Mrs M'Niddler was herself a witness at the trial, and spoke to the assault and to the fact, as she alleged, that her arm still bore a mark which was the result of the violence used upon her. She was asked if she was willing to show the bruise on her arm, to which question she returned an affirmative answer, but the matter was not pursued further during the proof. After the evidence on both sides had been closed, however, and after hearing argument, the magistrates, having retired to consider their decision, asked Mrs M'Niddler to come into the room to which they had retired, and examined her arm there, without the presence of the accused and of parties' solicitors—one of the magistrates being a medical man. Whether they asked her any questions we do not know, but I assume they did not.

This procedure, however well intended, and however harmless it may have been in this particular case, strikes at the principle—deeply rooted in the criminal law of Scotland—that no proceedings in a criminal trial, and particularly no proceedings connected with the taking of evidence can go on outwith the presence of the accused. The examination of the arm was just a means of taking evidence additional to that which was presented at the proof. The taking of such evidence, in the absence of the accused, is plainly an irregularity which vitiates the proceedings; and there is therefore nothing for it but to quash the conviction."

Appeal allowed.

NOTE

Not only must a summary trial always take place in the presence of the accused (except where trial in absence is otherwise competent, for example under section 338(b) of the 1975 Act), the prosecutor must also be present: see *Skeen* v. *Summerhill and Another* (1975) 39 J.C.L. 59. It is improper for a judge who has been at or near the *locus* at which the crime was committed to preside over a subsequent trial of a person arrested there, but it may not be oppressive: see *McDevitt* v. *McLeod*, 1982 S.C.C.R. 282, *supra*, Chap. 1.

(B)   UNSWORN STATEMENT FROM DOCK

Gilmour v. H.M. Advocate
1965 J.C. 45

An accused person was convicted after trial on indictment. The sheriff refused to allow the accused to make an unsworn statement from the dock. He appealed against conviction.

LORD JUSTICE-GENERAL (CLYDE): "In this case the applicant was found guilty by a jury in the Sheriff Court at Kilmarnock of assaulting his wife and striking her on the face with an axe or similar instrument to her injury.

At the close of the Crown evidence at the trial the solicitor appearing for the applicant informed the court that the accused 'wished to elect his right to make a statement from the dock.' The object of this motion was to enable the accused to avoid giving his evidence on oath and, in consequence, not to subject himself to cross-examination. This motion was refused by the Sheriff but thereafter the accused did not go into the witness-box to give evidence and the trial proceeded to a conviction.

The only ground argued to us in the present application is that the Sheriff erred in the course which he took in not permitting the accused to make a statement from the dock without giving evidence on oath. The basis put forward to justify this ground of appeal was section 1 (*h*) of the Criminal Evidence Act, 1898.

The Act in question is an Act applicable to Scotland and to England. The principal object of section 1 of the Act was to enable accused persons to be competent witnesses for the defence in a criminal case. Prior to that Act an accused person could not give evidence on his own behalf in the witness-box and the object of the Act was to remove this disability, which, in many cases, proved a real hardship to the accused. Section 1 (*h*) of the Act provides: 'Nothing in this Act shall affect the provisions of section eighteen of the Indictable Offences Act, 1848, or any right of the person charged to make a statement without being sworn.' The contention of the applicant in the present case is that the latter words in the subsection recognised his right to make a statement without going into the witness-box and taking an oath.

But it is to be observed in the first place that the subsection confers no new right of any kind on an accused. It merely preserves certain rights which he may have had when the 1898 Act came into operation. In the second place, the Indictable Offences Act, 1848, mentioned in section 1 (*h*) is an English Act, which does not, and never did, apply to Scotland. The outlook of the subsection is English in character and not Scottish. But, in the third place, the subsection does not preserve the right of an accused person to make a statement without being sworn. It is much more tentatively phrased. It does not recognise that there is such a right. It only preserves any right which there may be. It is consequently crucial to the success of the applicant's ground of appeal that he should be able to establish that such a right on the part of an accused to make a statement without being sworn, prior to the verdict of a jury, did exist in the law of Scotland in 1898. It appears that there is some such right in English criminal law (see Archbold, Criminal Pleading, Evidence and Practice, paragraph 553).

On the crucial matter, however, the applicant has completely failed to produce any decision or text-book in Scotland in support of such a right. The Crown informed us that they had been unable to find any warrant for the existence of such a right in Scotland.

I am satisfied that before 1898 an accused could make a judicial declaration before a magistrate, but that otherwise he had no right to give evidence in his own defence, either on oath or otherwise. It is quite impossible, if he had a right before 1898 to make a statement at the trial not on oath, that such a vitally important right would not have been referred to in the authorities or in the decided cases. Indeed, had there been such a right, it would obviously have frequently been invoked and there would have been little, if any, advantage in the main provisions of the 1898 Act, which, for the first time, entitled an accused to give evidence in his own defence. In my opinion, therefore, section 1 (*h*) of the 1898 Act applies only to England and has no application in Scottish criminal proceedings.

Since that Act came into operation an accused person who wishes to challenge any of the facts spoken to by the Crown witnesses has the opportunity, if he so wishes, of controverting these facts. But for that purpose he must go into the witness-box and, consequently, be liable to cross-examination. This is in accordance with our conception of fair play. If he does not take that course, he cannot give evidence at all. If he is represented by counsel or by a solicitor, he has, of course, the right, through them, to address the jury before they give their verdict. If he is not legally represented, he can himself address the jury. But these addresses can only be based on the evidence which has been led before the jury, and the judge is entitled to direct the jury to disregard facts alleged in these addresses which are not included in sworn testimony given at the trial. Any other rule can only lead to injustice.

We were informed that in recent years a practice has grown up in certain Sheriff Courts of allowing witnesses or accused persons to make statements without being put on oath or making a solemn affirmation before the statements were made. This practice is alleged to occur especially in summary cases. This court has had occasion to criticise such a practice in *Forbes* v. *H.M. Advocate*. If it does occur, it is quite an improper practice, whether in relation to witnesses or to accused parties. There is no warrant for it under our law either in summary or solemn proceedings and, indeed, *Forbes's* case is an illustration of how completely the court or the jury may be misled by slipshod procedure of this kind.

We were referred to the terms of an Act of Adjournal of 22nd March 1935, which deals with shorthand notes in criminal proceedings. Paragraph 1 of this Act of Adjournal does not recognise, nor imply, that any accused person has a right, prior to the verdict, to make a statement regarding the facts without going on oath. It merely includes within the expression 'proceedings at the trial' any statements made by or on behalf of the prisoner, whether before or after the verdict. It says nothing whatever as to the validity or competency of any such statement, but is merely intended to secure that the court has a clear record of all that has taken place in the court below them. This provision, therefore, is of no assistance to the applicant in the present case.

In my opinion the ground upon which this application for leave to appeal is made is unsound in law and the Sheriff was correct in rejecting it. The application must, therefore, in my opinion be refused."

Appeal refused.

NOTE

The law is thus clear, both in summary and solemn cases. Nevertheless mistakes have still occurred since this decision; clerks to lay magistrates sitting in the district court sometimes encounter this problem, particularly where the accused is unrepresented. It should also be noted that the accused is entitled, after conviction whether by trial or on a plea of guilty, to address the court in mitigation of sentence: *Falconer* v. *Jessop*, 1975 S.L.T. (Notes) 78.

(C) Is IT NECESSARY TO IDENTIFY THE ACCUSED?

By section 26(5) of the Criminal Justice (Scotland) Act 1980 it is provided: "At any trial of an offence under summary procedure it shall be presumed that the person who appears in answer to the complaint is the person charged by the police with the offence unless the contrary is alleged."

Smith v. Paterson
1982 S.L.T. 437

An accused person was acquitted of breach of the peace. The fiscal appealed by stated case. In the case the sheriff gave the following account of the evidence:

1. On 8 August 1981 a football match took place in Edinburgh between Hibernian and St Johnstone.

2. After the match a crowd of about 150 young Hibernian supporters set off from Easter Road, and walked along London Road.

3. There was unruly behaviour within this crowd; it split into various groups, of which one, numbering about 20 persons, walked on towards Princes Street.

4. Two police officers followed this crowd, and thereafter followed this group to Princes Street, where they observed its behaviour from a police vehicle.

5. At Princes Street this group sang songs, and swore and gestured at buses and pedestrians.

6. The police officers left their vehicle, moved forward and arrested a member of this group whom they had seen give a "V" sign at a passing vehicle.

7. This man was taken by the police officers to Gayfield Square police station, where he was cautioned and charged with the offence libelled in the complaint.

Neither of the two police officers who gave evidence was asked to identify the respondent.

LORD CAMERON: "This appeal by way of stated case from the sheriff court in Edinburgh raises sharply a short point of statutory interpretation. By s. 26(5) of the Criminal Justice (Scotland) Act 1980 it is provided that 'at any trial of an offence under summary procedure it shall be presumed that the person who appears in answer to the complaint is the person charged by the police with the offence unless the contrary is alleged'. The procedure for challenging the presumption is laid down in s. 334(1) of the Criminal Procedure (Scotland) Act 1975 as amended by para. 54 of Sched. 7 to the Act of 1980. No question as to the proper construction or application of these procedures arises in the present case as no such challenge was made by the respondent who was the accused. The appeal is at the instance of the prosecutor. The circumstances out of which the appeal arises are set out in the case. The respondent, along with some others, was charged on summary complaint with breach of the peace in that 'on 8 August 1981 in the street in Princes Street, Edinburgh [he] did conduct [him]self in a disorderly manner, shout and swear and commit a breach of the peace'. When the case called on 2 October 1981 the respondent was represented by a solicitor who tendered a plea of not guilty; his co-accused all pleaded guilty.

Trial took place on 8 January 1982 and evidence was led for the prosecution from two police officers. Their evidence is summarised by the sheriff as follows: [his Lordship quoted the findings-in-fact and continued:] Neither police officer was asked to identify the respondent. At the conclusion of the evidence for the prosecution the solicitor for the respondent submitted that in terms of s. 345A of the Criminal Procedure (Scotland) Act 1975 as now amended there was 'no case to answer'. The ground of the submission for the respondent was that there was no evidence identifying the respondent with the commission of the crime charged against him. Having heard parties the sheriff gave effect to the respondent's motion and acquitted him of the charge in the complaint. It is against this decision that the Crown have taken this appeal.

In his opinion the learned sheriff records that 'he had no reason to disbelieve the police officers and that the evidence which they gave was sufficient from which to infer that a breach of the peace had taken place'. It may therefore be accepted that there was corroborated and credible evidence sufficient to establish: (1) the fact of a breach of the peace being committed, (2) that the police arrested a person concerned in the commission of the offence, and (3) that this person after arrest was taken to a police station and there cautioned and charged with the offence libelled. The basis of the sheriff's judgment appears to be that, while rightly concluding that the provisions of s. 26 are dealing with matters of formal or routine evidence: 'identification of an accused person is not normally a formal matter, however. It is normally of the first importance requiring the best evidence and in a case like the present case it can be crucial'. Because the police officers did not formally identify the respondent the sheriff concluded that there was no evidence which would entitle him in this case to hold that the respondent had been identified as acting as alleged in the complaint. He therefore sustained the respondent's motion and acquitted him. For the Crown it was submitted that the sheriff erred. It was clear from the sheriff's narrative of the evidence that there was sufficient evidence of a breach of the peace being committed and of the arrest of a man and that man being taken to Gayfield Square and there charged. When the statutory presumption provided for in s. 26(5) was taken into account the identity of the accused as the person charged with the offence was established. That person was the respondent. That person was (if the police were believed) the person who was seen committing a breach of the peace and was arrested. Therefore the position was this: there was sufficient evidence of a breach of the peace; there was sufficient evidence that a person was seen committing such a breach; there was sufficient evidence that this person was arrested and taken to Gayfield Square; and there was no suggestion that a different person was subsequently charged as libelled. At this stage the presumption created by s. 26(5) which was, as its language and context plainly show, a limited presumption, came into play, there being no denial or challenge timeously made. In these circumstances there was certainly a 'case to answer' and the sheriff wholly misconstrued both the evidence and effect of the presumption in linking the respondent with the offender observed in the act of committing the offence and thereupon taken into and retained in custody until cautioned and charged with the offence. The chain of evidence linking the respondent to the offence charged was complete. Counsel referred to the case of *Muldoon* v. *Herron*. It was merely a coincidence that the witnesses to the incident and the officers who charged the respondent were the same individuals. The chain of evidence here was completed by the two police witnesses in the circumstances of the particular case. The sheriff had confounded identification of an accused as perpetrator of an offence and proof of the identity of the person in the dock as the individual charged. The question should be answered in the negative and the case sent back to the sheriff to proceed as accords. For the respondent, counsel submitted that identification of the perpetrator of an offence as the accused was vital. Here no witness identified the respondent as such and it was not to be assumed that in a question of 'routine evidence' the vital element of identification of the accused with commission of the offence could be 'presumed'. There was here a misuse of the presumption because the police could and should have been asked to identify the accused. The appeal should be refused.

In my opinion the learned sheriff has plainly erred in his construction of s. 26(5) of the Act of 1980. The provisions of s. 26(5) of the Criminal Justice (Scotland) Act 1980 are concerned with a presumption of limited operation and directed to matters of what are described in the side-note of the section as 'routine evidence'. Not only so but the presumption only applies in the absence of challenge by the accused. The right to exercise this challenge and precise time and circumstances in which it is be exercised are dealt with in s. 334(1) of the Criminal Procedure (Scotland) Act 1975 as amended by para. 54 of Sched. 7 to the Act of 1980. The presumption thus enacted is concerned solely with the identification of an accused on trial as the person whom the police have charged with the offence libelled against him in the complaint before the court. It does not therefore in terms or by any necessary implication create a presumption of identification of the person charged as the perpetrator of the offence libelled. In many cases the officers concerned in charging an accused can speak to no other relevant matter, far less be witnesses to identification of the accused as participants in the offence. It may happen, however, by coincidence that police witnesses give evidence which identifies or serves to identify the person charged by them as responsible for the criminal acts libelled. This however is a coincidence which may arise from the circumstances of the particular case. It is in no sense a necessary and conclusive consequence of the operation of this limited statutory presumption. Where the learned sheriff has fallen into error is in confusing the issue of identification of the culprit with that of identification of the accused as the person charged. The effect of the presumption in the circumstances of the present case however could have and did have no effect on the issue of the accuracy or credibility of the evidence of the police officers as to the actions of the culprit which led to his arrest and subsequent charge by them. It was therefore open to the defence to challenge the evidence of the police officers on the merits by cross-examination and, if felt such a course was possible or desirable, by leading evidence to controvert such evidence. In the present case the sheriff had before him unchallenged evidence—the credibility of which was for him to assess—which, if accepted, provided legal and sufficient proof of the commission of an offence and the arrest of the offender but in addition, and this is important, of the conveyance of the offender to a police station where that offender was charged with the particular offence libelled in the complaint. Now, subsequent to that charge a complaint was served on the respondent who answered to the complaint and was legally represented. He did not allege that he was not the person charged by the police and consequently the presumption applied. This, if the evidence, which the learned sheriff had no reason to disbelieve, was accepted completed an unbroken chain of proof linking the respondent with the commission of the offence charged. The presumption does no more and no less than provide one, but only one, step towards establishing the charges laid against an accused; the importance of that step in any particular case will depend on the circumstances of the case. Indeed it may have very little, depending again on the facts and nature of the particular case itself. Here the respondent by acceptance of the statutory presumption admitted that it was he who had been charged with the offence. The direct evidence of the police established, if accepted, that they had charged a person whom they had seen committing the offence charged on the date and in the place libelled. If then the accused not only makes no denial that he was the person charged but by his silence when appearing in answer to the complaint, admits that fact in the most formal way then in such circumstances the chain of evidence is complete. The sheriff's error here lay not so much in a misapprehension of the limited purpose of the new statutory presumption, but in his misapprehension of its effect as an element of proof in the identification of an accused with the commission of the offence libelled. In my opinion the sheriff fell into error in that he failed to note that if the respondent was by operation of the presumption held to be the person charged by the police there was evidence in law sufficient, if accepted, that this person was seen committing the offence libelled and arrested on the spot and thereafter taken to the police station and there charged with the offence. Therefore the person charged and the person who committed the offence libelled in the charge was one and the same—the respondent.

The respondent's motion should therefore have been refused by the sheriff. In these circumstances the questions in the case should be answered in the negative and the case remitted to the sheriff to proceed as accords."

Appeal allowed.

NOTE

It must be observed that section 26 (5) of the 1980 Act applies only to summary cases. If any denial that the accused is the person charged by the police is to be made, it should be made at the first calling of the case: section 334(2) of the 1975 Act, as amended by the 1980 Act, Sched. 7, para. 54. It will no longer be open to the defence to sit back and hope that the Crown witnesses are not asked or fail to identify the accused.

CHAPTER 14

APPEAL IN SOLEMN PROCEEDINGS

Prior to the Criminal Appeal (Scotland) Act 1926 the opportunities for review in solemn proceedings were very limited. A person convicted before the High Court had nothing in the nature of a general right of appeal against conviction or sentence (although an appeal court had been established under the Prevention of Crime Act 1908 to hear appeals against sentences of preventive detention). In solemn proceedings before the sheriff court the accused enjoyed a limited right of appeal on points of law by way of bill of suspension. Similarly, the prosecutor could, by bill of advocation, bring under review decisions on the competency and relevancy of the indictment. But apart from these cases the only method of review open to a convicted person was to petition the Secretary for Scotland for the exercise of the Royal Prerogative of Mercy.

In 1925 a committee on criminal appeals in Scotland recommended that a court of criminal appeal be established (along lines similar to the English Court of Criminal Appeal established in 1907) to review convictions on indictment in the High Court and sheriff court (Cmnd. 2456, 1925). Such a court was established by the Criminal Appeal (Scotland) Act 1926.

The provisions of the 1926 Act (as amended by the Criminal Appeal (Scotland) Act 1927) were re-enacted in section 228 *et seq.* of the 1975 Act. These provisions have been very substantially amended, or replaced by Schedule 2 to the 1980 Act. Throughout this chapter, therefore, references to the 1975 Act incorporate these changes, unless otherwise indicated.

a. Composition and status of the appeal court

Criminal Procedure (Scotland) Act 1975

"245.—(1) For the purpose of hearing and determining any appeal or other proceeding under this Part of this Act three of the Lords Commissioners of Justiciary shall be a quorum of the High Court, and the determination of any question under this Part of this Act by the court shall be according to the votes of the majority of the members of the court sitting, including the presiding judge, and each judge so sitting shall be entitled to pronounce a separate opinion.

262. Subject to the provisions of [section 263] of this Act, all interlocutors and sentences pronounced by the High Court under this Part of this Act shall be final and conclusive and not subject to review by any court whatsoever and it shall be incompetent to stay or suspend any execution or diligence issuing from the High Court under this Part of this Act."

NOTES

1. Section 263 confers on the Secretary of State the power to refer the case of a convicted person to the High Court for consideration. For a consideration of this power see *Leitch* v. *Secretary of State for Scotland, infra*, p. 457. Section 263 also provides that nothing in the appeals provisions shall affect the prerogative of mercy, for a consideration of which see *post*, Chap. 18.

2. Section 262 extends to the High Court as a court of appeal the finality of judgment enjoyed by the High Court at common law. There is, in particular, no further appeal from the High Court to the House of Lords in criminal cases. *Cf. Mackintosh* v. *Lord Advocate* (1876) 3 R. (H.L.) 34. The Thomson Committee (3rd Report) concluded that there was no strong demand for any change in this respect (para. 21.03). A contrary view has, however, been expressed, particularly in relation to the problem of divergent interpretation of United Kingdom legislation. See, *e.g.* Blom-Cooper and Drewry, *Final Appeal*, pp. 376-377. Of late, however, this problem has diminished in the face of the House of Lords' greater willingness to follow Scottish solutions. See, *e.g. Allan* v. *Patterson*, 1980 S.L.T. 77, *R.* v. *Lawrence* [1981] 1 All E.R. 974.

Section 262 may also exclude the possibility of an application to the *nobile officium* for review of a judgment of the appeal court. See *Ferguson* v. *H.M. Advocate*, 1980 J.C. 27, *infra*, p. 446. (The question was not actually decided in that case, the court being of the opinion that in any event the criteria for invoking the *nobile officium* were not satisfied.)

b.   *The ground of appeal and its effect on conviction*

1.   Criminal Procedure (Scotland) Act 1975

"228.—(1) Any person convicted on indictment may appeal in accordance with the provisions of this Part of this Act, to the High Court—

(*a*) against such conviction;

(*b*) against the sentence passed on such conviction;

or

(*c*) against both such conviction and such sentence:

Provided that there shall be no appeal against any sentence fixed by law.

(2) By an appeal under subsection (1) of this section, a person may bring under review of the High Court any alleged miscarriage of justice in the proceedings in which he was convicted, including any alleged miscarriage of justice on the basis of the existence and significance of additional evidence which was not heard at the trial and which was not available and could not reasonably have been made available at the trial.

254.—(1) The High Court may . . . dispose of an appeal against conviction by—

(a) affirming the verdict of the trial court;

(b) setting aside the verdict of the trial court and either quashing the conviction or substituting therefor an amended verdict of guilty:

Provided that an amended verdict of guilty must be one which could have been returned on the indictment before the trial court; or

(c) setting aside the verdict of the trial court and granting authority to bring a new prosecution in accordance with section 255 of this Act."

(2) In setting aside, under subsection (1) above, a verdict the High Court may quash any sentence imposed on the appellant as respects the indictment, and —

(a) in a case where it substitutes an amended verdict of guilty, whether or not the sentence related to the verdict set aside; or

(b) in any other case, where the sentence did not so relate,

may pass another (but not more severe) sentence in substitution for the sentence so quashed.

NOTE

The 1926 Act (whose provisions were reproduced in the 1975 Act) provided for three grounds of appeal against conviction, *viz.*, that the verdict was unreasonable or could not be supported having regard to the evidence, that there had been a wrong decision of law by the trial court, or that on any ground there had been a miscarriage of justice: 1975 Act (old) s. 254(1). These grounds of appeal were subject to "the proviso" which permitted the court to dismiss the appeal "notwithstanding that they were of opinion that the point raised in the appeal might be decided in favour of the appellant . . . if they considered that no substantial miscarriage of justice had actually occurred."

There is now only one ground of appeal—miscarriage of justice under section 228—and it applies both to appeal against conviction and appeal against sentence. The meaning of this term, and its effect upon conviction, are discussed in the following cases. Appeal against sentence is discussed *infra*, p. 442.

2. McCuaig v. H.M. Advocate
1982 S.L.T. 383;

An accused person appealed against conviction on the ground of miscarriage of justice. The alleged miscarriage lay in the inadvertent disclosure by the sheriff to the jury of the appellant's previous convictions prior to the verdict.

LORD JUSTICE-CLERK (WHEATLEY): "On the basis that the disclosure in the instant case was a breach of s. 160(1) of the Criminal Procedure (Scotland) Act 1975 as amended, I am of the opinion that the matter has to be looked at in the light of the new terms of s. 254(1) of that Act as amended. The disclosure arose out of a question put to a police witness by the presiding judge in an endeavour on his part to clarify the contents of a charge preferred against the appellant to which he had given an answer. The police witness had spoken to a charge which was in the terms of the charge in the indictment, but on being asked by the judge to be more specific he referred to his note-book and substantially repeated the words of the charge with the addition of the words 'and to conceal your true name and to avoid production of a reference to previous convictions relative to you and you did by said means attempt to defeat the ends of justice'. In these circumstances the question is whether or not that breach of s. 160(1) is sufficient to warrant the conviction being quashed. The matter in my view is now entirely one for the discretion of the court. In terms of s. 254(1) as amended the provision is that the High Court *may* subject to subs. (4) dispose of an appeal against conviction either by: (a) affirming the verdict of the trial court; or (b) setting aside the verdict and either quashing it or substituting therefor an amended verdict of guilty; or (c) setting aside the verdict of the court and granting authority to bring a new prosecution. This is in marked distinction to the original terms of s. 254 which provided that the appeal court '*shall* allow the appeal if they think . . . (*c*) that on any ground there was a miscarriage of justice' (my emphasis). There was a proviso, however, to the effect that the court 'may . . . dismiss the appeal if they consider that no substantial miscarriage of justice has actually occurred'. Thus an imperative requirement to allow the appeal and quash the conviction, subject to a proviso giving a discretionary power to the court not to do so in stated circumstances has been replaced by a discretionary power to the court inter alia to quash the conviction or amend the verdict of guilty. This seems to me to give wider power to the court than the previous legislation.

Looking at the circumstances of this case through the eyes of that amended subsection, I am of the opinion that the circumstances here do not warrant a finding that a miscarriage of justice has been sustained sufficient to warrant the setting aside of the verdict. I am accordingly of the opinion that the verdict which was returned should be affirmed and the appeal refused."

Appeal refused.

NOTES

1. Prior to the 1980 Act the relationship between the grounds of appeal recognised by the old section 254 and the disposal of the appeal was as follows. Once the appellant had established the

ground of appeal the appeal court was obliged to quash the conviction unless the Crown persuaded the court that there had been no substantial miscarriage of justice. The new appeal provisions as interpreted in *McCuaig* require the appellant to establish that there has been a miscarriage of justice. So that even if the appellant shows, for example, that there has been a misdirection or some other error of law, this may not of itself result in the conviction being quashed. There must also be a miscarriage of justice. The onus relating to miscarriage has, therefore, switched from a "negative" onus on the Crown, to a "positive" onus on the appellant.

2. But even where the court is satisfied that there has been a miscarriage of justice it would now seem that this will not necessarily result in the conviction being quashed. It must be a miscarriage of justice "sufficient to warrant the setting aside of the verdict". The Lord Justice-Clerk further developed this point in *Burns* v. *H.M. Advocate*, 1983 S.L.T. 38, a case involving a clear misdirection of a jury by a sheriff:

"In that situation have the appellants established a case for the quashing of the convictions? That the sheriff misdirected the jury is accepted on all hands. But did that misdirection create a miscarriage of justice, and, if so, was it so weighty as to warrant the quashing of the convictions? The phrase 'substantial miscarriage of justice' which found its place in previous legislation as a qualification of the otherwise mandatory direction to quash is no longer with us. But that mandatory direction to quash has been replaced by a permissive power to affirm, quash, or amend the verdict or authorise a new prosecution: s. 254(1) of the Criminal Procedure (Scotland) Act 1975, as amended. That permissive power has to be exercised having regard to all the circumstances of the case. Looking to all the circumstances of the instant case I do not consider that any miscarriage of justice resulted from the sheriff's unfortunate errors in law in directing the jury."

What has happened, in effect, is that the court has interpreted the new appeal provisions as meaning that the appellant is not entitled to succeed unless he shows that there has been, not simply a "miscarriage of justice" but a "substantial" or "material" or "weighty" miscarriage. That indeed was the formula adopted by the Lord Justice-Clerk in *Mackenzie* v. *H.M. Advocate*, 1983 S.L.T. 220 *infra*, p. 455 where he stated:

"Having regard to all these factors, I am of the opinion that the presiding judge erred in directing the jury . . . These errors resulted in such prejudice to the appellant that I have no alternative to holding that a substantial miscarriage of justice resulted and that the verdict of the court . . . must be set aside."

3. It is submitted that this is a most unfortunate interpretation of the new provisions. It is, however, inevitable once it is held that the court has a complete discretion under section 254 since it then becomes necessary to devise a formula to distinguish between those miscarriages which justify interfering with the verdict and those which do not. This interpretation is particularly unfortunate when one has regard to the provisions for re-trial. As will be seen from the case of *Mackenzie* even where the appellant shows that there has been a substantial miscarriage he may still be faced with the prospect of a fresh indictment.

4. Notwithstanding the very wide discretion now enjoyed by the court, it is submitted that there are some cases in which the quashing of a conviction is inevitable. In *McAvoy and Another* v. *H.M.Adv.*, 1982 S.C.C.R. 263, 1983 S.L.T. 16, Lord Hunter expressed the view (at 1982 S.C.C.R. 274) that "While the power to affirm a verdict is ex facie unfettered, it must, in my opinion, be qualified by certain implied limitations. Obviously a court would not affirm a verdict which seemed to the court to be perverse or not supported by the evidence." And see the following case:

3. Boyle v. H.M. Advocate
1976 J.C. 32

The appellant, an army deserter, pleaded guilty to a charge of assault and robbery. He was not in fact responsible for the offence in question, but pleaded guilty in an effort to avoid punishment for the military offence of desertion. He was sentenced to imprisonment for nine years, and lodged an application for leave to appeal on the ground that there had been a miscarriage of justice. He relied upon the former provisions of section 254(1) of the 1975 Act which provided, *inter alia*, that "the High Court on an appeal against conviction shall allow the appeal if they think . . . (c) that on any ground there was a miscarriage of justice".

LORD CAMERON: " . . . No question arises in the present case as to the possible application of the proviso. The miscarriage, if miscarriage there was and if this Court is competent to give a remedy, is one which plainly should result in the quashing of the conviction.

The language of section 254 (1) of the Criminal Procedure (Scotland) Act 1975 repeats that of section 2 (1) of the Criminal Appeal (Scotland) Act 1926 (cap. 15), which in turn repeats the wording of section 4 (1) of the Criminal Appeal Act 1907 (cap. 23). The particular words on which the applicant founded his argument on the competency of the application and on which the learned Solicitor-General also took his stand, are those of section 254 (1) (c) 'that *on any ground* there was a miscarriage of justice.'

The proposition which [counsel for the appellant] advanced is somewhat startling in its implications. Here is a case in which an applicant seeks to have set aside a conviction on a grave charge of armed assault and robbery to which he had, with legal advice and full knowledge of the nature of the crime, pleaded guilty. All that was or could be said in explanation was that he had done so under misapprehension as to the length of sentence likely to be imposed, and that he deliberately chose to plead guilty to a crime of which he was innocent and of which he had only learned in detail from a newspaper cutting in order to exchange the rigours of military punishment for prolonged absence from his regiment without leave, for the less severe regimen of a civil prison. The adequacy of the explanation may be open to doubt, but no other reason was suggested by [counsel for the appellant] for such otherwise inexplicable conduct. As, according to [counsel for the appellant's] information, confirmed by the Solicitor-General, the Crown was now satisfied that the applicant was in no way concerned in the crime to which he had falsely pled guilty then, whether his conduct was otherwise liable to prosecution and punishment, this conviction constituted a miscarriage of justice which could competently be corrected in this Court. It was a competent course because the language of section 254 (1) is sufficiently wide to include even an appeal against a conviction on a recorded plea of guilty which the applicant did not seek, if he could do so, to have recalled or withdrawn. The words in the section 'on any ground' were not limited in their application to grounds intrinsic to the proceedings out of which the application arose, but could include any ground extrinsic as well as intrinsic which demonstrated a miscarriage of justice in respect of the particular conviction.

In support of this contention, however, [counsel for the appellant] could cite no Scottish authority, but, in addition to his submission as to the inference to be drawn from the width of the language of the Statute, he placed reliance on certain decisions of the Court of Criminal Appeal in England interpreting the identical words used in section 4 (1) of the English Act of 1907 . . . [I]t is not, in my opinion, necessary in the peculiar circumstances of the present case either to canvass in detail the tract of English authority to which [counsel for the appellant] drew our attention, or to explore or attempt a precise delimitation of the circumstances in which it is competent for this Court to entertain an appeal against conviction on the comprehensive ground that the conviction resulted in a miscarriage of justice. The words of the Statute are admittedly wide and comprehensive— the only limit which they would appear to place upon the Court's power and duty to allow an appeal is that the Court should think there was a miscarriage of justice—but it must be substantial, according to the proviso to section 254 (1). It is obvious, however, that very grave difficulties must lie in the path of an applicant who seeks to complain of a miscarriage of justice in a case in which he himself has not only tendered a plea of guilty to the charge libelled against him on which the conviction sought to be appealed against is recorded, but has done so when acting with legal advice and in full knowledge of the nature and details of the charge to which deliberately and falsely he has tendered that plea and, further, has through the mouth of his counsel, presented a precise and detailed plea in mitigation of sentence. While that is necessarily so, it does not follow that there cannot be a case in which appeal against conviction following a recorded plea of guilty may not be competently submitted to this Court; all that it is possible to say is that the competence of such an application is neither specifically affirmed nor prohibited by the Statute. Thus, for example, a conviction on a plea of guilty to a charge which was fundamentally bad as libelling acts which did not constitute a crime could not in my view stand in the way of the Court's power to intervene on appeal to avoid a miscarriage of justice. But it is not necessary to multiply instances, as there are special and possible unique circumstances in the present case which, in my view, make it possible and competent for the Court to entertain the appeal to which the present application is directed. Not only does the prosecutor not oppose the application but he lends it full support, and does so on the specific ground that the conviction of the applicant constituted a miscarriage of justice. This is a very grave and weighty consideration. In his very frank disclosure of the unfortunate circumstances in which this came about, the learned Solicitor-General made it clear that investigation has now demonstrated that there was never in fact any evidence available to the Crown which could corroborate the applicant's admission of guilt or his circumstantial confession or confessions. Thus there was at no time legal evidence on which it would have been competent or proper for the Crown to initiate a prosecution even in face of the applicant's admission or confession, however detailed.

The Solicitor-General added that, had the initial investigation undertaken by the authorities disclosed the true situation, no charge could or would have been brought against the applicant. It was plain, also, from the Solicitor-General's statement that, had error not been made in the information which was before Crown counsel when, following the applicant's letter under section 102 of the 1975 Act and his subsequent appearance before the Sheriff, the applicant appeared on remit for sentence in the High Court, the plea therein offered would never have been accepted, nor, if the case had been fully precognosced, would the charge have been proceeded with. For the predicament in which he finds himself, however, the applicant must bear a heavy responsibility for his deliberate, detailed and repeated false admissions and confessions.

The intervention of the Crown in effect in support of the only ground of appeal open to the applicant introduces a unique element into a case for which since 1926 the reported decisions in this Court provide no precedent. The importance of that intervention in a Scottish criminal appeal is to be weighed in light of the constitutional position and responsibility of the Lord Advocate in our system of criminal administration.

[His Lordship outlined the powers and duties of the Lord Advocate as master of the instance in criminal proceedings (see above, p. 29) and continued:]

In the exercise of these formidable responsibilities the Lord Advocate has at his disposal the fullest available machinery of inquiry and investigation. The Statute provides that the Court *shall* allow the appeal if they think

. . . 'that on any ground there was a miscarriage of justice.' This phrase is to be contrasted with the two earlier grounds upon which an appeal shall be allowed which relate respectively to the quality of evidence or wrong decision of any question of law. From this it may legitimately be inferred that a miscarriage of justice therefore may be established from circumstances which lie outside the limits of the actual proceedings themselves and the jurisdiction of the Court in this last instance is not to be confined solely to consideration of the circumstances of the proceedings themselves. It is probably a unique circumstance of the present application that the Crown as master of the instance not only does not oppose it, but on behalf of the Lord Advocate the Solicitor-General has categorically and formally asserted that a miscarriage of justice has occurred and that recent inquiry has demonstrated that there is no evidence in existence upon which the applicant could or should have been charged, far less evidence upon which if led and accepted a proper and supportable conviction could have been recorded. In light of this the only remaining question is whether there is anything in the wording of the relevant provisions of the Act which inhibits the Court from entertaining or giving effect to the application which has been made? It appears to me that the words 'on any ground' are at least of such width as not to prevent this Court in circumstances so exceptional from giving a relief which in the interests of justice both prosecutor and accused concur in seeking at the hands of the Court.

There remains the practical question of how to give effect to these views. The accused's application is one for extension of time upon which to lodge an application for leave to appeal against conviction. [Counsel for the appellant] has drafted three grounds on which he would, if this application is granted, seek leave to appeal. The third of these alleges miscarriage of justice. In my opinion from what has been disclosed and admitted on behalf of the Crown in this unique case there can be no room for doubt that there has been miscarriage of justice, for which of course in large measure the reckless and deliberate action of the applicant himself is responsible. That, however, is not the question. The question is whether in fact a substantial miscarriage of justice has taken place. In my opinion that has been demonstrated and in my opinion also this Court can give a remedy. I would therefore move your Lordships that the present application be treated as a formal application for leave to appeal, that leave should be given and the appeal should be allowed and the conviction quashed."

Appeal allowed.

NOTES

1. It is clear from the above that the fact that the appellant himself is in large measure to blame for the miscarriage of justice does not of itself present a barrier to quashing the conviction.

2. Lord Cameron expressed the view that a miscarriage may be established "from circumstances which lie outside the limits of the actual proceedings themselves". The new section 228(2) (*supra*)

refers only to "any alleged miscarriage of justice in the proceedings" in which the conviction was obtained. Can any significance be attached to the difference between the statute and Lord Cameron's opinion? Was this a case of a miscarriage within the proceedings or outside them?

3. Although the decision in *Boyle* turns to a certain extent on the wording of the now repealed section 254(1), it is submitted that the wording of section 228(2) is sufficiently wide to encompass this sort of case, the words "any alleged miscarriage of justice" being at least as wide as the words "on any ground".

c. *The meaning of miscarriage of justice*

The extent to which the court is prepared to develop the notion of a miscarriage of justice independent of the pre-1980 Act cases is as yet unclear, although it would appear from *McCuaig* that they are unlikely to do so. The following cases are included as examples of the sort of issue which has in the past been presented to the court of appeal, and which for the future will be presented to the court as possible miscarriages of justice.

(i) Misdirection by the judge

1. McPhelim v. H.M. Advocate
1960 J.C. 17

The appellant was convicted on charges of assault and robbery committed in concert with three other men. He appealed to the High Court on the ground that certain omissions from the presiding judge's charge to the jury amounted to misdirection.

LORD JUSTICE-CLERK (THOMSON): "[His Lordship outlined the circumstances of the offence, and continued:] In these circumstances, the evidence being so recent, the competing stories being so clear and the jury having been addressed by counsel in what the presiding Judge described as two excellent speeches, it would not be surprising if the Judge were to say to the jury:—'This is a simple, straightforward issue of fact for you; you have heard the evidence and the speeches; are you satisfied beyond reasonable doubt that it has been brought home to the accused that he was one of the group who carried this thing out?' That is pretty much what the Judge did. I cannot help feeling that any detached and disinterested observer, who had sat through that trial, who had absorbed its atmosphere, and who had appreciated what the real issue was, would have agreed readily that there was little call for much more, and that there could be little doubt that the jury fully appreciated that the true issue at the trial was, whether the appellant was in the affair as a participator, or was the innocent victim of circumstances and propinquity.

The atmosphere in a Court of Appeal is apt to be a little different, and that, no doubt, is why this appeal has been taken. The criticism of the charge is that it was too brief, and that it failed adequately to instruct the jury on the way in which they should approach their consideration of the case.

In reviewing the proceedings at a criminal trial, a Court of Appeal has certain obvious advantages. It has before it a complete record of what has happened, and it has the time and opportunity to consider it dispassionately. The tension is over; it knows the result. It can be wise after the event. But these advantages are counterbalanced by obvious disadvantages. No Court of Appeal can truly recapture the feel and atmosphere of a trial. The drab record of proceedings cannot reproduce the ebb and flow of the trial, or the variations of emphasis. A Court of Appeal must therefore be constantly on its guard against failing to appreciate what were the vital issues—the matters to which those actively engaged in the trial were directing their attention. The very drabness of the record may lead the Court of Appeal to dwell unduly on matters which were perhaps taken for granted at the trial, or to pay undue attention to omissions which, while they are obvious enough on the written record, may have had little or no significance in the living context of the trial. Paradoxically enough, a Court of Appeal is quite as much in danger of getting the case out of focus as is the Judge who conducted the trial. For that reason, it is our duty to view with confidence and charity the course taken by an experienced Judge in charging a jury. If a charge is to be a good charge, it ought to be one addressed to the fifteen people in the jury-box, and not to the Court of Appeal. A charge, which meticulously covers every theoretical aspect, may be so complicated that the jury's capacity to appreciate what it is being told may be blunted long before the real matters with which it has to deal are reached. On the other hand, a vital and effective charge which brings the relevant issue squarely before the jury may on subsequent analysis be found to have technical weaknesses. No hard and fast rule can be laid down. Sometimes the charge must of necessity be technical, and the various legal issues must be fully and accurately defined; at the other extreme, little or no legal instruction is required. There are certain things which must be said, but the way in which they are said or the emphasis which need be laid on them, varies with the particular case."

Appeal refused.

NOTE

See also *McKenzie* v. *H.M. Advocate*, 1959 J.C. 32, *supra*, Chap. 1 and *Hamilton and Others* v. *H.M. Advocate*, 1938 J.C. 134, *supra*, Chap. 10, and *McIntyre* v. *H.M. Advocate*, 1981 S.C.C.R. 117. In the latter case the court expressed the opinion that "if on vital issues a direction given is so inadequate as to amount to a misdirection any conviction must be quashed." The court further expressed the view that what were "vital issues" would depend upon the circumstances of the case, and that "a judge must at least focus the vital issues in the context of the evidence" (p. 122). In *McAvoy and Another* v. *H.M. Adv.*, 1983 S.L.T. 16, 1982 S.C.C.R. 263, Lord Hunter stated: ". . . if the appeal is based, for example, upon a misdirection by the trial judge or the admission by the judge of inadmissible evidence and either of these grounds is established, then I am of opinion that the court is empowered to consider the materiality of that misdirection, or of the evidence which ought not to have been admitted, in relation to all the factors relevant to the verdict of guilty. If, having done that, the court is satisfied that neither the misdirection nor the admission of the inadmissible evidence, whatever it may be, was sufficiently material to cast doubt upon the guilty verdict, then the appeal should be dismissed." A failure to focus the "vital issues" may on the above views necessarily constitute a material miscarriage of justice. *Cf. Tonge and Others* v. *H.M. Advocate*, 1982 S.L.T. 506; 1982 S.C.C.R. 313, *supra* p. 177 and the following case.

2. McTavish v. H.M. Advocate
1975 S.L.T. (Notes) 27

The appellant, a nurse, was convicted of the murder of one of her patients by injecting into the latter an overdose of insulin. She appealed on the ground, *inter alia,* of misdirection. The nature of the alleged misdirection is set out in the opinion of the court.

OPINION OF THE COURT: " . . . Counsel for the appellant's argument can be summarised as follows. It was common ground that the appellant had given Mrs Lyon an injection. In this highly important respect the issue was whether she injected insulin, as the Crown contended, or sterile water as she maintained. In reviewing the Crown evidence in his charge to the jury the presiding judge made specific reference in detail to the replies attributed to her by the police witnesses when she was cautioned and charged. The charge at that time was simply one of assault. The relevant portion of that charge was that on 30th June 1973 in Ward 5, Ruchill Hospital, she assaulted Mrs Lyon, a patient in the hospital, and administered to her a substance which was to the procurator-fiscal unknown to her injury. According to the police witnesses the appellant's first reply was: 'I gave a half c.c. of insulin soluble to Mrs Lyon only because she wanted to be put out of her pain and misery and had trouble with her bowels.' Her second reply was: 'I gave Mrs Lyon a half c.c. of soluble insulin. She was taking a cerebral and was wanting out of her misery.' The presiding judge had prefaced his recital of this evidence by saying that the crucial statements made by the accused were those made in answer to the caution and charge. These statements, if accepted by the jury, were conclusive against the appellant in this vital issue in the case, and whereas the presiding judge had given prominence to them in his review of the Crown evidence, he made no reference whatsoever to the appellant's denial of them and her counter-account of what she said either when reviewing the defence case and the evidence in support of it, or indeed at any point in his charge. In the circumstances it was a fault of commission and not just one of omission. It was so highly prejudicial to the appellant that it constituted a misdirection in law on a vital matter which called for the quashing of the conviction on this murder charge.

In support of his submission counsel for the appellant founded strongly on various passages in the opinion of Lord Justice-Clerk Aitchison in the case of *H.M. Advocate* v. *Mills,* 1935 J.C. 77, 1935 S.L.T. 532. The one passage which seems most apposite to the present case is at p. 534 where his Lordship said: 'The charge proceeded on the view that the accuracy of Warnock's statement was not in doubt.' [Warnock was the police officer to whom the statement was made]. 'But the appellant himself gave evidence, and he disputed the accuracy of Warnock's evidence and gave a vitally different account of the words which he used. According to the appellant, it was Warnock who said: "We know you did not mean to murder her" and not himself who said: "I did not mean to murder her." The attention of the jury, in my view, ought to have been directed specifically to the appellant's evidence, and they ought to have been told that they must consider it in making up their minds whether the appellant had in fact used the words attributed to him by Warnock. No such direction was given. On the contrary, the charge was calculated to convey to the jury the impression that the statement as alleged by Warnock was indisputably proved.' Counsel for the appellant submitted that the present case was in pari casu, and that if one substituted the competing versions of the statements in the present case for the competing versions in *Mills'* case (supra) Lord Aitchison's words were exactly apposite. As the evidence on the point had been presented by the presiding judge to the jury, without any attention, specific or indeed otherwise, having been directed to the appellant's contradictory evidence, the charge was calculated to convey to the jury the impression that the statements as alleged by the police witnesses were indisputably proved. The omission to give proper direction on such a vital matter was, as he had argued, fatal to the conviction.

In his reply the Solicitor-General pointed out correctly that each case had to be considered on its own particular facts. He, accordingly, sought to distinguish the facts in the present case from those in *Mills.* We need not go into this in detail. It suffices to say that, in our opinion, the passage in Lord Aitchison's judgment quoted above is apposite to the present case. In both cases there was ample evidence to warrant a conviction. But in both cases the statement or statements were, on the Crown evidence, admissions of guilt, whereas the accused's version was a declaration of innocence. Nothing could be more vital. Faced with that situation, the Solicitor-General maintained that the attention of the jury to the appellant's denial of the police version of her statements need not be contained in a specific reference to what she said if it could be found by necessary inference from the charge read as a whole and under specific reference to certain passages therein. Without accepting that this is a legitimate extension of Lord Aitchison's phrase 'directed specifically' we are prepared to examine the Solicitor-General's argument on the basis that it is.

In limine, he argued that while the contents of the appellant's statements were in issue, this was not a vital issue in the case. We cannot agree. In our opinion this was a most vital issue. It related to a matter which could have swung the case one way or another.

Turning to the contents of the judge's charge, he first of all drew attention to some general and normal directions given by the presiding judge. These were that in the last analysis it was for the jury to make the final decisions; that it would be impossible in a case of this length to go into all the evidence in detail; that the facts were for them; that while he might indicate lines of approach, anything he said could be ignored or discarded by them; and that it was their recollection of the evidence, not his, which counted. The Solicitor-General then pointed out that throughout her evidence the appellant had maintained that it was sterile water which she had injected into Mrs Lyon, and that the presiding judge in his charge had made reference to appropriate passages where she said this. We pause to observe that while this is so, he nowhere made reference to the fact that she said that in her replies to the charge she denied the injection of insulin but talked about sterile water. His next point was that in dealing with statements to the police the presiding judge said: 'We have heard a good deal of evidence about certain statements which the accused made, or is alleged to have made to the police after the investigation into the death of Mrs Lyon was being carried out.' He argued that the use of the phrase 'or is alleged to have been made to the police' was a clear indication to the jury that the question of what the appellant said in any of her statements was an issue to be resolved, and that in turn involved consideration of what the appellant said she had said on any such occasion. That of necessity included a direction to consider what she said that she said in her replies to the charge. This is perhaps the strongest point in the Solicitor-General's argument. But at this point the presiding judge was dealing with all the statements made by the appellant after the police investigation had begun, and these included statements made before the charge was preferred against her as well as the statements made in reply to the charge. Not without some hesitation we have come to the view that the Solicitor-General's point is too fine a one, and that it cannot be said that the use of the phrase 'or is alleged to have been made to the police' is so unambiguous that any reasonable jury would have known that this was a clear invitation to them to have regard to the appellant's denial of the replies said by the police to have been made by her in reply to the charge. Here again the passage quoted is within a section of the charge where the issues being canvassed were the credibility of witnesses and the fairness or otherwise of the obtaining of the statements and not the contents of the statements. The same observation falls to be made in regard to the final excerpt quoted by the Solicitor-General, where the presiding judge said: ' . . . on the other hand, if you think what she says is correct or if you think that what she says puts any doubt on the matter, then

I direct you that you should exclude that evidence and these statements from your consideration.' But there his Lordship was dealing with the question whether the statements as spoken to by the police were truly voluntary or whether there was any unfairness about them, and not about the conflicting versions of the contents of the statements made in reply to the charge.

Of course, it is not sufficient to look at passages in a judge's charge in isolation. In respect of any point at issue the charge has to be read as a whole. We have given careful and anxious consideration to the charge. At the end of 13 days of evidence and two long and detailed speeches by counsel in a highly complicated case it was a far from easy task for the presiding judge to give a comprehensive, but clearly defined charge to the jury. In our opinion, but for a single omission which a few words could have cured, this was a well-constructed, clear and accurate charge. It is not disputed that in the course of it he failed to direct the jury specifically to consider whether in fact the appellant in her replies to the charge had made the statements attributed to her by the police which, if accepted, were vital pieces of evidence of a highly incriminating nature. On the authority of *Mills* such a failure would be fatal to a conviction. Even the most experienced judge may fail to give a direction which ought to have been given, particularly at the end of a long and exhausting trial. The judge here failed to give such a direction, and failed to draw the attention of the jury to the appellant's versions of the replies she gave. We are unable to find in the charge as a whole or in any of the selected passages therein which were cited to us sufficient to repair that deficiency by necessary inference or implication. We have reached the conclusion that in these circumstances counsel for the appellant was well founded in his submission that the charge was calculated, in the sense of being liable, to convey to the jury that the statements as alleged by the police witnesses were indisputably proved, and that the presiding judge's failure to give an adequate direction thereanent constituted a misdirection in law. The question then as always, is whether this omission was sufficiently material to vitiate the verdict. The answer to that can only be that it was. In so finding we echo the concluding words of Lord Aitchison in *Mills,* words which might have been coined for this very case. He said: 'I reach this conclusion with regret. It can never be a light thing to interfere with the verdict of a jury on a charge of murder, and, as I have already said, there is, in my view, ample evidence to support the verdict; but, by the law of Scotland, an accused person is entitled to have his case tried with an adequate direction to the jury, and, if on any vital matter the direction is inadequate, so as to amount to misdirection, it is our plain duty to set the verdict aside. We are not entitled to depart in any way from that imperative rule.' "

Appeal allowed; conviction quashed.

NOTES

1. The court could have applied the proviso and upheld the conviction on the ground that there had been no substantial miscar-

riage of justice. This is a course, however, which the High Court was always reluctant to adopt (see, for example, *Tobin* v. *H.M. Advocate*, 1934 J.C. 60 and *McKenzie* v. *H.M. Advocate*, 1959 J.C. 32). If this attitude were to be maintained today, therefore, it would seem that a misdirection of this sort would constitute a miscarriage of justice of sufficient materiality to justify interfering with the verdict.

2. The court was clearly unhappy with the outcome of the case. Would this be the type of case in which a fresh indictment could be brought under section 254(1)(*c*)?

(ii) Introduction of previous convictions

Section 160(1) of the 1975 Act provides that previous convictions against an accused shall not be laid before the jury, nor shall reference be made thereto in the presence of the jury before the verdict is returned. Breach of this provision has frequently been the subject of appeal to the High Court, on the ground of miscarriage of justice.

Cordiner v. H.M. Advocate
1978 J.C. 64

The appellant was charged, *inter alia,* with attempted extortion. The offence was alleged to have been committed during the month of June 1976. During that month the appellant was in prison. He lodged a special defence of alibi, which was read to the jury at the commencement of the trial (in accordance with normal practice). That charge was withdrawn by the Crown, but the appellant was convicted on two other charges contained in the same indictment. He appealed on the ground of miscarriage of justice, on the basis of a breach of section 160(1) of the 1975 Act. A second accused, Newby, also appealed on the ground of miscarriage. It was his contention that he had been tainted by association with Cordiner, and that his right to a fair trial had been prejudiced.

LORD JUSTICE-CLERK (WHEATLEY): " . . . Although there is a superficial similarity in the grounds stated by the two appellants there are important differences and we consider each case separately. Before we discuss Cordiner's appeal, we should mention that it was not disputed that Cordiner had been sentenced to 60 days' imprisonment in Edinburgh Sheriff Court on 24th May 1976, being released from Saughton prison on 2nd July 1976, and that this conviction did appear on the schedule of previous convictions. In the course of his evidence Cordiner himself, despite advice from the Court, made it clear that he had a 'criminal record' although the full details were not stated. His insistence on stating this was, he explained, because he had been 'framed' by the police and because 'the Crown has already forced me to produce my criminal records.' This reference to 'criminal records' was a distortion of the necessary reference to the one conviction of imprisonment for 60 days. We add that the trial Judge, in his charge to the jury, stressed that they should put out of their minds any references to previous records and ignore the fact that the appellant had been 'serving a minor prison sentence for what must have been a very minor offence' in June 1976.

It was conceded on behalf of the Crown that in the particular circumstances of this case, so far as relating to Cordiner, there had been a breach of section 160 (1) of the Criminal Procedure (Scotland) Act 1975 which provides: 'Previous convictions against the accused shall not be laid before the jury nor shall reference be made thereto in presence of the jury before the verdict is returned.' It was agreed that in lodging the special defence of alibi in answer to the second charge Cordiner was forced to disclose the fact that he was in prison in June 1976. This, it was conceded on behalf of the Crown, was equivalent to laying a previous conviction before the jury. In our opinion this concession could not have been withheld.

There was a difference of opinion on the effects of this breach of section 160 (1). For Cordiner, it was argued that this breach constituted prejudice which amounted to a substantial miscarriage of justice which vitiated the entire proceedings and must result in the allowance of the appeal and the quashing of his convictions. Reliance was placed on the observations of Lord Jamieson in *Bryce* v. *Gardiner* 1951 J.C. 134 at p. 142, where certain *dicta* in previous cases are considered, and on these *dicta* themselves. For the Crown, it was argued that although the breach amounted to a 'miscarriage of justice' it did not amount to a 'substantial miscarriage of justice,' and that accordingly the proviso to section 254 (1) of the Act of 1975 should be applied and the appeal dismissed. . . .

Reference was made to the opinions of various Judges in support of the contention that a breach of section 160 (1) or its equivalent was in itself sufficient to warrant the quashing of a conviction. The genesis of these opinions was the opinion of Lord Kyllachy in *Cornwallis* v. *H. M. Advocate* 3 Adam 604 where he said, when referring to previous convictions being laid before a jury: 'But I am bound to say that if the Sheriff or prosecutor had during the trial conveyed this information to the jury the action would have been bad.' Lord Young expressed a contrary view. Lord Anderson, in his dissenting opinion in *Corcoran* v. *H. M. Advocate* 1932 J.C. 42, when referring to the similar proviso in the Act of 1926, treats Lord Kyllachy's views in *Cornwallis* as meaning that 'there is always a substantial miscarriage of justice where a previous conviction has been disclosed by the prosecutor during trial . . . ' The Lord Justice-Clerk (Alness) also supported Lord Kyllachy but made no reference to the Act of 1926. In *Kepple* v. *H. M. Advocate* 1936 J.C. 76 Lord Justice-General Normand reserved his opinion on the question whether a breach of section 67 of the Criminal Procedure (Scotland) Act 1887 (corresponding to section 160 of the Act of 1975) necessarily leads to the quashing of a conviction. In *Bryce* v. *Gardiner, supra,* Lord Jamieson supported the view of Lord Anderson in *Corcoran, supra.* What has not been noticed is that the case of *Cornwallis* was decided before the passing of the Criminal Appeal (Scotland) Act

1926, and the introduction of the proviso in section 2 (1) thereof. Accordingly Lord Kyllachy could not be addressing his mind to the present question. *Bryce* v. *Gardiner* was a stated case on a summary complaint, to which section 2 (1) and its proviso did not apply, and so the issue could not arise and accordingly could not be discussed. In *Corcoran,* which was a case under solemn procedure, no reference was made to the proviso. Accordingly the support given to Lord Kyllachy in these cases has no relation to the point here.

In our opinion a breach of section 160 (1) of the Act amounts to a 'miscarriage of justice' but this does not necessarily lead to a quashing of the conviction. The proviso in section 254 (1) allows the Court to dismiss the appeal if they are of the opinion that the miscarriage of justice has not been 'substantial.' Taking an extreme illustration of the contrary view, we do not consider it conceivable that the wrongful disclosure of a conviction for a trivial motoring offence could be regarded as a substantial miscarriage of justice so as to vitiate a conviction on a charge of murder.

It was accepted on behalf of the Crown that the test for the application of the proviso was 'high and exacting' to quote the words of the Lord Justice-Clerk (Thomson) in *M'Kenzie* v. *H. M. Advocate* 1959 J.C. 32 in adopting the test of Viscount Simon in *Stirland* v. *D.P.P.* [1944] A.C. 315. That test was in these terms, *viz.*:—'the provision that the Court of Criminal Appeal may dismiss the appeal if they consider that no substantial miscarriage of justice has actually occurred in convicting the accused assumes a situation where a reasonable jury, after being properly directed, would, on the evidence, properly admissible, without doubt convict.' The basis of the argument for the Crown for the application of the proviso was the appellant's own evidence about his previous criminal record, which went far beyond the limited reference in the special defence, and the appellant's allegations that he had been 'framed' as a line of defence. Any possible prejudice which could have arisen from the disclosure that the appellant had been in prison in June 1976 was, it was said, 'swamped' by his own evidence which was deliberately exploiting the fact that the Crown had erred in regard to the enforced disclosure of a previous conviction. It has to be noted that the Crown's original error in including the offensive date in the charge when his list of previous convictions *prima facie* disclosed that he could not have committed the offence on that date was compounded by the fact that after the special defence had been lodged at the pleading diet the Crown took no steps to seek to have the charge amended so as to exclude the date which occasioned the special defence in this respect to be lodged. This failure to take appropriate action in the face of their attention being specifically drawn to a fact which was almost instantly verifiable, in the knowledge that otherwise the disclosure that the appellant had been in prison would inevitably be drawn to the attention of the jury, was in our opinion quite unjustifiable. It may well be that the appellant deliberately exploited the situation which had arisen from the inexcusable conduct of the Crown which had led to disclosure of the previous conviction, but we cannot dissociate the appellant's admission and line of defence from the initial error made by the Crown and ignore the possible prejudicial effect on the jury. We cannot say that the jury would have convicted if the Crown had not erred at the outset in forcing the appellant to admit that he was in prison in June 1976. The fact that, save in charge 1 (1) which was unanimous, the verdicts against the appellant were all by a majority reinforces that view. Accordingly we cannot apply the proviso here. For these reasons we have no alternative to quashing the conviction against Cordiner.

We turn to the appeal of Newby. We have earlier stated the first reason put forward in his application. The submission was that Newby was so closely associated with Cordiner that any prejudice sustained by Cordiner because of the breach of section 160 of the Act of 1975, involving Cordiner, must affect Newby. This association, it was said, related not only to the charges against them in the indictment, which were based on their acting in concert, but also to their private lives where there was evidence of a close association. It was furthermore argued that, even if Cordiner's appeal was refused because he had taken advantage of the Crown's initial error by expanding on his own criminal activities in support of his allegations of a 'frame up' by the police, Newby's appeal should succeed because of the resulting prejudice to Newby by Cordiner's actions. Reliance appeared to be placed on the fact that Newby did not have control of Cordiner's special defence and of any prejudicial evidence which Cordiner might give.

We cannot accept this submission for which no authority was produced. There was no breach of section 160 of the Act so far as Newby was concerned. The miscarriage of justice was in the breach of that section and only related to and affected Cordiner. The breach cannot, in our view, be founded on by a co-accused simply because they were charged together or were closely associated. An accused may suffer prejudice in the course of a trial in a number of ways but such prejudice may not amount to a 'miscarriage of justice.' An accused may prejudice a co-accused by giving evidence against the co-accused but that is not a miscarriage of justice. In a case like the present, an accused person might, voluntarily and for his own purposes, disclose a long list of previous convictions. A co-accused with whom that accused has a close association might say that he had no control of the accused and had been prejudiced thereby but he could not be heard to maintain that there was a miscarriage of justice as a result. We cannot see any basis for a transfer of prejudice against a co-accused amounting to a miscarriage of justice in this case."

Appeal by first appellant allowed.
Appeal by second appellant refused.

NOTES

1. The view that a breach of section 160(1) amounts to a miscarriage of justice but not necessarily a *substantial* miscarriage was probably what lay behind the decision in *McCuaig*. The court accepted that there had been a breach, and may therefore have been of opinion that there was a miscarriage of justice. If the court had not insisted on the discretionary nature of section 254, it would

have been faced with the prospect of holding that any breach of section 160(1) justified the quashing of a conviction on the ground of miscarriage. (The court could, of course, have held that the 1980 Act introduced completely new grounds of appeal, enabling it to develop a new line of authority on "miscarriage of justice" but it does not appear to have considered this possibility.)

2. In *McAvoy and Another* v. *H.M. Advocate*, 1983, S.L.T. 16; 1982 S.C.C.R. 263, however, the view was expressed (1983 S.L.T. at p. 20) that the view expressed in *Cordiner* (that a breach of section 160(1) amounts to a miscarriage) might not be of universal application. If this is so, then the assumption behind *McCuuig* flies off, and with it a substantial part of the reason for the decision.

3. The cases on section 160(1) are legion. For a general discussion of the authorities, see Renton and Brown, paras. 10-42 *et seq*.

(iii) Oppression by the trial judge

Oppressive conduct on the part of the trial judge may well constitute a miscarriage of justice of sufficient materiality to justify interference with the verdict. A typical case of oppression may arise where the judge abandons his role of impartial "referee" and takes on the role of inquisitor or prosecutor.

Tallis v. H.M. Advocate
1982 S.C.C.R. 91

The appellant was charged, along with his partner, Wands, with the theft of a quantity of rails. His partner pleaded guilty, and after trial the appellant was convicted. He appealed against conviction and sentence on the ground that the conduct of the trial judge may have constituted a miscarriage of justice.

LORD JUSTICE-GENERAL (EMSLIE): "In this appeal the appellant challenges his conviction upon the following ground: 'The sheriff interrupted the cross-examination of the procurator fiscal and proceeded to cross-examine the panel, and thereafter the terms of this charge were such as to show a bias and may have constituted a miscarriage of justice resulting in the panel being convicted by a majority of the jurors.' The appeal on this ground was presented under reference to the cases of *Nisbet* v *H.M. Advocate*, 1979 SLT (Notes) 5 and *Dobbins* v *H.M. Advocate*, as yet unreported save in Crown Office circular A28/80. In the former case the critical issue was whether the accused's admitted possession of certain articles was innocent or guilty. In the second it was whether the accused, who had admittedly caused the death of the deceased, was guilty of murder, as the Crown contended, or of culpable homicide. In both cases the credibility of the accused was of prime importance and conviction was challenged upon the ground that the conduct of the trial judge, who had himself questioned the accused at some length, had resulted in oppression of such a nature as to constitute a miscarriage of justice. In *Nisbet* Lord Thomson, with whose opinion Lords Robertson and Allanbridge agreed, said this: 'The law on this matter is not in dispute and was canvassed by this court iñ the case of *Ernest Livingstone* v *H.M. Advocate*, 22 March 1974. In that case the Lord Justice-Clerk said: "I must deprecate the practice of such constant interruptions by a presiding judge. Basically his function is to clear up any ambiguities that are not being cleared up either by the examiner or the cross-examiner. He is also entitled to ask such questions as he might regard relevant and important for the proper determination of the case by the jury, but that right must be exercised with discretion, and only exercised when the occasion requires it. It should not result in a presiding judge taking over the role of examiner or cross-examiner."' He [Lord Thomson] also pointed out that the question whether the conduct of a judge has so far strayed beyond the bounds of propriety as to result in oppression of such a nature as to constitute a miscarriage of justice, required to be resolved as a question of degree, and under reference to the particular issue before the court he said this: 'In our opinion, as it is was not disputed that the articles in question were found in the accused's possession, and the whole question for the jury to decide was whether his possession was honest or dishonest, it was particularly important for the sheriff to demonstrate and maintain his complete impartiality on that question. This in our view he failed to do.'

In this appeal the particular submission of counsel for the appellant came to be that the presiding sheriff took over the role of cross-examiner in the course of the evidence of the accused himself, that he conspicuously failed to demonstrate and maintain his complete impartiality upon the vital issue of the credibility of the accused and of Miss Veryan, and that he suggested to the jury that the Crown case might be such a strong one that they would be entitled to acquit the appellant only if they were satisfied with the explanation which he gave in the witness box.

In our opinion the submission of counsel for the appellant is well founded and must receive effect. In evidence certain police witnesses stated that before the appellant was charged he had explained his part in the removal of the rails and that he had believed that the work had been authorised by the order which Wands had shown him, which he had by that time discovered to be quite bogus. The appellant in evidence explained that he had then thought that both he and Wands had been the dupes of the author of the bogus order, and had only learned two months before the trial, that the 'order' had been prepared by Wands himself. During his cross-examination by the procurator fiscal the appellant stated: 'At the police station I was charged but before that they did tell you that I in fact explained my full position.' That was of course perfectly correct, and what the appellant was referring to was, clearly, 'his full position' as he had then understood it to be. The sheriff, alas, did not appreciate this, and intervened to cross-examine the appellant upon the basis that he was misleading the court, for he recalled that there had been no evidence from the police officers that the appellant had explained Wands' actings which had allegedly deceived him. There is, we think, little doubt that in the exchanges between the sheriff and the appellant they were at cross purposes, and that the sheriff's adverse view of the appellant's credibility was unfortunately made clear. The damage done by the sheriff's intervention could, of course, have been repaired by an impeccable charge. The sheriff's charge, however, cannot be so described, for he carried forward into his charge itself, in the short passage in which he introduced the question of the credibility of the appellant and Miss Veryan, the quite mistaken impression he had formed about the appellant's veracity. What he said was this: 'You have seen Mr Tallis giving evidence. It is a matter for you to assess whether you consider Mr Tallis to be a person who found it easy to shift his ground if he found a question a bit difficult or a bit tricky, ladies and gentlemen, and you will recall the point that I put to him, ladies and gentlemen—although it is a matter entirely for you whether you accept my version of the evidence—but you recall the point that he said he told the police all about it. Well, ladies and gentlemen, my recollection is that the police were not asked that and they certainly did not say that, but it is a matter entirely for you, ladies and gentlemen.' The only other thing he said was as follows: 'Then there is the girl Fiona Veryan, do you believe her, ladies and gentlemen? You may recall her dramatic exit line when asked why she had come to give evidence. She said that she had asked Wands, that is George Wands, what to say and that he had said, "Say that Tallis wrote the contract", and that she simply refused to do that because she wasn't prepared to let Tallis bear the brunt of something which she had in fact done. Well, ladies and gentlemen, as against that there is the alternative view that "Hell holds no fury like a woman's scorn". You may take that view, ladies and gentlemen. You recall that she said she was annoyed and had split up with Mr Wands because he had not visited her in hospital. These are all factors which you have to take into account when you make up your minds where you think the truth lies.' The observation of the sheriff about Miss Veryan was not only inaccurate; it was, at the very least, gratuitously unfortunate. The clear impression conveyed to the jury in this passage in the charge was that, in the sheriff's view, the credibility of the appellant and of Miss Veryan was suspect. That this is a fair interpretation of the passage we have so far considered is, we think, confirmed in a later and lengthier chapter of the charge in which, in the examination of the evidence led for the Crown, piece by piece, the sheriff repeatedly said to the jury, 'Why should he be involved at all if he wasn't in fact a party to the whole fiddle', or words to that effect. The matter does not, however, end there, because the sheriff severed the last link in the chain of impartiality required of him by giving to the jury what appears to us to be a serious misdirection in law. He said this: 'Though the situation may arise, ladies and gentlemen, that the Crown puts forward such a strong case that it is only if you are satisfied with the explanation given by the accused, that you would be entitled to acquit him and again that may very well be the situation here you feel, but again it is a matter for you to make up your minds about, ladies and gentlemen.' The gravity of this misdirection lies in the plain indication to the jury that in certain circumstances the onus of proof shifts to the accused and unless he can discharge it by an explanation which 'satisfies the jury', i.e., of his innocence, then conviction must follow. Upon a consideration of all these circumstances we are driven to the conclusion, without casting any doubt upon the accuracy of the guidance offered to judges in the cases of *Nisbet* and *Dobbins*, that in this case the sheriff's failure to demonstrate and maintain his complete impartiality upon the vital issue which was for the jury to resolve, may well have influenced the jury and resulted in oppression of such a nature as to constitute a miscarriage of justice. In the result we have no alternative but to allow the appeal and quash the conviction."

Appeal allowed; conviction quashed.

NOTES

1. Judicial interventions in the course of a trial may be objectionable, therefore, not only on the ground of their frequency, but also to the extent that they disclose bias or lack of impartiality. It is clear, also, from *Nisbet (supra)* that there are cases of interruption or intervention which cannot be cured by the judge's summing up. The summing up in *Nisbet*, for example, was said to be "quite adequate", and indeed no criticism was levelled at his general conduct of the trial.

2. *McMillan* v. *H.M. Advocate*, 1979 S.L.T. (Notes) 68 should also be noted in this context. In that case the trial judge allowed his views on the appellant's guilt to become known by canvassing before the jury the appropriate method of disposal of the offender, before a verdict had been returned. It was held that in the circumstances his conduct constituted a miscarriage of justice, even although he had not intended to be unfair, and was probably acting in what he considered to be the best interests of the accused.

(iv)   Unreasonable verdict

Section 254(1) of the 1975 Act formerly provided for an appeal on the ground that the verdict of the jury was unreasonable or could not be supported having regard to the evidence. The Thomson Committee (1st Report, Cmnd. 5038) recommended minor changes to these provisions, which would have removed the reference to the verdict being unsupportable having regard to the evidence (para. 12). The 1980 Act, of course, has removed all such references from the ground of appeal. The question remains as to whether the attitude of the courts will change.

Webb and Others v. H.M. Advocate
1927 J.C. 92

The appellant was convicted, along with two other men, of assaulting a man with a razor. He appealed to the High Court on the ground, *inter alia*, that the verdict of the jury was unreasonable or could not be supported having regard to the evidence.

LORD JUSTICE-CLERK (ALNESS): ". . .Now, it is necessary, in the first place, to apprehend the principles in accordance with which such an appeal as this falls to be determined, and then, having ascertained these principles, to apply them to the case in hand.

As regards the principles involved, some points, I apprehend, are clear. This is not a Court of review. Review, in the ordinary sense of that word, lies outside our province. We have neither a duty nor a right, because we might not have reached the same conclusion as the jury, to upset their verdict. The ambit of the Court of Criminal Appeal is circumscribed by narrower limits. We cannot interfere unless we think the verdict is unreasonable. The duty of this Court, in short, is similar to, if indeed it is not the same as, the duty devolving on a civil Court of appeal when considering the verdict of a jury on a motion for a new trial on the ground that the verdict is contrary to the evidence. In a civil Court the verdict of the jury is invulnerable, unless the Court of appeal thinks that it is perverse. I know of no better statement of the law relating to that topic than that contained in the opinion of Lord Kinnear in the case of *Campbell*, where his Lordship says: 'The verdict is not to be set aside merely because we disagree with it. If all we think of it is that we should not have agreed with it, then to set it aside would be to take upon ourselves the function of a jury. On the other hand, if it is apparent that the jury have not duly performed their functions, and have given a verdict which no reasonable jury, properly instructed, would have given, or, as the late Lord President put it, which is flagrantly wrong, the Court will set it aside, and that whether it be a verdict on a question of slander, or on any other question of fact. The question then is, Is the verdict before us so flagrantly wrong that no reasonable jury discharging their duty honestly under proper direction would have given it? In my judgment our duty in the Court of Criminal Appeal is indistinguishable from the duty of a civil Court in dealing with the verdict of a civil jury."

The court refused the appeal.

NOTES

1. The tone of the court's opinion echoes the views expressed by the Committee on Criminal Appeals who were very much concerned to preserve jury responsibility. The fear was that if juries became aware that their decisions could easily be reversed on appeal they would approach their task that much less seriously, which might have an adverse effect on the position of the accused (Cmnd. 2456, *supra*). The sanctity of the jury verdict was further enhanced by the highly restrictive approach adopted by the court to the admission of fresh evidence on appeal, as to which, see *infra*, p. 450.

2. The old ground of appeal has been swept away by the 1980 Act, and there are no new guidelines as yet. It is submitted that with the disappearance of the old statutory test the way is clear for the courts to adopt a new approach to this issue. Clearly it is undesirable that the verdict of the jury should be dislodged merely because the appeal court disagrees with it. But perhaps a test such as the following might effect a compromise between the strictness of the old law and the vagueness of the new provisions: "Has there been a miscarriage of justice in that the jury's verdict does not fairly reflect the evidence presented at the trial?"

(v) Other cases

It would be impossible in a work of this kind to cover the whole range of potential miscarriages of justice, and in any case it is to be hoped that even now a court might begin to develop some coherent principles governing the construction of section 228. In the meantime, however, it is likely that the views expressed in earlier decisions will remain influential in determining this issue. For a general account of the existing case law see Renton and Brown, para. 11-40.

d. Appeal against sentence

As was pointed out above (p. 420) the only ground of appeal against sentence is that there has been a miscarriage of justice (section 228(2)). Whether or not there has been a miscarriage of justice in relation to a sentence depends upon the rules and principles governing sentencing, and these matters are discussed *post*, Chap. 16.

So far as disposal of appeals against sentence is concerned, section 254(3) of the 1975 Act provides that the High Court may dispose of an appeal by: "(*a*) affirming such sentence; or (*b*) if the Court thinks that, having regard to all the circumstances, including any additional evidence such as is mentioned in section 228(2) of this Act, a different sentence should have been passed, quashing the sentence and passing another sentence whether more or less severe in substitution therefor." Again, the appropriate disposal will depend upon the rules governing sentencing, which are discussed *post*, Chap. 16.

e. Mentally abnormal offenders

In relation to any appeal under section 228(1), where it appears to the High Court that the appellant committed the act charged against him, but that he was insane when he did so, the High Court shall dispose of the appeal by (a) setting aside the verdict of the trial court, and substituting therefor a verdict of acquittal on the ground of insanity, and (b) quashing any sentence imposed on the appellant and ordering that he be detained in a state hospital (or such other hospital as for special reasons the court many specify): 1975 Act, s.254(4).

f. Procedure for appealing

The 1975 Act, as amended, contains detailed provisions governing the procedure for appealing, and the Act should be referred to for the terms of these procedures. This section deals with the principal steps in the procedure.

(i) Lodging the appeal and stating the grounds

1. Criminal Procedure (Scotland) Act 1975

"231.—(1) Subject to section 236B(2) of this Act, where a person desires to appeal under section 228(1)(a) or (c) of this Act, he shall, within two weeks of the final determination of the proceedings, lodge with the Clerk of Justiciary written intimation of intention to appeal and send a copy to the Crown Agent.

(2) Such intimation shall identify the proceedings and be in as nearly as may be the form prescribed by Act of Adjournal under this Act.

(3) On such intimation being lodged by a person in custody, the Clerk of Justiciary shall give notice thereof to the Secretary of State.

(4) For the purposes of subsection (1) above and section 270(2) of this Act, proceedings shall be deemed finally determined on the day on which sentence is passed in open court; except that, where in relation to an appeal under section 228(1)(a) of this Act sentence is deferred under section 219 of this Act, they shall be deemed finally determined on the day which sentence is first so deferred in open court."

NOTE

This section refers to intended appeals against conviction or conviction and sentence. Notice that at this stage the appellant is not required to state any grounds of appeal. It has been the practice in the past for the Justiciary Office to furnish a copy of the judge's charge on receipt of a note of appeal or application for leave to appeal (under the old law). That practice will continue (although there is no statutory provision for it) so that the appellant will have a copy of the charge before he formulates his grounds of appeal.

The availability of the charge at this stage prompted the following comment from the Lord Justice-Clerk (Wheatley) in *McAvoy and Another* v. *H.M. Advocate*, 1983 S.L.T. 16 (at p. 19): "I wish to add two post-scripts. Two of the five grounds of appeal, both of which alleged failure by the presiding judge properly to direct the jury, were not insisted upon. This sort of thing is happening far too often. Whatever difficulties existed previously in formulating grounds of appeal on inadequacies in the judge's charge because the charge was not available in time to be considered before the grounds of appeal had to be lodged, that cannot be said now. Since the judge's charge should now be available timeously, practitioners have a professional responsibility to see that criticisms of a judge's charge can be read out of the charge and do not stem from recollections which can be imperfect and unjustified. Whatever advantages unchecked and erroneous criticisms of a judge's charge may have for the defence, they constitute an unwarranted public criticism of the judge's professional competence and result in a waste of time and money."

2. Criminal Procedure (Scotland) Act 1975

"233.—(1) Subject to section 236B(2) of this Act, within six weeks of lodging intimation of intention to appeal or, in the case of an appeal against sentence alone, within two weeks of the passing of the sentence in open court, the convicted person may lodge a written note of appeal with the Clerk of Justiciary who shall send a copy to the judge who presided at the trial and to the Crown Agent: Provided that the first mentioned period may be extended, before expiry thereof, by the Clerk of Justiciary.

(2) Such a note shall identify the proceedings, contain a full statement of all the grounds of appeal and be in as nearly as may be the form prescribed by Act of Adjournal under this Act.

(3) Except by leave of the High Court on cause shown it shall not be competent for an appellant to found any aspect of his appeal on a ground not contained in the note of appeal.

(4) On a note of appeal against sentence alone being lodged by an appellant in custody the Clerk of Justiciary shall give notice thereof to the Secretary of State."

NOTES

1. Under the old procedure the appellant was obliged to lodge his appeal, or application for leave to appeal, within 10 days of conviction, and to intimate his grounds of appeal at the same time. Any later amendment or addition to these grounds could only be made

with the leave of the High Court. Furthermore, although a legal aid certificate granted for the purpose of the trial extended to advising on appeal, it did not extend to the framing of the grounds of appeal. To obtain a certificate for this purpose a fresh application had to be made for an appeal certificate. The net result of these rules was that grounds of appeal were "almost invariably" (Thomson Committee, 3rd. Report, para. 2.11) drafted by the appellant himself.

2. The new procedures allow up to six weeks from intimation of intention to appeal for the lodging of grounds of appeal, thereby overcoming much of the difficulty experienced in the previous law. Given the extended time allowed for formulating grounds of appeal it seems likely that the court will in future by very reluctant to allow an appellant to found any aspect of his appeal on a ground not contained in the note of appeal. For the position prior to the 1980 amendments, see *Reilly* v. *H.M. Advocate*, 1950 J.C. 52 and *Pool* v. *H.M. Advocate*, 1951 S.L.T. (Notes) 70.

3. There is no procedure for intimation of intention to appeal in cases of appeal against sentence alone. The time-limit for lodging the note of appeal in such cases is two weeks from sentence (s. 233(1)).

4. Section 236B(2) provides that any period mentioned in section 231(1) or section 233(1) may be extended at any time by the High Court in respect of any convicted person.

3. Criminal Procedure (Scotland) Act 1975

"236A.—(1) As soon as is reasonably practicable after his receipt of the copy note of appeal sent to him under section 233(1) of this Act, the judge who presided at the trial shall furnish the Clerk of Justiciary with a report in writing giving the judge's opinion on the case generally and on the grounds contained in the note of appeal; and the Clerk of Justiciary shall send a copy of the report to the convicted person or his solicitor, to the Crown Agent, and, in a case referred under section 263(1) of this Act, to the Secretary of State.

(2) Where the judge's report is not furnished as mentioned in subsection (1) above, the High Court may call for such report to be furnished within such period as it may specify or, if it thinks fit, hear and determine the appeal without such report.

(3) Subject to subsection (1) above, the report of the judge shall be available only to the High Court and the parties.

237. The High Court where hearing an appeal under this Part of this Act may require the judge who presided at the trial to produce any notes taken by him of the proceedings at the trial."

NOTE

These sections provide for the production of information which may assist the appellant in pursuing his appeal (236A(1)) or which may assist the court in disposing of the appeal (sections 236A(3) and 237). Formerly, although a trial judge's report was always required, the parties had no right to see it.

(ii)   Abandonment of appeal

1.   Criminal Procedure (Scotland) Act 1975

"244.—(1) An appellant may abandon his appeal by lodging with the Clerk of Justiciary a notice of abandonment in as nearly as may be the form prescribed by Act of Adjournal under this Act; and on such notice being lodged the appeal shall be deemed to have been dismissed by the court.

(2) A person who has appealed against both conviction and sentence may abandon the appeal in so far as it is against conviction and may proceed with it against sentence alone."

2.   Ferguson v. H.M. Advocate
1980 J.C. 27

The petitioner was convicted of assault and attempted robbery and sentenced to 21 months' imprisonment. He presented a note of application for leave to appeal against sentence, and this application was set down for hearing in 10 weeks time. He applied for, but was refused legal aid. Refusal was intimated to him six weeks before the hearing of his appeal. His solicitor informed him that he could see counsel at the court on the day of the hearing. Having spoken to counsel on the morning of the hearing, the petitioner instructed counsel to abandon his application for leave to appeal. But since his case was the first on the court's roll, there was no opportunity for him to lodge the appropriate notice of abandonment. When the case was called counsel moved the court for leave to abandon the application. This was refused, and counsel was invited to address the court on the question of sentence. Having heard counsel, the court quashed the sentence of 21 months and substituted a sentence of four years. He presented a petition to the *nobile officium* of the High Court for review of the decision of the appeal court.

LORD JUSTICE-CLERK (WHEATLEY): ". . .The applicant now submits that the sentence of 4 years' imprisonment was incompetent in respect that he had intimated to the Appeal Court the requisite abandonment of his Application for Leave to Appeal immediately after his case was called and before the Court has begun to consider the Application. He further submitted there was no appeal against sentence properly before the Court in terms of section 233 (5) of the Criminal Procedure (Scotland) Act 1975, and that in any event the procedure adopted by the Appeal Court and the increase in sentence were oppressive and unfair to him. He argues that if he had lodged a formal notice of abandonment timeously in terms of section 244 of the said Act the Application would not have been before the Appeal Court and would have been deemed to have been dismissed, and that by waiting to discuss the Application with counsel on 15th December 1977, he being in prison and not free to obtain advice earlier, he has been unnecessarily and unjustly punished by the Appeal Court.

Section 262 of the aforementioned Act is in the following terms: 'Subject to the provisions of the next following section of this Act, all interlocutors and sentences pronounced by the High Court under this Part of the Act shall be final and conclusive and not subject to review by any court whatsoever and it shall be incompetent to stay or suspend any execution or diligence issuing from the High Court under this Part of this Act.' Faced with this provision counsel for the petitioner submitted that this Court in the exercise of its inherent power under its *nobile officium* could overcome and over-ride the apparent finality of the Appeal Court's interlocutor and sentence of 15th December 1977 and determine the competency of those proceedings. He founded on a passage in Alison's Criminal Law, Vol. 2, at p.23 where the learned author says: 'The Court of Justiciary has the exclusive power of providing a remedy for all extraordinary or unforeseen occurrences in the course of criminal business whether before themselves or any inferior Court.'

We do not need to consider the general effect of this statement of the law in relation to the finality of the provisions of section 262 aforesaid, since we are satisfied that the circumstances narrated by the petitioner do not fall within the category of extraordinary or unforeseen occurrences. The petitioner knew by early November 1977 that he was not getting legal aid for his appeal. On his *ex parte* statement he was told by his solicitor that by some private arrangement he could see a counsel on the morning of the day when his Application was due to be heard. Even if that be so, he and those advising him were taking the risk that this might make it difficult though not impossible to lodge a notice of abandonment under section 244. It cannot be said that this was an extraordinary or unforeseen occurrence. Counsel submitted that it was quite common practice for motions for leave to abandon an appeal to be made verbally to the Court after the case had been called and this was presumably in the mind of the petitioner's legal advisers. This may be so, but for the reasons which we give later there is a distinction between a notice under section 244 which by statute results in the Application being deemed to have been dismissed by the Court and a verbal request to the Court after the case has been called asking the Court for leave to withdraw the Application. Even if the petitioner and his legal advisers did not appreciate this in law they ought to have appreciated it, and again it cannot be said that this constituted an extraordinary or unforeseen occurrence. For these reasons alone the petition would fall to be dismissed, since the criteria for invoking the *nobile officium* have not been established.

In view of what may be a common misapprehension about the procedure in relation to the withdrawal of Applications for Leave to Appeal or Appeals themselves we consider it desirable to state a further reason why this petition falls to be dismissed. Counsel for the petitioner submitted that up until the point when the argument in support of the Application had been started it is competent to withdraw the Application, and if a withdrawal is intimated to the Court before that point the Court has no option but to accept it and hold the Application to have been refused. When asked why if that be so it was necessary to have section 244 he submitted that it was simply there for administrative convenience and really did not matter. That is a startling proposition and in our opinion it is an entirely ill-founded one. Section 244 lays down a procedure which, if followed, results in a 'deemed' dismissal of the Application or Appeal by the Court when the notice is lodged. A 'deemed' dismissal cannot be obtained otherwise. No time limit is laid down in the section as to when the notice of abandonment has to be lodged. No such notice was lodged here. Once the case has called, the Court becomes master of the procedure. If any motion is made to the Court thereafter it is a matter for the discretion of the Court whether it should be granted or refused, unless there is statutory authority governing the matter. There is no statutory authority governing the situation here. In our view our Scottish procedure does not give an absolute right to an applicant or an appellant to withdraw an Application or an Appeal after the case has been called and is before the Court provided the motion is made before the argument in support of the Application or Appeal has started. Support for the opposite view was sought from the English case of *Rex* v. *Gibbon* [1946] 31 Cr. App. R. 143 and certain *dicta* by Lord Justice-General Clyde in *West* v. *H.M. Advocate* 1955 S.L.T. 425. In *Gibbon* the circumstances were identical with those in the instance case. Gibbon had appealed against sentence and the moment when the case called his counsel informed the Court that he wished to abandon his appeal. The Rule of Court regulating the abandonment of appeals was basically in the same terms as those in section 24. Lord Goddard L.C.J. said in that case: 'But if it be the fact that the appellant has the right to abandon his appeal at any time, the Court would not prevent him from exercising that right merely because, not having had the advantage of seeing counsel until the last moment, he has not had time to put that notice in writing. That would be taking too severe and too technical a view in a case of this sort. It seems to me clear under the statutory rule that the appellant can at any time abandon the appeal.' Lord Goddard, who was giving the opinion of the Court, went on to affirm that Counsel had a right to abandon the Appeal at the point when he did. The Appeal, which seemed basically to be one to canvas whether the sentence should be increased, was dismissed.

The opinion and judgment in *Gibbon ex facie* give full support for the argument advanced by counsel for the petitioner, but it is not an authority binding on this Court and we are not prepared to follow it. We prefer to consider this question in the light of our own procedure and our own statutory provisions. As previously indicated we consider that an abandonment which carries an automatic dismissal of an Application or an Appeal can only be achieved if the statutory procedure of section 244 is followed. If it is not, and the Application or Appeal is before the Court, as it is when the case is called, the applicant or appellant has no right under statute or at common law to abandon the Application or Appeal except with the leave of the Court.

In *West* v. *H.M. Advocate* the facts were quite different. The appellant had been given leave to appeal on the question of sentence. The appellant had been sentenced to 10 years' imprisonment, but in view of the nature of the offences the Court decided that consideration should be given to substituting a sentence of preventive detention. A report on the suitability of that form of disposal for the appellant was called for and when it was received it was adverse to the appellant and recommended that preventive detention should be imposed. On receiving a copy of this report the Appellant lodged a notice of abandonment of the appeal in terms of Rule 13 (a) of the Act of Adjournal 1926, which was the equivalent of section 244. When the hearing of the appeal was subsequently resumed the Court refused to admit the notice of abandonment and substituted a sentence of 12 years of preventive detention for the one of the 10 years' imprisonment. In the course of his opinion Lord Justice-General Clyde, with whom the other judges agreed, said: 'What the Rule is contemplating is an abandonment by an accused before the Court has begun to consider the appeal or application in question. In those circumstances there is no Court to dismiss the appeal or application, and the appeal or application is consequently deemed to have been dismissed. The situation is quite different where the Court has begun to hear the appeal or application. At that stage it is too late to invoke Rule 13(a). If the appeal or application is to be dismissed then it is the Court which must do it, and the situation where the appeal or application can be deemed to be dismissed does not arise. The Rule applies only up to the stage at which the actual hearing of the appeal or application begins and the accused or his Counsel begins to address the Court. I am confirmed in this view by the decision in England in *Rex* v. *Gibbon* on the interpretation of the Rule in England corresponding to Rule 13 (a). The appellant there was entitled to invoke the Rule and abandon his appeal because the moment the case was called the appeal was abandoned. That is not the situation here, for the appellant has presented in full to us the arguments in favour of his appeal against sentence.'

It has to be observed that in that case the Court was dealing with an entirely different situation. A full argument had been addressed to the Court before the attempt to abandon the appeal was made. The question whether the calling of the case and the invitation to counsel to address the Court or the start of the argument marked the point at which a statutory notice of abandonment was no longer competent did not arise and was not canvassed. It is true that, following *Gibbon*, Lord Justice-General Clyde said that the point of no return was the stage when the actual hearing of the appeal or application begins and the accused or his Counsel begins to address the Court. Since in the circumstances of that case this was not a point which was necessary for the decision of the case we do not consider that what was there said was a binding decision on the issue before the Court here. On the contrary we have reached the conclusion previously stated that the hearing of the Application or Appeal begins when the case is called and the applicant or appellant is called to address the Court on the Application or Appeal. From that point onwards the Court is the master of procedure and a written notice of abandonment and *a fortiori* a verbal intimation of abandonment comes too late to warrant an automatic dismissal of the Application or Appeal. It is then a matter for the discretion of the Court whether such a motion in either form should be granted.

It follows from this that in the instant case the Court of Appeal were entitled to refuse the request for leave to abandon the application, and for this further reason we shall dismiss the petition."

The court dismissed the petition.

NOTE

For a discussion of the *nobile officium* of the High Court see *post*, Chap. 18. Compare the fate of the petitioner in this case with that of the petitioner in *Mathieson, Petitioner*, 1980 S.L.T. 74, *post*, p. 594.

The importance of an effective abandonment of appeal against sentence lies, of course, in the fact that the court cannot increase a sentence on appeal unless it has before it an appeal against that sentence: section 254(3), *infra*.

(iii) Powers of the court in relation to appeals

1. Criminal Procedure (Scotland) Act 1975

"252. Without prejudice to any existing power of the High Court, that court may for the purposes of an appeal under section 228(1) of this Act—
(*a*) order the production of any document or other thing connected with the proceedings;
(*b*) hear any additional evidence relevant to any alleged miscarriage of justice or order such evidence to be heard by a judge of the High Court or by such other person as it may appoint for that purpose;
(*c*) take account of any circumstances relevant to the case which were not before the trial judge;
(*d*) remit to any fit person to enquire and report in regard to any matter or circumstance affecting the appeal;
(*e*) appoint a person with expert knowledge to act as assessor to the High Court in any case where it appears to the court that such expert knowledge is required for the proper determination of the case."

NOTE

This is a much-simplified re-working of the powers contained in the former section 252. The matters of greatest significance in section 252 are contained in paragraphs (*b*) and (*c*). In the past the court has shown great reluctance to admit fresh evidence. The attitude of the court to this question prior to the 1980 Act changes may be seen from the following cases.

2. Gallacher v. H.M. Advocate
1951 J.C. 38

The appellant was convicted of murder and sentenced to death. The deceased had been kicked to death by a group of men. The appellant was identified by three witnesses as having formed part of the group. Two other witnesses supported the appellant's account that he was not part of that group. In the course of the appeal the appellant applied to the court to lead evidence from three additional witnesses who would corroborate his version.

Lord Justice-Clerk (Thomson): ". . .It is in that state of evidence that we are asked to allow the evidence of three other witnesses to be heard. The terms of the application run that the appellant was not at the time of his apprehension assaulting the deceased but throwing stones at a material distance from the scene of the assault, and that such evidence would be an essential corroboration of the evidence given by the appellant at the trial.

Mr Milligan addressed us fully on the circumstances under which the fresh evidence had come to the knowledge of the appellant's solicitors since the conclusion of the trial. We are prepared to assume for the purposes of this case that the fact that the evidence is tendered only at this stage would not be a bar to our allowing it. The question remains whether, even on that assumption, we should allow it. We might observe, however, that the first question which the Court is bound to ask of any appellant who tenders fresh evidence is why it was not tendered at the trial. We do not propose to canvass the issue of what might or might not be an adequate explanation. No general rule can possibly be laid down and the explanation in any particular case must be viewed, not in the light of any technicality or rule of practice or of procedure, but solely in the light of the dominating consideration that we may order new evidence if we think it necessary or expedient in the interest of justice. . .

Section 6 [of the Criminal Appeal (Scotland) Act 1926] provides: 'For the purposes of this Act the Court may, if they think it necessary or expedient in the interest of justice— . . . (b) if they think fit, order any witnesses who would have been compellable witnesses at the trial to attend and be examined before the Court, whether they were or were not called at the trial.'

It is to be observed that this provision is of a highly discretionary character. It is permissive in form. The order is to be pronounced only if the Court think fit. The condition for the exercise of this discretionary power is that the Court must 'think it necessary or expedient in the interest of justice.' . . .

We cannot order a retrial by another jury. Further, it has been said by the Courts of Appeal, both in Scotland and in England, that we must not retry the case ourselves. That is to say, we must not consider afresh the whole case on the basis of the printed word and the new evidence. That would be substituting ourselves for a jury with none of the advantages of seeing and hearing the great bulk of the evidence which the jury possessed, substituting our assessment of the credibility of the witnesses whom the jury saw and heard for the assessment made by the jury.

If we are not to 'retry' the case in that sense, our function is to attempt to assess the value of the verdict in the light of the new evidence and to decide whether a verdict of guilty cannot now be supported or, it may be, to determine whether the result of its admission is to demonstrate that there has been a miscarriage of justice. This appears to involve weighing by some standard the possible verdicts to which a jury might come in the hypothetical circumstances of their having had the new evidence before them along with the old.

Counsel for the appellant argued that the standard for us was 'Are we satisfied that no reasonable jury, properly directed and having heard the new evidence, would or could have come to any other conclusion than that to which they did come and that no miscarriage of justice had actually occurred?' . . .

This does not seem to us to be the proper test. It would mean that if the new evidence was *ex facie* relevant and not obviously untruthful, the Court would be bound to say this might have affected the jury's minds and raised a reasonable doubt. Let us assume that in the present case the three new witnesses had appeared at the trial and said all that they are now expected to say. It is absolutely impossible on the facts of the present case to affirm with any confidence that, if the new evidence had been before the jury, they would have come to a different result. . . .

We cannot tell what sort of impression the three new witnesses might have made. They might have been impressive enough to raise a reasonable doubt but they might have been cast aside. When there are some witnesses one way and some another, the effect of the evidence of fresh witnesses, had they been at the trial, would depend not only on the impression given by the new witnesses but on the strength of the impression made by the old. One can imagine cases, and they are illustrated in the reports, where new evidence appeared which was so overwhelming as to leave no doubt that, had it been before the jury, it must have affected the verdict. In such circumstances, a miscarriage of justice can be confidently affirmed. But where, as here, the most that could possibly be said is that had the new evidence been before the jury the issue might have been rendered doubtful, its admission might lead to a miscarriage of justice by allowing to go free men whom a jury has convicted and whom even in the light of the new evidence they might well have still convicted.

Accordingly we do not think it is right to admit this new evidence, as we are not satisfied that it would, had it been before the jury, have had a decisive effect. To admit that evidence would be to give to late-coming evidence a greater force than is enjoyed by timeous evidence, for, if the additional evidence had been before the jury, we could quash only if no reasonable jury could have brought in a verdict of guilty, whereas, when the additional evidence is adduced for the first time before us, the defence argued that we must quash if a reasonable jury might or might not have brought in a verdict of guilty. If the new evidence had been at the trial and the jury had convicted, the verdict could not have been upset unless no reasonable jury could have arrived at such a verdict on the evidence. The proposed test would reverse the situation in cases where new evidence is allowed, and would result in convictions being quashed unless a reasonable jury was bound to convict on the evidence. This is not in accordance with the terms of section 2, and, if we were to accept the appellant's submission, we should be exceeding the powers conferred by that section. Unless we feel satisfied that a reasonable jury hearing the whole evidence old and new would have acquitted, we cannot say that a miscarriage of justice had taken place.

In weighing the considerations relevant to the exercise of such a highly discretionary function as this, previous instances of its exercise are not always helpful. The circumstances vary so much and sometimes the situation is so complicated that it is difficult for any report to present an adequate picture of the background of fact against which the application to lead new evidence was made. The *Slater* case [*Slater* v. *H.M. Advocate*, 1928 J.C. 94] proceeded under section 16 and, in any event, was entirely exceptional. The *Lowson* case [*Lowson* v. *H.M. Advocate*, 1943 J.C. 141] was hardly less so. Neither situation is likely to be repeated. In the more recent case of *Lennie* v. *H.M. Advocate*, 1946 J.C. 79 the Court allowed a witness to be tendered in supplement of a case of alibi, but it appears that they did so without the full argument of which we have had the benefit. The Crown did not oppose the examination of the one witness whose evidence was allowed. Further, the case throws no light on the problem of how new evidence is to be dealt with, as the Court was clearly of the view that it was unreliable. These cases do show, however, that the exercise of this power by our Court is to be made only in very exceptional circumstances. *Slater* and *Lowson* in general terms define the duty and function of the Court of Appeal in relation to additional evidence. We take the words of Lord Justice-General Normand (at p. 149) in the latter case, summarising the effect of the opinion of the Court in the former case: ' . . . that the Court of Appeal has no jurisdiction to retry the case; that the jury's verdict must be accepted, in considering the additional evidence, as a true verdict on the evidence before them; and that the Court of Appeal are the judges of the materiality and reliability of the additional evidence, and are required to decide whether that evidence is such as to satisfy the Court that the verdict was pronounced in the absence of matter material and relevant to lead to a contrary result.' We take this to mean that we must be reasonably satisfied that the jury's verdict would have been different. In other words we must be reasonably satisfied that the presence of the new evidence would have produced a contrary result and that a verdict pronounced in its absence amounts to a miscarriage of justice. We cannot read it as meaning that it is enough if we are satisfied that, if the new evidence had been heard by the jury in the original trial, it might have produced in their minds a reasonable doubt or that, having heard it they could have come to another verdict. As we have said, such a doctrine gives to new evidence a potency which is not enjoyed by the original evidence. Such a doctrine would open the door to the gravest abuses."

> The court refused the motion to
> lead additional evidence and
> refused the appeal.

NOTES

1. The decision in *Gallacher* has been followed in all the subsequent cases on this issue. See, *e.g. Higgins* v. *H.M. Advocate,* 1956 J.C. 69, *Thompson* v. *H.M. Advocate,* 1968 J.C. 61, *Temple* v. *H.M. Advocate,* 1971 J.C. 3, and *Lindie* v. *H.M. Advocate,* 1974 J.C. 1.

2. The Thomson Committee's view (1st Report, para. 26) was that this test was too restrictive, and concluded (para. 27) that the most appropriate test for the type of case in question would be: "Is the Appeal Court satisfied that a reasonable jury properly directed and having heard all the evidence, including the new evidence, would have convicted?"

3. Although the new section 252 is simpler and less restrictive than the old 252 (there is, for example, no requirement that new witnesses are restricted to those who would have been compellable witnesses at the trial) there is nothing in the new provisions which require the court to adopt a less restrictive test for the acceptance of fresh evidence.

4. It should be remembered that fresh evidence may be taken account of in appeals against sentence: section 254(3)(*b*) of the 1975 Act.

g.   Re-trial

The possibility of a re-trial was introduced by the new section 254(1)(*c*) of the 1975 Act. The procedures governing the re-trial are identical to those governing any other trial on indictment, although section 255 of the 1975 Act does contain certain supplementary provisions in respect of new prosecutions:

1.   **Criminal Procedure (Scotland) Act 1975**

"255.—(1) Where authority is granted under section 254(1)(*c*) of this Act, a new prosecution may be brought charging the accused with the same or any similar offence arising out of the same facts; and the proceedings out of which the appeal arose shall not be a bar to such new prosecution:

Provided that no sentence may be passed on conviction under the new prosecution which could not have been passed on conviction under the earlier proceedings.

(2) A new prosecution may be brought under this section, notwithstanding that any time limit (other than the time limit mentioned in subsection (3) below), for the commencement of such proceedings has elapsed.

(3) Proceedings in a prosecution under this section shall be commenced within two months of the date on which authority to bring the prosecution was granted; and for the purposes of this subsection proceedings shall, in a case where such warrant is executed without unreasonable delay, be deemed to be commenced on the date on which a warrant to apprehend or to cite the accused is granted, and shall in any other case be deemed to be commenced on the date on which the warrant is executed.

(4) Where the two months mentioned in subsection (3) above elapse and no new prosecution has been brought under this section, the order under section 254(1)(c) of this Act setting aside the verdict shall have the effect, for all purposes, of an acquittal."

NOTE

Sections 254(1) and 255 are both silent on the question of whether the court may grant authority for a new prosecution *ex proprio motu,* or whether this can only be done on the application of the prosecutor. In the absence of any requirement it would seem that such application is not necessary, and this is the course adopted by the court. What criteria govern the authorisation of a new prosecution? See the following case:

2. Mackenzie v. H.M. Advocate
1983 S.L.T. 220

The appellant was charged with murder. He tabled a special defence of self-defence, although in fact the true defence was one of accident. The trial judge directed the jury that they could not acquit on the ground of accident, but left the issue of self-defence for their consideration. The appellant was found guilty of culpable homicide and appealed on the ground of misdirection. The court held that there had been a material miscarriage of justice and quashed the conviction. They then considered the question of whether to authorise a new prosecution:

LORD JUSTICE-CLERK (WHEATLEY): " . . . Having decided that the verdict of the trial court must be set aside, I have now to consider what action should be taken thereon. Under the provisions of s. 254(1)(c) of the Criminal Procedure (Scotland) Act 1975 (as amended), instead of quashing the conviction this court can grant authority to bring a new prosecution in accordance with s. 255 of the Act. The new provision of allowing the court of appeal to grant such authority leaves the matter to the discretion of the court without specifying any grounds on which that course is warranted.

Each case will require to be dealt with on its own facts. Where it is not suggested that there was not sufficient evidence to warrant the conviction, or any fault on the part of the Crown, and the one thing which has led to the setting aside of the verdict is a material misdirection in law by the trial judge, that is something which, in the interests of justice and the public interest, must be seriously taken into account when deciding whether to grant authority to bring a new prosecution instead of simply quashing the conviction. In the instant case I consider that this consideration weighs heavily, and I am further influenced by the fact that the unnecessary introduction by the defence of the plea of self-defence in the terms tendered created a confusion which, although it should have been avoided, should not have been introduced. Accordingly I move your Lordships to set aside the verdict on charge 2 but to grant authority to bring a new prosecution in terms of s. 254(1)(c) aforesaid. This leaves to the Lord Advocate the decision whether such a new prosecution should be brought."

> Conviction quashed; authority to
> bring new prosecution granted.

NOTES

1. *Cf. McTavish* v. *H.M. Advocate, supra*, p. 429 in which the only ground for quashing the conviction was a material misdirection by the trial judge. It seems likely that in future such "technical" acquittals, even if they satisfy the miscarriage of justice test, will result in a new trial.

2. It is submitted that in determining whether or not to bring a new trial the Lord Advocate is governed by the rule that his discretion must not be exercised oppressively (*supra,* Chap. 2), and that the granting of authority to bring a new prosecution is a quite separate matter from whether such a prosecution should in fact be brought.

3. Re-trials are, in any event, a most unsatisfactory proceeding. Evidence once rehearsed loses its impact, and witnesses are in a position to adjust their testimony as necessary. It is curious that this objection, which has often been raised to the procedure of a trial within a trial, has not commended itself in this context.

4. Notice that the new charge may be one of the same "or any similar offence" arising out of the same facts. Suppose that a person is tried on a charge of culpable homicide, convicted and appeals successfully. If a new prosecution is authorised could he subsequently be indicted for murder (assuming the evidence warranted this)? And what are "the same facts"? Suppose that additional facts become known to the Crown when a fresh prosecution is being considered, can these be relied upon in determining the nature of the charge? It would seem not. The section states "arising out of the same facts" rather than "arising out of the same event".

h. Reference to the High Court by the Secretary of State

Leitch v. Secretary of State for Scotland
1982 S.L.T. (Sh. Ct.) 76

Section 263(1) of the Criminal Procedure (Scotland) Act 1975, as amended, provides (*inter alia*) that the Secretary of State on the consideration of any conviction of a person passed on a person who has been convicted, may, "if he thinks fit" refer the whole case to the High Court for consideration by that court, whether or not an appeal has been heard against that conviction. A prisoner convicted of armed robbery raised an action of damages against the Secretary of State alleging, *inter alia,* abuse of process and oppression on the latter's part. The pursuer founded, *inter alia,* on the defender's refusal to exercise his powers under section 263 to refer the pursuer's case to the High Court. The defender contended that his decision was not subject to review by the sheriff court, or indeed by any court. The sheriff dismissed the action as irrelevant. The pursuer appealed to the sheriff principal.

SHERIFF PRINCIPAL (GIMSON): " . . . I turn now to the pursuer's case of oppression contained in his averments regarding the Secretary of State's decision not to refer his case back to the High Court of Justiciary under s. 263 of the Criminal Procedure (Scotland) Act 1975. That case is indicated in the craves of the action by the references to oppression and abuse of legal process and in his second and fourth pleas-in-law.

The assumption of the pursuer's case is that the Secretary of State's decisions on the exercise of his powers under s. 263 are open to consideration by the courts. I share the sheriff's doubt whether such a question, if justiciable, could have been litigated in the sheriff court: but as I am satisfied that there can be no recourse to any court in respect of the powers conferred in s. 263, I need not consider that specialty.

There appears to be no reported decision in Scotland on this matter, and no authority was quoted to me on it. However, the statutory position in England is precisely the same as in Scotland, and I find that the courts there have held that they will not either act to require the Secretary of State to refer a case under the equivalent section (Criminal Appeal Act 1907, s. 19) or allow his decision to be questioned in the court (*Ex parte Kinally* [1958] Crim. L.R. 474 per Goddard L.C.J., Cassels and Diplock L.JJ.; *Hanratty* v. *Lord Butler of Saffron Walden* (1971) 115 S.J. 386 per Lord Denning M.R., Salmon and Stamp L.JJ.). The second of these cases was put on grounds similar to those averred here.

While these decisions may not be formally binding on the courts in Scotland, they are of strongly persuasive force on the question of the correct interpretation of the statutory words 'the Secretary of State . . . *may, if he thinks fit*' (refer a case to the High Court). The English decisions support what I consider to be the primary and correct view: that these words confer an absolute discretion on the Secretary of State."

Appeal dismissed.

NOTES

1. Section 263 also provides that the appeal provisions of the 1975 Act have no effect on the prerogative of mercy. The reference to the appeal court is quite distinct from the Secretary of State's functions with regard to the latter. The prerogative of mercy is discussed *post*, Chap.18.

2. Leitch subsequently appealed to the Court of Session against the decision of the sheriff principal, but this appeal was also refused.

i. Advocation

Advocation is a procedure whereby a party may bring under review irregularities in the preliminary stages of a case. It cannot be employed to obtain a review of the merits. It is a competent method of review in solemn and summary proceedings, but since it is most frequently encountered today in the latter it is discussed in the following chapter on review and appeal in summary proceedings, *post*, pp. 493-499.

j. Lord Advocate's reference

Criminal Procedure (Scotland) Act 1975

"263A.—(1) Where a person tried on indictment is acquitted of a charge, the Lord Advocate may refer a point of law which has arisen in relation to that charge to the High Court for their opinion; and the Clerk of Justiciary shall send to the person and to any solicitor who acted for the person at the trial, a copy of the reference and intimation of the date fixed by the Court for a hearing.

(2) The person may, not later than seven days before the date so fixed, intimate in writing to the Clerk of Justiciary and to the Lord Advocate either—

(*a*) that he elects to appear at the hearing; or

(*b*) that he elects to be represented thereat by counsel;

but, except by leave of the Court on cause shown, (and without prejudice to his right to attend), he shall not appear or be represented at the hearing other than by and in conformity with an election under this subsection.

(3) Where there is no intimation under subsection (2) (*b*) above, the High Court shall appoint counsel to act at the hearing as *amicus curiae*.

(4) The costs of representation elected under subsection (2) (*b*) above or of an appointment under subsection (3) above shall, after being taxed by the Auditor of the Court of Session, be paid by the Lord Advocate.

(5) The opinion on the point referred under subsection (1) above shall not affect the acquittal in the trial."

NOTES

1. This section was inserted in the 1975 Act by section 37 of the 1980 Act. It remains to be seen to what extent the procedure will be used in Scotland. Even in England, from which system it has been adopted, it is used on less than a dozen occasions per year. Given the High Court's reluctance to tackle so-called "academic" points of law it seems unlikely that this new procedure will make any substantial contribution to Scottish jurisprudence.

2. Notice that the procedure is not a procurator's appeal against acquittal. The opinion on the point referred to the court has no effect on that acquittal. It is also an interesting feature of this procedure that it will only be instituted on *acquittal*. No doubt the argument is that the accused will appeal if he wishes to challenge a point of law arising out of his conviction, or on a preliminary matter such as competency or relavancy.

3. In *Attorney-General's Reference (No.1 of 1975)* [1975] Q.B. 773 the court held that the procedure should be used for "short but important points which require a quick ruling . . . before a potentially false decision of law has too wide a circulation in the courts."

k. Appeal in connection with preliminary diets

Criminal Procedure (Scotland) Act 1975

"76A — (1) Without prejudice to any right of appeal under section 228 or 280A of this Act, a party may, with the leave of the court of first instance (granted either on the motion of that party or *ex proprio motu*) and in accordance with such procedure as may be prescribed by Act of Adjournal under this Act, appeal to the High Court against a decision at a preliminary diet; but any such appeal must be taken not later than 2 days after such decision.

(2) Where an appeal is taken under subsection (1) above, the High Court may postpone the trial diet for such period as appears to them to be appropriate and may, if they think fit, direct that such period (or some part of it) shall not count towards any time limit applying in respect of the case.

(3) In disposing of an appeal under subsection (1) above, the High Court may affirm the decision of the court of first instance or may remit the case to it with such directions in the matter as they think fit; and where the court of first instance has dismissed the indictment or any part of it, may reverse that

decision and direct that the court of first instance fix a trial diet if it has not already fixed one as regards so much of the indictment as it has not dismissed.

NOTES

1. Since the object of the preliminary diet is to enable matters of a preliminary nature to be disposed of prior to the actual trial, it is necessary to have an expedited form of pre-trial appeal to deal with disputed decisions at the preliminary diet. This is provided for by section 76A.

2. The right of appeal provided for is without prejudice to the accused's right of appeal against conviction or sentence under section 228, or the prosecutor's right of appeal by way of advocation under section 280A. This presumably means that a matter which could have been appealed under section 76A but which was not so appealed may still be appealed after conviction. What it probably does not admit (but does not in terms exclude) is the possibility of two appeals — one pre-trial and the other post-conviction — on the same point.

3. There is no absolute right of appeal. Appeal is only permitted with the leave of the court of first instance. There appears to be no provision for a party to challenge a refusal of leave to appeal.

4. Procedures for appeal are governed by the Act of Adjournal (Procedures under Criminal Justice (Scotland) Act 1980 No. 3) 1981.

CHAPTER 15

APPEAL AND REVIEW IN SUMMARY PROCEEDINGS

The materials in this chapter discuss the following methods of appeal and review in summary proceedings: appeal by stated case, suspension, advocation, appeals from decisions on competency and relevancy and appeal against sentence by note of appeal. Extraordinary methods of review such as petitions to the *nobile officium* of the High Court, applications to the European Commission on Human Rights and references to the Court of Justice of the European Communities are dealt with in Chap. 18, *post*.

a. Right of appeal and ground of appeal in summary proceedings

Criminal Procedure (Scotland) Act 1975

"442.—(1) Without prejudice to any right of appeal under section 453A of this Act—

(*a*) any person convicted in summary proceedings may appeal under this section to the High Court—

(i) against such conviction;

(ii) against the sentence passed on such conviction; or

(iii) against both such conviction and such sentence;

(*b*) the prosecutor in such proceedings may so appeal on a point of law—

(i) against an acquittal in such proceedings; or

(ii) against a sentence passed in such proceedings.

(2) By an appeal under subsection (1)(*a*) of this section or, as the case may be, against acquittal under subsection (1)(*b*) of this section, an appellant may bring under review of the High Court any alleged miscarriage of justice in the proceedings, including, in the case of an appeal under the said subsection (1)(*a*), any alleged miscarriage of justice on the basis of the existence and significance of additional evidence which was not heard at the trial and which was not available and could not reasonably have been made available at the trial."

NOTES

1. An appeal under section 442(1)(*a*)(i) or (iii) (appeal against conviction or conviction and sentence) or under section 442(1)(*b*) (prosecutor's appeal against acquittal or sentence) is made by way

of application for a stated case, in accordance with the procedures set out in sections 444 to 453 and 453D and 453E of the 1975 Act: *ibid.*, s. 442A(1).

An appeal against sentence alone under section 442(1)(*a*)(ii) is made by means of a "note of appeal" in accordance with the procedures set out in sections 453B to 453E of the 1975 Act: *ibid.*, s. 442B. "Provided that nothing in this section shall prevent a convicted person from proceeding by way of bill of suspension in respect of any alleged fundamental irregularity relating to the imposition of the sentence" (1975 Act, s. 442B).

2. Section 453A, which provides for appeal by way of bill of suspension or advocation on the ground of miscarriage of justice where an appeal under section 442 would be incompetent or inappropriate, is set out *infra*, p. 488.

3. Note that the prosecutor's appeal under section 442(1)(*b*) (whether against acquittal or sentence) can only be brought on a point of law. Note also that the ground of appeal under section 442—miscarriage of justice—does not apply to the prosecutor's appeal against sentence.

b.   Appeal by stated case

This method of appeal was introduced by the Summary Prosecutions Appeals (Scotland) Act 1875. Amended by subsequent legislation, the law relating to the stated case has been radically reformed by Schedule 3 to the 1980 Act. The nature of these changes is indicated, where appropriate, below.

(i)   Competency

As was pointed out above, a stated case is a competent method of appeal against conviction, conviction and sentence or, at the instance of the prosecutor against acquittal or sentence. It is not a competent method of appeal against sentence alone by a convicted person. Where there has been neither an acquittal nor sentence pronounced, a stated case is not competent:

1.   **Tudhope v. Mathieson**
1981 S.C.C.R. 231

An accused person was charged on summary complaint with various contraventions of the Road Traffic Act 1972. The sheriff dismissed the complaint as incompetent, on the ground that it was time-barred under section 331(1) of the 1975 Act. The prosecutor applied to the sheriff for a stated case:

SHERIFF KEARNEY: "In this cause under the Criminal Procedure (Scotland) Act 1975 I dismissed the complaint as time-barred by interlocutor dated 5th October 1981 to which interlocutor was appended a note which explained, as fully as I was able, my reasons for my decision. The prosecutor by note of appeal dated 9th October 1981 and lodged with the sheriff clerk's department on 12th October has craved the court to state a case for the opinion of the High Court of Justiciary under the said Act. So far as I am aware the only provision entitling the prosecutor to request a stated case under the said Act is to be found in sub-paragraph (b) of section 442(1) of the Act. The said sub-paragraph reads as follows:

'(b) The prosecutor in such proceedings may so appeal on a point of law—
(i) against an acquittal in such proceedings; or
(ii) against a sentence passed in such proceedings.'

The instant proceedings were terminated by dismissal. It clearly could not be contended that a dismissal was a form of sentence. As to the possible contention that dismissal is a form of acquittal I have always understood acquittal to imply the absolving of the accused from the charge in a manner comparable to a jury's verdict of 'not guilty'. When I became seized of the difficulty I asked the sheriff clerk to ventilate the matter and the prosecutor, the agent for the defence not objecting, asked for a hearing, and, at very short notice, Mr Lowe, assistant procurator fiscal, and the accused's agent, Mr Gordon, were able to attend at my chambers at 4 p.m. on 21st October.

Mr Lowe submitted that it was reasonable in the whole context of section 442 of the said Act to treat dismissal as being a form of acquittal. He also pointed out that in the circumstances of the present case the accused was, if the dismissal were justified, as immune from prosecution as he would have been had a verdict of 'not guilty' been returned in respect that the Crown could no longer initiate a prosecution as the case was time-barred.

The accused's agent informed me that his client was not greatly concerned either way but he did draw my attention to the wording of section 447 (1) of the 1975 Act as now amended which states, inter alia, 'Within three weeks of the final determination of proceedings in respect of which an application for a stated case is made under section 444 of this Act . . . the judge who presided at the trial, shall prepare a draft stated case.' Mr Gordon suggested that the mandatory language of the statute perhaps carried the consequence that the judge of first instance had no option but to state a case when requested to do so even if he thought it was incompetently asked for. Mr Lowe indicated that he was not happy to adopt this line of reasoning and in any event I think it is fallacious. It seems reasonably clear to me that the mandatory obligation on the judge to state a case arises only in the event of the case being lawfully requested and accordingly that it always remains open to the judge of first instance to decline to state a case if he is of opinion that the case has not been lawfully requested.

Although the word 'acquittal' has never, according to my researches (or indeed according to Mr Lowe's researches), been formally defined in Scottish legal literature or case-law it has, in my experience, always been used as equivalent of a complete absolvitor which frees the accused forever of the pending charge and lays a firm foundation for a possible plea of tholed assize or res judicata in exactly the same way as a jury's verdict of 'not guilty' would. I have now ascertained that the word is so used in the marginal note at p. 297 of the second volume of Benjamin Robert Bell's edition of *Hume's Commentaries on the Law of Scotland Respecting Crimes*, published in Edinburgh by Bell and Bradfute in 1844. This definition also derives support from the definition of 'acquittal' appearing at p. 12 of *The Oxford Companion to Law* recently published by Professor D. M. Walker, Q.C. The word is also used in this sense in section 140A of the 1975 Act as now amended. I would also mention, quantum valeat, that the same usage is adopted at para. 15.07 of Criminal Appeals in Scotland (3rd report) Cmnd 7005/1977 (being the 3rd report of the Thomson Committee). The consideration that the accused in the present case cannot now be prosecuted seems to me to be irrelevant since the reason for a new action not being able to be raised against this accused flows not from the instant action having been dismissed but from the lapse of six months from the date of the initial offence in terms of section 331 (1) of the said 1975 Act.

I have always understood that the correct method of bringing under review alleged procedural irregularities, including those arising in the preliminary stage of a case, was by bill of advocation (see Renton & Brown on Criminal Procedure, 4th edn, para. 16-128) and section 453A of the said 1975 Act, as now amended, would seem to preserve such method of appeal.

I have no wish unnecessarily to hold up this already delayed matter, but as I conceive that it would be incompetent for me to state a case I have concluded that I have no proper option but to decline to do so."

Application refused.

NOTES

1. Prior to the 1980 Act amendments, section 442 of the 1975 Act provided that appeal by stated case could be taken "on the final determination of any summary prosecution". Under the new section 442 the prosecutor's appeal is only competent on "acquittal" or against a "sentence".

2. It would have been competent for the prosecutor to have appealed by way of advocation (as to which, see *infra*, p. 493). The procedure for appeal from a decision on competency or relevancy provided for by section 334(2A) of the 1975 Act is also now available, although it had not been brought into force at the time of the case.

3. For a discussion of the appropriateness (as opposed to the competency) of this method of appeal, see *infra*, pp. 487-492.

2. MacNeill v. MacGregor
1975 J.C. 55

A plea of guilty was entered by a solicitor on behalf of an accused person. The following day (26 July 1974) the solicitor appeared before the sheriff and explained that that plea had been entered in error and should have been one of not guilty. The sheriff recalled the sentence and order of the court, allowed the plea of guilty to be withdrawn and, a plea of not guilty having been intimated, adjourned the diet until a later date. No objection was entered by the prosecutor. The accused duly appeared at the adjourned diet, and after trial was found not guilty. At the request of the procurator fiscal the sheriff stated a case for the opinion of the High Court.

LORD JUSTICE-CLERK (WHEATLEY): ". . . *In limine* this Court raised the question of the competency of the proceedings on 26th July 1974, since if these were *ultra vires* the present appeal which arose from, and was consequential upon, those proceedings would also be incompetent.

The Advocate-depute stated that he could not defend or justify the procedure which had taken place on 26th July 1974 and what had followed thereon, and that accordingly he could not insist on the present appeal. Since a finding that the order of the Court of 26th July was *ultra vires* and inept would restore the order of the Court of 25th July 1974 which found the respondent guilty and imposed the sentence above noted on him, we allowed Mr Younger, who appeared for the respondent, the opportunity of defending the *vires* of the proceedings on 26th July 1974. Mr Younger was unable to point to any precedent which authorised the procedure which the Sheriff followed here.

It has to be observed that what took place on 25th July 1974, as recorded in the Minutes of Procedure was that the Sheriff convicted the respondent of the charge and proceeded to sentence him. The Sheriff, in our view, thereby became *functus*, and had no authority thereafter to alter the finding *quoad* conviction. This he did, however, by recalling the order pronounced on 25th July 1974. There is statutory provision for a Sheriff to alter or modify a sentence under certain conditions—Summary Jurisdiction Act 1954, section 57. There is, incidentally, statutory power given to a Sheriff to review a previous decision on bail—Criminal Justice (Scotland) Act 1963, section 37. But there is no statutory provision for a Sheriff to review, amend or recall a conviction once it has been passed and recorded.

In view of the statutory provisions enabling him to amend or vary a sentence, this is significant. Since once he had convicted the respondent and this was recorded the Sheriff was *functus*, and his actions on 26th July 1974 were *ultra vires*, as was all that followed thereon. This in effect means that the only valid order standing is that of 25th July 1974.

It was in recognition of that situation that the Advocate-depute intimated that he could not ask the Court to answer the questions raised in the Stated Case. This is inevitably so, since the facts on which the questions are based arose from a trial which on the ground of our decision was *ultra vires* and inept.

We shall accordingly formally find that the order of 26th July 1974 was incompetent and must be quashed. That being so, and for the reasons stated we must dismiss the appeal which is an appeal against an order of the court which was itself incompetent.

We fully recognise the anomalous position in which the respondent may now find himself, but if he has a remedy it is not in this process.

While the view we have taken might appear to be a highly technical one, there seems to be justification for the technicality not only in the statutory provisions regulating the procedure but in the fact that if the course followed in this case was authorised as legitimate, it might well result in that course becoming commonplace and the subject of abuse by accused persons dissatisfied by the sentence imposed following a plea of guilty. If it is thought that provision should be made for exceptional cases, that would appear to be a matter for the legislature. As we have previously noted, the fact that the legislature has not made provision for this heretofore is not without its significance in the context of this case."

Appeal dismissed.

NOTE

For the final outcome of this case see *MacGregor* v. *MacNeill, infra*, p. 485.

(ii) Questions of fact and questions of law

Prior to the 1980 Act the decision of the trial judge on questions of fact was, in the ordinary run of cases, final. This meant that appeal by stated case was only competent on points of law, so that it was necessary in all cases to distinguish between questions of fact and questions of law. So far as appeal by a convicted person is concerned it is no longer necessary to make this distinction since appeal under section 442 is competent at the instance of the convicted person on grounds of fact as well as law. This is not so, however, in the case of appeals by the prosecutor, where the fact/law distinction remains relevant. The following cases are examples of this problem:

1. **Fraser v. Anderson**
(1899) 2 Adam 705

The appellant was convicted of theft and appealed by stated case. The question of law for the opinion of the High Court was "Whether, on the facts as stated, an act of theft was committed by the appellant".

Lord Kinnear: "I have some difficulty in answering the question put to us in this case. The question really at issue is rather one of fact than of law. But when we read the Sheriff's statement of the case, it seems to me that his conception of the matter was that, having found certain facts as proved, they appeared to him to raise a question of law, viz., whether these facts amounted to the crime of theft. Taking these facts, we have to consider whether or not the necessary legal inference is that the appellant was guilty of theft.

As I read the facts stated by the Sheriff to have been proved, there was a completed sale of certain heifers to Mr Chisholm on 16th June, but the cattle were by arrangement left in the possession of the appellant until the price should be paid. I agree with the Solicitor-General that although the cattle were left in the appellant's possession they were the property of Mr Chisholm, and were in the appellant's possession on a qualified title and for a limited purpose. Upon 22nd June the appellant not having received the price of the cattle, which according to arrangement he ought to have received, goes to his bank and finds that the money has not been paid into his account. I am not sure whether the Sheriff means us to take that as a fact which he finds as proved, or whether he only means to state it as a fact alleged by the accused in defence. But, however that may be, he does not find that in fact the appellant knew or believed that the money had been remitted. In these circumstances it is found that the appellant removed the cattle from his field and handed them over to a relative of his own with instructions to sell them, and the cattle having been sold the price so obtained was entered to the credit of the appellant in his bank account at Beauly. In so acting the appellant was doing what he was plainly not entitled to do, and if I were satisfied that he had so acted with any felonious intent, I should have no difficulty in holding that he had been guilty of theft. But the real question is whether any felonious intention was in fact proved. Now, it is said for the appellant that he believed on reasonable grounds that the purchaser had broken his contract, and the Sheriff does not find in fact that he did not so believe. It may quite well be on the facts found to be proved that the appellant acted as he did in ignorance of his legal remedy in the circumstances, and that he thought that the money not having reached him, he had a right to proceed to sell the cattle at his own hand. Such a supposition would have been negatived if the Sheriff had found as matter of fact that the accused acted as he did with felonious intent. But he has not done so. The things he finds that the appellant did may or may not have been done with felonious intent; that is a matter of fact and not of law. Therefore, when he asks us whether on the facts as stated an act of theft has been committed, my answer is that that is not proved. The facts proved may or may not amount to theft according as the appellant's intention was theftuous or not; and the Sheriff does not find that it was theftuous. I cannot infer that he meant so to find from the mere fact that he convicted the appellant, for the one question he puts in the case is whether that conviction rested on valid grounds; and the specific grounds on which it in fact rested are set forth in the case, and not in the conviction itself. The question stated is in effect whether the judge required to be satisfied of anything more than the bare facts specified in order to justify a conviction, and if anything further is necessary to complete the crime of theft, it appears to me that the defect cannot be supplied by inference from the very conviction that is put in question.

LORD ADAM (*diss*): "In these cases stated on appeal we have only to deal with questions of law. We do not deal with questions of fact. We are here asked whether on the facts stated an act of theft was committed? When it is said that, looking to the facts proved, the crime may have been committed if a certain inference is drawn from those facts, then I say that that inference is a matter of fact, and is therefore a question for the Sheriff, and we will only interfere with his decision if it can be made out that on no possible view of the facts are they capable of bearing out the inference he has drawn . . . Now, I can understand that one inference from these facts may be that the appellant, not knowing that the price had been already paid into his account on 22nd June, thought he might legitimately sell the cattle, but there is another inference, and that is that he acted as he did with felonious intent. Which of these inferences is correct is matter of fact and therefore for the Sheriff. Either inference may be drawn from the facts stated in the case."

> The court answered the question in the negative and allowed the appeal.

2.   Waugh v. Campbell
1920 J.C. 1

The respondent was charged with driving a vehicle recklessly and negligently contrary to section 1 of the Motor Car Act 1903. The sheriff found him not guilty and at the request of the procurator fiscal stated a case for the opinion of the High Court. The question for the opinion of the court was "Ought the respondent have been convicted?"

LORD DUNDAS: "I think there is no doubt that the question stated in this case will not do in the form in which it is stated. We are asked: 'Ought the respondent to have been convicted?' This is not a question that should be put to us. I think the proper form of the question would have been—Did the facts stated afford legal evidence on which the Sheriff-substitute was entitled to acquit? or something like that.

I have had some doubt and difficulty, but I have come to the conclusion that there was not such evidence. It is certain that we cannot review an inferior judge in a case of this sort upon facts, but we can, and, I think, ought to, interfere in any case in which we consider the evidence does not legally warrant the judgment at which he has arrived. I am bound to say that not only do I think the acquittal by the Sheriff-substitute was wrong, but I am really unable to see any evidence which could warrant it at all. The evidence seems to me to be all the other way.

The facts, to put them briefly, disclose that, as the respondent was going along this public road, with which he was well acquainted, and approaching Kirkdale Bridge, he was driving at about 14 miles an hour. Just at the end of the bridge there is a very sharp turn shown on the map—a blind turn, as it appears that, owing to the parapet wall and foliage, no one can see round it. Then when he got about halfway across this bridge he deliberately crossed to the wrong side of the road. He sounded no horn, but, proceeding on his way, although the road was admittedly broad enough easily to have allowed two cars to pass one another if each was on its proper side, he collided with a motor car coming in the other direction upon its own proper side of the road. These facts seem to me to involve a contravention of the section of the Act we are considering.

The learned Sheriff-substitute explains his ground of judgment in this way. He says that the respondent would probably be liable for the civil consequences of the collision. We have nothing to do with that, but probably the surmise is right. He goes on to say: 'There was nothing in the nature, condition, or use of the road, nor anything on account of the amount of traffic which was actually on it at the time or which might reasonably be expected to be on it at the time, which entitled me to hold that the respondent, in crossing from his left or proper side of the road to his right hand side under the circumstances and in the manner above described, was driving his motor car recklessly and negligently.' I cannot understand that. As regards the nature of the road, we have the facts I have summarised; this blind turn, and the other conditions. As regards the use of the road, we have this silent unheralded swerve at considerable speed round a right-angled turn. Then, as regards the traffic, I should have thought that the duty of the respondent was to anticipate that there might be traffic on this road coming in the other direction. We have it stated that the road is the public highway between Creetown and Gatehouse of Fleet, known as the Mail Coach Road, a comparatively quiet road, but one on which motor cars and other vehicular traffic pass along from time to time every day.

I do not hesitate to say that, upon this evidence, if I had been sitting as judge of first instance, I should have convicted. That is not enough by itself to warrant me in interfering in the matter; but I am constrained to go further and say that, viewing the evidence, it seems to me to be all one way, and that I am unable to see what facts can be laid hold of as affording any evidence at all to justify an acquittal. In other words, it seems to me not only that one differs—as I understand both your lordships differ—in opinion from the result arrived at by the learned Sheriff-substitute, but that really it amounts to this that he misdirected himself in law, and said to himself that the accumulated mass of evidence all in one direction warranted a verdict in the other. I do not see how we can avoid interfering in such a case; and, accordingly, in my opinion, we should find on the facts stated that the Sheriff-substitute was not entitled to acquit."

LORD SALVESEN: ". . . My greatest doubt in connexion with the case was whether after all it was not a question of fact, with regard to which we have no right to interfere. The Sheriff-substitute, I think, has not treated it as a question of fact, but has stated for us a question of law arising upon the facts; and on that question of law I am constrained to hold, though I confess I do it reluctantly in the case of an acquittal, that he misdirected himself, and that the statutory offence may be constituted merely by negligence, although the judge who tries the case thinks the negligence was not gross negligence and involved no moral blame. In that view of it I concur in the judgment, although I hope it will not lead to many appeals on what are primarily questions of fact, just because the prosecutor does not concur with the Sheriff in the verdict—for it is really a verdict—at which he arrives. I hope nothing we do in this case will encourage such a practice."

LORD GUTHRIE: "I agree on both points to which your Lordships have referred, first, that there are no facts here to support the verdict, and second, that the Sheriff-substitute has misdirected himself in law. On the first point Mr Jameson referred to the case of *Cromwell* v. *Renton* [(1911) 6 Adam 498], and to the Lord Justice-Clerk's opinion where he says:— 'Whether, in these circumstances, the appellant was rightly convicted is a pure question of fact on which we cannot interfere with the Sheriff-substitute's decision.' "

> The court answered the question in the
> negative and allowed the appeal.

NOTE

The absence of an effective means of challenging the trial judge's findings-in-fact was one of the criticisms voiced to the Thomson Committee (3rd Report, para. 8.09). The committee did not, however, accept this criticism. In considering whether or not there should be a right to a re-hearing in summary proceedings the committee expressed the view that "on the evidence before us, we see no need for such a radical departure from the principle that in summary procedure the trial judge is the final arbiter on questions of fact" (*ibid.*, para. 7.06). For an example of an appeal by stated case on a question of fact, see *Wilson* v. *Carmichael*, 1982 S.C.C.R. 528 and the commentary thereon at p. 532.

(iii) Limitations on appeal

1. Criminal Procedure (Scotland) Act 1975

"454. No conviction, sentence, judgment, order of court or other proceeding whatsoever under Part II of this Act shall be quashed for want of form or, where the accused had legal assistance in his defence, shall be suspended or set aside in respect of any objections to the relevancy of the complaint, or to the want of specification therein, or to the competency or admission or rejection of evidence at the trial in the inferior court, unless such objections shall have been timeously stated at the trial by the solicitor of the accused."

NOTE

Section 454 must be read subject to the rule that the High Court may quash a conviction on the ground of fundamental nullity even though no preliminary objection has been stated. See *O'Malley* v. *Strathern*, 1920 J.C. 74, *supra*, p. 397 and other authorities there cited, and *Robertson* v. *Aitchison*, 1981 S.L.T. (Notes) 127, *infra*, p. 477.

Section 454 does not refer in terms to acquittals, but see the following case:

2. Skeen v. Murphy
1978 S.L.T. (Notes) 2

The respondent was charged with a contravention of section 6(1) of the Road Traffic Act 1972. The appropriate analyst's and doctor's certificates were produced by the fiscal at the beginning of the trial. No objection was taken to these certificates by the respondent's solicitor at any time. During the trial the sheriff, *ex proprio motu*, raised the question of the competency of these certificates, and held that since it had not been proved that they had been served on the respondent in accordance with section 10(3) of the 1972 Act, their contents had not been properly proved in evidence. In the absence of the evidence provided by the certificates, the sheriff held the prosecution had not proved their case, and he acquitted the respondent. The prosecutor appealed by stated case.

LORD JUSTICE-CLERK (WHEATLEY): "It was argued by the advocate-depute that the tendering of these certificates by the procurator fiscal at the beginning of the trial was, by virtue of the statutory provisions relating thereto under s. 10 (1) of the 1972 Act, the factual presenting of evidence to the court, and that if any objection was to be taken to the admission of that evidence it should have been taken at the time the evidence was presented or at least before the end of the Crown case. He relied on s. 354 (1) of the Criminal Procedure (Scotland) Act 1975 in support of his argument. Counsel for the respondent submitted that in the absence of a prior agreement, which presumably would have to be recorded, s. 354 (1) did not apply to documents such as those we are concerned with here. He submitted that in the circumstances the sheriff was right in holding that the contents of the certificates had not been properly admitted in evidence and that the facts therein had not been proved, and this whether or not an objection had been taken at the time, because such a consideration was not relevant. That being so, the Crown had not proved all the essential evidence for a conviction on the charge, and accordingly there was bound to be an acquittal. We are of the opinion that the question here falls to be answered by reference to general principles without any reference to s. 354 (1) of the 1975 Act. In terms of s. 454 (1) of the Act of 1975 it is provided: 'No conviction, sentence, judgment, order of court or other proceeding whatsoever under this Part of this Act shall be quashed for want of form or, where the accused had legal assistance in his defence, shall be suspended or set aside in respect of any objections to the relevancy of the complaint, or to the want of specification therein, or to the competency or admission or rejection of evidence at the trial in the inferior court, unless such objections shall have been timeously stated at the trial by the solicitor of the accused'.

While that section relates to convictions etc., and not to acquittals, the underlying reasoning is that unless objection to the competency or admission of evidence is timeously taken, it cannot be subsequently taken, and, if not, such evidence becomes part of the evidence in causa. We do not see why such evidence should not be regarded as evidence in causa simply because an acquittal and not a conviction resulted. It is on the evidence in causa that the question of conviction or acquittal has to be determined. In any event it is a general rule that objections to the competency and admissibility of evidence should be taken when that evidence is tendered. That being so, what is the position here? The prosecutor tendered the reports as evidence in terms of the statute, together with the appropriate certificate of posting. No objection was taken at the time to the validity or competency of the evidence thus tendered. It was only during the hearing on evidence that the sheriff ex proprio motu raised the question whether the Crown had proved that these reports had been timeously served, and if not, whether the evidence contained therein should be excluded from the case. In our opinion, it was then too late for this point to be taken. The defence had not taken any objection to the competency or admissibility of that evidence when it was tendered, because the reports were not timeously served, and it was then properly before the court. On that short ground alone we can sustain the appeal."

Appeal allowed.

(iv) Miscarriage of justice

As was pointed out above, with the exception of the prosecutor's appeal against sentence, the sole ground of appeal in a stated case is that there has been a miscarriage of justice. Prior to the 1980 Act's amendments, a stated case could be brought to review the relevancy of the complaint, any irregularity in procedure, any alleged error of the court in point of law and, generally, any matter which immediately prior to the 1975 Act could have been competently reviewed by suspension (see infra, p. 481), advocation (see infra, p. 493) or appeal under the Heritable Jurisdictions (Scotland) Act 1746 (which had been obsolete for many years) or otherwise. (See the former terms of section 442 of the 1975 Act.)

Section 454(2) of the 1975 Act (now repealed by the 1980 Act) provided that no conviction, sentence, judgment, order of court or other proceeding could be quashed except on the ground of incompetency, corruption, malice or oppression, or unless the High Court was of opinion that the accused had been misled as to the true nature of the charge against him or been prejudiced in his defence on the merits, and that a miscarriage of justice had resulted thereby.

The question arises as to the relevancy of the old law to the new ground of appeal. It is submitted that those matters which constituted a miscarriage of justice under the provisions of section 454(2) should continue to be so considered. It is further submitted that cases of incompetency ("an inability in the Court to deal with the matter in hand . . . any case with which the Court, as a Court, had not power to deal," *per* Lord Justice-General Dunedin in *Robson* v. *Menzies* (1913) 7 Adam 156 at p. 161), corruption, malice and oppression must necessarily amount to miscarriages of justice, and for a discussion of these matters see Renton and Brown, paras. 16-25 to 16-59.

It would appear, however, that not every irregularity in procedure or error of law on the part of the court will be fatal to a conviction or acquittal. In every case the question is whether there has been a miscarriage of justice, and this must be established by the appellant, whether he be convicted person or prosecutor. On this point compare *Pettigrew* v. *Ingram*, 1982 S.L.T. 435; 1982 S.C.C.R. 259, and *McCuaig* v. *H.M. Advocate*, 1982 S.L.T. 383; 1982 S.C.C.R. 125, *supra*, Chap. 14.

Whether or not there has been a miscarriage of justice in relation to sentence (which is the test to be applied in the case of a convicted person's appeal) will depend upon the rules and principles governing sentencing. These matters are discussed *post*, Chap. 16.

(v) Method and time of appeal

Criminal Procedure (Scotland) Act 1975
"444. (1) An appeal under section 442(1)(*a*)(i) or (iii) or (*b*) of this Act shall be by application for a stated case, which application shall—

(*a*) be made within one week of the final determination of the proceedings;

(*b*) contain a full statement of all the matters which the appellant desires to bring under review and where the appeal is also against sentence, a statement of that fact; and

(*c*) be signed by the appellant or his solicitor and lodged with the clerk of court;

and a copy of the application shall within the period mentioned in paragraph (*a*) above be sent by the appellant to the respondent or the respondent's solicitor."

NOTES

1. Where an application is made under section 444(1) the court prepares, within three weeks of final determination of the proceedings in respect of which the application is made, a draft stated case which is issued to the appellant and a copy provided for the respondent (section 447(1)). During this three-week period the appellant may amend any matter stated in his application or add a new matter (section 444(1B)).

2. Where the appellant is in custody, the court may grant bail, grant a sist of execution or make any other interim order (section 446(1)). The requirement that the appellant should find caution to meet any fine and expenses imposed, which was formerly demanded by section 445 has, in accordance with the recommendations of the Thomson Committee (3rd Report, para. 8.24), been abolished by the 1980 Act.

(vi)   Adjustments

Criminal Procedure (Scotland) Act 1975

"448. (1) Subject to subsection (6) below, within three weeks of the issue of the draft stated case under section 447 of this Act, each party shall cause to be transmitted to the court and to the other parties or their solicitors a note of any adjustments he proposes be made to the draft case or shall intimate that he has no such proposal:

Provided that adjustments proposed shall relate to evidence heard (or purported to have been heard) at the trial and not to such additional evidence as is mentioned in section 442(2) of this Act.

(2) Subject to subsection (6) below, if the period mentioned in subsection (1) above has expired and the appellant has not lodged adjustments and has failed to intimate that he has no adjustments to propose, he shall be deemed to have abandoned his appeal; and subsection (4) of section 446 of this Act shall apply accordingly.

(2A) If adjustments are proposed under subsection (1) above or if the judge desires to make any alterations to the draft case there shall, within one week of the expiry of the period mentioned in that subsection or as the case may be of any further period afforded under subsection (6) below, be a hearing (unless the appellant has, or has been deemed to have, abandoned his appeal) for the purpose of considering such adjustments or alterations.

(2B) Where a party neither attends nor secures that he is represented at a hearing under subsection (2A) above, the hearing shall nevertheless proceed.

(2C) Where at a hearing under subsection (2A) above—

(*a*) any adjustment proposed under subsection (1) above by a party (and not withdrawn) is rejected by the judge; or

(*b*) any alteration to the draft case proposed by the judge is not accepted by all the parties,

that fact shall be recorded in the minute of the proceedings of the hearing.

(2D) Within two weeks of the date of the hearing under subsection (2A) above or, where there is no hearing, within two weeks of the expiry of the period mentioned in subsection (1) above, the judge shall (unless the appellant has been deemed to have abandoned the appeal) state and sign the case and shall append to the case—

(*a*) any adjustment, proposed under subsection (1) above, which is rejected by him, a note of any evidence rejected by him which is alleged to support that adjustment and the reasons for his rejection of that adjustment and evidence; and

(*b*) a note of the evidence upon which he bases any finding of fact challenged, on the basis that it is unsupported by the evidence, by a party at the hearing under subsection (2A) above."

NOTES

1. There was an obligation under the former section 448(2) for the trial judge to consider proposed adjustments, but he was not obliged to hear parties on such proposals, nor was he obliged to incorporate them into the final stated case, or even give grounds for rejecting them. The Thomson Committee (3rd Report, para. 8.18), recognising the difficulties this presented for those advising appellants when the case as finally stated "was so completely within the discretion and control of the judge", recommended a hearing on adjustments, which should be compulsory, and which both parties should have the right to attend.

2. It remains the case, in accordance with the views of the Thomson Committee, that the court is not obliged to accept proposed adjustments, but is obliged to indicate any adjustments which it has rejected, and its grounds for doing so. For an example of the High Court taking account of a rejected adjustment under the new procedure, see *Wilson* v. *Carmichael*, 1982 S.C.C.R. 528.

3. Section 448(6) makes provision for the High Court to extend time-limits provided for in relation to adjustments.

(vii) Form of the case

The case must be stated in the form provided for by the Act of Adjournal (Procedures under Criminal Justice (Scotland) Act 1980 No. 2) 1981, and must "set forth the particulars of any matters competent for review which the appellant desires to bring under review of the High Court, and of the facts, if any, proved in the case, and any point of law decided, and the grounds of the decision. Findings-in-fact must be just that. Mere assertions that the guilt of the appellant is established will not suffice": *Mitchell and Others* v. *Smith*, High Court, 21 January 1981, unreported, C.O.C. A2/81.

Galt v. Goodsir
1981 S.C.C.R. 225

The respondent was charged with contraventions of sections 6 and 22 of the Road Traffic Act 1972. At the close of the Crown case the respondent's solicitor made a submission that there was no case to answer. This was sustained by the sheriff who, at the request of the fiscal, stated a case for the opinion of the High Court. In his stated case the sheriff made no findings-in-fact, but simply set out the evidence for the prosecution. In his note to the case he explained why he had adopted this course:

SHERIFF CHRISTIE: "I would wish first of all to explain why I have not made findings in fact but merely stated the evidence which I heard. Since this appeal arises out of my decision that there is no case to answer in terms of section 345A of the Criminal Procedure (Scotland) Act 1975 I am concerned that should your Lordships be of the opinion that I was wrong in my decision the case would presumably be referred back to me and I would be required to hear the evidence for the defence, if any were tendered. If I make findings in fact at this stage I would be closing the door on the defence case. There were points put in cross-examination which if established by defence evidence would cast doubt on the prosecution evidence. Furthermore, since section 345A is dealing with sufficiency of evidence it seems to me that this should be tested by reference to evidence led."

NOTE

The High Court remitted the case to the sheriff for trial, but without expressing any opinion on the form of the stated case. The only other form of review in a case such as this would be by advocation under section 453A of the 1975 Act (*infra*, p. 488). But whether or not the sheriff rightly exercised his discretion under section 345A on the question of no case to answer is a question of law to be determined in the light of the facts. The facts could only be made available to the High Court by means of a stated case, and for this reason the latter procedure would seem to be appropriate.

(viii) Form and statement of the questions

1. Prentice v. Skeen
1977 S.L.T. (Notes) 21

Two accused were found guilty of stealing a quantity of meat. A stated case was applied for and the sheriff duly stated the case which in findings-in-fact 1 to 6 incorporated the evidence on which he based his finding that the appellants were guilty as libelled. In finding 7 he found as follows: "the meats in the possession of the appellants had been stolen by them from the deep freeze unit." The first question stated in the case for the opinion of the High Court was: "On the facts stated was I entitled to find the appellants guilty as libelled?" At the stage of adjustment the solicitor for the appellants asked the sheriff to incorporate a question to the following effect: "was there sufficient evidence to entitle me to make finding-in-fact No. 7?", but the sheriff refused.

OPINION OF THE COURT: "It has been stated time and time again in this court that when the issue raised in a stated case is incorporated in a finding-of-fact conclusive or at least indicative of guilt and the point sought to be argued is that there was not sufficient evidence in law to warrant that finding, it is not appropriate merely to pose a question of law in general form such as 'On the facts stated was I entitled to find the appellants guilty as libelled?' The proper method of stating the question in such circumstances is in the form proposed by the appellants' solicitor to the sheriff above quoted. Legal advisers for appellants have been criticised in the past by the court for not seeking to have such a question in proper form incorporated in the stated case. There is no reason why the same salutary rule should not be applied to judges in the inferior courts.

The court wishes to draw attention to the fact that when such an issue is the only issue in the case, or is a crucial issue in the case, it is imperative that the judge in the inferior court should incorporate a question in the appropriate form either ex proprio motu or on request. Failure to do so may well frustrate the whole method of this form of appeal. I cannot understand why the sheriff refused to incorporate such a question in the instant case."

NOTE

Cf. Waugh v. *Campbell, supra.*

2. Robertson v. Aitchison
1981 S.L.T. (Notes) 127

The appellant was charged with driving while disqualified, and a co-accused was charged with aiding and abetting him, contrary to sections 99(*b*) and 176 of the Road Traffic Act 1972. They were convicted and appealed by stated case.

OPINION OF THE COURT: "The sheriff in the very full and clear note appended to his findings-in-fact and his conclusions, draws attention to the fact that an extract conviction referable to the first accused was produced and proved in the course of the trial, and that the extract conviction demonstrated not only that the appellant mentioned had previously been convicted of a contravention of s. 8 (1) and (3) of the Road Traffic Act but also of a further contravention of s. 9 (3). In so doing he was careful to add in a case which, as he said 'turned solely on the question of credibility' that his judgment had been in no way influenced by the production of a potentially prejudicial piece of evidence, the production of which was in plain contravention of s. 357 of the Criminal Justice (Scotland) Act 1975.

It is in these circumstances that the present appeal comes before the court, but upon a series of questions which do not specifically raise the issue of fundamental nullity of a conviction where, in the course of proceedings, a previous conviction or convictions have been laid before the court in circumstances other than those covered by the precise terms of s. 357 (5) of the Act of 1975.

The point which counsel for the appellant sought to raise is short, but it is not one to which any of the questions posed in the stated case appear to relate unless it be, as counsel maintained, that it is covered by the wording of the third question relating to Sinclair. We are not persuaded that it can be said that any of the questions do precisely relate to this issue, but the matter has been presented by counsel as one which, if the argument is well-founded, goes to the root of the conviction and reduces it to a nullity. For the Crown it was not disputed that, if a true issue of fundamental nullity was disclosed in the proceedings that could properly be submitted for decision, even though not expressed or implied in any of the questions in the stated case. This is clearly right. The sheriff in his note has brought it to our notice, and while he himself did not apparently regard the reference to a previous conviction of the appellant Robertson of contravention of s. 8 (3) of the Road Traffic Act 1972, as nullifying the whole proceedings, the point has now been taken and we are in no doubt that where it appears on the face of the proceedings that a conviction is affected by a fundamental nullity it is for the court to take notice of it, however and in whatever form it comes to notice and, if that is found to be the case, to take the necessary action and quash the conviction so tainted."

Conviction quashed.

NOTES

1. *Cf. O'Malley* v. *Strathern*, 1920 J.C. 74, *supra* Chap. 13. For the terms of section 454 see *supra*, p. 470.

2. The court went on to hold that the conviction was fatally flawed by a fundamental nullity as a result of the introduction of the previous conviction. They also held that the conviction of the co-accused was similarly flawed:

"The appellants in this case were charged in one complaint, the charges arose out of one transaction in which both are alleged to have been simultaneously engaged. There is therefore no means or measure by which a different conclusion can be arrived at in their individual cases. The 'proceedings' are those in this complaint and, as the statute has been breached, the conviction obtained cannot stand."

Cf. Boustead v. *McLeod*, 1979 J.C. 70 and *Mitchell* v. *Dean*, 1979 J.C. 62. So far as the fate of the co-accused is concerned, compare this case with *Cordiner* v. *H.M. Advocate*, 1978 J.C. 64, *supra*, Chap. 14.

(ix) Hearing and disposal of appeals

Criminal Procedure (Scotland) Act 1975

"452.—(1) A stated case under this Part of this Act shall be heard by the High Court on such date as it may fix.

(2) For the avoidance of doubt, where an appellant, in his application under section 444(1) of this Act (or in a duly made amendment or addition to that application), refers to an alleged miscarriage of justice, but in stating a case under section 448(2D) of this Act the inferior court is unable to take the allegation into account, the High Court may nevertheless have regard to the allegation at a hearing under subsection (1) above.

(3) Except by leave of the High Court on cause shown, it shall not be competent for an appellant to found any aspect of his appeal on a matter not contained in his application under section 444(1) of this Act (or in a duly made amendment or addition to that application).

(4) Without prejudice to any existing power of the High Court, that court may in hearing a stated case—

(*a*) order the production of any document or other thing connected with the proceedings;

(*b*) hear any additional evidence relevant to any alleged miscarriage of justice or order such evidence to be heard by a judge of the High Court or by such other person as it may appoint for that purpose;

(*c*) take account of any circumstances relevant to the case which were not before the trial judge;

(*d*) remit to any fit person to enquire and report in regard to any matter or circumstance affecting the appeal;

(*e*) appoint a person with expert knowledge to act as assessor to the High Court in any case where it appears to the court that such expert knowledge is required for the proper determination of the case;

(*f*) take account of any matter proposed in any adjustment rejected by the trial judge and of the reasons for such rejection;

(*g*) take account of any evidence contained in a note of evidence such as is mentioned in section 448(2D) of this Act.

(5) The High Court may at the hearing remit the stated case back to the inferior court to be amended and returned.

452A.—(1) The High Court may, subject to section 453D(1) of this Act, dispose of a stated case by—

(a) remitting the cause to the inferior court with their opinion and any direction thereon;

(b) affirming the verdict of the inferior court;

(c) setting aside the verdict of the inferior court and either quashing the conviction or substituting therefor an amended verdict of guilty:

Provided that an amended verdict of guilty must be one which could have been returned on the complaint before the inferior court; or

(d) setting aside the verdict of the inferior court and granting authority to bring a new prosecution in accordance with section 452B of this Act.

(2) In an appeal against both conviction and sentence the High Court shall, subject to section 453D(1) of this Act, dispose of the appeal against sentence by exercise of the power mentioned in section 453C(1) of this Act.

(3) In setting aside, under subsection (1) above, a verdict the High Court may quash any sentence imposed on the appellant as respects the complaint, and—

(a) in a case where it substitutes an amended verdict of guilty, whether or not the sentence related to the verdict set aside; or

(b) in any other case, where the sentence did not so relate,

may pass another (but not more severe) sentence in substitution for the sentence so quashed.

(4) Where an appeal against acquittal is sustained, the High Court may—

(a) convict and sentence the respondent;

(b) remit the case to the inferior court with instructions to convict and sentence the respondent, who shall be bound to attend any diet fixed by the inferior court for such purpose; or

(c) remit the case to the inferior court with their opinion thereon:

Provided that the High Court shall not in any case increase the sentence beyond the maximum sentence which could have been passed by the inferior court.

(5) The High Court shall have power in an appeal under this Part of this Act to award such expenses both in the High Court and in the inferior court as it may think fit."

NOTES

1. Where authority is granted to bring a new prosecution, such prosecution may be brought charging the accused with the same or any similar offence arising out of the same facts: section 452B. For the analogous provisions with regard to solemn proceedings, see, *supra*, Chap. 14.

2. Where an appeal has been taken against conviction or conviction and sentence, the prosecutor may, if he is not prepared to maintain the judgment appealed against, consent to the conviction and sentence being set aside, either in whole or in part. In such a case the High Court may set aside the conviction. Where the High

Court refuses to do so, the matter is returned to the clerk of the inferior court and the appellant may proceed with his appeal: section 453.

(x) Abandonment of appeal

Criminal Procedure (Scotland) Act 1975
"449.—(1) An appellant in an appeal such as is mentioned in section 444(1) may at any time prior to lodging the case with the Clerk of Justiciary abandon his appeal by minute signed by himself or his solicitor, written on the complaint or lodged with the clerk of the inferior court, and intimated to the respondent or the respondent's solicitor, but such abandonment shall be without prejudice to any other competent mode of appeal, review, advocation or suspension.

(2) Subject to section 453A of this Act, on the case being lodged with the Clerk of Justiciary, the appellant shall be held to have abandoned any other mode of appeal which might otherwise have been open to him."

NOTES
1. For alternative methods of appeal, etc., see *infra*. Under 448(2) an appellant may also be deemed to have abandoned his appeal if he fails to comply with the procedure therein: see *supra*. He may also abandon his stated case after lodging, or abandon an appeal against conviction (but proceed with an appeal against sentence), all in accordance with the procedures laid down in Act of Adjournal (Procedures under Criminal Justice (Scotland) Act 1980 No. 2) 1981.

2. Abandonment of an appeal may , in exceptional circumstances, be subject to recall by an application to the *nobile officium* : *Mathieson, Petitioner*, 1980 S.L.T. 74, *post*, Chap. 18. (but *cf. Ferguson* v. *H.M. Advocate* 1980 J.C. 27, *supra*, Chap. 14).

c. Suspension

"Suspension is the appropriate mode of bringing under review of the High Court an illegal or irregular warrant, conviction, or judgment of an inferior Court" (Moncreiff on *Review in Criminal Cases*, pp. 169-170). As a form of review it is not open to the prosecutor, whose corresponding remedy is advocation (*infra*, p. 493).

(i)   Competency

High Court proceedings cannot be made the subject of a suspension (see Moncreiff, *loc. cit.*). Section 230 of the 1975 Act states that it shall not be competent to appeal to the High Court by bill of suspension against any conviction, sentence, judgment or order pronounced in any proceedings on indictment in the sheriff court. Where, however, a sheriff exercises a summary power of punishment for contempt in solemn proceedings the sentence imposed may be reviewed by suspension notwithstanding section 230: *Butterworth* v. *Herron*, 1975 S.L.T. (Notes) 56.

Before a suspension can be brought, however, there must be something in the way of an unlawful warrant, judgment, etc., to suspend:

1.   Jupp v. Dunbar
(1863) 4 Irv. 355

The suspender appeared in court, charged with a contravention of the Day Poaching Act. He pleaded not guilty to the charge. The minute of proceedings was as follows: "Thereafter, the following witnesses were examined on oath in support of the complaint:—1. Andrew Cleugh, junior, residing at Ochclate, on the estate of Thrumpster.

The Justices having considered the complaint, with the evidence adduced, finds the"—(No more of the sentence was written out.)

The suspender presented a bill of suspension in which he stated that, notwithstanding the omission of any finding of guilt or note of sentence, the magistrates imposed a fine of £2 and informed him that unless he paid the fine instantly he would be sent to prison. He paid the fine.

LORD JUSTICE-CLERK (INGLIS): ". . . There is nothing to suspend. The suspender complains that the fine has been extorted from him on the representation that he had been sentenced, while in fact no sentence had been pronounced. On that ground he may or may not have a remedy in another form; but it cannot enable the Court to quash a sentence which never existed. The suspension must be refused as incompetent."

Suspension refused
as incompetent.

NOTE

As was pointed out above, suspension may be employed to bring under review matters other than the judgment of a court, such as a warrant. For a modern example of this see *Wilson* v. *Milne*, 1975 S.L.T. (Notes) 26.

2.   Morton v. McLeod
1982 S.L.T. 187

An accused person was charged on summary complaint with a contravention of section 2(1) of the Food and Drugs (Scotland) Act 1956. A plea to the competency of the complaint was presented on his behalf and repelled by the sheriff. The accused then presented a bill of suspension to the High Court seeking review of the sheriff's decision on competency.

LORD CAMERON: ". . . It is in respect of the sheriff's decision that the present bill of suspension has been presented. The ground on which the competency of the complaint was challenged before the sheriff is set out in his note which is also appended to this bill. It was submitted on behalf of the accused that: 'As the bottle of milk was a sample and had been procured under the provisions of the Food and Drugs Act, proceedings in respect of the contents of the bottle should have been commenced before the expiry of two months from the date on which the sample was procured in compliance with the provisions of s. 41 (3) of the Act'. This plea was not accepted by the sheriff [ante, 1981 S.L.T. (Sh. Ct.) 107] and trial has been fixed for 7 September.

Prima facie the complaint, which makes no reference to the procurement of any sample or to the consequences of the analysis of any sample, would appear to be both competent and relevant.

The question which now sharply arises is whether this bill should be permitted to proceed further and a first order granted.

In the course of the debate before the sheriff certain statements of fact were made by the prosecutor as to the actual course of events on the date libelled in the complaint and as the sheriff records: 'a consignment of milk was delivered to Springside Primary School at 7.30 a.m. on 10 February 1981. The consignment was distributed round the classes and some surplus was left in the office. The janitor took one of the surplus bottles from the office to the kitchen staff. He noticed a drinking straw inside the bottle. He showed it to the school secretary who informed the local environmental health department at Irvine. At about 2.45 p.m. an assistant environmental health officer and a senior assistant environmental health officer called at the school. They saw the bottle still unopened with the straw inside. They took possession of the bottle and sent a letter concerning the matter to the defender on 11 February asking for his comments. The public analyst was not asked to analyse the contents of this bottle. The argument submitted to me was on the basis of these facts.'

This narrative however does not and could not constitute a minute of admissions of all the facts relevant to this complaint.

For the suspender, counsel maintained that he was entitled to a first order and to an interim suspension of proceedings as the issue between the parties was one of competency alone and the argument would be solely one on matters of law. He agreed that the complaint as libelled was both relevant and competent ex facie, but maintained that on the facts agreed, as set out in the passage in the sheriff's note which I have quoted, the bottle of milk itself forming the subject of the complaint—the corpus delicti—was to be held to be a 'sample' within the meaning of the statutory provisions in that when the officers of the local authority obtained possession of the offending bottle they were 'procuring a sample' within the meaning of s. 28 (1) of the Act of 1956, and that consequently as the proceedings had not been initiated within the period prescribed by s. 41 (3) the complaint was incompetent. This, he said, was placing a legal interpretation on the admitted actions of the officers of the local authority and therefore the issue of competency could and should be determined at this stage. The observations of the Lord Justice-General in *Fairley* v. *Muir*, 1951 S.L.T. 237 were in point in his favour. The issue was 'crisp' in the words of Lord Cooper, was purely one of law, and the first order should be granted.

For the Crown it was submitted that the bill was premature and the first order should be refused. Admittedly there was a depending process and the remedy of suspension was not available at this stage—only after trial and conviction, if conviction followed. In support of his general proposition the advocate-depute referred to Hume on *Crimes*, ii, 513 and 515, which made it clear that this remedy was only available after the conclusion of the trial and opened up all the proceedings. Alison, ii, 27-30 was to the same effect, as was Moncreiff at p. 170 who made it clear also that incidental warrants, i.e. those which do not form part of the main proceedings could be subject of suspension pendente processu (see Moncreiff, p. 186). The same views were expressed in Trotter at p. 62 and Renton and Brown, paras. 16.95 and 98. These principles do not admit of exceptions. In *Fairley* v. *Muir* the court was not dealing with a suspension in the course of proceedings, but after conviction and the judgment of Lord Cooper must be read in that context. The order sought should be refused and the bill dismissed. In any event, the suspender would still have his remedy if at the end of the day he were convicted on the present charge which admittedly was ex facie both relevant and competent.

In my opinion the argument presented for the suspender fails. The general rule is not in doubt; suspension as a mode of review is competent only after the conclusion of the trial. Nothing which was said in *Fairley* v. *Muir* casts any doubts on the general principle which was enunciated by Hume, ii, 513 in the simple phrase: 'The remedy of suspension applies after conclusion of a trial in the inferior court'. To this general rule it is recognised that an exception exists in respect of 'incidental warrants which do not form part of the case' (cf. Renton and Brown (4th ed.), para. 16.99).

In the present case the suspender seeks to review a decision of the sheriff on the competency of the complaint itself, a decision on which could dispose once and for all of the whole subject-matter of the charge. In my opinion there is no warrant or authority for such a procedure at this stage. The suspender will not lose his remedy if a conviction is recorded against him, while if he is acquitted the issue will not arise.

In any event, and apart from any question of general principle it was clear enough from the submissions of counsel for the suspender that the interpretation which he would seek to place on the facts of the case would necessarily depend on the findings which the sheriff would have to make as to the actions of various individuals and officers of the local authority—so that in no sense could it be said that 'the relevant circumstances are instantly, or almost instantly, verifiable, and the point sought to be raised is . . . a crisp issue of. . . competency' (*Fairley* v. *Muir*, 1951 S.L.T. at p. 238, per Lord Cooper). Indeed, while I appreciate the clarity and ingenuity with which counsel for the suspender presented his argument, I find it difficult to understand how a bottle of milk which is alone said to form the offending article of food can in any sense of the word be held in fact or in law to be a 'sample' of something which does not itself figure anywhere in the complaint. However, it is not necessary to pursue this because for reasons which I have already given I am of opinion that this is an incompetent application and the motions for a first order and for interim suspension of the proceedings in the lower court will be refused."

First order on bill and interim
suspension refused as incompetent.

NOTE

The appropriate procedure now for challenging decisions on competency (and relevancy) before the final determination of the cause is provided by section 334(2A) of the 1975 Act (*infra*, p. 500). And *cf. Hefferan* v. *Wright* (1910) 6 Adam 321.

3.   MacGregor v. MacNeill
1975 J.C. 57

For earlier proceedings related to this case see *MacNeill* v. *MacGregor, supra*, p. 465.

The complainer brought a bill of suspension for review of the sentence imposed by the sheriff, that sentence having been imposed as a result of a guilty plea tendered in error.

LORD JUSTICE-CLERK (WHEATLEY): ". . . The first question to be decided is whether in the circumstances the bill of suspension is competent. Mr Younger submitted that it was and the learned Advocate-depute conceded that it was. Suspension is a competent method of review when some step in the procedure has gone wrong, or some factor has emerged which satisfies the court that a miscarriage of justice has taken place, resulting in a failure to do justice to an accused. In the case of *Spowart* v. *Burr* (1895) 1 Adam 539 Lord Adam at 545-6 made it clear that a bill of suspension would not be entertained in the ordinary case where the panel has pleaded guilty, and after sentence wishes to go back on his plea. I endorse that view. If it were otherwise the doors would be opened wide to people seeking review because the sentence imposed following a plea of guilty was more than they had bargained for. In the same case Lord M'Laren said this at p. 546: 'But in the present case the statement for the complainer really amounts to nothing more than this, that the record of his plea is untrue. He says that he never gave such a plea. If enquiry were allowed on a mere circumstantial statement of this kind, I do not see how it could be refused in any case where the accused came forward and said that he had not in fact tendered the plea which the record bears that he had tendered. Where relief is asked on the ground that there has been an error in the proceedings, or some mistake on the part of the judge, there must be clear averments as to how the error or mistake originated, and unless upon such averments, enquiry cannot be allowed.' Again I would endorse what was there said. In that case the accused appeared on his own behalf at the trial and tendered the plea of guilty according to the record of the proceedings, but what Lord M'Laren said is, in my opinion, equally applicable where the accused is legally represented.

The present case has to be considered on the basis of the case as it stood when the conviction and sentence were passed and recorded on 25th July 1974. The submission on behalf of the complainer is that these proceeded on the vital mistake of a plea of guilty being tendered when the instructions given were to tender a plea of not guilty. This is accepted by the Crown. The complainer further submits that the miscarriage of justice here is under-lined by the fact that in the inept trial which followed upon the inept proceedings on 26th July 1974 he was found not guilty. The learned Advocate-depute again frankly and fairly conceded that in the circumst-ances here present, prejudice had been suffered by the complainer.

I am of the opinion that in all the circumstances placed before the court, this bill of suspension is competent and there has been disclosed such prejudice to the complainer as to have resulted in justice not having been done to him. It is true that the error or mistake which caused this was not due to anything done by the judge or prosecutor, but in my view the court is entitled to look at all the circumstances in deciding whether an injustice has resulted to an accused person.

I would like to point out, however, that there were very special circumst-ances here present, that a very full explanation has been given to the court, and that the explanation has been fully accepted by the Crown. I would not like it to be thought that this decision can be regarded as a precedent which would allow any claim that a wrong plea had been tendered automatically to result in proceedings being quashed. Each case will depend on its own circumstances, and very special circumstances will be required to justify the remedy which the complainer seeks in this case. In the very special circumstances of this case I am prepared to grant the complainer the remedy he seeks. I would accordingly move your Lordships to pass the bill, to quash the proceedings of 25th July 1974, and to remit the case back to the Sheriff to proceed as accords, if the Crown are so minded to proceed with the complaint."

The court passed
the bill.

4. O'Hara v. Mill
1938 J.C. 4

The complainer was convicted on summary complaint of an offence under the Prevention of Crimes Act 1871. He brought a bill of suspension in which he alleged, *inter alia*, that there was no evidence sufficient in law to support the conviction.

LORD JUSTICE-CLERK (AITCHISON): ". . . The question which the suspender now seeks to raise in this bill of suspension is whether the magistrate had evidence before him which was sufficient in law to entitle him to convict the suspender. I think it is obvious that, whenever a question of that kind is sought to be raised, the appropriate process in which to raise it is a stated case . . . If the suspender had proceeded by way of stated case, we should have had before us in the stated case the facts as found by the magistrate, and we should then have been able to say whether, on the facts found by the magistrate, there was sufficient evidence in law to entitle the magistrate to find the suspender guilty. It has always been recognised that this Court will not review the magistrate, either in a suspension, or in a stated case, so far as the facts found are concerned. 'To settle the fact is the peculiar province of every assize in what Court soever the trial be.' (Hume, ii, 514.) Accordingly, it is not open to us, even if we desired to do so, to review the magistrate upon the facts. But then, there are cases in which the Court has in a suspension entertained the question whether the evidence was sufficient in law to warrant a conviction. When one looks at these cases, of which *M'Shane* is an example, it appears that they were cases in which there was no dispute between the parties as to what the facts were, and the cases could be taken upon that footing. In the present case there is some agreement between the suspender and the respondent as to the facts, but in some material respects there is disagreement. That being the position, Mr Guthrie for the suspender conceded that he must take the case upon the statement of the respondent, as set out in the respondent's answers. [His Lordship then examined the averments contained in the respondent's answers, and stated his reasons for holding that they established that the evidence was sufficient to warrant the magistrate in finding the suspender guilty of the offence charged.]

The bill of suspension will, accordingly, be refused; but I desire to repeat that, when it is desired to raise a question of this kind, the appropriate form of appeal is a stated case, so that the Court may have before it the facts found by the magistrate. Although the Court has allowed in this case the question to be argued in a suspension, it must not be assumed that a similar indulgence will be granted in the future."

The court refused
to pass the bill.

NOTE

1. Lords Pitman and Wark agreed. The latter stated that "Nothing is better settled in our criminal law than that the merits of a

conviction cannot be reviewed in a process of suspension." See also *Moffat* v. *Skeen*, 1963 J.C. 84, *James Y. Keanie* v. *Laird*, 1943 J.C. 73 and *Fairley* v. *Muir*, 1951 J.C. 56, *infra*, p. 489.

2. Notwithstanding the above, the High Court has power under section 452(4)(*b*) of the 1975 Act to remit to any fit person to inquire and report in regard to any matter or circumstance affecting the appeal: section 453A(2). In *Neilands* v. *Leslie*, 1973 S.L.T. (Notes) 32 there was a dispute on matters of fact between the bill and the answers lodged thereto. The High Court gave the following general indication of its approach in such cases: "Where there is conflict between the bill and answers the court will usually accept the latter and although there may be cases where a remit to a reporter would be justified when there is a degree of doubt as to the accuracy of a respondent's answers the instant bill did not reveal such a case."

5.   Criminal Procedure (Scotland) Act 1975

"453A.—(1) Notwithstanding section 449(2) of this Act, a party to a summary prosecution may, where an appeal under section 442 of this Act would be incompetent or would in the circumstances be inappropriate, appeal to the High Court, by bill of suspension against a conviction, or as the case may be by advocation against an acquittal, on the ground of an alleged miscarriage of justice in the proceedings:

Provided that where the alleged miscarriage of justice is referred to in an application, under section 444(1) of this Act, for a stated case as regards the proceedings (or in a duly made amendment or addition to that application) an appeal under subsection (1) above shall not proceed without the leave of the High Court until the appeal to which the application relates has been finally disposed of or abandoned. . . .

(3) The foregoing provisions of this section shall be without prejudice to any rule of law relating to bills of suspension or advocation in so far as such rule of law is not inconsistent with those provisions."

NOTES

1. The competency of appeals by stated case is discussed above, p. 462. The appropriateness of that method of appeal has generally been discussed in the context of proceedings by way of bill of suspension. See *infra*, p. 487.

2. Section 444(2) of the 1975 Act provides that it shall be competent for an appellant to proceed by way of bill of suspension where an application for a stated case cannot proceed because the judge by whom he was convicted cannot sign the case owing to death or illness. In such a case "it shall be competent for the convicted person . . . to bring under review . . . any matter which might have been brought under review by stated case."

(ii) Appropriateness

Even where review by bill of suspension is competent, it may not necessarily be the appropriate method of review. It should be noted also that in many cases the issues of competency and appropriateness cannot always be kept clearly apart.

1. Fairley v. Muir
1951 J.C. 56

LORD JUSTICE-GENERAL (COOPER): "This bill of suspension relates to a conviction for alleged contravention of the Food Rationing Regulations obtained in Edinburgh Sheriff Court on 30th November 1950. The statement of facts contains three or four pages of type devoted to a description of the evidence oral and documentary which was adduced, and the point sought to be raised by the bill is whether the proceedings at the trial were vitiated by the illegal admission of incompetent evidence. In the course of the statement of facts it is disclosed that the complainer applied for a stated case, and evidently got it, but that in the course of the adjustment of the stated case he was advised that the question involved would be more appropriately dealt with in a bill of suspension. The present bill of suspension was presented to this Court on 20th January, when I declined in chambers to take the responsibility for pronouncing a first order, and directed that the case should be heard by this Court.

Within the last thirteen years there have been, I think, no fewer than nine cases before this Court in which pointed attention has been drawn to the requirements of our law and practice as regards the review of summary convictions, and the two considerations by reference to which the competency or propriety of a bill of suspension should be judged, (first) the delay in presentation of the bill, and (second) the nature of the question sought to be raised.

In the case of *O'Hara* v. *Mill* [*supra*] the matter was the subject of comment by a Court presided over by Lord Justice-Clerk Aitchison, and the views there expressed were subsequently reinforced by the Court as differently constituted in the case of *Dawson* v. *Adair* [16 Sept. 1941, unreported.] Two years later in the case of *James Y. Keanie, Limited* v. *Laird* [1943 J.C. 73] this Court, again differently constituted, took occasion for the third time to stress the different types of review which were appropriate to a stated case and to a bill of suspension respectively. I need not read from my own judgment in that case, in which I pointed out that a bill of suspension and a stated case are not alternative and equivalent methods of submitting to this Court questions determined in Courts of summary jurisdiction; but I would draw attention to the observation of Lord Wark who said (at p. 77): 'I think it is high time that it should be quite clearly understood by the profession that the rule laid down in *O'Hara* and *Dawson* is one which will be enforced, and that the indulgence which was given in some of the cases prior to *O'Hara* will not be allowed in future cases.' There have been a number of other cases which are not reported, but I need not deal further with the general question except to say this, that, from the point of view of the due administration of justice, there are certain types of question capable of being brought for review from a summary Court which are essentially appropriate only to a stated case, in which we are given the benefit of the considered views of the Court of first instance formed at a time when the evidence is fresh in the memory of the Sheriff or magistrate, and that (while I do not say that the function of a bill of suspension is strictly confined to cases of this kind) the type of case to which a bill of suspension is truly appropriate is the case where the relevant circumstances are instantly, or almost instantly, verifiable, and the point sought to be raised is raised promptly, a crisp issue of, say, jurisdiction, competency, oppression, or departure from the canons of natural justice.

Returning to this case, the issue which the complainer desires to raise is the competency of the admission by the Sheriff-substitute of certain items of documentary evidence. That raises an issue in law peculiarly appropriate to a stated case, and one which, broadly speaking, could never be determined satisfactorily, so far as I can see, without a narrative of the conclusions on the evidence on which the Sheriff-substitute proceeded, so that we might discover, amongst other things, how far the documents challenged were indispensable to the conviction, and whether in the words of section 75 their admission if incompetent inferred a miscarriage of justice. The complainer evidently recognised that by applying for a stated case. Why he was advised that the question involved would be more appropriately dealt with in a bill of suspension I am still, I regret to say, unable to understand. The Dean of Faculty has informed us that the case as drafted raised a number of other issues which he could not have maintained with success. If so, it would be no new thing in this Court for counsel to have so stated, and to have confined his attention to the matters upon which he did desire to present argument. It has been suggested that a difficulty, the nature of which I cannot appreciate, would have been encountered, or was encountered, in obtaining from the Sheriff-substitute a stated case properly directed to the question which it is desired to raise. If such a difficulty arose, or may yet arise, it is a difficulty of a type by no means unfamiliar in this Court, and for which we are always ready, if necessary, to afford a remedy in a remit to the Sheriff-substitute with instructions as to the nature of the findings and information which we require.

In the result I find myself unable to discover either within the four corners of the bill or in the candid explanation offered by the Dean of Faculty any sufficient explanation for a delay of roughly two months in presentation of the bill, still less for the substitution of a bill of suspension as a means of reviewing this issue in place of the stated case which is to my mind manifestly the more appropriate, if not the only appropriate, method of raising the issues sought to be determined. In view of the repeated judgments which have been directed to questions of this type I do not feel any hesitation in suggesting to your Lordships that our proper course in this case is to decline to pronounce the first order."

The court refused to let the bill proceed.

NOTE
There is no statutory time-limit for bringing a suspension, but delay may be fatal as indicating acquiescence in the judgment or order complained of. Whether or not a delay will be considered undue, and thus operate as a bar, will depend upon the facts and circumstances of each case. See, for examples, Renton and Brown, para. 16-152 and the following case.

2. Handley v. Pirie
1977 S.L.T. 30

An accused person was charged with a contravention of section 6(1) of the Road Traffic Act 1972. He was convicted on the sheriff's acceptance of an analyst's certificate tendered under section 10 of the 1972 Act. The accused had pled not guilty at the first diet and was ordained to appear for trial on 3 November. On that date he again appeared and pleaded not guilty. The prosecutor, however, moved the court to adjourn the diet, the reason being that he had omitted to serve upon the accused the analyst's certificate or to cite the analyst as a witness. Despite objections by the accused the diet was adjourned to 28 November 1975, by which time the prosecutor served upon the accused a copy of the analyst's certificate in accordance with section 10(3) of the 1972 Act. The accused presented a bill of suspension to the High Court.

LORD JUSTICE-GENERAL (EMSLIE): ". . . The single question with which this bill is concerned is whether in the particular circumstances disclosed therein the certificate relied on by the sheriff was by itself competent evidence of the matters which it purported to certify. . . .
Although the bill appears to raise a separate question relating to the allowance of the adjournment this question was not insisted in and in the result the short sharp issue is whether the certificate was served upon the complainer not less than seven days before his trial began. The complainer contends that it was not upon the submission that the trial began on 3 November 1975 before the diet was adjourned. The respondent contends that it had not begun and that it did not begin until 28 November. There is no dispute or doubt about the facts and it is clear that this issue falls to be resolved upon a consideration of the events which happened and the terms of s. 10 (3).
At the hearing on the bill the Crown argued in limine under reference to the case of *Fairley* v. *Muir*, 1951 S.L.T. 237, 1951 J.C. 56, that we should refuse the bill as incompetent, upon the ground that a challenge of the merits of a conviction is essentially appropriate only to a stated case and, in any event, upon the view that the complainer had delayed too long in presenting the bill. We reject this submission in the peculiar circumstances of this case, and in so doing we wish to cast no doubt upon the general rule which will be enforced, that a challenge of a conviction on its merits will,

save in exceptional circumstances, only be entertained when the matter is brought before the court by a stated case in which the considered views of the trial judge will be expressed. In this case, however, to quote what was said by the Lord Justice-General in *Fairley*: 'the relevant circumstances are instantly . . . verifiable and the point sought to be raised is . . . a crisp issue of . . . competency' of the certificate as evidence of its contents. For this reason the bill is an appropriate and competent method of raising the issue and since we have been satisfied that there was no undue delay in presenting it the grounds of objection relied on by the Crown have not been made out."

The court passed the bill and quashed
the conviction.

3.   Galloway v. Smith
1974 S.L.T. (Notes) 63

The complainer pled guilty to a contravention of section 143(1) of the Road Traffic Act 1972 and was fined £10 and disqualified from holding or obtaining a driving licence for a period of six months. He presented a bill of suspension to have the sentence of disqualification quashed. It was argued on his behalf that the sheriff had proceeded on misleading information given to the court on behalf of a co-accused, but denied by the complainer's solicitor at the trial. There was nothing in the bill to indicate that the sheriff had proceeded on such a basis.

LORD JUSTICE-CLERK (WHEATLEY): "All that counsel for the complainer said was that it was a matter of inference that the sheriff had so proceeded. I cannot see how this court can be expected to accept that as a matter of inference. I wish to reiterate something which I have said from time to time in this court, which is that if an appeal is taken against a sentence, and allegations are going to be made that the presiding judge proceeded on a certain basis and had misdirected himself on that basis, then the proper method of appeal is by way of stated case, which would enable the judge in the court below to present to this court a full statement of the reasons why he disposed of the case in a certain manner. I trust that this will be noted by people who are wishing to proceed by way of appeal on such a basis. When it proceeds by way of bill of suspension we are then presented with an ex parte statement that is not capable of being checked by the best authority possible, namely, the presiding judge himself.

Accordingly, I am unable to proceed on the basis that the sheriff in reaching his decision to disqualify relied on the misleading information given on behalf of the co-accused, but denied by the complainer's agent. On the merits of the appeal I am of the opinion that in all the circumstances it cannot be said that the sentence of disqualification imposed was harsh and oppressive."

The court refused to
pass the bill.

NOTE

Since stated case is no longer a competent method of appeal against sentence alone (see *supra*, p. 462), the proper method of appeal today in such a case would be by way of note of appeal under section 453B.

(iii) Grounds of appeal

It will be apparent from the above that suspension may be brought on a variety of grounds, including miscarriage of justice (under section 453A). It would be impracticable to give examples of all of the grounds so far recognised in this book. Reference is made, therefore, to the foregoing cases, and the list of grounds in Renton and Brown at para. 16-149.

(iv) Limitations on appeal

The limitations on appeal imposed by section 454 apply in the case of suspension (see *supra*, p. 470.)

(v) Disposal of appeals

In disposing of an appeal by way of suspension, the High Court may pass the bill and suspend the sentence, order, etc., repel the reasons of suspension and refuse the bill, or amend any conviction or sentence. The court may also remit the case to the inferior court, with instructions to proceed if necessary.

In the case of an appeal against conviction under section 453A, the powers of hearing and disposal provided for by sections 452(4)(*a*) to (*e*), 452A(1)(*d*), 452A(3) and 452B apply in the same way as in the case of appeals under section 444(1): section 453A(2). These powers, which apply only to appeals under section 453A, are without prejudice to any rule of law relating to bills of suspension in so far as such rule of law is not inconsistent with those powers.

The provisions of section 453, as amended, relating to the prosecutor's consent to the setting aside of a conviction apply to appeals by way of suspension.

d. *Advocation*

Advocation originally denoted the removal of a case from an inferior court (of summary or solemn jurisdiction) to the High Court. Section 280A of the 1975 Act now provides that the prosecutor's right to bring a decision under review of the High Court by way of bill of advocation "in accordance with existing law and practice" shall extend to the review of a decision of any court of solemn jurisdiction. Decisions of the High Court itself as a court of first instance are now subject to review by advocation.

Section 280A refers in terms to the "prosecutor's right" to bring a bill of advocation. Apart from this provision, advocation is, in theory, a procedure available to accused persons as well as the prosecutor. In practice, however, it is only available to the accused in exceptional circumstances and is generally regarded as a prosecutor's remedy, equivalent to the accused's right to bring a suspension.

1. **Muir v. Hart**
1912 S.C. (J.) 41

An accused person was charged on indictment with fraud. At the first diet the sheriff repelled objections to the relevancy of the indictment, lodged on behalf of the accused. The accused then brought an advocation of that interlocutor before the trial diet.

LORD JUSTICE-CLERK (MACDONALD): ". . . Had this question arisen for the first time, my view therefore would have been that as regards what the complainer proposes to do in this case there is no law, as there is no practice, to support it. But I am supported in this view by the case of *Jameson* v. *Lothian* [(1855) 2 Irv. 273], when this very question was brought before a bench of five Judges, and was decided on the competency, as I think this case ought to be decided. From that day to this no similar case has been brought before the Court. Neither has any such attempt been made under the Act of 1887, to which I shall refer presently. Thus no advocation such as this has been attempted for more than fifty years. I say nothing as to what might be done in any special case, such as was suggested in *Jameson's* advocation, where action might be taken at an early stage of procedure, if, as Lord Justice-Clerk Hope said, something was done 'which outraged all the principles of the liberty of the subject,' or if, as Lord Ivory said, there was 'an objection to the jurisdiction *funditus*.' Such a case, if it ever occurs, must be dealt with as it presents itself. . . . Here we are asked to intervene, not because by any action of the Judge there has been a stoppage of proceedings before him, not because there has been any fundamental nullity by which the course of justice has been stopped. Nothing has been done which can be impugned as not being according to practice, or that in itself stopped procedure under the indictment. All has been regular and according to statute. All that is said is that the Sheriff has formed a wrong opinion on a point of relevancy. In my opinion we have no duty or right to interfere at such a stage."

LORD JOHNSTON (*diss.*): ". . . To refuse advocation at the stage in question would, as appears to me, be to obliterate the process of advocation from our criminal procedure, and to make suspension the sole mode of review of proceedings in an inferior Court. Advocation can only be resorted to *pendente processu*, and was introduced for the very purpose of correcting errors in procedure of the inferior Court Judge at a stage prior to final sentence. Suspension, with or without liberation according to the form of the sentence, can only be brought of a sentence, and is the only process by which such can be reviewed, though on the ground of error in law or procedure only, and not of fact. The one is the advocation of a process for correction of procedure before sentence—the other is the suspension of a sentence after the process is concluded.

It is for these reasons that I have ventured to maintain that the judgment in *Jameson's* case ought not to be regarded as binding in the somewhat altered circumstances. The considerations which these circumstances present have led me to the conclusion that to refuse this advocation as incompetent would be to reject the opportunity, which the passing of the Acts of 1853 and 1887 has afforded, of facilitating procedure, and instead to perpetuate inconvenience and expense."

LORD SALVESEN (*diss.*): ". . . We were not referred to any authority, apart from the decision in the case of *Jameson*, which supports the view that advocation of an interlocutor pronounced by a Sheriff finding the libel relevant is incompetent. The institutional writers seem to take it for granted that such a process is competent. Thus Hume says (p. 509) that there are three forms of process in which decrees of the inferior Courts may be submitted to the revisal of the Lords of Justiciary, namely, advocation, suspension, and appeal, and he goes on to point out that advocation is the proper remedy before a trial has taken place, just as suspension is that which applies after conclusion of the trial in the inferior Court to hinder execution of the sentence. With regard to advocation he says,—'This form of redress seems to be universally applicable with the exception only of the sentences of the Court of Admiralty, with respect to which all advocation is absolutely forbidden by the statute of 1681, cap. 16.' It is true he does not expressly mention that advocation is competent in order to review a finding upon relevancy, but he says that 'the manner of the process seems to have been thus. That on a bill offered to the Lords of Privy Council, or Council and Session, an order was made and intimated enjoining the inferior Judge not to proceed.' This was before the Court of Justiciary was established; and shortly after that Court came into existence Hume says,—'The Lords of Justiciary attained to the quiet and exclusive possession of the right of passing bills of advocation for themselves in all cases which fall properly within their charter.' Further, there are two recent decisions which seem not entirely consistent with the case of *Jameson*. In *Craig* v. *Galt* [4 Coup. 541] the Sheriff had dismissed a criminal libel at the instance of a private prosecutor with concurrence of the public prosecutor, because of the non-production, the day before the first diet at which the case was called, of an article libelled as to be produced at the trial. The complainer thereupon brought a bill of advocation and contended that 'in criminal cases before the Sheriff productions did not require to be lodged till the day before the trial,

and that the trial was now regarded in practice as being at the second diet.'
The Court were of opinion that the Sheriff had erred; and they sustained
the advocation, recalled the interlocutor complained of, and remitted to
the Sheriff to proceed according to law. Now, under the old practice, as
there was only one diet, it is plain that the objection would have been a
good one; but it was held to be bad, not because of any new act of adjournal
regulating the time for production of documents, but because of the
introduction of two diets, and the practice which had followed upon that
introduction. In the subsequent case of *Macrae* v. *Cooper* [4 Coup. 561] the
Sheriff had deserted the diet *simpliciter* in a criminal trial, because at the
first diet the prosecutor was not personally present, although a person
holding a commission from him was in attendance. On a bill of advocation
being presented, the Court advocated the cause, reversed the judgment of
the Sheriff, and remitted to him to proceed according to law.

It would thus appear that where at the first diet an interlocutor is
pronounced adverse to the prosecutor, it is competent for him to bring a bill
of advocation, and for the Court to remit to the Sheriff who has finally
decided the cause to proceed with the trial. If that be so, I can see no reason
in principle why the same privilege should not be accorded to the accused;
and there is nothing, so far as I know, either enacted by statute or in our
mode of administering justice in criminal causes which requires that we
should discriminate thus unfairly between the remedies open to the prosecutor and those open to the accused.

On the question of the expediency of advocating a deliverance sustaining
the relevancy of a libel I have already pointed out the advantage to the
accused of not having to undergo a trial on an irrelevant indictment. From
the public point of view the expediency is even more obvious. If a mistake
has been made in framing an indictment on which the accused has been
tried and convicted, the conviction may be quashed by the High Court. The
mistake may have been a formal one, and the conviction just on the facts
proved at the trial, but the accused person having tholed an assize cannot
again be indicted. If, however, the same decision had been pronounced in
an advocation on relevancy the prosecutor would have an opportunity of
serving a new and relevant indictment which would obviate the risk of a
guilty person escaping all punishment because of a formal and technical
defect in the original indictment.

On the whole matter, therefore, I am of opinion that this advocation is
not merely competent, but that it is expedient in the interests of both of the
accused and of the administration of justice, and that we should entertain
it."

> The court held the advocation
> to be incompetent.

NOTES

1. So far as appeal against a decision on relevancy (or competency) prior to final determination is concerned, the appropriate
procedure now is that provided by section 334(2) of the 1975 Act. In

so far as *Muir* v. *Hart* (and *Jameson*) prevent recourse to advocation prior to final determination, they remain unaffected by section 334(2).

2. The majority of the court (four judges) thought that the advocation was incompetent. Of the remaining three judges two (Lords Salvesen and Johnston) thought it both competent and expedient in the circumstances. The Lord Justice-General thought it was competent but inexpedient.

2. MacLeod v. Levitt
1969 J.C. 16

The respondent was disqualified for holding or obtaining a driving licence for a total of seven years and six months. He applied under section 106(1) of the Road Traffic Act 1960 for removal of that disqualification. His application was granted by the sheriff, and the procurator fiscal presented a bill of advocation for recall of the sheriff's interlocutor.

LORD JUSTICE-GENERAL (CLYDE): ". . . A preliminary matter arises first of all as to the competency of our entertaining the present bill of advocation at all, as a means of reviewing the Sheriff-substitute's order in Mr Levitt's petition.

It is important in the first instance to see what section 106 envisages. It contemplates not a continuation of the original complaint process, but the start of a totally new and independent application to the Court which ordered the disqualification. That application is made by way of a petition, and the petition is at the instance not of the procurator-fiscal, but of the disqualified person. Service is not required on the procurator-fiscal, although in practice this is done, so that he can place before the Court any information in the possession of the Crown relative to the matters mentioned in section 106 (1). Thus he is not a party to the process, although in practice he usually attends as a purveyor of information if the Sheriff-substitute requires it. The process is of a discretionary and administrative character, and no provision is made for an appeal from the decision of the Sheriff-substitute in such process. Section 105 of the 1960 Act provides for an appeal against an order of disqualification, but in marked contrast to this section 106 says nothing about any appeal from an order removing a disqualification. We are here in the realm of statutory provisions and not common law, and in the absence of a statutory provision for appeal in such an application I am of opinion that an appeal by stated case . . . would not be competent.

It is in this situation that the question of the competency of a bill of advocation arises. In modern times this procedure has become very rare, and for practical purposes is really out of date. It was invoked more frequently before appeals by stated case were competent. In my view the very limited sphere in which it could be invoked is accurately summed up in

Trotter on Summary Jurisdiction, p. 68, where a bill of advocation is described as a process by which review is sought of a decision pronounced in a preliminary part of a prosecution and prior to final judgment. (Compare Renton and Brown's Criminal Procedure, (3rd ed.) p. 324.) The order removing the disqualification from driving in the present case was not pronounced in a preliminary part of a prosecution: it was not pronounced in a part of a prosecution at all, but in a separate petition to which the prosecutor was not a party and indeed in which there was no prosecutor: and in any event it was not pronounced prior to final judgment, and it was in fact itself the final end of the matter. In these circumstances, in my opinion, the bill of advocation is incompetent."

LORD CAMERON: ". . . The process of advocation, though not wholly obsolete . . . has been almost entirely superseded in practice as a method of appeal by the introduction of appeal by way of stated case in summary procedure and by the forms of appeal applicable to procedure on indictment provided by the Act of 1926. The limited sphere of competence of the process of advocation lies in the correction of irregularities in the preliminary stages of a case, though recourse to the process is incompetent until the cause is finally determined, unless in very special circumstances—see *Muir* v. *Hart* [*supra*], *Strathern* v. *Benson* [1925 J.C. 40], and Renton and Brown's Criminal Procedure, (3rd ed.) p. 324. It cannot be used to obtain review on the merits—see *List* v. *Pirie* [(1867) 5 Irv. 559]."

The court dismissed the bill.

NOTES
1. The court's views on the obsolescence of advocation were a little premature. In recent years the procedure has undergone something of a revival in popularity. See, for example, *Skeen* v. *Skerret*, 1976 S.L.T. (Notes) 6, *Skeen* v. *McLaren*, 1976 S.L.T. (Notes) 14, *Tudhope* v. *Lawrie*, 1979 S.L.T. (Notes) 13, *Skeen* v. *Fullarton*, 1980 S.L.T. (Notes) 46.
2. The rule that advocation cannot be employed to obtain a review on the merits may be qualified by section 453A of the 1975 Act which allows an appeal by advocation on the ground of miscarriage of justice in limited circumstances. There are also cases in which the High Court appears to have reviewed the merits of decisions on adjournment when these have been brought before it by means of advocation; see, *e.g.* *Tudhope* v. *Lawrie, supra*.
3. In *Mackinnon* v. *Craig & Anr.*, 1983 S.L.T. 475, it was held on the authority of *Alison*, ii, 26 that a Bill of Advocation was properly applicable not only to an "order or judgment" but to a "proceeding", so that it was a competent method of review in the absence of any minuted interlocutor putting an end to the proceedings brought

under review. But *cf.* the styles of Bills of Advocation in *Trotter* on *Summary Jurisdiction* and the early editions of *Renton and Brown*.

4. In disposing of the appeal the High Court may pass or refuse the bill, in whole or in part. It may also remit the case to the inferior court, if necessary with instructions. Where an appeal is taken on the ground of miscarriage of justice under section 453A, the court enjoys the same powers of hearing and disposal as where an appeal is taken by bill of suspension under that section: 1975 Act, s. 453A(2).

e. Appeals against sentence by note of appeal

Criminal Procedure (Scotland) Act 1975

"453B.—(1) An appeal under section 442(1)(*a*)(ii) of this Act shall be by note of appeal, which shall state the ground of appeal.

453C.—(1) An appeal against sentence by note of appeal shall be heard by the High Court on such date as it may fix, and the High Court may, subject to section 453D(1) of this Act, dispose of such appeal by—

(*a*) affirming the sentence; or

(*b*) if the Court thinks that, having regard to all the circumstances, including any additional evidence such as is mentioned in section 442(2) of this Act, a different sentence should have been passed, quashing the sentence and passing another sentence, whether more or less severe, in substitution therefor:

Provided that the Court shall not in any case increase the sentence beyond the maximum sentence which could have been passed by the inferior court."

NOTES

1. The note of appeal must be lodged with the clerk of the court from which the appeal is taken within one week of the passing of sentence. On receipt of the note of appeal the clerk sends a copy to the respondent or his solicitor and obtains a report from the sentencing judge: section 453B(3) and (3).

2. See *Galloway* v. *Smith*, 1974 S.L.T. (Notes) 63, *supra*, p. 492. For further details of the procedures governing this form of appeal see sections 453B and 453C of the 1975 Act and Renton and Brown, Chap. 16.

f. Appeals against decisions on competency and relevancy

The Thomson Committee (3rd Report, para. 13.15) recommended that both the prosecutor and the accused should have rights of appeal on issues of competency and relevancy in summary proceedings as soon as the issue was determined. They were influenced in this view by the fact that where an issue of competency or relevancy was decided against an accused who maintained a plea of not guilty, the issue of competency or relevancy might yet be decided in his favour after the time and expense of a trial. The following provision goes some way to meeting that objection:

Criminal Procedure (Scotland) Act 1975

"334.—(2A) Without prejudice to any right of appeal under section 442 or 453A of this Act, a party may, with the leave of the court (granted either on the motion of that party or *ex proprio motu*) and in accordance with such procedure as may be prescribed by Act of Adjournal under this Act, appeal to the High Court against a decision of the court of first instance (other than a decision not to grant leave under this subsection) which relates to such objection or denial as is mentioned in subsection (1) above; but such appeal must be taken not later than two days after such decision.

(2B) Where an appeal is taken under subsection (2A) above, the High Court may postpone the trial diet (if one has been fixed) for such period as appears to them to be appropriate and may, if they think fit, direct that such period (or some part of it) shall not count towards any time limit applying in respect of the case.

(2C) If leave to appeal under subsection (2A) above is granted by the court it shall not proceed to trial at once under paragraph (*a*) of section 337 of this Act; and paragraph (*b*) of that section shall be construed as requiring sufficient time to be allowed for the appeal to be taken.

(2D) In disposing of an appeal under subsection (2A) above the High Court may affirm the decision of the court of first instance or may remit the case to it with such directions in the matter as they think fit; and where the court of first instance had dismissed the complaint, or any part of it, may reverse that decision and direct that the court of first instance fix a trial diet (if it has not already fixed one as regards so much of the complaint as it has not dismissed)".

NOTE

A party seeking review of a decision on competency and relevancy does not have the right to appeal to the High Court, but must obtain the leave of the court.

CHAPTER 16

PUNISHMENT AND OTHER FORMS OF DISPOSAL

This chapter examines the range of penalties and other forms of disposal available to the Scottish courts when dealing with those brought before them on criminal charges. The matters dealt with in this chapter have recently been made the subject of a study by Sheriff Nicholson, and for detailed discussion of the topics in this chapter reference is made to that work: Nicholson, *The Law and Practice of Sentencing in Scotland.*

It should be remembered that not every measure available to the courts can be described as a penalty or a punishment. The philosophy behind certain methods of disposal (*e.g.* community service, probation and deferred sentence) is quite distinct from the simple objective of punishment or retribution. Furthermore, there are certain cases in which punishment is quite inappropriate, as, for example, in the case of mentally disordered offenders.

Finally it should be noted that this chapter is concerned with measures applicable to persons over the age of 16. The special procedures governing disposal of children under that age are discussed *post*, Chap. 17.

a. Custodial sentences

At the time of writing, a custodial sentence may take the form of imprisonment, Borstal training or detention in a detention centre. However the latter two forms of sentence has been abolished by s. 45 of the 1980 Act, which has not yet been brought into force. The following discussion assumes however that the 1980 amendments are now effective, and deals with the sentences of imprisonment and detention.

(i) Imprisonment

The powers of the courts to impose imprisonment are subject to certain restrictions. While the High Court may, subject to any statutory limitations, impose up to life imprisonment in appropriate cases, the powers of the sheriff and district courts are more limited. The sheriff may, in solemn proceedings, impose up to two years' imprisonment (1975 Act, s. 2(2)). In summary proceedings the sheriff may normally only impose a maximum of six months' imprisonment, but this power may be increased to a maximum of six months in respect of certain second or subsequent convictions (1975 Act, s. 289 and s. 290). The district court's powers are limited to a maximum of 60 days' imprisonment, for both common law and statutory offences (1975 Act, s. 284). For the relationship between these limited powers of sentence, and the power to order consecutive sentences, see *Thomson* v. *Smith*, 1982 S.L.T. 546.

The 1975 Act and the 1980 Act impose further restrictions on the power of the courts to impose a sentence of imprisonment:

1.   Criminal Procedure (Scotland) Act 1975

"207.—(1) It shall not be competent to impose imprisonment on a person under 21 years of age."

2.   Criminal Justice (Scotland) Act 1980

"*Restriction on passing sentence of imprisonment or detention on person not legally represented*

41.—(1) A court shall not pass a sentence of imprisonment or of detention in respect of any offence, nor impose imprisonment, or detention, under section 396 (2) of the 1975 Act in respect of failure to pay a fine, on an accused who is not legally represented in that court and has not been previously sentenced to imprisonment or detention by a court in any part of the United Kingdom, unless the accused either—

(*a*) applied for legal aid and the application was refused on the ground that he was not financially eligible; or

(*b*) having been informed of his right to apply for legal aid, and having had the opportunity, failed to do so.

(2) The court shall, for the purpose of determining whether a person has been previously sentenced to imprisonment or detention by a court in any part of the United Kingdom—

(*a*) disregard a previous sentence of imprisonment which, having been suspended, has not taken effect under section 23 of the Powers of Criminal Courts Act 1973 or under section 19 of the Treatment of Offenders Act (Northern Ireland) 1968;

(*b*) construe detention as meaning—

(i) in relation to Scotland, detention in a young offenders institution or detention centre;

(ii) in relation to England and Wales, borstal training or detention in a detention centre; and

(iii) in relation to Northern Ireland, detention in a young offenders centre.

(3) Subsection (1) above does not affect the power of a court to pass sentence on any person for an offence the sentence for which is fixed by law.

Restriction on passing sentence of imprisonment on person not previously so dealt with
42.—(1) A court shall not pass a sentence of imprisonment on a person of or over twenty-one years of age who has not been previously sentenced to imprisonment or detention by a court in any part of the United Kingdom unless the court considers that no other method of dealing with him is appropriate; and for the purpose of determining whether any other method of dealing with such a person is appropriate the court shall obtain (from an officer of a local authority or otherwise) such information as it can about the offender's circumstances; and it shall also take into account any information before it concerning the offender's character and physical and mental condition.

(2) Where a court of summary jurisdiction passes a sentence of imprisonment on any such person as is mentioned in subsection (1) above, the court shall state the reason for its opinion that no other method of dealing with him is appropriate, and shall have that reason entered in the record of the proceedings.

(3) Subsections (2) and (3) of section 41 of this Act shall apply for the purposes of this section as they apply for the purposes of that section."

NOTES
1. Although the court should have regard to the background reports required by section 42(1), it is not obliged to accept them as determining the issue of sentence. In *Scott and Another* v. *MacDonald*, 1961 S.L.T. 257, Lord Clyde, repeating a statement he had made in an earlier unreported decision said: "In this country it is still the judge and not the probation officer who has to determine what is the appropriate penalty to impose, even upon first offenders. Although the court should pay great regard to the conclusions or expressions of opinion of the probation officer, the Court, nonetheless, has the ultimate task of determining what is the appropriate penalty."
2. The requirement under section 42(2) should be closely observed, and a failure to do so may imperil the sentence of imprisonment.

3. **Binnie v. Farrell**
1972 J.C. 49
The complainer, a man of 22 who fell to be treated as a first offender, was convicted on summary complaint of housebreaking and theft. Having obtained a social inquiry report the sheriff sentenced the complainer to 30 days' imprisonment, telling the accused that he thought that no other method of dealing with him

was appropriate, and giving his reason for this view. In recording the sentence, the clerk of the court omitted the reason. The complainer presented a bill of suspension to the High Court.

LORD JUSTICE-GENERAL (EMSLIE) (His Lordship considered the relevant statutory provisions and related authorities, and continued): "I return now to the first argument for the complainer in this case. It is in my opinion clear that the relevant statutory procedure has been enacted in peremptory terms for the protection of first offenders. Each of the steps in that procedure is important, and it is plain that a failure to carry out any one of them will place any sentence of imprisonment imposed on a first offender in peril. Each step is mandatory, and the object of the requirements that the Sheriff shall state his reason for sentencing a first offender to imprisonment and that that reason shall be recorded, is to leave the first offender in no doubt why he is not being dealt with in any other way and to provide him with the material which he is entitled to have in order to bring the sentence under review. A failure to take both of these steps, and even a failure to record the Sheriff's reason, cannot in my opinion be regarded as a mere want of form. Any sentence of imprisonment recorded against a first offender will be inept if the reason for that sentence has not been stated and recorded along with it. Even a failure to take the last step, that of recording the reason, will normally demonstrate such prejudice or potential prejudice to the first offender as to be fatal to the sentence, unless it is clearly shown that the failure has in fact deprived the individual concerned of none of the essential protection which the subsection intended him to have.

Having said all this, however, the question for us is whether in the circumstances of this case we must pass the bill by recalling the sentence imposed on the complainer and by substituting another sentence. The temporary Sheriff, it is agreed, took correctly every step required of him save the last step of causing his reason for the sentence to be recorded. The complainer and the court are admittedly in possession of the whole information which the statutory sentencing procedure was designed to secure for them. The failure to record the reason for the sentence has in fact deprived the complainer and this court of nothing which is necessary to a consideration of the sentence. In this situation I am of opinion that there is no justification in this bill of suspension for recalling the sentence, defective though the procedure has been in the respect which I have explained. A bill of suspension is designed to allow this court, in a situation in which relief cannot readily be secured by the statutory means of review, to grant relief where there may have been oppression amounting to a miscarriage of justice, or significant prejudice suffered by an accused person. In this case the complainer does not and cannot maintain prejudice of any kind, far less miscarriage of justice, and there accordingly appears to me to be no sound basis on which, in the exceptional circumstances of this case, we could or should pass this bill upon the first branch of the complainer's argument."

LORD CAMERON: ". . . In my opinion, compliance with the statutory injunction cannot be regarded as something in the nature of a mere technicality or a matter of form, failure in which can be readily overlooked or dispensed with. When there is such failure, as here, in my opinion the whole sentence in the particular case is put in peril of being set aside, and must be set aside as incompetent or oppressive unless it may be that in very exceptional circumstances it can be demonstrated by the prosecutor to the satisfaction of the court that the appellant must necessarily concede, on facts found or admitted, that the appropriate procedure was followed out in its entirety up to the recording of the court's decision, and in particular that the opinion of the court was expressed in open court and was expressed and understood in terms which are agreed and in respect of which there is no suggestion of dispute or doubt. In such circumstances it may be possible for a court of review to accept that there has not been any such failure in the machinery as to be fatal to the sentence under review."

The court refused to pass
the bill.

NOTES

1. Since "sentence" is defined in the 1975 Act as not including an order for committal in default of payment of any sum (such as a fine) (see the 1980 Act, Sched. 7, para. 76(*c*)), it would appear that section 42(2) does not apply where a sentence of imprisonment is imposed in default of payment of a fine. See on this point *Sullivan* v. *McLeod*, 1980 S.L.T. (Notes) 99.

2. Provided that the statutory restrictions and procedures are observed, there is nothing incompetent in imposing an immediate custodial sentence on a first offender. The circumstances in which this may be justified are discussed *infra*, p. 545.

(ii) Detention

As was pointed out above, it is not competent to impose a sentence of imprisonment on a person under 21 years of age. Section 45(3) and (4) of the 1980 Act abolished the distinct sentence of Borstal training. When these sections are in force, detention will be the only competent custodial sentence for a person over 16 but under 21. For the old law relating to Borstal training and detention centre training, see the 1975 Act (unamended) ss. 204, 209, 210, 211, 414, 418, 419, 420.

Section 207 of the 1975 Act provides that a court may impose detention on a person "who is not less than 16 but under 21 years of age, where but for subsection (1) . . . the court would have power to impose a period of imprisonment; and the period of detention imposed under this section shall not exceed the maximum period of imprisonment which might otherwise have been imposed".

The restrictions on imprisonment of unrepresented accused persons contained in section 41 apply equally to sentences of detention. Section 207(3) contains provisions analogous to those contained in section 42(2) of the 1980 Act (*supra*) except that (1) the provisions of section 207(3) apply to courts of solemn and summary jurisdiction, and (2) the High Court is not required to record its reasons for holding that no other method of dealing with the offender is appropriate.

Where detention is imposed on a male person for a period of at least 28 days but not exceeding four months the court must normally order that the detention be in a detention centre. In any other case the court must order the detention to be served in a young offenders' institution.

(iii) Punishment for murder

Criminal Procedure (Scotland) Act 1975
"*Punishment for murder*
205.—(1) Subject to subsections (2) and (3) below, a person convicted of murder shall be sentenced to imprisonment for life.

(2) Where a person convicted of murder is under the age of 18 years he shall not be sentenced to imprisonment for life but to be detained without limit of time and shall be liable to be detained in such place, and under such conditions, as the Secretary of State may direct.

(3) Where a person convicted of murder has attained the age of 18 years but is under the age of 21 years he shall not be sentenced to imprisonment for life but to be detained in a young offenders institution and shall be liable to be detained for life.

Recommendation as to minimum period of detention for person convicted of murder
205A.—(1) On sentencing any person convicted of murder a judge may make a recommendation as to the minimum period which should elapse before, under section 61 of the Criminal Justice Act 1967, the Secretary of State releases that person on licence.

(2) When making a recommendation under subsection (1) above, the judge shall state his reasons for so recommending."

NOTES
1. The proviso to section 228 of the 1975 Act provides that there shall be no appeal against any sentence fixed by law. Notwithstanding that proviso, an appeal may be brought against any recommendation made under section 205A: section 205A(3).

2. The death penalty for murder was abolished by the Murder (Abolition of Death Penalty) Act 1965. For discussion of the

penalties for homicide, see the *Report of the Interdepartmental Committee on the penalties for Homicide* (the Emslie Committee), Cmnd. 5137, 1972.

b. Non-custodial disposals

(i) Absolute discharge

Courts of solemn and summary jurisdiction may dispose of an offender's case by making an order discharging him absolutely: sections 182 and 383 of the 1975 Act. Normally absolute discharge will not be treated as a conviction for any purpose other than the purposes of the proceedings in which the order is made, and of laying it before a court as a previous conviction in subsequent proceedings: 1975 Act, ss. 191(1) and 392(1).

(ii) Admonition

A court of summary or solemn jurisdiction may, "if it appears to meet the justice of the case" dismiss with an admonition any person found guilty by the court of any offence: 1975 Act, ss. 181 and 382.

(iii) Community service by offenders

Community Service by Offenders (Scotland) Act 1978

"*Community service orders*

1.—(1) Subject to the provisions of this Act, where a person of or over 16 years of age is convicted of an offence punishable by imprisonment, other than an offence the sentence for which is fixed by law, the court may, instead of dealing with him in any other way, make an order (in this Act referred to as 'a community service order') requiring him to perform unpaid work for such number of hours (being in total not less than forty nor more than two hundred and forty) as may be specified in the order.

(2) A court shall not make a community service order in respect of any offender unless—

(*a*) the offender consents;

(*b*) the court has been notified by the Secretary of State that arrangements exist for persons who reside in the locality in which the offender resides, or will be residing when the order comes into force, to perform work under such an order;

(*c*) the court is satisfied, after considering a report by an officer of a local authority about the offender and his circumstances, and, if the court thinks it necessary, hearing that officer, that the offender is a suitable person to perform work under such an order; and (*d*) the court is satisfied that provision can be made under the arrangements mentioned in paragraph (*b*) above for the offender to perform work under such an order.

(4) Before making a community service order the court shall explain to the offender in ordinary language—

(*a*) the purpose and effect of the order and in particular the obligations on the offender as specified in section 3 of this Act;

(*b*) the consequences which may follow under section 4 of this Act if he fails to comply with any of those requirements; and

(*c*) that the court has under section 5 of this Act the power to review the order on the application either of the offender or of an officer of the local authority in whose area the offender for the time being resides.

Obligations of persons subject to community service orders

3.—(1) An offender in respect of whom a community service order is in force shall—

(*a*) report to the local authority officer and notify him without delay of any change of address or in the times, if any, at which he usually works; and

(*b*) perform for the number of hours specified in the order such work at such times as the local authority officer may instruct.

(2) Subject to section 5 (1) of this Act, the work required to be performed under a community service order shall be performed during the period of twelve months beginning with the date of the order; but, unless revoked, the order shall remain in force until the offender has worked under it for the number of hours specified in it.

(3) The instructions given by the local authority officer under this section shall, so far as practicable, be such as to avoid any conflict with the offender's religious beliefs and any interference with the times, if any, at which he normally works or attends a school or other educational establishment.

Failure to comply with requirements of community service orders

4.—(1) If at any time while a community service order is in force in respect of any offender it appears to the appropriate court, on evidence on oath from the local authority officer, that that offender has failed to comply with any of the requirements of section 3 of this Act (including any failure satisfactorily to perform the work which he has been instructed to do), that court may issue a warrant for the arrest of that offender, or may, if it thinks fit, instead of issuing a warrant in the first instance issue a citation requiring that offender to appear before that court at such time as may be specified in the citation.

(2) If it is proved to the satisfaction of the court before which an offender appears or is brought in pursuance of subsection (1) above that he has failed without reasonable excuse to comply with any of the requirements of the said section 3, that court may—

(*a*) without prejudice to the continuance in force of the order, impose on him a fine not exceeding £50;

(*b*) revoke the order and deal with that offender in any manner in which he could have been dealt with for the original offence by the court which made the order if the order had not been made; or

(c) subject to section 1 (1) of this Act, vary the number of hours specified in the order."

NOTES

1. The above Act also provides for the performance of unpaid work by persons on probation. See *infra*, p. 513.

2. At the time of writing there appear to be no reported decisions of the courts on the construction of these provisions. The central issue in community service is likely to be that of the offender's suitability under section 1(2)(c). The court is required by that subsection to take into account information concerning "the offender and his circumstances." The Act does not expressly mention the nature of the offence as a factor in judging suitability, but, it is submitted, this ought to be a relevant factor, and one which should be considered. The English courts have, on the other hand, made community service orders even in the case of violent offenders (*McDiarmid* (1980) 2 Cr. App. R (S.) 130 — young man of previously good character convicted of inflicting grievous·bodily harm) or offenders with serious records (*Afzal* (1980) 2 Cr. App. R (S.) 93.) It would appear from English decisions that the suitability of the offender to perform community service is an issue distinct from the appropriateness of that sentence. In *Luke* (1980) 2 Cr. App. R. (S.) 232 the appellant committed a serious wounding on his victim. The court accepted that he was a suitable person to perform community service, but imposed a custodial sentence on the ground that community service would not be appropriate having regard to the nature of the offence.

(iv) Fines

This is perhaps the commonest form of disposal available to the courts. In solemn proceedings the court may impose a fine of any amount. This was always so in respect of common law offences, and the common law power was effectively extended to all offences by section 193A of the 1975 Act. In summary proceedings the maximum fine which the sheriff can impose is £1,000 (1975 Act, s. 289B(6)). A similar limit is set on the powers of a stipendiary in the district court: District Courts (Scotland) Act 1975, s. 3(2). A district court justice may impose a fine of up to £200 in respect of common law (1975 Act, s. 284(b)) and statutory (1980 Act, s. 7(1)) offences.

Formerly the procedures governing the enforcement of fines in solemn and summary proceedings differed. Section 47 of the 1980

Act broadly assimilates the two procedures by extending to solemn procedure the existing provisions for the enforcement of fines in summary procedure. The provisions which now govern fines are those mentioned in section 47 of the 1980 Act, *viz.*, sections 395 to 401, 403 to 404, 406 to 409, 411 and Schedule 7.

1.   Criminal Procedure (Scotland) Act 1975

"**395.**—(1) A court in determining the amount of any fine to be imposed on an offender shall take into consideration, amongst other things, the means of the offender so far as known to the court. . . .

396.—(1) Where a court has imposed a fine on an offender . . . the court shall, subject to the provisions of the next following subsection, allow him at least seven days to pay the fine or the first instalment thereof. . .

(2) If on the occasion of the imposition of a fine—

(*a*) the offender appears to the court to possess sufficient means to enable him to pay the fine forthwith; or

(*b*) on being asked by the court whether he wished to have time for payment, he does not ask for time; or

(*c*) he fails to satisfy the court that he has a fixed abode; or

(*d*) the court is satisfied that for any other special reason that no time should be allowed for payment,

the court may refuse him time to pay the fine and, if the offender fails to pay, may exercise its power to impose imprisonment and, if it does so, shall state the special reason for its decision."

NOTES

1. A court may allow time for payment even where this has not been requested by the accused: *Fraser* v. *Herron,* 1968 J.C. 1.

2. The court may, in fining an offender impose a period of imprisonment in default of payment. The maximum periods which may be imposed are as follows (s. 407(1A) of the 1975 Act):

Amount of Fine or of Caution	Maximum Period of Imprisonment
Not exceeding £25	7 days
Exceeding £25 but not exceeding £50	14 days
Exceeding £50 but not exceeding £200	30 days
Exceeding £200 but not exceeding £500	60 days
Exceeding £500 but not exceeding £1,000	90 days
Exceeding £1,000 but not exceeding £2,500	6 months
Exceeding £2,500 but not exceeding £5,000	9 months
Exceeding £5,000	12 months

3. A fine should not be set at such a figure that, having regard to the means of the offender an excessive period of payment would be involved, and the offender would be left with virtually no disposable income after the payment of necessaries: *Glen* v. *McLeod* 1982 S.C.C.R. 449.

2. **Barbour v. Robertson**
Ram v. Robertson
1943 J.C. 46

The first appellant was convicted of knowingly permitting a house to be used for the purposes of prostitution, contrary to section 13(2) of the Criminal Law Amendment Act 1885. She was fined £50, with a sentence of two months' imprisonment in default of immediate payment. Ram was convicted of keeping, managing or assisting in the management of a brothel, contrary to section 13(1) of the 1885 Act. He was fined £100, with a sentence of three months' imprisonment in default of immediate payment. The magistrate refused time to pay in view of the nature of the offence. Barbour and Ram appealed against conviction and sentence, and argued that even if the convictions were to be upheld the sentences were excessive and they should be given time to pay.

LORD JUSTICE-CLERK (COOPER) (Having upheld the convictions and the sentences): "There is, however, one last point common to both cases which deserves a word of comment. In both instances the learned police judge having imposed [the fines] refused time to pay, and in both cases he gives as his reason for so doing the nature of the offence. I feel that this method of procedure complies neither with the letter nor the spirit of the statutory provisions dealing with the allowance of time for the payment of a monetary penalty. Those provisions, which we find in the Criminal Justice Administration Act 1914, section 42(2) and 42(6) seem to me to make it plain that the question of time for payment is one which ought always to be prominently before the Court when a substantial monetary fine is imposed, and that the nature of the offence, to which the police judge in this case has twice referred, can rarely be a relevant consideration upon the question of whether time should be allowed for payment or not. The relevant matters on the question of allowing time for payment are, as is laid down by section 42(2) and 42(6), the means of the offender, his ability to make immediate payment and similar considerations, and I feel that, where the offence is of such a grave character as to warrant the imposition of a term of imprisonment, the proper course is definitely to impose such a sentence, either without the option of a fine or with a fine in addition; and not to purport to impose a merely pecuniary penalty, but, by making that penalty of large amount and by refusing to allow time for payment, as in effect to convert the imposition of the fine into the imposition of a sentence of imprisonment without the option of a fine."

NOTES

1. Where time *is* allowed for payment the court may impose imprisonment for future default at the time of imposing the fine the offender is before the court and the court decides that "having regard to the gravity of the offence or to the character of the offender, or to other special reason" it is expedient that he should be imprisoned without further inquiry in default of payment: section 396(4), 1975 Act. Why should the gravity of the offence be relevant to this situation, when the nature of the offence is not (or only rarely) relevant to the granting of time in the first place?

2. For a detailed discussion of fines, see Nicholson, *op. cit.* For guidance on the use of maximum fines, see *Edward & Sons Ltd.* v. *McKinnon*, 1943 J.C. 156, *infra*, p. 548.

(v) Probation

Criminal Procedure (Scotland) Act 1975

"*Probation*

384.—(1) Where a person is charged before a court of summary jurisdiction with an offence (other than an offence the sentence for which is fixed by law) and the court is satisfied that he committed the offence, the court, if it is of opinion having regard to the circumstances, including the nature of the offence and the character of the offender, that it is expedient to do so, may, without proceeding to conviction, ... make a probation order, that is to say an order requiring the offender to be under supervision for a period to be specified in the order of not less than one nor more than three years.

(2) A probation order shall be as nearly as may be in the form prescribed by Act of Adjournal, and shall name the local authority area in which the offender resides or is to reside and the order shall make provision for the offender to be under the supervision of an officer of the local authority of that area . . .

(4) Subject to the provisions of the next following section, a probation order may in addition require the offender to comply during the whole or any part of the probation period with such requirements as the court having regard to the circumstances of the case, considers necessary for securing the good conduct of the offender or for preventing a repetition by him of the offence or the commission of other offences.

(5) Without prejudice to the generality of the last foregoing subsection, a probation order may include requirements relating to the residence of the offender:

Provided that—

(*a*) before making an order containing any such requirements, the court shall consider the home surroundings of the offender; and

(*b*) where the order requires the offender to reside in any institution or place, the name of the institution or place and the period for which he is so required shall be specified in the order, and that period shall not extend beyond 12 months from the date of the requirement or beyond the date when the order expires.

(6) Before making a probation order, the court shall explain to the offender in ordinary language the effect of the order . . . and that if he fails to comply therewith or commits another offence during the probation period he will be liable to be convicted of and sentenced for the original offence and the court shall not make the order unless the offender expresses his willingness to comply with the requirements thereof.

Failure to comply with requirement of probation order
387.—(1) If, on information on oath from the officer supervising the probationer, it appears to the court by which the order was made or to the appropriate court that the probationer has failed to comply with any of the requirements of the order, that court may issue a warrant for the arrest of the probationer, or may, if it thinks fit, instead of issuing such a warrant in the first instance, issue a citation requiring the probationer to appear before the court at such time as may be specified in the citation.

(2) If it is proved to the satisfaction of the court before which a probationer appears or is brought in pursuance of the foregoing subsection that he has failed to comply with any of the requirements of the probation order, the court may—
(*a*) without prejudice to the continuance in force of the probation order, impose a fine not exceeding £20; or
(*b*) (i) where the probationer has been convicted for the offence for which the order was made, sentence him for that offence;
　　(ii)where the probationer has not been so convicted, convict him and sentence him as aforesaid; or
(*c*) vary any of the requirements of the probation order, so however that any extension of the probation period shall terminate not later than three years from the date of the probation order.

Supplementary provisions as to probation
391.—(1) Any court, on making a probation order, may, if it thinks that such a course is expedient for the purpose of the order, require the offender to give security for his good behaviour."

NOTES
1. A probation order generally has the same effect as an absolute discharge in relation to conviction: sections 191(1) and 392(1), 1975 Act.

2. A court in making a probation order may include in that order a requirement that the offender shall perform unpaid work for a specified number of hours in accordance with the provisions of sections 183(5A) or 384(5A) of the 1975 Act (as inserted by section 7 of the Community Service by Offenders (Scotland) Act 1978).

Such a requirement is similar to, but distinct from, a community service order, which cannot be linked to any other form of disposal (see section 1(1) of the 1978 Act).

(vi) Compensation orders

1. Criminal Justice (Scotland) Act 1980

"Compensation order against convicted person
58.—(1) Subject to subsection (3) below, where a person is convicted of an offence the court, instead of or in addition to dealing with him in any other way, may make an order (in this Act referred to as 'a compensation order') requiring him to pay compensation for any personal injury, loss or damage caused (whether directly or indirectly) by the acts which constituted the offence:

Provided that it shall not be competent for a court to make a compensation order—
(*a*) where, under section 182 of the 1975 Act, it makes an order discharging him absolutely;
(*b*) where, under section 183 of that Act, it makes a probation order; or
(*c*) at the same time as, under section 219 or 432 of that Act, it defers sentence.

(2) Where, in the case of an offence involving the dishonest appropriation, or the unlawful taking and using, of property or a contravention of section 175 (1) of the Road Traffic Act 1972 (taking motor vehicle without authority etc.) the property is recovered, but has been damaged while out of the owner's possession, that damage (however and by whomsoever it was in fact caused) shall be treated for the purposes of subsection (1) above as having been caused by the acts which constituted the offence.

(3) No compensation order shall be made in respect of—
(*a*) loss suffered in consequence of the death of any person; or
(*b*) injury, loss or damage due to an accident arising out of the presence of a motor vehicle on a road, except such damage as is treated, by virtue of subsection (2) above, as having been caused by the convicted person's acts.

Amount of compensation order
59.—(1) In determining whether to make a compensation order against any person, and in determining the amount to be paid by any person under such order, the court shall take into consideration his means so far as known to the court:

Provided that where the person is serving, or is to serve, a period of imprisonment or detention no account shall be taken, in assessing such means, of earnings contingent upon his obtaining employment after release.

(2) In solemn proceedings there shall be no limit on the amount which may be awarded under a compensation order.

(3) In summary proceedings—
(*a*) a sheriff, or a stipendiary magistrate appointed under section 5 of the

District Courts (Scotland) Act 1975, shall have power to make a compensation order awarding in respect of each offence an amount not exceeding the prescribed sum (within the meaning of section 289B of the Criminal Procedure (Scotland) Act 1975);

(b) a judge of a district court (other than such stipendiary magistrate) shall have power to make a compensation order awarding in respect of each offence an amount not exceeding £200.

Guidance as to whether compensation order or fine should be preferred

61. Where a court considers that in respect of an offence it would be appropriate to impose a fine and to make a compensation order but the convicted person has insufficient means to pay both an appropriate fine and an appropriate amount in compensation the court should prefer a compensation order.

Precedence of compensation order over fine

62. Where a convicted person has both been fined and has a compensation order made against him in respect of the same offence or different offences in the same proceedings, a payment by the convicted person shall first be applied in satisfaction of the compensation order.

Appeal as regards compensation order

63.—(1) For the purposes of any appeal or review, a compensation order is a sentence.

(2) Where a compensation order has been made against a person, a payment made to the court in respect of the order shall be retained until the determination of any appeal in relation to the order."

NOTES

1. In *R.* v. *Inwwod* [1974] 60 Cr. App. R. 70, the Court of Appeal explained the function of compensation orders in the following terms: "Compensation orders were not introduced . . . to enable the convicted to buy themselves out of the penalties for crime. Compensation orders were introduced . . . as a convenient and rapid means of avoiding the expense of resort to civil litigation when the criminal has means which would enable the compensation to be paid . . . Compensation orders should certainly not be used when there is any doubt as to the liability to compensate, nor should they be used when there is real doubt as to whether the convicted man can find the compensation."

In *R.* v. *Vivian* [1979] 1 All E.R. 48 the Court of Appeal took this fairly narrow view rather further and held that "no order of compensation should be made unless the sum claimed by way of compensation is either agreed or has been proved."

2. It is fairly clear that the Scottish courts are taking a much wider view of their powers under the 1980 Act (as may well have been

expected from the rather different emphasis in the Scottish provisions). See, for example, the following case:

2. Stewart v. H.M. Advocate
1982 S.C.C.R. 203

LORD HUNTER: "This is a note of appeal by Alan Stewart. The appellant pled guilty to a charge that, along with two other men, he entered a lock-up garage occupied by the complainer and stole a motor-car, and we were told that in effect the car became a write-off. This of course was a charge not merely of theft but of theft by housebreaking [sic]. In respect of the plea of guilty the learned sheriff made a compensation order for £500. For this purpose he took £400 as being the value of the car when it was stolen and £100 as a figure to make allowance for inconvenience suffered by the complainer. I cannot for myself say that such an order was open to justifiable criticism having regard to secton 58(1) of the Criminal Justice (Scotland) Act 1980 which authorises the making of such an order requiring the person convicted to pay compensation for any personal injury, loss or damage caused either directly or indirectly by the acts which constituted the offence. Accordingly, apart from the question of means, I do not think any successful attack has been made on the compensation order. The learned sheriff also imposed a fine of £250, which under the Act comes lower in priority for payment than the compensation order. It is apparent that, although this disposal was designed to teach the appellant a sharp lesson and to hurt him in his pocket, it is not beyond his means even at the rate of payment which was imposed, namely £30 per week. In the whole circumstances I find myself unable to say, even having regard to the size of the compensation order, that the size of the fine was excessive and I am not prepared for myself to say that the sentence of the learned sheriff should be interfered with by this court. I would accordingly suggest to your Lordships that the appeal should be dismissed."

The court dismissed
the appeal.

NOTES

1. Very little guidance is given by the Act as to the assessment of the amount of compensation which it is appropriate to award. The only factor that the court is required to take into consideration is the means of the offender. It is submitted, however, that it is proper for the court to have regard to other factors, such as the degree of responsibility of the accused for the loss suffered. *Cf. Tudhope* v. *Furphy, infra,* p. 517. In the instant case the court held the appellant liable for the whole loss, apparently on the basis that his co-accused was not in employment and could not, therefore, contribute to the compensation order.

2. The English courts have repeatedly stressed the need for realism in the making of compensation orders. A compensation order should not be made "if there is no realistic possibility of the compensation order being complied with" (*per* Cantley J., *R. v. Webb and Davis* (1979) 1 Cr. App. R. (S.) 16) at least within a reasonable time (*R. v. Brown* (1979) 1 Cr. App. R. (S.) 189). In *R. v. Daly* (1973) 58 Cr. App. R. 333 Lord Widgery C.J. held that a repayment period extending to six years was unreasonable.

There may be cases, however, in which an order requiring a lengthy period of payment may be justified. In *R. v. Workman* (1979) 1 Cr. App. R. (S.) 335 the appellant remained in possession of the proceeds of her criminal activities, which she had used to finance the purchase of her house. In these circumstances the court held that a substantial order for compensation, requiring a lengthy repayment period was justified.

3. "Means" are not defined for the purposes of these provisions. Do they extend to the totality of the offenders assets? In *Harrison* (1980) 2 Cr. App. R. (S.) 313 it was held that a compensation order could not be made on the assumption that the offender's matrimonial home could be sold to satisfy the order.

4. The decision in *Stewart* should be contrasted with *R. v. Donovan* (1981) 3 Cr. App. R. (S.) 192. In that case the defendant was convicted of taking a conveyance without the consent of the owner, contrary to s.12 of the Theft Act 1968. The vehicle was a car which he had hired from a car hire firm, and which he had failed to return. A compensation order was made to include an element of loss of use by the company. The Court of Appeal held that that element could not be included. Such loss was, in view of the Court, "notoriously difficult to assess".

5. A compensation order cannot be combined with probation since the former may only be imposed on conviction of the offender: 1980 Act, S. 58(1). The payment of compensation may, however, be made a condition of probation.

6. To whom may compensation be payable? As to this, see the following case:

3. **Tudhope v. Furphy**
Glasgow Sheriff Court, 1 December 1982,
unreported, C.O.C. A48/82

SHERIFF KEARNEY: "This is a case under the Criminal Procedure (Scotland) Act 1975 wherein the accused was charged that he did on 1 or 2 January 1982 while acting along with others outside 91 Cockmuir Street, Glasgow, steal motor vehicle registered number FLS 594S.

After sundry procedure the cause came before me on 10 September 1982 when the accused was represented by his solicitor Mr Brown and when the plea of not guilty previously tendered was withdrawn and a plea of guilty as libelled entered on behalf of the accused who turned out to be a first offender.

I was told by the prosecutor that several hundred pounds' worth of damage had been done to the vehicle which the accused and the other persons had stolen and, being minded to grant a compensation order, I asked the procurator fiscal to obtain more detailed information as to loss and adjourned the diet until 29 September for this purpose.

When the cause came before me on the latter date the procurator fiscal laid before me a letter dated 14 September 1982 from Messrs Hutchison and Craft, insurance brokers, Glasgow, and the letter was in the following terms:—

'Our Claim Number: 82/1/59 — Our Client: Mr A. Dallas

Theft of a Motor Vehicle on the 2nd January 1982

We have been asked by our client's Insurers, Anchor Underwriters, 17 Station Road, Ilford, Essex IG1 4DS., to take steps to press for Compensation Order for the sum of £560·00 on their behalf.

We have made it clear to them that the Compensation Order is granted only at the discretion of the Court and that there is no guarantee that it will be enforced.

The accused in this particular case is one G. Furphy of 22 Menzies Road, Glasgow, the case is being dealt with by Clydebank C.I.D. under their Crime Number DA 0017/01/82. We trust this information will allow you to trace your file of papers and note our principals request for the Compensation Order.

Should you require any further information please contact the writer immediately.

Yours faithfully
for HUTCHISON & CRAFT LIMITED,

G. Fraser,
Claims Department.'

It was evident from the terms of this letter that it had been written by Messrs Hutchison & Craft on their initiative and not in reply to my own call for information but, of course, it contained the necessary information.

In all the circumstances I decided that it would be very desirable indeed for the accused to compensate the owner of the car for his loss, even although it might turn out to be the legal duty of the owner of the car to repay the compensation to the insurers who had borne the loss. This seemed to me to be entirely in accord with both the letter and the spirit of Pt. IV of the Criminal Justice (Scotland) Act 1980. In considering the amount of compensation I kept in mind the accused's resources, which were exiguous, and the consideration that, according to such information as I possess, he had apparently been a junior partner in the joint adventure of stealing the car. I accordingly fixed £150 as the compensation payable by the accused and, as this was for him a considerable penalty in itself, I did not separately fine him but simply admonished and ordered the £150 compensation to be paid to the sheriff clerk at the rate of £5 per week. The minute recording this disposal reads as follows: 'The court admonished and dismissed the accused and ordered the accused to pay £150 compensation by instalments of £5 per week commencing on 6/10/82.'

Following upon the sentence being pronounced the sheriff clerk, in accordance with normal practice, issued a payments card to the accused and also wrote to the complainer advising him that compensation had been ordered and informing him inter alia that if he had already received any form of compensation in the same connection from any other source such as insurance companies, Criminal Injuries Compensation Board, Department of Health and Social Security, etc., he should check as to whether he was obliged to inform them of any payments received under the compensation order.

On or about 4 October 1982 the sheriff clerk's said letter addressed to the complainer was returned by the post office marked 'deceased' and I understand that the complainer had in fact died before my interlocutor granting compensation had been pronounced. The sheriff clerk brought the matter to my attention and, as the situation was a novel one, I asked the sheriff clerk to advise all interested parties that I would hold a hearing in chambers at which I would consider written or oral submissions. I asked the sheriff clerk to intimate to the solicitors for the accused, to Messrs Hutchison & Craft Ltd., insurance brokers, who had submitted the initial request for compensation, and to the procurator fiscal in the public interest. The hearing duly took place and the procurator fiscal was represented by Mr N. G. O'Brien, assistant procurator fiscal and Messrs Hutchison & Craft Ltd. were represented by Mr G. Fraser of their claims department. Mr Fraser, of course, is not a solicitor and would not have a voice in any formal court hearing but as the hearing I had fixed was not such a formal hearing (and indeed, I am afraid, was without explicit statutory warrant) I considered it would not be improper to allow myself to have the benefit of any assistance that Mr Fraser could give me. The accused's solicitors did not appear personally but made a written submission in the following terms: 'In our experience this is a completely novel situation and that being so the only suggestion that we could forward would be to have the Compensation Order rescinded and further imposing a similar monetary penalty substituted'.

Mr O'Brien drew my attention to the wording of s. 60 of the Criminal Justice (Scotland) Act 1980. This section reads as follows:
Payment under compensation order
60.—(1) Payment of any amount under a compensation order shall be made to the clerk of the court who shall account for the amount to the person entitled thereto.

(2) Only the court shall have power to enforce a compensation order.' Mr O'Brien also drew to my attention c. 8(2) of the Act of Adjournal (Procedures under Criminal Justice (Scotland) Act 1980 No. 2) 1981 which reads as follows:

'(2) Entries shall be made in the record or minutes of proceedings by the clerk of court on the making of a compensation order, specifying the terms of the order and in particular—

(a) the name of the convicted person or persons required to pay compensation;

(b) the amount of compensation required to be paid by such person or such persons;

(c) the name of the person or persons entitled to the compensation payable;

(d) where there is more than one such person, the amount of compensation each is entitled to and the priority, if any, among those persons for payment.'

It is to be remarked in limine that the minute in the instant case did not comply strictly with the specification desiderated in this act of adjournal in that the minute did not specifically name the complainer as the person entitled to the compensation. I am, however, clearly of opinion that this is not a fatal flaw in the minuting since, in a case where there is only one complainer, there could be no doubt that the person in whose favour the order was being pronounced was that complainer. It goes without saying, however, that such matters should not be left to inference and that the minute should always name the person entitled specifically.

The interesting question which arises is, of course, what effect, if any, the death of the complainer before the compensation order was pronounced is to have on the implementation of the order. Mr O'Brien submitted strongly that irrespective of who might be held entitled in due course to receive the benefit of the compensation order, the person primo loco empowered to collect the amount was the sheriff clerk and that the sheriff clerk should be allowed to do so and thereafter, if and when any amount had been collected, to face up to the problem of deciding to whom he should pay the proceeds: in the normal way this would present no problem but in the present case it might be argued that those standing in right of the deceased by having already paid him for the damage (i.e. the insurance company represented by the insurance brokers) would be the persons so entitled.

Mr Fraser associated himself with Mr O'Brien's point of view and indicated a general concern with trying to maximise the possibility of making offenders pay for the damaging results of their crimes—very much in the spirit of Pt. IV of the 1980 Act.

The first problem to be resolved is the locus of the sheriff to hear argument and rule upon what should be done in the situation which has arisen here. Section 66(1) of the 1980 Act substantially equiparates compensation orders with fines and s. 395A of the 1975 Act provides inter alia that a fine may at any time be remitted in whole or in part by the court which imposed the fine. While I have some doubt whether the legislature envisaged a compensation order being varied or reduced to nil on the basis that it was alleged to be void ab initio as opposed to remitting it for some reason connected with the accused (e.g. that he had started a long prison term after the imposition of the compensation order) the language of the statute is nevertheless so wide that I have come to the conclusion that I have power to reduce or extinguish a fine or a compensation order in a wide variety of circumstances including those applicable in the instant case.

As the procedure to be adopted s. 395(A) of the 1975 Act empowers the court to act 'without requiring the attendance of the accused' but I do not read this as prohibiting the course of action which I took in convening parties to an informal hearing and indeed I am satisfied that this was clearly the correct course to take.

The next matter to be resolved is whether, on the information that the complainer was deceased before the compensation order was pronounced, I should regard this as having rendered the order void ab initio and recognise this by remitting the compensation order completely. (I use the words 'regard' and 'recognise' advisedly since I am clear that, within the context of the present process, I have no legal powers to pronounce a formal declarator or to 'rescind' the compensation order in the sense of declaring it to be of no legal effect.) I have been able to find no authority which is of direct assistance. Archbold's *Criminal Pleading Evidence and Practice* (40th ed.) deals with the English experience of compensation orders at paras. 768(e) to (g) but this particular problem does not seem to have arisen. In my judgment the compensation order is a creature of statute and sui generis so that analogy with other forms of compensation would not be very helpful. It seems to me, from the general thrust of Pt. IV of the 1980 Act, that the clear intention of the legislature was to make the offender pay for his crime in a way which was more constructive than would be achieved by the mere imposition of a fine. As Sheriff Gordon points out in his commentary on s. 66 of the Act, 'This section equiparates compensation orders with fines, subject to some minor modifications. Taken along with s. 62 *supra,* it means in general terms that where a court makes a compensation order it is in effect imposing a fine payable (through the clerk of court) to the victim'. In regarding whether or not the death of the victim might be regarded as invalidating the order, one should not, in my view, approach the matter in a technical but in a pragmatic manner. I think the test is whether, had the death been known when the compensation order was pronounced, this would have made any difference to the presiding judge pronouncing the order. Applying that test to the instant case I have no difficulty in deciding that, given that I had the letter dated 14 September 1982 from Messrs Hutchison & Craft Ltd. before me, I would still have pronounced the same compensation order except that Messrs Hutchison & Craft Ltd. and not the late Mr A. Dallas would have been the 'person entitled' in terms of the act of adjournal. I am accordingly not in favour of reducing the compensation order to nil unless by so doing I would be producing an impossible situation for the sheriff clerk, namely, the ing-athering of a fund which could not be paid out to anyone.

Section 60 of the 1980 Act reserves to the court (as opposed, presumably, to the beneficiary) the power to enforce a compensation order and obliges the clerk of the court to 'account for the amount to the person entitled thereto'. The problem therefore arises as to what is to happen when for one reason or another the 'person entitled' in terms of the act of adjournal is unavailable and, again, the question of whether, and if so by what authority, the sheriff is to resolve the problem when it arises. In my view the leading provision is that of the Act itself which obliges the clerk of court to 'account for' the amount of the compensation order to 'the person entitled thereto'. I do not read the Act as using the phrase 'the person entitled thereto' as any term of art but as simply meaning what it says and, that being so, I do not think the sheriff clerk is necessarily and on every occasion to be bound by the interlocutor naming a given individual as the 'person . . . entitled to the compensation payable'. The accounting which the sheriff clerk will have to undertake will always take place after, and sometimes very long after, the pronouncing of the compensation order and (although I am aware that this did not happen in the instant case) and supervening death of the person named in the compensation order is an obvious possible contingency. Another possible contingency is if the person in right of the compensation disappears before the accounting can take place thus leaving the sheriff clerk with some cash on his hands which he is unable to distribute to any obvious party.

Once again, the prior question is the sheriff's competency to rule on the matter. The Act has not made any specific provision for these contingencies and the sheriff, as opposed to the High Court of Justiciary, has no power ex nobile officio to supply a lacuna in a statutory provision. Nor, perhaps unfortunately, does the sheriff have any power to report or remit the matter to the High Court by way of special case or otherwise for an authoritative opinion. Once again I think the matter must be approached pragmatically and with regard to the spirit as well as the letter of Pt. IV of the 1980 Act. While appreciating that in solemn proceedings there is no limit to a compensation order, it is self-evident that by far the majority of compensation orders will be for comparatively small amounts, hundreds rather than thousands of pounds and frequently below £100: indeed, s. 59(1) of the Act with its emphasis on having regard to the means of the accused to pay and the bar on speculating on possible employment after a prison term, appear to suggest that the courts should be moderate in assessing the quantum of compensation orders and so far as I am aware this is the spirit in which the sheriffs tend to operate the Act. It therefore seems to me that the legislature must be regarded as having been well aware that comparatively small amounts would often be involved and that therefore any formal or elaborate (and therefore legally expensive—one thinks of a multiplepoinding) procedure was to be eschewed. I therefore take the view that s. 60(1) of the 1980 Act can properly be read as empowering the sheriff clerk to pay out any compensation gathered in to the person who, on the best information available to him, is the person entitled to that fund. When the named 'person entitled' is available then he must be paid and his receipt will constitute a valid and sufficient discharge for the sheriff clerk. If a problem arises such as has happened in the present case or as might happen in the other examples mentioned already, then the sheriff clerk has to decide on the information available to him who has the best claim to the fund. No doubt in a difficult case the sheriff clerk will wish, as part of the normal exercise of his function within the sheriff court structure, to seek legal guidance from the sheriff as has happened in the instant case. I can see no impropriety in this and, indeed, consider it to be the only proper course of action and I therefore conclude that it is right in such circumstances for the sheriff, after such inquiry as he considers appropriate and reasonable, to issue appropriate directions to the sheriff clerk as to how the fund should be distributed and as to whose receipt should constitute a valid and sufficient discharge.

Applying these considerations to the present case I have no difficulty in concluding that the person in right of the amount of any compensation order which may be recovered from the accused is the person who, on the best information available to me, paid for the damage which the complainer's property suffered. I cannot think that any further investigation of the matter would, having regard to the amount involved, be warranted and I have therefore directed the sheriff clerk to continue to ingather the compensation all in terms of the interlocutor of 29 September 1982 and in due course to account to Messrs Hutchison & Craft Ltd. for the amount recovered.

I should perhaps add, with respect to the accused's solicitors' suggestion that I might 'rescind' the compensation order and substitute a fine of equivalent amount, that I am clear that I have no power to convert a compensation order into a fine in this way. I have, of course, power to reduce or discharge the order under s. 64 of the 1980 Act (which is not apposite to the facts of this case) and I have the power, referred to already, to remit in whole or in part under s. 395A of the 1975 Act as applied to compensation orders by s. 66 of the 1980 Act but this, for the reasons outlined supra, I am not prepared to do."

NOTE

The sheriff appears to have given due weight both to the means of the accused and to his part in the loss of the vehicle. The question arises, however, whether payment of compensation to an insurance company in this way is really what was intended by the Act. It should be recalled, after all, that such payments take precedence over any fine. And in what sense had the insurance company suffered any real loss or damage? They may have paid out that sum under a contract of insurance, but is that "loss or damage" within the meaning of the Act? It would be an odd insurance company which did not cover such "loss" by appropriate adjustment of its premiums.

(vii) Deferred sentence

It is competent for a court of solemn or summary jurisdiction to defer sentence after conviction for a period and on such conditions as the court may determine: 1975 Act, ss. 219 and 432.

Lennon v. Copeland
1972 S.L.T. (Notes) 68

An accused person was charged with (1) having in his possession a drug, namely cannabis, contrary to Regulation 3 of the Dangerous Drugs (No. 2) Regulations 1964 and (2) having in his possession capsules containing LSD contrary to the provisions of the Drugs (Prevention of Misuse) Act 1964. Both offences were alleged to have occurred at the same place and on the same date. The accused was found guilty of both charges. The sheriff imposed a sentence of three months' imprisonment on the second charge and deferred sentence on the first charge. A bill of suspension was brought against the sentence of imprisonment. It was argued for the complainer that the sheriff had failed to dispose of the case in a proper manner, that it was contrary to justice and inconsistent to impose a sentence of imprisonment on one charge and defer sentence on the other, and that the sentence of imprisonment was, in any event, harsh and oppressive. (*Downie* v. *Irvine,* 1964 S.L.T. 205).

OPINION OF THE COURT: —"After careful consideration of the arguments presented to us on the oppressiveness of the sentence of imprisonment on the second charge we see no reason to interfere therewith. The offence is clearly a serious one, the punishment imposed is within the limits laid down in the statutory provisions and no valid ground has been stated to us to show why we should disturb the sentence which the sheriff decided to impose for this offence.

The only other point raised before us was the propriety of deferring sentence on the other charge regarding cannabis. The question of the sentence on this latter charge (charge 1 in the complaint) is not strictly before us in this bill and we cannot therefore dispose of it. But the method which the sheriff adopted of sentencing on the LSD charge and deferring sentence on the cannabis charge is contrary to ordinary practice. Moreover it would fetter the discretion of the sheriff if he ever comes to impose a sentence on this charge at some future date. His proper course would have been to have imposed appropriate sentences on each of the two charges which he held to be proved, or to have imposed a sentence on the LSD charge and if he thought fit to have admonished the complainer on the cannabis charge. It does not appear to us that he could properly impose a further sentence on the deferred charge at some future date, after he has imposed a sentence already on the second charge relating to LSD."

Suspension refused.

(viii) Endorsement and disqualification in driving offences

The Road Traffic Act 1972, as amended by the Road Traffic Act 1974 and, most recently and significantly, by the Transport Act 1981 provides on conviction of certain offences for the penalty of disqualification from driving. Disqualification may be obligatory or discretionary. The category into which an offence falls—obligatory or discretionary disqualification—is determined by Schedule 4 to the 1972 Act as amended.

The above legislation also provides for the endorsement on the offender's licence of the particulars of the offence, conviction, etc. Unlike disqualification, endorsement, if it is provided for at all, is obligatory. Again, the offences for which endorsement is applicable (and thus obligatory) are to be found in Schedule 4 to the 1972 Act as amended.

Formerly a driving offender who collected more than a certain number of endorsements on his licence within a specified period was liable to disqualification, under what was known as the "totting up" procedure (as to which, see Nicholson, *op. cit.*, Chap. 6). The old "totting up" procedure has now been replaced by a table of "penalty points", contained in Schedule 7 to the Transport Act 1981, *infra*, p. 527. The change is intended to allow greater scope for the court in imposing endorsement to reflect the gravity of the offence. Formerly, no distinction was made between, say, endorsement of a speeding offence and one for reckless-driving. Under the new scheme the former offence carries with it three penalty points, while the latter carries 10.

1. Transport Act 1981

"Disqualification for repeated offences

19.— (1) When a person is convicted of an offence involving obligatory or discretionary disqualification and the court does not order him to be disqualified (whether on that or any other conviction) but orders particulars of the conviction to be endorsed under section 101 of the 1972 Act, the endorsement ordered shall include—

(*a*) particulars of the offence, including the date when it was committed; and

(*b*) the number of penalty points shown in respect of the offence in Schedule 7 to this Act (or, where a range of numbers is so shown, a number falling within the range);

but if a person is convicted of two or more such offences the number of penalty points to be endorsed in respect of those of them that were committed on the same occasion shall be the number or highest number that would be endorsed on a conviction of one of those offences.

(2) Where a person is convicted of an offence involving obligatory or discretionary disqualification and the penalty points to be taken into account under subsection (3) number twelve or more, the court shall order him to be disqualified for not less than the minimum period defined in subsection (4) unless the court is satisfied, having regard to all the circumstances not excluded by subsection (6), that there are grounds for mitigating the normal consequences of the conviction and thinks fit to order him to be disqualified for a shorter period or not to order him to be disqualified.

(3) The penalty points to be taken into account on the occasion of a person's conviction are—

(a) any that on that occasion will be ordered to be endorsed on any licence held by him or would be so ordered if he were not then ordered to be disqualified; and

(b) any that were on a previous occasion ordered to be so endorsed, unless the offender has since that occasion and before the conviction been disqualified, whether under subsection (2) or under section 93 of the 1972 Act;

but if any of the offences was committed more than three years before another the penalty points in respect of that offence shall not be added to those in respect of the other.

(4) The minimum period referred to in subsection (2) is—

(a) six months if no previous disqualification imposed on the offender is to be taken into account; and

(b) one year if one, and two years if more than one, such disqualification is to be taken into account;

and a previous disqualification imposed on an offender is to be taken into account if it was imposed within the three years immediately preceding the commission of the latest offence in respect of which penalty points are taken into account under subsection (3).

(5) Where an offender is convicted on the same occasion of more than one offence involving obligatory or discretionary disqualification—

(a) not more than one disqualification shall be imposed on him under subsection (2); and

(b) in determining the period of the disqualification the court shall take into account all the offences; and

(c) for the purposes of any appeal any disqualification imposed under subsection (2) shall be treated as an order made on the conviction of each of the offences.

(6) No account is to be taken under subsection (2) of—

(a) any circumstances that are alleged to make the offence or any of the offences not a serious one;

(b) hardship, other than exceptional hardship; or

(c) any circumstances which, within the three years immediately preceding the conviction, have been taken into account under that subsection in ordering the offender to be disqualified for a shorter period or not ordering him to be disqualified.

Schedule 7

PENALTY POINTS

PART I

OFFENCES WHERE DISQUALIFICATION OBLIGATORY
EXCEPT FOR SPECIAL REASONS

Description of offence	Number of penalty points
Any offences involving obligatory disqualification (within the meaning of Part III of Road Traffic Act 1972).	4

PART II

OFFENCES WHERE DISQUALIFICATION DISCRETIONARY

A—Offences under Road Traffic Act 1972

Section of 1972 Act creating offence	Description	Number of penalty points
2	Reckless driving	10
3	Careless or inconsiderate driving	2-5
5 (2)	Being in charge of motor vehicle when unfit through drink or drugs	10
6 (1) (b)	Being in charge of motor vehicle with alcohol above prescribed limit	10
7 (4)	Failing to provide specimen for breath test	4
8 (7)	Failing to provide specimen for analysis	10
16	Carrying passenger on motor cycle contrary to section 16	1
22	Failing to comply with traffic directions	3
24	Leaving vehicle in dangerous position	3
25 (4)	Failing to stop after accident	5-9
25 (4)	Failing to give particulars or report accident	4-9
40 (5)	Contravention of construction and use regulations	3

Section of 1972 Act creating offence	Description	Number of penalty points
84 (1)	Driving without licence	2
88 (6)	Failing to comply with conditions of licence	2
91 (1)	Driving with uncorrected defective eyesight	2
91 (2)	Refusing to submit to test of eyesight	2
99 (b)	Driving while disqualified as under age	2
99 (b)	Driving while disqualified by order of court	6
143	Using, or causing or permitting use of, motor vehicle uninsured and unsecured against third-party risks	4-8
175	Taking in Scotland a motor vehicle without consent or lawful authority or driving, or allowing oneself to be carried in, a motor vehicle so taken	8

B—Offences under other Acts
(or, where stated, attempts)

Act and section creating offence or providing for its punishment	Description	Number of penalty points
Road Traffic Regulation Act 1967 s. 13 (4)	Contravention of traffic regulations on special roads	3
Road Traffic Regulation Act 1967 s. 23 (5)	Contravention of pedestrian crossing regulations	3
Road Traffic Regulation Act 1967 s. 25 (2)	Failure to obey sign exhibited by school crossing patrol	3
Road Traffic Regulation Act 1967 s. 26 (6), s. 26A (5)	Contravention of order prohibiting or restricting use of street playground by vehicles	2
Road Traffic Regulation Act 1967 s. 78A	Exceeding a special limit	3

| Theft Act 1968 s. 12 | Taking or attempting to take conveyance without consent or lawful authority or driving or attempting to drive a motor vehicle so taken or allowing oneself to be carried in a motor vehicle so taken | 8 |
| Theft Act 1968 s. 25 | Going equipped for stealing with reference to theft or taking of motor vehicle | 8 |

C—Thefts and attempted thefts

Description of offence	Number of penalty points
Stealing or attempting to steal motor vehicle.	8

Note: The descriptions of offences under A and B above indicate only their general nature."

NOTES

1. The references to the "1972 Act" in section 19 are to the Road Traffic Act 1972, as amended.

2. Note that while the points for certain offences are fixed by the statute, conviction for certain other offences offers a range of points. No doubt there will be room for dispute in relation to the appropriate sentencing range here.

3. Where more than one endorseable offence is charged it is important to determine whether or not the offences were committed "on the same occasion" within the meaning of s.19(1)(b). Consider the following example: A takes a vehicle without consent or lawful authority and drives it while under disqualification by order of a court. The first offence attracts 8 points, the second 6, making a total of 14 points to be endorsed on conviction. The endorsement of 14 points would (in absence of mitigating circumstances) result in obligatory disqualification under section 19(2). But if the offences were committed "on the same occasion" then by virtue of section19(1)(b) the number of penaly points endorseable would only be 8 — which would not result in disqualification.

4. What constitutes "the same occasion" for these purposes is, it is submitted, a matter of circumstance and degree. Many cases will

present no problems. A, for example, is seen driving carelessly at 10 p.m. in Edinburgh, and at 11 p.m. on the same evening on the Forth Road Bridge. This would constitute two separate occasions. On the other hand, B, driving recklessly, goes through a red light. There would appear to be two offences here which coincide on one occasion.

A number of endorseable offences are "continuing" offences — driving while disqualified, uninsured, etc. Each period of driving would appear to constitute an "occasion", but only one occasion within (and for the duration of) each period of driving. But what would be the case where, for example, A drives while uninsured, stops to post a letter, and resumes driving? One or two occasions?

In *Johnson* v. *Finbow*, The Times, March 21 1983 the Divisional Court held that the construction of the words "on the same occasion" was a matter of common sense. In that case the appellant was convicted of failing to stop after an accident, and failing to report the accident. Up to 24 hours is allowed for the reporting of an accident, and consequently the *offences* were separated by that period of time (although the events giving rise to them occured at the same time). The court held that the offences were committed on the same occasion.

5. The question arises as to whether or not endorsement, and now penalty points, constitute a "penalty" at all. The significance of the question is that section 311(5) of the 1975 Act requires service of a notice of penalties for a statutory offence along with the complaint, and in the absence of such notice of possible penalties such penalties cannot be imposed. The matter has been discussed in a number of recent cases:

2.   Scott v. Annan
1981 S.L.T. 90

An accused person was convicted of a contravention of section 6 of the Road Traffic Act 1972, an offence carrying obligatory disqualification and endorsement in the absence of special reasons. The sheriff imposed a fine and disqualification, and ordered the accused's licence to be endorsed. No notice of penalties had been served on him in terms of section 311(5) of the 1975 Act. He appealed on the ground, *inter alia,* that the sentence imposed was incompetent.

OPINION OF THE COURT: " . . . There remains question 3 and this turns upon the fact, because it is a fact that no notice of penalty was served upon the appellant. It follows, accordingly, that although the conviction must stand no penalty was competent and the question is what must be done about the disposal of the case by the sheriff? The sheriff fined the appellant and disqualified him. He also ordered that his licence should be endorsed. There is no doubt that the fine and the disqualification were penalties, and that in the absence of a notice of penalties were incompetently imposed and must be quashed. For the Crown the argument was that endorsement on the other hand is merely a record of a conviction which is entered upon a licence, and is not therefore a penalty. In making that submission the learned advocate-depute drew our attention to what he described as a well-reasoned judgment by Sheriff Nicholson in the case of *Pirie* v. *Rivard,* 1976 S.L.T. (Sh. Ct.) 59. In reply to the submission that endorsement is not a penalty counsel for the appellant, who was somewhat taken by surprise, merely asserted that it is. Having read Sheriff Nicholson's opinion we see no reason to doubt the soundness of his view. We are prepared to hold that endorsement is not a penalty. It is merely the entering of a record of conviction upon a licence. In the result therefore the endorsement which we understand has already been made upon the licence will stay there."

Appeal allowed in part.

3. Tudhope v. Stirrup
Glasgow Sheriff Court, 19 November 1982, unreported,
C.O.C. A40/82

SHERIFF KEARNEY: "This is a cause under the Criminal Procedure (Scotland) Act 1975 wherein the accused was charged that on 24 April 1982 from Ardoch Street in the Possilpark area of Glasgow he took and drove away a motor vehicle namely the Vauxhall Viva car registration mark NVS 141G without having either the consent of the owner or other lawful authority and thus contravened s. 175(1) of the Road Traffic Act 1972.

After sundry procedure a trial took place before me on 2 November 1982 which was the day after s. 19 of the Transport Act 1981 had been brought into force by statutory instrument. I had no difficulty in dealing with the merits of the case. There was evidence which I accepted that the accused had made an unequivocal confession of guilt to the police shortly after apprehension and there was sufficient evidence from independent sources to provide the necessary corroboration. I preferred the evidence led by the Crown to that adduced by the accused and found him guilty.

Miss Barr, solicitor, addressed me in mitigation of penalty and told me that the accused was single, aged 21 and was unemployed receiving benefits of £21.15 per week of which he gave £11 per week to the house. He was trying to obtain employment but was not the holder of a driving licence. In all the circumstances I decided that disqualification from driving would not be an appropriate disposal and my inclination was to impose a fine and probably couple this with a compensation order to go some way to make good the £50 repair bill which the car owner Mr John Burton had to face. In former days that, with endorsement of the licence (or rather endorsement of any licence which the accused may come to have) would have been the end of the matter, but, as already narrated, the new 'penalty points' section of the Transport Act had come into force and I had to apply my mind as to its effect, if any, on my disposal of the case. The notice of penalties served with the complaint contained the usual intimation that endorsement of licence would follow upon conviction but it contained no reference to the penalty points introduced by s. 19 of the 1981 Act although it would presumably have been an easy enough matter to append to notices of penalties an anticipatory reference to these penalty points since the Transport Act received the Royal Assent on 31 July 1981 which is one-and-a-quarter years before the coming into force of the statutory instrument.

Both Mr McLaughlin and Miss Barr addressed me briefly on the matter but I took the view, with which I understood Miss Barr, at least, concurred, that the matter was important and urgent enough to merit a fuller debate than was practicable at the time. I accordingly fixed a hearing for 11 November and adjourned the cause to that date without proceeding to conviction.

On said 11 November the accused was represented by Mr Harper, solicitor, and the procurator fiscal by Miss McMenamin, procurator fiscal-depute. Mr Harper's basic submission was presented with attractive simplicity, namely, that there was no mention of penalty points in the Schedule, that the law required such notice before any penalty could be imposed that, penalty points were clearly of the nature of a penalty and that therefore penalty points could not be recorded against his client in this case. Mr Harper recognised however that standing the decision in *Scott* v. *Annan*, 1982 S.L.T. 90, 1981 S.C.C.R. 172 following *Pirie* v. *Rivard*, 1976 S.L.T. (Sh. Ct.) 59 he would require to amplify his argument since these cases laid down, and in the case of *Scott* v. *Annan* authoritatively, that endorsement of a licence was not in the nature of a penalty but simply a record of the offence: and in introducing the penalty points system s. 19 of the Act, on one reading at least, equiparates the recording of penalty points with endorsement.

Mr Harper submitted that, apart from the peremptory provisions of s. 311(5) of the Criminal Procedure (Scotland) Act 1975 considerations of fairness demanded that an accused person should be aware of the penalties which he faced. He pointed out that, although s. 19(1) of the 1981 Transport Act introduced the concept of penalty points by the phrase 'The endorsement ordered shall include', the Act had greatly enlarged and substantially changed the concept of endorsement in such a way as to make earlier case law inapplicable. The changes comprised: the concept of variable numbers of points depending upon the gravity of the offence; the discretion vested in the court in certain offences (e.g. failing to stop after an accident) to vary the number of penalty points in the light of the seriousness of the offence; and the concept, introduced according to Mr Harper by subs. (3) of s. 19, of the penalty points becoming 'spent' after the expiry of three years.

In reply Miss McMenamin submitted quite simply that s. 19(1) of the 1981 Act introduced what was in substance, even if not in words, a refinement of the concept of endorsement and she of course relied upon the wording of s. 19(1): 'The endorsement ordered shall include'. She also drew my attention to the case of *Urry* v. *Gibb* 1979 S.L.T. (Notes) 19 wherein, in a 'totting up' situation no notice of previous convictions had been served and no specific reference had been made in the notice of penalties to the subsection dealing with 'totting up' although there had been a general reference to the possibility of disqualification. I do not think that the case of *Urry* v. *Gibb,* is directly in point and, if anything, it tends to support the line of argument of the accused in this case in that s. 101(8) of the 1972 Road Traffic Act as amended by the 1974 Road Traffic Act enacts: 'Nothing in the provisions of sections 15(5) and 31(1) of the Summary Jurisdiction (Scotland) Act 1954 (complaint and notice of penalty and previous convictions) shall affect the power of the court under subsection (4A) of this section to take into consideration a previous conviction or disqualification endorsed on the licence of the accused.' In short the 1974 Act appeared to recognise the possibility that the court might regard itself, in the absence of specific statutory clarification, as debarred from using the previous convictions to produce a 'totting up' result if they had not been libelled. It is a pity that the legislature, in enacting the 1981 Act, did not display a similar foresight in clarifying whether it was obligatory upon the prosecutor to give explicit note in the 'notice of penalties' of the application of the points system. Perhaps Parliament took the view that it was too obvious to need stating that 'penalty points' would have to be included in a statutory notice of penalties. Perhaps, on the other hand, Parliament, standing the decision of *Scott* v. *Annan* took the view that the penalty points system was simply a refinement of the concept of endorsement and therefore fell within the rule in *Scott* v. *Annan* and required no further clarification.

I regret to say that I do not find the answer to be at all clear. I can appreciate the attractiveness of the argument which presents the recording of penalty points as having many of the features of the imposition of a punishment, namely: (1) it is imposed by a court; (2) it is imposed as a consequence of an offence; (3) it is within the power of the court to withhold the points if special reasons exist for so doing; (4) the number of points varies, sometimes by statute, sometimes within the discretion of the court within a statutory band, depending upon the gravity of the offence; (5) it is unwelcome to the offender and is undoubtedly regarded as a penalty by him; (6) it has, by virtue of insisting upon the recording of the points on the licences as opposed to elsewhere a disabling effect on the offender as he will find if he attempts to hire a car or applies for certain types of occupation; (7) it is described by a phrase, viz. 'penalty points' which common sense and common usage would tend to associate with the imposition of punishment; and (8) it brings the offender a step nearer a graver punishment (disqualification) in the event of the commission, in appropriate circumstances, of certain other offences. I can also, however, appreciate that by introducing the penalty points system by stating 'The endorsement ordered shall include', the legislature appears to be bringing the points system within the rule in *Scott* v. *Annan.* I also find it striking that all of the eight elements of punishment listed above with the exception of (4) and (7) applied equally to the old style endorsement as to the new style endorsement with penalty points although none of these considerations was apparently argued either in the case of *Pirie* v. *Rivard* or the case of *Scott* v. *Annan*: indeed the matter of whether or not an endorsement was a penalty does not seem to have been argued at any length either before the sheriff in *Pirie* v. *Rivard* or before the High Court of Justiciary in the case of *Scott* v. *Annan*.

Mr Harper's argument before me hinged upon the contention that I could distinguish the case of *Scott* v. *Annan* on the basis that the new legislation had introduced such a fundamentally new concept that a case interpreting the old legislation was no longer in point. In approaching the task of deciding whether I can make such a distinction I think I should ask myself the question whether the changes introduced by the new legislation are substantial and fundamental as opposed to comparatively minor. Approaching the question in this light it will be seen that of the eight characteristics of the new system which I have enunciated the old system already embraced six. Mr Harper laid stress on the element of discretion involved in the cases under the new system wherein the court could award penalty points within a band. The instant case, as it happens, is not one in which the court has any such choice but I do not think too much can hang upon this consideration since it would in my judgment be completely unacceptable to have to conclude that some penalty points disposals had to be included in the notice of penalties and that some others did not so require. I accordingly approached this matter on the same basis as if the instant case had been a case wherein penalty points within a band were to be applied. The argument here is that the court is being given a discretion and therefore it is anomalous to contend that it is merely exercising a recording function. Against that argument there is the consideration that there was always a degree of exercise of discretion in deciding whether or not to endorse a licence: even in the most serious cases (e.g. cases falling within s. 6(1) of the 1972 Act the court had and has a discretion, if it finds special reasons for so doing, to refrain from endorsing the licence). This is, in common with the other considerations, not a matter which was specifically canvassed by the court either in *Pirie* v. *Rivard* or *Scott* v. *Annan* but I do not think it is open to me to speculate on whether, certainly in relation to the latter case, the High Court would have come to a different decision had this matter been explicitly raised. I therefore conclude that the element of discretion in selecting the number of penalty points in the cases wherein this is competent is not of itself a change so substantial and fundamental as to entitle me to distinguish the case of *Scott* v. *Annan*.

There remains the consideration that Parliament has christened the unwelcome points as 'penalty points' thus rendering it paradoxical, not to say Gilbertian, to hold that what Parliament had thus described as a 'penalty' should not be included in the list which Parliament had, in form no. 1 of Pt. III of the Summary Jurisdiction (Scotland) Act 1954 headed up as a 'notice as to penalty for statutory offences'. Miss McMenamin had no ready answer to this problem and was compelled, as it were, to look at it squarely and then pass on.

It seems to me that the court is put in an unenviable position. The 1981 Act has, by the use of the introductory phrase, 'The endorsement ordered shall include', deemed penalty points to be an aspect of an endorsement, which does not require specific mention in the statutory notice of penalties but has proceeded to christen the unwelcome points with the adjectival noun 'penalty'. As I see it, on the basis of the reasoning supra, the vast majority of the characteristics of the old endorsement apply to the new penalty points and it has been authoritatively ruled that the old endorsement does not require to appear on the notice of penalties. By selecting the term 'penalty points' Parliament has cast doubt on whether the new endorsement can still be treated as before but since Parliament has enacted the new concept within the context of endorsement it respectfully seems to me that the correct course for the court of first instance is to treat the new points as part of the endorsement and therefore as exempt from inclusion in the statutory notice of penalties until and unless the matter is reconsidered by the High Court of Justiciary.

I will accordingly deal with this case as follows: the accused is fined £100, is ordered to pay £50 compensation to the car owner, Mr John Burton with endorsement of the particulars of the driving licence including eight penalty points as prescribed by the Transport Act 1981."

NOTE

It may be possible to distinguish between penalty points and endorsement on the basis of the element of discrimination embodied in the points system. The differentiation between offences suggests something rather more in the nature of a penalty than the simple recording of a conviction. It should also be remembered that the court has in respect of certain offences discretion as to the number of penalty points to be endorsed. This discretion, it is submitted, is more akin to the court's sentencing powers and tends to reinforce the view that penalty points are what they say they are.

(A) SPECIAL REASONS FOR NOT DISQUALIFYING

The court may be called upon to consider whether or not there are reasons for not disqualifying a driver, where disqualification would otherwise be obligatory, in two situations:
—where the accused has been convicted of an offence involving obligatory disqualification (s. 93(1) of the 1972 Act).
—where disqualification is obligatory under the "totting up" provisions of section 19 of the Transport Act 1981.

In the first case, the court must disqualify for at least 12 months, unless it considers that there are "special reasons" for not disqualifying, or for disqualifying for a shorter period:

1. Copeland v. Sweeney
1977 S.L.T. (Sh. Ct.) 28

SHERIFF I. A. DICKSON: "There is no dispute about the facts which are, simply, that the accused was in charge of licensed premises during his wife's absence and, after hours, he had no need to use or intention of using his car, since he lived above the licensed premises. His wife's mother was staying with him, and in the course of the evening his wife telephoned from Balmaha to say that the daughter of the marriage between her and the accused had been stung by, it was thought, a wasp. Normally, this would not create anything remotely resembling a medical emergency but there was a history of allergy which was spoken to by a doctor whose evidence— and this was unchallenged—was that on a previous occasion a sting sustained by this child had threatened to create a serious situation and there was fear lest the swelling could not be localised and that it might reach the trachea and cause suffocation. The accused sought to console his wife and agreed that poulticing should be effective, but on further consideration, the accused, mindful of the isolation of the caravan site at Balmaha and of the alarming possible complications which were liable to follow a sting to his daughter, decided to leave his home in Bellshill to obtain medication in Glasgow and then to proceed to Balmaha with the medicine. It was whilst driving his car between Bellshill and Glasgow that the accused was stopped and, after normal procedure had been adopted, was charged with driving his car with more than the permitted proportion of alcohol in his blood. No challenge as to procedure was made, but it was established that the car had a lighting defect and that this, combined with a more-than-normal speed, persuaded the police to stop the accused.

The question therefore arises—and it is the only question in issue—was this a medical emergency which would entitle the accused to retain his licence? The approach to this question is laid down in *McLeod* v. *Scoular*, 1974 S.L.T. (Notes) 44 where four situations are envisaged. The present case appears to me to fall neatly into the third of the four situations enumerated namely that the prosecution disputed the fact that a special reason arose, i.e. a material fact. The fact here disputed is not whether in the particular instance of allergy the sting amounted to a medical emergency. In such a case, there has been adopted here the procedure regarded as correct by the court in *McLeod* v. *Scoular* namely to order a further hearing 'to allow the defence to lead evidence in support of [the] facts, with the right to the prosecution to cross-examine'.

It is clear throughout the series of cases which form our law on this matter that personal considerations—that is, considerations personal to the accused—are not special reasons: *Adair* v. *Brash*, 1940 J.C. 69, 1940 S.L.T. 414, where Lord Justice-General Normand said at p. 74 that the court had a double function—first, to see if there were, in the circumstances, 'special reasons' and secondly, but only secondly, to exercise a discretion. In the same case Lord Justice-Clerk Aitchison said at p. 77 that if a relaxation can be granted consistent with public safety an entitlement to exercise discretion might emerge and 'I should be very slow to affirm that considerations of hardship are not relevant and proper'.

Again in *Fairlie* v. *Hill*, 1944 J.C. 53, 1944 S.L.T. 224, Lord Fleming at p. 58 lays down as a prerequisite 'safety of the public'—a consideration more fully discussed in *Brown* v. *Dyerson* (to which I refer later). As to the matter of 'medical emergency' which was the plea put forward here, that was also the subject of consideration in *R.* v. *Baines* [1970] Crim. L.R. 590. This was a case where a man—having no intention of driving—felt impelled to do so in response to a call for help from his partner who, with an aged and ailing mother, was stranded. There, alternatives which did not involve driving were available and it was accordingly held that the circumstances did not amount to a 'medical emergency'. There is of course a danger in relying on English authority, as was clearly indicated in *Irvine* v. *Pollock*, 1952 J.C. 51, 1952 S.L.T. 195 where at p. 52 the Lord Justice-General referred to the 'slightly different view . . . adopted in England'. It is also relevant to observe that once more—and in the same passage—reference is made to the fact that cases fall to be distinguished on their facts. The same stress on possible alternatives which should be exhausted before recourse is had to driving were also referred to in the unreported case of *Copeland* v. *Pollock* in 1976, where the use of a telephone (or even a letter) was postulated as a correct approach before the driving of a vehicle when the permitted amount of alcohol was excessive. I have referred to *Brown* v. *Dyerson* [1969] 1 Q.B. 45 in which Bridge J. spells out at p. 52 what may be regarded as a medical emergency, and at p. 53 speaks of safety to the public in a context of driving behaviour very much the same as the circumstances accepted as occurring in the present case, but once again it was the particular circumstances of the case (vide the dicta of Bridge J. in the last paragraph at p. 54) on which the case truly turned. Notwithstanding the position envisaged by Lord Widgery in *Taylor* v. *Rajan* [1974] R.T.R. 304 where at p. 309 he stated that: 'if a man in the well-founded belief that he will not drive again puts his car into the garage . . . drinks and there is afterwards an emergency which requires him . . . to take his car out . . . that is a situation which can in law amount to a special reason for not disqualifying a driver', the true test seems to be: 'Was there an alternative?' Here there was—the police, a hospital or even local help from a nearby car driver rather than a drive of some 30 miles. As McKenna J. said at p. 311: 'the reason must be compelling' and that means not what may seem compelling to what may be an impaired person but in the cold light of consideration of all the alternatives available.

I am therefore left with no option but to hold that, there having been alternatives, I am bound to disqualify."

NOTE

Cf. Graham v. *Annan*, 1980 S.L.T. 28, *infra*, p. 542.

2. McLeod v. Scoular
1973 J.C. 28

LORD JUSTICE-CLERK (WHEATLEY): "The respondent in this stated case pleaded guilty to a charge under section 5 (1) of the Road Traffic Act, 1972, that she was driving a motor car when unfit to drive through drink or drugs. Certain facts relating to the offence were placed before the Sheriff by the appellant. The respondent's solicitor submitted further facts, which were designed to establish special reasons in terms of section 93 (1) of the Act for not imposing the otherwise mandatory disqualification.

In presenting the appeal the learned Advocate-depute stated that he was not disputing that on the facts of this case the court was entitled to hold that special reasons had been constituted, provided always that the court was entitled to proceed on the *ex parte* statements of the respondent's solicitor which the prosecution was not at that time in a position to accept or contradict. The Crown was only concerned to get the proper procedure established for the future. It is accordingly unnecessary to recite the statements made by the Procurator-fiscal Depute and the solicitor for the appellant, since all that this court is concerned with now is the question of defining the proper procedure.

It appears from the stated case that, on inquiry from the Sheriff, the Procurator-fiscal Depute said that she had no information available to contradict the statements made on the respondent's behalf, since she had received no notice that a plea was to be made in the terms placed before the court to establish special reasons. In these circumstances the Sheriff decided to accept the information given by the respondent's solicitor *pro veritate*, without requiring what he calls a proof in mitigation. He then invited both parties to make submissions on whether these facts constituted special reasons. The Sheriff has explained that he considered that he was entitled to accept the account given on behalf of the respondent (which he did) as sufficient without the necessity for what he describes as corroboration to establish special reasons. Having taken this approach he held that there were special reasons.

It is manifestly desirable that the proper procedure in such circumstances should be authoritatively determined. It is not disputed, not could it be, that the onus is on an accused to establish special reasons in terms of section 93 (1). In two English cases it has been said that the court ought to hear evidence on that matter, and not merely to accept statements made by the defendant's legal representative—*Jones* v. *English* [[1951] 2 All E.R. 853] and *Brown* v. *Dyerson*, [[1968] 3 All E.R. 39]. It was submitted by respondent's counsel here that these expressions of judicial views in England were of no value in Scotland because they were linked to statutory provisions pertaining in England whereby a court could not order disqualification in the absence of the defendant. We find no force in this submission. On the contrary, we find in the views expressed in these cases fortification for the basic principle which must underlie the procedure which should be followed in Scotland.

Since the onus is on an accused to satisfy the court that there are special reasons, it is for the defence to place before the court evidence to justify the court in holding that special reasons have been established. The interests of justice, and indeed the public interest, require that the prosecution should have the opportunity of placing before the court evidence which contradicts or qualifies that other evidence. It is only then that the court is in a proper position to decide whether the onus has been discharged by the accused, who must otherwise suffer the mandatory punishment of disqualification.

Four situations might arise. The first is when the prosecution is in the position to agree that the facts as stated by the defence are true. In that situation the court is entitled to proceed on the facts so stated, but could always adjourn for fuller particulars if such were thought to be necessary for the proper disposal of the plea. It is conceivable that if the case has gone to trial, the facts founded upon have been explored in evidence, in which case it might not be necessary to have any further inquiry, and the issue could be decided forthwith. That would be the second situation. The third is when the prosecution disputes any of the material facts relied on by the defence. Unless the court is of the opinion that these latter facts do not constitute special reasons, the proper course is for the court to order a further hearing of the case to allow the defence to lead evidence in support of these facts, with the right to the prosecution to cross-examine on such evidence, or to lead evidence in rebuttal of it. The fourth situation is where at the time of the trial the prosecution is not in a position to admit or deny or qualify the facts submitted by the defence. In that case, the proper course is for the court to follow the procedure adumbrated in the third situation.

That being so, the proper procedure was not followed in this case, and the first question in law falls to be answered in the negative. The second question accordingly does not require an answer.

The learned Advocate-depute said that in the event of the first question being answered in the negative, as it has been, he would not move this court to remit the case back to the Sheriff with a direction to disqualify, since the Crown was only concerned to have the procedure established. In these circumstances it is not necessary to make any further order."

The court answered the first question in the negative and found it unnecessary to answer the second question.

NOTES

1. The question of special reasons also arises under section 101 of the 1972 Act in relation to endorsement. For a discussion of the issue in that context, see *infra*, p. 542.

2. So far as "totting-up" disqualification is concerned, s. 19 of the Transport Act 1981 provides for obligatory disqualification unless the court is satisfied, having regard to all the relevant circumstances, that there are grounds for mitigating the normal consequences of conviction. For these purposes the court cannot have regard to the circumstances set out in s. 19(6) (*supra*). This means, for example, that circumstances which might mitigate the seriousness of an offence are relevant only to the number of points to be awarded (where the court has a discretion in this matter) and not to the issue of disqualification.

3. **Smith v. Craddock**

1979 J.C. 66

LORD CAMERON: "This stated case arises out of prosecution of the respondent alleging a breach of the Road Traffic Regulation Act 1967, section 71 and 78A, and section 203 of the Road Traffic Act 1972. When the case was called the respondent appeared with a law agent, tendered a plea of guilty and admitted certain previous convictions which disclosed that he was subject to disqualification in terms of what are commonly called the 'totting up' provisions of section 93 (3) of the Road Traffic Act 1972. The learned Sheriff, who is a very experienced Sheriff, goes on to say in the case the facts stated in mitigation by the appellant's law agent, in whom the Sheriff had complete confidence, were first, that the respondent is a driver by trade and this is his only trade, second, the disqualification from holding a driving licence would result in his losing his employment and, third, the respondent had dependent upon him a wife and four young children. The Sheriff adds that so far as the actual offence was concerned there were no mitigating circumstances nor indeed in his previous driving record. The Sheriff, exercising his powers under section 93 (3), considered that the permissible grounds for mitigating the normal consequences of the conviction were not necessarily restricted to matters in connection with the offence itself but that he could take into account also the hardship which would be imposed upon the respondent's wife and family by disqualifacation. He therefore exercised his discretion by imposing a substantial fine of £75 endorsing his licence but refrained from disqualification and the question for the opinion of the court is whether on these facts the Sheriff was bound to disqualify the respondent for a period of at least six months in terms of section 93 (3) of the Act of 1972. Now it is important to notice the distinction between the language of section 93 (1) and that of the subsection under consideration, because under the former subsection where a person is convicted of an offence involving obligatory disqualification the court shall order him to be disqualified for such period not less than 12 months as the court thinks fit unless the court for special reasons thinks fit to order him to be disqualified for a shorter period or not to order him to be disqualified, and what are special reasons have been developed and discussed in a large number of cases. Now subsection (3) provides that where the necessary conditions have been satisfied the court shall order the person convicted to be disqualified for such period not less than six months as the court thinks fit unless the court is satisfied having regard to all the circumstances that there are grounds for mitigating the normal consequences of the conviction and thinks fit to order the accused to be disqualified for a shorter period or not to order him to be disqualified. Now the distinction is clear. The learned Advocate-Depute in asking the court to answer the question in the affirmative, having drawn attention to the difference in language in the two subsections, argued that hardship alone without any special or qualifying circumstances attached to that hardship was not a sufficient reason for refraining from imposing a period of disqualification. What the Sheriff has done, according to the argument for the Crown, is really to excuse the respondent from disqualification solely because he is a driver and therefore by disqualification his employment will be interrupted or terminated, and the Advocate-Depute therefore maintained that upon this view of the matter it was clear that this was not enough, because in every case the plea of hardship could be put forward with greater or less force. Every driver who is disqualified can well say that disqualification involves him in hardship. The question, however, being a question of law is whether or not the Sheriff misdirected himself in the exercise of his discretion. This clear distinction in language between subsection (3) and subsection (1) suggests very plainly that the ambit of the discretion entrusted to a Sheriff in cases falling within subsection (3) is materially wider than the limited discretion which is reposed in the Sheriff in cases falling within subsection (1). In the course of debate the Advocate-Depute referred to certain passages in a well-known work on traffic offences, known as Wilkinson's Road Traffic Offences, and certain passages on pp. 764 and onwards. He also referred to an English case of *Baker* v. *Cole*, reported in [1971] 1 W.L.R. 1788 in which the then Lord Chief Justice, Lord Parker, pointed out that hardship to an accused may properly be taken into account. The learned Advocate-Depute was not able however to say that the Sheriff had misdirected himself in taking into account first of all the particular degree of hardship which this respondent would suffer in the event of disqualification being imposed, or indeed in the having regard to the family circumstances and what would happen to the family as a result of disqualification. Viewing the matter purely as a question of law, as we must, there having been no misdirection of himself by the Sheriff we are clearly of the opinion that the Sheriff was entitled in the circumstances to take these considerations into account and to give them such proper weight as he thought fit. On the facts stated we are of opinion that the Sheriff was entitled to have regard to the matters he said he took into account. There is nothing in the case itself to indicate that these were in themselves matters of insufficient weight to permit him to exercise that discretion which Parliament has reposed in him. It would be difficult, if not indeed impossible as well as undesirable, to attempt to lay down rigid rules or guide-lines as to the degree of hardship in individual cases personal, circumstantial or professional which would entitle a Sheriff to exercise this very important discretion. It is sufficient to say that in this case the Sheriff did not misdirect himself in law and that he had before him material on which he could legitimately exercise his discretion; and therefore the appropriate answer to the question which is put is in the negative."

The court answered the question of law in the negative.

NOTE

The test under section 19 is now *exceptional* hardship, and since loss of a driving licence, or any disadvantage arising therefrom, would constitute hardship for any driver it is probably necessary to show something which is peculiar to the accused, and possibly involving hardship to others as well.

(B) Special reasons for not endorsing

Graham v. Annan
1980 S.L.T. 29

Opinion of the Court: "In this case the appellant is William White Graham who pleaded guilty to two charges contained in a summary complaint. The charges were that on 15 January 1979 he drove a motor car whilst disqualified in terms of an order dated 15 August 1978 and further, arising out of same event, that he was driving on that occasion without the requisite insurance cover. The real issue in these circumstances for the sheriff was, firstly, as to the matter of penalty and, secondly, as to the matter of the possible endorsement of the appellant's licence. What the sheriff had to do therefore was to decide what monetary penalty was appropriate and whether any period of disqualification ought to be ordered in the circumstances which were established in the proof in mitigation of penalty. It was only after a proper decision had been come to, on the question of penalty, that the sheriff should have addressed his mind to the question of endorsement. In particular, if the sheriff decided in the exercise of his discretion to disqualify, he was bound to endorse the licence. If, on the other hand the sheriff decided not to disqualify in the proper exercise of his discretion then he was bound to go on and consider whether in terms of s. 101 (2) of the Road Traffic Act 1972, special reasons had been established why an otherwise obligatory endorsement should not be ordered.

The facts established at the proof in mitigation demonstrate that since the order of disqualification on 15 August 1978 the appellant had made comprehensive arrangements to make sure that he did not drive his own motor car. These are set out in finding 4 and we do not rehearse them. Furthermore the particular act of driving while disqualified occurred, as the findings show, in special and unusual circumstances. There is no doubt that the appellant and his wife had a business appointment in Edinburgh in connection with their children's schooling. Both attended an interview with the headmistress of the school and to reach that school for that interview they travelled in their motor car which, of course, was driven by the appellant's wife. At the end of the interview, at about 11 o'clock in the morning, they set off to return home and it is perfectly clear that the intention was that the appellant's wife would drive all the way back and at no time would there be any question of the appellant driving the motor car at all. What happened was, putting the matter very shortly, for it is set out in great detail between findings 5 and 13, the appellant's wife became unwell to such an extent that the appellant directed her on to a relatively quiet road instead of the motorway. Thereafter the appellant's wife was forced to stop the car so that she might get out of it and be sick. At all events she was so unwell that a question arose as to what was to happen. In the result, the appellant decided to drive her by a route which took them near a hospital, if that proved to be necessary, and towards their home. Shortly after that the car was observed to be driven by the appellant by police, who knew the appellant, and was stopped. There is no question in this case of any inadequacy in the driving of the car on the part of the appellant.

In all these circumstances the first question is whether the sheriff approached his task correctly for he disqualified for a period of 18 months and he endorsed the licence of the appellant. We are able by looking at the sheriff's note and the minute of proceedings for 4 June to see that the sheriff appeared to approach his task in the wrong way. Instead of considering primarily whether this was a case in which to exercise a discretion in favour of disqualification he appears to have examined first, the question of whether special reasons had been established why no endorsement should be ordered and, having decided that special reasons had not been established to his satisfaction to that end, only then did he proceed to consider whether or not to disqualify. We are satisfied that having approached his task in that way the sheriff misdirected himself and that if he had approached his task in the correct way and, let us say, had reached the conclusion that there should have been no disqualification in this case he might well have taken a different view upon the question of special reasons for the purpose of s. 101 (2) of the Act.

It follows from what we have said that the matter is at large for us and we have to approach the task correctly by asking ourselves first of all whether in the circumstances of this case, having regard to the public interest and the prospect of any repetition of an act which was irresponsible but understandable, disqualification was necessary. Without going into detail on this matter we are satisfied that this was not a case in which disqualification should have been ordered. Clearly the appellant was faced with a totally unexpected crisis. Although he may have reacted wrongly to it, as we have said already his reaction to it was understandable, and it seems quite unlikely, having regard to finding 4 in the case, that there is the slightest prospect of his attempting to drive his motor car again at least until the expiry of the period of disqualification which has still eight months to run under the order of August 1978. Now having taken that view we must ask ourselves whether we are satisfied on the findings in this case that there were special reasons why endorsement should not be ordered. In the particular circumstances of this case which we have rehearsed sufficiently we are satisfied that we should find that special reasons were established with the result that endorsement should not be ordered. The special reasons arise out of the particular circumstances which gave rise to the offence against the background of the arrangement which the appellant had made to avoid the commission of just such an offence. In all the circumstances we do not consider that the public interest will be in any way adversely affected by the decision which we have reached. In the result we shall answer question two first of all in the affirmative, and having done that, we shall then in the correct order answer question one in the negative. In the result the appeal succeeds, the disqualification will be quashed, and in so far as endorsement was ordered that order will be quashed also."

Appeal allowed.

(ix)   Recommendation for deportation

Willms v. Smith
1982 S.L.T. 163; 1981 S.C.C.R. 257

LORD JUSTICE-CLERK (WHEATLEY): "This is a note of appeal against sentence by Gunter Willms who complains about a recommendation for deportation which was made by the sheriff in Edinburgh when sentencing the noter for an offence of assault. I pause to point out that the charge was a simple charge of punching the victim on the face to his injury. There is no suggestion that the assault was to severe injury. The sheriff's reason for making the recommendation for deportation, as appears from his note, was that the complainer was punched in the face more than once, albeit on the face of the complaint it was a single assault. The gravamen of the criticism of the sheriff is that it would appear that he was motivated by the extent of the injuries which had been caused as a result of the assault, which he regarded as a very serious one, despite the fact that 'to severe injury' was not libelled in the charge. It was accordingly submitted on behalf of the noter that the sheriff had misdirected himself in fact and in the result had misdirected himself in law in making that recommendation. The circumstances and considerations which ought to govern the making of a recommendation of this nature were considered by the Court of Appeal in England in two cases, namely, *Caird* [1970] 54 Cr. App. R. 499 and *Nazari and Others* [1980] 71 Cr. App. R. 87. In my opinion what was said there properly represents the considerations that ought to be taken into account and the nature of the facts on which a recommendation would be justified. Briefly, the facts should relate either to a serious charge or a succession of charges indicating a course of conduct. The test at the end of the day is whether to allow the offender to remain in this country would be contrary to the national interest. Having regard to these criteria it seems to me that a simple assault of this nature by a person whose only previous conviction was for a breach of the peace which resulted in a fine of £5 does not qualify for such a recommendation, and thus clearly demonstrates that the sheriff had misdirected himself in regard to the nature of the offence which would merit such a recommendation and to the possible danger to the safety of the country which such conduct and such a record would suggest. I accordingly am of the opinion that this note of appeal is well-founded and I would move your Lordships to grant the appeal and to quash the recommendation for deportation which the sheriff made."

NOTES

1. See also *Faboro* v. *H.M. Advocate*, 1982 S.C.C.R. 22 and *Salehi* v. *Smith*, High Court 13 January 1983, unreported, C.O.C. A45/82. In *Faboro* the High Court refused to interfere with a recommendation for deportation where the accused had engaged in "calculated frauds, brazenly carried out" which "struck at the root of one aspect of the banking system" of this country.

2. The power to recommend deportation (which is exercisable

only by the High Court or the sheriff) stems from s. 3(6) of the Immigration Act 1971 as amended by Sched. 4 of the British Nationality Act 1981. Under the section a person who is not a British citizen is liable to deportation if, having attained the age of 17, he is convicted of an offence punishable with imprisonment and, on his conviction, is recommended for deportation.

c. Sentencing guidelines

The following are examples of the criteria applied by the courts in determining the appropriateness or otherwise or certain types of sentence. They are not intended to be an exhaustive account of the sentencing process. For a detailed examination of modern sentencing criteria, see Nicholson, *op. cit.* Chap. 10.

It should be recalled that since the ground of appeal against sentence in solemn and summary proceedings is that there has been a miscarriage of justice (or that there has been a fundamental irregularity relating to the imposition of the sentence), the measure of an appropriate sentence is whether or not it constitutes a miscarriage of justice. This is rather different from the test under the old law, at least in respect of summary appeals where the criterion was "harsh and oppressive". It remains to be seen what effect the new test will have in practice, but it is submitted that, in principle at least, a sentence could constitute a miscarriage of justice without necessarily being harsh and oppressive.

(i) First offenders

As was pointed out above, there is nothing incompetent *per se* in imposing an immediate custodial sentence on a first offender.

Smith v. Adair
1945 J.C. 103

The complainer was convicted of driving a vehicle while incapable through drink of having proper control of it, contrary to section 15(1) of the Road Traffic Act 1930. He had had a collision with a traffic island which did substantial damage to his car, but which did not involve any actual personal injury. The sheriff sentenced him to imprisonment for 30 days, suspended his driving licence for six months, and ordered his licence to be endorsed. He appealed by bill of suspension on the ground of oppression. The complainer was of previous good character.

LORD JUSTICE-GENERAL (NORMAND): ". . . As there seems to be some misapprehension about the attitude of this Court towards the punishment of a first offence by imprisonment without the option of a fine, I think it may be useful if I said that, in those cases which have come before us and in which we have intervened, the offence was not one which was likely to create danger to members of the public and was comparatively a venial offence, even if it involved dishonesty. But I do not recollect that we have a modified sentence of imprisonment for a first offence if the offence was one, like this, which was likely to involve members of the public in danger to life and limb."

NOTES

1. *Cf. Simpson* v. *Morrison*, 1951 J.C. 82.

2. *Cf. Stewart* v. *Cormack*, 1941 J.C. 75 in which the High Court upheld a sentence of 30 days' imprisonment, without the option of a fine imposed upon an 18-year-old youth, described as being, until the commission of the offence, as "an exemplary character". The offence in question was one of theft of some goods whose value was "not great". The court was unable to hold that the sentence was "oppressive". An oppressive sentence was defined as one which: "is not properly related to the crime . . . but is either to be regarded as merely vindictive or as having proceeded upon some improper or irregular consideration, or . . . upon some misleading statement of facts put before the sheriff by the prosecutor, or the like." Such a degree of oppression would, it is submitted necessarily satisfy the "miscarriage of justice" test.

3. A custodial sentence on a first conviction may also be justified by the need to impose an exemplary sentence. See, for example, the following case:

(ii) Exemplary sentences

Blair v. Hawthorn
1945 J.C. 17

LORD JUSTICE-GENERAL (NORMAND): "The appellant was convicted of stealing handkerchiefs to the value of 5s. 6d. It was her first offence, and she was previously of good character. She was sentenced to forty days' imprisonment without the option of a fine, and she asks for suspension of that sentence as oppressive.

It appears that while her solicitor was urging in her favour her good character and representing that she had suddenly succumbed to the temptation to steal, the learned Sheriff-substitute interjected the remark that she must have been aware of cases of a similar nature which had occurred and of the sentences of imprisonment which had been imposed in many of these cases. That is all the information which we have about the Sheriff-substitute's reason for taking the unusual course of inflicting a period of imprisonment without the option of a fine for a first offence where the value of the articles stolen was small. It is sometimes proper for a Court to take into consideration the frequency of particular crimes in the district, and it may be necessary, in order to bring to an end the commission of such crimes, to inflict an exemplary sentence, preferably after some warning has been given. But, even then, it is necessary that the Court should take into consideration any circumstances which are urged in mitigation of the sentence to be passed on the prisoner before it. Here, however, it was not explicitly on the ground of frequency of theft within the jurisdiction of the Sheriff Court of Stirling or in any other particular locality that the Sheriff-substitute dealt as he did with the case. He seems to have assumed that this woman was aware of other similar cases which had occurred and of the sentences of imprisonment which had been imposed in many of them. He means, no doubt, in the neighbourhood of Stirling, although his observation is not limited in that way. I think, however, that he was not entitled to assume that any particular prisoner necessarily had knowledge of the facts relating to other offenders, and he ought to have been prepared to listen to representations which might have satisfied him that this was not a case on all fours with other cases of theft which had recently taken place in or near Stirling, but that the appellant had yielded to a temptation which was explainable by her special circumstances. I cannot but feel that the learned Sheriff-substitute has not given full attention to the individual case and to the individual circumstances, and that his mind was distracted from the considerations which should have weighed with him in the serious task of passing sentence, especially on a first offender.

The court passed the bill and substituted a fine of £3.00.

NOTES

1. Compare *Selfridge* v. *H.M. Advocate*, 1981 S.C.C.R. 223. The appellant, a 43-year-old female first offender pleaded guilty to 16 charges of shoplifting. All were committed as part of a planned scheme of shoplifting. She was sentenced to six months' imprisonment. The opinion of the court stated: ". . . let it be said at once that it would be difficult to describe as excessive a sentence of six months' imprisonment, even upon a first offender in a case such as this . . . Offences of this kind are all too easy to commit and they are committed all too often and it is as well that those who commit them should know, first offenders or not, that they are quite likely to receive severe sentences at the hands of the court."

2. The courts are prepared to use the exemplary sentence as a response to a general problem (such as "football hooliganism": *Blues* v. *MacPhail*, 1982 S.C.C.R. 247) as well as in response to a more localised issue: *Campbell* v. *Johnston*, 1981 S.C.C.R. 179 (prevalence of a certain type of motoring offence in a particular locality).

(iii) Maximum penalties

Edward & Sons Ltd. v. McKinnon

1943 J.C. 156

Section 23 of the Finance (No. 2) Act 1940 imposed on certain manufacturers an obligation to register under that Act. By section 23(5) the penalty for failing to register was £100, plus £10 for each day during which such failure continued. Under section 35 of the same Act it was an offence for any person knowingly or recklessly to make false statements in furnishing information required under the Act. The maximum penalty for this offence was £500. A company pleaded guilty to a contravention of section 23, by failing to register and continuing in that failure for a period of approximately two years. The company was fined £5,100 (the maximum it could have been fined was £7,200). The manager pleaded guilty to four contraventions of section 35 and was fined £2,000.

The company and the manager appealed against sentence by bill of suspension. The High Court, applying the dictum of the court in *Stewart* v. *Cormack* (*supra*) reduced the fines to £150 and £500 respectively. In disposing of the appeal the Lord Justice-Clerk made the following general comments:

LORD JUSTICE-CLERK (COOPER): ". . .There remains one general observation. The heavy penalties so frequently specified in recent statutes, regulations and orders, ought normally to be regarded as the limit set on the powers of the Court when dealing with the gravest type of offence which the Legislature contemplated as likely to arise in practice. In all proceedings under the Summary Jurisdiction (Scotland) Act, 1908, the Court has, in addition, the express power to mitigate the statutory penalty . . . If that latter power is not used, and if in the early stages maximum, or nearly maximum, penalties are imposed in cases where few or no features of aggravation are present, there is grave risk that, if and when much more serious cases later arise, the Court may find itself powerless to exercise that just discrimination in the award of penalties which is indispensable to the due administration of criminal justice."

NOTES

1. Although the court was addressing itself to the question of fines, it is submitted that the principle would be applicable to other forms of penalty where the court's power is subject to an express upper limit. This, however, is uncommon in relation to non-statutory penalties, although the courts may themselves set the generally appropriate maxima in such cases.

2. The power to mitigate penalties is now contained in section 193 and 394 of the 1975 Act. And see *Lambie v. Mearns* (1903) Adam 207.

(iv) The comparative principle

The court will have regard to the principle of comparative justice. Persons with widely differing criminal records should not, normally, receive the same sentence.

Davidson and Another v. H.M. Advocate
1981 S.C.C.R. 371

The appellant Davidson was convicted of armed robbery using weapons which included a sawn-off shotgun. £4,500 was stolen. The appellant had a bad criminal record. The appellant Muldoon was convicted of theft, along with a third accused, McReynolds. Both Muldoon and McReynolds were sentenced to four years' imprisonment for the theft, although there was a wide disparity in their previous records. On the charge of armed robbery Davidson was sentenced to 14 years' imprisonment. Davidson and Muldoon appealed against conviction and sentence. In disposing of the appeals against sentence the court made the following comments:

OPINION OF THE COURT: ". . . The sentence imposed upon the appellant James Davidson upon his conviction of armed robbery under charge 2 was one of fourteen years' imprisonment. That sentence is attacked as being excessive upon the ground that it is substantially out of line with sentences which have been imposed over the last two years and, indeed, since 1978 for single crimes of armed robbery and the range is said to have been, on average, of the order of six to nine years. In presenting his submission Mr Kerrigan indicated that perhaps not enough weight had been given to the personal circumstances of the appellant and the particular circumstances of this crime of armed robbery; and that, on the other hand, too great weight had been given to the element of general public deterrence. We know, of course, why the trial judge selected the sentence which he did. He described armed robbery and possession of firearms as a serious crime, as indeed it is. He then went on to say that this was a deliberate and planned crime and that the fact that one of the guns was defective seemed to be of little moment as the other was fully operative and loaded. When found later that day by a street cleaner the loaded weapon discharged itself, fortunately without causing any personal injury. In his view the imposition of comparatively lenient sentences for armed robbery has not had the effect of reducing the numbers of such crimes or the carrying and use of firearms. Having said that he drew attention to Davidson's record which he described as a bad one. These then were the reasons for selecting fourteen years as the appropriate period of imprisonment in this case. It is impossible to quarrel with the trial judge's approach to the imposition of sentence in this case. It appears that the level of sentences which have been imposed has been insufficient to discourage the carrying of weapons in the course of crime, or to discourage armed robbery. We are nevertheless of opinion that the trial judge in selecting a realistic sentence for the particular circumstances of this crime went somewhat further than was necessary or appropriate. He was perfectly right to have regard to the nature of the weapons carried and the planning which went into the enterprise. We are dealing here, as the trial judge recognised, with armed robbery involving the carrying of sawn-off shotguns, one at least of which was working and was loaded, and a bayonet. We have, however, come to be of opinion that the sentence of fourteen years imposed was excessive. On the other hand we are quite satisfied that a very substantial sentence was merited in the public interest. What we regard as the appropriate sentence in the public interest, having regard to the circumstances of the appellant and of the crime, is a sentence of eleven years' imprisonment which we shall substitute.

So far as the appellant Muldoon is concerned he was convicted of charge 3, a charge of theft involving a well-planned crime and proceeds of just upwards of £4,000. For our purpose it is not necessary to consider the sentence imposed on Davidson on charge 3. What is important is to notice the sentences imposed on Muldoon and McReynolds. Each was sent to prison for four years for his part in the theft. Mr Taylor's submission was a short one. Comparative justice requires that the sentence upon Muldoon should be reduced for it was quite wrong that the same sentence should have been imposed upon him and McReynolds. In making that submission he drew our attention to Muldoon's record which discloses only three previous convictions of a minor character, none leading to a custodial sentence. McReynolds, on the other hand, has an appalling record, eight previous convictions, many involving serious crimes of dishonesty, and many sentences of imprisonment in the highest courts of the land up to periods of seven years at a time. No doubt the record of McReynolds ended in 1974 but, said Mr Taylor, you cannot shut your eyes to the very different past of McReynolds and Muldoon. We think there is force in that submission and in the interest of comparative justice what we propose to do, largely on the strength of the history of Muldoon and McReynolds, is to reduce the sentence imposed on Muldoon to a sentence of three years' imprisonment."

Sentences varied accordingly.

NOTES

1. In *Lambert* v. *Tudhope*, 1982 S.C.C.R. 144 the court applied the comparative principle to different offences (reckless driving and maliciously damaging property) arising out of the same incident. See also *Brodie* v. *H.M. Advocate*, 1982 S.C.C.R. 243.

2. Note in the case of *Davidson* the issue of protection of the public.

(v) **Public outrage**

The court may take into acccount public revulsion or outrage at an offence, so as to justify what would otherwise be an excessive sentence:

Dewar v. H.M. Advocate
1945 J.C. 17

The appellant was the manager of a crematorium. He was convicted of the theft of two coffins and the lids of a number of coffins which, along with their contents, had been delivered to the crematorium for cremation. He had no previous convictions and was sentenced to three years' imprisonment. He appealed against conviction and sentence. Having refused his appeal against conviction, the court then addressed the matter of the sentence:

LORD JUSTICE-GENERAL (NORMAND): "We have now to deal with the appeal against sentence. The [trial judge] sentenced the appellant to three years' penal servitude. It was represented to us that that was an excessive sentence, and our attention is called to sentences which have been passed upon persons convicted for the first time of theft. No doubt, if this were an ordinary case of theft, the sentence of three years' penal servitude would be a severe and unusual sentence. But it is far from an ordinary or a usual case of theft. I do not suppose that a case has come into these Courts which contained details so horrifying, so outrageous to public feeling, so repugnant to ordinary decency as this case has been. The Court is not only entitled to, but it must in justice, take into account such aggravating circumstances as have been proved in the present case. I think the sentence is justly merited, and I hope it will deter other persons in the like position from repeating such acts as have been established in the present instance."

Appeal dismissed.

NOTE

The case had indeed caused widespread distress in the area in and around Aberdeen where the offences were committed. There was also a serious element of breach of duty on the part of a public employee in this case.

(vi) Guilty plea and co-operation with the Crown

There is no authority in Scotland to the effect that a guilty plea *per se* will entitle the accused to more lenient treatment. Nicholson *op. cit.*, p. 218, suggests, however, that where the guilty plea makes a positive contribution to the clearing up of the offence, or prevents witnesses from being put through the ordeal of giving evidence, or otherwise provides some ground for mitigation, it should be taken into account. It is pointed out however (p. 219) that in such cases the mitigation must lie in these surrounding factors and not in the plea itself.

This view is based partly, it would seem, on a dislike of the notion of "plea-bargaining", which is described as being "wholly alien to the Scottish system". It is submitted, however, that such bargains are not at all alien—as indeed has been recently recognised by the Lord Advocate (see 1983 S.L.T. (News) 47). What is alien, of course is a bargain in which the judge participates. An adjustment of sentence on a guilty plea would seem to have less relevance rather because of the arrangements which may be made between the Crown and the accused. It may well be, for example, that higher penalties are avoided by adjustment of plea rather than sentence in Scotland.

In any event, there are suggestions that, in conjunction with other factors, co-operation with the Crown is a factor which may tend to mitigate: see *Brodie* v. *H.M. Advocate*, 1982 S.C.C.R. 243.

d. Mentally disordered offenders

Persons who are "insane", or who are found to be suffering from a "mental disorder" are subject to special disposals provided for by the 1975 Act:

Criminal Procedure (Scotland) Act 1975

"Procedure at trial of persons suffering from mental disorder
Insanity in bar of trial or as the ground of acquittal

174.—(1) Where any person charged on indictment with the commission of an offence is found insane so that the trial of that person upon the indictment cannot proceed, or if in the course of the trial of any person so indicted it appears to the jury that he is insane, the court shall direct a finding to that effect to be recorded.

(2) Where in the case of any person charged as aforesaid evidence is brought before the court that that person was insane at the time of doing the act or making the omission constituting the offence with which he is charged and the person is acquitted, the court shall direct the jury to find whether the person was insane at such time as aforesaid, and to declare whether the person was acquitted by them on account of his insanity at that time.

(3) Where the court has directed that a finding be recorded in pursuance of subsection (1) of this section, or where a jury has declared that a person has been acquitted by them on the ground of his insanity in pursuance of the last foregoing subsection, the court shall order that the person to whom that finding or that acquittal relates shall be detained in a State hospital or such other hospital as for special reasons the court may specify.

(4) An order for the detention of a person in a hospital under this section shall have the like effect as a hospital order (within the meaning of section 175 (3) of this Act) together with an order restricting his discharge, made without limitation of time; and where such an order is given in respect of a person while he is in the hospital, he shall be deemed to be admitted in pursuance of, and on the date of, the order.

(5) Where it appears to a court that it is not practicable or appropriate for the accused to be brought before it for the purpose of determining whether

he is insane so that his trial cannot proceed, then, if no objection to such a course is taken by or on behalf of the accused, the court may order that the case be proceeded with in his absence.

Power of court to order hospital admission or guardianship

175.—(1) Where a person is convicted in the High Court or the sheriff court of an offence, other than an offence the sentence for which is fixed by law, punishable by that court with imprisonment, and the following conditions are satisfied, that is to say—

(*a*) the court is satisfied, on the written or oral evidence of two medical practitioners (complying with the provisions of section 176 of this Act) that the offender is suffering from mental disorder of a nature or degree which, in the case of a person under 21 years of age, would warrant his admission to a hospital or his reception into guardianship under Part IV of the Mental Health (Scotland) Act 1960, and

(*b*) the court is of opinion, having regard to all the circumstances including the nature of the offence and the character and antecedents of the offender, and to the other available methods of dealing with him, that the most suitable method of disposing of the case is by means of an order under this section.

the court may by order authorise his admission to and detention in such hospital as may be specified in the order or, as the case may be, place him under the guardianship of such local authority or of such other person approved by a local authority as may be so specified:

Provided that, where his case is remitted by the sheriff to the High Court for sentence under any enactment, the power to make an order under this subsection shall be exercisable by that court.

(2) Where it appears to the prosecutor in any court before which a person is charged with an offence that the person may be suffering from mental disorder, it shall be the duty of such prosecutor to bring before the court such evidence as may be available of the mental condition of that person."

NOTES

1. For a discussion of the plea of insanity, whether in bar of trial or as a defence, see Gordon, *Criminal Law,* Chap. 10. Relevant cases on these matters are set out in Gane and Stoddart, *Casebook on Criminal Law* at pp. 185 *et seq.*

2. There is no provision for appeal against a finding of insanity (it being in effect an acquittal). The making of the hospital order under section 174(3) is mandatory. Appeal against the hospital order is provided for by section 280 of the 1975 Act.

3. The court should not specify a state hospital in a hospital order unless the court is satisfied on medical evidence that he requires treatment under special conditions of security, and cannot be suitably cared for in a hospital other than a state hospital: section 173(4).

CHAPTER 17

PROCEDURES INVOLVING CHILDREN

The matters discussed in this chapter are principally—but not exclusively—concerned with children as offenders. The involvement of children in criminal offences is rightly a matter of great concern, whether that involvement be as offender, victim, or even in a less central role as witness. This concern is reflected not only in the existence of special procedures for young offenders, but also in the existence of rules protecting young persons who have become involved in the criminal process from publicity and, in some cases, from being subjected to potentially harmful or distressing court appearances.

As offenders, children may be dealt with, broadly, in one of two ways: by prosecution under the Criminal Procedure (Scotland) Act 1975, as modified or adapted by special provisions and administrative practice, or by the non-criminal procedure of reference to a children's hearing provided for by Part III of the Social Work (Scotland) Act 1968, as amended.

a. Prosecution of children

1. Criminal Procedure (Scotland) Act 1975

170./369. "It shall be conclusively presumed that no child under the age of eight years can be guilty of any offence."

2. Social Work (Scotland) Act 1968

"**31.**—(1) No child shall be prosecuted for any offence except on the instructions of the Lord Advocate, or at his instance; and no court, other than the High Court of Justiciary and the sheriff court, shall have jurisdiction over a child for an offence. . . .

30.—(1) Except where otherwise expressly provided, a child for the purposes of this Part of this Act means—

(a) a child who has not attained the age of sixteen years;

(b) a child over the age of sixteen years who has not attained the age of eighteen years and in respect of whom a supervision requirement of a children's hearing is in force under this Part of this Act;

(c) a child whose case has been referred to a children's hearing in pursuance of Part V of this Act.

(2) For the said purposes the expression 'parent' includes a guardian."

(3) Where a child attains the age of sixteen years after the date on which a children's hearing first sit to consider his case, but before the date of the conclusion of the proceedings on his case, the provisions of this Part of this Act and of any statutory instruments made thereunder shall continue to apply to him in relation to that case as if he had not attained that age.

NOTE

The definition of "child" contained in s. 30 applies, broadly speaking, for the purposes of the 1975 Act: 1975 Act, s. 462(1).

3. **M. v. Dean**
1973 J.C. 20

The appellant, a 14-year-old boy, was charged on a summary complaint, along with three other persons, with assault. He pleaded not guilty. An objection to the competency of the proceedings was lodged on his behalf on the ground that there was no evidence of instructions having been given for the prosecution by the Lord Advocate. That objection was repelled and the appellant was convicted. At the appellant's request the sheriff stated a case for the opinion of the High Court.

LORD JUSTICE-CLERK (WHEATLEY): ". . . The essence of the argument advanced on behalf of the appellant is this. Since the appellant is aged 14 he is a child within the meaning of the Social Work (Scotland) Act, 1968. [His Lordship quoted the terms of section 31 (1) of the Act and paragraph 3 of the Act of Adjournal (Summary Proceedings) (Children), 1971 and continued—] There is no provision that the complaint against a child should bear to be on the instructions of the Lord Advocate. On the contrary, paragraph 4 of the Act of Adjournal provides that the forms used in such proceedings (which would include the complaint) shall be, *mutatis mutandis*, those applicable to proceedings under the Summary Jurisdiction (Scotland) Act, 1954, with such variations as circumstances may require. In other words, the complaint in the present case should be, as in fact it was, in accordance with the common form set out in Part 2 of the Second Schedule to the Summary Jurisdiction (Scotland) Act, 1954. If in summary proceedings in the Sheriff Court the complaint did not bear *ex facie* to be on the instructions of the Lord Advocate, the Court should be satisfied by some means or other that it was proceeding on the instructions of the Lord Advocate before the Court could entertain it as competent. In the present case no such information was laid before the Court, and the proceedings were accordingly incompetent. Counsel for the appellant maintained that there was a marked distinction between cases proceeding on indictment and cases proceeding by way of summary complaint so far as a 'child' is concerned. In indictable cases the indictment is at the instance of the Lord Advocate, and accordingly there is *ex facie* of the indictment in a 'child' case sufficient to satisfy the requirement that the proceedings have been initiated on the instructions of the Lord Advocate. When the indictment is in the Sheriff Court, and is signed by the Procurator-fiscal, the words 'By authority of Her Majesty's Advocate' must be prefixed to his signature.

But summary prosecutions are in a different position. They are conducted by the Procurator-fiscal and in his own name—Lord Justice-General Clyde in *Hester* v. *MacDonald* [1961 S.C. 370 at p. 378, *supra*, Chap. 2]. As this complaint did not bear to be authorised by or to proceed on the instructions of the Lord Advocate, and there was no information before the Court regarding the Lord Advocate's instructions, as could have been produced by an appropriate statement by the Procurator-fiscal depute, the complaint is incompetent.

The point raised is one of general application and importance. The position is quite clear in indictable cases, since the indictment itself produces *ex facie* evidence of the Lord Advocate's instructions. In summary cases the complaint could bear on the face of it that it was proceeding on the instructions of the Lord Advocate and that would suffice to meet the requirements. That, however, might be a cumbersome procedure in some cases, such as the present one where there are several accused some of whom are and some of whom are not 'children,' and I do not consider this style of complaint to be necessary. In my opinion the presumption *omnia rite acta* applies to a complaint at the instance of a Procurator-fiscal where the instructions of the Lord Advocate are required by statute. This is only a presumption and it can be rebutted. If an accused challenges the competency of the proceedings on the ground that such instructions do not appear *ex facie* of the complaint, the presumption will fly off and the Procurator-fiscal will have to satisfy the Court on the point *aliunde*. If no challenge is made, then the presumption is sufficient to regularise the proceedings. But if such a challenge is to be made, at what point in the proceedings should it be taken? Normally it would be at the first diet as a challenge to the competency of the proceedings—section 26 of the Summary Jurisdiction (Scotland) Act, 1954. How can the Procurator-fiscal satisfy the Court *aliunde*? He could, of course, produce written authority. This might be a communication under the hand of the Lord Advocate himself, or of an accredited representative—*Stevenson* v. *Roger* [(1914) 7 Adam 571]. But in my opinion it is not necessary for the Procurator-fiscal to produce written authority. It would be sufficient if he simply made an oral statement. In fact the instructions of the Lord Advocate could be given orally and there would be no written evidence of them. The next question is whether there requires to be individual instructions in each case. In my opinion this is not necessary. General instructions given by the Lord Advocate to cover groups of cases would be sufficient authority for any case within any of the groups. There is nothing in section 31 of the 1968 Act to indicate that the instructions require to be individual and not general.

The learned Advocate-depute informed the Court that at the material time when this prosecution was initiated there were in existence general instructions by the Lord Advocate authorising proceedings in various groups of offences, and the charge was comprehended within one of the groups. This statement was not made by the Procurator-fiscal depute when the challenge was made at the conclusion of the evidence, but then the challenge came too late. That in itself would be sufficient to dispose of this appeal, and I have less hesitation in relying on such a technical solution when it is clear that the requisite instructions had in fact been given by the Lord Advocate. The learned Advocate-depute stated that while such a situation was unlikely to arise, he would like to reserve the Crown's position as to what was required in a case which was not covered by general instructions.

I, too, would prefer to reserve my views on such a situation until it rose as a practical question in relation to actual circumstances. It does not arise here, and on the facts of the present case, viewed in the light of the procedure which I envisage should apply in these circumstances, I am of opinion that the appeal fails."

The court refused
the appeal.

NOTES

1. The Lord Advocate's instructions contain general guidance as to the considerations governing the prosecution of children. Thus, no child under the age of 13 can be prosecuted except on the specific instructions of the Lord Advocate, and all very serious offences, which would normally be tried in the High Court (murder, rape, etc., see *supra*, Chap. 2) will be brought to the attention of the fiscal.

Where the powers of the children's hearing may not be adequate, it may be appropriate to take criminal proceedings. So, for example, it may be appropriate to prosecute in a case involving offensive weapons since the court has the power to order forfeiture of the weapon, whereas the children's hearing does not.

For a general account of such considerations, see Moore and Wood, *Social Work and Criminal Law in Scotland*, pp. 63 *et seq.* and Crown Office Circulars 1970/1095 and 1974/1268.

2. Where a child is to be brought before a court on a criminal charge, notification of the time of the appearance and the nature of the charge must be made by the chief constable of the area in which the offence is alleged to have been committed to the local authority for the area in which the court will sit. On receipt of such notification the local authority makes certain investigations into the background of the child (home surroundings, school record, health and character of the child). These matters are reported to the court to the extent that the local authority considers that they will assist the court in the disposal of the case: 1975 Act, ss. 40 and 308.

4.   Act of Adjournal (Summary Proceedings) (Children) 1971

"3. Proceedings in a Court against or in respect of a child charged with an offence shall be commenced on the instructions of the Lord Advocate by complaint at the instance of the procurator fiscal, and shall thereafter proceed as regards citation, service, finding of security, the issue of warrants, and other steps of procedure, as nearly as may be in accordance with the provisions of [Part II of the 1975 Act] and by this Act of Adjournal. . . .

5. (1) In any such proceedings as are referred to in paragraph 3 hereof, the Court shall, except when the child is represented by solicitor or counsel, allow the parent or guardian of the child to assist him in conducting his defence to the complaint or in presenting his case, including the examination or cross-examination of witnesses.

(2) Where in any such proceedings the parent or guardian cannot be found or cannot in the opinion of the Court reasonably be required to attend, the Court may allow any relative or other responsible person to take the place of the parent or guardian for the purposes of this Act of Adjournal.

6. In any case where a child is brought before a Court charged with an offence the following procedure shall be followed, viz.:

(1) The Court shall explain to the child the substance of the charge in simple language suitable to his age and understanding, and shall then ask the child whether he admits the charge.

(2) If the child has been brought before the Court on apprehension, the Court shall inform him that he is entitled to an adjournment of the case for not less than 48 hours.

(3) If the child does not admit the charge the Court may adjourn the case for trial to as early a diet as is consistent with the just interest of both parties, and in that event shall give intimation or order intimation to be given of such adjourned diet to such child and his parent or guardian: but the Court may proceed to trial forthwith if the Court considers this to be advisable in the interests of the child or to be necessary to secure the examination of witnesses who would not otherwise be available.

(4) (a) At the trial of the case the Court shall hear the evidence of the witnesses in support of the charge. At the close of the evidence-in-chief of each witness the witness may be cross-examined by or on behalf of the child.

(b) If, in any case where the child is not represented by solicitor or counsel or assisted in his defence as provided by this Act of Adjournal, the child, instead of asking questions by way of cross-examination, makes assertions, the Court shall then put to the witness such questions as it thinks necessary on behalf of the child and may for this purpose question the child in order to bring out or clear up any point arising out of any such assertions.

(5) At the close of the case for the prosecution, the Court shall tell the child that he may give evidence or make a statement, and the evidence of any witness for the defence shall be heard.

(6) Where the Court is satisfied, after trial or otherwise, that the child has committed an offence, the Court shall so inform the child and,

(a) he and his parent or guardian, or other person acting in accordance with this Act of Adjournal, shall be given an opportunity of making a statement;

(b) the Court shall obtain such information as to the general conduct, home surroundings, school record, health and character of the child as may enable it to deal with the case in his best interests, and shall if such information is not fully available consider the desirability of remanding the child for such inquiry as may be necessary;

(c) the Court shall take into consideration any report which may be made or obtained by a local authority in pursuance of section 43 of the Act of 1937;

(d) any written report of a local authority, education authority, or registered medical practitioner may be received and considered by the Court without being read aloud, provided that

(i) the child shall be told the substance of any part of the report bearing on his character or conduct which the Court considers to be material to the manner in which he should be dealt with;

(ii) the parent or guardian, or other person acting in accordance with this Act of Adjournal, shall, if present, be told the substance of any part of the report which the Court considers to be material as aforesaid and which has reference to his character or conduct, or the character, conduct, home surroundings or health of the child; and

(iii) if the child or his parent or guardian, or other person acting in accordance with this Act of Adjournal, having been told the substance of any part of any such report, desires to produce evidence with reference thereto, the Court, if it thinks the evidence material, shall adjourn the proceedings for the production of further evidence, and shall, if necessary, require the attendance at the adjourned hearing of the person who made the report;

(e) if the Court acting in pursuance of this paragraph of the Act of Adjournal considers it necessary in the interests of the child, it may require the parent or guardian, or other person acting in accordance with this Act of Adjournal, or the child, as the case may be, to withdraw from the court.

(7) The Court shall thereupon, unless it thinks it undesirable to do so, inform the parent or guardian, or other person acting in accordance with this Act of Adjournal, of the manner in which it proposes to deal with the child and shall allow the parent or guardian, or other person acting in accordance with this Act of Adjournal, to make a statement. . . .

(9) The Court shall take steps so far as possible to prevent children attending sittings of the Court from mixing with one another."

NOTES

1. The 1975 Act contains a number of provisions designed to protect the interests and welfare of children brought before the courts, both in solemn and summary proceedings. The most important of these is to be found in sections 172 and 371: "Every court in dealing with a child who is brought before it as an offender shall

have regard to the welfare of the child and shall in a proper case take steps for removing him from undesirable surroundings".

2. Where a child is charged with an offence, his parent or guardian may, and if he can be found and resides within a reasonable distance, shall be required to attend all stages of the court proceedings against the child, unless the court is satisfied that it would be unreasonable to require such attendance: 1975 Act, s. 39(1) and 307(1).

b. Disposal of child offenders

(i) Custodial measures

Three provisions of the 1975 Act should be noted here: Section 205, the terms of which are set out *supra*, p. 506 concerns the punishment for murder. Section 206 makes general provision for the detention of children convicted on indictment, and section 413 makes provision for children in respect of whom a finding of guilt has been made in summary proceedings.

Criminal Procedure (Scotland) Act 1975

206.—(1) Subject to section 205 of this Act, where a child is convicted and the court is of the opinion that no other method of dealing with him is appropriate, it may sentence him to be detained for a period which it shall specify in the sentence; and the child shall during that period be liable to be detained in such place and on such conditions as the Secretary of State may direct.

(2) Subject to subsection (3) below, the Secretary of State may release on licence, on such conditions as may for the time being be specified in the licence, a person detained under subsection (1) above.

(3) Where a person has been sentenced under subsection (1) above to be detained for a period exceeding 18 months, the Secretary of State—

(*a*) shall not release him on licence under subsection (2) above except on the recommendation of the Parole Board for Scotland (in this section referred to as "the Board"; and

(*b*) shall consult the Board with regard to the inclusion or subsequent insertion of any condition in the licence or the variation or cancellation of any such condition; but for the purposes of this paragraph the Secretary of State shall be treated as having consulted the Board about a proposal to include, insert, vary or cancel a condition in any case if he has consulted the Board about the implementation of proposals of that description generally or in that class of case.

413. Where a child charged summarily before the sheriff with an offence pleads guilty to, or is found guilty of, that offence the sheriff may order the child to be committed for such period not exceeding two years as may be specified in the order to such a place as the Secretary of State may direct for

the purpose of undergoing residential training, and where such an order is made the child shall during that period be liable to be detained in that place subject to such conditions as the Secretary of State may direct.

NOTES

1. A licence granted under s. 206(2) may be revoked by the Secretary of State on the recommendation of the Parole Board or at his own instance where it appears to be in the public interest to do so before consultation with the Board is practicable. A person subject to such recall has the right to make written representations to the board, who may require the Secretary of State to release him: s. 206(5) and (6).

2. If not previously revoked under s. 206(5), a licence remains in force for 12 months or until the expiry of the period of detention imposed under 206(1) whichever is the longer: s. 206(4).

3. Where a licence is revoked by the Secretary of State, the licensee is liable to be detained in pursuance of this sentence until the expiry of the period of detention imposed under s. 206(1), or for three months from the date of his re-detention, whichever is the later: s. 206(7). Where a licence has been revoked, the Secretary of State may, at any time prior to the expiry of the original period of detention, release the child once again on licence: s. 206(7).

4. The words "conviction" and "sentence" are not to be used in relation to children dealt with summarily, and any reference in any enactment to a person convicted, a conviction or a sentence is in the case of a child to be construed as including a reference to a person found guilty of an offence, a finding of guilt or an order made upon a finding of guilt: 1975 Act, s. 429.

(ii) Non-custodial measures

Broadly speaking, the non-custodial measures available to the court when dealing with adult offenders are available when dealing with child offenders, and the more important of these measures are set out in Chap. 16, *supra*. There are, however, certain exceptions and modifications to be noted when dealing with children:

(A) COMMUNITY SERVICE ORDERS

These may only be employed in respect of offenders aged sixteen or over. This will exclude most, but not all, of those offenders falling within the definition of a "child".

(B) FINES

Generally, the provisions of the 1975 Act governing fines apply in respect of children. Where a child would, if he were an adult, be liable to imprisonment in default of payment of a fine (as to which see Chap. 16, *supra*) the court may, if it considers that none of the other methods by which the case may legally be dealt with is suitable, order that the child be detained for such period, not exceeding one month, as may be specified in the order in a place chosen by the local authority in whose area the court is situated: 1975 Act, s. 406. This section applies to solemn and summary proceedings: 1975 Act, s. 194.

As in the case of an adult, a child may be allowed time to pay a fine, and where this has been allowed, the court shall not order detention in default of payment unless the child has been placed under supervision in respect of the fine, or the court is satisfied that it is impracticable to place him under supervision. Where the court orders detention, it must state the grounds on which it is satisfied that supervision is impracticable: 1975 Act. s. 400(4) and (5) and s. 194.

(c) PROBATION

The making of probation orders in respect of children is subject to the same rules as adult probation. The following procedures apply in the case of breach of probation by a child:

Act of Adjournal (Summary Proceedings) (Children) 1971

7. In any case where a child is to be brought before a Court upon information given on oath that he has failed to comply with any of the requirements of a probation order, the following procedure shall be followed, viz.:

(1) The person under whose supervision the child has been placed shall immediately upon making oath as aforesaid give intimation of the fact to the procurator fiscal;

(2) The citation (if any) requiring the appearance of the child shall be accompanied by a notice giving the reasons for the issue of such citation and stating in what respects it is alleged that any one or more of the requirements of the order has or have not been complied with by him, and in any case where the child has been apprehended without prior citation such notice shall be handed to him in court.

(3) The court shall explain to the child in simple language suitable to his age and understanding the effect of the notice and shall then ask him whether he admits having failed to comply with the requirements of the order as alleged: provided that where the notice has been handed to the child in court, the Court may, if it thinks it desirable, adjourn the proceedings for 48 hours before so interrogating him.

(4) If the child does not admit the alleged failure to comply with the requirements of the order, the proceedings shall thereafter be conducted and the matter shall be determined by the Court in like manner as if the

same were a matter which had arisen for determination upon the original complaint.

(D) COMPENSATION ORDERS
A compensation order may be made against a child, but the limited means of most children are likely to inhibit the making of such orders.

(iii) Remits to hearings
The 1975 Act contains provision for the involvement of the children's hearings in the disposal of children and certain young offenders brought before the ordinary courts. These provisions do not apply where the offence in question is one for which the sentence is fixed by law: 1975 Act, s. 173(5) and 372(5).

(A) CHILDREN ALREADY SUBJECT TO A SUPERVISION REQUIREMENT
Where a child who is subject to a supervision requirement (within the meaning of section 44(1) of the Social Work (Scotland) Act 1968) is found guilty of an offence, the sheriff court shall (whether in summary or solemn proceedings) and the High Court may request the reporter of the local authority to arrange a children's hearing for the purpose of obtaining their advice as to the treatment of the child. On consideration of that advice the court may, as it thinks proper, dispose of the case itself, or remit the case to the reporter to arrange for the disposal of the case by a children's hearing: 1975 Act, ss. 173(3) and 372(3).

(B) CHILDREN NOT ALREADY SUBJECT TO A SUPERVISION REQUIREMENT
Where a child who is not subject to a supervision requirement is found guilty of an offence, the court may, instead of dealing with the case itself, remit the case to the reporter to arrange for its disposal by a children's hearing, or to arrange a hearing for the purposes of obtaining advice as to the treatment of the child. Where such advice is obtained, the court may, as it thinks fit, dispose of the case itself or remit it to the reporter for disposal by a hearing: 1975 Act, ss. 173(1), (2) and 372(1) and (2).

(C) PERSONS OVER 16 BUT UNDER 18 YEARS OF AGE
Where a person over the age of 16 who is not within six months of being 18, and who is not subject to a supervision requirement, is found guilty before a summary court, that court may request the reporter to arrange a hearing to obtain advice as to the treatment of that person. On consideration of that advice, the court may dispose

of the case itself or, where the hearing so advises, remit the case to the reporter to arrange for its disposal by a hearing: 1975 Act, s. 373.

(c) *Protection of children in criminal proceedings*

1.   Criminal Procedure (Scotland) Act 1975

"169.—(1) No newspaper report of any proceedings in a court shall reveal the name, address or school, or include any particulars calculated to lead to the identification, of any person under the age of 16 years concerned in the proceedings, either—

(*a*) as being a person against or in respect of whom the proceedings are taken; or

(*b*) as being a witness therein;

nor shall any picture which is, or includes, a picture of a person under the age of 16 years so concerned in the proceedings be published in any newspaper in a context relevant to the proceedings:

Provided that, in any case—

(i) where the person is concerned in the proceedings as a witness only and no one against whom the proceedings are taken is under the age of 16 years, the foregoing provisions of this subsection shall not apply unless the court so directs;

(ii) the court may at any stage of the proceedings if satisfied that it is in the public interest so to do, direct that the requirements of this section (including such requirements as applied by a direction under paragraph (i) above) shall be dispensed with to such extent as the court may specify;

(iii) the Secretary of State may, after completion of the proceedings, if so satisfied by order dispense with the said requirements to such extent as may be specified in the order.

(2) This section shall, with the necessary modifications, apply in relation to sound and television broadcasts as it applies in relation to newspapers."

NOTES

1. This section applies to solemn and summary proceedings, and section 365 of the 1975 Act, which applied to publicity in respect of summary proceedings is repealed.

2. Any person who publishes matter in contravention of this section is guilty of an offence, punishable on summary conviction with a fine not exceeding £500.

3. The former section 169 was permissive in its terms: "In relation to any proceedings in any court, the court *may* direct that" (our emphasis). The present provisions are mandatory, in the sense that no publicity of the kind referred to is allowed, unless covered by proviso (i), (ii) or (iii).

4. Although section 169 does not apply to reports of proceedings before courts in England and Wales or Northern Ireland (s. 169(4)), it does apply to reports of Scottish proceedings published in those parts of the United Kingdom: 1980 Act, s. 84(5) and (6).

2. Thomson Committee, 2nd Report

"Evidence of children in cases of sexual offences

43.31 Finally we considered whether children who have been the victims of sexual offences should be required to give evidence in court. Some of our witnesses thought that such children are so seriously affected by having to narrate the circumstances of the offence in evidence in court that the practice should be discontinued. The majority of witnesses, however, were firmly of the view that such evidence should continue to be heard in court. They argued that children are not so seriously affected by giving evidence of this kind as is generally assumed. This view is supported by psychiatrists and social workers who do not think that there is any solid evidence of children being harmed by their court experience. They claim that any damage that does occur arises prior to court appearance from the delay and the multiplicity of questions, including those from parents, which the child is sometimes subjected to over a long period. It is also argued by some witnesses that there is no acceptable alternative to the present procedure in such cases. They maintain that if there is one type of offence where the credibility and reliability of the witness is particularly in issue it is in the realm of sexual offences, and it is therefore essential, in fairness to the accused, that the child witness should be seen and heard by the court when giving evidence.

43.32 Our own view is that while the present procedure is not ideal, and children are inevitably caused a certain amount of distress by having to give evidence in court, we are not aware of any alternative procedure which would satisfy both the interests of justice and be fair to accused persons. We have considered a number of alternative procedures, such as the provision of hearsay evidence to the court, whereby an adult would narrate to the court the gist of an account of the circumstances given to him spontaneously and informally by the child. Another suggestion is that the child's statement made to the police in the presence of the parents could be lodged with the court and the police and the parents could be examined thereon in court. As already indicated we do not think that any of the alternative proposals we considered would satisfactorily resolve the problem or serve the interests of justice. We therefore propose that the present procedure should be retained. We would, however, point out that a great responsibility rests on the legal profession in this matter, and prosecution and defence counsel should never be aggressive in their examination or cross-examination of children. We suggest too that everything possible should be done—as we believe is happening at present in many courts—to create an atmosphere of reassurance when children are being examined. We are impressed too by the evidence of our psychiatrist and social worker witnesses to the effect that much of the damage that occurs in these cases arises prior to the court proceedings, and we would express the hope that steps will be taken to avoid all unnecessary delay in bringing such cases to court. We also consider that parents of children involved in sexual assaults are very much in need of guidance in dealing with the child in this situation, and should be given expert child guidance and other such help from social work departments both during the pre-court and immediate post-court period."

NOTES

1. Generally, no child under 14 years of age (other than an infant in arms) is permitted to be present in court during the trial of any other person, or during any proceedings preliminary thereto, except during such time as his presence is required as a witness or otherwise for the purposes of justice: sections 165 and 361, 1975 Act.

2. Where a child is called as a witness in proceedings relating to an offence against decency or morality, the court may direct that persons not directly concerned in the case shall be excluded during the taking of the evidence: 1975 Act, ss. 166 and 362, provided that nothing in these sections authorises the exclusion from court of bona fide representatives of a newspaper or news agency: *ibid.*

3. In the case of certain proceedings (such as cases of offences against the Sexual Offences (Scotland) Act 1976) in which the alleged victim is under 17, the case may be proceeded with and determined in the absence of that person if the court is satisfied that his or her attendance is not essential to the just hearing of the case: 1975 Act, s. 167.

4. Whether a child or young person called as a witness should be required to take the oath before giving evidence is a matter for the discretion of the trial judge: *Anderson* v. *McFarlane* (1899) 1 F.(J.) 36.

d. Children's hearings

In line with the recommendations of the Interdepartmental Committee on Children and Young Persons (Scotland) (Cmnd. 2306, 1964), Part III of the Social Work (Scotland) Act 1968 established a framework for the treatment and disposal of young persons in need of compulsory measures of care. These procedures are not restricted to disposal of young offenders, although such cases necessarily represent a substantial proportion of the work of those involved in operating the system. The provisions governing the operation of the children's hearings system are lengthy, complex, and not always satisfactory. Any account of criminal procedure in Scotland would, however, be incomplete without at least an outline of the system. The materials in this section attempt to do no more than that, and for a full account of the system the reader is referred to the accounts contained in Renton and Brown, Chap. 19, Martin and Murray, *The Scottish Juvenile Justice System,* Moore and Wood, *op. cit.,* Martin, Fox and Murray, *Children out of Court,* and the articles by J.P. Grant at 1971 J.R. 149, 1973 S.L.T. (News) 190, 1974 S.L.T. (News) 213, 1975 J.R. 209, 1978 S.L.T. (News) 301.

1.   Social Work (Scotland) Act 1968

"*Children in need of compulsory measures of care*

32.—(1) A child may be in need of compulsory measures of care within the meaning of this Part of this Act if any of the conditions mentioned in the next following subsection is satisfied with respect to him.

(2) The conditions referred to in subsection (1) of this section are that . . .

(*g*) he has committed an offence . . .

(3) For the purposes of this Part of this Act 'care' includes protection, control, guidance and treatment.

Formation of children's panels

33.—(1) A panel (to be called 'the children's panel') shall be formed for every local authority area for the purposes of this Part of this Act . . .

Children's hearings

34.—(1) Sittings of members of the children's panel, hereinafter referred to as children's hearings, shall be constituted from the panel in accordance with the provisions of this section to perform, in respect of children who may require compulsory measures of care, the functions assigned to those hearings by this Part of this Act.

(2) A children's hearing shall consist of a chairman and two other members and shall have both a man and a woman among the members.

The reporter and deputies

36.—(1) For the purpose of arranging children's hearings and for the performance of such other functions in relation to the children's panel or to children's hearings as may be assigned to him by this Part of this Act, a local authority shall, appoint an officer, whole-time or part-time, to be known as the reporter, and such other officers as deputies of the reporter as may be required."

NOTES

1. Children's hearings are conducted in private, in accommodation which must be dissociated from criminal courts and police stations: (1968 Act, ss. 35(1) and 34(3). Where a child is notified that his case has been referred to a children's hearing he is obliged to attend that hearing (1968 Act, s. 40(1)). The parent of such child has a right to attend, and is required to attend unless the hearing are satisfied that it would be unreasonable to require such attendance,

or that such attendance would be unnecessary to the consideration of the case: section 41.

2. Where there is a risk of conflict between the child's interests and those of the parent, it is the duty of the chairman to ensure that the interests of the child are safeguarded. This may be done by the appointment of a person to safeguard the child's interests: section 34A.

3. The reporter may receive information from any person or source that a child may be in need of compulsory measures of care: sections 37 and 38. On receiving such information the reporter conducts an initial investigation. The duty imposed on the police of reporting offences to the appropriate prosecutor has effect so as to include a duty to make reports to the appropriate reporter: section 38(2).

2. Social Work (Scotland) Act 1968
"Action on initial investigation by reporter

39.—(1) Where the reporter decides that no further action on the case is required, he shall, where he considers this to be the proper course, so inform the child and his parent and the person who brought the case to his notice, or any of those persons.

(2) Where the reporter considers it to be the proper course, he shall refer the case to the local authority with a view to their making arrangements for the advice, guidance and assistance of the child and his family in accordance with Part II of this Act.

(3) Where it appears to the reporter that the child is in need of compulsory measures of care, he shall arrange a children's hearing to whom the case shall stand referred for consideration and determination.

(4) Where the reporter has arranged a children's hearing in pursuance of the last foregoing subsection, he shall request from the local authority a report on the child and his social background and it shall be the duty of the authority to supply the report which may contain information from any such person as the reporter or the local authority may think fit.

(5) Where the reporter has decided that no further action on the case is required, or has taken action in pursuance of subsection (2) of this section, he shall not thereafter take action under subsection (3) of this section in relation to the same facts.

NOTE

There is no obligation on the part of the reporter to notify the child or its parents that the reporter has received information concerning the child, nor is there any obligation, where he decides that no further action is required, to inform the child or its parents that he has conducted an initial investigation.

Conduct of children's hearing and application to sheriff for findings

42.—(1) Subject to the provisions of subsections (7) and (8) of this section, at the commencement of a children's hearing, and before proceeding to the consideration of the case, it shall be the duty of the chairman to explain to the child and his parent the grounds stated by the reporter for the referral of the case for the purpose of ascertaining whether these grounds are accepted in whole or in part by the child and his parent.

(2) Thereafter—

(*a*) where the child and his parent accept the grounds stated by the reporter for the referral the hearing shall proceed;

(*b*) where the child and his parent accept those grounds in part and where the children's hearing consider it proper so to do the hearing may proceed in respect of the grounds so accepted; and

(*c*) in any other case, unless they decide to discharge the referral, the children's hearing shall direct the reporter to make application to the sheriff for a finding as to whether such grounds for the referral, as are not accepted by the child or his parent, are established having regard to the provisions of section 32 of this Act.

(3) It shall be the duty of the chairman of a children's hearing who have made a direction under the last foregoing subsection to explain to the child and his parent the purpose for which the application to the sheriff is being made, and to inform the child that he is under an obligation to attend the at hearing of the application, and where a child fails to attend the hearing of the application the sheriff may issue a warrant for the apprehension of the child; and any warrant so issued shall be authority for bringing him before the sheriff and for his detention in a place of safety until the sheriff can hear the application, but a child shall not be detained under this subsection for a period exceeding seven days or after the sheriff has disposed of the application.

(4) An application under subsection (2) of this section shall be heard by the sheriff in chambers within twenty-eight days of the lodging of the application and, without prejudice to their right to legal representation, a child or his parent may be represented at any diet fixed by the sheriff for the hearing of the application.

(5) Where a sheriff decides that none of the grounds in respect of which the application has been made has been established for the referral of a case to a children's hearing, he shall dismiss the application and discharge the referral in respect of those grounds.

(6) Where the sheriff is satisfied on the evidence before him that any of the grounds in respect of which the application has been made has been established he shall remit the case to the reporter to make arrangements for a children's hearing for consideration and determination of the case, and where a ground for the referral of the case is the condition referred to in section 32 (2) (*g*) of this Act, the sheriff in hearing the application shall apply to the evidence relating to that ground the standard of proof required in criminal procedure.

(7) Where a children's hearing are satisfied that the child for any reason is not capable of understanding the explanation of the grounds of referral

required by subsection (1) of this section, or in the course of, or at the conclusion of that explanation, it appears not to be understood by the child, the hearing shall, unless they decide to discharge the referral, direct the reporter to make application to the sheriff for a finding as to whether any of the grounds for the referral have been established, and the provisions of this section relating to an application to the sheriff under subsection (2) (c) thereof shall apply as they apply to an application under that subsection.

(8) The acceptance by a parent of the grounds of referral shall not be a requirement to proceeding with a case under this section where the parent is not present."

NOTES

1. The reporter need not be legally qualified. In the past this created problems since he or she had no right of audience *qua* reporter before the sheriff on an application under section 42(2)(c): *Kennedy* v. *O'Donnell*, 1975 S.L.T. 235. The matter is now governed by section 36A of the 1968 Act (inserted by section 82 of the Children Act 1975) and regulations made thereunder. The Reporters (Conduct of Proceedings before the Sheriff) (Scotland) Regulations 1975 (S.I. 1975 No. 2251) provide that any officer appointed under section 36, and having held an appointment under that section for any period or periods amounting to not less than one year may conduct before the sheriff any proceedings under Part III of the Act which are heard by the sheriff in chambers, or any application under sections 37 or 40 in relation to a warrant.

2. Proceedings before the sheriff are not criminal proceedings, but civil proceedings, to which the ordinary civil rules of evidence apply:

3. M'Gregor v. T. and P.
1975 S.C. 14.

LORD PRESIDENT (EMSLIE): "These are two appeals by stated case under section 50 of the Social Work (Scotland) Act 1968. The appellant is the Reporter for the County of Dunbarton. The respondents in the first appeal are T., a child within the meaning of Part III of the statute, and his father. In the second the respondents are a child, P., and his mother.

As the stated case in the first appeal discloses, the reporter referred the child to a children's hearing. The grounds of referral, to use the jargon of the statute, were that the child had committed 19 separate offences. These grounds of referral were not accepted by the child or his father. In short they did not accept that the child had committed any of the alleged offences. The reporter was thereupon directed by the children's hearing, acting under section 42 (2) (c) of the statute, to apply to the Sheriff for a finding as to whether the grounds of referral or any of them were established.

At the hearing of the application before the Sheriff, the child and his mother appeared and were represented by the same solicitor. The reporter then intimated that he did not intend to proceed with 13 of the alleged offences. The child and his mother did not accept the remaining six grounds of referral which are set out in the stated case. In five of these alleged offences the child T. was said to have acted together with two other boys. One of these was P. He also had been referred to the children's hearing and there was before the Sheriff a similar application for a finding as to whether certain grounds of referral in the case of P. were established. These grounds included the five alleged offences in which he is said to have acted together with T. At the hearing before the Sheriff, P. also appeared with his mother and they were represented by the same solicitor who appeared for the T.s. On the motion of all parties the two applications were heard together and evidence was led by the reporter. At the conclusion of the evidence led by the reporter the Sheriff found that none of the grounds of referral in the case of T. had been established. He accordingly dismissed the application and discharged the referral. He also found that the five grounds of referral common to the two applications had not been established in the case of P.

The short point in these appeals arises from what happened during the proof for the reporter. He had duly cited the mothers of T. and P. and tendered them as witnesses. An objection was taken by the solicitor representing the T.s and the P.s. The Sheriff sustained the objection, holding that neither mother was a competent and compellable witness against her own child. It is the reporter's contention that the Sheriff erred in law in so holding. The first question of law in the cases is accordingly in these terms—'Was I entitled to hold that said Mrs T. and Mrs P., the mothers of said children, were not competent and compellable witnesses at the instance of the appellant?'

Shortly stated the Sheriff's decision proceeded upon the view that although the mother of a child is by the general law of evidence of Scotland both a competent and compellable witness against her child in all criminal proceedings, and is also competent and compellable as a witness at the instance of the opposing party against the interest of her child who is a party to civil proceedings, the provisions of Part III of the Social Work (Scotland) Act 1968, and the terms of the Act of Sederunt (Social Work) (Sheriff Court Procedure Rules) 1971 clearly imply that in hearings of applications by a Sheriff under section 42 of the statute, the mother of a child is neither a competent nor a compellable witness for the reporter.

There is no doubt that before the Sheriff it was not disputed that the hearing before him was a judicial proceeding and that, by the law of Scotland, subject to the alleged innovation introduced by the Social Work (Scotland) Act 1968, the competency and compellability of a mother against the interest of her child in all judicial proceedings is clear. It is, however, necessary at the outset, in view of certain arguments canvassed in the appeals before us, that we should examine briefly these two assumptions on which the hearing before the Sheriff proceeded.

The first question accordingly is as to the nature of the hearing by the Sheriff of an application under section 42 of the Social Work (Scotland) Act 1968. For the respondents, T., Mr Craik at one point appeared to contend that it did not qualify for the description 'judicial proceeding' because of its special nature. In my opinion this contention is quite without substance. The hearing is conducted by the Sheriff *qua* Sheriff under the direction that it must take place in chambers. It is governed by Rules of Court. If he takes a certain view of the facts the Sheriff is empowered to dismiss the application and to discharge the referral in whole or in part. Although he must give his decision orally at the conclusion of a hearing, that decision is then to be embodied in an interlocutor which must be transmitted by the Sheriff Clerk to the parties involved.

In these combined circumstances, the hearing of an application by a Sheriff, notwithstanding its lack of formality, can be regarded as nothing but a 'judicial proceeding.'

The next question is whether this judicial proceeding ought to be regarded as a criminal proceeding. It arises because in an alternative submission, Mr Philip for the respondents in the P. case, sought to persuade us that it ought so to be regarded and, if it were so regarded, that we should accept that by the Law of Scotland, a mother is at least not a compellable witness against her accused child in criminal proceedings in respect that she has an option to decline to give evidence against her child if she is called as a witness by the prosecutor.

In my opinion whatever else this judicial proceeding is it is not a criminal proceeding. Hearings may take place in relation to all or any of the grounds set out in section 32 (2) of the Act, many of which have or may have nothing to do with offences of a criminal character. Although the ground set out in section 32 (2) (*g*) is that the child referred has committed an offence, and the standard of proof to be applied by the Sheriff in a hearing directed to that ground is that required in criminal procedure (see section 42 (6)), a hearing of an application involving ground 32 (2) (*g*) is not a criminal proceeding, since it is not concerned with a prosecution and it can lead to no conviction. In any event, even if contrary to my opinion, such a hearing were to be regarded as a criminal proceeding it is not now the Law of Scotland, and for over 130 years at least has not been the Law of Scotland, that a parent may decline, if called as a witness against his or her accused child, to give evidence against him. By the early years of the nineteenth century it was clear that a parent was a competent witness against his or her child. I recognise, however, that at that time there was some basis in authority for the proposition that a parent called by the prosecutor was entitled to decline to give evidence against his child. Whatever the scope of the proposition, however, and whether or not it rested upon any sound foundation, the law since 1840 has recognised no such entitlement in such a parent. By section 1 of the Evidence (Scotland) Act 1840 3 and 4 Victoria cap. 59 it was enacted as follows—

'That from and after the passing of this Act it shall by the Law of Scotland be no objection to the admissibility of any witness that he or she is the father or mother, or son or daughter, or brother or sister, by consanguinity or affinity, or uncle or aunt, or nephew or niece, by consanguinity, of any party adducing such witness in any action, cause, prosecution, or other judicial proceeding, civil or criminal; nor shall it be competent to any witness to decline to be examined and give evidence on the ground of any such relationship.'

The important words are these—'nor shall it be competent to any witness to decline to be examined and give evidence on the ground of any such relationship.' By one reading the expression 'such relationship' might, as Mr Philip contended, be restricted to relationship to the 'party adducing' the witness. This, however, is not the only reading which the expression will bear, nor is it the reading which was approved in the case of *HMA* v. *Cairns* 2 Swin 531 decided in 1841. In that case the Court plainly regarded the important words of the section which I have quoted as taking away any option which may formerly have been available to, *inter alios,* parents, to decline to be examined on the ground of parental relationship to the accused. This construction found contemporary support in Bell's Notes to Hume's Commentaries, Vol. 2, p. 249 and has never been questioned since. Further in Dickson on Evidence, as edited by Grierson in 1887, Vol. 2, p. 866, the following categorical statement is made. 'By the Act 3 and 4 Vict. c. 59, the privilege enjoyed by the parents and children of accused persons of declining to give evidence against them was abolished; and, in consequence, the pupil children are competent witnesses against the prisoner.' I have only to add that not only has the interpretation placed upon section 1 of the Act of 1840 by the Court in *Cairns* stood unchallenged for over 130 years, but it is, in my opinion, the only reasonable interpretation which it can bear.

In light of the opinion which I have to this point expressed, the remaining question to be resolved is whether, as the Sheriff has held, Part III of the Social Work (Scotland) Act 1968 and the Rules made in the relevant Act of Sederunt, innovate upon the otherwise universal rule applicable to all judicial proceedings with the result that neither parent of any child may be called as a witness by the reporter in the hearing of any application to secure a finding as to whether any grounds of referral are established.

As I understand them the Sheriff's reasons are these. His first is that the Act of 1968 makes the parent a party to the various proceedings contemplated by Part III. In support of this proposition, he refers to the parent's right under section 41 to attend at all stages of a hearing and, indeed, a parent must attend unless in certain circumstances the hearing rules to the contrary. He also notices that not only must the child accept the grounds of referral if the hearing is to proceed without an application to the Sheriff under section 42 but the parent must accept them as well. In addition he draws attention to the right given to a parent to be represented either separately or jointly with his child and the rights of appeal available to a parent under sections 49 and 50. In my opinion the Sheriff is probably right in saying that a parent is, or in some instances may be, a party in proceedings for the purposes of Part III of the Act. Having said that, however, the fact that a person is a party to judicial proceedings which are not criminal proceedings does not make it incompetent for another party to call him as a compellable witness and by itself, accordingly, this reason does not advance the matter in the respondents' interest. To be fair to the Sheriff I do not understand him to say that it does and he contents himself by saying that because of the special position of the parent prescribed by Part III the 'competency of calling the parent of an accused child as a witness for the prosecution in ordinary criminal procedure is not necessarily applicable.'

The Sheriff's second reason is that the main object of Part III of the Act is the welfare of the child; that the compellability of the parent as a witness for the reporter might often be contrary to the interests of the child; that the interest of the child in having the advice and guidance of his parent in the statutory proceedings, even where a solicitor is employed, and the confidentiality of communications between them, might suffer; and that to allow the parent to be a compellable witness for the reporter before the Sheriff would put a strain upon the parent-child relationship. In my opinion this reason is unsound.

It is no doubt the case that Part III of the Act is designed to secure the welfare of children in the sense that, subject to the provisions of section 31, they are not to be prosecuted for offences and that those children in need of compulsory measures of care should have the appropriate measures applied in their interests. To say, however, that these laudable objects may be frustrated if the parent of a child who has not been prosecuted may be called as a compellable witness by a reporter at a Sheriff's hearing is, with respect to the learned Sheriff, absurd. The better view is that, if the parents were neither competent nor compellable the attainment of the objects of Part III of the Act would in many cases be seriously impeded and children who, *ex hypothesi*, may require compulsory measures of care under direction of a children's hearing may be deprived of them when they are most needed. One has only to look at the various grounds of referral listed in section 32 (2) to see that the evidence of a parent may be essential to the establishment of some of them, and if a parent is not to be a competent and compellable witness where the ground is the alleged commission of an offence, that ground would be incapable of being established in many cases, including, in particular, cases where the parent was the victim of the alleged offence. In such situations if the law is as the Sheriff declares it to be, the result might well be that the Lord Advocate would be forced in the public interest and in the interest of the child concerned to prosecute in circumstances in which the aim of the Act is to avoid prosecution.

It is no doubt also the case that Part III of the Act and the relevant Rules recognise that it is in the interests of a child to have the advice and guidance of his parents in course of the statutory proceedings, but there is nothing new in this. These interests of a child may be supposed to have existed as matter of fact before 1937 and although they received statutory recognition in the Children and Young Persons (Scotland) Act 1937, section 42, and in the Act of Adjournal (Summary Proceedings) (Children) 1971, it has never been suggested that these interests afforded any ground of objection to the competency and compellability of a parent as a prosecution witness. I am therefore quite unable to see that they should constitute such a ground of objection in a hearing before the Sheriff under section 42 of the Social

Work (Scotland) Act which can in no circumstances result in findings of guilt within the meaning of the criminal law or in conviction of the child of any crime. If, because of the position of the parent as guide and counsellor of the child in connection with any proceedings under Part III of the Act, it could be shown that certain communications made to the parent actually representing a child would, if made to a solicitor in the same situation, be protected by confidentiality, then no doubt objection could be taken to disclosure of the alleged confidential communication, but this in no way goes to the competence or compellability of such a parent as a witness and there is no good reason in law or fairness why it should. As to the strain which might be put upon the parent-child relationship if the parent were to be a competent and compellable witness at the instance of a reporter, I have only to say that such a strain could be expected in even greater measure in many cases whenever a parent is required to give evidence for the prosecution in a criminal trial.

In so far, therefore, as the Sheriff's decision depends upon the provisions of the Social Work (Scotland) Act 1968, I am unable to find in these provisions any colourable justification for it.

The Sheriff's third reason is derived from the Act of Sederunt (Social Work) (Sheriff Court Procedure Rules) 1971 and in particular rule 8 thereof. It can be briefly disposed of. I do not in the first instance understand that an Act of Sederunt made under the powers conferred on the Court by section 34 of the Administration of Justice (Scotland) Act 1933 could competently alter the general law governing the competency and compellability of witnesses in any judicial proceedings in the Sheriff Court for which Rules of Court are required. In any event the Rules in question are plainly procedural only. If an intention to change the law as to the competency and compellability of a parent as a reporter's witness in proceedings under section 42 of the Act of 1968 cannot be discovered in that Act, it certainly cannot be derived from a consideration of the terms of these Rules. In particular, I see nothing difficult in reconciling the right of a parent provided by rule 8 (2) to confine himself to making an unsworn statement, with the right of a reporter to call him as a witness if his evidence is required in proof of a ground of referral.

In the whole matter I am of opinion that as was said by the Lord Justice Clerk (Grant) in *Kennedy* v. *B. and Another* 1973 S.L.T. 38 at 41—'the basic rules of evidence must be observed.' I am therefore for answering question 1 in the negative. It follows that the appeals should be allowed and the cases should be remitted back to the Sheriff to enable the reporter to lead the evidence which was wrongly excluded. I regret the necessity for the remit back but it is inevitable. It might have been avoided with obvious advantages in time and expense had the Sheriff taken the course of hearing the evidence to the admission of which objection was successfully taken. This is plainly the course which ought properly to be followed in future in similar circumstances."

NOTE

The sheriff has no power to amend the grounds of referral which are brought before him by the reporter: *McGregor* v. *D.,* 1977 S.L.T. 183.

4. Social Work (Scotland) Act 1968

"**44.**—(1) Subject to the provisions of this Part of this Act a children's hearing, where, after the consideration of his case, they decide that a child is in need of compulsory measures of care, may make a requirement, in this Act referred to as a supervision requirement, requiring him—

(*a*) to submit to supervision in accordance with such conditions as they may impose; or

(*b*) to reside in a residential establishment named in the requirement and be subject to such conditions as they may impose;

and a condition imposed by virtue of head (*a*) of this subsection may be a condition as to the place where the child is to reside, being a place other than a residential establishment, and the place may be a place in England or Wales where arrangements have been made in that behalf."

NOTES

1. No child may continue to be subject to a supervision requirement for any time longer than is necessary in his interest, and where the local authority think that in the interests of the child a requirement should be varied or brought to an end, they shall refer the case to their reporter for review of that requirement by a children's hearing. The hearing may continue the requirement, vary it, or terminate it: 1968 Act, s. 47.

2. In any event the supervision requirement is subject to review under section 48 of the 1968 Act by the children's hearing, and no supervision requirement shall remain in force for a period extending beyond one year. Where a requirement is not reviewed within the period of one year from the making or continuing of the requirement it ceases to have effect at the expiration of that period: s. 48(3).

3. Within the time-table provided for by section 48(4) a child or its parent may require a review of the requirement.

4. A child or parent or both may, within three weeks of the date of any decision of a children's hearing appeal to the sheriff in chambers against that decision, provided that it is a decision as to the final disposal of the hearing: s. 49(1); *H.* v. *McGregor,* 1973 S.C. 95.

5. Appeal lies to the Court of Session by way of stated case on a point of law or in respect of any irregularity in the conduct of the case, at the instance of a child or its parent or both or a reporter acting on behalf of a children's hearing, from any decision of the sheriff under Part III of the 1968 Act: 1968 Act, s. 50.

6. Section 50 cannot be employed to bring under review the

decision of the hearing to impose a supervision requirement where the sole ground of the objection to that requirement is that the treatment prescribed thereby is inappropriate for the child: 1968 Act, s. 50(4).

CHAPTER 18

EXTRAORDINARY REMEDIES

a. The nobile officium of the High Court

"In addition to its powers of review, the High Court of Justiciary, as the supreme Court in criminal matters, has, in respect of its *nobile officium*, the power of interfering in extraordinary circumstances, for the purpose of preventing injustice or oppression. although there may not be any judgment, conviction, or warrant brought under review." (Moncreiff on *Review in Criminal Cases*, p.264.) Procedure is by way of petition to the *nobile officium* of the High Court, and such petitions may be taken by an accused or convicted person, the Crown (see, *e.g.* H.M. Advocate v. Greene, 1976 S.L.T. 120) or other aggrieved party (see, *e.g. Wan Ping Nam* v. *Federal German Republic Minister of Justice and Others, post*, and *Lloyds and Scottish Finance Ltd.* v. *H.M. Advocate*, 1974 S.L.T. 3). A single judge of the High Court cannot entertain an application to the *nobile officium*. It must be presented to a quorum of the High Court (three judges): *H.M. Advocate* v. *Lowson*, (1909) 2 S.L.T. 329.

1. **Wan Ping Nam v. Federal German Republic Minister of Justice and Others**
1972 S.L.T. 220

OPINION OF THE COURT: "This is a petition presented under the nobile officium to the High Court by one Wan Ping Nam, who has been committed as a fugitive offender to the prison of Barlinnie by the sheriff at Greenock. The order so committing him was made under s. 10 of the Extradition Act 1870. The prayer of the petition in effect seeks relief, by way of suspension of the committal order, it being alleged in the petition that it was unlawful, in respect that the petitioner is a British subject. It should be explained that by the Federal Republic of Germany (Extradition) Order (S.I. 1375), which gave effect to the subsisting agreement between Her Majesty's Government and the Federal German Republic for the extradition of fugitive criminals, it is provided inter alia by art. 4 of the First Schedule thereof, that no British subject shall be delivered up by the Government of the United Kingdom to the Government of the Federal Republic of Germany. It follows from these terms of the statutory instrument, under reference to s. 6 of the Extradition Act 1870, that where the alleged criminal is a British subject the Act does not apply in the case of the Federal Republic of Germany; and that no British subject is a person 'liable to be apprehended and surrendered in manner provided by' the Act.

The background against which the petition falls to be considered is briefly as follows. In February 1972 the petitioner was a member of the crew of the motor vessel *Taiping* registered in Bremen in the Federal Republic of Germany. This ship, which may be owned by the Island Navigation Company, Hong Kong, was then on charter to a West German company. While the ship was at sea the chief steward, one Ho On Hing, was the victim of an incident, as the result of which he later died. On 11th February 1972, when the ship called at Campbeltown, the petitioner, who was suspected of the murder of Ho On Hing, was removed from the ship by the police. On 12th February 1972, he appeared on petition before the sheriff at Campbeltown upon a charge of murder, and was committed to prison for further examination. On 18th February 1972, the petitioner was committed to prison until liberated in due course of law. Subsequently, when it was ascertained that the crime with which the petitioner had been charged had been committed on the high seas, he was formally liberated by administrative action. He was, however, at once rearrested and the proceedings with which this petition is concerned were begun. These were proceedings under the Extradition Act 1870.

Essentially what happened was that a warrant for the apprehension of the petitioner as a fugitive criminal was issued by the sheriff at Greenock acting under s. 8 of the Extradition Act 1870. An order from the Secretary of State was then presented to the sheriff signifying that a requisition for the surrender of the petitioner under the Extradition Act 1870 had been made by the Federal German Republic. Thereupon, the sheriff, after a hearing on 3rd May 1972, committed the petitioner to the prison at Barlinnie pending his possible surrender to the Federal German Republic. It is against the order so committing him, which purported to be made under s. 10 of the Act, that this petition is directed.

This petition was served upon the Minister of Justice of the Federal Republic of Germany, the Secretary of State for Scotland and Her Majesty's Advocate. At the hearing before us all three respondents were represented and the primary question for our decision was whether the relief sought by the petitioner was available at the hands of this court.

It is clear from an examination of the Extradition Act 1870 (and the problem before us is not affected by any of the subsequent amendments to that Act) that it was contemplated that proceedings with a view to the extradition of a fugitive criminal would normally be before a police magistrate in England. Indeed the statute is couched in language which plainly has the jurisdiction and the procedure of the English courts primarily in mind. In particular, s. 10, which deals with the stage of committal of the alleged fugitive criminal to prison, is in the following terms:—'10. In the case of a fugitive criminal accused of an extradition crime, if the foreign warrant authorising the arrest of such criminal is duly authenticated, and such evidence is produced as (subject to the provisions of this Act) would, according to the law of England, justify the committal for trial of the prisoner if the crime of which he is accused had been committed in England, the police magistrate shall commit him to prison, but otherwise shall order him to be discharged.

'In the case of a fugitive criminal alleged to have been convicted of an extradition crime, if such evidence is produced as (subject to the provisions of this Act) would, according to the law of England, prove that the prisoner was convicted of such crime, the police magistrate shall commit him to prison, but otherwise shall order him to be discharged.

'If he commits such criminal to prison, he shall commit him to the Middlesex House of Detention, or to some other prison in Middlesex, there to await the warrant of a Secretary of State for his surrender, and shall forthwith send to a Secretary of State a certificate of the committal, and such report upon the case as he may think fit.'

Where a person has been committed under s. 10 the procedure under s. 11 then comes into play. This section, which deals with the surrender of the fugitive criminal upon a warrant granted by the Secretary of State, opens thus:—'If the police magistrate commits a fugitive criminal to prison, he shall inform such criminal that he will not be surrendered until after the expiration of 15 days, and that he has a right to apply for a writ of habeas corpus.'

From what we have said so far it is plain that had the petitioner been committed to prison by a police magistrate in England, relief by way of application to the court for a writ of habaes corpus would have been available to him. As we understand it, this prerogative writ provides, in England, the means by which unlawful detention can be brought to an end by the High Court. It need hardly be said that it does not run in Scotland and is wholly unknown to our law.

We come now to s. 16 of the Act which deals with extraditable crimes committed on the high seas. So far as is relevant to the problem before us it is in the following terms:—

"16. Where the crime in respect of which the surrender of a fugitive criminal is sought was committed on board any vessel on the high seas which comes into any port of the United Kingdom, the following provisions shall have effect:

1. This Act shall be construed as if any stipendiary magistrate in England or Ireland, and any sheriff or sheriff-substitute in Scotland, were substituted for the police magistrate throughout this Act, except the part relating to the execution of the warrant of the police magistrate:

2. The criminal may be committed to any prison to which the person committing him has power to commit persons accused of the like crime'. It is as the result of these provisions of s. 16 that the sheriff at Greenock came to commit the petitioner to prison under s. 10 of the Act.

When, however, s. 11 is construed as provided by s. 16, paras. 1 and 2, it will be seen at once that the only form of relief expressly mentioned as being available to a person who has been committed by a sheriff under s. 10, is one which is unknown to the law of Scotland. In this situation, and since the statute, read as a whole, provides no means whereby a person committed by a sheriff in Scotland can seek his release from detention under an unlawful order purporting to be made under s. 10, the question is whether this court can and should under its inherent power to prevent injustice, supply the apparent omission in the Act by affording a remedy to the petitioner. It is to be noted in passing that this is not the only point at which, in the statute, there is an omission to deal with the consequences of a committal order pronounced in Scotland. There appears, indeed, to be a similar omission as regards Scotland in the procedure provided by s. 12 for the discharge of persons committed but not surrendered within two months. By s. 17 (4) Parliament expressly recognised the need to secure that his power of discharging a criminal should be available to a judge of any court exercising, in a British possession, the like powers as the court of Queen's Bench exercises in England. As in the case of s. 11, however, the Act gives no recognition to the contingency that a fugitive criminal may have been committed under s. 10 within the jurisdiction of the courts in Scotland.

The answer to this question depends essentially upon the intention of the Act. In our opinion the intention that relief shall be available to all persons committed under s. 10 is plain. This we discover from the express reference to habeas corpus procedure in s. 11. In any event, we cannot decern in the statute any indication of an intention that persons committed by a sheriff in Scotland should be in any less advantageous position than those committed by a police magistrate in England. In these circumstances we are in no doubt that, the statute having disclosed the intention, this court has ample power to provide what the statute has omitted to provide, namely, the means of giving effect to that intention. As we were reminded recently in the case of *Wylie and Another* v. *H.M. Advocate,* 1966 S.L.T. 149, at p. 151 — 'This court, of course, is not a mere creation of recent statutes; it has as Alison, *Criminal Law of Scotland,* Vol. II, p. 23, states: "The exclusive power of providing a remedy for all extraordinary or unforeseen occurrences in the course of criminal business whether before themselves or any inferior court. Akin to the well-known nobile officium of the Court of Session is a similar power enjoyed by Justiciary Court". Moncreiff on *Review in Criminal Cases,* p. 264, states: "In addition to its power of reviewing, the High Court of Justiciary as the Supreme Court in criminal matters has in respect of its nobile officium the power of interfering in extraordinary circumstances for the purpose of preventing injustice or oppression although there may not be any judgment, conviction or warrant brought under review". The same proposition is to be found in Macdonald on *Criminal Law,* at p. 193'. In our opinion, the circumstances of this case to which we have drawn attention are, on any view, extraordinary and we are satisfied that in the exercise of the nobile officium this court may properly examine the allegation of injustice made by the petitioner, and suspend the order under which the petitioner is committed if it should be established that it is unlawful in the respect set out in the petition. In the whole matter, we shall order the respondents to lodge answers to this petition, if so advised, within seven days, when the case will be put out by order for further procedure. This procedure may involve inquiry into the petitioner's claim to be a British subject. Any necessary inquiry will take place before one of our number. In so saying we observe that a similar claim was investigated, de novo, in England, by the court itself, in the case of *Re Guerin* (1889) 58 L.J. 42."

Answers were lodged. After inquiry it was held that the petitioner had failed to prove that he was a British subject. The court then refused the prayer of the petition.

NOTE

The *nobile officium* was invoked by a person in custody where no other remedy existed. The problem arose because the remedy envisaged by the Extradition Act 1870 (*habeas corpus*) is not available in Scotland — a classic *casus improvisus* attributable to the draftsman omitting to bear in mind Scottish procedures when drafting United Kingdom legislation. A similar problem arose in *Lloyds and Scottish Finance Ltd.* v. *H.M. Advocate* (*supra*). The petitioners hired a vehicle to P. under a contract of hire purchase. P. was subsequently convicted of reset, the stolen goods being found in the car. The sheriff made a forfeiture order in respect of the car, under section 23 of the Criminal Justice Act 1972. As the 1972 Act applied to England, section 23(3) afforded the true owners of property forfeited an opportunity to vindicate their rights to the property. That subsection did not apply in Scotland. The court held since Parliament had clearly expressed the intention that the rights of third parties should be protected, but had merely omitted to provide the appropriate machinery for Scotland, the *nobile officium* could be invoked to protect the rights of the petitioners.

2. Bernard Heslin, Petitioner
1973 S.L.T. (Notes) 56

The Act of Adjournal (Criminal Legal Aid Fees) 1964 (as amended by the Act of Adjournal of 29th November 1968) provided by s. 13 (2):—

'It shall be competent immediately on conclusion of the trial for the counsel or solicitor who appeared for the accused to make oral application to the court for a certificate that the case has necessarily been one of exceptional length, complexity or difficulty.

If such a certificate shall be granted, then any limitation contained in the foregoing paragraphs, or such of them as are referred to in such certificate, on the amount of any fee payable shall not apply and such fees shall be allowed, after taking into account all the relevant circumstances of the case, in respect of the work done, as appears to represent fair remuneration according to the work actually and reasonably done, due regard being had to economy.'

The petitioner had acted as solicitor for a man accused of murder, who pleaded not guilty and tendered a special defence of self-defence. In preparing the case the petitioner precognosced 42 Crown witnesses and 16 defence witnesses, in addition to carrying out a great deal of other work. As questions of forensic medicine arose, he instructed a pathologist to attend the post-mortem. The trial occupied three days, and the accused was eventually convicted of culpable homicide. At the conclusion of the trial counsel, who had been instructed by the petitioner, applied for a certificate under s. 13 (2). The trial judge stated that in his opinion the case was no more difficult, complex or longer than the usual murder trial, and refused the application. He also refused to adjourn the hearing of the application to chambers.

There being no provision for appeal, the petitioner presented a petition to the High Court of Justiciary craving the court to exercise its nobile officium by reviewing the trial judge's decision.

The court (Lord Justice-Clerk (Wheatley), Lords Milligan and Kissen) heard the petition on 24th May 1973.

In arguing that the petition was competent and that the decision of the trial judge should be reviewed in respect that he had wrongly exercised his discretion in refusing to adjourn to chambers and in refusing to grant the application, counsel for the petitioner referred to *H.M. Advocate* v. *Gray*, 1969 J.C. 35; *J. P. Hartley* [1968] J.C.L. 191; and *H.M. Advocate* v. *Wylie*, 1966 S.L.T. 149. Counsel for the Crown argued that while the court might exercise its nobile officium where there was a casus improvisus or a lacuna in a statute, as in *Wan Ping Nam*, 1972 S.L.T. 220, in the instant case it could not do so, as there was no casus improvisus but merely an intention in the Act of Adjournal that the trial judge alone should decide. The petition was therefore incompetent.

Eo die the court held that the Act of Adjournal intended that the decision on applications under s. 13 (2) should be entirely in the discretion of the trial judge and *refused* the petition as incompetent.

Petition refused.

3. Rae, Petitioner
1982 S.L.T. 233

OPINION OF THE COURT: "This petition invites the court to exercise its nobile officium by reviewing the refusal of the trial judge to grant to the petitioner a certificate under para. 13 (2) of the Act of Adjournal (Criminal Legal Aid Fees) 1964 as amended.

The petitioner acted as solicitor for a youth named William Albert Speirs, who, with five co-accused, stood trial on indictment in the High Court upon a charge of murder and a charge of attempted murder. All were in receipt of legal aid. At the conclusion of the trial which lasted for eight days, Speirs and four of his co-accused were convicted as libelled.

According to the petition the petitioner carried out a great deal of work in preparation for this trial, in which Speirs lodged a special defence of alibi, and claims, no doubt correctly, that the maximum fees available to her under para. 6 of the act of adjournal represent wholly inadequate remuneration for her professional services. In these circumstances junior counsel on her instructions moved the trial judge, when the trial had ended, to grant a para. 13 (2) certificate on the grounds of the exceptional length, complexity and difficulty of the case, or, alternatively, on the grounds of exceptional length alone. Similar motions were made on behalf of the solicitors acting for all Speirs' co-accused on the single ground that the case had necessarily been one of exceptional length. The motions on behalf of these solicitors were granted at once. The motion on behalf of the petitioner was not.

In the petition it is averred that the senior counsel who was instructed by the petitioner to represent Speirs was a Member of Parliament and was absent on Parliamentary business for some days during the trial. According to the petition it appears that at the hearing of the application on the petitioner's behalf, and thereafter, what happened was as follows:

[His Lordship then narrated the following facts as set out in the petition:]

"In respect of the application made on behalf of the petitioner his Lordship made an observation to the effect that the agents themselves could not have considered the case to be one of exceptional complexity if they had instructed as senior counsel someone who was to be absent for such a significant proportion of the trial. Junior counsel explained to his Lordship that he understood from the agents that senior counsel had confirmed his availability to them for the trial, and that at no time prior to the commencement of the trial were the agents given to understand that senior counsel would be absent for such a proportion of the trial. It was further submitted to his Lordship that notwithstanding his observations regarding complexity, the case was one of exceptional length and at least merited certification on that ground alone. His Lordship indicated that he was not prepared to grant said application to any extent and junior counsel then requested him to adjourn the application for a further hearing in chambers in terms of said paragraph. This request was granted. His Lordship indicated that in his view the petitioner was making very serious allegations against senior counsel whereupon junior counsel indicated that he wished to lodge written submissions in support of the application. In the interim junior counsel would himself speak to the partner in the petitioner's firm who had personally checked in advance on senior counsel's availability and would include in said written submissions a full account of the circumstances in which senior counsel had come to be instructed. A written submission was accordingly prepared and submitted to his Lordship. Said submission dealt with inter alia the circumstances in which senior counsel was instructed and his Lordship indicated that he was willing to hear junior counsel in further amplification thereof. Junior counsel explained that he had thoroughly investigated the matter. He had spoken to Mr Ross Harper, the senior partner of the petitioner's firm and had ascertained that Mr Harper had spoken to senior counsel on 24 November 1978 regarding his availability for the case, on which occasion senior counsel had confirmed his availability apart from the possibility that he might require to leave the court around mid-afternoon on one day of the trial to attend an evening engagement in Oxford. It was explained that Mr Harper was prepared to give evidence on oath to that effect, and that junior counsel was now specifically instructed to seek certification only on the ground of exceptional length. His Lordship indicated that it would not be necessary for Mr Harper to give evidence on oath, but that he considered the matter as very serious and wished further amplification in writing of the circumstances in which senior counsel came to be instructed as spoken to by junior counsel in support of the written submissions. He specifically indicated that if further specification were forthcoming, he would be prepared to grant the restricted application which was now being made. It was agreed that further written submissions would be prepared, and that a date would be arranged between junior counsel, the petitioners firm and his Lordship's clerk for a hearing in respect of the further written submissions. Further written submissions were prepared and were duly lodged and junior counsel appeared by arrangement with his Lordship's clerk on 21 December 1978 in chambers to review the earlier application. On said occasion his Lordship again refused said application."

Against the background of this narrative the petitioner avers that the whole written submissions submitted to the trial judge in support of the application dealt with the matters which had been raised by the trial judge as fully as could reasonably have been expected. She further avers that, in any event, the case in respect of Speirs was, in the matter of its length, indistinguishable from that of his co-accused. Her complaint is that, in refusing her application 'His Lordship exercised his discretion unreasonably and oppressively; and that he misdirected himself as to the elements in the case to which it was appropriate to have regard when considering an application for certification'.

At the hearing of the petition the petitioner's submissions were presented by the learned Dean of Faculty and were supported by counsel on behalf of the Law Society of Scotland. To the learned advocate-depute we are indebted for a brief submission made for our assistance.

In presenting his argument the learned Dean of Faculty recognised that it was expressly held in *Heslin, Petr.* that this court will not, in the exercise of its nobile officium, entertain an application seeking review of the refusal by a trial judge to grant a certificate under para. 13 (2) of the act of adjournal. The reasons for that decision are to be found in the full text of the opinion of the court in *Heslin* to which we have had access and we do not rehearse them here. Suffice it to say that it has not been suggested to us that the judgment in *Heslin* was not perfectly well founded. The submission was, however, that that judgment does not preclude us from interfering in the extraordinary circumstances of this case. Under reference to the discussion of the scope of the nobile officium of this court in the opinion of the court in the case of *Wan Ping Nam* v. *Federal German Republic Minister of Justice* it is clear that the power will be exercised to interfere in extraordinary circumstances for the purpose of preventing injustice or oppression. This petition is not to be regarded an an attempt to defeat the intention of the act of adjournal that there should be no right of appeal against a trial judge's discretionary decision in a para. 13 (2) application. The complaint which it makes is of an extreme nature and the petition, properly understood, discloses a decision taken in quite extraordinary circumstances, a decision which amounted to an abuse of the discretion confided to the trial judge, and which constituted an act of oppression leading to injustice.

We have no difficulty in accepting that the High Court of Justiciary as the supreme court in criminal matters has, in respect of its nobile officium, the power of interfering in extraordinary circumstances for the purpose of preventing injustice or oppression. We bear in mind, however, that this power may never be invoked when to do so would conflict with statutory intention clear or implied. These propositions which formed the background against which the decision in *Heslin, Petr.* was taken emerge clearly in the opinions of the court in the case of *Wan Ping Nam* and in the later case of *Anderson* v. *H.M. Advocate* and require no amplification here.

The real primary question to be decided in this case is however not as to the scope of the nobile officium of this court but whether we are precluded by the judgment of this court in *Heslin, Petr.* from entertaining the petitioner's complaint against the decision of the trial judge when it is properly understood. Upon consideration of the history disclosed in the petition and a report by the trial judge which he provided for us on our invitation, we have come to be of opinion, not without hesitation, that we should give effect to the learned Dean's submission. On consideration of all the circumstances in so far as they can be ascertained from these sources we conclude that this case is to be regarded essentially as one in which the trial judge did not, in the event, exercise his discretionary judgment at all upon the application, which in its final form, sought the grant of a certificate upon the ground of exceptional length alone. He refused the application but, when one considers the circumstances, it is reasonably clear that he did so, simply because he had formed a certain view of the behaviour of senior counsel for the accused Speirs. Initially, when he was moved to grant the application on all three grounds specified in para. 13, the conduct of that senior counsel might properly have been taken into account as a relevant consideration in relation to the issue of complexity. In its final form, however, the issues of complexity and difficulty disappeared and if, as seems likely, the trial judge proceeded to reject it only because of the absence of senior counsel for Speirs during part of the course of the trial, it may be said with justification that he did not apply his mind at all to the only issue before him, namely, whether to grant or refuse the application on the ground that the case had necessarily been one of exceptional length. It will be recalled that applications upon the same ground, made by solicitors for the co-accused of Speirs, were granted by him without hesitation at the conclusion of the trial.

The circumstances of this case are exceptional and we are prepared to take the view that to neglect to consider the petitioner's application on its merits (for this is in effect and substance what the trial judge appears to have done) constituted oppression resulting in injustice. Notwithstanding the decision in *Heslin* that this court will not in the exercise of the nobile officium embark upon any review of a trial judge's decision of the issue before him in the exercise of his discretion, we are persuaded that our exceptional power should be exercised in this case to secure that the trial judge will address his mind to, and dispose of, the petitioner's application for a para. 13 certificate on the ground of exceptional length alone. We shall accordingly remit the petitioner's application with a direction to the trial judge to dispose of it on its merits. There can be no question of its disposal by this court because disposal is for the trial judge alone and because a certificate of a trial judge is the only certificate which may be recognised for the purpose of para. 13."

> Application remitted to trial judge who, after considering the application on its merits, granted the application.

NOTES

1. *Heslin* and *Rae* should be read along with *Harper, Petitioner*, 1982 S.L.T. 232 and *Lloyds and Scottish Finance Ltd.* v. *H.M. Advocate* (*supra*). These cases make it clear that a distinction should be drawn between the case of the true *lacuna* or *casus omissus* in legislation and the case where it is the intention of the legislator not to provide for a method of review or other remedy. Thus in the case of para. 13(2) the absence of a method of review was not due to an oversight, but rather it was the intention of the legislation that the court's discretion should not be subject to review. This may be contrasted with the situation in *Lloyds and Scottish Finance Ltd.* v. *H.M. Advocate* where the lack of protection for third party rights arose not from the intention of Parliament but from an oversight on its part. Where the intention of the legislator is clearly expressed it cannot be avoided by an application to the *nobile officium*. (For a further discussion of this point, see *Anderson* v. *H.M. Advocate, infra.*)

2. The *nobile officium* of the High Court cannot be invoked to review the merits of a decision taken on a matter which falls within the sole discretion of a judge or court. Where, however, the court fails to address its mind to the real issues (as in *Rae*) or refuses to decide the case at all (as in *Harper*) such failure or refusal may be reviewed by the High Court so as to ensure a proper exercise of that discretion. This principle applies even where the refusal to entertain a case is based on the well-founded view that it would not be competent to do so (*Harper*).

3. Where the High Court is prepared to intervene on the above grounds it is clear that it will not substitute its own decision on the merits (*Rae, Heslin*).

4. The particular problem raised by these cases has now been provided for by an amendment to paragraph 13: see Act of Adjournal (Criminal Legal Aid Fees Amendment) 1982 (see 1982 S.L.T. (News) 67). This amendment does not, of course, affect the general principles derived from these cases.

4.   Anderson v. H.M. Advocate
1974 S.L.T. 239

The petitioner was charged on summary complaint with breach of the peace. He tendered a plea of not guilty and lodged a special defence of alibi. He was convicted after trial and thereafter required the sheriff to state a case for the opinion of the High Court of Justiciary. The stated case was pursued to its conclusion when the court answered the only question of law in the affirmative and dismissed the appeal. The sole question raised by the appellant concerned the evaluation of evidence and the credibility of witnesses in the summary trial before the sheriff. Thereafter the appellant presented a petition to the *nobile officium* of the High Court craving that his conviction be quashed on the ground that there had been a miscarriage of justice in that the sheriff had failed in his appreciation of the evidence adduced before him and in his preparation of the stated case.

LORD JUSTICE-GENERAL (EMSLIE): "The petitioner was charged on summary complaint under the Summary Jurisdiction (Scotland) Act 1954 with breach of the peace during the hours of darkness on 18th December 1972. The complainers were two 14-year-old girls. To this charge the petitioner tendered a plea of not guilty and lodged a special defence of alibi. He was convicted after trial, and thereafter required the sheriff to state a case for the opinion of the High Court. The petitioner, being dissatisfied with the draft stated case, proposed extensive adjustments which the sheriff, to all but an insignificant extent, refused to incorporate in the case in its final form. The stated case was duly lodged and was pursued by the petitioner to its conclusion when the High Court, havng refused to remit the case back to the sheriff to amplify the findings-in-fact as they had been moved by counsel for the petitioner to do, answered the only question in the case in the affirmative and dismissed the appeal.

At the trial the only point at issue was the identification of the petitioner as the person involved in the offence and the sheriff convicted, as the stated case shows, because he believed and accepted as reliable the evidence of the two complainers, and because he must have disbelieved the evidence given by the petitioner. Notwithstanding the straightforward nature of the sole question for decision at the trial — a question essentially of credibility and reliability well within the competence of an experienced sheriff to resolve upon the evidence — the petitioner in this petition of quite remarkable length avers that a substantial miscarriage of justice has occurred and prays that the High Court in the exercise of its nobile officium should quash the conviction. The alleged substantial miscarriage of justice is said to be the result of (i) alleged failures in duty on the part of the sheriff in his appreciation and evaluation of the evidence led before him; (ii) alleged failures in duty on the part of the sheriff in the preparation of the stated case, in the course of which he declined to adjust the case on the lines desiderated by the petitioner; and (iii) alleged prejudice suffered by the petitioner in the conduct of his defence on the merits by reason of the method used by the police to identify him before he was charged, and by reason of the failure of the sheriff to find as proved facts certain evidence given by certain defence witnesses which, it is said, was not subject to express challenge in cross-examination on behalf of the Crown.

For the moment we shall say of these allegations only this: it is obvious that essentially they amount to no more than assertions that no reasonable sheriff should have held the identification of the petitioner by the two credible complainers as reliable in light of the whole evidence led at the trial, and that it was the duty of the sheriff not only to state his findings upon the sole question of disputed fact at issue in the trial but to incorporate in the stated case other facts which emerged in evidence which were relevant only to the assessment of the credibility of the petitioner and of the reliability of the complainer's evidence of the identification of the petitioner upon which the critical findings-in-fact depends. In short, it is plain from this petition that the petitioner is seeking once more to have the merits of his conviction reviewed.

With this introduction we now turn to the question of the competency of this petition which has been challenged by the Crown.

At the outset it is as well to remind ourselves of the true scope and purpose of the valuable but exceptional jurisdiction which the petitioner has invited us to exercise. As is stated by Alision, *Criminal Law of Scotland*, Vol. II, in the well-known passage beginning on p. 23: 'Akin to the well-known nobile officium of the Court of Session, is a similar power enjoyed by the Justiciary Court, of providing a remedy for any extraordinary or unforseen occurrence in the course of criminal business in any part of the country. This is an unusual remedy, not to be called into operation when any of the ordinary courts are adequate to the matter; but still abundantly established wherever no other means of extricating it appears. . . . In short, the principle is, that wherever the interposition of some authority is necessary to the administration of justice, and there exists no other judicature by whom it can competently be exercised; or which has been in use to exercise it, the Court of Justiciary is empowered and bound to exert its powers, on the application of a proper party, for the furtherance of justice.' To the same effect is Moncreiff in *Review in Criminal Cases*, p. 264, who says 'In addition to its power of reviewing, the High Court of Justiciary as the Supreme Court in criminal matters has in respect of its nobile officium the power of interfering in extraordinary circumstances for the purpose of preventing injustice or oppression although there may not be any judgment, conviction or warrant brought under review.' These classical descriptions of the power have been accepted by this court as authoritative in all cases in which the scope of its power under the nobile officium has been called in question, and as the cases show, have been interpreted to mean that the power will only be exercised where the circumstances are extraordinary or unforeseen, and where no other remedy or procedure is provided by the law. Examples of these cases which clearly show the approach which this court will follow in considering the competency of exercising this very special power are *Wylie and Another* v. *H.M. Advocate*, 1966 S.L.T. 149 and *Wan Ping Nam* v. *Minister of Justice of the Federal German Republic*, 1972 S.L.T. 220. In both of these cases the power was exercised because no procedure or remedy of any kind was available to the petitioners. To complete this review of the nature, scope and limits of the power we have only to add that the nobile officium of this court, and for that matter of the Court of Session, may never be invoked when to do so would conflict with statutory intention, express or clearly implied (see *Adair and Others* v. *Colville*, 1922 S.C 672, 1922 S.L.T. 532).

In light of this discussion of the law, what is the position of this application by this petitioner?

In the first place it cannot be said that the petition discloses any extraordinary or unforseen circumstances and it is clear that the primary justification for the exercise of the nobile officium cannot be said to exist. Summary prosecution and appeals have for long been governed by statute, and the relevant statute now in force is the Summary Jurisdiction (Scotland) Act 1954 as amended. Examination of that statute shows that for review of the merits of any summary conviction an adequate procedure was provided, and that is appeal by stated case. It is not in doubt that the intendment of the provisions of this Act is that although certain common law procedures were preserved to enable convictions to be challenged on grounds extraneous to the merits, the only mode of appeal competent where review of the merits of conviction is sought is appeal by stated case; and that in summary prosecutions the trial judge is to be final on all questions of fact. If authority were needed for the soundness of this interpretation of the statute it is to be found in *Rush* v. *Herron*, 1969 S.L.T. 211, in which the Lord Justice-General, in his opinion, stated the position thus: 'It is well settled in Scotland that, to quote the passage always referred to in this connection in Renton and Brown's *Criminal Procedure*, p. 316:—"The merits of a conviction cannot be reviewed in a suspension." There has been a long series of cases in which this principle has been laid down. The latest reported case is the decision in *Moffat* v. *Skeen*, 1963 J.C. 84, in which at p. 89, the following passage from Lord Wark is quoted from the case of *O'Hara* v. *Mill*, 1938 J.C. 4, at p. 7, 1938 S.L.T. 184, at p. 185: "Nothing", says Lord Wark, "is better settled in our criminal procedure than that the merits of a conviction cannot be reviewed in a process of suspension. Where it is the desire of a complainer against a conviction to evaluate the evidence his proper course is to apply for a stated case to the judge who has tried it, in order that the court may have before it an authoritative statement of what the evidence was and with the grounds upon which the judge proceeded." In the present case it is impossible to avoid the conclusion that the issue between the complainer and the respondent turns directly on a question of evaluation of evidence and the credibility of witnesses.

In the case of this petition it is just as impossible as it was in *Rush* (supra) to avoid the conclusion that the real issue between the petitioner and respondent turns directly on a question of the evaluation of evidence and the credibility of witnesses. For the ventilation of such a question Parliament has prescribed the sole remedy—a remedy, indeed, which the petitioner has resorted to and which has now been exhausted. On this ground alone we have no doubt that this petition is incompetent. Lest it be thought, however, that in so saying we have overlooked the petitioner's criticisms of the sheriff in relation to the preparation of the stated case we have to add that all these criticisms were advanced and rejected by the High Court of Justiciary which heard the petitioner's appeal. In delivering the opinion of the court the Lord Justice-Clerk said this:—

'It was forcibly submitted by appellant's counsel however, that the facts stated indicated that the sheriff had obviously accepted the evidence of identification given by the two girl complainers without due regard having been given to all the other evidence in the case which conflicted with the reliability of that identification. And that, in any event there were elements in the stated facts relating to their evidence which indicated that their identification was not reliable. On this latter point I confine myself to saying that the criticisms of the girls' evidence as stated were not well founded. These criticisms were valid matters of comment before the sheriff, and were admittedly made to him, but he did not regard them as affecting the reliability of their identification and that was a matter for him and not for this court. The stronger argument was that the sheriff had made no reference to the evidence adduced which reflected on, if not wholly contradicted, the accuracy of the girls' identification. This is perfectly true, and the question is whether his failure to do so vitiated the stated case as it stands, either to the extent of necessitating a quashing of the conviction, or at least remitting the case back to him, asking him to expand his note to explain why he had omitted to deal with this evidence in his note, and to make appropriate findings-in-fact relating to this evidence. When a case is being stated it is not necessary for every fact adduced in evidence to be incorporated. All that require to be included are the facts admitted or proved relevant to the charge under consideration. It is not necessary to state facts which are not relevant thereto. The judge stating the case has to provide a note explaining why he has reached his decision, but that does not require him to rehearse the whole of the evidence. He is not in the same position as a judge of first instance in a civil proof. The gravamen of the criticism by appellant's counsel was that the sheriff had believed the girls and had not taken into account the evidence adduced by the defence. This evidence was fully rehearsed before us, but we were informed that it has also been submitted to the sheriff. When submitting his alternative proposal that the case should be remitted back to the sheriff, for an explanation as to whether he took this evidence into account when he decided to accept the girls' evidence, appellant's counsel seemed to proceed on the assumption that the sheriff had not done so. I do not consider that the court is entitled to make this assumption. On the contrary, I think that there is a presumption that a sheriff, and indeed a very experienced sheriff, would take this elementary step in the administration of justice.'

With this opinion on the sheriff's duty in the circumstances of this case we entirely concur.

In the second place, however, the petition is clearly incompetent for quite a different reason. Section 68 of the Summary Jurisdiction (Scotland) Act 1954 is in the following terms:—

'(1) An appellant under s. 62 of this Act may at any time prior to lodging the case with the clerk of justiciary abandon his appeal by minute signed by himself or his solicitor, written on the complaint, or lodged with the clerk of court, and intimated to the respondent, but such abandonment shall be without prejudice to any other mode of appeal, review, advocation, or suspension competent. (2) On the case being lodged with the clerk of justiciary, the appellant shall be held to have abandoned any other mode of appeal which might otherwise have been open to him.'

By this section Parliament has provided expressly, in the interests of securing finality in summary criminal proceedings, that the right to follow any common law mode of appeal whatsoever should cease to be available the moment an appellant has elected to pursue the statutory mode of appeal, and election is of course, complete the moment a stated case has been lodged. In this case the petitioner not only lodged a stated case but pursued his chosen mode of appeal to an unsuccessful conclusion. In these circumstances, in the face of the clear and express statement of the intention of Parliament to which we have referred, it would be quite improper for this court to exercise its power under the nobile officium at the invitation of this petitioner. It is, no doubt, the fact, as the petitioner pointed out to us in argument, that this court has on one occasion exercised its power under the nobile officium to quash a conviction after a stated case had been lodged. The case was the case of *Patrick McCloy, Petitioner,* 1971 S.L.T. (Notes) 32. This case, however, does not assist the present petitioner since the question of competency was not considered at all, and all that can be said of the case of *McCloy* (supra) is that it disclosed a manifest, admitted, and quite exceptional miscarriage of justice before a magistrate who invented a witness to justify his alleged findings-in-fact. It did not, be it noted, involve in any way any question of review of the merits of conviction.

What we have said so far is sufficient for the disposal of the petition, but in the public interest there are certain observations we feel bound to make. We have already dealt with the ill-founded allegations of breach of duty on the part of the sheriff in connection with the preparation of the stated case. As to the remaining averments in the petition we are satisfied that they disclose no proper basis for the assertion that the sheriff failed in duty in any other respect. In this connection it is important to remember what was said by the Lord Justice-Clerk, in the passage which we have already quoted, in delivering the opinion of the court in this petitioner's appeal. It must not be forgotten that the credibility of the complainers is not disputed, and that the critical questions for the sheriff to resolve were as to the reliability of their evidence of identification of the petitioner which they undoubtedly gave in the witness box, and as to the credibility of the petitioner who denied having been the man involved. Both questions were essentially for decision by the sheriff who had the advantage, which no appellate court could have, of seeing and hearing the witnesses concerned. All the other evidence in the case, including the evidence of the way in which the police conducted their initial investigation, was relevant only to the solution of these two questions, and even if we were to assume that the petitioner's whole averments about this other evidence are true, it would be quite impossible for any appellate court to say that the sheriff was not entitled to reach the conclusion which he did. It is inconceivable that the experienced sheriff concerned in the case did not have regard to all this other evidence and to the arguments thereanent submitted to him by counsel for the petitioner, and there is accordingly no reason to suppose that, had this petition gone further, any 'oppression' or 'miscarriage of justice' would have been demonstrated."

The court held the
petition incompetent.

NOTES

1. This application was doomed from the start in that it was a virtually undisguised attempt to have the trial judge's decision on the facts reviewed by the High Court. This is not to say that the criticisms of the stated case procedure which lay behind this application were not well founded (although the Thomson Committee did not discover widespread demand for change in stated case procedure). Many of the defects highlighted by the *Anderson* case (the limitation to questions of law, the trial judge's absolute control over adjustments, etc., have been met by the changes to stated case procedure brought about by the 1980 Act; as to which, see *supra*, Chap. 15, and Renton and Brown, Chap. 16.

2. The *Anderson* case illustrates the point that the *nobile officium* cannot be invoked to supplement an established procedure, even where the defects in that procedure are recognised. The existence of a process of review was fatal. It would have been otherwise if there had been no such process. Thus in *Wylie and Another* v. *H.M. Advocate*, 1966 S.L.T. 149 it was held that the *nobile officium* could competently be invoked to appeal against the imposition of a three-year sentence for contempt of court where no other form of appeal was available. Notice also the court's insistence that the matter to be brought under review must be "extraordinary and unforeseen." As to this, see *Mathieson, infra.*

3. For an examination of this case and its wider implications, see *The Case of David Anderson*, a Report for Justice prepared by a Scottish Working Party, 1978.

5. Mathieson, Petitioner
1980 S.L.T. 74

An accused person appealed against a sentence of five years' detention in a young offender's institution and then abandoned his appeal. He subsequently presented a petition to the nobile officium craving the High Court to review his sentence. On 21 February 1980 the High Court granted the prayer of the petition and allowed the petitioner to be heard on the question of sentence.

OPINION OF THE COURT: "This is a petition presented to the nobile officium of this court by James Mathieson, presently a prisoner in H.M. Remand Unit at Longriggend. Mathieson is a young man, just 18 now, who pled guilty when charged on indictment to the crime of wilful fire-raising. After sundry procedure including the obtaining of a series of psychiatric reports Mathieson was remitted for sentence to the High Court. In the High Court, when further psychiatric reports had been considered and when the evidence of two psychiatrists had been led before the judge concerned with sentencing, the sentence imposed on Mathieson was one of five years' detention in a young offender's institution. Thereafter it was desired by Mathieson, with legal advice, to challenge that sentence as excessive. To that end an application for legal aid was made and granted and a note of application for leave to appeal against sentence was duly lodged. What happened thereafter was that without consulting his legal advisers, and it seems on the advice of his mother, this young man signed on his own behalf and lodged a note of abandonment of his proposed appeal against sentence. By statute the effect of the lodging of that note was of course that his appeal is deemed to have been dismissed and there is now no statutory means by which the sentence can be examined by this court. It is for this reason that the petitioner invites the court, in the exercise of its nobile officium, to take the extraordinary step, in spite of the lodging of the note of abandonment of his appeal, of allowing him to be heard on the question of his sentence. The law as to the scope and purpose of the valuable by exceptional jurisdiction which the court possesses is fully set out in the case of *Anderson* v. *H.M. Advocate*, 1974 S.L.T. 239. For that reason it is unnecessary to rehearse it here. From that case it is plain, we think, that the power which this court undoubtedly possesses will be exercised to avoid possible miscarriages of justice or to cure a miscarriage of justice in circumstances which are both extraordinary and unforeseen provided that to exercise the power would not defeat the intention of Parliament as that intention may appear in public general statutes. The question for us in this petition is whether the circumstances which have been disclosed, and these circumstances not only include what is contained in the petition itself but in the various reports to which our attention has been drawn, can be described as sufficiently extraordinary and unforeseen to justify us in granting the prayer of the petition. Without rehearsing the details of the matter we have come to be of opinion that the prayer should in this case be granted simply upon the very special ground that the circumstances are sufficiently extraordinary and unforeseen and unlikely to be repeated. For these reasons the petition succeeds and the opportunity to argue sentence will be permitted to the petitioner."

The court granted
the prayer of the petition.

NOTES

1. There is clearly a link between the *casus omissus* and the "extraordinary and unforseen" situation, and indeed the latter is capable of encompassing the former. This case illustrates the point that "extraordinary and unforeseen" circumstances may arise above and beyond the case of the *casus omissus*. Compare, on this point, *Fenton, Petitioner*, 1982 S.L.T. 164. A convicted person lodged a note of appeal against sentence, and at the same time applied for interim liberation pending his appeal. This was refused. An appeal against this refusal was also lodged, but not within the 24-hour time-limit required by section 446 (2) of the 1975 Act as amended. The appellant then presented a petition to the *nobile officium* seeking admission to bail. The High Court refused the petition:

"In our view it is not for the court to exercise its power under the nobile officium simply because an accused or his legal advisers have been mindless of a statutory time-table. If it were otherwise the court could be flooded with petitions to the nobile officium. If the legislature intended that failure to obtemper a strict time-table could be excused on cause shown, that could have been provided for in the statute, as is the case in other procedural matters. That was not done and there is no justification for considering that this was a casus omissus. A statutory procedure was enacted, and in the absence of any provision to excuse non-compliance, non-compliance is fatal. The exercise of the nobile officium should not be regarded as the kiss of life in such circumstances."

It could be said that if Parliament had intended that an abandonment of appeal could be withdrawn on cause shown that too could have been provided for. No doubt the flood-gates argument is as strong (or as weak) in relation to bail applications as anywhere else, but it seems difficult to justify the court's refusal of a remedy whatever the circumstances. What would have been the situation if, for example, the applicant in *Fenton* had been incorrectly advised by his legal advisers?

2. Compare the fate of the petitioner in *Mathieson* with that of the petitioner in *Ferguson, Petitioner* (*supra*, Chap. 14).

b.   The Royal Prerogative

H.M. Advocate v. Waddell
1976 S.L.T. (Notes) 61;
High Court, 29 November 1976, unreported
(For the background to this case see *H.M. Advocate* v. *Waddell.*
supra, p. 20.)

LORD ROBERTSON: ". . .A further matter of some importance appeared in the course of the argument. It seems that one of the witnesses elicited by the Crown in the present case, Patrick Connolly Meehan, has already been convicted of the robbery and murder which formed the basis of charge 2 against Waddell. On appeal the conviction was apparently upheld and has never been quashed by this court. The Crown however refer to the pardon granted to him 'in respect of the said conviction' under the Royal Prerogative. The terms of the pardon produced did not appear to go further than 'pardoning, remitting and releasing unto him all pains, penalties and punishments whatsoever', coming from the same conviction. It was argued by the Lord Advocate on behalf of the Crown that the effect of the pardon was to purge the offences and was equivalent to quashing the conviction. In reply it was submitted on behalf of Waddell that the pardon did not quash the conviction which remains standing and was extractable. Apparently there is no other case in which this point has been considered or has even arisen. It is to be noted that the Crown has not chosen in the Meehan case to proceed as it could have done to attempt to have the conviction quashed in the original appeal court. This procedure was carried out in the Oscar Slater case in 1928 (*Slater* v. *H.M. Advocate*, 1928 S.L.T. 602).
It seems to me that this matter may well be of critical importance at a later stage. The point has not formally been presented on behalf of Waddell as a plea in bar of trial and it is not prima facie clear at this stage that the Crown have proceeded incompetently in presentation of the indictment against Waddell. As the Lord Advocate said there is no rule of law which renders the procedure so far incompetent. It is therefore in my view premature to decide this point at this stage. I should add that it was expressly conceded by the Lord Advocate on behalf of the Crown, as I understood him, that he would be bound to withdraw charge 2 against Waddell if it were found that the conviction against Meehan stands.
In the result I shall repel the preliminary pleas on behalf of the panels."

> The preliminary pleas having
> been repelled, the accused
> tendered a plea of not guilty.
> The legal effect of the Free
> Pardon granted to Meehan
> was further considered at the
> trial:

LORD ROBERTSON: "When the Crown led a police officer as a witness to speak to charge 2 of the indictment, counsel for the accused Waddell objected on the ground that it was incompetent for the Crown to lead evidence in relation to this charge as there is a conviction standing against Patrick Connolly Meehan, witness no. 94 on the Crown list. Extract conviction defence production no. 7 was referred to. It showed that Meehan was convicted of the crime libelled in charge 2 of the present indictment, no notice being made of any pardon in the margin of the record of conviction to which it applies.

The argument presented on behalf of Waddell elaborated upon the argument presented in the course of the diet on 5 October 1976 when I repelled it as not truly a plea in bar of trial. In view of the importance attached to the argument by the Lord Advocate, I adjourned the trial for consideration of the objection by a larger court.

It was argued that the conviction of Meehan for the murder still stands as extractable and has indeed been extracted. The pardon, defence production No. 8, has not had the effect of quashing the conviction. What it says is that the Sovereign, by virtue of the Royal Prerogative, was graciously pleased to extend Her Grace and Mercy to the said Patrick Connolly Meehan and to grant him a Free Pardon in respect of said conviction, thereby pardoning, remitting and releasing unto him all pains, penalties and punishments whatsoever that from the said conviction may come.

The effect of this pardon, according to counsel for Waddell was not to quash the conviction. It was conceded on behalf of the Crown that there was no question of Meehan and Waddell acting together. It was incompetent now for the Crown, standing Meehan's conviction, to prosecute another person for the same crime. In my opinion, this argument is unsound. No principle or law or authority was put forward in support of it. I see no reason why the previous conviction of an individual upon a particular charge should, of itself, render incompetent subsequent prosecution of another person for the same offence.

Circumstances may readily be envisaged under which such a prosecution might be required in the interests of justice. It must be for the Lord Advocate, in his discretion, to decide whether such circumstances exist in any particular case. It is not necessary, in my view, to consider the exact meaning and effect of the Free Pardon, which is not a live issue, the decision of which is necessary for the proper conduct of this trial. The existence of such a pardon would no doubt be one of the circumstances which the Lord Advocate would take into account when exercising his discretion. This is enought to decide the point of competency taken by counsel for Waddell in his objection to the evidence.

Counsel for Waddell, however, took a further point that the Crown was now barred from proceeding further against his client in view of certain remarks made by the Lord Advocate at the first diet on the 5 October 1976 and in the course of argument following upon the present objection. These remarks were represented as amounting to a concession, that unless the effect of the Free Pardon was equivalent to a quashing of Meehan's conviction, he would not proceed further against Waddell on charge 2.

I have carefully considered the remarks in question and have studied the transcript of certain passages in the debate of 5 October 1976. These remarks, while they might be construed as conditional concessions, are couched in imprecise terms. In my view, they are not properly to be regarded as duly considered and accurately formulated concessions as to the circumstances in which the Lord Advocate might decide not to proceed. I do not think that they amount to such unequivocal statements as to justify the principle of *Thom* v. *H.M. Advocate*, 1976 S.L.T. 232, being applied.

In any event, I do not consider that it is the proper function of the court to give rulings on questions of law which do not have to be decided to the proper conduct of the trial, merely for the purpose of deciding whether concessions expressed as conditional are to be given a practical effect.

I should add that Lord Keith and Lord Maxwell, who heard the arguments, agree with what I have said. I shall repel the objection."

Objection repelled. The
jury returned a verdict of
not guilty.

NOTES

1. For a full discussion of the issues raised by this case see Gane, "The Effect of a Pardon in Scots Law," 1980 J.R. 18.

2. Lord Robertson returned to the question of the effect of the pardon during his charge to the jury (*supra*, p. 22). There he expressed the opinion that "in the ordinary use of language . . . if you pardon someone, you pardon them for something that they have done, and not for something that they haven't done. This indeed is an interpretation supported by the actual terms of the Free Pardon itself which appear to free Meehan from the consequences of the conviction and not from the conviction itself. It certainly doesn't quash the conviction by due process of law."

His Lordship may well be correct with regard to the "ordinary use of language" but it is clear that in several instances the Royal Pardon has been used to remedy clear miscarriages of justice, including wrongful conviction, (as to which, see Gane, *loc. cit.* and C.H. Rolph, *The Queen's Pardon*, Chap. 6). As regards the effect of the pardon, it appears that much of the confusion arises from the archaic language of the Free Pardon as presently expressed, and from the assumption that that term, as used in *English* law, has the same meaning in Scots law. In English law a "free pardon" is recognised as not only removing the consequences of conviction, but of removing the conviction itself: *Hay* v. *Justices of the Tower Division of London* [1890] 24 Q.B.D. 561. In Scotland, the term probably has no greater significance than the distinction between an unconditional ("free") pardon, and a conditional pardon. Even then, the pardon probably only extends to the consequences of conviction and not to the conviction itself, unless by its terms it expressly states otherwise.

Lord Robertson's opinion that the pardon cannot quash a conviction appears to be shared by the government (see the statement of the Solicitor-General during the Scottish Grand Committee Debate on the Hunter Report on the murder of Mrs Rachel Ross and its aftermath: (1983) 76 SCOLAG Bul. 7). It is submitted, however, that a properly worded pardon could, under Scots law, extend to the conviction itself.

The obvious solution is a revision of the wording of the present "Free Pardon" so as to make it clear what its effect is intended to be. The view has been expressed, however, that this might raise certain difficult issues as to the extent of the Royal Prerogative: Hunter Report, Comment No. 4, p. 1014.

3. As noted in Chap. 14, the appeal procedures contained in the 1975 Act have no effect on the prerogative of mercy: 1975 Act, s. 263(1), and see the case of *Leitch* v. *Secretary of State for Scotland* (*supra*, p. 457).

c.   The European Convention on Human Rights

The provisions of the Convention guaranteeing minimum procedural standards in the criminal process are set out in Chap. 1. The Convention is not limited, of course, to the regulation of procedures, but is intended also to secure certain substantive rights and freedoms. A discussion of these matters would be out of place in a work such as this, but it is felt that an outline of the procedures established to ensure the observance of the Convention by its signatories might usefully be included here.

The institutions

Article 19 of the Convention establishes two institutions whose function is "to ensure the observance of the engagements undertaken by the High Contracting Parties". The institutions are (1) the European Commission on Human Rights, and (2) The European Court of Human Rights (The Commission was set up immediately following upon the entry into force of the Convention. By article 56, however, election of judges to the Court was made conditional upon recognition of the Court's compulsory jurisdiction by at least eight states. This condition was not satisfied until five years after the entry into force of the Convention.)

The members of the Commission are elected by the Committee of Ministers of the Council of Europe for a period of six years. The Commission consists of a number of members equal to that of the high contracting parties (though there is no requirement that members be nationals of a high contracting party). No two members of the Commission may be nationals of the same state. Members of the Commission sit in their individual capacity, *i.e.* not as representatives of any state. No special qualifications are laid down in the Convention for membership of the Commission, although members of the Commission traditionally have held qualifications similar to those required of judges of the Court.

Members of the Court are elected for a period of nine years by the Consultative Committee of the Council of Europe from a list of persons nominated by the Members of the Council. Candidates for election "shall be of high moral character and must either possess the qualifications required for appointment to high judicial office or be jurisconsults of recognised competence" (article 39(3)). The Court consist of a number of judges equal to that of the Members of the Council of Europe (*i.e.* it is not limited to the number of high contracting parties) and no two judges may be nationals of the same state.

In addition to these specially created bodies, the Committee of Ministers of the Council of Europe exercises certain judicial functions in accordance with article 32 of the Convention.

European Convention on Human Rights

"Article 24
Any High Contracting Party may refer to the Commission, through the Secretary-General of the Council of Europe, any alleged breach of the provisions of the Convention by another High Contracting Party.

Article 25
1.	The Commission may receive petitions addressed to the Secretary-General of the Council of Europe from any person, non-governmental organisation or group of individuals claiming to be the victim of a violation by one of the High Contracting Parties of the rights set forth in this Convention, provided that the High Contracting Party against which the complaint has been lodged has declared that it recognises the competence of the Commission to receive such petitions. Those of the High Contracting Parties who have made such a declaration undertake not to hinder in any way the effective exercise of ths right.
2.	Such declarations may be made for a specific period. . . .

Article 26

The Commission may only deal with the matter after all domestic remedies have been exhausted, according to the generally recognised rules of international law, and within a period of six months from the date on which the final decision was taken.

Article 27

1.   The Commission shall not deal with any petition submitted under Article 25 which
(*a*) is anonymous, or
(*b*) is substantially the same as a matter which has already been examined by the Commission or has already been submitted to another procedure of international investigation or settlement and if it contains no relevant new information.
2.   The Commission shall consider inadmissible any petition submitted under Article 25 which it considers incompatible with the provisions of the present Convention, manifestly ill-founded, or an abuse of the right of petition.
3.   The Commission shall reject any petition referred to it which it considers inadmissible under Article 26.

Article 28

In the event of the Commission accepting a petition referred to it:
(*a*) it shall, with a view to ascertaining the facts, undertake together with the representatives of the parties an examination of the petition and, if need be, an investigation, for the effective conduct of which the States concerned shall furnish all necessary facilities, after an exchange of views with the Commission;
(*b*) it shall place itself at the disposal of the parties concerned with a view to securing a friendly settlement of the matter on the basis of respect for Human Rights as defined in this Convention.

Article 30

If the Commission succeeds in effecting a friendly settlement in accordance with Article 28, it shall draw up a Report which shall be sent to the States concerned, to the Committee of Ministers and to the Secretary-General of the Council of Europe for publication. This Report shall be confined to a brief statement of the facts and of the solution reached.

Article 31

1. If a solution is not reached, the Commission shall draw up a Report on the facts and state its opinion as to whether the facts found disclose a breach by the State concerned of its obligations under the Convention. The opinions of all the members of the Commission on this point may be stated in the Report.
2.   The Report shall be transmitted to the Committee of Ministers. It shall also be transmitted to the States concerned, who shall not be at liberty to publish it.

3.   In transmitting the Report to the Committee of Ministers the Commission may make such proposals as it thinks fit.

Article 32

1.   If the question is not referred to the Court in accordance with Article 48 of this Convention within a period of three months from the date of the transmission of the Report to the Committee of Minister, the Committee of Ministers shall decide by a majority of two-thirds of the members entitled to sit on the Committee whether there has been a violation of the Convention.
2.   In the affirmative case the Committee of Minster shall prescribe a period during which the High Contracting Party concerned must take the measures required by the decision of the Committee of Ministers.
3.   If the High Contracting Party concerned has not taken satisfactory measures within the prescribed period, the Committee of Ministers shall decide by the majority provided for in paragraph (1) above what effect shall be given to its original decision and shall publish the Report.
4.   The High Contracting Parties undertake to regard as binding on them any decision which the Committee of Ministers may take in application of the preceding paragraphs.

Article 44

Only the High Contracting Parties and Commission shall have the right to bring a case before the Court.

Article 45

The jurisdiction of the Court shall extend to all cases concerning the interpretation and application of the present Convention which the High Contracting Parties or the Commission shall refer to it in accordance with Article 48.

Article 46

1.   Any of the High Contracting Parties may at any time declare that it recognises as compulsory *ipso facto* and without special agreement the jurisdiction of the Court in all matters concerning the interpretation and application of the present Convention.
2.   The declarations referred to above may be made unconditionally or on condition of reciprocity on the part of several or certain other High Contracting Parties or for a specified period.

Article 47

The Court may only deal with a case after the Commission has acknowledged the failure of efforts for a friendly settlement and within the period of three months provided for in Article 32.

Article 48

The following may bring a case before the Court, provided that the High Contracting Party concerned, if there is only one, or the High Contracting Parties concerned, if there is more than one, are subject to the compulsory jurisdiction of the Court or, failing that, with the consent of the High

Contracting Party concerned, if there is only one, or of the High Contracting Parties concerned if there is more than one:
(a) the Commission:
(b) a High Contracting Party whose national is alleged to be a victim;
(c) a High Contracting Party which referred the case to the Commission;
(d) a High Contracting Party against which the complaint has been lodged."

NOTES

1. It might be concluded from the above provisions that the function of the Commission is to act as a "filter," ensuring that only appropriate cases reach the Court. In a sense this is true, and indeed "the figures show . . . that the Commission has functioned as a fine-meshed filter" (Mikaelsen, *European Protection of Human Rights*, p. 15). Over 95 per cent. of cases registered with the Commission are held to be inadmissible by that body. But the Commission is also charged with a primary function under article 28 of seeking a "friendly settlement" between the parties. Such settlements are in practice rare, and indeed the first was not achieved until 1962 (*Boeckmans* v. *Belgium*, 1727/62; 8 Yearbook 410).

2. Procedure is by way of a simple application stating details of the applicant, the country against which the application is made, the facts, the alleged violations of the Convention, the objects of the claim, and a statement of the remedies pursued before the appropriate domestic judicial and administrative bodies.

3. Applications may be made by any person, non-governmental organisation, or group of individuals as well as by any high contracting party. This right of individual petition, which is the cornerstone of the system established by the Convention depends on the high contracting party against whom the complaint is taken recognising the competence of individual petition. The United Kingdom government has recognised this right since 1966, for periods of five years at a time. This recognition was renewed recently, with effect until 13 January 1986. (See the *Declarations* relative to the Commission and the Court at Cmnd. 8488.)

4. Substantial procedural hurdles are contained in article 26. In particular the requirement of exhaustion of local remedies should be noted. In many cases this would require an applicant to exhaust all local avenues of appeal, though an exception is recognised where the existing state of the local law offers no reasonable prospect of success. (See, further, Jacobs, *The European Convention on Human Rights*, pp. 235 *et seq.*) The applicant may be required to resort to administrative remedies, such as, for example, remedies afforded to a prisoner under the Prison Rules (*Courcy* v. *U.K.*, 2749/66; 10 Yearbook 388).

5. It has been stated (Jacobs, *op. cit.*, p. 24) that "incompatibility" under article 27(2) arises if a complaint is "altogether outside the scope of the Convention". On the other hand, a complaint is "manifestly-ill founded" within the same article if "while it falls *prima facie* within the scope of the Convention, a preliminary examination of the merits shows that there is no need for any further such examination. This may be because the applicant has made wholly unsubstantiated allegations, . . . Or it may be because the allegations which he makes, even if substantiated, would not suffice to establish a violation" (*ibid.*).

6. Only where the Commission has declared an application admissible and has acknowledged the failure of efforts for a friendly settlement may the Court deal with a case. The high contracting parties undertake to abide by the decisions of the Court in any case to which they are parties (article 53) and the judgment of the Court is final (article 52). The Court may, where it finds that there has been a violation of the Convention and where local remedies are inadequate, "afford just satisfaction to the injured party" (article 50). However, the Court has no power to enforce its judgments directly.

7. For detailed discussions of the Convention and the procedures for enforcing the rights and freedoms secured by it, see Mikaelsen, *op. cit.*, Jacobs, *op. cit.*, Nedjati, *Human Rights under the European Convention*; Beddard, *Human Rights and Europe*.

d. Reference to the Court of Justice of the European Communities

The possibility of a reference to the Court of Justice of the European Communities may arise where a ruling is required on the interpretation of the EEC Treaty (the Treaty of Rome), the interpretation of the treaty establishing the European Atomic Energy Community, or interpretation of acts of the institutions of the Communities. By article 177 of the EEC Treaty, and article 150 of the EURATOM Treaty such questions of interpretation when arising before a court of a member state, may be referred to the Court of Justice. Where, however, that local court is one from which there is no appeal (as, for example, in the case of the High Court sitting on appeal in summary or solemn proceedings, or hearing an application to the *nobile officium*) the question must be referred to the Court of Justice for a ruling on interpretation.

The procedures are governed by Act of Adjournal (References to the European Court) 1973. For a discussion of these procedures see Renton and Brown, Chap. 16.

INDEX

Absolute discharge. *See* Sentence
Advocation. *See* Bill of advocation
Appeal. *See* Appeal in solemn
  proceedings; Bill of advocation; Bill
  of suspension; Competency; Nobile
  officium; Note of appeal against
  sentence; Preliminary diet;
  Relevancy
Appeal in solemn proceedings,
  abandonment of, 446-450
  fresh evidence in, 451-454
  ground of, 419-427
    introduction of previous
      conviction as, 433-437
    miscarriage of justice, 419-442
    misdirection of jury as, 437-440
    oppression by trial judge as,
      437-440
    unreasonable verdict, 440-442
  High Court as court of appeal in,
    418-419
  powers of court in relation to, 450-
    454
  procedure for,
    lodging appeal, 443-444
    stating ground of appeal, 444-446
Arrest, 104-131, 141-156
  access to legal advice following,
    142-144
  admissibility of statements made
    under, 157-190
  appearance before court, following,
    141-142
  citizen's power of, 110
  common law powers of, 104-106,
    107-110
  definition of, 122-129
  detention and, distinguished, 104-
    105
  entry to effect,
    common law powers, 118
    statutory powers, 19-122
  fingerprinting of persons following,
    145-148
  intimation of fact of, 142-144
  magistrates' powers of, 105
  matrimonial interdict, 153-156
  police powers of, 104-122
  questioning of persons following,
    157-190
  search following, 144-145
  search prior to, 144-145, 200-205
  statement of grounds for, 129-131

Arrest — *cont.*
  with warrant, 104-106
  without warrant, 104-117
    common law offences, 107-110
    common law powers of, 107-110
    statutory offences, 109
    statutory powers,
      Civic Government (Scotland)
        Act 1982, under, 111
      exercise outwith Scotland,
        114-117
      types of, 110-111
    suspicion, on, 110, 112-114

Bail, 214-227
  breach of conditions of, 282-285
  commission of offence while on,
    282-285
  discretion of court and, 214-218
  guidelines for granting, 222-224
  money deposit as precondition of,
    214
  murder cases in, 219-220
  pending appeal, 220-221
  prosecutor's attitude to, 214-218
  rape cases, in, 217
  refusal of,
    appeal against, 224-227
    review of, 224-227
  standard conditions of, 218
  treason cases, in, 219
  "Wheatley guidelines" for, 222-224
Bill of advocation, 493-499
  availability of,
    prior to final determination,
      497-498
    to accused, 494
    to prosecutor, 493-494
  High Court proceedings in, 493-494
  merits, review of, 498
  proceedings, review of, 498
  relevancy, review of, 494-496
Bill of suspension, 481-493
  appropriate, where, 489-493
    "crisp issue", 489-493
    review of merits, 487-488
  availability of,
    prior to final determination,
      483-485
    to prosecutor, 481
  competent, where, 482-489
  delay in bringing, 491-492
  disposal of, 493

Verdict, — *cont.*
  consistency with indictment, 346
  inconsistency of, 350-355

Warnings to accused persons, 42-44